An Inclusive Academy

An Inclusive Academy

Achieving Diversity and Excellence

Abigail J. Stewart and Virginia Valian

The MIT Press
Cambridge, Massachusetts
London, England

This book was set in Stone Serif by Westchester Publishing Services. Printed and bound in the United States of America.

Library of Congress Cataloging-in-Publication Data

Names: Stewart, Abigail J., author. | Valian, Virginia, author.
Title: An inclusive academy : achieving diversity and excellence / Abigail J. Stewart and Virginia Valian.
Description: Cambridge, MA : The MIT Press, 2018. | Includes bibliographical references and index.
Identifiers: LCCN 2017047689 | ISBN 9780262037846 (hardcover : alk. paper)
Subjects: LCSH: College teachers--Selection and appointment--United States. | College teachers--Rating of--United States. | Minority college teachers--United States. | Faculty integration--United States. | College personnel management-- United States.
Classification: LCC LB2332.72 .S74 2018 | DDC 378.1/25--dc23 LC record available at https://lccn.loc.gov/2017047689

10   9   8   7   6   5   4   3   2

To Seth Katz
To the memory of Jerrold J. Katz
and to Nick, Tim, and future generations of faculty

Contents

Acknowledgments

We have benefited from many conversations with colleagues and friends about the material covered in this book. Among our many interlocutors some particularly important ones include Lotte Bailyn, Sabrica Barnett, Diana Bilimoria, Nancy Cantor, Mark Chesler, Paul Courant, Kay Deaux, Sarah Fenstermaker, Julia Fulghum, Alec Gallimore, Michelle Hebl, Alice Hogan, Wayne Jones, Diana Kardia, Laura Kramer, Randi Martin, Terrence McDonald, Annemarie Nicols-Grinenko, Vita Rabinowitz, Elizabeth Travis, Karla Vineyard, Janet Weiss, Shaun Wiley, and David Winter. We are also grateful to the associates, sponsors, speakers, and advisors affiliated with the Gender Equity Project at Hunter College, and the staff at UM ADVANCE, especially Shawn Beard, Cynthia Hudgins, Keith Herzog, and Janet Malley, as well as Jennifer Linderman, Karin Martin, Denise Sekaquaptewa, Lilia Cortina, Mark Chesler, and the members of the STRIDE committee over many years. We are also grateful for timely advice from and discussion with Francine Blau, Philip Laughlin, Katherine Almeida, and Hilary Levinson.

In addition, many people read part or all of this manuscript in draft form and provided us with invaluable feedback and advice. These include Richard Aslin, Francine Blau, Charles Brown, Molly Carnes, Jessie DeAro, Julia Fulghum, Donna Ginther, Alice Hogan, Michelle Hebl, Madeline Heilman, Shulamit Kahn, Laura Kramer, Danielle LaVaque-Manty, Sandra Masur, Terrence McDonald, Richard McGee, Beth Mitchneck, Scott Page, Mary C. Potter, Paul Rozin, Martin Ruck, Jennifer Saul, Kimberlee Shauman, Jennifer Sheridan, Janet Weiss, Alison Wylie, and two anonymous reviewers for MIT Press. Finally, we have both benefited from discussion of issues of institutional change over many years, not only with many of those already named, but also with Augusto Blasi, Ned Block, Susan Carey, David Chalmers, Anne Cutler, Francine Deutsch, Karen Fournier, Donna Henderson-King,

Eaaron Henderson-King, Nancy Hopkins, Gail Hornstein, Christian Matijas-Mecca, Domna Stanton, Keivan Stassun, Susan Sturm, Tim Stewart-Winter, Meg Urry, and Nick Winter, among others. We are grateful to all of these friends and colleagues.

We have been stimulated by the challenging questions asked at the talks we have given, and we have been both amused and chagrined by the stories we have heard at different colleges and universities. Here's a favorite: at one university we learned that a department had hired a woman for the first time. This department had a tradition of having a retreat in the woods before each academic year. The faculty rented a cabin and stayed together in the cabin. The faculty recognized that it was an important experience that the new faculty member should somehow be a part of, but they couldn't figure out how to include her. She couldn't stay in a cabin with all the men, but it wouldn't be right for her to be in a completely separate cabin. Stymied, they finally suggested that her husband attend the retreat instead of her and tell her what had transpired! These stories give life to the experiments we discuss in our book—in this case, of a good intention that misfired.

We have also been delighted to meet, and be instructed by, the many people we have discussed diversity with—people who are eager to improve their institution's inclusiveness, and who have told us about practices that worked and didn't work for them. We hope that they will find this book useful.

Acknowledgments for Funding

Virginia Valian acknowledges the support of the National Science Foundation, the National Institutes of Health, and the Sloan Foundation. Her contribution to this book is based upon work supported by the National Science Foundation under Award No. 0123609, Grant No. 0620083, and Grant No. 1023165. Any opinions, findings, and conclusions or recommendations expressed in this material are those of the author(s) and do not necessarily reflect the views of the National Science Foundation. Her contribution is also based upon work supported by the National Institutes of Health Grant No. GM088530. Any opinions, findings, and conclusions or recommendations expressed in this material are those of the author(s) and do not necessarily reflect the views of the National Institute of Health. Her contribution is also based on work supported by the Sloan Foundation. Any opinions, findings, and conclusions or recommendations expressed in this material are those of the author(s) and do not necessarily reflect the views of the Sloan Foundation. Hunter College and the City University of New York provided a much-appreciated and timely sabbatical. Finally, the Department of Psychology at Hunter College and the PhD Programs in Psychology, Linguistics, and Speech-Language-Hearing Sciences at the CUNY Graduate Center have offered the kind of working environment that we recommend in this book.

Abigail Stewart acknowledges support from the National Science Foundation, the Sloan Foundation, and the University of Michigan. Her contribution to this book is based upon work supported by the National Science Foundation under SBE-0123571 and SBE-0620022. Any opinions, findings, and conclusions or recommendations expressed in this material are those of the author(s) and do not necessarily reflect the views of the National Science Foundation. It is also based on work supported by the Sloan Foundation on Supporting Women Scientists and Engineers in Leadership Positions (B2007-61). Any opinions, findings, and conclusions or recommendations expressed in this material are those of the author(s) and do not necessarily reflect the views of the Sloan Foundation. Finally, she is grateful to the University of Michigan for financial support for her research, as well as for a sabbatical and funded leaves of absence that enabled her to complete her work on this book.

Preface: Why This Book?

Why We Wrote This Book

Efforts to increase equity and diversity evoke a wide range of reactions—from enthusiastic embrace to outright antagonism. Most people are in the middle, intending to do the right thing, slightly skeptical, open to suggestions. We are committed to providing an evidence-based approach, grounding our conclusions and recommendations in the best available research. In part I we review a lot of evidence! We discuss the extent to which universities do and do not live up to their ideals. We present data about the value of diversity. We examine the ways that we fall short of judging individuals fairly and the reasons for our misevaluations. Part II of our book makes recommendations in a wide variety of areas: the search for job candidates, the process of evaluating job, tenure, and promotion candidates, the role of the department in helping people succeed or fail, ways to broaden rewards and recognition.

Despite its suggestions and recommendations for how to create an inclusive and fair institution, this book is not a manual. Rather, we concentrate on principles. Our recommendations are examples of how to give concrete form to those principles. We have seen, and there are data to suggest, that there are many routes to success—and to failure. Different institutions, and different units within those institutions, may need different approaches. Our recommendations distill what we think is common to workable solutions.

Who We Are

We, Abigail Stewart and Virginia Valian, are psychologists. Although we had both worked on gender before meeting for the first time in 2001 in San Francisco at a tiny conference, we had not made any systematic effort to change our institutions. That idea was stimulated by the National Science Foundation's (NSF's) ADVANCE program. The program began late in 2001, funding nine colleges and universities with large Institutional Transformation (IT) awards. The aim was—and remains—to increase the representation and advancement of women in the natural and social sciences, math, engineering, and technology.

NSF began the program with the idea that women's underrepresentation in the sciences did not require "fixing the woman." Instead, it required understanding and changing how institutions worked. The goal was to create a better and more inclusive college or university, one that would make use of everyone's talents and resemble the population in all its diversity. That was a radical idea in 2001, and in 2018, even after dozens of schools have received funding through a variety of different NSF ADVANCE awards, it continues to be a radical idea, one to which we subscribe.

The University of Michigan (AJS's home institution) and Hunter College—CUNY (VVV's home institution) were two of the nine schools funded by ADVANCE in that first round of grants. This book distills what we have learned in the past 17 years. We have learned a great deal, thanks to NSF and ADVANCE, thanks to ADVANCE's then program director, Alice Hogan, thanks to the women and men who have been working to make NSF's vision a reality, and thanks to the skyrocketing volume of research on diversity and equity. We have worked on our own campuses, and we have spoken, collectively, at over 150 schools and conferences in the United States, Canada, Australia, Europe, and Asia. Although ADVANCE focuses on gender, it has increasingly attended to other types of underrepresentation, especially the underrepresentation of people of color. We, too, have a wider lens in this book than a gender lens.

We also have a wider lens than a psychologist's lens. We understand the need to offer analyses at both the individual level and the institutional level, and to show how those two levels are connected. We try to do both.

Finally, we draw on our own experiences for examples and proposed remedies. As a result we often cite our own institutions' programs and practices, though we also refer to programs and practices we have learned about at other institutions. We know that many other institutions have developed important innovations to achieve inclusion, and ours are neither perfect nor comprehensive. We do not take our institutions as "exemplary"; we cite them because they are the institutions we know best.

Is This Book for You?

This book is for people who want to increase the diversity, inclusiveness, and excellence of their college or university. They want to make a difference— whether the difference is at the level of their immediate work group, their department, their college, or their university. To succeed in making a difference requires both understanding and action. On the understanding end, we need to understand how diversity and inclusiveness contribute to excellence, and we need to understand how our thoughts and behaviors and our institutions' procedures make change difficult. On the action end, we need to put concrete changes in place. It's not enough to think about change, or talk about change, or plan for change. We have to, well, change.

Our aim is to change institutions to make them more inclusive, stronger, and better. We see inclusiveness and excellence as going hand in hand. They are not in competition. Administrators can play a positive, neutral, or negative role in that effort. This book is partly for administrators, so that they will be better able to play a positive role and effect institutional change. But this book is also for individuals who are not administrators but still want to make positive changes in the academy. We recognize that different people want different amounts of information, so we have placed details that provide more background and justification in notes and an appendix. If your favorite study is not present in the text, check the notes; it may be there. But we may have missed it. Let us know.

In one way it is easiest to make changes locally, because the smaller the group, the more say each person has. But local changes can also be hard to create: we lack a distanced perspective on our own behavior, seeing ourselves as benign individuals who only want to do our jobs as well as possible. We can thus be unaware of the voices we are failing to bring out and the talents we are failing to develop. Soliciting and attending to new suggestions while keeping our work going in a positive direction, being open to other perspectives while being the leader of a group and making the final decisions about what to do—those are difficult balancing acts. This book is designed to show the advantages of inclusiveness and diversity and provide principles for how to go about realizing them. We think it is salutary for those who direct any sort of group, no matter how small, to see that it isn't always easy to be open and flexible, or to bring out the best of everyone in the group, or to realize how much their rank matters.

For example, one of us read a newspaper article about business managers who believe that they are funny, using as evidence the fact that the people working under them laugh at their jokes. Oh, she thought, is that me? I think I'm funny, and at research group meetings the students and assistants laugh at my jokes. Are they just laughing because they know I want them to laugh? The next day, when talking to a student and an assistant, she brought this up, and they nodded. She was hoping that they would say, "No, you really are funny," but they didn't. A little later in the conversation she said something she thought was funny, they laughed, and after she looked at them inquiringly, one of them kindly said, "That really *was* funny." That example brought home to her how difficult it is to appreciate how much rank matters when one has the higher rank.

The department is the next level where individuals can play a role. Someone does not need to be the chair of a department in order to make suggestions, argue for the value of their suggestions, and follow through on them. Chairs should welcome new ideas and create an environment that makes it easy for people to offer them, but individuals also have a responsibility to learn to speak up effectively. This book highlights institutional changes, such as how recruiting of new faculty is accomplished, while recognizing that individuals contribute to such changes and have the job of implementing them.

Most faculty spend most of their time in their department. The department is an intermediary between an individual faculty member and the higher level administration (the deans, provosts, and presidents). What happens at the level of the department has an enormous effect on faculty morale and productivity. Good departments can help faculty weather severe budget cuts, changes in upper level administrations, and apathy or worse from upper level administrations. Department chairs or heads[1] are doing a good job if they are attuned to maximizing everyone's potential and creating a place that faculty enjoy working.

Many faculty have little or no interaction with administrators above the level of their chair or head. They may not know who their dean or provost is, even by name, and may have little idea of what those administrators do.

In their turn, deans and provosts and presidents may be far removed from faculty concerns. In some ways, being an administrator of any office or department is a thankless job. Projects and initiatives that one has started may be undone or abandoned by the next person in that role. One person we know who had designed an interdisciplinary honors program that he thought managed to be both broad and deep was chagrined to see that his successor had a completely different idea of what an honors program should be like and thus removed all the interdisciplinary elements.

And so it can happen with diversity and inclusiveness. One higher level administrator might make great strides in those areas but find that his or her successor has abandoned those projects. Thus, although our book is aimed at improving higher education's diversity and inclusiveness, and that means providing administrators with principles and specific recommendations about how to enact those improvements, we want to emphasize that everyone can do something, no matter what position they occupy in the institution. Everyone can identify an area that needs improvement. Everyone can work effectively to realize and maintain those improvements. Improvements that become part of the way a department or school or institution operates are improvements that may last, no matter who the president or provost is.

We think that teams are a key to success. Teams have more ideas than a single person does, teams have more connections than a single person does, and teams have a broader range of expertise than a single person does. Changes that are the result of team activity are more likely to endure than changes that are the result of a single person's actions. The more people involved in making a change, the more likely it is that the change will stick. For that reason, we encourage individuals to work with others.

We start with six principles, some of which we have already mentioned.

Six Principles

1. *Use universal design.* This principle was first proposed in connection with buildings and environments, in order to make them usable for everyone, or as many people as possible, regardless of their age or mobility. Street cutouts (or curb cuts) are the most obvious example. Although they were intended largely for people in wheelchairs, they help people with grocery carts, strollers, aging people who prefer ramps to even one step, and so on.

Another example—too seldom employed—is the legible name tag.[2] Most name tags at academic conferences have print so small that no one can read them without peering closely. Although people with limited vision would particularly benefit from name tags with the first or last name written very large and in a sans serif font, the change would benefit everyone.

In the case of diversity, universal design means treating everyone equally, but in a way that is responsive to difference. That balance, which at first seems self-contradictory, is critical. Here's an example. Deans at one university asked for advice about the following problem. When they told female assistant professors that their performance wasn't on track for promotion and tenure, the women were very disturbed and discouraged and felt it was hopeless to continue. When they told male assistant professors the same thing, the men brushed it off and didn't take it seriously. The deans asked whether they should approach men and women differently, given the differences in how the women and men responded to the information about their status.

Our view is no. The deans' current procedure was not meeting their goal of helping junior faculty improve so that they would be good candidates for promotion and tenure. What they needed was a universal design solution, one that took into account the differences between their female and male faculty but treated them the same. One solution—not, we emphasize, the only one—is to tell the faculty member that the dean (or other appropriate administrative official) wants to work with him or her to ensure a good outcome. The dean can ask the faculty member (perhaps along with the chair of the relevant department) to return in three to four weeks (or some other period) with a plan for improvement that they can review together. That solution tells faculty members that the dean wants them to succeed and that they need a plan to do better. It simultaneously reassures the woman and tells the man that the issue is serious. Although the dean had identified women as having one type of response and men as having another, there might be women with the "male" response and men with the "female" response. People, including people within groups that are known to have certain responses "on average," are different. The solution to aim at is one that takes into account the variability in human response and encompasses that variability. (We pass no judgment here about whether the university's criteria for promotion and tenure were good criteria.)

Our suggestions in part II are aimed at making life better for everyone. The impetus for a change may be related to gender or race or ethnicity,[3] but the result of the ensuing change should benefit the community as a whole.

2. *Maximize each individual's potential.* This can be seen as the inverse of *the squeaky wheel gets the grease.* Many of our specific suggestions—for example, those concerning the job interview—are aimed at bringing out the best that a person has to offer. Some people are "good" interviewees and some aren't. Within any department or school, some people are deft negotiators and some aren't. Those differences exist both within sex and within ethnicity and between genders and ethnicities. We can help people develop skills to be a "better" interviewee or negotiator on their own behalf, but we can also help interviewers develop the skills to bring out the best in people and help those who control the resources provide them in a way that maximizes the number of people who can do their best work. Having a good idea doesn't necessarily go along with being able to talk about it well. Of course, people can and should develop their verbal skills, but it's the leader's job to detect the good idea.

3. *Take a different perspective.* At one institution, we heard the following story. Two people were brought in to interview for a position as director of one of three important divisions. The woman worked in England and flew to the United States—more than five time zones away—for the interview. The man worked in the United States in the same time zone. There was much enthusiasm for the woman's candidacy among the postdocs and junior scientists, but the institution offered the job to the male candidate, giving as one reason that the female candidate didn't seem interested in the job. The individuals who related the story said, "She's British! She doesn't express enthusiasm in the same way Americans do. She flew over here for the interview; doesn't that show interest? She discussed our work with us at length; doesn't that show interest?" (As of this writing, all three directors are still men.)

We have no way of knowing whether the people who told us the story were accurately relating what had transpired, nor whether there were other reasons for preferring the male candidate. A single example is only food for thought. And one thought is that the interviewers were indeed failing to see things from another perspective. This is where getting diverse opinions is very helpful. Finding out how other people see a situation can change one's own perceptions, and one is more likely to get a diverse range of opinions if one samples a diverse group of people.

4. *Be alert to, and be willing to change, structural factors.* When we observe others' behavior, we tend to attribute it to their individual characteristics—often, their personality—rather than to structural or situational factors. From the outside, it looks as if the individual responded in a certain way because of who he or she is; we see the person as having made a choice to respond as he or she did. From the inside, however, the individual may feel constrained to behave in a particular way.

For example, a senior male administrator at one institution described the extensive steps taken to interest a female faculty member in an administrative position. Regardless of what they offered her, and it was a lot, including the possibility of working fewer hours for a period of time, she said no, explaining that her children required too much of her attention at that moment. The administrator's admiration of the woman was patent, as was his desire to figure out a solution. As presented, there seemed little to recommend other than to search for other talented women who might fill the position.

Afterward, a female faculty member approached one of us and said, "She said that because her excuse was socially acceptable. It wasn't her real reason. She's definitely interested in academic leadership. Her real reason is that the administration is toxic here. But she couldn't say that."

This is a difficult situation for everyone. The well-meaning senior person has no idea what is happening—in part because of lack of attention to a range of views about the administration (see principle 3 above)—and attributes the woman's refusal to her stated personal reasons. The woman, feeling powerless to change what she sees as an administration that makes life hard for its members, says no to a position that, with a different cast of characters, she would like to take on.

At a less personal level, a similar situation arises when a department posts a job search and has very few female or underrepresented minority applicants. It is tempting for the department to see the lack of applications as individual choices that individual women and underrepresented minorities are making. One common attribution at research-intensive institutions is that women and minorities are more interested in institutions that emphasize teaching. We recommend that the department also consider how it is going about its search. Is it really *searching*, is it really *recruiting*? Is the job description written broadly enough? Does the department look like an appealing place to a wide range of people? Does the departmental website make the department look like a place that treats people well? Change can't happen unless people take responsibility for change.

In the chapter on recruiting, we make recommendations about how to increase the pool of women and underrepresented minorities. Our broader point is that when there is an obstacle to a desired outcome involving diversity, people should focus on finding out what structural and procedural factors are preventing diversity, and start changing them.

5. *Try things out.* Some of the things people try may work and some of them may not. When something doesn't work, try something else. There is no single one-time wave of a wand that will increase the hiring, retention, and promotion of women and people of color. One colleague described a situation at her university: after a salary analysis in her school, the dean determined that women were being underpaid relative to men. He raised the women's salaries to levels that seemed appropriate, given their accomplishments. He figured he had solved the salary problem and could move on to other issues. But when he did another salary analysis two years later, he discovered that there was again a gender disparity. The reason? Male faculty, especially White male faculty, were entertaining offers of employment at other universities. To keep those male faculty, chairs were raising their salaries. That recreated a disparity between White men and everyone else.

What else could the dean try? When the late Denice Denton was dean of engineering at the University of Washington, she told her faculty that outside offers would not be a way to get a salary hike. If they wanted more money, they should come to see her and make their case. If they were unhappy at the university, they should tell her what their concerns were. What they should not do was use an outside offer as a bargaining tool. When asked if she was able to stick to her word, she said, "Mostly."

We like Denton's approach. It solves a problem by treating everyone the same (see principle 1), and it goes to the root of a problem. We also like her approach because it saves everyone a lot of time and money. The outside school mounts a long and expensive effort, involving many people, to attract the faculty member. The home school similarly spends a lot of person-hours mobilizing a counteroffer. Whichever school loses has spent resources that might be better deployed elsewhere.

Another problem with outside offers is that not only may women and minorities court them less than White men do, but they may be treated differently when they do receive an outside offer. Two women we know told their chair and dean about their outside offers. In one case, the dean said, "That sounds like a great offer. I think you should take it." She did. In the other case, the dean said, "That school is not ranked nearly as high as we are. Why would you want to go?" That dean was betting that the prestige of her home institution would be sufficient to retain her. It wasn't. She left. In both cases the deans saved time and effort by saying no, but they also lost people who became major figures in their fields. In the case of the second woman, the institution later regretted its decision and tried to hire her back. She declined.

Sometimes external factors can seem insurmountable, making change impossible. At institutions in rural locations, we have heard people say that women and minorities do not want to live in such a rural place: the community is isolated, it does not provide a lot of cultural opportunities other than the ones provided by the college or university, and it does not provide employment for a partner. They may add that the community does not welcome minorities, or gays, or some other group. At institutions in urban locations, we have heard people say that the cost of living is too high, housing is difficult, traffic is bad, and the public schools aren't good. Or we hear that their school cannot compete with school X, which has more of some quality that people value. Or that their school is very competitive, and women and people of color do not want that kind of pressure. It begins to seem miraculous that schools hire any faculty at all.

What is positive about such responses is that the schools are identifying structural issues (though they are also making assumptions on the basis of gender and ethnicity that may not be warranted). At one rural university, an employee in human resources told one of us that it was very difficult to attract African American faculty. There was nowhere for African Americans to get their hair cut and styled, and nowhere for African American women to buy hosiery or makeup appropriate for their skin tone. Those are real problems. One solution the university had entertained was hiring a bus to take their African American faculty to a larger town where such services would be available. (Yes, we have heard everything.) They were stymied.

A White male faculty member at another rural university, who, with his White wife, had adopted an African American girl, spoke poignantly of their steep learning curve in figuring out how to help their daughter have a positive identity. Both parents had taken lessons in how to braid their child's hair into cornrows, and had sought out local African American families. There were class issues as well as ethnicity issues. The university had no office to help.

What could these universities do? They could experiment with different possibilities. For example, they could create an office that will help faculty who represent rare groups on campus and in the community. Another example is to work with local merchants and service providers to supply the needed items and skills. A third is to hire enough people in a given group so that they are not so rare.

6. *Hold people accountable.* If a given outcome is part of a job description, people can be evaluated in part on the basis of how well they have met that outcome.

Claims People Make

There are two polar opposite claims we hear people make frequently. The first is that there really isn't a problem, anymore. There *used* to be a problem. Women and people of color *used* to face obstacles in academia, but those times are behind us. This book argues that although there has been clear and important progress, the advancement of women and people of color in academia is still too slow. The problem used to be bigger and more overt, but there remains a problem, noticeable in the slower advancement of women and people of color compared to men and Whites, and in the more marginal position women and people of color occupy in their professional communities.

One example concerns the identity of invited speakers at conferences. In 2016, the University of Windsor had a conference directed toward undergraduates, who could present their work to the university community. There were six keynote speakers—all men. Four were faculty—four White men. One speaker was a First Nations man who coordinates the Aboriginal Education Centre at the university. One speaker was a Black man who was the president of the university's Students Alliance. We choose this example—among several we could have described—because the conference was aimed at undergraduates and had encouraged undergraduates to make presentations.

We know that people's aspirations are affected by whom they see in different positions. The failure to include a single woman in a group of six speakers sends an unwelcoming message to young women. And that unwelcoming message is repeated at academic conferences. One website is dedicated to notices about all-male panels and periodically posts examples of conferences all of the speakers of which are male; most contributors are from Europe, perhaps giving a misleading idea of the geographical scope of the problem.

The United States is not home free: the Eastern Psychological Association—an association of academic psychologists that one of us is a member of—included 14 invited speakers for its conference in March 2017, of whom 2 were women. On the (conservative) assumption that half the candidate pool was female (based on the percentage of women in academic psychology; gender data are not available for members), the odds of having so few women are 6 in 1,000. Women were similarly underrepresented in 2016 and 2015, but things are looking up: the 2018 list of invited speakers currently includes 6 women and 4 men, which is what one would expect if the percentage of female speakers reflected the available pool. Sometimes it takes very little for evaluators and judges to search further for excellence in all genders and ethnicities. Sometimes a brief and polite word or note will do the trick.

These are, of course, only examples. Throughout the book, we use examples to illustrate issues, but we do not rely on them to make the case that there is an issue to illustrate. In part I, we present observational and experimental data from many sources to back up the claim that a problem remains. We interpret the data by integrating theories from cognitive psychology, social psychology, economics, sociology of education, sociology of science, organization science, and women's and gender studies. In part II, we recommend procedures for hiring and promoting, running a department, helping all faculty thrive and receive recognition, and making changes last.

We are optimistic about change, while seeing it as still too slow. The polar opposite claim we encounter is that academia is hostile to women and people of color, more so as their careers progress, and that administrators and colleagues are not working for change. Even if one puts sexual harassment to one side, the continuing existence of male-dominated conference line-ups is depressing evidence of the lack of proper attention to diversity and equity.

Our optimism comes in part from successful changes that we have witnessed or read about and from our experiences where we have given talks and workshops. We think that there has been measurable progress, but that people often do not know exactly how to attend to diversity and equity. In discussions with university administrators, chairs, and faculty, we have found that people lack the background information they need to understand why women and people of color are underrepresented at research-intensive universities and are unaware of research showing the importance of structural factors that they take for granted—features like the typical procedures of search committees or promotion and tenure committees, and the importance of small, daily differences in their treatment of different groups of people. In our experience, in the absence of adequate information on such issues, people are genuinely baffled by the phenomena in front of them.

Here are some of the conclusions that influenced the content and form of this book.

• Many people are open to creating a more inclusive professoriate but unsure how to go about it. Some people worry that not all of their values can coexist. For example, some people worry that their institution will sacrifice excellence in its attempts to be more inclusive. In part I we emphasize that equity and excellence go hand in hand. More inclusive groups are better groups. There is remarkable uniformity among faculty and administrators about what a university *should* be like. We describe those ideals in *chapter 1*. Faculty value the search for truth and the freedom to pursue all ideas, whether popular or not. Faculty prize knowledge and evidence, creativity and innovation.

• Faculty are committed—at least in the abstract—to judging people on the basis of merit. Faculty believe in including everyone who works to uphold the virtues of academia. Faculty strive to pass on those values to students, to teach students how to evaluate claims, and to encourage students to develop their own ideas.

• Most people—not all, but most—are unaware of the intellectual benefits of diversity. Among those benefits is greater innovation. We describe those benefits in *chapter 2*.

• Everyone espouses the merit principle, and many people think it is already operating: standards are appropriate and fair, they think, and applied equitably, independently of anyone's gender or race-ethnicity (or social class, sexual orientation, handicap status, political persuasion, or religious group membership). People intend to judge fairly and believe that they are successful in judging fairly. In *chapters 3 and 4*, we show that despite people's good intentions, they do not always judge fairly. We also question whether all the standards in use are appropriate. In *chapters 6 and 9*, we discuss how to improve the evaluation of job candidates and promotion and tenure candidates. In *chapter 10*, we discuss how to recognize people's accomplishments and achievements.

• Most people—not all, but most—do not know the demographics of the availability pool or how their school's hiring and promotion rates compare with those of other schools. They do not know what a reasonable goal is. Departments that have not hired many women or people of color tend to think that there aren't any.

One of us, for example, remembers visiting an institute after giving a talk to about 250 women who specialized in a particular subfield. The institute was searching for a new head for one of its sections. The director told her that he would like to hire a woman, but there were so few in that subfield that he didn't think it would be possible. She mentioned the 250 women in that subfield that she had just encountered, some of whom might be appropriate candidates. Having good data helps search processes. We discuss how to search and recruit candidates in *chapter 5*.

• Most people—not all, but most—are not knowledgeable about the underlying structural and psychological factors that influence who applies for a position, who is interviewed for a position, who is offered a position, and who is promoted and tenured. One comment we have heard is "I don't judge people by their gender or the color of their skin. I don't care who they are." We think the evidence shows that people's judgments and evaluations are indeed affected by the demographic group someone belongs to, and we deal with this explicitly in *chapters 3 and 4*. People are misled by their good intentions into thinking that their judgments are unbiased.

• Most people—not all, but most—are unaware of the cumulative effects of small instances of unequal treatments of groups. Another comment we have heard is "Pick your battles." People are primed to notice and decry outright overt discrimination, but they are less able to see and effectively respond to unintentional actions that put some classes of people at a disadvantage. (And we hope that being heard and attended to in a meeting isn't a battle.) What happens in people's academic department—their home—influences how committed and productive they are. We discuss creating a beneficial environment in *chapters 7 and 8*.

An Old Story and a New Ending

In Valian's 1998 book, *Why So Slow? The Advancement of Women*, she relates a phenomenon she had observed at faculty meetings. Susan, say, makes a suggestion. Everyone ignores it. Ten minutes later Joe makes the same suggestion. People say, "Joe, what a great idea!" Susan thinks, what just happened? If she brings up the incident to a colleague, they are likely to say, "Don't make a mountain out of a molehill." Valian has repeated that description to various audiences, academic and nonacademic alike, for 20 years, and it continues to be greeted by rueful chuckles. In mid-2016, a male audience member came up to her and said, "That happened to my wife just last week!"

Being ignored in a meeting is a molehill, but molehills matter, because advantage accumulates via molehills. Mountains *are* molehills, piled one on top of the other. Joe exits the meeting having been credited with a good idea. He's had a tiny success that he can build on. He has a small advantage. We discuss the importance of the accumulation of advantage in *chapter 3*.

It's possible to intervene. In the department of one of us, a colleague thought he had seen that phenomenon occur in faculty meetings. He decided to do something about it. He now watches for moments when someone's idea is ignored. When it happens, he says something like, "Susan (or Harry) made a suggestion that I think we should discuss." He might then repeat her (or his) suggestion. He doesn't necessarily say it was a great suggestion. Nor does he castigate his colleagues for not noticing it. His aim is to ensure that people are heard. Everyone can contribute in such a way. It's a small step, and it won't solve every problem, but it's a step in the right direction.

More systematic remedies for unequal influence at faculty meetings are also possible. Chairs can ensure that everyone is heard. In the department of one of us, a former chair arranged faculty meetings so that in every meeting there were small group discussions of issues, a record of important points from each conversation, and a report of those points without attribution to the individuals who made them. That approach increased the number of different people who had input into the department's policies (at least while the person who began the policy was in charge) and put into practice the idea that everyone should be able to participate. This way of running faculty meetings did not take up more time than the more typical way. It also avoided two phenomena that we have sometimes observed at faculty meetings: one person (sometimes the chair!) goes on at too great length, or a protracted and unproductive back-and-forth takes place between the chair and a faculty member.

Our dual point here is that small inequities and incivilities, the effects of which mount up over time, continue to exist in most workplaces and take a toll. It is possible to reduce those inequities at various levels. One change we have seen over the past 20 years is greater alertness to small losses and greater willingness to intervene to change them, either at the individual level or at the institutional level.

Our Approach

We integrate two different perspectives on the still too slow advancement of faculty who are women and people of color—individual and institutional. At the individual level, as we discuss in *chapter 1*, observers are cognitively fallible evaluators. People make mistakes in judgments that have nothing to do with gender or ethnicity. We are, for example, likely to pay too much attention to our own experience and not enough attention to statistics. If we fly on an outmoded plane on a long trip, we will have a bad opinion of that airline and vow never to fly them again, even if the airline has few planes of that type. A single rude salesperson at a new store weighs more heavily for us than the judgments of hundreds of people who have had good experiences. These kinds of fallibilities, well-known in cognitive psychology, are exacerbated when we make judgments of other people.

The often-unarticulated views we have about men and women, about African Americans and Whites, affect our evaluations and judgments of others, even while we believe that we are being impartial. *Chapters 3 and 4* describe how this works, using the notion of gender schemas and ethnicity schemas. In the domain of gender, both men and women judge other men and women similarly, slightly overrating men and slightly underrating women.

The vagaries of human judgment, when combined with schemas about classes of people, lead to the construction of policies and procedures that unintentionally exclude individuals whose inclusion would benefit our colleges and universities. Policies and procedures, once developed, are difficult to change. It is difficult for people who have operated successfully within them even to consider the possibility that the policies might need changing.

For example, some academics think that success in academia requires a certain style of self-presentation and a certain style of interacting with others. One of us, upon teaching for the first time a cognitive psychology course with an attendant lab, was told by the usual instructor that he tried to cover statistics in the first two classes so that he could weed out students who didn't realize how math- and science-intensive psychology was. He expected her to follow suit. She didn't, because she did not want to intimidate students who would be able to do well in the course even if they were not already statistically informed. Some of our institutional procedures are of that ilk—similar to hazing rituals.

Aggressive and borderline insulting questions or comments, sometimes in the question session after a talk, are a form of rudeness that happens to everyone and need not have any sexist or racist content. (Such incivility is, however, more likely to happen to women and people of color than to White men.) The people who ask such questions can defend them on the grounds that speakers who cannot handle such questions should go into a different line of work. We take a different view. We think schools can lose out on needed talent because of beliefs about how people should respond to certain types of challenges. Instead of thinking about what's wrong with an individual who doesn't handle provocation well, we should think about how to create institutions that will bring out the best work people can do.

We need, for example, to interview people in a way that allows them to demonstrate their potential, and we need to treat them as valuable once we hire them. We need to divide resources and responsibilities so that everyone has a shot at doing his or her best work. We need to help people become successful in their own way, rather than in a preordained way determined by the behavior of previous jobholders. In part II we give examples of how to do this—how to formulate a job description, how to interview candidates, how to evaluate people for promotion and tenure, how to create an environment where everyone can thrive, and how to improve the disciplinary organizations that academics belong to.

Certain themes recur throughout this book—themes such as the role of schemas in evaluations and judgments of others, the importance of a feeling of belonging, the notion of "choice," and creating procedures that will bring out the best in people.

A Final Word

Throughout this book we talk in broad terms about men and women, and about different races and ethnicities. We know that those categories are rough and broad. They represent statistical regularities, not essential qualities characterizing a group as a whole. We reject the idea of essences, beyond the essence of being human. First and foremost, people are people. When we point out statistical regularities and generalizations, we are not making any claims about essences.

What is it like to be a woman? A lot of things, with much variation from person to person and from time to time. Still, women in academia are, *on average*, likely to rise through the ranks more slowly than are men. That regularity holds even though there are some women who have meteoric rises. Underrepresented minorities, as a group defined in a particular way, are underrepresented at elite institutions. That regularity is not negated by the fact that some underrepresented minorities work at elite institutions. One cannot disconfirm a regularity by pointing to exceptions.

We are, then, dealing with generalizations that may not apply to a particular person at a particular time. One cannot object to a generalization about one's group on the grounds that it doesn't apply to oneself. Maybe it does—one's employees may be laughing at one's jokes primarily because one is their employer—and maybe it doesn't. Still, the generalization holds.

The categories that we use throughout this book—male, female, African American, Hispanic, White—are too all-inclusive to represent the complexities of individual people's felt experiences. Everyone has more than one identity, different identities come to the fore in different situations. How one behaves, or is treated, when one's identity as a father is salient is different from how one behaves, or is treated, when one's identity as an employee is salient. And different fathers behave differently.

Equally, people are not simply the sum of their different identities. Being an African American woman doesn't mean adding together being African American and being a woman. People have a sense of who they are that transcends the different categories they fit; they may even reject some of the categories they demographically fit as applying to them. When we discuss "men" and "women," or any other set of categories, we do not mean to suggest that people *are* their gender, or their ethnicity, or even the intersection of their identities. People are more than the sum of their parts. There is, nevertheless, value in showing that people are perceived, evaluated, and treated on the basis of their demographic group. While that demonstration may not help us understand a single individual, it does help us understand the behavior of most people in a group, and it gives us a better idea of how to improve institutions to make them fair and inclusive.

Notes

1. Chairs are elected and heads are appointed according to one convention, but usage varies.

2. This example was used in a talk by Sheryl Burgstahler, the founder and director of the DO-IT Center at the University of Washington. "*Inclusion of individuals with disabilities: Accommodations and universal design.*" Workshop of Excellence Empowered by a Diverse Academic Workforce: Chemists, Chemical Engineers, and Materials Scientists with Disabilities, Washington D.C., February 2009.

3. We sometimes use the terms race, ethnicity, or race and ethnicity, or race-ethnicity interchangeably. We primarily use the term African American rather than Black, but use White and European American interchangeably, and Hispanic and Latino interchangeably.

I   Why an Inclusive Academy Is Difficult to Achieve: Individual and Institutional Perspectives

1 Academic Ideals: What Keeps Some Out of Reach?

What are our academic ideals? Faculty, students, and members of the public agree that an ideal college or university provides a space that promotes and secures six central virtues: a search for truth, the freedom to explore all ideas, a respect for knowledge and expertise, a valuing of creativity and innovation, a commitment to meritocracy, and a willingness to open its doors to all groups in society.

Despite this consensus, some people perceive actual institutions of higher education as bastions of elitism or irrelevance. For them, colleges and universities have failed to live up to one or more ideals. At the same time, others fiercely defend the relative success of academic institutions in safeguarding those virtues. Ideas about the six academic virtues, and their relative importance, have varied over time and in different locations, and the depth of commitment to them varies in different kinds of institutions. We believe that these virtues are nevertheless valued in all institutions of higher education, including community colleges, liberal arts colleges, comprehensive universities, and research universities; in an important sense, they define our ideal academic culture.

How those different institutions address these virtues varies, though. For example, new ideas and the freedom to discuss them are important in all of these institutions, but only some of them are in a position to provide faculty and students with resources to generate new scholarship and innovations as well as to learn about them. Finally, we recognize that colleges and universities could do a better job of showing or explaining why it is necessary to pursue and teach about some kinds of scholarship that may appear unnecessary or difficult to understand. While there is less consensus about many details, there is also long-standing shared agreement on the part of everyone from novelists to former students to faculty themselves about the academic virtues. For that reason we review both precisely how people generally understand these virtues and why we fall short of realizing some of them.

We will sometimes discuss these virtues as they apply to both students and faculty, but we note that it is the faculty in our institutions of higher education who are responsible for ensuring that these virtues are realized. Because faculty are the stewards of the institutions, and the actors who ensure that in the day-to-day operation of classrooms, laboratories, libraries, and meeting rooms we are doing our best to live up to these ideals, it is the faculty who are the focus of our attention throughout this book.

This chapter first reviews all six of the ideal academic virtues and what makes some of them hard to achieve, including constraints on our ability to judge or evaluate "merit," so critical to attaining a true meritocracy. The rest of this book concentrates on the last two ideals: meritocracy and inclusion. It is here that institutions of higher education—despite their clear intention to live up to all of the ideals—too often fall short. And in failing to live up to those ideals, the academy makes the other ideals harder to achieve.

Although there are no longer laws against the full participation of everyone in society in the academy, we will show that actual colleges and universities can do more to approximate the ideals of meritocracy and inclusiveness with respect to faculty. The standards for merit are too vague and still too saturated with inherited or unearned qualities, like the social class of our families. Individuals from different demographic groups are still insufficiently included or rewarded when they are inside the borders of academia. Moreover, the ideals of inclusion and merit are often perceived as in tension with one another—that is, that inclusion of all groups will risk or dilute merit, and that demanding merit will require exclusion of some groups, thereby limiting inclusion.

Like most of our colleagues in academic higher education, we are firmly committed to merit as the only basis for inclusion and recognition of faculty. At the same time, we reject the notion that these two valued virtues are opposites or even in necessary tension. In short, we believe that it is possible to attain a genuinely meritocratic *and* inclusive academic world. We also recognize that higher education is substantially more meritocratic and inclusive than it once was. Our hope, in writing this book, is that we can help speed up the process of change, allowing us all to operate within institutions that are more inclusive and meritocratic in the future than they are now. That is, we hope both to show why it can be difficult to actualize our commitments to meritocracy and inclusion on the ground and to provide specific remedies for some of those difficulties.

The Academic Virtues

Search for Truth

In the ideal academic setting scholars have the time and resources to search for truths within their fields. Among scientists, developing theories that will explain how the world works is a fundamental part of that search for truth. In other fields, there may be skepticism about whether there are capital-T Truths to be discovered. But most academics in the United States would agree with some of the views expressed by the German Nobel Prize–winning novelist Hermann Hesse in his post–World War II novel *The Glass Bead Game*, or *Magister Ludi*, celebrating a well-ordered intellectual world protecting knowledge against chaos and threat. For example, he wrote,

> To sacrifice the sense of truth, intellectual probity and loyalty to the laws and methods of the spirit to any other interest is treachery. If, in the struggle of interests and slogans, truth is imperiled, devalued, mutilated and violated … then it is our duty to resist and to rescue the truth, i.e., to persist in striving after truth—the highest canon of our faith. (Hesse, 1949, p. 325)

The ideal academic setting for many is one in which striving after truth is the first and most important responsibility of scholars. In fact, Hesse excoriates the "scholar who, as an orator, author or teacher, wittingly utters falsehood and supports lies and perjuries," suggesting that such scholars are "of no use to [other] people whatever," causing them "nothing but harm" (p. 325). The ethical standards guiding many disciplines, most university research offices, and many mission statements of academic institutions explicitly or implicitly articulate the centrality of striving after truth. It is unstated, but nevertheless accurate, that the search for truth is best served by having diverse seekers; an inclusive institution would help attain this goal.

Freedom to Pursue All Ideas

Strongly related to the quest for truth is a second feature of the ideal academic setting: it is a space in which people are free to pursue *all* ideas—those that are popular and those that are unpopular, those that are familiar and those that are novel, those that are probable and those that are improbable. Robert Hutchins, the visionary and controversial president of the University of Chicago, put it this way: "The claim of academic freedom is based on the high and serious calling of the academic profession. That calling is to think. *A university is a center of independent thought*" (Hutchins, 1953, p. 87; our emphasis).

Equally, the American Association of University Professors (AAUP, 2013) states,

Academic freedom is the indispensable quality of institutions of higher education. As the AAUP's core policy statement argues, "institutions of higher education are conducted for the common good and not to further the interest of either the individual teacher or the institution as a whole. *The common good depends upon the free search for truth and its free exposition*" (1940 *Statement of Principles on Academic Freedom and Tenure*; our emphasis).

There is, then, broad agreement that academic freedom, understood as the "free search for truth and its free exposition," is an essential academic virtue. It is clear both that institutions must better explain why this is so important to the public, and that real tests of academic freedom arise when institutions are more inclusive.

Respect for Knowledge and Expertise
In ideal academic institutions expert knowledge is valued and respected by both students and faculty. In her autobiography, Supreme Court Justice Sonia Sotomayor (2013) recalled feelings of respect and reverence for knowledge as she described her reactions as a new student to Princeton University's library:

I reveled in the vastness of the main catalog room, riffling through the drawers full of cards, rows and rows of cabinets running almost the length of the ground floor. And above them, like cathedral spires, rose the stacks, shelf after shelf, carrying a book for every card below, books ranging in subject from the majestic to the comically arcane. Here, in one of the world's greatest libraries, was my first exposure to the true breadth of human knowledge, the humbling immensity of what was known and thought.... (pp. 128–129)

Jonathan Cole, a professor and former provost at Columbia University, expressed similar feelings about Columbia College:

Traversing the tree-lined Columbia Walk, I thought of George Santayana's possibly apocryphal observation that when he walked the...campus he felt in the company of great minds. There was something inspiring about looking up at the façade of Butler Library and seeing carved in stone the names of Homer, Sophocles, Plato, Aristotle, Cicero, and Virgil, and those of Shakespeare, Milton, and Goethe, among many others whose work we would read in Columbia's required Humanities course. (Cole, 2016, p. ix)

Few would question that a deep respect for the "humbling immensity of what was known and thought" is at the core of academic institutions and must be preserved. At the same time, anxiety about the value of what Sotomayor characterizes as "comically arcane" research is almost always near the surface of statements valuing "majestic" knowledge and expertise. As a crucial counterpoint to this anxiety, Hanna Gray, a recent President of the University of Chicago, points out that *unquestioning* acceptance of traditional knowledge is not implied by the valuing of expertise in the contemporary university. Instead, there is a "focus on scholarly investigation and discovery, a wide embrace of all the emerging and newly created fields of knowledge…." (Gray, 2012, p. 43).

Legislatures also frequently comment on what seems to them to be arcane and unimportant intellectual pursuits, thereby questioning whether it makes sense to "respect expertise" that does not make intuitive sense to those outside of academic institutions. Part of respecting expertise and valuing truth and knowledge for its own sake includes understanding that people cannot predict ahead of time what might turn out to be an important discovery, and that we must protect the ability of scholars to pursue ideas that may seem improbable but *might* provide a crucial key to our understanding. Another part of valuing truth and knowledge is accepting that it is difficult to determine, in fields outside one's specialty, whether a particular line of research is promising.

Finally, all researchers know that even dead ends often teach the field something. It can be difficult to make these larger points within academia as well as outside it, but an important component of the system of higher education in the United States and other countries with similar systems is commitment to the free and open pursuit and exchange of ideas, with reviews by one's peers providing some constraints on the wildness of our speculations. Clearly these values are best served when the faculty is inclusive of a wide range of kinds of knowledge and expertise.

Embrace of Creativity and Innovation

Today's ideal academic institution embraces creativity and innovation as much as it respects a secure grounding in past understanding. Hesse's vision included the idea that "we may under certain circumstances also be innovators, discoverers, adventurers, pioneers, and interpreters" (p. 324). As Gray argues, exposure to the liberal arts in the university is "liberating" because it frees

the mind from unexamined opinions and assumptions to think independently and exercise critical judgment, to question conventional doctrines and inherited claims to truth, to gain some skill in analysis and some capacity to deal with complexity, to embrace a certain skepticism in the face of dogma, and to be open to many points of view. (Gray, 2012, p. 43)

Students and faculty in all academic institutions are expected, then, both to respect acquired knowledge and to value the intellectual skills and gifts that enable individuals to challenge existing beliefs and develop truly new ideas and understanding. In chapter 2 we will see that creativity and innovation are fostered by inclusive diversity.

Merit

In the ideal college or university, success is a function solely of someone's capacity and desire to do the work. Hesse's (1949) vision here is apt: "[A]ll the students, irrespective of descent and prospects, are on a completely equal footing: the hierarchy is graded entirely according to the aptitudes and qualities of the students, in respect of intellect and character" (p. 101). This meritocratic ideal posits that demonstrated "merit" (here, the aptitudes and qualities of the student), rather than inherited position or wealth, determines academic value. Admissions policies that emphasize evidence of past learning and the capacity for further intellectual growth reflect this meritocratic ideal, as do tenure and promotion policies that rely on evidence of intellectual accomplishment in teaching and research.

Nevertheless, colleges and universities have never been and are not now entirely meritocratic, either in the admission of students or in the selection and promotion of faculty (see Clark Kerr, 1963/2001). For example, many institutions give an advantage in admissions to students whose parents or other relatives are alumni; such legacy students are viewed in admissions as having a special kind of "merit" that students from different kinds of families cannot access or demonstrate. Similarly, many faculty members prefer to hire colleagues with credentials from prestigious institutions, independent of their other qualifications (Karabel, 2005). Although faculty tend to think that merit is in one way like obscenity in the mind of Supreme Court Justice Potter Stewart (*Jacobellis v. Ohio*, 1964)—they know it when they see it—there are frequent debates about what counts as merit. In later chapters we will consider the importance of the vagueness around our definitions of merit in enabling us to act on irrelevant preferences rather than judgments of merit. Although it is difficult to ensure that our academic institutions are truly meritocratic, that commitment is central to the ideal vision.

Inclusiveness

Finally, and tightly related to the ideal of meritocracy, is the notion that academic institutions should be inclusive. That is, membership on the faculty or in the student body should not be reserved, as it once was, to a single group, whether defined by gender, race or ethnicity, religion, economic means, those without disabilities, or other personal characteristics. Instead, our ideal academic institutions are open to everyone and should include a wide range of kinds of people who share only their quest for knowledge and commitment to pursuing truth, creativity and innovation, and the other virtues of higher education. Jonathan Cole, while admiring Columbia's scholarly seriousness, also notes who was not present in his class of 600: "When I entered the college [in 1960], there were no women (Barnard was the women's college at Columbia), only two African Americans—both talented academics and athletes—and no Hispanics in my class."

In later years all institutions of higher education in the United States were challenged to be more inclusive. As Richard Rodriguez wrote, "When educators promised to open their schools [to those previously excluded], it was partly because they couldn't imagine another response; *their schools were rooted in the belief that higher education should be available to all*" (Rodriguez, 1981, p. 154; our emphasis).

Most people agree that the ideal college or university should not resemble the original institutions of higher education in America that refused to consider admission of women and other groups as a categorical matter. Women and advocates for women's education had to fight for the notion that women should be able to demonstrate that they had the qualities of mind and knowledge that suited them for higher education. The "junior girls" of 1876 wrote a poignant letter to their successors 100 years later at the University of Michigan, expressing

[o]ur hope that the next Centennial may find in our University a larger band of girls than we: wiser for all the progress which the world will make in these hundred years to come, but still as enthusiastic and earnest as we are to whom the admission of women to colleges is a new thing and for whom it required some heroism to enter upon a university course. (Farrand & Marston, 1876)

Just as women were only grudgingly admitted to higher education, racial and ethnic minorities faced many obstacles to higher education, perhaps stemming in the United States from the spirit of pre–Civil War laws that prohibited teaching slaves how to read and write. In the wake of slave rebellions, several states passed laws fining those who might teach slaves to read and write, tacitly acknowledging the subversive potential of reading and writing. The ideal academic institution now takes a very different approach, repudiating all demographic limits on who is "fit" to be educated.

Realization of Academic Virtues

Institutions of higher education worldwide, and perhaps especially in the United States, have a great deal to be proud of, in terms of their success at living up to the six ideals we have outlined. College and university campuses remain centers of a love of the search for knowledge and understanding, of freedom to pursue all kinds of ideas and insights, of respect both for acquired expertise and knowledge and for creativity and the capacity to innovate and produce new understanding and new knowledge. Each accomplishment has also been challenged. For example, academics who supported left-wing causes were persecuted during the McCarthy era (see, e.g., Karabel, 2005; Schrecker, 1986). The sixties and seventies saw demands for "relevance" (Gitlin, 1987). More recently, attempts to introduce inclusive terminology have met charges of "political correctness" (Bloom, 1987; Friedman & Narveson, 1995). Each change must be articulated and supported by evidence and argument in every generation of faculty, students, and administrators. In the main, we believe that most faculty and most students experience colleges and universities as living up to these ideals—especially the first four—more often than not. And we concur.

How and Why We Fall Short of Our Ideals

Differential Access and Failures of Inclusion

We know that higher education is not equally available to everyone who could benefit from it, and we know that some people who have access to it are sometimes alienated by it. Differential access, differential inclusion, and differential benefits have been documented over and over for both faculty and students, despite our best intentions and the progress we have made (Bowen & Bok, 1998; Chesler, Lewis, & Crowfoot, 2005; Fryberg & Martinez, 2014a; Gutiérrez y Muhs, Flores Niemann, González, & Harris, 2012; Karabel, 2005). For example, 60% of the American high school sophomores in 2002 who came from the top socioeconomic quartile of families earned college degrees by 2012, compared to only 14% of the sophomores raised in families in the bottom quartile, and to only 29% of those in the middle two quartiles (Bowen & McPherson, 2016, pp. 37–38).

Further, even if we limit the analysis to those students who *begin* a course of study at four-year colleges and universities, college completion within six years is accomplished by only 27% of those students whose parents did not attend college, while the completion rate is 42% for those students whose parents did (DeAngelo, Franke, Hurtado, Pryor, & Tran, 2011). There are parallel differences by race and ethnicity. For example, over 40% of White and Asian American first-year students completed college in six years, while only 26% of Latinos, 21% of African Americans, and 17% of Native Americans did. As we will see in detail in later chapters of this book, the same kinds of patterns apply to faculty: women, racial and ethnic minorities, and other groups do not advance to faculty positions in numbers proportionate to their presence in the population, or even among those with substantial higher education. Why do some groups of students and faculty have better educational outcomes than others?

The Problem of Belonging

One might imagine that not entering the institutions is one problem, and not completing a degree is another. Both problems are the result of many factors we will explore, but both are exacerbated by the sense of "not belonging" that some individuals expect to experience in those institutions, and actually do experience if they get to them. Certain kinds of students anticipate that they will fit in when they get to college: students whose families have attended college in the past and whose life experiences before higher education suggested to them that they have a right to be in educational settings. First-generation college students, students from poor and working-class families, racial-ethnic minorities, some women, students with disabilities, and immigrants are all less likely to have experiences that lead them to expect to fit in, or to actually fit in, at these institutions. And members of those groups are then less likely to become members of the faculty in those same institutions. When we differentially exclude groups from participating as students, we set up a situation that will also exclude them as faculty.

One powerful account of feeling like an "outsider" as a student is provided by an Asian American immigrant to the United States (quoted in Xiong & Tatum, 1999). The experience of not belonging is what is meant when people talk about the importance not only of "access" (the door is open), but of "inclusion" (a sense of full participation and belonging). Mai's story shows how important experiences of not belonging and exclusion— including observing the even greater exclusion of others—can be:

I was one of a few Asian students in my school for a long time. And then there were more and more Hmong refugees coming in…. But during that time, my English was getting better and their English was still different from mine…. So my classmates distinguished the difference between [my cousins] and me. Even though they discriminated against me, it was a different kind of discrimination that they had against my cousins…. I thought if they hate me why do they hate my cousins more? (p. 234)

This student, Mai, struggled in high school. She said,

I knew I could do better in school. I just had so many questions and just never felt comfortable. I mean now I understand…. you never had Asian American studies and I always thought, "why aren't we in the book?" …I just always felt uneasy…. And when we studied world history we never got to Laos and I just felt really bad about it. So I just had a very difficult time. (p. 235)

Interestingly, Mai did go to college, and there she found some help:

I met professors who were activists…. And I was really inspired by that…and then learning about race issues in this country. And all that made sense to me…. Now there are words for how I was feeling…. Before I was just feeling things and I didn't have any words to describe it. (p. 237)

In the end, although Mai articulates how little she felt she belonged, she also points out that education was a powerful tool that helped her articulate her experience better. Thus, this is in part a story of how higher education can be successful and can provide people with solutions to their problems. But it also points to some of the structures and processes that make it hard for that success to happen for everyone.

Social Stratification and Access

As both the data we have outlined and Mai's story show, the larger U.S. population is itself not merely diverse and heterogeneous, but is also stratified in terms of gender, race and ethnicity, social class, immigration status, disability status, and other forms of privilege and disadvantage that map onto the acquisition of the kind of expertise that is necessary to gain access to higher education. This broader social stratification means that some groups have more rapid, automatic, and complete access to information and other forms of social capital that help create a meritorious record, and hence have a greater likelihood of inclusion in selective institutions. Because social capital is accumulated beginning early in life and throughout every life stage, unequal distribution of resources tends to be replicated across generations despite the reality of some social mobility for some individuals. Thus, structures of sex segregation in the workplace (Blau, Gielen, & Zimmerman, 2012; Kmec, McDonald, & Trimble, 2010; Roth, 2004), of residential and educational racial-ethnic segregation (Reskin, 2012), and of income and wealth inequality (Reardon & Bischoff, 2011) are all reproduced in every generation (Smeeding, Erikson, & Jäntti, 2011).

These larger social structures create unequal access to the high-quality preschools and primary and secondary educations (to say nothing of world travel, art, music and language lessons, and leadership opportunities) that are prerequisites to higher education and the broad range of career choices associated with that education (Alon, 2009; Borman & Dowling, 2010; Mayer, 2010).

Richard Rodriguez (1981) famously criticized practices he felt were inaccurately labeled as "affirmative action" because they ignored the requirement that affirmative action should only be taken when individuals are qualified for a given position or admission, and because they failed to address appropriate attention to class and race-based inequalities in preparation. He argued that this institutionalized inattention to inequities in students' actual situation—despite recognition of those students' potential—constituted cruelty:

The conspiracy of kindness [among well-intentioned faculty and administrators] became a conspiracy of uncaring. Cruelly, callously, admissions committees agreed to overlook serious academic deficiency.... [A]mong those students with very poor academic preparation, few completed their courses. Many dropped out, most blaming themselves for their failure. One fall, six nonwhite students I knew suffered severe mental collapse. None of the professors who had welcomed them to graduate school were around when it came time to take them to the infirmary or to the airport. And the university officials who so diligently took note of those students in their self-serving totals of entering minority students finally took no note of them when they left. (pp. 154–155)

There is, then, no substitute for serious attention to the unequal preschool, primary, and secondary educational systems that left Mai feeling she didn't belong and couldn't succeed, despite her talent and eagerness to learn. Higher education cannot rapidly or easily rectify the inequalities in preparation that are the result of earlier inequities in schooling. It can, however, get better at recognizing talent when it presents itself in people who have not had certain kinds of advantages that are indicators of relative prosperity and privilege rather than the capacity to learn. It can also take steps to reduce the likelihood that students feel that the inequities in their background education and exposure render them unsuitable for educational opportunities and can never be overcome or addressed.

Impact of Social Stratification on Academic Experience
Many of the practices of de facto segregation by gender, race and ethnicity, and social class are replicated within all educational institutions, making it less likely that students will aim to be included in colleges and universities, and less likely that they will feel accepted if they do get there. For example, the phenomenon of relatively low teacher, parent, and peer expectations held for girls in math and science (Eccles, 2011), and for African Americans in school more generally, depresses academic performance, beginning at an early age (Diamond, Randolph, & Spillane, 2004).

Students who internalize low expectations often fear that others will view them through the lens of those expectations. That anxiety interferes with their performance, creating a vicious cycle of anxiety, lower performance, confirmation that they are not talented, and lesser confidence (Steele, 2011). These phenomena help ensure that school is widely perceived as a domain for Whites and Asians/Asian Americans, and math and science as reserved for White and Asian/Asian American men, while athletics are reserved for African American men.

Justice Sotomayor outlined the corrosive effect of these expectations for her and other Latino students at Princeton:

The Daily Princetonian routinely published letters to the editor lamenting the presence on campus of "affirmative action students," each one of whom had presumably displaced a far more deserving affluent white male and could be expected to crash into the gutter built of her own unrealistic aspirations. There were vultures circling, ready to dive when we stumbled. The pressure to succeed was relentless, even if self-imposed out of fear and insecurity. For we all felt if we did fail, we would be proving the critics right, and the doors that had opened a crack to let us in would be slammed shut again. (p. 145)

Contrast her account of feeling under surveillance, and not belonging, with the recollection of American playwright Arthur Miller (1953) when he attended the University of Michigan in the 1930s. Miller came from an east coast family of modest means and had a weak academic record ("I had flunked algebra three times in my Brooklyn high school." [p. 68]). Some combination of his personal drive and confidence, and perhaps his status as a White man, led him to apply to the university *three times* (overcoming two rejections), despite that record. Once he got there, he felt he was in the right place. He wrote that he found himself very much "at home":

I loved the place...because it was just big enough to give one the feeling that his relative mediocrity had real meaning, and yet not so big as to drown one in numbers.... It was a little world and it was man-sized. My friends were the sons of die-makers, farmers, ranchers, bankers, lawyers, doctors, clothing workers, and unemployed relief recipients." (p. 70)

Miller viewed the world he found at Michigan as diverse, felt he fit in, and didn't particularly miss the presence (for example) of women at the University. In contrast, Mai didn't feel "at home." But it was enormously helpful to her to learn how to articulate and understand her experience, and she was lucky to find professors in college who helped and inspired her, after years of having teachers who made her feel left out.

Impact of Social Stratification on De Facto Segregation
Other practices—like the tendency for groups to form around social identities—lead to segregation in the lunchroom, at recess, in study halls, and in locker rooms by race and ethnicity and gender, thereby limiting

cross-group contact (Chesler, Lewis, & Crowfoot, 2005; Tatum, 2003). Add to that the well-known practice of "tracking" in U.S. public schools, which starts ever-earlier in a child's school experience, and the likelihood that even children attending "diverse" schools will ever really know children quite different from themselves is very low (Mickelson & Everett, 2008).

Within universities, we see the same patterns of group-based segregation of activities, and, even more problematic, differential distribution into fields by gender and race and ethnicity of both faculty and students. Though some argue that "preference" dictates some of these differential patterns, some fields with very similar academic content (e.g., nursing and premedicine) nevertheless show quite different patterns of "choice" by men and women. We discuss choice at greater length in later chapters.

Impact of Social Stratification on "Role Models"

Social science evidence makes clear that students' choices are constrained by what they have observed as possible in the world and by what others encourage them to be, as well as by their own talents, interests, and accomplishments (Eccles, 2011). As Supreme Court Justice Sotomayor pointed out,

> When a young person, even a gifted one, grows up without proximate living examples of what she may aspire to become—whether lawyer, scientist, artist, or leader in any realm—her goal remains abstract. Such models as appear in books or on the news, however inspiring or revered, are ultimately too remote to be real, let alone influential. But a role model in the flesh provides more than an inspiration; his or her very existence is confirmation of possibilities one may have every reason to doubt, saying, "Yes, someone like me can do this." (p. 178)

Dasgupta (2011) has labeled this phenomenon "stereotype inoculation" and argues that the presence of experts who come from your social group and affirm your talent inoculates you against the group-based stereotype that people like you cannot do well in that field. Consistent with this idea, women in a political psychology class were more likely to view women, and themselves, as potential leaders if they participated in sections where examples of women leaders were included along with examples of men, rather than in sections with the conventional nearly exclusive focus on the activities of men leaders (Rios, Stewart, & Winter, 2010).

One of us read books as a child in a series on the childhoods of famous Americans. Her parents bought her these books, which included both women and men. The other was often encouraged by her mother to complete school assignments like "write about a great New Yorker" by learning about an accomplished woman. Those experiences probably contributed to our belief that we could aspire to an education and life that our parents had not had.

Gender, racial and ethnic, and class segregation also operate across generations. Mentors and teachers are most likely to encourage and support children who appear to fit their ideas about who is academically successful (Rosenthal, 1992). This tendency leads to the development of "old boys' networks" known to underlie the far greater social capital of some (usually White male) students who attended prestigious undergraduate institutions (Dutton, Ashford, Lawrence, & Miner-Rubino, 2002; Gamba & Kleiner, 2001). Teachers and mentors, sometimes without even knowing they are doing it, elevate those students' chances over others' by calling on their networks of connections on their behalf. Interestingly, some academic practices (like issuing formal job advertisements) arose as higher education became somewhat more diverse. As a result, the reliance on old boys' networks has been reduced.

When women, minorities, first-generation college students, and students with disabilities rarely see faculty like them in front of the classroom, it is not unreasonable for them to conclude that they are unlikely to end up there themselves. Indeed, in a rare experimental study of the impact of taking an introductory math course from a female versus a male instructor, researchers were able to randomly assign men and women to particular sections (Carrell, Page, & West, 2010). They found not only that women were more likely subsequently to take more math courses if they had a female instructor, and were more likely to major in math or science fields, but that men were unaffected by the gender of the instructor. Thus, for the women students this early exposure to a situation in which they could see themselves made a big difference, and it did not harm the men, who presumably were not in doubt.

Similarly, when the overwhelming majority of people whose work is discussed in courses, or whose achievements are mentioned, are affluent White men, it is easy for everyone (faculty and students of all backgrounds) to conclude that the stratification of accomplishment by gender, race, and class that they observe is inevitable and "natural," rather than the result of certain social processes.

Naturalization of the Status Quo and Belonging

The combination of forces that we have just described results in "naturalization of the status quo." That is, it leads some people to believe that the current situation arose "naturally," that they have "a place" that is preordained, and that their job in school is to prepare to take up that place. It also leads both the privileged and their less privileged counterparts to believe that other groups do not particularly fit in or "belong" in that place. Considerable research demonstrates the powerful impact of the feeling of "belonging" or "not belonging" on students' and faculty members' capacity to thrive in our institutions (Dasgupta, 2011; Ostrove, Stewart, & Curtin, 2011; Walton & Carr, 2012; Walton & Cohen, 2007).

One ingenious study created an intervention designed to increase students' feelings of belonging on a selective college campus (Walton & Cohen, 2011). Students read survey data indicating that uncertainty about belonging was common and short-lived at that campus. The students then wrote and orally presented an essay in which they described their own experiences pertaining to that evidence. As predicted, African American students were deeply affected by this intervention, showing not only a greater sense of belonging three years later, but also a significantly higher grade point average than comparable control students. In contrast, there were no effects for European American students exposed to this intervention, presumably because the issue of belonging was much less salient and fraught for them.

It is impressive that this relatively brief and modest intervention made such a difference, but evidence also shows that even the inanimate objects in an environment can signal either that you belong or that you don't. In a remarkably straightforward study, psychologists found that substituting "neutral" objects in a classroom (a nature poster, phone books) for objects that were stereotypically associated with men (a Star Trek poster, video games) shifted women's interest in computer science from well below men's to equal (Cheryan, Plaut, Davies, & Steele 2009). In the presence of cues of "ambient belonging," the women developed an interest in this masculine stereotyped field that they did not develop in the absence of those cues. Male students were unaffected by the different cues. Colleges and universities are filled with cues that some students and faculty belong—in general and in particular places—while others do not. Crucially, those who feel they do belong rarely even notice them. We will return to this issue in later chapters.

Naturalization of the status quo—the creation of expectations that the academic world is and always will be dominated by certain kinds of people—in turn leads to unintentional reproduction of that very status quo. The tendency toward institutional inertia—that things remain as they are rather than changing—is very strong in the absence of a compelling pressure or reason for change. As noted above, the presence of a more heterogeneous student population motivated substantial changes in higher education. In describing the history of America's flagship public universities, Tobin (2009) noted,

As universities actively recruited women, Blacks, Hispanics, Asians and other ethnic minorities, faculties responded with the introduction of multi-disciplinary courses in African American, women's and ethnic studies. Institutions responded to the growth of undergraduate enrollments with support services to address the needs of first-generation college-goers and students from disadvantaged backgrounds. (p. 258)

Thus, changes in the student body resulted in changes in academic institutions: in their curricula and the services they offered (see Stockdill & Danico, 2012). And, of course, a different curriculum requires a different faculty. So there has been change in the demographic makeup of the American professoriate: slower than the change in the student body, but change nonetheless.

The increase in inclusiveness and breadth of opportunity shows that change has happened and therefore is entirely possible. But the progress has been slow, and that slow development can be (incorrectly) taken as evidence that faculty of color and faculty from other traditionally excluded groups have yet to demonstrate their excellence (Fryberg & Martinez, 2014b). The implication is that the slow rate of change is the result of deficiencies in those most subject to exclusion rather than due to institutional features that discourage and devalue those individuals. As such, talk of "slow progress" can demoralize the very people who already feel marginal in the institution.

Making matters worse is that the hopeful message of slowly increasing diversity in faculty demographics in universities is often undermined with a not-so-subtle suggestion that excellence may be at risk if change were to happen more quickly. This false opposition of diversity and excellence is not only a brake on motivation for change among the dominant groups in academic institutions, but it erodes the sense of belonging and institutional value among those who represent "diversity" (see also Sekaquaptewa, 2014).

Individuals and Institutional Structures

In this book, as in the accounts we have offered to this point, we will focus on this perceived tension between meritocracy and inclusion, a tension that can slow change in realizing the ideals of meritocracy and inclusion and result in the wide variation we see in how inclusive different institutions actually are. In examining how this tension has become so important in slowing change, we will examine two broad kinds of factors: features of human psychology that make it difficult for us as *individuals* to make good judgments of merit and to be inclusive and features of our *institutions* that reflect and even exaggerate those human frailties, giving them greater force through convention and policy. Although we use the term "institution," we use it broadly, to include those institutional features that may attach not only to an entire college or university but also to a department, committee, research center, laboratory, or other unit within a larger institution.

It is sobering to recognize that there are important internal individual and external institutional obstacles to achieving our ideal academic institutions, and that both kinds of obstacles enhance the view that two of our cherished academic virtues are mutually exclusive. However, we believe that examining the power of the perceived tension between two valued goals will help motivate us to adopt new practices and policies that both mitigate some unfortunate psychological tendencies *and* avoid setting them in institutional stone. In short, our experience has made us optimistic that change in institutions' policies and procedures to make them more inclusive is possible.

Judging Merit: Critical to Meritocracy

As just outlined, we argue that there is an important and unrecognized role for flawed, error-prone cognitive processes in the many evaluations, or judgments of merit, that are at the center of our academic institutions. We will describe these individual psychological processes and their impact throughout this book.

If these processes are indeed flawed in systematic ways, then the fact that our institutions are not strict meritocracies is the result not only of individual psychological processes, but of the institutionalized acceptance and solidification of those processes. In the second part of this book we argue that flawed individual judgments are at the core of college and university processes of hiring and promotion of faculty, as of admission and graduation of students. Those judgments are structured into our selections and into our reward systems at every level of the institution. We do not claim that either individual judgment or institutional process is "primary"; both operate and they reinforce each other.

We need, then, to begin by thinking about both how the judgments are made and what problems might arise in making them. We also need to understand how those flawed judgments are structured into our institutions in ways that create, cement, and reproduce inequities instead of ensuring what we're after: merit. Once we have examined the individual judgment processes that are a part of our assessments of merit, as well as the obstacles to inclusiveness, we will turn to institutional processes that establish, reflect, and enhance them.

In admitting students and hiring faculty, evaluating them at transition points, and promoting and advancing them, over and over we judge their work. We judge individual products and overall records of accomplishment. When we make these gatekeeping judgments, we are generally quite confident that we know excellence when we see it, and that our estimates of excellence are reliable and accurate (Thorngate, Dawes, & Foddy, 2009). Subjectively, we rarely doubt our capacity to separate wheat from chaff in the domain of academic achievement.

One academic told ethnographer Michèle Lamont that there was no need for "special training" for people to do peer review, because "It's the kind of stuff we do all our lives. Teaching, criticizing other people's work, reading articles for courses…. I mean, all we do is criticize and pick apart people's arguments…" (Lamont, 2009, p. 44). As this faculty member points out implicitly, faculty members' subjective confidence grows over the course of a career. In our experience, new faculty often feel less certain than more experienced ones about what an "A" paper looks like when compared with a "B" and also feel less certain than senior colleagues about which job candidates meet "our standards." But senior faculty grow ever more certain of their ability to make accurate evaluations.

Cognitive psychologist Daniel Kahneman pointed out that experts are very confident of their opinions (and academics are experts in our fields), but that expert intuition is not always reliable. Specifically, expertise "works" intuitively (to make accurate, quick, nondeliberative judgments) when the expert has had a chance to learn about errors in a "high-validity" environment—that is, when the expert gets rapid feedback about the correctness or incorrectness of the judgment.

Kahneman contrasts anesthesiology and radiology. When a patient is in surgery, there is rapid feedback from the various instruments that monitor the patient's body's responses about whether dosage and delivery of anesthesia are going well. In contrast, in radiology, the accuracy of interpretation of images may never be assessed in the form of feedback to the radiologist (Kahneman, 2011, chapter 22). We suggest that faculty predictions about job candidates' long-term success are rarely evaluated in terms of actual long-term outcomes. Searching for colleagues is more like radiology than anesthesiology in this respect.

The evidence from students of cognition like Kahneman is that our confidence is unrelated to our accuracy. All human beings, including academic faculty and administrators, are prone to some common kinds of errors in making judgments. At the same time, our extensive academic training and experience build our confidence and make it very unlikely that we will worry about those potential errors or take steps to overcome the well-known but faulty conclusions we are prone to drawing.

Kahneman suggested not only that "we are often confident when we are wrong," but that we can "improve the ability to identify and understand errors of judgment and choice, in others and eventually in ourselves, by providing a richer and more precise language to discuss them." He suggests that "an accurate diagnosis may suggest an intervention to limit the damage that bad judgments and choices often cause" (Kahneman, 2011, p. 4). We provide a brief outline of Kahneman's three paradigmatic kinds of errors in order to examine how they may be crucial elements blocking the attainment of the truly ideal university we seek (see also Nisbett & Ross, 1980; Thorngate, Dawes, & Foddy, 2009, for other accounts of how difficult it is for us to judge merit accurately).

Decision-making Strategies

Some key experience-based strategies we use for solving problems and making decisions (sometimes called *heuristics* in the literature) were first identified in Tversky and Kahneman's (1974) paper about making judgments under conditions of uncertainty. They pointed out then, and decades of research cited in Kahneman's book have confirmed, that these strategies enable us to convert complex decision-making tasks into relatively simple judgments—judgments that reflect "thinking fast" or in a relatively non-deliberative manner. As Kahneman notes, the problem is that "these heuristics [or strategies for making judgments] are quite useful, but sometimes they lead to severe and systematic errors" (p. 419). The three key strategies rely on *representativeness, availability*, and *anchoring and adjustment*. Each strategy is both useful and dangerous in the core processes of evaluating faculty and students in the academy.

It is important to note that the strategies we will discuss apply to our estimates of the likely weather, of the riskiness of a drive along a highway without a guardrail, and of how many marbles are in a jar, as much as they apply to our judgments of other people. They are used not because we are motivated to make bad decisions about people, but because we are motivated to make lots of different kinds of rapid decisions based on the evidence at hand—not to spend too much time on judgments that must be rapid, or may not be consequential, or in which we cannot easily obtain further evidence. Moreover, we don't keep a running tally of our judgments in order to assess how accurate they were in retrospect. As a result, we can mistakenly rely on such strategies under conditions that *are* consequential and where they can lead to seriously biased outcomes. These outcomes then contribute to a highly stratified status quo that is experienced as natural and as reflecting some kind of underlying true merit.

Representativeness

We use the *representativeness* strategy when faced with a decision about whether an individual (person or event) belongs in a particular group. It comes up when intelligence professionals try to decide how likely it is that a particular person is a terrorist, or when we try to decide whether a new neighbor is likely to become a friend, or (more relevantly for our purposes) when faculty try to decide whether a young scholar is likely to be a productive and collegial colleague. In making these decisions, we are in effect estimating the probability of a particular outcome, and it may make a difference—though we rarely think about it—to consider how common that outcome is. If the outcome is quite common, then the probability that *anyone* will have that outcome is inevitably higher than if the outcome is quite rare.

How might this matter in judgments of faculty who are applying for a job or of students applying for admission? First, evaluators rating applications do not consider, generally, the frequency of a given outcome in the pool as relevant. Thus, in a pool of applicants for a position or in a pool of students for admission, we might ask first *how many of the people within that pool will become successful students or faculty somewhere, or at schools that are our peers?* It could be that only a few will be successful, in which case our careful consideration of whom to admit is appropriate and leads us to find the few "good ones" in the pool. However, it also could be that most of the applicants will be successful, and we are simply choosing from a pool that is very talented, in which most people will succeed. This is actually an empirically answerable question about our past pools of faculty applicants. But to our knowledge search and admissions committees do not generally begin with an expectation about how many people in the pool are likely to meet their standards, based on past outcomes.

If we learned that everyone that we considered seriously for a faculty position (i.e., that we "short-listed") over the past ten years actually became successful in the field, we might wonder if our criteria for choosing the one person we chose really mattered.[1] Instead, we move immediately to the question of evidence in the record that the individual is similar to our idea of a successful faculty member (or is "representative" of a category we are interested in). When we do that, it is clear that one critical question is whether the evidence in the record is actually good evidence for making the judgment at hand or, as in Tversky and Kahneman's examples, poor evidence that we nevertheless use simply because we have it. As we will see, to a surprising degree we rely on evidence that is not particularly good when we hire faculty—evidence that reflects institutional structures that are highly stratified, segregated, and the result of differential access.

Research has shown that when we move to considering "evidence," we rely heavily on *representativeness*, or the degree to which a person appears to us to be similar to existing members of the relevant category (terrorists, friends, successful faculty). On the face of it, that seems logical. If the person shares characteristics of other members of a category, then the person must belong (or could belong) in that category. But in fact, as Kahneman details, similarity is not a particularly good predictor of probability, even though people heavily rely on it. Thus, for example, if most faculty in my department got their PhDs at a particular institution (and this is indeed common in higher education), I could conclude that getting a degree at that institution is an appropriate criterion for assessing whether a candidate would make a good scholar/colleague. Obviously, some people trained at that institution might, but many people trained at other institutions also might. The fact that a person is similar to the people who are currently in my department in terms of that background may be reasonable evidence that they are likely to be successful in my department, but it is *not* good evidence that they will be more successful than people who have different training. I may draw that conclusion, anyway, in part because that criterion has become associated in my mind with that outcome, and I've lost track of the way in which it is a function of differential access and stratification processes, among other irrelevant factors.

Interestingly, when people are asked to make predictions about near-term success and more remote success, they tend to make identical predictions, based on the similarity of the outcome to a single current indicator (e.g., representativeness), even though the predictability of remote success from any current indicator is much lower than near-term success. Thus, the presence of a current record of having published research is a pretty good predictor of the likelihood of publishing more research next year, but is a less good predictor of whether the person will accumulate a tenure-worthy record several or many years from now. When events are far in the future—for example, the several years until a tenure decision—many factors will have contributed to someone's publication record, including events in both their personal and professional lives (will their parents or partners suffer illnesses or death? will they confront health challenges? will they pursue a novel line of research that gains acceptance only slowly or stick with the mainstream, contributing uncontroversial scholarship?) and in their lives in their institution (how rapidly their laboratory is built, whether they have collaborators or mentors who are supportive, whether their department is riven by factions, etc.).

Some departments focus on trying to predict outstanding accomplishments, like entrance into a national academy, or winning rare awards for exceptional achievement. Many people accumulate tenure-worthy records and indeed attain tenure. Only a few are ever awarded Nobel Prizes. Basing the prediction of common (tenure) or rare (outstanding prizes won) outcomes on the same data is clearly faulty reasoning.

We are also often misled by the illusion of the validity of the predictions we make based on faulty application of strategies. This arises because of our confidence in the apparent fit between current performance (inputs such as number of publications or presence of publications in first-tier journals) and the hoped-for outcome (tenure worthiness or outstanding accomplishment 6 or 20 years from now). Exacerbating our reliance on poor evidence is our tendency to rely on redundant pieces of evidence (several good publications) rather than pieces of evidence from independent domains (e.g., good publications, impressive service, reports of good teaching), which produce higher quality predictions.

In this case, if we think that an important criterion for getting tenure is publishing in a particular journal in our field, then it may appear to make sense to assume that someone who has "already" (while in graduate school or a postdoc) published in that journal is a better bet for tenure than someone who has not yet published in that journal. But perhaps the person's advisor was really the driving force behind the prestigious journal acceptance for one person, and another has not yet submitted a paper to such a journal but is building a strong research program that in fact will be publishable in that journal soon.

Equally plausibly, perhaps the individual's research program is not particularly well suited to publication in that journal in the field. However, if we only assess the journal in terms of its "merit" (i.e., its quality), we may fail to notice that it has different standards for different areas of research. It may use one set for assessing research in areas already seen as important in the field because many senior people in the field work in that area and use another set for research in newly emerging fields in which women and racial-ethnic minority scholars may be interested. Seeing some similarity between someone's current performance on a particular indicator and the outcome desired in the future is actually *not* a solid basis for prediction of future outcomes, but sometimes it feels like it is to us. Thus, if all of the tenured faculty in our department had published in the flagship journal of the discipline before tenure, that does not mean that every future faculty member must publish in that journal in order to get tenure, especially if we hire people whose work crosses interdisciplinary boundaries or breaks new ground. In short, our practice of relying on various forms of representativeness in making judgments leads us to risk low accuracy in our judgments.

Availability

Let us imagine that one of the job applicants in a pile of applications is Native American. If my field is Native American Studies, then I can think of quite a few Native American scholars. If my field is Classics, I may never have met a Native American scholar in my field, so it may be difficult for me to think of any exemplar of the category Classical Scholar who has a Native American background. In this case, because of the differential distribution of scholars with particular backgrounds in various disciplines, as well as the highly differentiated nature of our social networks (we tend to know people "like us" even within our fields, a phenomenon sometimes called "homophily"), *availability* of exemplars might differentially operate on our selection of faculty colleagues. Here we rely on the degree to which we can easily think of an example of an outcome (i.e., how quickly it comes to our minds or is "available"), or how easily we can think of reasons for an outcome in deciding how probable it is. Relying on availability can be sensible since more frequent events probably are often those that are more available, but it can also lead to well-documented biases or errors.

Perhaps the example of availability that is most obviously relevant to judgments of faculty candidates is familiarity, since examples that are familiar come more quickly to mind (are "available"). In addition, people estimate familiar groups to be larger than unfamiliar groups, regardless of the specific evidence they are given. Thus, we overestimate the size of groups that are familiar (White male applicants likely to be successful physicists in our pool of applicants) and underestimate the size of groups that are unfamiliar (African American female applicants likely to be successful physicists in our pool of applicants). We generalize from our own experience (familiarity) to the actual world. If we know a lot of people in a category we think there *are* a lot of people in that category. If we know few, we assume there really are few. Similarly, we overestimate the frequency of events (e.g., bombing, crime) if they have happened recently or we have recently observed them.

It is availability that is at the base of the well-known "implicit association test," which measures the speed of our associations between distinct categories (gender and math ability or leadership capacity, race and intelligence; see Banaji & Greenwald, 2013, for a popular treatment, or Greenwald, Poehlman, Uhlmann, & Banaji, 2009, for a review). The test assesses our "intuitive" or "fast" judgments, not our deliberative or slow views. When we make associations between unrelated categories rapidly—and we do that when exemplars of that association are very familiar, even if they are rare and not logically connected—we are particularly vulnerable to errors of judgment based on illusory correlation.

If these availability processes, like the representativeness processes, can lead to serious errors of judgment, why do we rely on them? Research has shown that in thinking of exemplars, and making connections or associations between two unrelated concepts (like gender and math), we rely on availability as a tool for rapid judgments. That tool, which is useful in increasing our speed and confidence, nevertheless only sometimes leads us to accurate judgments; its very speed may be part of its power to lead us astray (Kahneman, 2011, p. 427).

Adjustment and Anchoring

Whoever we finally hire in the job search becomes our colleague and is in our department for several years. At the end of a few of those years, we have an opportunity, if we are tenured faculty, to evaluate them again for tenure and promotion. When we do that, we are vulnerable to the *adjustment and anchoring* heuristic. There is strong evidence that our second judgment is very likely "anchored" by our first judgment. That is, we begin—when we are estimating someone's value as a scholar, teacher, and colleague (or their tenurability)—from a starting point and then make relatively little "adjustment" based on subsequent evidence. In the case of faculty hiring, this could also come up when a committee member believes, based on review of files, that it is a mistake to interview a candidate but goes along with the group decision to offer an interview (thus, her anchoring judgment is less favorable than others'). Even if she is influenced by the outstanding job talk to "adjust" her judgment, that adjustment will likely only be modest, anchored as it is by the first judgment, such that it is still less favorable than others'.

Fallible Cognition: How Much Harm Can It Do in Judging Merit?

If errors of judgment are common, then how problematic could they really be? Moreover, aren't faculty in colleges and universities less prone to making such errors than other people, given their extensive training in reasoning? The troubling and surprising answers to these questions, as we have seen, are that the errors are problematic not only because they are frequent, but because they are not random, and trained academic minds make errors when they are making judgments of people, perhaps more than when they are thinking about research problems. Most dangerous of all, those with specialized intellectual training and expertise have unwarranted faith in their judgments (Kahneman, 2011).

We propose that reliance on these common, but fallible, strategies leads academic evaluators to make individual judgments that are not merely inaccurate in a random way, but are inaccurate in ways that benefit the people we are used to seeing in certain roles. That is, our use of the strategies contributes to the continued presence of some kinds of people in our social environment in certain roles, and the absence of others. We are more likely to overestimate talent in people who belong to a group from whom we expect talent and to underestimate talent in people who belong to a group from whom we do not expect talent. This systematic bias in our errors means that we end up believing that we see more talent in people who have frequently been in positions of power, authority, and prestige, and less in people who have rarely been in those positions.

Thus, what appear to us to be sound judgments of individuals, based on good evidence, end up in fact being error-ridden judgments based on schemas, or ideas about groups. In this way our judgments of individuals are saturated with our expectations about groups, our own past experience, and the status quo. If unexamined, these judgments will lead us to reproduce what is: a norm of the faculty member who is White, male, at least middle-class, and likely also able-bodied and heterosexual, and a university that is most comfortable for people with those characteristics. We will outline in more detail how these common cognitive errors get in the way of evaluating individuals who come from some groups more than others. Before we turn to that issue, though, we need to consider a common set of psychological processes that impede not so much our judgments of merit, but our genuine *comfort* with diversity and *capacity* for inclusion, regardless of our avowed valuing of them.

Homophily and Diversity: Why It Can Be Difficult to Accomplish Inclusion

The cognitive strategies just reviewed operate to make us likely to base our judgments of merit on our own past experience and on the status quo in ways that will lead us systematically to overestimate merit in some and underestimate it in others. Beyond that, there is considerable evidence that people tend to associate with others who resemble them, and they expect to be more comfortable when they do. Their experience thus leads them to greater familiarity not just with *some* groups, but with their *own* group. Of course, we are members of groups defined in many different ways; according to one study, the dimensions on which resemblance is based include age, religion, education, occupation, and gender (McPherson, Smith-Lovin, & Cook, 2001), among many others.

Which similarity feature feels relevant depends on where we are and what we are doing. When we are at a conference of psychologists, our subfield "group" comes to matter. When we are in another country, people who speak English seem more like us than people who do not. When we are discussing tenure or retirement, the faculty around us who are in the same career and at the same life stage are more often the people we want to spend time with.

Such variables also influence people's long-term networks: who people's friends are, who they confide in, who they have long-term romantic relationships with, who they exchange information with, and who they collaborate with. Race and ethnicity are other variables that affect the composition of someone's network. People tend to marry others of similar age, social class, education, intelligence, and, to a lesser degree, attractiveness (see the summary in Zietsch, Verweij, Heath, & Martin, 2011).

Homophily in Academic Life

Although similar principles operate in all networks, we are concerned here with professional networks—who talks to whom within a department or school or at meetings; who chooses to work with whom; who invites whom to give a talk or be on a thesis committee. In 2002, the then dean of engineering at MIT, Thomas Magnanti, wrote in the foreword to the school's report on the status of women that part of his attraction to engineering as a child had been its promise that anyone with merit could succeed. He was disappointed to discover that, at MIT, that was not so (Boyce et al., 2002):

We learn, for example, about some of our women faculty colleagues, who despite their superb professional standing and despite the fact that they are highly valued by their faculty colleagues, have never been asked to serve on the Ph.D. committee of even one of their colleagues' students in their own research area. Stunning.

Thus, "homophily"—or a preference for people we perceive to be similar to us—is a factor limiting inclusion in networks that in turn undermines our capacity to achieve meritocracy. Two of our institutional virtues or goals—meritocracy and inclusion—are closely linked as outcomes of both similar and separate processes.

Homophily seems "natural" and inevitable. Infants prefer individuals who speak the same language or have the same accent as their primary caretakers, even before they themselves are producing or understanding speech (Kinzler, Dupoux, & Spelke, 2007). These preferences for "similarity" are, of course, learned since we are not born knowing what similarities will matter in our social worlds. For example, nine-month-olds, but not six-month-olds, show more strongly differentiated reactions to same-race than other-race stimuli (Anzures, Quinn, Pascalis, Slater, & Lee, 2010). Infants' preference for looking at faces of the same race develops as a function of familiarity; when younger infants see a mix of races in infancy they show no preference (see the review in Anzures, Quinn, Pascalis, Slater, & Lee, 2013; see also Hirschfeld, 2012). The development of same-race *preference* (independent of language) occurs even later, though before age five (Dunham, Baron, & Banaji, 2008; Kinzler & Spelke, 2011).

Although homophily is ubiquitous, the consequences of some forms of homophily are pernicious. One apparent consequence is segregation (Clark & Fossett, 2008; Schelling, 1971). Once segregation exists, it also raises the likelihood that it will increase some forms of familiarity and lessen others, thereby increasing segregation. It sets up a vicious cycle. A playable computer simulation based on Schelling's work demonstrates that even a relatively small preference on an individual's part to interact with like others will yield system-wide segregation (Hart & Case, n.d.). The simulation also demonstrates that segregation on one dimension can be reversed by exercising a relatively small preference for diversity on the same dimension. The message is clear: exercise a small preference for diversity over homophily to create a more diverse social environment. Recognition of these facts underlies affirmative action as a policy, even as it has been unevenly understood and implemented (see Walsh, 2014).

In academia, homophily, rather than a preference for diversity, can enter the picture at every point in the assessment of merit, from hiring to promotion to tenure. When members of a search committee say that a candidate is not "a good fit," they may be expressing a homophilous preference. When symposium organizers plan whom to invite to participate, homophily can limit the range of people they think of. One example of homophily at a large research-intensive university comes from a survey of male and female scientists (Belle, Smith-Doerr, & O'Brien, 2014). The men's and women's networks of colleagues were similar in size, and they reported equal resources and opportunities for collaboration. However, the networks differed in composition. Both groups had more men than women in their networks, presumably reflecting the fact that the natural sciences are male dominated; opportunity to have a gender-mixed network is limited. But men's networks had a higher proportion of men than women's networks did, and women's networks had a considerably higher proportion of women than men's networks did. The fact that women report having more women in their network than men do shows that it is possible for men to include more women. Although we know of no studies that examine homophily with respect to race or ethnicity in academia, we would expect the same phenomenon there. Again, the message is clear: if we examine the content of our networks, we are likely to observe a small homophilous preference that operates to limit their diversity, not the small preference for diversity that might lead to different outcomes.

Homophily plus Aversive Racism

As with many preferences, homophily tends to operate outside awareness. One's own racism is so painful and socially costly to acknowledge (i.e., aversive) for professionals in general and academics in particular that they will create rationales to justify their preferences that have nothing to do with race or ethnicity, even when the data suggest that ethnicity is indeed the basis for their behavior. For example, White individuals are more likely to show a preference for Whites if they have previously been in a position where they made a token gesture that indicated support for a Black person. Individuals who said that they supported Barack Obama were more likely to then say that Whites were more suitable for a job than Blacks (Effron, Cameron, & Monin, 2009; Monin & Miller, 2001). It appears that simply announcing that one is progressive gives one more license to be less progressive than if one had not made such an announcement. Self-congratulation on one's good intentions and past "progressive" actions makes one freer to act at variance with those espoused beliefs.

Further, though it is counterintuitive, people's egalitarian goals, and their beliefs that they *are* egalitarian, can lead to their making nonegalitarian choices, again without realizing that they are doing so. For example, when participants—primarily White and Asian—are given false feedback telling them that they are progressing in becoming more positive toward Blacks, they then sit further away from Black individuals and closer to

White individuals than do participants who do not receive such feedback (Mann & Kawakami, 2012). Our knowledge of our high ideals has two effects: it fools us into thinking we live up to our ideals, and it frees us to live up to them less.

When Whites are given more rationales for not helping someone, they are less likely to help Blacks than they are to help Whites (Saucier, Miller, & Doucet, 2005). If, for example, helping someone would take time or involve risk, Whites can justify not helping on those grounds. But they are more likely to invoke such grounds to avoid helping Blacks than to avoid helping Whites. And, ironically, Whites sometimes distance themselves from Blacks because they are afraid of appearing racist in an interaction (Goff, Steele, & Davies, 2008). If, however, Whites see an interaction with Blacks as an opportunity to learn, rather than as a test they might fail, they are somewhat more likely to engage in interaction (Goff et al., 2008).

It is difficult for people to be aware of all the ways in which their behavior reflects their nonconscious beliefs and attitudes. One study with White undergraduate participants in conversation with White or Black confederates found that their *explicit* (expressed and conscious) attitudes predicted their verbal behavior, but their *implicit* attitudes (those outside of their awareness but reflected in preferences and comfort level) predicted their nonverbal behavior. Explicit attitudes were measured by a set of questions the participants answered; implicit attitudes were measured by how quickly they assigned value-laden adjectives (like smart, likable, and good; or stupid, unpleasant, and bad) to White or Black faces. Independent observers who did not know whether the student had interacted with a White or Black confederate assessed behaviors such as how friendly a participant was. The participants themselves could predict their verbal behavior, but not their nonverbal behavior (Dovidio, Kawakami, & Gaertner, 2002). This is one of several experiments suggesting that aspects of behavior that are outside conscious awareness reflect beliefs and attitudes we may not only be unaware of, but dislike.

What we have learned so far suggests that our intentions, and genuine egalitarian principles, are not enough to guide our behavior. The combination of small preferences for people like us—homophily—and trust in our good intentions yields behavior that isolates or marginalizes people who are not like us and impedes our capacity to create institutions that are diverse and inclusive. The good news, though, is that we will create more diverse environments and teams—and benefit from that diversity—if we make a constant small effort in the direction of diversity and inclusion.

Overcoming Individual Tendencies That Limit Meritocracy and Inclusion

In the cases of both meritocracy and inclusion, then, we are optimistic that we can mitigate the individual limitations that can lead to undesirable outcomes and unintentionally augment preexisting inequities. Awareness about how those limitations work is an important first step, and social science research has offered abundant evidence about that.

But mere knowledge of how we misevaluate and exclude others does not lead automatically to successful avoidance of such misevaluation and exclusion. Instead, we need to identify specific practices that will buffer the errors we might otherwise make and increase our use of our best capacities. Happily, these practices can make a difference even if they are not applied in all of the judgments we make. (It is probably impossible, and not even desirable, to completely shed our faulty cognitive strategies or our tendency toward homophily.)

If we identify the key gatekeeping judgments that are consequential in determining who enters and thrives in our institutions, then we can develop policies and practices that improve our judgments and limit the operation of our homophilous tendencies in creating the climate and culture of institutional settings like departments, research centers, laboratories, as well as the larger structure. (This strategy is well-illustrated in the legal system for prosecutorial decision-making by Carbone, 2013.)

In the next chapters we examine the benefits of diversity and of equity or reliance on merit, we discuss the operation of "schemas" as a special problem that combines reliance on cognitive strategies as well as homophily (or familiarity and experience) in further limiting our judgments of merit and our success at inclusion, and we consider alternate explanations for the lack of ideal levels of inclusion. In part II, we detail institutional policies and practices that can limit our reliance on faulty cognitive processes by prescribing good practices and proscribing risky or dangerous ones, bringing us closer to realizing our ideal of meritocratic, inclusive institutions. Many others have noted that it is only through examining and changing the core policies and practices of the institution that the institution is likely really to change (see, e.g., Alston & Cantor, 2014; Plaut, 2014). Moreover, measuring and monitoring those changes provides us with crucial information about how successful we are in meeting our ideals. Finally, developing new practices can give us direct feedback that would allow us to change our faulty assumptions.

Note

1. Our reasoning here assumes that people whom we do not select will have equally good opportunities elsewhere, which we realize is not always the case. For many reasons, a worthy candidate may have an opportunity that is worse, in the sense of not providing all the resources the person needs to do his or her best work. If we knew about the person's outcome, we might then falsely decide that we had made the right choice, failing to take into account the extent to which the environment contributed to that person's success.

References

Alon, S. (2009). The evolution of class inequality in higher education: Competition, exclusion and adaptation. *American Sociological Review, 74*(5), 731–755.

Alston, K., & Cantor, N. (2014). Valuing the world, valuing diversity. In S. A. Fryberg & E. J. Martinez (Eds.), *The truly diverse faculty: New dialogues in American higher education* (pp. 25–34). New York, NY: Palgrave MacMillan.

American Association of University Professors. (2013, May 15). Mission and description. http://www.aaup.org/about/mission-description (accessed October 23, 2017).

Anzures, G., Quinn, P. C., Pascalis, O., Slater, A. M., & Lee, K. (2010). Categorization, categorical perception, and asymmetry in infants' representation of face race. *Developmental Science, 13*(4), 553–564.

Anzures, G., Quinn, P. C., Pascalis, O., Slater, A. M., & Lee, K. (2013). Development of own-race biases. *Visual Cognition, 21*(9–10), 1165–1182.

Banaji, M. R., & Greenwald, A. G. (2013). *Blindspot: Hidden biases of good people*. New York, NY: Delacorte Press.

Belle, D., Smith-Doerr, L., & O'Brien, L. M. (2014). Gendered networks: Professional connections of science and engineering faculty (pp. 153–175). In V. Demos, C.W. Berheide, & M.T. Segal (Eds.), *Gender transformation in the academy (Advances in gender research, Volume 19)*. Emerald Group Publishing Limited.

Blau, F. D., Gielen, A., & Zimmerman, K. F. (Eds.). (2012). *Gender, inequality and wages*. Oxford, UK: Oxford University Press.

Bloom, A. (1987). *The closing of the American mind*. New York, NY: Simon & Schuster.

Borman, G., & Dowling, M. (2010). Schools and inequality: A multilevel analysis of Coleman's Equality of Educational Opportunity data. *Teachers College Record, 112*(5), 1201–1246.

Bowen, W. G., & Bok, D. (1998). *The shape of the river*. Princeton, NJ: Princeton University Press.

Bowen, W. G., & McPherson, M. S. (2016). *Lesson plan: An agenda for change in American higher education*. Princeton, NJ: Princeton University Press.

Boyce, M. C., Chisholm, P., Crawley, E. F., Gibson, L. J., Gleason, K. K., Lynch, N. A., & Vander Sande, J. B. (2002, March). Report of the committee on women faculty in the school of engineering at MIT. Massachusetts Institute of Technology. http://facultygovernance.mit.edu/sites/default/files/reports/2002-03_Status_of_Women_Faculty-All_Reports.pdf

Carbone, C. S. (2013, April). Putting it in context: The opportunity structure for bias within prosecutorial decision-making. Paper presented at Conference on Implicit Bias, Philosophy and Psychology, Sheffield, England.

Carrell, S. E., Page, M. E., & West, J. E. (2010). Sex and science: How professor gender perpetuates the gender gap. *Quarterly Journal of Economics, 125*(3), 1101–1144.

Cheryan, S., Plaut, V. C., Davies, P. G., & Steele, C. M. (2009). Ambient belonging: How stereotypical cues impact gender participation in computer science. *Journal of Personality and Social Psychology, 97*(6), 1045–1060.

Chesler, M., Lewis, A., & Crowfoot, J. (2005). *Challenging racism in higher education*. Lanham, MD: Rowman & Littlefield.

Clark, W. A., & Fossett, M. (2008). Understanding the social context of the Schelling segregation model. *Proceedings of the National Academy of Sciences of the United States of America, 105*(11), 4109–4114.

Cole, J. (2016). *Toward a more perfect university*. New York, NY: PublicAffairs.

Dasgupta, N. (2011). Ingroup experts and peers as social vaccines who inoculate the self-concept: The stereotype inoculation model. *Psychological Inquiry, 22*(4), 231–246.

DeAngelo, L., Franke, R., Hurtado, S., Pryor, J. H., & Tran, S. (2011). *Completing college: Assessing graduation rates at four-year institutions*. Los Angeles, CA: Higher Education Research Institute.

Diamond, J. B., Randolph, A., & Spillane, J. P. (2004). Teachers' expectations and responsibility for student learning: The importance of race, class, and organizational habitus. *Anthropology & Education Quarterly, 35*(1), 75–98.

Dovidio, J. F., Kawakami, K., & Gaertner, S. L. (2002). Implicit and explicit prejudice and interracial interaction. *Journal of Personality and Social Psychology, 82*(1), 62–68.

Dunham, Y., Baron, A. S., & Banaji, M. R. (2008). The development of implicit intergroup cognition. *Trends in Cognitive Sciences, 12*(7), 248–253.

Dutton, J. E., Ashford, S. J., Lawrence, K. A., & Miner-Rubino, K. (2002). Red light, green light: Making sense of the organizational context for issue selling. *Organization Science, 13*(4), 355–369.

Eccles, J. (2011). Gendered educational and occupational choices: Applying the Eccles et al. model of achievement-related choices. *International Journal of Behavioral Development, 35*(3), 195–201.

Effron, D. A., Cameron, J. S., & Monin, B. (2009). Endorsing Obama licenses favoring Whites. *Journal of Experimental Social Psychology, 45*(3), 590–593.

Farrand, E. M., & Marston, M. O. (1876). Greetings from the Women of the University in 1876. In book of greetings compiled by the Ladies Library Association of Ann Arbor on the occasion of the University Centennial contained at the Bentley Historical Library, University of Michigan.

Friedman, M., & Narveson, J. (1995). *Political correctness: For and against.* Lanham, MD: Rowman & Littlefield.

Fryberg, S. A., & Martinez, E. J. (Eds.). (2014a). *The truly diverse faculty: New dialogues in American higher education.* New York, NY: Palgrave MacMillan.

Fryberg, S. A., & Martinez, E. J. (2014b). Constructed struggles: The impact of diversity narratives on junior faculty of color. In S. A. Fryberg & E. J. Martinez (Eds.), *The truly diverse faculty: New dialogues in American Higher education* (pp. 3–24). New York, NY: Palgrave MacMillan.

Gamba, M., & Kleiner, B. H. (2001). The old boys' network today. *International Journal of Sociology and Social Policy, 21*(8–10), 101–107.

Gitlin, T. (1987). *The sixties: Years of hope, days of rage.* New York, NY: Bantam.

Goff, P. A., Steele, C. M., & Davies, P. G. (2008). The space between us: Stereotype threat and distance in interracial contexts. *Journal of Personality and Social Psychology, 94*(1), 91–107.

Gray, H. H. (2012). *Searching for utopia.* Berkeley, CA: University of California Press.

Greenwald, A. G., Poehlman, T. A., Uhlmann, E., & Banaji, M. R. (2009). Understanding and using the Implicit Association Test: III. Meta-analysis of predictive validity. *Journal of Personality and Social Psychology, 97*, 17–41.

Gutiérrez y Muhs, G., Flores Niemann, Y., González, C. G., & Harris, A. P. (2012). *Presumed incompetent: The intersections of race and class for women in academia.* Boulder, CO: University of Colorado Press.

Hart, V., & Case, N. (n.d.). Parable of the polygons: A playable post on the shape of society. Accessed 9 October 2017 from ncase.me/polygons/

Hesse, H. (1949). *Magister Ludi* (M. Savill, Trans.). New York, NY: Frederick Ungar.

Hirschfeld, L. A. (2012). Seven myths of race and the young child. *Du Bois Review, 9*(01), 17–39.

Hutchins, R. M. (1953). *The university of utopia.* Chicago, IL: University of Chicago Press.

Jacobellis v. Ohio (1964). https://supreme.justia.com/cases/federal/us/378/184/case.html

Kahneman, D. (2011). *Thinking, fast and slow.* New York, NY: Farrar, Straus and Giroux.

Karabel, J. (2005). *The chosen: The hidden history of admission and exclusion at Harvard, Yale, and Princeton.* Boston, MA: Mariner Books.

Kerr, C. (2001). *The uses of the university.* Cambridge, MA: Harvard University Press. (Original work published 1963)

Kinzler, K. D., Dupoux, E., & Spelke, E. S. (2007). The native language of social cognition. *Proceedings of the National Academy of Sciences of the United States of America, 104*(30), 12577–12580.

Kinzler, K. D., & Spelke, E. S. (2011). Do infants show social preferences for people differing in race? *Cognition, 119*(1), 1–9.

Kmec, J. A., McDonald, S., & Trimble, L. B. (2010). Making gender fit and "correcting" gender misfits: Sex segregated employment and the nonsearch process. *Gender & Society, 24*(2), 213–238.

Lamont, M. (2009). *How professors think: Inside the curious world of academic judgment.* Cambridge, MA: Harvard University Press.

Mann, N. H., & Kawakami, K. (2012). The long, steep path to equality: Progressing on egalitarian goals. *Journal of Experimental Psychology. General, 141*(1), 187–197.

Mayer, S. E. (2010). The relationship between income inequality and inequality of schooling. *Theory and Research in Education, 8*(1), 5–20.

McPherson, M., Smith-Lovin, L., & Cook, J. M. (2001). Birds of a feather: Homophily in social networks. *Annual Review of Sociology, 27*, 415–444.

Mickelson, R. A., & Everett, B. J. (2008). Neotracking in North Carolina: How high school courses of study reproduce race and class-based stratification. *Teachers College Record, 110*(3), 535–570.

Miller, A. (1953, December). University of Michigan. *Holiday Magazine, 14*(6), 68–71; 128–136

Monin, B., & Miller, D. T. (2001). Moral credentials and the expression of prejudice. *Journal of Personality and Social Psychology, 81*(1), 33–43.

Nisbett, R., & Ross, L. (1980). *Human inference: Strategies and shortcomings in social judgment.* New York, NY: Prentice Hall.

Ostrove, J. M., Stewart, A. J., & Curtin, N. L. (2011). Social class and belonging: Implications for graduate students' career aspirations. *Journal of Higher Education, 82*(6), 748–774.

Plaut, V. (2014). Models of success in the academy. In S. A. Fryberg & E. J. Martinez (Eds.), *The truly diverse faculty: New dialogues in American higher education* (pp. 35–60). New York, NY: Palgrave MacMillan.

Reardon, S. F., & Bischoff, K. (2011). Income inequality and income segregation. *American Journal of Sociology, 116*(4), 1092–1153.

Reskin, B. (2012). The race discrimination system. *Annual Review of Sociology, 38*, 17–35.

Rios, D., Stewart, A. J., & Winter, D. G. (2010). "Thinking she could be the next President": Why identifying with the curriculum matters. *Psychology of Women Quarterly, 34*(3), 328–338.

Rodriguez, R. (1981). *Hunger for memory.* Boston, MA: David R. Godine.

Rosenthal, R. (1992). *Pygmalion in the classroom (Expanded edition).* New York, NY: Irvington.

Roth, L. M. (2004). Engendering inequality: Processes of sex-segregation on Wall Street. *Sociological Forum, 19*(2), 203–228.

Saucier, D. A., Miller, C. T., & Doucet, N. (2005). Differences in helping Whites and Blacks: A meta-analysis. *Personality and Social Psychology Review, 9*(1), 2–16.

Schelling, T. C. (1971). Dynamic models of segregation. *Journal of Mathematical Sociology, 1*(2), 143–186.

Schrecker, E. (1986). *No ivory tower: McCarthyism and the universities.* New York, NY: Oxford University Press.

Sekaquaptewa, D. (2014). On being the solo faculty member of color: Research evidence from field and laboratory studies. In S. A. Fryberg & E. J. Martinez (Eds.),

The truly diverse faculty: New dialogues in American higher education (pp. 99–120). New York, NY: Palgrave MacMillan.

Smeeding, T., Erikson, R., & Jäntti, M. (Eds.). (2011). *Persistence, privilege and parenting: The comparative study of intergenerational mobility.* New York, NY: Russell Sage.

Sotomayor, S. (2013). *My beloved world.* New York, NY: Alfred A. Knopf.

Steele, C. M. (2011). *Whistling Vivaldi: And other clues to how stereotypes affect us.* New York, NY: Norton.

Stockdill, B. C., & Danico, M. Y. (Eds.). (2012). *Transforming the ivory tower.* Honolulu, HI: University of Hawaii Press.

Tatum, B. D. (2003). *Why are all the Black kids sitting together in the cafeteria?* New York, NY: Basic Books.

Thorngate, W., Dawes, R. M., & Foddy, M. (2009). *Judging merit.* New York, NY: Psychology Press.

Tobin, E. M. (2009). The modern evolution of America's flagships. In W. G. Bowen, M. M. Chingos, & M. S. McPherson (Eds.), *Crossing the finish line: Completing college at America's public universities* (pp. 239–264). Princeton, NJ: Princeton University Press.

Tversky, A., & Kahneman, D. (1974). Judgment under uncertainty: Heuristics and biases. *Science, 185*(4157), 1124–1131. doi:10.1126/science.185.4157.1124. Reprinted in Kahneman (2011).

Walsh, D. M. (2014). *Employment law for human resource practice* (5th ed.). Boston, MA: Cengage Learning.

Walton, G. M., & Carr, P. B. (2012). Social belonging and the motivation and intellectual achievement of negatively stereotyped students. In M. Inzlicht & T. Schmader (Eds.), *Stereotype threat: Theory, process, and application* (pp. 89–106). New York, NY: Oxford University Press.

Walton, G. M., & Cohen, G. (2007). A question of belonging: Race, social fit, and achievement. *Journal of Personality and Social Psychology, 92,* 82–96.

Walton, G. M., & Cohen, G. (2011). A brief social-belonging intervention improves academic and health outcomes of minority students. *Science, 331,* 1447–1451.

Xiong, T., & Tatum, B. D. (1999). "In my heart I will always be Hmong": One Hmong American woman's pioneering journey towards activism. In M. Romero & A. J. Stewart (Eds.), *Women's untold stories: Breaking silence, talking back, voicing complexity* (pp. 227–242). New York, NY: Routledge.

Zietsch, B. P., Verweij, K. J., Heath, A. C., & Martin, N. G. (2011). Variation in human mate choice: Simultaneously investigating heritability, parental influence, sexual imprinting, and assortative mating. *American Naturalist, 177*(5), 605–616.

2   The Benefits of Diversity and Inclusion

In this chapter we review the benefits of diversity and inclusion for a range of institutional and organizational outcomes. Many people approach the issue of diversity from the standpoint of fairness. For these people, the inclusion of a wide range of people in colleges and universities is required by the institutions' responsibility for fairness: everyone should have the same chance and the same opportunities to excel. This responsibility is a critical part of the commitment to equitable and meritocratic treatment. As a basic good, fairness needs no justification. Thus, for some people, fairness is by itself enough of a reason to achieve diversity because those people assume that excellence is uniformly distributed across different groups. For others, who may think that talent is more likely in some groups than others, an appeal to fairness may not be persuasive.

We think that diversity is not only fair but smart, because diversity promotes excellence. All institutions prize excellence, and so do we. Diversity and inclusion yield benefits that extend in many directions: embracing innovation and creativity, welcoming challenges to received wisdom or traditional knowledge, increasing the visibility of our dedication to the free pursuit of truth, inspiring students to have high aspirations and to explore new ideas, and so on. We review those benefits in this chapter, along with the challenges in bringing about diversity that works.

Leaders are responsible for diversity, and they must solve two puzzles, regardless of the size of the group that they lead. The first is how to overcome the tendency for groups to be homogeneous. The second is how to bring out the best efforts of everyone in the group. This book has a broad conception of leaders. A leader may lead a class, a small group of students, a large lab, a committee, a department, a school, or a university. Whatever form leadership takes, leaders will benefit from knowing what makes groups work well. The research we present suggests that diversity increases positive outcomes, but only if everyone in the group can contribute his or her best. Leaders affect whether the benefits of diversity will outweigh the costs.

Benefits of Diversity

Demographic Diversity Increases Innovation
Developing and testing new ideas is one of the six "virtues" of ideal academic institutions, and it is at the core of a great deal of scholarship and research. In some fields, with problems that are well-defined by previous knowledge, the goal is clear and there may even be a formula, or algorithmic procedure, for reaching the goal. But for most of the problems that researchers, scholars, and change agents want to solve, it is not clear how to get to the solution. Indeed, it often is not clear how to formulate the problem to begin with. The form and possible content of a solution are also not clear. This is what is meant by calling a problem space ill-defined (Simon, 1973).

Many games, like chess or tic-tac-toe, are examples of well-defined problem spaces. What makes chess hard is not the problem space, but following the chain of the myriad possible outcomes of a given move to decide on the best move. The initial state—the location of the pieces on the board—and the final state—checkmate (or stalemate)—are both known. In addition, the possible moves each piece on the board can make are specified in advance. Players can't devise new moves for pieces.

Most scholarly problems, and problems on a global scale, are not like chess or tic-tac-toe. Is the problem of understanding the origins of modernism, or the causes of the Civil War, or election results, or cancer, one problem or many problems? Is sexual assault in the U.S. military in the same problem space as sexual abuse of children, or are those phenomena only distantly related? Even for a much narrower "academic" question—does bilingualism have cognitive benefits?—the researcher faces an ill-defined problem space. What counts as being bilingual? What counts as a cognitive benefit? Are all cognitive benefits on a par? Is bilingualism only one of many challenging activities that could equally benefit cognition? Setting up the problem is daunting. Achievement of a good statement of the problem, and of a good statement of what the final state should be, helps to structure the problem but does not dictate how to approach the problem.

Diversity—Demographic and Otherwise

Diverse groups *should* produce more innovative solutions and products, given that most problems are ill-defined. If all members of a group specify an ill-defined problem in the same way and come up with similar solutions, they will fail to see other approaches, some of which may be preferable (Hong & Page, 2004; Page, 2007). Having a group of highly trained experts, all of whom look at a problem in a similar way, might seem a priori like the best way to approach a problem, but that will only be true for problems that are already well-defined.

Intellectual diversity is thus highly desirable, though primarily for complex problems (van Dijk, van Engen, & van Knippenberg, 2012). It is possible to achieve diversity of perspective and approach without demographic diversity. A group of White men can have diverse ideas and diverse intellectual backgrounds. People are not clones of each other, no matter how similar their gender, race, ethnicity, class, age, religion, sexual orientation, and education. People differ in their openness to new experiences (a characteristic that is strongly correlated with creativity; McCrae & Greenberg, 2014), their extraversion (another characteristic that is correlated with creativity; Furnham & Bachtiar, 2008), their willingness to challenge received opinion, their ability to stimulate thinking in other people, their fields of knowledge, and so on. Variation in those characteristics contributes to intellectual diversity. Because of the active suppression of women and people of color from academic research until the late twentieth century, the sciences and other fields were primarily populated by White men. The fields nonetheless progressed with innovative approaches to scientific problems.

The important question we address here is whether demographic diversity adds to intellectual diversity (or is valuable for other reasons) or has no positive effect. There is evidence that demographic diversity does contribute to innovation and better ideas (Schiebinger, 2014; van Dijk et al., 2012; see also van Dijk, Meyer, van Engen, & Loyd, 2017). The data are complicated and suggest that a fine-grained analysis of a fairly large range of variables is needed to understand the complex findings, and we review some of them here. From the historical record, we cannot tell whether academic research might have been even more innovative and whether progress would have been faster had women and people of color been working on the problems. We can only make use of the data on innovation in organizations, and those data suggest that the answer is a qualified yes: research in general benefits from diversity. When we consider restrictions now recognized as ridiculous—such as the exclusion of Jews from physics in Nazi Germany—we can get an idea of what we might be missing by excluding women and people of color.

Just as demographic uniformity does not prevent innovation, demographic diversity does not guarantee it. Demographic diversity does, however, make innovation more likely, and we can understand some of the reasons why. Demographic diversity is a proxy for other types of diverse thinking, and diverse thinking is useful for solving ill-defined problems. Even people who know little or nothing about an area—such as students at the beginning of a course—can ask questions that stimulate instructors to look at a problem in a new light. Experts "know" what questions to ask and thus tend to stay within established outlines. Diversity yields intellectual and creative benefits not because people reason differently as a function of their sex or race, but because their somewhat different interests and experiences give rise to different perspectives and ideas. A diverse group increases the likelihood of a range of solutions. In addition, the acceptance of innovations is more likely among a diverse group of people (Østergaard, Timmermans, & Kristinsson, 2011, for educational and gender diversity).

Impact of Diversity in Different Areas

The impact of diversity has been studied more extensively in areas with a focus on problem-solving rather than in areas such as the humanities where many forms of understanding are valued even if they do not lead to new "solutions," but instead to a new appreciation of factors that produced the problem. In these fields, though innovation is highly prized, it takes somewhat different forms than it does in other fields, and it is much less studied by social scientists. One factor producing this outcome is that it is by definition easier to study diversity when research is conducted in groups rather than by solo scholars, and team activities are more common in the social and natural sciences than in the humanities.

Although some social scientific research is aimed at assessing the creativity of artistic products (Joy, 2012) and the contextual factors that increase creativity (Amabile & Pillemer, 2012), the focus has been on individual works of art or the creativity of individuals. We hope that social scientists will turn their attention to studying teams in the arts and humanities and to understanding how a field may function as a proxy "team" with many different individual scholars contributing to understanding a phenomenon. We need to understand the impact of diversity of perspective within all fields, whether work is designed or studied by individuals or groups.

It is striking that in the arts, where creativity and fresh outlooks are de rigueur, it remains difficult for women and people of color to be seen and heard. A well-known poster from 1987/88 by the Guerrilla Girls lists the "advantages" of being a woman artist, such as working without the pressure of success and not having to undergo the embarrassment of being called a genius. (See http://www.guerrillagirls.com/projects/ for representations of all Guerrilla Girls projects, including a short video on the Guerrilla Girls' *Guide to Behaving Badly*.) The poster was created in the 1980s, but contemporary women artists and artists of color continue to be scarce in exhibitions at major museums (though firm statistics are hard to come by).

According to the National Endowment for the Arts (2011), in 2005–2009, women were almost half of artists (construed broadly) but earned 81% of what men earned. Ironically, exhibitions of Guerrilla Girls posters seem to get more attention than women artists do; even women's protest signs from the Women's March in 2017 are being collected by museums (Ryan, 2017). In 2015 the magazine *ArtNews* put out a list of the 100 most influential people in the international contemporary art world—a list including artists, museum directors, curators, gallery owners, and so on. The list was 68% male and 32% female; 70% White, 16% Asian, 5% African American, and 7% Hispanic; and 51% European (Artsy, 2016). The percentage of Hollywood directors who are female or African American is similarly small. In the same way, writing, directing, producing, and photographing in television has few women and people of color (Lauzen, 2017), with little change over a ten-year period.

Diversity and Innovation

Whether innovations are for solving social or medical problems like cancer or dementia or for more modest problems like developing new products, they are more likely to occur with diverse teams. A survey of 1,775 Danish firms of different sizes examined the roles of gender, age, ethnicity, and education in predicting how innovative a firm would be (Østergaard, Timmermans, & Kristinsson, 2011). An innovation was defined as an "introduction of a new product or service, excluding minor improvements on already existing products and services" (p. 504). Gender diversity was linked to greater innovation. Ethnicity did not play a role, perhaps because, by U.S. standards, the employees were not very diverse: they came primarily from Nordic countries and other countries in Western Europe. No mention was made of people of color. Subsidiary analyses suggested that neither males nor females should predominate in an organization if the goal is to maximize innovation.

As another example, although women are a small, underrepresented percentage of patent holders (Frietsch, Haller, Funken-Vrohlings, & Grupp, 2009; Hunt, Garant, Herman, & Munroe, 2013; Meng & Shapira, 2010; Rosser, 2009), their presence on a patent team leads to more citations of the patent (Ashcraft & Breitzman, 2007), testifying to the value of mixed-gender teams. Similarly, in the ecological sciences, articles with at least one woman among the coauthors are cited more than male-only articles (Campbell, Mehtani, Dozier, & Rinehart, 2013).

A field study that experimentally examined the role of ethnic diversity found that diverse teams were less likely than homogeneous teams to accept inflated prices in trading (Levine, Apfelbaum, Bernard, Bartelt, Zajac, & Stark, 2014). Diverse teams may make better judgments in part because members of homogeneous groups are more likely to trust each other even when they shouldn't (Levine et al., 2014). That may in turn account for why scientific papers by U.S. researchers show the influence of homophily: Whites (people with "English"-sounding names) tend to collaborate with Whites, and Asians (people with "Asian"-sounding names) tend to collaborate with Asians, more often than a random assortment would predict. Researchers have a closer connection to others with the same ethnicity. Papers with authors of different ethnicities are, however, cited more often than those with similar ethnicities (Freeman & Huang, 2014).

Other data about the benefits of gender diversity for group work provide mixed results. The effects of women on boards of directors have varied from study to study, sometimes being positive, sometimes negative, and sometimes neutral (Carter, D'Souza, Simkins, & Simpson, 2010; Crédit Suisse Research Institute, 2012; Dobbin & Jung, 2011; Triana, Miller, & Trzebiatowski, 2013). A meta-analysis of 146 studies concludes that the presence of women as chief executive officers and board members is weakly positively related to long-term company performance and weakly negatively related to short-term company performance (Jeong & Harrison, 2017).

Effects of the presence of women among management are somewhat more clearly positive, but only for companies that put a premium on innovation (e.g., Dezsö & Ross, 2012; see also Crédit Suisse Research Institute, 2014). Women in Congress deliver more funding to their districts than do men, after various controls are included (Anzia & Berry, 2011), and, when women are in the minority party, they are more effective than their male peers (Volden, Wiseman, & Wittmer, 2013). Finally, and relatedly, some data suggest that women particularly contribute to helping a group work well by contributing a cooperative climate (Bear & Woolley, 2011; Woolley, Chabris, Pentland, Hashmi, & Malone, 2010).

To summarize so far, diverse groups tend to come up with more innovative solutions to problems. One reason is that the group members in diverse groups have a large range of perspectives and approaches. Another reason is that group members *expect* people who are demographically different from them to have different perspectives. They are thus more open to hearing a range of ideas. Perhaps for that reason, when groups of diverse people learn that the members are more alike than different, the result can be counterproductive (Phillips & Loyd, 2006).

Not all innovations succeed. By their nature, innovations and new directions are risky. Stasis, however, is also risky. Some innovations will fail, just as some standard approaches will fail. Innovations might even be expected to fail at a higher rate than standard approaches exactly because their methods and frameworks are less well-established. Innovations are also likely to spark resistance at the outset, before it is clear that they will lead to intellectual or artistic benefits. And to the extent that fields are less ready to accept innovations that come from women and people of color, it will be harder to demonstrate the worth of new approaches. Progress in any field, however, requires innovation, raising the issue of how best to ensure productive innovative efforts.

Demographic Diversity Enlarges, Changes, and Improves Areas of Study

There are direct benefits to knowledge from greater demographic diversity. We offer three examples. The first example is the development of subfields that either did not exist or barely existed before women and people of color entered the discipline. In the field of psychology, for example, work on the ways that social status affects perceptions of others antedated the increase of women in the field, but the ways that gender affects evaluations were largely ignored until the influx of women into psychology. That work has led to a wide range of subfields: work on identity—how the identity of the observer and the observed shape perceptions; work on what happens when multiple identities are in play; work on cross-national differences in sex disparities in science and math achievement, and the significance of variation. Also in the field of psychology, work on stereotype threat, particularly as it affects African Americans, was introduced by an African American (Steele & Aronson, 1995). There are questions one doesn't think to ask unless one is a member of one or another demographic group.

Equally, scholarship about writers and composers was altered and enhanced by the presence of female, racial-ethnic, and sexual minority scholars in the fields examining their work (Awkward, 1995; Brett, 2006; Hubbs, 2004; Showalter, 1977). Women writers, or African American writers (such as Toni Morrison), or gay composers (such as Benjamin Britten) became better known as a broader diversity of scholars began taking such artists seriously. In history, the role of women, children, and the poor was better and differently understood as women, minority, and working-class-origin scholars more often wrote about the history of past events, events that had previously been written about by a relatively narrowly defined group of men and from a limited perspective (Hewitt, 1969; Lerner, 1971; Pinchbeck, 1930). In addition, some events previously treated as unimportant have been taken up as significant historical subjects by new entrants to the field (e.g., second-wave feminism, Echols, 1989; Rosen, 2000; motherhood, Badinter, 1981; including motherhood and race; Feldstein, 2000).

One acute instance of the neglect of women and minorities, and one that is acutely damaging to science itself, is in medical- and health-related research. Congress passed an act in 1993 directing that research that was funded by the National Institutes of Health (NIH) include women and minorities as participants in health studies. In 2001, NIH updated the policy as follows:

The guidelines ensure that all NIH-funded clinical research will be carried out in a manner sufficient to elicit information about individuals of both sexes/genders and diverse racial and ethnic groups and, particularly in NIH-defined Phase III clinical trials, to examine differential effects on such groups. Since a primary aim of research is to provide scientific evidence leading to a change in health policy or standard of care, it is imperative to determine whether the intervention or therapy being studied affects women or men or members of minority groups and their subpopulations differently. (NIH, 2001)

It is astounding that an act of Congress was needed to forcefully present the idea that studies of people's health should not be confined to studies of White men's health and White men's reactions to medications.

NIH grant recipients do not always honor their duty to study and report on women (Carnes, Morrissey, & Geller, 2008; Geller, Koch, Pellettieri, & Carnes, 2011). Researchers do not routinely report the sex of cultured cells in cardiovascular studies (Taylor, Vallejo-Giraldo, Schaible, Zakeri, & Miller, 2011), nor do they report sex differences in efficacy of drugs for dementia (Mehta, Rodrigues, Lamba, Wu, Bronskill, Herrmann, Gill, et al. 2017). Researchers do not include minorities at appropriate rates in cancer clinical trials and do not routinely report the results when they are included (Chen, Lara, Dang, Paterniti, & Kelly, 2014), nor do they include women at the appropriate rates (Klein, Schiebinger, Stefanick, Cahill, Danska, De Vries, Kibbe, McCarthy, Mogil, Woodruff, & Zucker, 2015). Failing to include the full range of human variation in studies leads to mistakes (Nielsen, Alegria, Börjeson, Etzkowitz, Falk-Krzesinski, Joshi, Leahy, Smith-Doerr, Woolley, & Schiebinger, 2017).

The authors of the studies pointing out such failures are primarily women and minorities. That is not to say that White men are not involved in pointing out such failures, nor is it to say that women and members of underrepresented minorities do not contribute to such failures. Rather, we are pointing out that the inclusion of a broader range of people is likely to appropriately broaden the areas of inquiry.

The work of women—Ruth Kirschstein and Geraldine Woods—was important in moving NIH to include women and minorities among those studied (Davis, 2011). Ruth Kirschstein was White and Jewish, and Geraldine Woods was African American. As a female Jew applying to every medical school in the United States in 1947, Kirschstein was rejected by all but two, Tulane and New York University. A staff member at one school suggested she change her name to increase her odds of acceptance (Davis, 2011). Both women worked to include women and people of color among reviewers as well as among those studied. Since we do not have access to an alternate universe in which women and people of color were included in positions of authority in academic science and NIH, we cannot know whether their inclusion would have precluded sex and ethnicity disparities in research from the outset. But it seems likely that a more diverse group would have reduced the extent of disparities in research.

Although research by women and people of color has demonstrated how far medical research still has to go in inclusiveness, we want to avoid creating sharp boundaries related to sex and ethnicity since they may disguise other aspects of variation. There may, for example, be apparent sex differences in response to medications that are actually due to other factors, such as weight, that correlate with gender (Richardson, Reiches, Shattuck-Heidorn, LaBonte, & Consoli, 2015; see also discussion by Schiebinger & Klinge, 2015; Maney, 2016, and other papers in a themed issue on neural sex differences and their significance in *Philosophical Transactions of the Royal Society B, Biological Sciences*, 2016, Volume 371, Issue 1688, compiled and edited by Mary M. McCarthy). Similarly, differences that are on their surface due to race or ethnicity may be due to other factors (Grandner, Williams, Knutson, Roberts, & Jean-Louis, 2016; Roberts, 2013), and conditions may be underdiagnosed for individuals in one or another ethnic group because of beliefs that those conditions only occur or do not occur in "their" group (Yudell, Roberts, DeSalle, & Tishkoff, 2016).

Thus, we see inclusiveness as a goal that is best met by—being inclusive! Women and people of color have been instrumental in opening topics of scholarly discussion and in bringing up the full range of human diversity. The most recent studies referred to above caution against locking human and animal diversity into neat categories.

The second example of how diversity benefits knowledge is more subtle (see, for discussion, Crasnow, Wylie, Bauchspies, & Potter, 2009/2015; Fausto-Sterling, 2012; Schiebinger, 2014; Wylie, 1997). Diversity leads to less reliance on contemporary folk notions of gender and ethnicity differences as guiding metaphors for faulty science. In biology, for example, research on the sex-determining factor and the roles of X and Y chromosomes were initially wrongheaded, seeing the sperm as active and dominant and the egg as passive (Fujimura, 2006; Martin, 1991). Here, science has largely corrected itself, thanks in part to work by scientists who were not in the grip of folk beliefs about gender. But the role of gender schemas is evident in the first theories scientists developed.

Similar examples are the hypothesis that an extra Y chromosome makes males more aggressive and, hence, more likely to be imprisoned for violent crimes, even though XXY and XYY males have similar incarceration rates (Richardson, 2010, 2012, 2013). Here, too, science corrected itself. However, biologists themselves continue to use metaphors of male "agency" and female "allure" in talking about chromosomes (Richardson, 2012, 2013). In archeology and anthropology, researchers run the risk of projecting pictures of present-day male-female arrangements onto an understanding of the past (Wylie, 1997; see also Hays-Gilpin & Whitley, 1998; Nelson, 2007; Wright, 1996).

Folk notions about gender also continue in claims about differences between male and female brains (see critiques by, among others, Fine, 2010, 2013, 2017; Jordan-Young, 2010). Here, too, we can expect that science will eventually correct itself, and work proposing that the human brain is a mosaic and cannot be definitively categorized as "male" or "female" should help in that effort (Joel, Berman, Tavor, Wexler, Gaber, Stein et al., 2015; Joel & Fausto-Sterling, 2016). Further, the importance of the fact that different brain mechanisms can mediate the same behavioral outcome will be better appreciated (De Vries, 2004; Fausto-Sterling, 2012), as will the role of the environment in mediating and organizing the expression of hormones (see the discussion in Valian, 1998). But while we are waiting for science to correct itself, we can lament the need for it to do so. We can see that the inclusion of a broader diversity of researchers could have headed off some mistaken directions at the outset.

A third example comes from fields that are more remote from gender, such as theoretical mathematics and theoretical physics. Here, the fields may be losing out in two ways—by not including women and underrepresented minority members and by paying too little attention to the subfields— "niches"—where women are more numerous (Wylie, 2012). In the first case, there is an arbitrary restriction of the talent that is capitalized on. Even if one thought that the pool of White men was large and intellectually diverse enough to allow those fields to move forward (an assumption that is increasingly untenable as fewer and fewer U.S.-born White men enter into or stay in math and science fields), any exclusion of half the available pool—in the case of women—or 30% of the available pool—in the case of African Americans and Hispanics—looks foolhardy and wasteful. In the second case, fields that women and minorities are more numerous in can be slighted simply because they are fields that women and minorities are more numerous in. Insights from such fields may be harder to achieve because of lack of support and because the implications of the insights may be insufficiently appreciated.

To make our claims clear: we are *not* saying that only women or people of color will introduce new perspectives or frameworks, even when those perspectives and approaches are linked to gender or ethnicity issues. We *are* saying that any field will maximize new perspectives and approaches by including a demographically diverse group of people. We *are* saying that new ideas should receive constructive, rather than destructive, critiques.

Demographic Diversity Has Broad Benefits
for Institutions and Individuals
Better Outcomes for Undergraduate and Graduate Students   An intellectual advantage of a diverse faculty for students is that a diverse range of academic interests will be available. Students will be exposed to a broader range of questions than they would with a demographically limited faculty. Budding interests that students might have in a wide set of areas are more likely to find receptive responses if the faculty are diverse.

Another advantage of a diverse professoriate is the demonstration that there is room in the professions and in academia for aspiring students, regardless of their sex and ethnicity. Young people are unlikely to enter fields where they see no possibility for advancement. Aspirants do not need to see people exactly like them in senior positions and among the faculty, but they do need to see that there is room for them if they are going to continue. One way to demonstrate that there is room is by hiring excellent and diverse faculty. Another way to demonstrate that is by having White male faculty who take an interest in the intellectual development of all students, regardless of gender or race and ethnicity. Being taken seriously and being constructively challenged by a diverse group of faculty makes it clear to students that the field as a whole wants them to be successful.

Although anyone can encourage students to succeed, several pieces of evidence suggest that diversity encourages participation and aspiration. In one study, college men and women who were interested in science saw mock videos of a supposed summer science conference (Murphy, Steele, & Gross, 2007). In one video, the ratio of males to females was 1:1; in the other it was 2:1. Women students who saw the 2:1 video showed heightened physiological vigilance (such as faster heartbeat) and a lower sense of belonging compared to women who saw the 1:1 video. Both groups of female students reported a preference for attending the conference with equal ratios. Men were largely unaffected by the ratios, except that they too preferred a conference with an even ratio (though not necessarily for the same reasons as women had).

The presence of a variety of social groups in positions of authority should have two effects. First, diversity suggests that there is room for the aspirant: where there is a lot of variety it is plausible to think that there is room for more. Second, and relatedly, diversity will make the roles of English professor, scientist, surgeon, or successful businessperson ones which are not sex or race specific. Diversity in a group makes it easier for everyone to make accurate judgments of the qualifications and value of nontraditional applicants for positions. If you no longer think "male" or "White" when you think "surgeon," an African American female surgeon will not be burdened in your evaluations by being African American and female.

One implication of the importance of cues like the ratio of males to females is the different perspective it provides about *choice*. Individuals do not necessarily freely *choose* to have or not to have certain careers (see, inter alia, Dasgupta, Scircle, & Hunsinger, 2015, for addressing this point). If White men, White women, and people of color are responding to subtle cues about the appropriateness and rightness of their presence in a field, their choices are not the product of a pure preference, but are constrained by cues suggesting that they do or do not belong. Both observers and participants may see choices as the product of preferences, even when the environment has narrowed or directed choice. Preferences and interests are internal states that are affected by external contexts.

We emphasize what we have already indicated: the same holds for White men. To those whose environment supports their aspirations and ambitions, the environment may simply appear neutral rather than supportive. Thus, men, especially White men, look as if they are choosing, and perceive themselves as choosing, to be doctors and mathematicians and scientists, although their choices are also constrained and directed. In the case of females, as we detail in following chapters, the environment with respect to math and science does not support aspirations and ambitions in childhood, where girls are seen as doing well because of effort, even when their standardized test scores are equal to boys'. The subtle cues that high school girls and college women are faced with become all the more important as determinants of "choice."

Although it is helpful to see that people similar to oneself are in the positions one aspires to, the effect of role models can be debilitating as well as inspiring. If the role model's behavior and achievements seem achievable, then the role model is inspiring (Lockwood & Kunda, 1997, 1999, 2000). If the stars in a field seem to be almost inhumanly talented and hardworking, their existence may instead confirm the impossibility of achievement for an ordinary mortal. In the case of demographic groups that are underrepresented in positions of power and prestige, the presence of an outstanding minority member may serve only to undermine potential aspirants. The person may evaluate the distance between themselves and the star as too great. Since the women and people of color who occupy positions of power and prestige *are* exceptional, both in their numbers and in their achievements, it can seem as if those exceptional qualities are necessary for achievement if one is a woman or person of color. Instead of thinking, "I'm like her, I can do it, too," the person thinks, "I'm not like her, so I probably can't do it."

But when people can identify with those who have achieved success in a field, or see themselves as similarly capable, they are more likely to aspire to that success. In one experiment, college women who were in math classes taught by female instructors had a range of positive outcomes that women in classes with the same content that were taught by men did not have (Stout, Dasgupta, Hunsinger, & McManus, 2011). Women with female instructors increased their interest in and liking for science-related fields and showed greater confidence about their abilities in those fields. Women in the U.S. Air Force Academy prosper in science-related classes when women are instructors, while male students are unaffected (Carrell, Page, & West, 2010). Elementary schoolchildren of color benefit from the presence of teachers of color (Goldhaber, Theobald, & Tien, 2015), and high school students of color receive higher expectations from teachers of color than from White teachers (Gershenson, Holt, & Papageorge, 2016). The data on the beneficial effects of teacher diversity on students of all ages are clear: females and individuals of color benefit in performance and motivation.

Although the notion of a critical mass is too narrow to account for the decisions that women—and men—make about whether to pursue particular careers, the data suggest that a combination of factors, including critical mass and other features of the environment, convey to potential students the extent to which they fit or belong in the discipline (Creamer, 2012; Fox, Sonnert, & Nikiforova, 2009; Sonnert, Fox, & Adkins, 2007). Having women and minority faculty well represented demonstrates to students that they can belong. Interestingly, even male students are more interested in engineering when female students are more numerous (Creamer, 2012).

All students benefit from diversity, regardless of their eventual field. After students graduate, they will work in a diverse world. The mental flexibility that is necessary for success in that diverse world will be developed in part through experiences with a diverse student body and a diverse group of faculty and administrators. A diverse faculty gives students a head start in learning how to appreciate and interact with a range of coworkers and authority figures.

Improving the Job Applicant Pool   Broad inclusion increases the range and size of any candidate pool: the larger the qualified pool, the greater the choice and the higher the likelihood of finding well-qualified candidates. A few individual institutions might be seen as so desirable as places to work that they can afford to eliminate half their potential talent pool, but most institutions are not in that category, nor is the nation as a whole. It also seems inconsistent to make less of an effort to include women and people of color on the faculty than one makes to include them in the student body. The advantages that women and people of color bring to the student body should extend to the professoriate (Gurin, 2004; Gurin, Dey, Hurtado, & Gurin, 2002). Further, whatever responsibilities institutions have to educate women and people of color should extend to hiring them after educating them.

Why the Composition of Teams Is Important

Increasingly, published work in the sciences (broadly conceived) is pursued by teams, where a "team" consists of any group larger than one. Science contrasts with the arts and humanities, where there has been little or no increase in collaborations (Jones, Wuchty, & Uzzi, 2008; Wuchty, Jones, & Uzzi, 2007). The growth from 1955 to 2000 in the extent to which teams dominate published papers has occurred in all broadly conceived science fields—natural sciences, engineering, and social sciences. In contrast, in the arts and humanities most papers (90%) are single-authored. Teams in medicine, biology, physics, chemistry, and materials science all averaged more than three persons.

Work produced by teams is also cited more often than single-authored papers, even after controlling for self-citations and excluding editorials and letters to the editor (Wuchty et al., 2007). Thus, teams produce more and more of the published work in science, and their work is cited more often than single-authored work. (That does not mean that the work is better, only that it is more influential.)

Along with an increase in team size there has been an increase in cross-institution collaborations in the natural and social sciences (but not in the arts and humanities; Jones et al., 2008). An analysis of who collaborates with whom across institutions shows the equivalent of assortative matching: when schools are placed into tiers based on how often their publications are cited,[1] one sees that individuals in the top tier tend to collaborate with each other more often than one would expect if individuals were randomly matched across institutions.[2] The same is true for individuals in the bottom tier of schools. That is probably due to three factors. One is the composition of professional networks and homophily—people tend to know people like themselves. Another factor may be a reluctance on the part of individuals at higher ranked institutions to collaborate with individuals at lower ranked institutions, and perhaps a reluctance (motivated differently) for those at lower ranked institutions to approach those in the top tier. The third factor is that top-tier schools have resources at their disposal that lower tier schools lack.

Most cross-institution collaborations in the natural sciences involve the 5% of schools that are in the top tier of citation rates. That 5% accounts for 59% of cross-institution collaborations. The schools in the top tier collaborate at similar rates with other schools in the top three tiers but collaborate less with schools in the bottom tier. The bottom tier, which consists of 80% of institutions, accounts for only 30% of cross-institution collaborations (Jones et al., 2008).

When individuals in the top 5% collaborate with others in the top 5% of schools, they benefit; the publications resulting from those collaborations are cited even more than publications resulting from within-institution collaborations at those schools. In contrast, when the 80% of schools in the bottom tier collaborate with other schools in the bottom tier, they reap no advantage from cross-institution collaboration. The bottom 80% only reaps a benefit (as measured by citations) when they collaborate with higher tier schools. The fact that top-tier schools have resources ranging from support for graduate students to well-maintained physical plants to highly experienced staff may be a large part of the reason that the bottom 80% only benefits when it collaborates with higher tier schools.

Thus, diversity in the prestige of institution plays a role in collaborations. Individuals at very high-prestige institutions preferentially collaborate with researchers in the first and second tier (defined by number of citations), even though 80% of schools are in the bottom tier. Since women and people of color are overrepresented at low-prestige institutions, demographic diversity is less likely among top-tier collaborations. That hardens the isolation of women and people of color.

This is an example where the benefits of diversity that would arise from cross-institution collaboration across prestige boundaries appear to be undercut by the lower resources of lower prestige institutions.

When and Why Diverse Groups Fail

When diverse teams work well, they tend to outperform homogeneous groups and produce innovative solutions. But some diverse teams implode. What determines whether a team will work well or badly?

Three bodies of research are particularly relevant. One set of studies examines "identity congruence" theory (e.g., Swann, Johnson, & Bosson, 2009), another examines "psychological safety" and opportunities for learning (e.g., Edmondson, 1999), and a third examines effects of diversity on "nondiverse" group members (e.g., Phillips, Northcraft, & Neale, 2006). (See also van Knippenberg & Schippers, 2007; articles in Brief, 2008; see Galinsky, Todd, Homan, Phillips, Apfelbaum, Sasaki, et al., 2015, for a succinct overview, including policy suggestions.)

"Identity congruence" theory suggests what can go wrong in groups (Polzer, Milton, & Swann, 2002; Swann, Polzer, Seyle, & Ko, 2004). In any group, each member has an idea of what he or she can contribute, of what his or her strengths are; members want other group members to verify those strengths. And in any group, each member has an idea of what the other members can contribute, of what their strengths are. When those ideas are in alignment, the group flourishes. If, in short, you and I agree about what strengths we each bring to the group, if our identities converge, the group will prosper. When the ideas are not in alignment (if what I think I can contribute differs from what you think I can contribute), the group does badly. Group members may not volunteer solutions to problems if they believe that the group will not value their contributions. Equally, some group members may simply be skeptical about the value of particular other group members.

One study that demonstrates the importance of identity (also sometimes called interpersonal) congruence tested 83 groups of MBA students who performed semester-long group projects (Polzer et al., 2002). The students were placed into groups that varied in how diverse they were. In groups where members' views of others coincided with those others' views of themselves, the products received higher grades than those that were not congruent. Further, those groups worked better together. Finally, group members' views of each other after ten minutes of interaction predicted the outcome well.

The implication from this study and others in this vein is that having one's identity verified and confirmed by other group members leads to superior performance and intact groups. Identity confirmation creates a sense of belonging. Leaders can potentially make use of such information by interviewing group members ahead of time to determine what they think they have to offer the group and explicitly conveying that information when introducing group members to each other. The role of leaders in assembling teams, and the role of team members, is thus clear: work to ensure that group members recognize each other's strengths and potential contributions. That will make it more likely that those strengths come to the fore and that potential contributions become actual contributions.

The work on identity congruence is related to work on "psychological safety." In a field study of 51 work teams in a manufacturing company, investigators found that teams where members thought they were respected and liked and could express their views freely—teams with high "psychological safety"—performed better than teams where that was not the case. Such teams could also learn from their mistakes better than other teams. High psychological safety led to better learning, which in turn led to better performance (Edmondson, 1999; Edmondson & Lei, 2014; Nembhard & Edmondson, 2011). Again, the notion of belonging comes in: in teams with high psychological safety, members feel that they belong, and belongingness creates flexibility. Further, psychological safety seems to be even more important for the performance of racial and ethnic minorities than of Whites (Singh, Winkel, & Selvarajan, 2013).

This research is particularly helpful for two reasons. The first is that it deals with work teams where the team members are known to each other. In much of the laboratory research that we discuss, the team members are meeting each other for the first time when the experiment begins, and their expected duration of interaction is at most a semester or a year and is generally considerably shorter. The research just described shows that even in groups where the members are known to each other, psychological safety improves group performance. The second reason the research is helpful is that the results hold independent of diversity. *All* groups, not just diverse groups, work better under conditions of psychological safety. Related work shows the relevance of psychological safety for racially diverse groups (Ely, Padavic, & Thomas, 2012; Ely & Thomas, 2001). Team leaders can thus see that helping teams, especially diverse teams, to collaborate well requires a respectful atmosphere that is tolerant of error.

One department's experience in creating a respectful atmosphere, an atmosphere that would increase psychological safety and facilitate more creative discussion, resulted in a list of guidelines for respectful philosophical discussion at colloquia (http://as.nyu.edu/philosophy/climate/initiatives/nyu-guidelines-for-respectful-philosophical-discussion.html). Examples include the following: "Don't be incredulous, roll your eyes, make faces, laugh at a participant, or start side conversations" (which we particularly like); "Objections are fine, but it's also always OK to build on a speaker's project. Even objections can often be cast in a constructive way, and even destructive objections can often be usefully accompanied by a positive insight suggested by the objection"; "Chairs should attempt to balance discussion between participants, prioritizing people who haven't spoken before, and keeping in mind the likelihood of various biases (e.g., implicit gender biases) when calling on questioners and applying these guidelines."

The third stream of studies (e.g., Phillips & Loyd, 2006; Phillips et al., 2006; Phillips, Rothbard, & Dumas, 2009) investigates group members' expectations about the conditions under which new ideas will surface. Group members *expect* people who are demographically different from them to have different perspectives. Although one might think that such expectations would lead group members to dismiss the opinions of those who are demographically different, the data suggest that they are instead more open to hearing a range of ideas when they are faced with people who occupy a range of demographic niches. A dissenting view expressed by

African American participants led White college students to engage in more complex thinking than when that same view was expressed by White participants (Antonio, Chang, Hakuta, Kenny, Levin, & Milem, 2004). One possible reason for the effect is that Whites, for example, know that African Americans have had different experiences and thus have a different basis for their contributions. But whether the data from these experiments can be generalized widely is unknown.

Some data suggest that women particularly contribute to helping a group work well, as we will describe. In one experiment, researchers recruited 40 teams of three people each from the general public via advertisements (Woolley et al., 2010). Before each group began the suite of tasks that the researchers provided, they took a ten-minute test of general intelligence. The team then completed four different tasks over five hours. The tasks recruited a wide range of different abilities, such as brainstorming together, performing a reasoning task together, coordinating a shopping trip to make it as efficient as possible within a set of constraints, and coordinating a typing task. All groups also played a game of checkers together against a computer as a criterion task. How well the group did on one task was correlated with how they performed on the other tasks, despite the diversity of the tasks. A combined value representing that overall performance—c—correlated well with the group's performance on the criterion task. Similar results occurred in a follow-up experiment that had a wider range of tasks and a more complex criterion task. The follow-up included 152 groups of different sizes ranging from two to five.

In both experiments, c was a much better predictor of the criterion task than was the group's average intelligence as measured by an intelligence test, or the score of the person in the group with the highest intelligence score, suggesting that groups are greater than the sum of their parts (Woolley et al., 2010). Both the average group intelligence score and the maximum group intelligence score were correlated with c, but three other factors were much more strongly correlated. One was how socially sensitive group members were, as measured by an independent test. Another was the extent to which group members shared equally in the discussion—the more even the speaking turns, the better the results. The third was the percentage of women in the groups—the more women, the better the results. Since women had higher social sensitivity scores than men did, it is likely that social sensitivity was the critical factor.

To summarize, diverse teams can be very effective in producing innovative solutions, more innovative than the solutions produced by individuals or by homogeneous teams. Diversity can be achieved in a variety of ways, including demographic status, which can include factors like sex and ethnicity. (Although age and other forms of diversity have not been systematically manipulated as a variable, all forms of diversity could yield benefits.) But the success of diverse teams rests on a mutual appreciation of what each group member has to offer, an openness to others' views, and the creation of an atmosphere where people feel free to express their opinions, even if their opinions are incorrect. Women appear at present to have an advantage in facilitating group harmony, but the ability to foster equal discussion is presumably equally achievable (perhaps with effort) by all genders and ethnic groups.

Institutional leaders and agencies supporting all scholarship, including those supporting scientific advancement, need to be concerned about arbitrary restrictions on who pursues scholarship in order to maximize the likelihood of innovation. Moreover, individual researchers will benefit from looking at all the available talent and diversifying their groups.

In this chapter we have emphasized the importance of diversity and inclusion for innovation and for better theories. We have done so because we see development of innovative solutions to scholarly and public policy problems and deeper understanding of intellectual issues as the key research values that an institution has. Our emphasis on the pragmatic value of diversity should not, however, detract from an understanding that an ongoing active commitment to equal access to all of society's demographic subdivisions is the fair thing to do.[3] Academic institutions pride themselves on their equal access. But access is meaningless if everyone's presence is not valued and appreciated. We think institutions can do better at creating the conditions for true inclusion, and learning how to develop successful diversity is one avenue to equality and excellence.

Notes

1. The citations exclude publications resulting from cross-institution collaborations, in order to have "clean" groups for measuring citations.

2. Because the quartiles are determined by number of citations per school, there are unequal numbers of schools in the different quartiles (Jones et al., 2008). The top quartile consists of 5% of the schools examined.

3. By emphasizing that diversity is "good for the organization" over diversity is "fair," one broadens one's conception of diversity (Trawalter, Driskell, & Davidson, 2016). The result of including more groups, such as older people, in one's conception of diversity is that some groups, such as African Americans, become a lower priority.

References

Amabile, T. M., & Pillemer, J. (2012). Perspectives on the social psychology of creativity. *Journal of Creative Behavior, 46*(1), 3–15.

Antonio, A. L., Chang, M. J., Hakuta, K., Kenny, D. A., Levin, S., & Milem, J. F. (2004). Effects of racial diversity on complex thinking in college students. *Psychological Science, 15*(8), 507–510.

Anzia, S. F., & Berry, C. R. (2011). The Jackie (and Jill) Robinson effect: Why do congresswomen outperform congressmen? *American Journal of Political Science, 55*(3), 478–493.

Artsy. (2016, October 20). We broke down *ArtReview*'s Power 100 by race, gender, profession, and place of birth. Retrieved on March 5, 2017, from https://www.artsy.net/article/artsy-editorial-we-broke-down-the-art-world-s-100-most-powerful-people-by-race-gender-profession-and-place-of-birth

Ashcraft, C., & Breitzman, A. (2007). Who invents IT? An analysis of women's participation in Information Technology patenting. University of Colorado: The National Center for Women & Information Technology. http://www.ncwit.org/sites/default/files/resources/patentreport_wappendix.pdf

Awkward, M. (1995). *Negotiating difference: Race, gender, and the politics of positionality.* Chicago, IL: University of Chicago Press.

Badinter, E. (1981). *The myth of motherhood: An historical view of the maternal instinct.* London, UK: Souvenir.

Bear, J. B., & Woolley, A. W. (2011). The role of gender in team collaboration and performance. *Interdisciplinary Science Reviews, 36*(2), 146–153.

Brett, P. (2006). *Music and sexuality in Britten.* Berkeley, CA: University of California Press.

Brief, A. P. (Ed.). (2008). *Diversity at work.* Cambridge, UK: Cambridge University Press.

Campbell, L. G., Mehtani, S., Dozier, M. E., & Rinehart, J. (2013). Gender-heterogeneous working groups produce higher quality science. *PLoS One, 8*(10), e79147.

Carnes, M., Morrissey, C., & Geller, S. E. (2008). Women's health and women's leadership in academic medicine: Hitting the same glass ceiling? *Journal of Women's Health, 17*(9), 1453–1462.

Carrell, S. E., Page, M. E., & West, J. E. (2010). Sex and science: How professor gender perpetuates the gender gap. *Quarterly Journal of Economics*, *125*(3), 1101–1144.

Carter, D. A., D'Souza, F., Simkins, B. J., & Simpson, W. G. (2010). The gender and ethnic diversity of US boards and board committees and firm financial performance. *Corporate Governance*, *18*(5), 396–414.

Chen, M. S., Lara, P. N., Dang, J. H., Paterniti, D. A., & Kelly, K. (2014). Twenty years post-NIH Revitalization Act: Enhancing minority participation in clinical trials (EMPaCT): Laying the groundwork for improving minority clinical trial accrual. *Cancer*, *120*(S7), 1091–1096.

Crasnow, S., Wylie, A., Bauchspies, W. K., & Potter, E. (2009/2015). Feminist perspectives on science. In E. N. Zalta (Ed.), *The Stanford encyclopedia of philosophy* (Summer 2015 Edition). http://plato.stanford.edu/archives/sum2015/entries/feminist-science/

Creamer, E. G. (2012). Effects of numeric representation of women on interest in engineering as a career. *American Journal of Engineering Education*, *3*, 1–12.

Crédit Suisse Research Institute. (2012). Gender diversity and corporate performance. Available online at https://publications.credit-suisse.com/tasks/render/file/index.cfm?fileid=88EC32A9-83E8-EB92-9D5A40FF69E66808

Crédit Suisse Research Institute. (2014). The CS gender 3000: Women in senior management. Available online at https://publications.credit-suisse.com/tasks/render/file/index.cfm?fileid=8128F3C0-99BC-22E6-838E2A5B1E4366DF

Dasgupta, N., Scircle, M. M., & Hunsinger, M. (2015). Female peers in small work groups enhance women's motivation, verbal participation, and career aspirations in engineering. *Proceedings of the National Academy of Sciences of the United States of America*, *112*(16), 4988–4993.

Davis, A. F. (2011). *Always there: The remarkable life of Ruth Lillian Kirschstein, M.D.* Bethesda, MD: National Institutes of Health.

De Vries, G. J. (2004). Minireview: Sex differences in adult and developing brains: Compensation, compensation, compensation. *Endocrinology*, *145*(3), 1063–1068.

Dezsö, C. L., & Ross, D. G. (2012). Does female representation in top management improve firm performance? A panel data investigation. *Strategic Management Journal*, *33*(9), 1072–1089.

Dobbin, F., & Jung, J. (2011). Corporate board gender diversity and stock performance: The competence gap or institutional investor bias. *North Carolina Law Review*, *89*, 809–838.

Echols, A. (1989). *Daring to be bad: Radical feminism in America, 1967–1975*. Minneapolis, MN: University of Minnesota Press.

Edmondson, A. (1999). Psychological safety and learning behavior in work teams. *Administrative Science Quarterly, 44*(2), 350–383.

Edmondson, A. C., & Lei, Z. (2014). Psychological safety: The history, renaissance, and future of an interpersonal construct. *Annual Review of Organizational Psychology and Organizational Behavior, 1*(1), 23–43.

Ely, R. J., Padavic, I., & Thomas, D. A. (2012). Racial diversity, racial asymmetries, and team learning environment: Effects on performance. *Organization Studies, 33*(3), 341–362.

Ely, R. J., & Thomas, D. A. (2001). Cultural diversity at work: The effects of diversity perspectives on work group processes and outcomes. *Administrative Science Quarterly, 46*, 229–273.

Fausto-Sterling, A. (2012). *Sex/gender: Biology in a social world.* New York, NY: Routledge.

Feldstein, R. (2000). *Motherhood in black and white: Race and sex in american liberalism, 1930–1965.* Ithaca, NY: Cornell University Press.

Fine, C. (2010). *Delusions of gender: How our minds, society, and neurosexism create difference.* New York, NY: Norton.

Fine, C. (2013). Neurosexism in functional neuroimaging: From scanner to pseudoscience to psyche. In M. K. Ryan & N. R. Branscombe (Eds.), *The Sage handbook of gender and psychology* (pp. 45–60). London, UK: Sage.

Fine, C. (2017). *Testosterone rex: Myths of sex, science, and society.* New York, NY: Norton.

Fox, M. F., Sonnert, G., & Nikiforova, I. (2009). Successful programs for undergraduate women in science and engineering: Adapting versus adopting the institutional environment. *Research in Higher Education, 50*, 333–353.

Freeman, R. B., & Huang, W. (2014). *Collaborating with people like me: Ethnic co-authorship within the US* (NBER Working Paper 19905). Cambridge, MA: National Bureau of Economic Research.

Frietsch, R., Haller, I., Funken-Vrohlings, M., & Grupp, H. (2009). Gender-specific patterns in patenting and publishing. *Research Policy, 38*(4), 590–599.

Fujimura, J. H. (2006). Sex genes: A critical sociomaterial approach to the politics and molecular genetics of sex determination. *Signs (Chicago, Ill.), 40*(1), 49–82.

Furnham, A., & Bachtiar, V. (2008). Personality and intelligence as predictors of creativity. *Personality and Individual Differences, 45*(7), 613–617.

Galinsky, A. D., Todd, A. R., Homan, A. C., Phillips, K. W., Apfelbaum, E. P., Sasaki, S. J., et al. (2015). Maximizing the gains and minimizing the pains of diversity: A policy perspective. *Perspectives on Psychological Science, 10*(6), 742–748.

Geller, S. E., Koch, A., Pellettieri, B., & Carnes, M. (2011). Inclusion, analysis, and reporting of sex and race/ethnicity in clinical trials: Have we made progress? *Journal of Women's Health, 20*(3), 315–320.

Gershenson, S., Holt, S. B., & Papageorge, N. W. (2016). Who believes in me? The effect of student–teacher demographic match on teacher expectations. *Economics of Education Review, 52,* 209–224.

Goldhaber, D., Theobald, R., & Tien, C. (2015). The theoretical and empirical arguments for diversifying the teacher workforce: A review of the evidence. *The Center for Education Data & Research, University of Washington Bothell.* Retrieved January 27, 2018, from http://www.cedr.us/papers/working/CEDR%20WP%202015-9.pdf

Grandner, M. A., Williams, N. J., Knutson, K. L., Roberts, D., & Jean-Louis, G. (2016). Sleep disparity, race/ethnicity, and socioeconomic position. *Sleep Medicine, 18,* 7–18.

Gurin, P. (Ed.). (2004). *Defending diversity: Affirmative action at the University of Michigan.* Ann Arbor, MI: University of Michigan Press.

Gurin, P., Dey, E. L., Hurtado, S., & Gurin, G. (2002). Diversity and higher education: Theory and impact on educational outcomes. *Harvard Educational Review, 72*(3), 330–367.

Hays-Gilpin, K., & Whitley, D. S. (Eds.). (1998). *Reader in gender archaeology.* New York, NY: Routledge.

Hewitt, M. (1969). *Children in English society.* London, UK: Routledge & Kegan Paul.

Hong, L., & Page, S. E. (2004). Groups of diverse problem solvers can outperform groups of high-ability problem solvers. *Proceedings of the National Academy of Sciences of the United States of America, 101,* 16385–16389.

Hubbs, N. (2004). *The queer composition of America's sound: Gay modernists, American music and national identity.* Chicago, IL: University of Chicago Press.

Hunt, J., Garant, J. P., Herman, H., & Munroe, D. J. (2013). Why are women underrepresented amongst patentees? *Research Policy, 42*(4), 831–843.

Jeong, S. H., & Harrison, D. A. (2017). Glass breaking, strategy making, and value creating: Meta-analytic outcomes of women as CEOs and TMT members. *Academy of Management Journal, 60*(4), 1219–1252.

Joel, D., Berman, Z., Tavor, I., Wexler, N., Gaber, O., Stein, Y., et al. (2015). Sex beyond the genitalia: The human brain mosaic. *Proceedings of the National Academy of Sciences of the United States of America, 112*(50), 15468–15473.

Joel, D., & Fausto-Sterling, A. (2016). Beyond sex differences: New approaches for thinking about variation in brain structure and function. *Philosophical Transactions of the Royal Society B, 371*(1688), 20150451.

Jones, B. F., Wuchty, S., & Uzzi, B. (2008). Multi-university research teams: Shifting impact, geography, and stratification in science. *Science, 322*(5905), 1259–1262.

Jordan-Young, R. M. (2010). *Brain storm*. Cambridge, MA: Harvard University Press.

Joy, S. P. (2012). Origins of originality: Innovation motivation and intelligence in poetry and comics. *Empirical Studies of the Arts, 30*(2), 195–213.

Klein, S. L., Schiebinger, L., Stefanick, M. L., Cahill, L., Danska, J., De Vries, G. J., et al. (2015). Opinion: Sex inclusion in basic research drives discovery. *Proceedings of the National Academy of Sciences of the United States of America, 112*(17), 5257–5258.

Lauzen, M. M. (2017). *Boxed in 2016–17: Women on screen and behind the scenes in television*. San Diego, CA: Center for the Study of Women in Television and Film, San Diego State University; http://womenintvfilm.sdsu.edu/wp-content/uploads/2017/09/2016-17_Boxed_In_Report.pdf. Accessed January 27, 2018.

Lerner, G. (1971). *Women in American history*. Menlo Park, CA: Addison-Wesley.

Levine, S. S., Apfelbaum, E. P., Bernard, M., Bartelt, V. L., Zajac, E. J., & Stark, D. (2014). Ethnic diversity deflates price bubbles. *Proceedings of the National Academy of Sciences*, online prepublication.

Lockwood, P., & Kunda, Z. (1997). Superstars and me: Predicting the impact of role models on the self. *Journal of Personality and Social Psychology, 73*(1), 91–103.

Lockwood, P., & Kunda, Z. (1999). Increasing the salience of one's best selves can undermine inspiration by outstanding role models. *Journal of Personality and Social Psychology, 76*(2), 214–228.

Lockwood, P., & Kunda, Z. (2000). Outstanding role models: Do they inspire or demoralize us? In A. Tesser, R. B. Felson, & J. M. Suls (Eds.), *Psychological perspectives on self and identity* (pp. 147–171). Washington, DC: American Psychological Association.

Maney, D. L. (2016). Perils and pitfalls of reporting sex differences. *Philosophical Transactions of the Royal Society B, 371*(1688), 20150119.

Martin, E. (1991). The egg and the sperm: How science has constructed a romance based on stereotypical male-female roles. *Signs (Chicago, Ill.), 16*, 485–501.

McCrae, R. R., & Greenberg, D. M. (2014). Openness to experience. In D. K. Simonton (Ed.), *The Wiley handbook of genius* (pp. 222–243). Chichester, UK: Wiley.

Mehta, N., Rodrigues, C., Lamba, M., Wu, W., Bronskill, S. E., Herrmann, N., et al. (2017). Systematic review of sex-specific reporting of data: Cholinesterase inhibitor example. *Journal of the American Geriatrics Society, 16*, 2213–2219.

Meng, Y., & Shapira, P. (2010). Women and patenting in nanotechnology: Scale, scope, and equity. In S. E. Cozzens & J. M. Wetmore (Eds.), *Nanotechnology and the challenges of equity. Yearbook of Nanotechnology in Society 2* (pp. 23–46). Dordrecht, the Netherlands: Springer.

Murphy, M. C., Steele, C. M., & Gross, J. J. (2007). Signaling threat: How situational cues affect women in math, science, and engineering settings. *Psychological Science, 18*(10), 879–885.

National Endowment for the Arts. (2011, October). Artists and arts workers in the United States: Findings from the American Community Survey (2005–2009) and the Quarterly Census of Employment and Wages (2010). Retrieved January 27, 2018 from https://www.arts.gov/sites/default/files/105.pdf

National Institutes of Health. (2001). NIH policy and guidelines on the inclusion of women and minorities as subjects in clinical research—Amended, October, 2001. https://grants.nih.gov/grants/funding/women_min/guidelines_amended_10_2001.htm

Nelson, M. (Ed.). (2007). *Women in antiquity: Theoretical approaches to gender and archaeology.* Walnut Creek, CA: AltaMira Press.

Nembhard, I. M., & Edmondson, A. C. (2011). Psychological safety: A foundation for speaking up, collaboration, and experimentation in organizations. In G. M. Spreitzer & K. S. Cameron (Eds.), *The Oxford handbook of positive organizational scholarship* (pp. 490-503). Oxford, UK: Oxford University Press.

Nielsen, M. W., Alegria, S., Börjeson, L., Etzkowitz, H., Falk-Krzesinski, H. J., Joshi, A., et al. (2017). Opinion: Gender diversity leads to better science. *Proceedings of the National Academy of Sciences of the United States of America, 114*(8), 1740–1742.

Østergaard, C. R., Timmermans, B., & Kristinsson, K. (2011). Does a different view create something new? The effect of employee diversity on innovation. *Research Policy, 40*(3), 500–509.

Page, S. E. (2007). *The difference: How the power of diversity creates better groups, firms, schools, and societies.* Princeton, NJ: Princeton University Press.

Phillips, K. W., & Loyd, D. L. (2006). When surface and deep-level diversity collide: The effects on dissenting group members. *Organizational Behavior and Human Decision Processes, 99*(2), 143–160.

Phillips, K. W., Northcraft, G. B., & Neale, M. A. (2006). Surface-level diversity and decision-making in groups: When does deep-level similarity help? *Group Processes & Intergroup Relations, 9*(4), 467–482.

Phillips, K. W., Rothbard, N. P., & Dumas, T. L. (2009). To disclose or not to disclose? Status distance and self-disclosure in diverse environments. *Academy of Management Review, 34*(4), 710–732.

Pinchbeck, I. (1930). *Women workers and the Industrial Revolution, 1750–1850.* London, UK: Routledge & Sons.

Polzer, J. T., Milton, L. P., & Swann, W. B., Jr. (2002). Capitalizing on diversity: Interpersonal congruence in small work groups. *Administrative Science Quarterly, 47,* 296–324.

Richardson, S. S. (2010). Feminist philosophy of science: History, contributions, and challenges. *Synthese, 177*(3), 337–362.

Richardson, S. S. (2012). Sexing the X: How the X became the "female chromosome." *Signs (Chicago, Ill.), 37*(4), 909–933.

Richardson, S. S. (2013). *Sex itself: The search for male and female in the human genome.* Chicago, IL: University of Chicago Press.

Richardson, S. S., Reiches, M., Shattuck-Heidorn, H., LaBonte, M. L., & Consoli, T. (2015). Opinion: Focus on preclinical sex differences will not address women's and men's health disparities. *Proceedings of the National Academy of Sciences of the United States of America, 112*(44), 13419–13420.

Roberts, D. (2013). *Fatal invention: How science, politics, and big business re-create race in the twenty-first century.* New York, NY: The New Press.

Rosen, R. (2000). *The world split open: How the modern women's movement changed America.* New York, NY: Viking.

Rosser, S. (2009). The gender gap in patenting: Is technology transfer a feminist issue? *NWSA Journal, 21,* 65–84.

Ryan, L. (2017, January 11). Museums across the world are collecting Women's March signs. *New York Magazine.* Retrieved January 27, 2018, from http://nymag.com/thecut /2017/01/museums-across-the-world-are-collecting-womens-march-signs.html

Schiebinger, L. (2014). Gendered innovations: Harnessing the creative power of sex and gender analysis to discover new ideas and develop new technologies. *Triple Helix, 1*(9). doi:10.1186/s40604-014-0009-7

Schiebinger, L., & Klinge, I. (2015). Gendered innovation in health and medicine. *Gender, 7*(2), 29–50.

Showalter, E. (1977). *A literature of their own: British women novelists from Brontë to Lessing.* Princeton, NJ: Princeton University Press.

Simon, H. A. (1973). The structure of ill-structured problems. *Artificial Intelligence, 4,* 181–201.

Singh, B., Winkel, D. E., & Selvarajan, T. T. (2013). Managing diversity at work: Does psychological safety hold the key to racial differences in employee performance? *Journal of Occupational and Organizational Psychology, 86*(2), 242–263.

Sonnert, G., Fox, M. F., & Adkins, K. (2007). Undergraduate women in science and engineering: Effects of faculty, fields, and institutions over time. *Social Science Quarterly, 88,* 1333–1356.

Steele, C. M., & Aronson, J. (1995). Stereotype threat and the intellectual test performance of African Americans. *Journal of Personality and Social Psychology, 69*(5), 797–811.

Stout, J. G., Dasgupta, N., Hunsinger, M., & McManus, M. A. (2011). STEMing the tide: Using ingroup experts to inoculate women's self-concept in science, technology, engineering, and mathematics (STEM). *Journal of Personality and Social Psychology, 100*(2), 255–270.

Swann, W. B., Jr., Johnson, R. E., & Bosson, J. K. (2009). Identity negotiation at work. *Research in Organizational Behavior, 29*, 81–109.

Swann, W. B., Jr., Polzer, J. T., Seyle, D. C., & Ko, S. J. (2004). Finding value in diversity: Verification of personal and social self-views in diverse groups. *Academy of Management Review, 29*, 9–27.

Taylor, K. E., Vallejo-Giraldo, C., Schaible, N. S., Zakeri, R., & Miller, V. M. (2011). Reporting of sex as a variable in cardiovascular studies using cultured cells. *Biology of Sex Differences, 2*(1), 1–7.

Trawalter, S., Driskell, S., & Davidson, M. N. (2016). What is good isn't always fair: On the unintended effects of framing diversity as good. *Analyses of Social Issues and Public Policy (ASAP), 16*, 1–31.

Triana, M. D. C., Miller, T. L., & Trzebiatowski, T. M. (2013). The double-edged nature of board gender diversity: Diversity, firm performance, and the power of women directors as predictors of strategic change. *Organization Science, 25*(2), 609–632.

Valian, V. (1998). *Why so slow? The advancement of women.* Cambridge, MA: MIT Press.

van Dijk, H., Meyer, B., van Engen, M., & Loyd, D. (2017). Microdynamics in diverse teams: A review and integration of the diversity and stereotyping literatures. *Academy of Management Annals, 11*(1), 517–557.

van Dijk, H., van Engen, M. L., & van Knippenberg, D. (2012). Defying conventional wisdom: A meta-analytical examination of the differences between demographic and job-related diversity relationships with performance. *Organizational Behavior and Human Decision Processes, 119*(1), 38–53.

van Knippenberg, D., & Schippers, M. C. (2007). Work group diversity. *Annual Review of Psychology, 58*, 515–541.

Volden, C., Wiseman, A. E., & Wittmer, D. E. (2013). When are women more effective lawmakers than men? *American Journal of Political Science, 57*(2), 326–341.

Woolley, A. W., Chabris, C. F., Pentland, A., Hashmi, N., & Malone, T. W. (2010). Evidence for a collective intelligence factor in the performance of human groups. *Science, 330*, 686–688.

Wright, R. P. (Ed.). (1996). *Gender and archaeology*. Philadelphia, PA: University of Pennsylvania Press.

Wuchty, S., Jones, B. F., & Uzzi, B. (2007). The increasing dominance of teams in production of knowledge. *Science, 316*, 1036–1039.

Wylie, A. (1997). The engendering of archaeology: Refiguring feminist science studies. *Osiris, 12*, 80–99.

Wylie, A. (2012). Feminist philosophy of science: Standpoint matters. *Proceedings and Addresses of the American Philosophical Association, 86*(2), 47–76.

Yudell, M., Roberts, D., DeSalle, R., & Tishkoff, S. (2016). Taking race out of human genetics. *Science, 351*(6273), 564–565.

3   Understanding Inequities: The Role of Schemas

"I don't care who they are; I just want the best person."

Perhaps the most common statement we hear from faculty and administrators is their commitment to the merit principle. Everyone affirms that people's advancement should be based purely on their merit, not their gender, color, sexual orientation, religion, class, or any other feature that is irrelevant to merit. Hiring and advancement should be based solely on excellence. We agree.

In this chapter we introduce the notion of schemas (especially gender and race schemas) and the role they play in our perceptions and evaluations of people (for review, see Valian, 1998).[1] In brief, gender and race schemas result in our slightly undervaluing the accomplishments and competence of women and people of color, and slightly overvaluing the accomplishments and competence of White men. Many of the examples we discuss are small and can occur outside awareness. We note the covert nature of many of our perceptions and discuss the importance of even small examples of erroneous judgments. Schemas, and their effect on the policies and procedures that affect hiring, retention, and promotion, explain how, despite good intentions, colleges and universities end up hiring and promoting fewer women and underrepresented minorities than would be expected on the basis of the available pool.

We agree that decisions should be based solely on excellence. We disagree when people tell us that the social group someone belongs to plays no role in their evaluations. We think the data are clear that someone's social group does play a role, overall, whether people think it does or not. We say "overall" because many factors affect evaluations. On any given occasion, it can be hard to know what the effect of someone's social group is.

Three Mistakes in Judgment That People Make

We think people make three mistakes (at least!) about their judgments.

Mistake 1: People Think That Their Explicit Intentions to Be Fair Completely Determine Their Behavior

People incorrectly believe that their explicit intentions completely guide their evaluations and observations of others. People think that consciously saying and believing something—in the area of evaluation—make it so. At least, they think it is so for *them*: *they* are not biased, or, even if they are slightly biased, they do not behave in a biased way. They have a blind spot where their own behavior is concerned (Pronin, Lin, & Ross, 2002; West, Meserve, & Stanovich, 2012). Nor are people aware of the studies we describe in this chapter that indicate that good intentions are not enough. Those studies suggest that all of us at least occasionally make decisions influenced by the gender, race, ethnicity, and other characteristics of the person we are assessing. Perhaps the worst aspect of our belief in our good intentions is that the very belief that we can evaluate people independently of the group to which they belong can actually make it easier to judge people on the basis of those irrelevant characteristics. We present data on belief in one's own good intentions.

Mistake 2: People Think That Judging Merit Is Straightforward—At Least for Them

People see the criteria they are using as valid on the face of it and transparent, even though their criteria may be somewhat idiosyncratic. They do not consider that some of their criteria may be subjective nor that their criteria might shift so that they choose someone who seems like a "good fit"—that is, someone who will fit in well with *them*, as we described when discussing homophily. People also seldom ask whether their criteria inadvertently exclude people whose contributions they would value. Finally, people do not see that their own behavior may affect how others display their merit. We present data on judgments of merit.

Mistake 3: People Do Not Understand How Success Happens

People associate success with banner-headline achievements, tending not to see the slow accumulation of small successes that make large achievements possible. They also fail to see how a steady drumbeat of small bits of praise or criticism can encourage or suppress people's efforts to be successful in a given field. If, more often than not, you receive praise for doing a good job, only profound modesty will prevent you from concluding that you are capable and talented. Conversely, if, more often than not, your efforts are either ignored or criticized, only profound aplomb will protect you from concluding that your aspirations are too high.

Data Examined in This Chapter

In this chapter we draw on experimental data—some that were collected in the field and some that were conducted in the laboratory—to determine whether and how people get advantages on the basis of irrelevant characteristics. The data show that Whites are advantaged compared to people of color, and that men are advantaged compared to women, especially in domains related to work. Those asymmetries in advantage occur even if others think they are judging on the basis of merit alone.

Although we have just spoken of "Whites" and "people of color," of "women" and "men," we realize that people fit multiple categories simultaneously, and that the groups are large and very heterogeneous. In short, we realize that there are subtleties that the experimental data we report do not always capture and that experiments have both strengths and limitations. Our general strategy is to use both experimental and observational data. When the two converge in their findings, we are more confident that the phenomena we are examining are strong. In this chapter we concentrate on experiments. In chapter 4 we concentrate on observational data—data on numbers and percentages of men, women, and people of color in different types of academic institutions, and data on salaries.

Three Studies to Set the Stage

The three studies we begin with all use real-life events, such as employer responses to people applying for a job, faculty responses to people requesting an appointment, and bus driver responses to people with insufficient fare.

Study 1

Excellent credentials do not fully offset the disadvantages that African Americans experience in job hunting. That was tested by submitting identical job applications to employers that differed in the kind of first name the applicant had. The names Lamar or Ebony suggest a different race than the names Ronny or Anne. But although prospective employers pay attention to the prestige of a candidate's degree, a prestigious degree (from, say, Harvard) for an African American is similar in effect to a less prestigious degree (from, say, the University of Massachusetts at Amherst) for a White (Gaddis, 2015). Lamar from Harvard receives the same number of responses as Ronny from UMass (13% of the time). African Americans with *low*-prestige degrees received a response only 7% of the time.

When applying for jobs, candidates submit their dossiers and hope for the best. Prospective employers use various cues to ethnicity and gender (consciously or nonconsciously), along with information about job-relevant characteristics, and judge accordingly.

Social class matters too, though there is less research on it, and our first example here does not concern employment. Mental health practitioners, in another audit study (Kugelmass, 2016), replied positively to ostensibly middle-class people who requested an appointment on average 23% of the time but replied positively to ostensible working-class people only 8% of the time. Some of those class effects may be driven by a reluctance to deal with the bureaucracy of Medicaid (Asplin, Rhodes, Levy, Lurie, Crain, Carlin, & Kellermann, 2005). Within the group of apparently middle-class people, African Americans received an offer of an appointment 17% of the time, while Whites received an appointment 28% of the time. Another suggestion that race is more important than class comes from the finding that, within race, names associated with higher social class are likely to receive as many invitations for a job interview as names associated with lower social class (Bertrand & Mullainathan, 2004).

Study 2

Lest faculty think that they are immune to cues about race, ethnicity, and gender, they can absorb the sobering results of a study of 6,548 professors showing a preference for Whites (Milkman, Akinola, & Chugh, 2012). Fictitious e-mails, purportedly from prospective doctoral students, were sent under different names. Some names sounded Caucasian, some African

American, some Hispanic, some Indian, and some Chinese. Some were from women and some were from men. In one condition, the prospective students asked for a meeting that same day; in the other they asked for a meeting in a week. The e-mails were otherwise identical.

The experimenters predicted little or no preferences on the basis of race, ethnicity, or gender for a same-day request, on the grounds that the faculty member would think primarily about whether they had time in their schedule. As predicted, faculty treated different groups the same when they were asked for a same-day meeting. For the more distant request, the experimenters predicted a preference for White males, on the grounds that the faculty member would probably try to control how they allocated their time a week hence and could thus think about whether they actually wanted to meet the person. That prediction was confirmed.

Note that in both Study 1 and Study 2, prospective employers or faculty had no information about the applicant other than what was provided in the applicant's dossier or e-mail. Thus, they had no additional information that gave them a sense of what the person was like, information that will be particular to that person. That information is sometimes called individuating information. Many real-life situations are exactly like the conditions in Studies 1 and 2: evaluators have little to go on, so they rely on preconceptions that they would deny that they have. Study 3 examined what happened when observers had some individuating information.

Study 3

In a field study of bus drivers in Australia, the drivers actually saw an individual who boarded the bus and said they did not have enough fare for the trip they wanted to take (Mujcic & Frijters, 2013). White bus drivers gave a free ride to Whites twice as often as they gave a free ride to Blacks (76% vs. 38%). Drivers gave both Whites and Blacks more free rides when they were dressed in business clothes instead of casual clothes, but they still gave Whites more free rides. Thus, business clothes offset some of the disadvantage Blacks face but did not eliminate the cost of being Black. Here, too, although the drivers saw the individuals, they had only cursory information about them, as is common in real life. There are many cases where one gives or withholds opportunities, politeness, and kindness on the basis of minimal cues.

What if You Have Even More Information about the Person? Gender Still Matters

The cautious reader will note that we often have richer information about people than that presented in the previous studies. So we might think that if an observer has enough information to get a full idea of the person, then the person's gender, race, and ethnicity would be relatively unimportant. People would be judged on the basis of who they are.[2] And, indeed, "stereotypes typically have no … effects when the individual is also known to have engaged in an unambiguous behavior that is clearly diagnostic of the trait in question" (Kunda & Thagard, 1996, p. 291). The problem is that in most situations in academia (and in many situations in life more generally), we do not encounter unambiguous behaviors that are "clearly diagnostic of the trait in question." We are usually faced with ambiguous behaviors that can be interpreted in multiple ways.

Research on parents' impressions of their children and teachers' impression of their students give two examples showing that even when people have a great deal of individuating information, they are still affected by their beliefs about gender differences.[3]

The simplest example comes from a study of mothers' impressions of 11-month-old infants' crawling abilities. There are no gender differences in early motor development. Crawling and walking, for example, occur at similar ages in boys and girls and develop in a similar way (see Mondschein, Adolph, & Tamis-LeMonda, 2000, for a review).[4] During the toddler years, boys' motor skills outshine girls', but in infancy the two are equal.

Infants' mothers offered estimates of their children's crawling ability and estimates of how well the infants would navigate a sloped walkway (Mondschein et al., 2000). Despite their personal experience with their children's behavior, mothers of boys overestimated and mothers of girls underestimated how well their children would perform on the slope. Boys and girls made the same number of attempts, they navigated the same degree of slope, and they were equally unlikely to attempt slopes that were too steep for them. Yet mothers of boys thought their sons would succeed when the likelihood of success was actually 0%, and mothers of girls thought their daughters would fail when the likelihood of success was actually 100%.

Individuating information may nevertheless be having an effect on mothers. The experiment did not test how adults without children would rate infant girls and boys. Mothers may be more accurate than nonparents, while still being inaccurate along the lines that schemas would predict. The information they have may reduce, even though it does not eliminate, the impact of schemas.

The cautious reader may bring up another point: not everyone responds the same. We are reporting group averages. People vary from one to another, and within themselves from one occasion to another. For that reason researchers try to have large samples, so that the variability will not obscure the regularities. Even though there is variability, there are also average differences. Men are on average taller than women, for example. That phenomenon does not vanish because there are some very short men and some very tall women. Similarly, we tend to judge men and women, boys and girls, differently, even though we do not judge them differently on every occasion. One of us has often enough observed herself making judgments favoring White men to think that the experiments apply to her as well as to participants in experiments. See box 3.1 for one example.

The parents in the study we described spent months viewing their children's crawling and were likely motivated to think the best of their children. Nevertheless, their children's gender influenced evaluations of their children's abilities. Parents' beliefs about what children are capable of in turn influences what parents expect of their children; that in turn influences what children think they can do. Parents want to, and believe they do, assess their children simply as individuals. And in many areas they

Box 3.1
Gender Enters Perception, but Effort Can Prevent Its Influence on Behavior

One of us is embarrassed to report the following example:

I walked into a computer store in search of an arcane peripheral. As I approached the relevant department I saw two salespeople, a young man and a young woman, standing and chatting together. I had to stop myself from addressing only the man. I had to force myself to look equally at both salespeople as I asked my question. I could see that I thought the man was likely to be more knowledgeable about computers than the woman, even though they were both working in the same department. Had it not been for my knowledge of the literature, I probably would have been unaware of my assumption that the man would be more knowledgeable and I would have focused my attention on him without thinking about it. (Neither of them, it turned out, had any knowledge of the arcane peripheral—but it did take the man quite some time to say so.)

do (see Valian, 1998, for a review). But not all. In the case of motor development, parents may be basing their judgment about different motoric skills on differences that will eventually distinguish boys and girls. Parents' knowledge about general gender differences makes it difficult for them to see their children neutrally, even if they have individuating information about their children that would support correct estimates of their abilities.

Crawling might not matter much. But math and science matter a great deal. If a little girl is an astounding whiz at math—and assuming that she has had an opportunity to demonstrate and develop her proficiency—she will probably correctly be perceived by her parents and teachers as a whiz. In that sort of case, the girl's outstanding characteristics may outweigh any beliefs about gender differences in math that her parents and teachers have. (The same holds for adults. People who are astounding and outstanding are likely to be perceived as such. Most of the people in any population, however, are by definition not astounding and outstanding.) But in the case in which the girl is simply very good at math, she may not be exceptional enough to override adults' beliefs that girls do not excel at math. A boy who is equivalently good will be recognized because he confirms his parents' beliefs that boys do excel at math.

Data on White middle-class parents in both the United States (Yee & Eccles, 1988) and Finland (Räty, Vänskä, Kasanen, & Kärkkäinen, 2002) are suggestive. Parents view their young sons as better at math than their daughters (which they may be, but school grades show an advantage for girls, Voyer & Voyer, 2014). And parents are more likely to see their sons as excelling because of their ability. When explaining the performance of children whom they had rated as highly competent at either math *or* reading, parents tended to understand the children's achievements differently. Parents were more likely to attribute boys' very high competence to talent, but ascribe girls' very high competence to effort (Räty et al., 2002). Thus, boys are talented and girls work hard. Regardless of the domain, parents see boys' and girls' academic excellence differently, despite the large amount of individuating information they have. Similarly, as we describe later, college students are more likely to view their male (vs. their female) professors as brilliant.

Girls do in fact possess better work habits than boys, habits like paying attention, working hard, and being self-disciplined (Duckworth & Seligman,

2006; Lubienski, Robinson, Crane, & Ganley, 2013). However, parents and teachers appear to be overinfluenced by girls' good work habits when they rate children's abilities. They seem to see talent and effort as inversely related to each other, even though they are compatible (Dweck, 1999). Parents are fond of talking about how different each of their children is, without considering the extent to which their treatment of their children, or subtle ways that they talk to their children, might have contributed to those differences.

To summarize the results about individuating information for gender: people attend to individuating information, but they attend differently, depending on the sex of the child or person who is displaying the behavior (Chan & Mendelsohn, 2010) and depending on the nature of the information (Kunda & Thagard, 1996). Gender can play a role even when we are evaluating individuals about whom we have a great deal of information. Nevertheless, individuating information—of the right kind and in the right amount—will serve to reduce inaccuracies based on schemas. It thus behooves evaluators to seek as much diagnostic information as possible, and it behooves those who are being evaluated to provide as much diagnostic information as possible.[5]

In the case of race and ethnicity, the data are more equivocal than the data for gender, with more work suggesting that individuating information overrides beliefs about race and ethnicity for some types of judgments (e.g., Chan & Mendelsohn, 2010). One difference between gender and ethnicity is that men and women are equally represented in the population, have had many interactions with each other, and dress and behave in ways that differentiate them on the basis of their gender. The same is not true for race or ethnicity.

We conjecture that it is difficult to counter gender in part because our view about gender differences are exceptionally detailed. If, for example, we ask people who is more likely to take baths, men or women, people answer, "women," without hesitation, even if their personal experience is very limited. And the question seems natural. But if we ask people who is more likely to take baths, African Americans or Whites, people are likely to say "Huh?" The very question seems odd. Gender pervades every area of existence, but race and ethnicity do not. Even in areas where there are known differences, people are unlikely to be able to say more than what they themselves do and extrapolate from there. Thus, if asked who is more likely to refrigerate their ketchup, Whites or African Americans, people will answer on the basis of what they themselves do. (It appears that Whites in general refrigerate their ketchup more than African Americans do; Page, 2007.)

Schemas—How We Evaluate Others

How can we understand our judgments about people? We emphasize the role of schemas.[6] Schemas are hypotheses that we use to interpret people and social events (Fiske & Taylor, 1991). Schemas are cognitive constructs that represent knowledge and beliefs about social groups and roles (such as scientist). They can be accurate and predictive (Jussim, 2017; McCauley, Stitt, & Segal, 1980). Gender schemas are hypotheses about what it means to be male or female; race and ethnicity schemas are hypotheses about what it means to be a particular race or ethnicity. In our use of the term, schemas are similar to stereotypes. We prefer the term "schema" because it is broader and more neutral. The term "stereotype" often carries with it the idea of a negative evaluation (though there are positive as well as negative stereotypes) while the term "schema" does not. All stereotypes are schemas, but not all schemas are stereotypes.

The term "schemas" brings out the protoscientific nature of the social hypotheses that we all share. Categorizing objects and events helps us keep track of them and understand them. We have schemas about everything, including inanimate objects. We have a schema for what a chemistry lab looks like.

Why We Have Schemas

We need schemas to make sense of our world. When applied to people, they help us have expectations of others, predict others' behavior, and orient our own behavior. Schemas do some valuable work for us. For example, if we twist our ankle and someone in medical scrubs walks by, we are more likely to ask them for help than another random stranger. The person may not be a doctor, but our schema about doctors will be invoked. We can't respond to every person we see as if we know nothing about the social groups to which they belong. Schemas are at least partially diagnostic: they do tell us something about people. Students have schemas about professors: faculty are knowledgeable about their subject matter, they come to class prepared and on time, they write exams that aren't "tricky," and they grade fairly. When professors violate any of those expectations, students complain. Schemas can thus be both descriptive and prescriptive—they describe what is generally so and they describe what should be so.

The Role of Physical Appearance

People's physical appearance helps us categorize them. For example, when either of us talks to university audiences, we have a pretty good chance of picking out the upper level administrators, just on the basis of their dress and hair. Administrators on the whole dress in a more corporate and formal style than most academics; they look as if they spent time and money to create their appearance. Their garments are coordinated and pressed, their hair is tidy, and they are well-groomed. The men tend to wear ties and suits. The women tend to wear skirt suits more than pants suits, but either way there are a lot of jackets; they wear scarves and jewelry, especially necklaces and earrings. Those cues do not *always* identify upper level administrators. There are exceptions in both directions. But they work often enough for us to keep on categorizing. People may use cues like dress without being aware of them. The fact that such cues are not part of people's conscious awareness does not prevent people from using them. In general, much of the content of schemas is nonconscious.

The physical differences between men and women help underpin the idea of a psychologically "nurturant" woman: women, unlike men, can literally breastfeed an infant (see Valian, 1998, for a hypothesis about the cognitive basis of gender schemas). Similarly, women's lesser physical strength can help underpin the idea of women as "the weaker sex," not only physically but in other domains as well. There is also some evidence that women who are less feminine looking are viewed as more competent than women who appear more feminine (Heilman & Stopeck, 1985). The physical differences among different ethnicities, in contrast, have more limited extensions. The physical characteristics of Jewish individuals, for example, have no relation to the contents of schemas about Jews. It is possible, however, to create an arbitrary link between visual cues and beliefs about personality, behavior, and intelligence. People can, for example, come to associate how Asians "look" with math and science ability, even though there is nothing in how Asians look that directly supports the association.

At the negative end, both African Americans and Whites see African American men who look more "African-American" (e.g., by having darker skin) more negatively than they perceive African American men who are less racially phenotypical (Maddox, 2004). African Americans who "look" African American receive harsher sentences for the same crimes than do African Americans who "look" less African American (e.g., Burch, 2015). (In connection with our earlier statement that stereotypes are neutralized in the presence of a clearly diagnostic event, it appears that commission of a crime need not be seen as clearly diagnostic.) Non–African Americans are also more likely to feel threatened when interacting with African Americans compared to non–African Americans (Mendes, Blascovich, Lickel, & Hunter, 2002). The perceptions extend to school personnel's observations of children: African American children receive more punishment in school than White children of equivalent social class who show similar behaviors (Skiba, Michael, Nardo, & Peterson, 2002; Skiba, Horner, Chung, Rausch, May, & Tobin, 2011). Immigrant workers with lighter skin tones earn higher wages than those with darker skin tones, even when controlling for education, proficiency in English, and other relevant factors (Hersch, 2008).

Although schema formation is ubiquitous and helpful *overall*, schemas are a form of "fast" thinking (Kahneman, 2011) that can lead to error and, when applied to people, can lead to inappropriate perception and treatment of others. Once we know the results of experiments demonstrating the ways in which schemas lead to errors, we can sometimes catch ourselves in the act of drawing inappropriate conclusions.

Are Schemas Shared between Groups?

In the case of gender, men and women are similar in how they see the sexes. The content of male schemas, as we describe below, is shared by both men and women, as is the content of female schemas. That is probably a function of the fact that men and women grow up together as part of the same community. In the case of race and ethnicity, however, the groups in question sometimes make similar judgments and sometimes differ. For example, while the schemas of African Americans and Whites about Whites include some elements in common (e.g., "good at school"), they may not share others (e.g., "likely to be racist"; see also Conley, Rabinowitz, & Rabow, 2010).

Similarly, African Americans and Whites do not necessarily have identical schemas about African Americans. Studies of Hispanics and Asian Americans similarly find conflicting evidence, but there is some evidence that members of both groups internalize—to some extent—the views of themselves that Whites have of them (Jones, 2001; Pittinsky, Shih, & Ambady, 1999; Steele, 2011).[7]

The Available Data and Our Account

We are concerned in this book primarily with people in professional life. Scholars have investigated the objective performance of women and men as well as women's and men's perceptions of their performance. That research is both quantitative and qualitative and includes both objective measures and reports of subjective experiences. Considerably less research exists on the professional performance of different races and ethnic groups and on perceptions of their performance. Nevertheless, the accounts that we offer to explain the lower prestige and power of women and of non-Whites are similar in four ways.

1. People perceive others in terms of surface characteristics that are often unrelated to actual achievement.

2. Surface characteristics activate schema-based perceptions and evaluations.

3. Schemas allow quick decisions but also result in inaccurate judgments and the unintentional advantaging of one group over another in professional settings.

• Some of the different treatments and evaluations are major, such as failures to hire or promote.

• Many of the different treatments are small, daily incivilities (Cortina, Magley, Williams, & Langhout, 2001) that may not be noticed or may be seen as unimportant by either the person experiencing them or the person who engages in them.

• Disadvantages accrue to women and people of color more often than to White men.

4. Different treatments and evaluations, including the ones that are small and hard to detect, not only directly create different outcomes when they should not, but can create different performances.

Schemas have a broad range of consequences, some of which we describe in this chapter, and some of which we describe in our discussions of hiring and promotion in part II.

Stereotype Threat

One consequence for people of being seen as not having the abilities that are necessary for success is lower performance. When people's knowledge of a negative stereotype about them is activated, and the stereotype is in an area that is important to them, their performance suffers. That phenomenon is called stereotype threat. Women for whom math is important perform less well on a math test when they are told that women typically perform worse on it than when they are told that there are no gender differences (Spencer, Steele, & Quinn, 1999). Tests of intellectual performance also pose stereotype threat to African Americans and Hispanics who value academic achievement, reducing their performance (see reviews in Spencer, Logel, & Davies, 2016; Steele, 2011).[8]

Part of the insidiousness of stereotype threat is that it can lead to confirmation and amplification of the contents of the stereotype. If women or minorities who are susceptible to stereotype threat perform poorly, that confirms their lack of ability both to others and to themselves. Expectations do not need to be directly communicated to people to impair their performance.

Gender and ethnicity work somewhat differently, in that subtle cues lead to larger effects for women in math than do more blatant cues, while the reverse is true for ethnicity (Nguyen & Ryan, 2008). Gender and ethnicity also combine to produce complex effects (Gibson, Losee, & Vitiello, 2014; Pittinsky et al., 1999; but see Moon & Roeder, 2014). For example, if Asian women are primed with their ethnicity (i.e., given a cue that brings their ethnicity to mind), they tend to perform above expectation (stereotype "lift"), but if they are primed with their gender, they tend to perform below expectation (stereotype threat).

Explanations for the effects invoke three different underlying mechanisms, all of which consume cognitive resources that would otherwise be used to perform at capacity (Schmader, Johns, & Forbes, 2008). There is a physiological stress reaction, a tendency to think about one's performance as one is doing it, and an attempt to suppress negative thoughts (Murphy, Steele, & Gross, 2007). All of those processes take attention and resources away from the task itself, reducing performance.

The presence of stereotype threat is itself evidence of schemas. If there were no stereotype or schema, or if people were unaware of it, or did not care whether or not it was true, there could be no threat. Thus, the dimensions on which stereotype threat operates tell us something about the content of schemas.

Stereotype threats—or their absence—also affect the extent to which people feel they belong in a setting. If you *do* belong, it is hard to appreciate how much it matters not to belong. Research stemming from belongingness theory (Baumeister & Leary, 1995) has delineated the importance of a feeling of belonging for academic success (e.g., Glass & Westmont, 2014). Most people, regardless of their gender, race, or ethnicity, want to feel that they belong, and a positive feeling of belonging is correlated, among college students, with academic success.

Stereotype threat effectively announces that the person does not belong. For example, environmental cues that indicate that a given domain is "White" or "male" affect how much women and racial-ethnic minorities feel that they belong in academic settings (Cheryan, Plaut, Davies, & Steele, 2009; Murphy et al., 2007; Walton & Cohen, 2007, 2011). A corrosive sense of not fitting in, of being unwelcome, is usually accompanied by depressed performance—and confirmation of negative stereotypes. White men can feel similarly uncomfortable and out of place in a group of African American women. That is not to say that people cannot overcome stereotype threat. They can. But it requires cognitive resources to do so. People who are in environments where they feel—and observers feel—that they fit have an easier time.

When African Americans and Whites are having a conversation together, different threats are activated. African Americans are concerned about appearing competent, believing as they do that Whites are likely to think they are not competent, while Whites are concerned about appearing likable and nonracist, believing as they do that African Americans are likely to think they are racist (Bergsieker, Shelton, & Richeson, 2010). Both Whites and African Americans have different goals in cross-race interactions than in same-race interactions. And their concerns about what impression they are making takes a cognitive toll for both parties (Richeson & Shelton, 2007).

Both gender and race-ethnicity produce complex expectations in ourselves and in observers about what we are good at and what we can achieve (Steele, 2011). Those expectations in turn can enhance or diminish our performance. Because the dimension of competence or intelligence is so consistently important in the construction of gender and racial-ethnic stereotypes, the academy—where this kind of talent is the one at stake—is a particularly charged domain.

The Specific Content of Gender Schemas

We have spoken generally thus far about schemas. Gender schemas are hypotheses about what it means to be male or female, hypotheses that we all share, male and female alike. Gender schemas assign different psychological traits to males and females (Martin & Halverson, 1987; Spence & Helmreich, 1978). We think of males as capable of independent action (agentic), as focused on the task at hand (task oriented), and as doing things for a reason (instrumental). Thus, we expect men to demand compensation for their activities. As mentioned earlier, we think of females as nurturant; we also see them as being expressive and behaving communally. Thus, we expect women to "labor for love" and see them as selfish if they demand compensation; they have violated the schema that women are nurturant and communal. In brief: men act; women feel and express their feelings.

Our beliefs about gender differences have some support. First, people differ in how strongly they see different characteristics as applying to them. While men and women overall are roughly similar on the characteristics we associate with men—traits like "stands one's ground," women do endorse more of the characteristics we associate with women—traits like "kind"— than men do. Second, the sexes agree on what *other* people are like, seeing college students as more polarized in "masculine" and "feminine" characteristics than they have said they themselves are. There is a gap between how people see themselves and how they see the average person (Ridgeway, 2011).[9]

Since men are associated with the competent capable norm, it is safe for women to acquire some of the hallmarks of the male gender schema, and in fact women must do so if they are going to be perceived as competent. However, if women do not include some of the hallmarks of the female gender schema in their behavior, they will experience backlash (Heilman, 2012; Heilman & Okimoto, 2007; Ridgeway, 2011; Rudman & Phelan, 2008). Men run the risk of seeming incompetent if they appear too "feminine," and they experience backlash if they appear modest (Moss-Racusin, Phelan, & Rudman, 2010) or succeed at "feminine" tasks (Rudman & Fairchild, 2004).

Men who succeed at "feminine" tasks are also seen as wimpy (Heilman & Wallen, 2010).

As a result of schemas, people overrate men's performances and under-rate women's. The differences are usually small but consistent. For example, college students see male college professors as having more innate ability than female college professors. An analysis we ran of adjectives used in Rate My Professors descriptions shows that the word *brilliant* is used more often for men than women in every academic field, even those like account-ing, where *brilliant* is seldom used (sorry, accountants). Similarly, the word *genius* is more often used for men than women, with an even bigger gender disparity than *brilliant*. As one might expect, women are rated as "helpful" and "sweet" more than men are—in every field. But negative adjectives related to student treatment, such as "mean" and "strict," are also more com-mon for women, possibly because women who are not "helpful" and "sweet" are violating gender schemas. Men are rated as much more "arrogant" than women in every field. (See http://benschmidt.org/research-portfolio/, Gen-dered Language in Teacher Reviews, to put in your own search terms.)[10]

The more male dominated a field is, the greater the belief about the importance of innate ability compared to motivation and hard work (Leslie, Cimpian, Meyer, & Freeland, 2015). Faculty and graduate students in differ-ent academic disciplines rated how much their field required abilities that could not be taught. The fewer women that the field contained, the more people thought their discipline required innate talent. Our field, psychol-ogy, which grants PhDs primarily to women (more than 70%), was rated by people in the field as requiring little field-specific ability compared to hard work. In contrast, philosophy, which has a relatively low proportion of women PhDs compared to other humanities fields (around 30% of 2011 PhDs), was rated as requiring more field-specific innate ability than any other field.

Overall, then, gender schemas skew our perceptions and evaluations of men and women, causing us to overrate men and underrate women. Gender schemas affect our judgments of people's competence, ability, and personal characteristics. Many of our judgments are small everyday events, such as not listening when a woman talks to us or not congratulating a woman on an achievement. Moreover, these small but frequent occurrences, which seem too petty to notice, accumulate to advantage men and disadvantage women.

Experimental Data about Perceptions of Sex Differences

Experimental data demonstrate that we do not see other people simply as people; we see them as males or females. Once gender schemas are invoked, they work to disadvantage women by directing and skewing our perception, even in the case of objective characteristics like height. In one example (Biernat, Manis, & Nelson, 1991), the experimenters exploited the fact that our schemas include the—of course correct—information that men are on average taller than women. In this experiment, college students saw photographs of other students and estimated their height in feet and inches. The photos always contained a reference item, such as a desk or a doorway, so that height could be accurately estimated.

Unbeknownst to the students who were doing the estimating, the experimenters had matched the photographs so that for every photograph of a male student of a given height there was a female student of the same height. But the students were affected by their knowledge that men are on average taller than women. They judged the women as slightly shorter than they really were, and the men as taller. This finding is reminiscent of the study we referred to earlier, where parents underestimated their 11-month-old daughters' motor ability and overestimated their sons' (Mondschein et al., 2000).

In the experiment on height, there were no differences in male and female observers. That is the usual finding. We all have hypotheses, some conscious and some not, about males and females, and we all use those hypotheses in perceiving and evaluating others. The important point about these two studies is that genuinely objective characteristics—height and motor ability—are not immune from the effects of gender schemas. Observers are influenced by what is generally the case, as in the height example, or what *will* generally be the case, as in the example concerning infants' motor ability. And it makes cognitive sense to be influenced by the average. Absent other information, the average is a good measure to go by. At the same time, that strategy has a cost for the individuals who are misjudged. When one underestimates people's abilities or skills, one tends to give those people less credit than they deserve, to ask less of them, and to rob them of the potential for growth.

Four Examples of Judgments of Professional Competence

In the case of professional competence, which differs from height in being harder to measure, our perceptions are similarly prone to error. We are likely to overvalue men and undervalue women. We can see why that would be the case: gender schemas will play a large role in evaluations (1) whenever schemas make a clear differentiation between males and females, and they do for professional competence as much as for height, and (2) when evidence is ambiguous and open to interpretation, as is the case with professional competence. It is tempting to think excellence is straightforward, but it is not. Four experiments on judgments of women's competence demonstrate the effects of gender schemas and the costs for women in professional life.

The first study investigated how males and females rated people who were described as being an Assistant Vice President in an aircraft company (Heilman, Wallen, Fuchs, & Tamkins, 2004). The evaluators read background information about the person, the job, and the company. The information they read about the person included the person's birthplace, the college they attended, their grades, how long they had worked in the company, how much management training they had received, how many employees they currently supervised, and their personal interests. In half the cases, the person was described as about to have a performance review. Thus, in this condition, evaluators did not know how well the person was doing in the job. In the other half of the cases, the person was described as having been a stellar performer. The evaluators' job was to rate the employees' competence and likability.

When evaluators had no information about how well people were doing in the job, they rated the man as more competent than the woman and rated them as equally likable. The finding that both men and women rate women as less competent than men, even when given identical information, is a typical finding in the social psychology literature. What was new about this experiment was looking at what happened to likability.

When the background information made clear that the individuals were extremely competent, evaluators rated the man and the woman as equally competent, showing that evaluators are responsive to clear information. It is only when the information is ambiguous that men have an advantage in competence ratings. But evaluators rated the competent woman as much less likable than the competent man. They also perceived the woman as considerably more hostile than the man.

Thus, in evaluating a woman in a male-dominated field, male and female observers alike see her as less competent than a similarly described man unless there is clear information that she is competent. And in that case, they see her as less likable than a comparable man. Both males and females see competence as the norm for men and as something that has to be demonstrated unequivocally for women. Both males and females see competent men as likable. Neither males nor females see competent women in male-dominated positions as likable.

And likability matters: in a follow-up experiment, the experimenters described the people to be evaluated as high or low in competence and high or low in likability. People rated those who were high in likability as better candidates for being placed on a fast track and as better candidates for a highly prestigious upper level position. It would be poor advice to tell women just to be competent because likability can make the difference in whether or not people get rewards. Again, there were no male-female rater differences.

A second study shows that there is a trade-off for women between competence and femininity (Phelan, Moss-Racusin, & Rudman, 2008). Observers heard fictitious interviews for a computer lab manager job in which both the interviewer and interviewee were actors who used exactly the same scripts. The observers were told that the job required strong technical skills as well as social skills—because of the need to help students and faculty. In one condition, the interviewees adopted an assertive style emphasizing their competence; in the other, they adopted a style that emphasized how communal they were. Observers rated the interviewees on their competence, their social skills, and how hireable they were.

Evaluators generally gave more weight to competence than social skills. The notable exception was women who were assertive. In that case observers gave more weight to social skills. Since assertive women were seen as not having social skills, they were also seen as less hireable than assertive men. Again, there was no difference in judgments on the part of female versus male observers. Women are thus in a difficult position. If they are not perceived as competent, they will not get the job. But if they make their competence clear by behaving assertively, they will be seen as lacking social skills and will be downgraded for that reason.[11]

The third study demonstrated how people shift their standards in order to justify a choice that seems a priori reasonable to them (Norton, Vandello, & Darley, 2004). In this experiment, gender schemas determined what seemed reasonable. The experimenters asked male undergraduates to select a candidate for a job that required both a strong engineering background and experience in the construction industry. The evaluators rated five people, only two of whose résumés were competitive. One candidate had more education—both an engineering degree and certification from a concrete masonry association—than the other, who only had an engineering degree. The other candidate had more experience—a total of nine years—than the first, who only had five years. Thus, there was a trade-off between accreditation and experience.

In the control condition, the candidates were identified only by initials. Here, the evaluators chose the candidate with more education three-quarters of the time and education was the reason most often cited as important for their decision. In one of the two experimental conditions, a male name was given to the résumé that had more education and a female name to the résumé that had more experience. Here, too, evaluators chose the candidate with more education three-quarters of the time and also rated education as very important. In the second experimental condition, a female name was given to the résumé with more education and a male name to the résumé with more experience. Now, less than half of the evaluators picked the person with more education and less than a quarter cited education as the most important characteristic.[12]

Men look more appropriate than women for the job of construction engineer, whether they have more education *or* more experience. The standards by which we judge people shift depending on our a priori judgments about their goodness of fit. Gender schemas help determine goodness of fit. This study demonstrates how easily people can shift their standards if they have not antecedently decided what the criteria are.

The fourth study bears on a possible objection to the studies just reviewed: the participants are (generally) college students who are not trained in evaluating others. Working scientists, the thinking goes, would be able to judge men and women accurately, both because scientists are trained to objectively and dispassionately evaluate data and because they subscribe to the merit principle. Thus, any differences in the representation of men and women in science would be due to the different choices that men and women make, due to factors that are internal to men and women, rather than due to the social structure or evaluators' judgments. But it turns out that scientists—chemists, physicists, and biologists—are just like undergraduates.

University scientists were given a description of a possible lab manager—an undergraduate student who would manage a laboratory (Moss-Racusin, Dovidio, Brescoll, Graham, & Handelsman, 2012). The description of the candidate was ambiguous, indicating weaknesses as well as strengths. An ambiguous description was used because, as we have noted, observers are able to recognize outstanding talents in women. It is when people are less than outstanding (which most people are) that schemas have more room to operate. Given the ambiguous description, we would expect scientists to respond by overrating the man and underrating the woman. And that is what they did—they rated the female candidate less positively than the identical male candidate.[13] As usual, there were no differences between male and female scientists in the ratings.

The scientists also completed a Modern Sexism Scale designed to tap subtle beliefs about gender equality (Swim, Aikin, Hall, & Hunter, 1995). It included eight items on which the scientists indicated the extent of their agreement, such as "Society has reached the point where women and men have equal opportunities for achievement" and "Women often miss out on good jobs due to sexual discrimination."

The scale taps "modern" sexism in two ways. First, participants indicate the extent to which they think that problems related to gender and achievement are in the past, and second, beliefs like equality of opportunity do not appear sexist on their face. They are not the same as believing that women are intellectually inferior to men. Scientists are reluctant to voice such attitudes, but thinking that sexual discrimination is in the past seems like a benign belief. Despite how mild such sentiments seem to be, the more the scientists endorsed statements indicating that women faced no particular hurdles, the more likely they were to rate the female candidate poorly. (Scientists' evaluation of the male candidate was unaffected by their score on this scale.) There were no differences between men and women scientists in the extent to which they believed sex discrimination was a thing of the past.

These results suggest that beliefs that women and men are on an equal footing make it more likely that an evaluator will judge a woman poorly. It appears that people go from endorsing the desirability of judging people without regard to gender to believing that the world actually does judge people without regard to gender.[14] Part of the problem, then, is that people's conviction that gender equality is a fact, and not simply a desired state, impairs their judgment of women. Their very belief in the existence of equality is associated with more negative evaluations of women.

Perceptions of Outstanding Women

We have alluded several times to the differences between people's responses to outstanding individuals and individuals who are closer to the average. There are signs of progress in the perception of leaders, at least among some people in some settings. For example, in a survey that was available online to visitors to the MSNBC site, people were invited to rate their boss. Over a ten-day period, roughly 60,000 people contributed usable data (Elsesser & Lever, 2011). Although differences in ratings were very small, women with male managers rated them as more competent than did women with female managers; men were more evenly split, but men with female managers rated them as very slightly more competent than did men with male managers. That effect appeared to be driven by competition: whichever gender people reported competing with at work was the gender that got lower competence ratings. Those results suggest that people do not necessarily rate their manager's competence along gender lines.

However, a somewhat different picture emerged when people were asked to indicate which sex they would prefer to work for. Among the slightly less than half who indicated a preference, men were preferred at more than double the rate at which women were preferred. The preference for men was even stronger in male-dominated occupations, with no difference between male and female participants.

Why might people's preferences in the abstract differ from their evaluations of their own managers? It may be easy for people to see their own manager as an exception to a more general tendency—to engage in subtyping (Richards & Hewstone, 2001). In subtyping, seeing someone who is very different from one's expectations may result in an accurate perception of that person without a change in one's overall view. The person is an exception who leaves the rule intact. And that is a rational way to behave: a single experience should not overturn a view based on multiple experiences. In the domain of social perception, however, where perceptions are affected by a person's group membership, and where beliefs can substitute for firsthand experience, the "rule" may itself be incorrect.

Businesspeople's perceptions of men and women as leaders suggest that women are seen as excelling in some of the traits associated with the gender schema for women, such as supporting and rewarding others, while men are seen as excelling in traits associated with the gender schemas for men, such as delegating and influencing one's superiors (Prime, Carter, & Welbourne, 2009). Other traits, such as the "masculine" trait of problem-solving, are seen by women as more common for women but are seen by men as more common for men. A meta-analysis of 99 studies of perceptions of male and female leaders suggests that, overall, both men and women rate their female leaders more highly than their male leaders, but when rating themselves as leaders, men rate themselves much more highly than women rate themselves (Paustian-Underdahl, Walker, & Woehr, 2014). One reason for the superior rating of women in top positions may be that women in those positions are seen as having overcome, and may actually have overcome, strong odds against them through superior competence (Foschi, 2000; Paustian-Underdahl et al., 2014).

Taken together, the results suggest that people can acknowledge outstanding female performance under certain conditions. Consider, for example, a study in which students rated individuals applying for a position of either a football or a tennis photographer on a magazine (Heilman, Martell, & Simon, 1988). Football photography is considered a male-dominated field compared to tennis photography. In one condition, the dossier was labeled as awaiting review, and in the other the person was labeled as a finalist, having been chosen by experts as worthy of being in final consideration.

In both the tennis case and the football case, when evaluators had no information about how the candidates had been rated, female candidates were seen as less competent than male candidates. Absent information to the contrary, people rate men more highly than women. However, when evaluators had information that the women were finalists, ratings of tennis and football photographers were not the same. When women were finalists in tennis, there was no difference in ratings for male and female candidates; legitimation by experts made men and women equal. When women were finalists in football, they received ratings that were *more* favorable than men's (Heilman et al., 1988). Evaluators seemed to think that the woman must be a star to have received a favorable rating from experts in a highly male-dominated field.

A similar finding arose in a study of rankings of job candidates for a professorial position in science (Williams & Ceci, 2015), where evaluators were presented with descriptions of three candidates, two of whom had already received very high ratings from a search committee. One of the two was male, and one was female. In line with the study on sports photographers, evaluators—in this case academics—ranked the woman as the person to hire.[15] When women are stars, they will be recognized.

This review of gender schemas in action demonstrates that both men and women are likely to overrate men and underrate women in settings where professional competence is at issue. Different reactions to the same behavior, occurring because of the sex of the person displaying the behavior, happen among college students, business school students, working adults, and working scientists. Part of what makes schemas so powerful is their very subtlety. On implicit measures, both men and women evaluate men more positively than women, even though most individuals demonstrate a commitment to judging individual merit rather than basing judgments on group membership.

Laboring for Love

A female full professor, whom we will call Carol, provided the following example. Carol had spoken to her chair, whom we will call John, about the differential treatment of two new faculty who had been hired two years earlier and whose research overlapped. John was a friend of Carol's; she liked him and respected him. The male assistant professor had taught the same two courses every semester, one of which was a graduate seminar in his area. He recruited students to work with him from that seminar. The female assistant professor had taught different courses every semester, always undergraduate "service" courses. Carol suggested that John should make more equitable assignments. John agreed that the inequity was helping the junior male and hurting the junior female. But, he said, the junior male hadn't been very cooperative and had resisted John's request that he teach other courses. The junior male also wasn't a great teacher. The junior female didn't put up a fight about her teaching and did a good job at it. He had to think about the department and the students.

Relatively little quantitative data from 2010 on are available to show how teaching and service responsibilities are divided among women and men, but women appear to teach more (Carrigan, Quinn, & Riskin, 2011) and perform more service, regardless of rank (Guarino & Borden, 2017; for a review, see Mitchell & Hesli, 2013). White women and men and women of color perceive that they spend more time than their White male colleagues mentoring women and students of color and spend more time, relatively speaking, on committees so that those committees can be more diverse. One study of over 1,000 faculty in political science found that women say no to committee assignments less often than men do (Mitchell & Hesli, 2013). Women are asked to serve more often than men are, and they accept more invitations than men do. They do not volunteer more often than men. In addition to serving on more internal committees, the women also had more undergraduate students than the men (though they did not supervise more projects) and fewer postdocs. Examination of faculty workload reports across a range of disciplines at a single university found similar results: women performed more service than men (O'Meara, Kuvaeva, & Nyunt, 2017). Women are also asked to perform more service, according to diary entries of individual faculty at 13 of the 14 Big Ten universities (O'Meara, Kuvaeva, Nyunt, Waugaman, & Jackson, 2017).

Time allocation studies provide inconsistent reports about whether men and women of color spend more time teaching and mentoring than their White peers (for discussion, see Martinez & Toutkoushian, 2014). Latinx faculty are similar to White faculty in their time allocations, except that Latinx faculty spend more time than do Whites on unpaid work in the community (Martinez & Toutkoushian, 2014).

The request for women's services is expected since the schema for women portrays them as nurturant and communal. Women are expected to, and will, labor for love. We see this explanation as part of the gender schema story. Institutions can ameliorate the problem of unequal demands on different demographic groups by reviewing their teaching and committee assignments for fairness. Chairs can learn how to handle refractory faculty. If White women and men and women of color are doing more than their fair share of committee service, they can be compensated for that extra service via course releases or research assistance.

When Good Intentions Go Awry

What is most sobering for evaluators who wish to be fair is that simply explicitly disagreeing with an overtly sexist statement makes it more likely that an individual will then go on to pick a man for a stereotypically male job (Merritt, Effron, & Monin, 2010). People were asked to say whether a job in the construction industry—a job typically associated with men—would be better for men, better for women, or equally suited to either sex. One group of participants was first asked to agree or disagree with statements like "Most women are not very smart." Another group did not read any sexist statements ahead of time. Male participants who read the statements were likely to disagree with them, but that very disagreement made them more likely to choose a male for the construction job than the participants who had not read any statements (Monin & Miller, 2001). (Women were unaffected.)

It appears that once individuals have announced their bona fides, they think they have demonstrated a lack of bias. That in turn makes it more likely that, on their next opportunity in a situation that activates gender schemas, they will demonstrate bias. People can reassure themselves that their decision was made on the basis of merit because they have at hand judgments that they had just made that suggested to them that they were free of bias. Since academics routinely espouse the merit principle, this moral "licensing" should give everyone pause. The statement with which we opened the chapter—"I don't care who they are; I just want the best person"—is a good example. Once people have assured themselves that they judge fairly, they are less concerned about their behavior in any particular case.

Again, the propensity to make errors in evaluation can best be handled by having explicit valid criteria and procedures.

Race and Ethnicity Schemas

In the same way that individuals are egalitarian and meritocratic in their explicit comments about women, they are egalitarian and meritocratic in their explicit views of African Americans, Hispanics, and other underrepresented minorities. And, as with gender, subtle tests suggest a more complicated picture. When people say that they "don't see race," they are not taking into account data about how evaluations work. Whether judging males or females, or African Americans or Whites or Hispanics, we generally take people's social identities into account. Yet it is hard to say what the content of our race and ethnicity schemas is. In the case of gender, we can articulate the core of each schema. For the male gender schema, agency is the core; for the female gender schema, nurturance is the core. For ethnic groups, it is more difficult to say what the core is. For example, what is the core of the White ethnicity schema?

Different schemas characterize different racial-ethnic groups. African Americans and Hispanics are viewed as lower than Whites on competence and warmth, while Asians are rated as high on competence but low on warmth (see, e.g., Zhang, 2015). Schemas about different ethnic groups are related to schemas about job prestige. Hispanics are assumed to hold lower status jobs than non-Hispanics, and in turn to have less of a work ethic and to be more "traditional," that is, in having a greater family orientation and religiosity (Jones, 2001). Both African Americans and Whites see Whites as having high status (see the review in Fiske, Dupree, Nicolas, & Swencionis, 2016). Similarly, in a study of adolescents' stereotypes, beliefs that African Americans were not successful in school, and that Hispanics engage in manual labor occupations, underlay adolescents' stereotypes about their intelligence, compared with those of Asians (Kao, 2000).

Status enters via the terms used to describe different groups. Whites evaluate "Blacks" more negatively than "African Americans" or "Whites," and see them as having lower status and as being less competent (Hall, Phillips, & Townsend, 2015). Whites also see "Blacks" as having less education than "African- Americans" and as making less money. Further, in newspaper articles, "Blacks" are associated with more negative emotions than "African Americans," especially more terms conveying anger. For Whites, the term "Black" conveys less respect than the term "African American."

Americans of African descent are about evenly split in their preferences between "Black" and "African American," but different subgroups show a strong preference for "African American" (Sigelman, Tuch, & Martin, 2005). For example, the combination of having been in a grammar school that was roughly 50–50 African American and White, plus being younger, plus living in a city, plus not living in the South, plus identifying strongly with an African American identity was associated with a strong preference for

"African American." (See Agyemang, Bhopal, & Bruijnzeels, 2005, who argue that there are health treatment consequences to what labels are used, and Philogène, 1999.)

Ethnicity in the Workplace

Since we are primarily concerned with professional competence, we can concentrate on the data concerning schemas of different ethnicities in the workplace. In rating a series of adjectives taken from various studies of race schemas, a group of business school students (African Americans, Whites, Asians, Hispanics, and other ethnicities) perceived hypothetical African American and White managers differently. Whites were seen as more competent, ambitious, and manipulative; African Americans were seen as more skillful interpersonally but less polished. (There were not enough participants to determine whether African Americans and Whites examined separately would differ in their judgments.) When the participants were asked to rate successful managers, rather than just managers, Whites continued to be seen as more manipulative and African Americans as more skillful interpersonally and less polished (Block, Aumann, & Chelin, 2012). In a related study, similar perceptions of Whites came from ratings by minority students—African Americans, Asians, and Hispanics. Some of the positive traits that all three ethnic groups saw as characteristic of Whites were having more opportunities, being intelligent, being confident, and being outgoing (Conley et al., 2010).[16]

Since competence is the key characteristic for professional success—at least when White men possess it—the fact that Whites are seen as more competent gives them an advantage in the same way that the perception of men as more competent than women gives them an advantage. For example, when men and women of varied ethnicities (but primarily White) believed that they had performed poorly on a task, they were more likely to relinquish leadership to a White male than to an African American male (Ratcliff, Vescio, & Dahl, 2015).[17] Similarly, participants were more likely to cede power to a White man than a White woman (Ratcliff et al., 2015).

Differential assumptions about ability have implications for evaluations of success and failure. In one study, participants read about a company that had succeeded or failed either because of a leader's performance or because of external conditions that were independent of anything the leader did

(Rosette, Leonardelli, & Phillips, 2008). The company leader was sometimes given a "Black" name (Tyrone) or a "White" name (Todd). A picture was provided of the leader. Thus, evaluators had some detailed information about the leader. Observers rated the leader on competence, confidence, intelligence, and competitiveness.

In the condition in which the organization had been successful, Whites were rated as more effective than African Americans when internal reasons were given for the success, but when external reasons were provided for success, the two groups were rated as equally effective. Thus, Whites are seen as having earned their success, even when identical language is used to indicate that African Americans are responsible for their success. When the organization had not been successful, there were no differences in ratings for Whites and African Americans. In this study, there were no differences as a function of the participant's race. Thus, it appears that non-Whites are as likely as Whites to see successful leadership as White.

However, race does not have uniform effects on non–African Americans' perceptions of African American men and women. Non–African American participants rated a leader in one of eight conditions: the leader was White or African American, male or female, and showed dominant or communal behavior. Participants rated the leader's effectiveness on several dimensions (Livingston, Rosette, & Washington, 2012).

African American female leaders were seen as equally effective whether they were dominant or communal, but White female leaders were penalized for showing dominant behavior rather than communal behavior. Among male leaders, African Americans were penalized for being dominant rather than communal, but Whites were rated equally highly whether they were dominant or communal. Thus, non–African American observers "allow" African American women and White men to be dominant or communal but do not allow African American men or White women to be dominant (Livingston et al., 2012).

It is worth noting that—partly because of the long and painful history of slavery and race relations between African American and White Americans—more is known about African American stereotypes than about those of other racial and ethnic groups. One meta-analysis found that in the three social psychology journals that published much of the research on schemas about different races and ethnic groups, only 7% of that research focused on stereotypes about Hispanics, while 61% focused on stereotypes about African Americans, even though Hispanics are a larger percentage of the population (Dovidio, Gluszek, John, Ditlmann, & Lagunes, 2010).

Why We Need to Pay Attention to Race and Ethnicity

We understand why Whites find the idea of paying attention to race aversive. At first blush, attending to race seems like a violation of the merit principle. Shouldn't one judge people completely on their merits? If one could really be blind to race, color, and ethnicity, wouldn't the world be a better place?

We have argued that it is not possible to perceive people independently of their social identities. For that reason, it is better to be on one's guard about the perceptions one is likely to have than to deny their existence. Until the world really *is* fair, we should not act as if it is. When there are clear and valid standards for performance, and when it is possible to evaluate people without knowledge of their social identity, then people can judge impartially (e.g., Goldin & Rouse, 2000; Self, Mitchell, Mellers, Tetlock, & Hildreth, 2015). However, in keeping with our earlier discussion of the importance of visual cues, listeners rely on them even when they are evaluating musical performance (Tsay, 2013). As long as there are cues to social identity, social identity has an impact on judgments.

Trying to adopt a race-neutral approach in a world that sees race and ethnicity can backfire (Apfelbaum, Norton, & Sommers, 2012). For example, children who heard a story about a teacher who adopted a color-blind approach were less likely to subsequently recognize overt discrimination than were children who heard a story about a teacher who did not adopt a color-blind approach (Apfelbaum, Pauker, Sommers, & Ambady, 2010).

If we think that race and ethnicity *can't* play a role, we are unlikely to see the occasions when it is playing a role. We recognize that one is not always correct in seeing a role for social identity. If one is always looking for evaluation errors, one may see some where they do not exist. Whatever hypothesis we hold is likely to affect how many confirming examples we see. We argue that it is healthy to start with the possibility that one is choosing the White over the African American for reasons that are incidental to their actual performances. That will make it more likely that we perceive evidence in favor of the hypothesis. Whites are already highly motivated to find that hypothesis to be wrong, so they need consciously to look for evidence that the hypothesis is right.

Another reason for Whites to pay attention to race and ethnicity is that underrepresented minorities prefer to have differences acknowledged rather than ignored and prefer a multicultural approach in which different orientations are valued, rather than a color-blind approach or an assimilationist approach in which minorities are assimilated to the majority culture (Dovidio, Gaertner, Ufkes, Saguy, & Pearson, 2016; Ryan, Casas, & Thompson, 2010; Ryan, Hunt, Weible, Peterson, & Casas, 2007). Whites could thus recognize difference and value it instead of denying its existence or effects.

When Leaders Fail

All leaders occasionally fail. When women or people of color fail, their failure is likely to be attributed to their gender or ethnicity. When White men fail, in contrast, they are more likely to be seen as failing as individuals (or as failing because the task was very difficult). People do not say, "Oh, so-and-so was a poor president because he was White." They say, "Oh, so-and-so was a poor president because he lacked initiative," or "He didn't have people skills," or "He was a poor delegator." When women or people of color fail, they are seen as failing because of their group membership (Miller, Taylor, & Buck, 1991). They failed because they were women (and women as a group don't have the qualities necessary for success), or because they were African American (and African Americans as a group don't have the qualities necessary for success).[18]

Accumulation of Advantage

Many of the slightly too negative evaluations that women receive and the slightly too positive evaluations that men receive seem minor. Women and men notice some of them but not others in daily life. As we mentioned in the preface, the most commonly noticed examples arise in meetings. A woman makes a suggestion, and no one pays any attention to it. A little later a male colleague makes the same suggestion, and everyone says, "Joe, what a great idea." What makes it hard for the woman herself to evaluate this event is that everyone's ideas are ignored some of the time; she doesn't want to be paranoid. Neither she nor anyone else has been keeping a running tally. Is it really a systematic phenomenon? Did she not express her idea in an optimal way? Did the idea just need time to percolate through the group? And, should she mention the phenomenon to a colleague, that colleague might or might not agree that women weren't attended to quite as much but would probably suggest that it's not worth her time to think about it, let along protest it. She shouldn't make a mountain out of a molehill (Valian, 1998).

One woman told us about giving a keynote address at a major international conference. Her department put that honor on their website for two days. It was then superseded by an announcement about a male colleague who would be giving a keynote address at a much smaller conference the following year. His notice stayed up for over a week. (In fact it stayed up until she approached her chair about the reason for his being featured.) Her major achievement was briefly recognized; his minor achievement—which had not even happened yet—was given much more attention. In another website example, a woman was elected as a board member for a prestigious, national board. Although the department was informed about the honor, it did not put it on the website. Later, when a man was a candidate for the same board, his candidacy was put on the website. (He did not get elected.) Since these data are not systematic, we do not know if there were equally many examples that went in the opposite direction; the accumulated data we have presented thus far would suggest not.

Again, someone might say about such events, don't make a mountain out of a molehill. Giving the keynote was the honor; being elected was the honor. Those were the important things. It doesn't matter that much that your department hardly noticed.

One feature of small negative effects is that they tend to be more frequent than big negative effects. They are chronic. They may be like gnats, but the effort of swatting away gnats on a frequent basis is stressful. A meta-analysis comparing the negative effects of subtle and overt discrimination found that both were correlated with negative effects in a variety of areas (Jones, Peddie, Gilrane, King, & Gray, 2016). Subtle discrimination referred to the kinds of small events we have been discussing (Hebl, Foster, Mannix, & Dovidio, 2002). The negative effects ranged from decreased success in one's job (as measured by promotions and productivity) to substance abuse. Correlations were as high for the subtle measures of discrimination as for the more overt measures. Small negative experiences turn out to have negative effects on the person that are comparable to those from large negative experiences.

But they also have negative effects over time. That is where the notion of the accumulation of advantage becomes relevant. The Matthew effect (Merton, 1988; Zuckerman, 1997) was developed to explain disparities in scientific recognition: to oversimplify, the rich (or recognized) get richer (even more recognized). (See Rigney, 2010, for a recent summary of effects in a range of fields and for a discussion of the limits of the accumulation of advantage; see also DiPrete & Eirich, 2006.) It lets us see that mountains *are* molehills, piled one on top of the other (Valian, 1998). Most success is the accrual of small gains that compound over time, like interest on investments. If one fails to get one's fair share of the interest, one ends up with less in the long run.

A computer simulation of this phenomenon showed that a tiny amount of bias—an amount accounting for only 1% of the variability in determining who would get promoted—resulted in a striking difference over time in the composition of the uppermost level of the simulated organization (Martell, Lane, & Emrich, 1996). The simulation assumed an eight-level hierarchically organized company, with 500 positions at the lowest level and 10 positions at the highest. It was staffed initially by the same number of men and women.[19] There was an attrition process, so that 15% of incumbents were periodically removed. The promotion process assumed equal performance by men and women, but men received bonus points—for being men—that amounted to 1% of the variance in scores. The promotion process was repeated until the organization had completely turned over. At that point, the uppermost level was 65% male. (Twenty iterations were run, so that the average was 65%.) Thus, even a tiny amount of bias, an amount most institutions would be delighted to achieve, adds up over time to a mountain of disadvantage.

Summary

Our presentation of the literature on gender schemas and race and ethnicity schemas shows that, without intending to, we treat people differently on the basis of their gender, their race, their ethnicity, and a number of other factors. We are likely to undervalue the competence and professional ability of women and members of underrepresented groups. An analysis of schemas looks underneath the more common reasons suggested for the relative paucity of certain groups and shows how some of those apparent differences—including apparent differences in interests—could arise. Those differences have consequences for the opportunities that we make available to people, the expectations that we have of them, the support that we provide them, and the evaluations that we give them. Although we believe we are attending only to merit when we evaluate others, our impressions are shaded by our schemas. We are unlikely to eradicate the cognitive strategies that give rise to those impressions. The first step is to become aware of them. The second step is to create procedures that will protect us from the mistakes resulting from those strategies.

Notes

1. Early sources of information about schemas in the sense that they are being used here include Bakan, 1966; Fiske & Taylor, 1991; Martin & Halverson, 1987; and McCauley, Stitt, & Segal, 1980. These researchers link schemas or probabilistic stereotypes to general cognitive concept formation.

2. In Bayesian terms, schemas are the equivalent of what people in some fields call "priors" or expectations. They can thus be modified, in any individual case, by the information presented, depending on the strength of the priors, the nature of the information, and other factors. We thank Charles Brown for pointing out this parallel.

3. In characterizations of people's personalities, race and ethnicity seem to recede in importance as more information is provided, but race and ethnicity remain important when judging leadership abilities, as we discuss below.

4. When possible, we refer to very recent studies, so that we can avoid discussing previously observed phenomena that may no longer hold. It seems unlikely, however, that parents have shifted their views about the motoric abilities of their 11-month olds since 2000.

5. A study of male conscripts in the Norwegian Armed Forces found that minimal individuating information did not alter their lower evaluations of a woman as a possible squad leader, but that intense exposure by sharing a room and working in the same squad as a female soldier did (Finseraas, Johnsen, Kotsadam, & Torsvik, 2016).

6. Schemas are somewhat different from implicit attitudes, as measured by, for example, the Implicit Association Test (IAT; Banaji & Greenwald, 2013). We emphasize the cognitive content of schemas and the continuity between social schemas

and schemas for inanimate objects and asocial events that lack intrinsic affect. Affect may be attached to schema content and often is in the case of schemas about human groups. There is disagreement in the literature about whether content and affect can be separated (e.g., Fiske, 2015). IAT measures correlate with behaviors toward members of different groups, though the extent of the relation and its importance is debated (Greenwald, Banaji, & Nosek, 2015; Oswald, Mitchell, Blanton, Jaccard, & Tetlock, 2015). It is difficult to alter IAT judgments (Lai et al., 2014, 2016), though some approaches have appeared successful (Carnes et al., 2015; Devine, Forscher, Austin, & Cox, 2012). Short-term procedures that have been used to change IAT performance have not reliably mediated changes in behavior (Forscher et al., 2017).

Whether the IAT measures associations, propositions, beliefs, attitudes, or some other mental structure, is not clear. For discussion of the nature of implicit bias, see, inter alia, Gendler (2008), Levy (2015), Madva and Brownstein (in press), and Mandelbaum (2016). We do not use the term *implicit bias*, despite its popularity and utility, and despite our agreement that much of human cognition is not conscious. The reason is that we do not equate rapid associations with bias.

7. People also make judgments about people's warmth and competence (for more detail, see the stereotype content model of Fiske, Cuddy, & Glick, 2007) and their moral character (Goodwin, 2015; Goodwin, Piazza, & Rozin, 2014). All three attributes are at least partially independent. People can, for example, have a fine moral character but be cold and incompetent. Status is highly correlated with perceived competence, especially by those who believe that people get what they deserve, with the result that low-status individuals are seen as incompetent. Gender and ethnicity play a role. In the United States, Asians, Jews, the rich, and professionals, even if they are female or ethnic minorities, are seen as competent and cold (Fiske et al., 2007). In contrast, older people, and the physically and mentally disabled, are seen as incompetent and warm. Higher-status groups, such as middle-class people, Christians, and straights, are perceived as both competent and warm. Lower-status groups, such as poor Whites, Hispanics, and Blacks, are seen as incompetent and cold.

8. The extent to which people are knowledgeable about the stereotype, the extent to which they believe it, the subtlety with which the stereotype is activated, and other factors affect the strength of the phenomenon (see Kiefer & Sekaquaptewa, 2007; see papers in Inzlicht & Schmader, 2012).

9. In the 1970s the differences in how men and women rated themselves on various traits were more marked than they were in 2000 (Spence & Buckner, 2000). The change over time was due primarily to women's seeing themselves as having more characteristics that we associate with men—such as "has leadership." Men changed less in the extent to which they endorsed "feminine" characteristics. One reason for women to have changed more than men is that men define the norm in the professions, where it is not just acceptable but desirable to be capable of independent

action, oriented to the task at hand, and doing things for a reason. Even though kindness is socially desirable, our schemas about what is required to be a successful professional do not represent kindness as a useful characteristic. Another reason for women to have changed more is that they became a larger and larger percentage of the workforce between the 1970s and 2000.

People apply gender schemas less to themselves than to others (see also Gill, 2004; Heilman, 2012; Ridgeway, 2011). Males and females describe their traits more similarly than people's beliefs about gender differences would suggest. Even as the sexes move closer together in reporting that they share traits classically associated with one sex or the other, schemas continue to guide our perceptions and evaluations of others. We see people as more different than they actually are and penalize people when they deviate from what is expected.

10. Teaching evaluations of instructors by students show that when students in an online course believe their instructor is male, the instructor is rated more highly than when the students believe their instructor is female (MacNell, Driscoll, & Hunt, 2015). See also Boring, Ottoboni, and Stark (2016) for further analysis of these U.S. data and French data, plus analyses showing that student evaluations do not measure teaching effectiveness. A meta-analysis similarly suggests that student evaluations do not correlate well with teaching effectiveness (Uttl, White, & Gonzalez, 2017).

11. A related study also found that women appear to be punished if they make their skills clear. Undergraduate participants read a résumé for a candidate for a job as a project manager. In one condition, the résumé presented the candidate in terms that were stereotypically masculine (competitive and self-aggrandizing); in another condition, it was stereotypically feminine (sensitive to others' needs). The same qualifications were present in both conditions. Participants evaluated a single candidate on multiple dimensions: likability, competence, social skills, interview probability, and hireability. Since the résumé was identical in all conditions, participants' evaluations of the candidate were based on the candidate's sex and whether the description "fit" the candidate's sex (Tyler & McCullough, 2009). If women's problem is a failure to promote themselves as strongly as men do, they should receive higher evaluations when their cover letter is stereotypically masculine rather than stereotypically feminine. Men rated the female applicant more negatively on each measure compared to the male applicant if her cover letter displayed typically masculine characteristics. On every dimension, men rated the stereotypical male candidate highest and the counterstereotypical female lowest. When the cover letter was more communal in tone, men still tended to rate the male applicant more highly on every dimension. Women aren't as good job candidates as men, period, where men are concerned. Women participants, however, were unaffected in their judgments of the candidates by the nature of the cover letter and showed no consistent preference for a male or female candidate. (The difference between male and female reactions in this study may be due to women's heightened sensitivity about job applications.)

12. A related experiment used a community sample of people in a public park instead of undergraduates. The findings were similar, except that women were less likely to shift their standards than men were (Uhlmann & Cohen, 2005). This is one of the rare studies in which women and men responded differently.

13. The scientists rated either a male or a female candidate. Scientists who saw the male candidate's qualifications rated him as more competent and more hireable than did those who rated the female candidate. Scientists were willing to provide more career mentoring for the male candidate than for the female candidate. Scientists said they would pay the male more than the female, on average $3,000 more.

14. A related finding is that people who do not see beliefs as sexist are also more likely to endorse them (Swim, Mallett, Russo-Devosa, & Stangor, 2005).

15. There were several methodological limitations to the study, as well as a lack of full presentation of the findings, making the study difficult to fully evaluate. For example, the study also varied descriptors used for each of the two competitive candidates, using either male- or female-stereotyped terms, sometimes for the male and sometimes for the female. Data were not presented separately for those conditions. As another example, ranking, which the investigators used, is a less preferable system than rating because it forces a search for extraneous reasons in candidates who might otherwise be evaluated as the same. As another example, both candidates were described and rated unrealistically highly, and to the same degree, in the paragraph that was the basis for ranking; similarly, in a control condition where evaluators saw CVs, the accomplishments were also unrealistically high. There was, unfortunately, no baseline condition—a condition without gender-based descriptors. There were no questions probing evaluators' understanding of the task. The descriptions of the candidates included irrelevant (and illegal) information about their marital and parental status. See Williams and Smith (2015) for methodological points.

Another study, in France, suggested that women were more likely to be chosen as instructors than equivalently competent men in fields where women were underrepresented (Breda & Hillion, 2016). The instructors were by and large being chosen for subuniversity (high school) positions, where they are referred to as professors but are not professors in the sense understood in the United States. It is not clear that evaluators would use the same metrics for judging university faculty. In addition, the report lacked necessary information about the structure of the examinations and the basis for evaluators' decisions. It is thus difficult to determine whether there are any implications of the study for college and university hiring.

16. Most studies examining race and ethnicity schemas do so with the aim of understanding more general attitudes that different groups hold of each other. Thus, investigators have concentrated on how positively or negatively people view others of the same and different ethnicities, how prone they are to interpret an ambiguous photo

(e.g., where an individual is holding something) in a way that suggests fear (e.g., as a weapon rather than a cell phone), and the extent to which Whites are implicit racists. We will discuss such studies when we consider the perceptions and behaviors of interviewers and other gatekeepers.

17. No data on ethnicity differences among participants were provided, but the majority of participants were White.

18. Although one experiment we reviewed earlier suggested that people saw Whites and African Americans similarly when they failed in leadership roles, that experiment explicitly provided evaluators with reasons. Either the failure was the fault of the person being evaluated, or the failure was due to external circumstances. The hypothesis we are presenting here is that when evaluators have to decide themselves what is behind a failure, they are likely to see Whites as responsible for specific reasons and African Americans as responsible because they are African Americans.

19. The two types of individuals were arbitrarily labeled males and females. They could have been labeled anything. The results are as applicable to race-ethnicity as to gender. Small amounts of preference amount, over the long haul, to large differences.

References

Agyemang, C., Bhopal, R., & Bruijnzeels, M. (2005). Negro, Black, Black African, African Caribbean, African American or what? Labelling African origin populations in the health arena in the 21st century. *Journal of Epidemiology and Community Health*, 59(12), 1014–1018.

Apfelbaum, E. P., Norton, M. I., & Sommers, S. R. (2012). Racial color blindness: Emergence, practice, and implications. *Current Directions in Psychological Science*, 21, 205–209.

Apfelbaum, E. P., Pauker, K., Sommers, S. R., & Ambady, N. (2010). In blind pursuit of racial equality? *Psychological Science*, 21, 1587–1592.

Asplin, B. R., Rhodes, K. V., Levy, H., Lurie, N., Crain, A. L., Carlin, B. P., & Kellermann, A. L. (2005). Insurance status and access to urgent ambulatory care follow-up appointments. *Journal of the American Medical Association*, 294(10), 1248–1254.

Bakan, D. (1966). *The duality of human existence*. Chicago, IL: Beacon Press.

Banaji, M. R., & Greenwald, A. G. (2013). *Blindspot: Hidden biases of good people*. New York, NY: Delacorte Press.

Baumeister, R. F., & Leary, M. R. (1995). The need to belong: Desire for interpersonal attachments as a fundamental human motivation. *Psychological Bulletin*, 117(3), 497–529.

Bergsieker, H. B., Shelton, J. N., & Richeson, J. A. (2010). To be liked versus respected: Divergent goals in interracial interactions. *Journal of Personality and Social Psychology*, *99*(2), 248–264.

Bertrand, M., & Mullainathan, S. (2004). Are Emily and Greg more employable than Lakisha and Jamal? A field experiment on labor market discrimination. *American Economic Review*, *94*(4), 991–1013.

Biernat, M., Manis, M., & Nelson, T. E. (1991). Stereotypes and standards of judgment. *Journal of Personality and Social Psychology*, *60*(4), 485–499.

Block, C. J., Aumann, K., & Chelin, A. (2012). Assessing stereotypes of Black and White managers: A diagnostic ratio approach. *Journal of Applied Social Psychology*, *42*(S1), E128–E149.

Boring, A., Ottoboni, K., & Stark, P. (2016). Student evaluations of teaching (mostly) do not measure teaching effectiveness. *ScienceOpen Research*, 1–11. https://www.scienceopen.com/document/read?vid=818d8ec0-5908-47d8-86b4-5dc38f04b23e

Breda, T., & Hillion, M. (2016). Teaching accreditation exams reveal grading biases favor women in male-dominated disciplines in France. *Science*, *353*(6298), 474–478.

Burch, T. (2015). Skin color and the criminal justice system: Beyond Black-White disparities in sentencing. *Journal of Empirical Legal Studies*, *12*(3), 395–420.

Carnes, M., Devine, P. G., Manwell, L. B., Byars-Winston, A., Fine, E., Ford, C. E., et al. (2015). Effect of an intervention to break the gender bias habit for faculty at one institution: A cluster randomized, controlled trial. *Academic Medicine*, *90*(2), 221–230.

Carrigan, C., Quinn, K., & Riskin, E. A. (2011). The gendered division of labor among STEM faculty and the effects of critical mass. *Journal of Diversity in Higher Education*, *4*(3), 131–146.

Chan, W., & Mendelsohn, G. A. (2010). Disentangling stereotype and person effects: Do social stereotypes bias observer judgments of personality? *Journal of Research in Personality*, *44*(2), 251–257.

Cheryan, S., Plaut, V. C., Davies, P. G., & Steele, C. M. (2009). Ambient belonging: How stereotypical cues impact gender participation in computer science. *Journal of Personality and Social Psychology*, *97*(6), 1045–1060.

Conley, T. D., Rabinowitz, J. L., & Rabow, J. (2010). Gordon Gekkos, frat boys and nice guys: The content, dimensions, and structural determinants of multiple ethnic minority groups' stereotypes about White men. *Analyses of Social Issues and Public Policy (ASAP)*, *10*, 69–96.

Cortina, L. M., Magley, V. J., Williams, J. H., & Langhout, R. D. (2001). Incivility in the workplace: Incidence and impact. *Journal of Occupational Health Psychology*, *6*(1), 64–80.

Devine, P. G., Forscher, P. S., Austin, A. J., & Cox, W. T. (2012). Long-term reduction in implicit race bias: A prejudice habit-breaking intervention. *Journal of Experimental Social Psychology, 48*(6), 1267–1278.

DiPrete, T. A., & Eirich, G. M. (2006). Cumulative advantage as a mechanism for inequality: A review of theoretical and empirical developments. *Annual Review of Sociology, 32,* 271–297.

Dovidio, J., Gluszek, A., John, M., Ditlmann, R., & Lagunes, P. (2010). Understanding bias toward Latinos: Discrimination, dimensions of difference, and experience of exclusion. *Journal of Social Issues, 66,* 59–78.

Dovidio, J. F., Gaertner, S. L., Ufkes, E. G., Saguy, T., & Pearson, A. R. (2016). Included but invisible? Subtle bias, common identity, and the darker side of "we." *Social Issues and Policy Review, 10*(1), 6–46.

Duckworth, A. L., & Seligman, M. E. P. (2006). Self-discipline gives girls the edge: Gender in self-discipline, grades, and achievement test scores. *Journal of Educational Psychology, 98*(1), 198–209.

Dweck, C. S. (1999). *Self theories: Their role in motivation, personality, and development.* Philadelphia, PA: Psychology Press/Taylor and Francis.

Elsesser, K. M., & Lever, J. (2011). Does gender bias against female leaders persist? Quantitative and qualitative data from a large-scale survey. *Human Relations, 64,* 1555–1578.

Finseraas, H., Johnsen, Å. A., Kotsadam, A., & Torsvik, G. (2016). Exposure to female colleagues breaks the glass ceiling—Evidence from a combined vignette and field experiment. *European Economic Review, 90,* 363–374.

Fiske, S. T. (2015). Intergroup biases: A focus on stereotype content. *Current Opinion in Behavioral Sciences, 3,* 45–50.

Fiske, S. T., Cuddy, A. J., & Glick, P. (2007). Universal dimensions of social cognition: Warmth and competence. *Trends in Cognitive Sciences, 11*(2), 77–83.

Fiske, S. T., Dupree, C. H., Nicolas, G., & Swencionis, J. K. (2016). Status, power, and intergroup relations: The personal is the societal. *Current Opinion in Psychology, 11,* 44–48.

Fiske, S. T., & Taylor, S. E. (1991). *Social cognition,* 2nd edition. New York, NY: McGraw-Hill.

Forscher, P. S., Lai, C., Axt, J., Ebersole, C. R., Herman, M., Devine, P. G., & Nosek, B. A. (2017, October 5). A meta-analysis of change in implicit bias. Retrieved from http://psyarxiv.com/dv8tu

Foschi, M. (2000). Double standards for competence: Theory and research. *Annual Review of Sociology, 26,* 21–42. doi:10.1146/annurev.soc.26.1.21

Gaddis, S. M. (2015). Discrimination in the credential society: An audit study of race and college selectivity in the labor market. *Social Forces, 93*(4), 1451–1479.

Gendler, T. (2008). Alief and belief. *Journal of Philosophy, 105*(10), 634–663.

Gibson, C. E., Losee, J., & Vitiello, C. (2014). A replication attempt of stereotype susceptibility (Shih, Pittinsky, & Ambady, 1999). *Social Psychology, 45*, 194–198.

Gill, M. J. (2004). When information does not deter stereotyping: Prescriptive stereo-typing can foster bias under conditions that deter descriptive stereotyping. *Journal of Experimental Social Psychology, 40*(5), 619–632.

Glass, C. R., & Westmont, C. M. (2014). Comparative effects of belongingness on the academic success and cross-cultural interactions of domestic and international students. *International Journal of Intercultural Relations, 38*, 106–119.

Goldin, C., & Rouse, C. (2000). Orchestrating impartiality: The impact of blind audi-tions on female musicians. *American Economic Review, 90*(4), 715–741.

Goodwin, G. P. (2015). Moral character in person perception. *Current Directions in Psychological Science, 24*, 38–44.

Goodwin, G. P., Piazza, J., & Rozin, P. (2014). Moral character predominates in person perception and evaluation. *Journal of Personality and Social Psychology, 106*, 148–168.

Greenwald, A. G., Banaji, M. R., & Nosek, B. A. (2015). Statistically small effects of the Implicit Association Test can have societally large effects. *Journal of Personality and Social Psychology, 108*(4), 553–561.

Guarino, C. M., & Borden, V. M. (2017). Faculty service loads and gender: Are women taking care of the academic family? *Research in Higher Education, 58*, 672–694.

Hall, E. V., Phillips, K. W., & Townsend, S. S. (2015). A rose by any other name? The consequences of subtyping "African-Americans" from "Blacks." *Journal of Experimental Social Psychology, 56*, 183–190.

Hebl, M. R., Foster, J. B., Mannix, L. M., & Dovidio, J. F. (2002). Formal and inter-personal discrimination: A field study of bias toward homosexual applicants. *Personality and Social Psychology Bulletin, 28*, 815–825.

Heilman, M. E. (2012). Gender stereotypes and workplace bias. *Research in Organiza-tional Behavior, 32*, 113–135.

Heilman, M. E., Martell, R. F., & Simon, M. C. (1988). The vagaries of sex bias: Con-ditions regulating the undervaluation, equivaluation, and overvaluation of female job applicants. *Organizational Behavior and Human Decision Processes, 41*(1), 98–110.

Heilman, M. E., & Okimoto, T. G. (2007). Why are women penalized for success at male tasks? The implied communality deficit. *Journal of Applied Psychology, 92*(1), 81–92.

Heilman, M. E., & Stopeck, M. H. (1985). Attractiveness and corporate success: Different causal attributions for males and females. *Journal of Applied Psychology, 70*(2), 379–388.

Heilman, M. E., & Wallen, A. S. (2010). Wimpy and undeserving of respect: Penalties for men's gender-inconsistent success. *Journal of Experimental Social Psychology, 46*(4), 664–667.

Heilman, M. E., Wallen, A. S., Fuchs, D., & Tamkins, M. M. (2004). Penalties for success: Reactions to women who succeed at male gender-typed tasks. *Journal of Applied Psychology, 89*, 416–427.

Hersch, J. (2008). Profiling the new immigrant worker: The effects of skin color and height. *Journal of Labor Economics, 26*(2), 345–386.

Inzlicht, M., & Schmader, T. (Eds.). (2012). *Stereotype threat: Theory, process, and application.* New York, NY: Oxford University Press.

Jones, K. P., Peddie, C. I., Gilrane, V. L., King, E. B., & Gray, A. L. (2016). Not so subtle a meta-analytic investigation of the correlates of subtle and overt discrimination. *Journal of Management, 42*(6), 1588–1613.

Jones, M. (2001). Stereotyping Hispanics and Whites: Perceived differences in social roles as a determinant of ethnic stereotypes. *Journal of Social Psychology, 131*(4), 469–476.

Jussim, L. (2017). Accuracy, bias, self-fulfilling prophecies, and scientific self-correction. *Behavioral and Brain Sciences, 40*, 1–65.

Kahneman, D. (2011). *Thinking, fast and slow.* New York, NY: Farrar, Straus and Giroux.

Kao, G. (2000). Group images and possible selves among adolescents: Linking stereotypes to expectations by race and ethnicity. *Sociological Forum, 15*, 407–430.

Kiefer, A., & Sekaquaptewa, D. (2007). Implicit stereotypes and women's math performance: How implicit gender-math stereotypes influence women's susceptibility to stereotype threat. *Journal of Experimental Social Psychology, 43*, 825–832.

Kugelmass, H. (2016). "Sorry, I'm not accepting new patients": An audit study of access to mental health care. *Journal of Health and Social Behavior, 57*(2), 168–183.

Kunda, Z., & Thagard, P. (1996). Forming impressions from stereotypes, traits, and behaviors: A parallel-constraint-satisfaction theory. *Psychological Review, 103*(2), 284–308.

Lai, C. K., Marini, M., Lehr, S. A., Cerruti, C., Shin, J. L., Joy-Gaba, J. A., et al. (2014). A comparative investigation of 17 interventions to reduce implicit racial preferences. *Journal of Experimental Psychology. General, 143*, 1765–1785.

Lai, C. K., Skinner, A. L., Cooley, E., Murrar, S., Brauer, M., Devos, T., et al. (2016). Reducing implicit racial preferences: II. Intervention effectiveness across time. *Journal of Experimental Psychology. General, 145*(8), 1001–1016.

Leslie, S. J., Cimpian, A., Meyer, M., & Freeland, E. (2015). Expectations of brilliance underlie gender distributions across academic disciplines. *Science, 347*(6219), 262–265.

Levy, N. (2015). Neither fish nor fowl: Implicit attitudes as patchy endorsements. *Noûs, 49*(4), 800–823.

Livingston, R. W., Rosette, A. S., & Washington, E. F. (2012). Can an agentic Black woman get ahead? The impact of race and interpersonal dominance on perceptions of female leaders. *Psychological Science, 23*(4), 354–358.

Lubienski, S. T., Robinson, J. P., Crane, C. C., & Ganley, C. M. (2013). Girls' and boys' mathematics achievement, affect, and experiences: Findings from ECLS-K. *Journal for Research in Mathematics Education, 44*(4), 634–645.

Maddox, K. B. (2004). Perspectives on racial phenotypicality bias. *Personality and Social Psychology Review, 8*(4), 383–401.

Madva, A., & Brownstein, M. (in press). Stereotypes, prejudice, and the taxonomy of the implicit social mind. *Noûs.*

Mandelbaum, E. (2016). Attitude, inference, association: On the propositional structure of implicit bias. *Noûs, 50*(3), 629–658.

Martell, R. F., Lane, D. M., & Emrich, C. (1996). Male-female differences: A computer simulation. *American Psychologist, 51*, 157–158.

Martin, C. L., & Halverson, C. F. (1987). The role of cognition in sex role acquisition. In D. B. Carter (Ed.), *Current conceptions of sex roles and sex typing: Theory and research* (pp. 123–137). New York, NY: Praeger.

Martinez, S., & Toutkoushian, R. K. (2014). Decomposing the differences in time allocation and research output between Latino and non-Latino White faculty. *Latino Studies, 12*(4), 566–595.

MacNell, L., Driscoll, A., & Hunt, A. N. (2015). What's in a name: Exposing gender bias in student ratings of teaching. *Innovative Higher Education, 40*(4), 291–303.

McCauley, C., Stitt, C. L., & Segal, M. (1980). Stereotyping: From prejudice to prediction. *Psychological Bulletin, 87*(1), 195–208.

Mendes, W. B., Blascovich, J., Lickel, B., & Hunter, S. (2002). Challenge and threat during social interactions with White and Black men. *Personality and Social Psychology Bulletin, 28*(7), 939–952.

Merritt, A. C., Effron, D. A., & Monin, B. (2010). Moral self-licensing: When being good frees us to be bad. *Social and Personality Psychology Compass, 4,* 344–357.

Merton, R. K. (1988). The Matthew effect in science. II: Cumulative advantage and the symbolism of intellectual property. *Isis, 79*(4), 606–623.

Milkman, K. L., Akinola, M., & Chugh, D. (2012). Temporal distance and discrimination: An audit study in academia. *Psychological Science, 23*(7), 710–717.

Miller, D. T., Taylor, B., & Buck, M. L. (1991). Gender gaps: Who needs to be explained? *Journal of Personality and Social Psychology, 61*(1), 5–12.

Mitchell, S. M., & Hesli, V. L. (2013). Women don't ask? Women don't say no? Bargaining and service in the political science profession. *PS, Political Science & Politics, 46*(02), 355–369.

Mondschein, E. R., Adolph, K. E., & Tamis-LeMonda, C. S. (2000). Gender bias in mothers' expectations about infant crawling. *Journal of Experimental Child Psychology, 77*(4), 304–316.

Monin, B., & Miller, D. T. (2001). Moral credentials and the expression of prejudice. *Journal of Personality and Social Psychology, 81,* 33–43.

Moon, A., & Roeder, S. S. (2014). A secondary replication attempt of stereotype susceptibility (Shih, Pittinsky, & Ambady, 1999). *Social Psychology, 45,* 199–201.

Moss-Racusin, C. A., Dovidio, J. F., Brescoll, V. L., Graham, M. J., & Handelsman, J. (2012). Science faculty's subtle gender biases favor male students. *Proceedings of the National Academy of Sciences of the United States of America, 109*(41), 16474–16479.

Moss-Racusin, C. A., Phelan, J. E., & Rudman, L. A. (2010). When men break the gender rules: Status incongruity and backlash against modest men. *Psychology of Men & Masculinity, 11*(2), 140–151.

Mujcic, R., & Frijters, P. (2013). Still not allowed on the bus: It matters if you're Black or White! (Institute for the Study of Labor [IZA] Discussion Paper No. 7300). Bonn, Germany: IZA.

Murphy, M. C., Steele, C. M., & Gross, J. J. (2007). Signaling threat: How situational cues affect women in math, science, and engineering settings. *Psychological Science, 18*(10), 879–885.

Nguyen, H. H. D., & Ryan, A. M. (2008). Does stereotype threat affect test performance of minorities and women? A meta-analysis of experimental evidence. *Journal of Applied Psychology, 93*(6), 1314–1334.

Norton, M. I., Vandello, J. A., & Darley, J. M. (2004). Casuistry and social category bias. *Journal of Personality and Social Psychology, 87,* 817–831.

O'Meara, K., Kuvaeva, A., & Nyunt, G. (2017). Constrained choices: A view of campus service inequality from annual faculty reports. *Journal of Higher Education*, *88*(5), 672–700. doi:10.1080/00221546.2016.1257312.

O'Meara, K., Kuvaeva, A., Nyunt, G., Waugaman, C., & Jackson, R. (2017). Asked more often: Gender differences in faculty workload in research universities and the work interactions that shape them. *American Educational Research Journal*. Advance online publication. doi:10.3102/0002831217716767

Oswald, F. L., Mitchell, G., Blanton, H., Jaccard, J., & Tetlock, P. E. (2015). Using the IAT to predict ethnic and racial discrimination: Small effect sizes of unknown societal significance. *Journal of Personality and Social Psychology*, *108*(4), 562–571.

Page, S. E. (2007). *The difference: How the power of diversity creates better groups, firms, schools, and societies*. Princeton, NJ: Princeton University Press.

Paustian-Underdahl, S. C., Walker, L. S., & Woehr, D. J. (2014). Gender and perceptions of leadership effectiveness: A meta-analysis of contextual moderators. *Journal of Applied Psychology*, *99*(6), 1129–1145.

Phelan, J. E., Moss-Racusin, C. A., & Rudman, L. A. (2008). Competent yet out in the cold: Shifting criteria for hiring reflect backlash toward agentic women. *Psychology of Women Quarterly*, *32*, 406–413.

Philogène, G. (1999). *From Black to African American: A new social representation*. Westport, CT: Praeger/Greenwood.

Pittinsky, T. L., Shih, M., & Ambady, N. (1999). Identity adaptiveness: Affect across multiple identities. *Journal of Social Issues*, *55*, 503–518.

Prime, J. L., Carter, N. M., & Welbourne, T. M. (2009). Women "take care," men "take charge": Managers' stereotypic perceptions of women and men leaders. *Psychologist Manager Journal*, *12*(1), 25–49.

Pronin, E., Lin, D. Y., & Ross, L. (2002). The bias blind spot: Perceptions of bias in self versus others. *Personality and Social Psychology Bulletin*, *28*(3), 369–381.

Ratcliff, N. J., Vescio, T. K., & Dahl, J. L. (2015). (Still) waiting in the wings: Group-based biases in leaders' decisions about to whom power is relinquished. *Journal of Experimental Social Psychology*, *57*, 23–30.

Räty, H., Vänskä, J., Kasanen, K., & Kärkkäinen, R. (2002). Parents' explanations of their child's performance in mathematics and reading: A replication and extension of Yee and Eccles. *Sex Roles*, *46*(3–4), 121–128.

Richards, Z., & Hewstone, M. (2001). Subtyping and subgrouping: Processes for the prevention and promotion of stereotype change. *Personality and Social Psychology Review*, *5*, 52–73.

Richeson, J. A., & Shelton, J. N. (2007). Negotiating interracial interactions: Costs, consequences, and possibilities. *Current Directions in Psychological Science, 16,* 316–320.

Ridgeway, C. L. (2011). *Framed by gender: How gender inequality persists in the modern world.* Oxford, UK: Oxford University Press.

Rigney, D. (2010). *The Matthew effect: How advantage begets further advantage.* New York, NY: Columbia University Press.

Rosette, A. S., Leonardelli, G. J., & Phillips, K. W. (2008). The White standard: Racial bias in leader categorization. *Journal of Applied Psychology, 93*(4), 758–777.

Rudman, L. A., & Fairchild, K. (2004). Reactions to counterstereotypic behavior: The role of backlash in cultural stereotype maintenance. *Journal of Personality and Social Psychology, 87,* 157–176.

Rudman, L. A., & Phelan, J. E. (2008). Backlash effects for disconfirming gender stereotypes in organizations. *Research in Organizational Behavior, 28,* 61–79.

Ryan, C. S., Casas, J. F., & Thompson, B. K. (2010). Interethnic ideology, intergroup perceptions, and cultural orientation. *Journal of Social Issues, 66*(1), 29–44.

Ryan, C. S., Hunt, J. S., Weible, J. A., Peterson, C. R., & Casas, J. F. (2007). Multicultural and colorblind ideology, stereotypes, and ethnocentrism among Black and White Americans. *Group Processes & Intergroup Relations, 10*(4), 617–637.

Schmader, T., Johns, M., & Forbes, C. (2008). An integrated process model of stereotype threat effects on performance. *Psychological Review, 115*(2), 336–356.

Self, W. T., Mitchell, G., Mellers, B. A., Tetlock, P. E., & Hildreth, J. A. D. (2015). Balancing fairness and efficiency: The impact of identity-blind and identity-conscious accountability on applicant screening. *PLoS One, 10*(12), e0145208.

Sigelman, L., Tuch, S. A., & Martin, J. K. (2005). What's in a name? Preference for "Black" versus "African-American" among Americans of African descent. *Public Opinion Quarterly, 69*(3), 429–438.

Skiba, R. J., Horner, R. H., Chung, C. G., Rausch, M. K., May, S. L., & Tobin, T. (2011). Race is not neutral: A national investigation of African American and Latino disproportionality in school discipline. *School Psychology Review, 40*(1), 85–107.

Skiba, R. J., Michael, R. S., Nardo, A. C., & Peterson, R. L. (2002). The color of discipline: Sources of racial and gender disproportionality in school punishment. *Urban Review, 34*(4), 317–342.

Spence, J., & Buckner, C. (2000). Instrumental and expressive traits, trait stereotypes, and sexist attitudes: What do they signify? *Psychology of Women Quarterly, 24*(1), 44–62.

Spence, J., & Helmreich, R. (1978). *Masculinity and femininity: Their psychological dimensions, correlates and antecedents*. Austin, TX: University of Texas Press.

Spencer, S. J., Logel, C., & Davies, P. G. (2016). Stereotype threat. *Annual Review of Psychology, 67*, 415–437.

Spencer, S. J., Steele, C. M., & Quinn, D. M. (1999). Stereotype threat and women's math performance. *Journal of Experimental Social Psychology, 35*(1), 4–28.

Steele, C. M. (2011). *Whistling Vivaldi: And other clues to how stereotypes affect us*. New York, NY: Norton.

Swim, J. K., Aikin, K. J., Hall, W. S., & Hunter, B. A. (1995). Sexism and racism: Old-fashioned and modern prejudices. *Journal of Personality and Social Psychology, 68*, 199–214.

Swim, J. K., Mallett, R., Russo-Devosa, Y., & Stangor, C. (2005). Judgments of sexism: A comparison of the subtlety of sexism measures and sources of variability in judgments of sexism. *Psychology of Women Quarterly, 29*, 406–411.

Tsay, C. J. (2013). Sight over sound in the judgment of music performance. *Proceedings of the National Academy of Sciences of the United States of America, 110*(36), 14580–14585.

Tyler, J. M., & McCullough, J. D. (2009). Violating prescriptive stereotypes on job resumes: A self-presentational perspective. *Management Communication Quarterly, 23*, 272–287.

Uhlmann, E. L., & Cohen, G. L. (2005). Constructed criteria: Redefining merit to justify discrimination. *Psychological Science, 16*, 474–480.

Uttl, B., White, C. A., & Gonzalez, D. W. (2017). Meta-analysis of faculty's teaching effectiveness: Student evaluation of teaching ratings and student learning are not related. *Studies in Educational Evaluation, 54*, 22–42.

Valian, V. (1998). *Why so slow? The advancement of women*. Cambridge, MA: MIT Press.

Voyer, D., & Voyer, S. D. (2014). Gender differences in scholastic achievement: A meta-analysis. *Psychological Bulletin, 140*(4), 1174–1204.

Walton, G., & Cohen, G. (2007). A question of belonging; Race, social fit, and achievement. *Journal of Personality and Social Psychology, 92*(1), 82–96.

Walton, G., & Cohen, G. (2011). A brief social-belonging intervention improves academic and health outcomes of minority students. *Science, 331*, 1447–1451.

West, R. F., Meserve, R. J., & Stanovich, K. E. (2012). Cognitive sophistication does not attenuate the bias blind spot. *Journal of Personality and Social Psychology, 103*(3), 506–519.

Williams, J., & Smith, J. (2015). The myth that academic science isn't biased against women. *Chronicle of Higher Education.* http://www.chronicle.com/article/The-Myth -That-Academic-Science/231413

Williams, W. M., & Ceci, S. J. (2015). National hiring experiments reveal 2:1 faculty preference for women on STEM tenure track. *Proceedings of the National Academy of Sciences of the United States of America, 112*(17), 5360–5365.

Yee, D., & Eccles, J. (1988). Parent perceptions and attributions for children's math achievement. *Sex Roles, 19,* 317–333.

Zhang, Q. (2015). Perceived ingroup stereotypes, threats, and emotions toward Asian Americans. *Howard Journal of Communications, 26*(2), 115–131.

Zuckerman, H. (1997). Accumulation of advantage and disadvantage: The theory and its intellectual biography. In C. Mongardini & S. Tabboni (Eds.), *Robert K. Merton and contemporary sociology* (pp. 139–161). London, UK: Routledge.

4 How Careers Progress for Different Groups: Observational Data and Alternate Accounts

In chapter 3 we presented laboratory data and results from field studies to support our two-part hypothesis about the evaluations of people who differ in terms of gender, race, and ethnicity. We concluded that gender, race, and ethnicity schemas result in a systematic small undervaluation of women and non-Whites and a systematic small overvaluation of White men in professional settings. The examples of undervaluation—such as being ignored, or rated lower, or given fewer opportunities to excel—are small but, we argue, frequent. Those small differences in advantage and disadvantage add up over time—like interest on investments—to create disparities in outcomes: molehills become mountains. Given our conclusions from the studies we reviewed in chapter 3, we expect to see differences in observational data as well.

In the first part of this chapter we examine hiring, salaries, and related outcomes. In the second part we consider additional hypotheses to those we presented in chapter 3. The underrepresentation of women and people of color in positions of power and prestige is a complex phenomenon that no single factor can explain. In some cases we think the additional hypotheses have merit and can be added to our interpretation in chapter 3 without supplanting it, while in other cases we think the hypotheses have at best weak evidence in their favor.

Generalizations

Some generalizations hold across different samples.

First, academia is not unique among the professions. White women and men and women of color fare worse than White men in law, medicine, and business: they make less money and they advance more slowly. Because of the similarity across professions, and because very large samples are available for fields outside academia, we draw on the accumulated data.

Second, academia in the United States is not unique among the world's colleges and universities: women fare worse than men; minority groups fare worse than majority groups.

Third, the data are similar across different samples: differences in careers start out small and get larger as careers progress. The finding of growing disparities over individuals' careers is expected if some individuals can accumulate advantage more rapidly than others.

Methodological Issues

In examining the reasons for the gender and race gaps that we observe, we face a central problem at the outset. It is impossible to include only variables that are not themselves a product of how people are treated. This is an important limitation, though it is often not considered in studies that "control" for the effect of variables that actually partially construct and reflect gender and/or race. Consider the following scenario. Whites are more successful in obtaining grants than are African Americans with the same qualifications (Ginther, Schaffer, Schnell, Masimore, Liu, Haak, & Kington, 2011); in addition, there is some evidence that female African Americans fare worse than male African Americans (Ginther, Kahn, & Schaffer, 2016). Now imagine that grant funding predicts salary (see, e.g., Kelly & Grant, 2012; Melguizo & Strober, 2007).

If we use grant funding as a predictor of salaries or as a factor we "control" for, we might diminish or eliminate the salary difference between African Americans and Whites. However, in using grant funding as a variable, we are using a measure that may itself be a product of inappropriate and disparate treatment. A finding that salary differences are reduced once funding is taken into account can make it seem as if a puzzle has been solved, when in fact the heart of the puzzle is still there, just further back in the causal chain. In other cases, we may be in the dark about whether a variable is the product of unequal treatment. For example, women are less likely to work in more remunerative areas, like engineering and economics, than men. Choice of field may be a preference but it may also or alternatively be a product of earlier disparate treatment.

The absence of a gap, by itself, does not entail the absence of unequal treatment, nor does the presence of an unexplained gap, by itself, entail the presence of unequal treatment.[1] For example, in the absence of a gap, women and men could fare equally well in a field because the women who remain are more highly selected than the men who remain in the field. Conversely, an unexplained disparity could be due to a factor that has not been measured.

Different studies consider different measures (such as prestige of degree-granting institution and propensity to compete) but seldom include estimates of the importance of each measure to the outcome (salary, rate of advancement, etc.), or the extent to which different groups (men and women, African Americans and Whites) vary on the measure, or the effect of the disparity on the outcome.

Finally, with a wealth of partial data—studies that are incommensurable because they do not measure the same variables—comes a wealth of competing interpretations of the data, depending on the theoretical framework of the investigator. We try to steer our way through the data by relying in part on the experiments we discussed in chapter 3.

Data on Professional Trajectories

With the methodological cautions in mind, we first consider some representative large- and medium-scale findings in order to illustrate real-world gender and race and ethnicity differences. We then present other data about gender, race, and ethnicity in academia.

Study 1—Wage Growth as Careers Progress

We begin with large-scale observational data from the United Kingdom on gender disparity (Manning & Swaffield, 2008). The study examined wage growth—how salaries increase over time—and shows (as do many studies) that the disparity between men's and women's wages develops gradually over people's careers. The United Kingdom data came primarily from the British Household Panel Study that covered the period from 1991 to 2002, and data from the New Earnings Survey, for a sample of more than 10,000 observations on roughly 3,500 people.

In this study, men and women had similar earnings when they first entered the labor market, but women's wages grew more slowly than men's, with the result that their incomes after ten years were lower than men's. Some of the gap could be explained by gender differences in time out from the labor market and other factors, but women were about 8% behind men even if they had been continuously employed full-time, had no children, did not plan to have any children, and had similar personality characteristics (Manning & Swaffield, 2008).

The British study's findings are similar to those in the United States: women progress more slowly than men. In some cases that have been analyzed, the slower progression can be accounted for completely by the variables that the investigators have used, such as in a study of MBAs (Bertrand, Goldin, & Katz, 2010), and in other cases there remains a gap which is not explained. (For a comprehensive review, see Blau & Kahn, 2017.)

Study 2—Salary

Our second example comes from the United States. In 2016, the National Science Board (which is a federal group that establishes policies of the NSF), in a report titled *Science and Engineering Indicators 2016*, compared salaries of men and women, and different racial and ethnic groups, in science and engineering fields (where science includes psychology and social sciences as well as biological, physical, and computing sciences). The most recent available data were from 2013. Looking across all employment sectors, the Board reports that women make less money than men, and non-Asian minorities make less money than Whites and Asians, whether the most advanced degree was a BA, an MA, or a PhD. (Sample sizes are not reported for these comparisons, but other data tables suggest that roughly four million data points exist for the entire sample.)

For PhDs, without any controls, women made 21.4% less than men. Non-Asian minorities with PhDs averaged 16% less money than did Whites and Asians. After controlling for field of degree, occupational category, employment sector, years since PhD, years since degree squared, Carnegie classification of the school that awarded the PhD, and status (private or public) of the institution awarding the PhD, the gender disparity was reduced from 21.4% to 7.4%.[2] Although these data are not for academia alone, the analyses found disparities when controlling for sector of employment. The minority disparity, when the same controls were introduced, was reduced from 16.2% to 5.7%.[3] Whether all the controls introduced were appropriate is arguable. For example, the sector in which an individual is employed might itself be determined by employer preferences rather than employee preferences.

After adding further controls for citizenship, race and ethnic status (for gender), sex (for minorities), marital status, disability status, number of children living in the household, geographic region, and parental education, the gender disparity was slightly reduced, from 7.4% to 6.9%,[2] and the minority disparity was reduced from 5.7% to 4.8%.[3] Whether the third model's controls are appropriate is also arguable, but they reduced the disparities only by small amounts, and there continued to be disparities.[4]

Gender disparities in salary exist among both science and nonscience faculty, even after controls for productivity and teaching are included, although the patterns are somewhat different in the two broad areas (Kelly & Grant, 2012, using national data from 8,350 full-time faculty in 2003–2004). For an example of one female scientist's attempt to increase her salary, see box 4.1. Married and single women without children earn less

Box 4.1
One Way Salaries Do Not Progress

The year was 2005. The place was a basic science department in a major midwestern medical school. The scene was a meeting between Karen, an associate professor with tenure, and John, the chair of her department. Karen had two children; her husband was a stay-at-home father. Karen wanted an increase in her salary so that she would make the same amount of money that her colleague Phil, who recently got a raise, made. She thought that they were comparable. She was productive, she had grant support, she sat on an NIH study section. John said, "When your CV looks like Phil's, then we can talk about a salary increase." Karen thought their CVs *were* comparable, which was why she had approached the chair to begin with. John went on to say, "Or if you get an offer from somewhere else, come see me." Karen knew it was common for chairs and deans to adopt the approach of responding to outside offers, but she thought it was not good policy, since it encouraged people to look elsewhere, was distracting, and wasted time. Finally, John said, "Anyway, Phil's wife was making more money than he was, so I had to give him a raise." To that, Karen had no answer. In 2016, Karen decided to take early retirement, despite her love for her research and her success in obtaining grants to fund the research. Her department had changed leadership but the underlying problems remained.

than married fathers, but the disparity is greater in nonscience than science fields. Individual fields differ somewhat: business schools, for example, do not show a gender disparity once subfield and rank are accounted for (Sutanto, Bell, Fei, & Scott, 2014). Gender disparities in salary were not found across the board in all ranks and all fields (Ceci et al., 2014). However, medical schools show gender disparities in young faculty's salaries even after a broad range of controls is included (Jagsi, Griffith, Stewart, Sambuco, DeCastro, & Ubel, 2013).

To summarize, in 2013, women with PhDs in the sciences (broadly construed) made 7% less money than comparable men. Although gender disparities are common in a number of fields, they are not universal. Non-Asian minorities made 5% less.

Study 3—Progress through the Ranks (Spain)

The third study examines promotion in academia in Spain (Anghel, de la Rica, & Dolado, 2011). These data are similar to U.S. data and show that the phenomenon is not limited to the United States. Near the beginnings of their careers men and women are much more similar than they are ten years after they have begun a career—even after one controls for a number of variables.

There are no gender differences in promotion to associate professor, whether one compares men and women in the aggregate or by specialization. However, there are gender differences in promotion from associate to full professor. When comparing men and women of the same age, with the same amount of time since their PhD, the same field of knowledge, the same recent academic publication record, and the same number of dissertations directed, men were 2.5 times more likely to be promoted than women.

There are also gender differences in the effect of having children on promotion from associate to full professor. When comparing men and women with the same personal and professional characteristics and the same productivity, fathers are 4 times more likely to be promoted to full professor than mothers. These data are reminiscent of those for the United States, showing the penalty that women with children face in universities (Mason & Goulden, 2004; Mason, Wolfinger, & Goulden, 2013), in corporations (Correll, Benard, & Paik, 2007), and in experimental simulations (Benard & Correll, 2010; Correll et al., 2007).

Interim Conclusion

Our interim conclusion is that, as the experimental data suggest, women and racial-ethnic minorities fare worse than White men in compensation and advancement. What about other differences like sexual identity or disability status? We cannot examine observational data about these important issues because those characteristics are typically not recorded in the large data sets that are available, and they are usually not available in institutional data sources for reasons of privacy. For that reason it is especially helpful that some experimental studies do exist.

Representation among Doctoral Degree Recipients

Who earns a doctoral degree? Although different tables from the NSF present slightly different numbers, the overall picture for different sexes and different races and ethnicities is similar. We concentrate on degrees to U.S. citizens and permanent residents, even though temporary residents currently obtain more than a quarter of all doctoral degrees and more than 50% of doctoral degrees in fields like engineering and economics. Women in all race and ethnic groups, African Americans, and Hispanics are represented more strongly among citizens and permanent residents than among temporary residents.

In 2015, about a quarter of doctorate recipients acquired their degrees in education, the humanities, or other nonscience fields. Most degrees are in the natural and social sciences, mathematics and computer sciences, and engineering.[5] Among U.S. citizens and permanent residents, as table 4.1 shows, Whites received most doctoral degrees, followed by Asians, Hispanics, and African Americans. The remainder consists of American Indians, native Hawaiians, those reporting more than one race, and those of unknown origin.[6] Among the different groups, Whites and Asians are overrepresented compared to their percentages of the population between ages 25 and 64, while African Americans and Hispanics are underrepresented.[7,8] Women and men are roughly equally represented among Whites, but men are underrepresented among African Americans, Asians,[5,9] and Hispanics.[6,7]

In all fields, from engineering to education, the percentage of women among doctorate recipients has slowly and steadily increased, partly because more women are receiving degrees and partly because fewer men are. For example, in 1995, women were 12% of PhD recipients in engineering. By 2015, that figure had risen to 23%. Women even became more numerous

Table 4.1

Percentage data for PhDs who are U.S. citizens or permanent residents in all fields (science and nonscience alike) in 2015, along with 2014 estimated census data for adults ages 25–64 in each ethnicity group; groups are mutually exclusive

	Percentage of 2014 population[a]	Percentage of 2015 PhD recipients[b]	Percentage of PhD recipients who are male[b]
Whites	63.3	72.3	51
African Americans	12.3	6.5	36
Hispanics	16.3	7.0	46
Asians	5.8	8.7	44[c]
All others	2.2	5.5	51
All groups	99.9	100	49

[a]See note 7. [b]See note 6. [c]See note 9.

in some fields where they were already numerous. For example, in 1995, women were 61% of PhD degrees in education. By 2015, that figure was even higher at 68%.[10] Despite that increase, women's degrees are less likely than men's to come from prestigious departments (Weeden, Thébaud, & Gelbgiser, 2017).

In contrast, the percentage of underrepresented minorities barely moved over that 20-year period. For example, in 1995, African Americans received 2% of conferred doctorates in engineering; in 2015, they received 3.9%.[11] Similarly, African Americans received 3% of doctorates in the life sciences in 1995; that rose to only 5.3% in 2015.[10]

Representation within Academic Institutions

After receiving their degrees, individuals who take jobs in academia achieve positions at institutions that vary in pay and prestige. The most prestigious institutions are those classified by the Carnegie Foundation as having very high research activity. In this section we investigate whether gender and ethnicity are related to having a job at the most prestigious institutions—those labeled as having *very high* research activity and those labeled as having *high* research activity. The most recent data available from the NSF are from 2013 and are limited to science, engineering, and health doctorates.[12] Table 4.2 displays the data. These data include all researchers, regardless of citizenship status. (Most PhDs are bestowed at institutions with very high research activity.)

Table 4.2
Proportional representation of men and women faculty, and different racial and ethnic groups, at institutions rated as having very high or high research activity

	Total sample size	Proportion (of group) at *very high* research activity institutions	Proportion at *high* research activity institutions
Male	163,600	.47	.16
Female	89,800	.44	.13
Total	253,400	.46	.15
White	187,800	.46	.15
Asian	41,500	.53	.16
African American	8,800	.34	.14
Hispanic	11,200	.45	.13
All others	4,600	.39	.11
Total	253,900	.46	.15
With disability	19,500	.43	.16
Without disability	234,000	.47	.15
Total	253,500	.46	.15

For gender, our calculations from NSF show significantly lower representation of women than men at *very high* (44% vs. 47%) and *high* (13% vs. 16%) research active institutions.[13] (Although the differences in percentages are small, the very large sample size provides enough power to determine that the difference is significant.) Women in science fare worse than men, in the sense that they are significantly less likely to be employed at the most prestigious academic institutions.

When we compare different ethnic groups,[14] the picture is more extreme. At very high research activity institutions, Asians are better represented than Whites, and Whites are marginally better represented than Hispanics and better represented than African Americans and all others. At high research activity institutions, Asians are again better represented than Whites and Whites are better represented than any other group. African Americans have a lower representation than any other group in institutions with very high and high research activity. In sum, African Americans fare particularly poorly in academic positions and Asians fare particularly well.

For individuals with and without disabilities, representation differs at the two types of institution. Individuals with disabilities have lower representation at institutions with very high research activity, and higher representation at institutions with high research activity.[15]

Rank and Tenure

One marker of success is the speed by which one attains the top two faculty ranks: full professor (the highest rank except for named professorships and distinguished professorships) and associate professor. NSF provides data for science, engineering, and health fields. We compared only men and women who were less than ten years post-PhD in 2013.[16] We also only included individuals who are in the ranks of assistant, associate, or full professor in the denominator. Since a higher percentage of women than men are in instructor or lecturer positions, this is a conservative estimate of the gender disparity in rising through the ranks. The data are shown in table 4.3.[17]

Across all three fields (science, engineering, and health), men were significantly more likely to achieve the top two ranks within ten years postdegree than women were: 28% versus 24%.[18] For science fields as a whole, men were also significantly more likely to achieve full and associate professor status

Table 4.3
Proportions of men and women at full and associate professor ranks within ten years post-PhD

	All fields	Science	Engineering	Health
Proportion of field that is male	.55	.54	.76	.27
Male	.28	.27	.28	.33*
Female	.24*	.22*	.21*	.37
Sample N	57,600	44,000	7,600	5,900

Note. The proportion of a field that is male is calculated from all those with degrees less than ten years old who are employed in four-year educational institutions in any capacity. The denominator for proportions of men and women at senior ranks includes full, associate, and assistant ranks, but excludes "instructor or lecturer," "all other faculty," and "rank not applicable" individuals (N excluded = 43,900 for all fields), in order to restrict the comparison to those with ranked positions. Comparisons with an asterisk are statistically significant. For engineers, data for full professors were too sparse to be reported; only associate professors comprise the numerator. See also note 19.

than were women: 27% of men versus 22% of women.[18] For engineering, the comparable percentages (for associate professor level only, due to sparse data for full professors) are 27% versus 21%, also a significant difference.[18] For health, however, the percentages are reversed: 33% of men versus 37% of women achieve the top two ranks within ten years, again a significant difference.[18,19]

To investigate different science fields, we conducted individual analyses for the percentages of individuals who reached the rank of associate professor within ten years, as shown in table 4.4. (In most fields, NSF does not list the number of individuals at the full professor rank, because there are so few.) The fields are presented in descending order of the proportion of men in the entire field (including all ranks). In math, physical sciences, biological and agricultural sciences, and social sciences (excluding psychology), men are more successful than women.[20] In computer science and psychology, men and women are equally successful.[21]

To summarize our findings about success in reaching the top two ranks in academia within ten years in 2013, our data are limited to different fields within science. We find that in five fields (engineering, math and

Table 4.4

Proportions of men and women at associate professor rank within ten years post-PhD in individual science fields

	Computer science	Math	Physical sciences	Biological/ agricultural sciences	Social sciences (excluding psychology)	Psychology
Proportion of field that is male	.77	.69	.67	.53	.51	.32
Male	.44	.24	.18	.17	.28	.25
Female	.40	.08*	.16*	.10*	.25*	.25
Sample N	2,300	4,100	5,800	10,900	12,800	6,800

Note. Comparisons with an asterisk are statistically significant. Fields are ordered by the proportion of the field that is male and thus include all those with degrees less than ten years old who are employed in four-year educational institutions in any capacity. The N includes only associate and assistant professors; it excludes "instructor or lecturer," "all other faculty," and "rank not applicable" individuals, in order to restrict the comparison to those with ranked positions. It also excludes full professors because the N is so small that it often does not appear in NSF tables. See also note 21.

statistics, physical sciences, biological and agricultural sciences, and social sciences) men are more successful. In two fields (computer science and psychology) men and women do not differ. In one field (health) women are more successful than men. (Since there are two fields in which the sexes do not differ, and one in which women are more successful, differing patterns of time away from the job between men and women are unlikely to account for the differences we observe.)

In general, women fare best in achieving associate and full professorship status in the two fields with the highest percentage of women (health and psychology), but they fare as well as men in computer science. In three of the four fields that have been characterized as "math intensive" (engineering, physical science, and math), women are less successful than men, but that is also true for other fields that are not generally classified as math intensive (biological and agricultural sciences and social sciences).

By restricting our analysis to individuals who are less than ten years postdegree, we have reduced (but of course not eliminated) the possible extent of variation in qualifications. Disparities are considerably greater between 10 and 19 years postdegree, as one would expect from the accumulation of advantage and disadvantage, but as one would also expect because of the many variables (such as matching of outside offers) that could produce such disparities.

We performed the same gender comparisons for achievement of tenure within ten years for 2013 and present the data in table 4.5.[22] For this comparison we excluded individuals who are not on a tenure track or to whom tenure does not apply. We are thus comparing only men and women who have achieved tenure out of all men and women with tenure plus those without tenure but on the tenure track. Since women are overrepresented among those not on a tenure track and those in positions to which tenure does not apply, the gender disparities in achievement of tenure are conservative estimates.

Tenure and rank are correlated (those with tenure are likely to be in the top two ranks, and those in the top two ranks are likely to have tenure), so one would expect gender disparities in tenure. Although the differences across all fields are numerically extremely small, men are significantly more successful than women are (26% of men vs. 24% of women); the same holds for science as a whole (26% of men vs. 23% of women). In engineering, however, there is no difference in tenure rates, even though women lag behind men

Table 4.5
Proportions of men and women who have achieved tenure within ten years post-PhD for all fields, science, engineering, and health

	All fields	Science	Engineering	Health
Proportion of field that is male	.55	.54	.76	.27
Male	.26	.26	.24	.25*
Female	.24*	.23*	.25	.33
Sample N	44,900	34,300	6,600	4,200

Note. Comparisons with an asterisk are statistically significant. The proportion of the field that is male includes all those with degrees less than ten years old who are employed in four-year educational institutions in any capacity. For tenure, the N excludes "not on tenure track" and "tenure not applicable" individuals (N excluded = 56,600 for all fields, N excluded = 46,300 for science fields).

in becoming associate and full professors (table 4.3). (The reasons for the differences in rank and tenure success are not clear.) In health, women are significantly advantaged in tenure, as they were for rank (table 4.3).[23]

We also examine broad fields within science; the data are shown in table 4.6.[24] In math and statistics, the physical sciences, and the biological sciences, men are significantly more likely to achieve tenure within ten years postdegree than are women, mirroring the results for achievement of associate professor status. These fields include ones where the total percentage of men in the field is high (e.g., mathematics and statistics) and one where it is similar to the percentage of women (biological and agricultural sciences). In computer science and the social sciences, there are no significant gender differences. In psychology, where women outnumber men, women are significantly advantaged; the same holds for health. In engineering, where men outnumber women 3:1, the two groups are nevertheless equal in tenure rates, similar to the social sciences, where men only slightly outnumber women (51%).

The data in tables 4.5 and 4.6 do not show a tight connection between the percentage of women in a field and their achievement of tenure within ten years. In both engineering and computer science, where women are not quite 25% of the field, there are nevertheless no differences in tenure rates. In biology, where young women are almost as numerous as young

Table 4.6
Proportions of men and women who have achieved tenure within ten years for each broad field within science: biological/agricultural/life sciences; computer/information sciences; mathematics/statistics, physical sciences, psychology, social sciences (excluding psychology), engineering, and health

	Computer science	Math	Physical sciences	Biological/ agricultural sciences	Social sciences (excluding psychology)	Psychology
Proportion of field that is male	.77	.69	.67	.53	.51	.32
Male	.44	.26	.21	.20	.28	.24*
Female	.40	.11*	.13*	.13*	.29	.27
Sample N	2,300	3,200	4,900	7,600	11,200	5,000

Note. Fields are ordered by the proportion of the field that is male and include all those with degrees less than ten years old who are employed in four-year educational institutions in any capacity. Comparisons with an asterisk are statistically significant.

men, men are more successful. But in psychology, health, and social science, where women are more numerous, they are either more successful than men or equally successful.

Our data are generally, but not always, consistent for achievement of rank and tenure across fields in science, engineering, and health. In math, physical sciences, and biological and agricultural sciences, men fare better than women in both rank and tenure. In engineering and social sciences, men have an advantage in rank but are equal with women in tenure rates. In computer science, men and women are on a par in rank and tenure. In psychology, men and women are on a par in rank, but women are advantaged in tenure. Fields may differ in whether rank or tenure is the more difficult achievement.

Overall, we would sum up our findings for men and women in the sciences as showing that women are only more advantaged relative to men if they are extremely highly represented in a field (health and, for tenure, psychology). Otherwise, men are either more advantaged in achievement of rank and tenure, or on a par with women. We also note that if we included all individuals, such as instructors and lecturers, gender disparities would be greater.

Not all studies are consistent with our findings. The differences across studies are difficult to evaluate but may be due to differences in methods, data set, and types of analyses. One gender analysis separated individuals by broad field (life and social sciences vs. natural sciences, engineering, and math) and found that women fare worse than men in the life and social sciences but do as well as men in the natural sciences, after a number of characteristics, including marital status, are controlled for (see Ceci et al., 2014, for a summary). (We would argue that controlling for marital status is overcontrolling. If employers treat married men and women differently, that is a problem that should not be masked by using marriage as a control.) A study limited to junior faculty in the natural sciences and math at 14 universities found no gender differences in time to tenure or in retention, except in math (Kaminski & Geisler, 2012); no factors were controlled for. A study of faculty in the social sciences found differences in time to tenure (Box-Steffensmeier, Cunha, Varbanov, Hoh, Knisley, & Holmes, 2015).

Earlier we reviewed data on rank progression in universities in Spain showing slower progression for women. The phenomenon of slower rank progression for women also occurs in the Netherlands, as shown in a study of young researchers in three social science fields (psychology, economics, and behavioral and educational research) roughly ten years post-PhD (van den Besselaar & Sandström, 2016). Researcher productivity predicted rank, and men published more than women (but had equal citation rates), but gender had an effect above and beyond productivity and other controls (van den Besselaar & Sandström, 2016). At the beginning of their careers, the young researchers did not differ in productivity. Men's productivity grew faster than women's over the ten-year period. That finding is susceptible to varying interpretations that are not mutually exclusive: women may be given fewer resources, including mentoring and collaboration, than men; women may work less intensively than men; women may produce work of lower quality; or women may perceive that they must reach a higher standard.

Summary

To conclude, women in the sciences are significantly less likely than men to have positions in universities with very high or high research activity; in several fields, they are significantly slower to achieve tenure within the first ten years post-PhD and are less likely than men to become an associate or full professor; they also make less money. African Americans are significantly less likely than Asians, Whites, or Hispanics to have positions in universities with very high research activity, while Hispanics are on a par with Whites. African Americans and other non-Asian minorities make less money than Whites and Asians.

In the workplace as a whole, including academia, men in general fare better than women in terms of promotion and salary, even after considering a number of factors that reduce gender disparities (Blau & Kahn, 2017). Similarly, White men fare better than non-Asian men and women of color.

Although we conclude that White men have more successful careers, as conventionally defined, than do White women or non-Asian men and women of color, we also reiterate that careers for White women in particular have markedly improved since 1970. That noticeable improvement can draw attention away from the stubborn inequalities that remain. We attribute the recalcitrance of those inequalities to two factors. One is the differences in evaluations of people, differences due to schemas that people hold about the abilities and performances of different groups, as described in chapter 3. The other factor is the absence of policies and procedures that will reduce the likelihood of incorrect evaluations, for which we recommend policy changes in later chapters. (We consider other possibilities in the next section.)

We also suggest that visible exceptions—very successful White women, very successful male and female African Americans—can disguise the inequalities that remain in the advancement of underrepresented groups. Our focus on the exceptions can mislead us into thinking that there is no problem; that logic implies that if there were a problem, then there would be no successful individuals from those groups. However, it is important to realize that the exceptions are exceptions, not the norm.

Accounts of the Observational Data

As detailed in chapter 3, people evaluate White men differently from White women and people of color, even when performances are the same. Many of those evaluations are small daily occurrences that can be barely visible but that mount up over time to accumulate advantage (White men) or disadvantage (White women and non-Asian men and women of color). Although the observational and experimental studies that we have cited support our explanation, there are other accounts that have been provided for the observational data.

We consider in turn seven additional accounts of the patterns of career advancement that we have detailed.[25] As we noted earlier, we think some of the accounts have merit and can be interpreted within the framework we developed in chapter 3. For others, the accounts adduce facts that are not well established.

Seven Accounts

1. Demographic inertia, based on the fact that there are so many more older White men than women, or so many more older Whites and Asians than people of color in various samples or populations:

• The problem will take care of itself in time; there is nothing that academia needs to do differently.

2. Disparities in distribution of *extra*-academic responsibilities, such as childcare within heterosexual couples or community work on the part of White women and African American and Hispanic men and women:

• There are societal and cultural issues preventing equal advancement that are outside the purview of academia; there is nothing that academia needs to do differently, but it could provide benefits making childcare more available and accessible.

3. Disparities in ability:

• Members of different social groups have different abilities; as a result, members of different social groups go into different fields and have different levels of success; there is nothing that academia needs to do differently.

4. Disparities in productivity:

• Members of social groups differ in their average productivity; as a result, members of different social groups have different levels of success; there is nothing that academia needs to do differently, but it could "mentor" groups to increase productivity.

5. Disparities in interest:

• Members of different social groups have different interests; as a result, members of different social groups go into different fields and have different levels of success; there is nothing that academia needs to do differently.

6. Disparities in attempts to negotiate, compete, or self-promote:

• Members of different social groups have different skills or interest in negotiating, competing, or self-promoting; as a result, members of different social groups go into different fields and have different levels of success; there is nothing that academia needs to do differently, but it could "mentor" individuals from those groups to increase their skills.

7. Overt bias:

• Academia needs to reduce bias.

1. Demographic Inertia

In the case of gender, the account draws on the fact that, in the past, the "pipeline"[26]—especially in the natural sciences and engineering—had many fewer women compared to men. Because White men in the past achieved advanced degrees at rates much higher than did White women or men and women of color, they automatically dominate the higher ranks of academia. According to this hypothesis, men are so numerous in higher ranks because there are a lot of older men around. Women are concentrated in lower ranks because there are so many young women (compared to older women) around. Under this hypothesis, the small number of women full professors is the consequence of a relatively recent increase of young women in the sciences (Hargens & Long, 2002). The same hypothesis can be advanced to explain the low representation of African Americans and Hispanics, whose representation among PhD recipients is still very low, and considerably below their representation in the population as a whole.

There is a statistical kernel of truth here. If an area continues to award only 20% of its PhDs to women, that field will never have more than 20% women at the highest ranks unless men drop out in very large numbers.[27] Similarly, if Hispanics and Blacks remain only 6% of PhD recipients in the sciences, it will be a very long time indeed before their representation among full professors increases.

Despite the kernel of truth, the inertia hypothesis does not account for all of the facts. With respect to gender, women's movement through transitions does not match what demographic inertia would predict (Ceci, Ginther, Kahn, & Williams, 2014, who also suggest that subfield differences exist; Shaw & Stanton, 2012; Thomas, Poole, & Herbers, 2015). Inertia predicts a higher percentage of women in graduate school, postdoc positions, and assistant professorships than is in fact the case,[28] though there may no longer be a drop-off between a bachelor's degree and a doctorate (Miller & Wai, 2015). Even in fields where women are well-represented, such as psychology, women do not succeed at the same rate as men. For example, women leave psychology after graduate school at roughly the same rate that they leave physics (Shaw & Stanton, 2012). Having a large number of women with the appropriate degrees does not guarantee that they will remain in that field. The "pipeline" leaks women. Only if policies and procedures change at every point in the pipeline, from recruitment to retention to promotion, will the leakage stop (Thomas et al., 2015).

We conclude that demographic inertia alone cannot account for the fact that different demographic groups progress through their careers at different rates.

2. Extra-academic Responsibilities

In most dual-earner two-sex households, women and men do not equally divide their household and childcare responsibilities. Further, few universities provide adequate parental leave or childcare facilities for parents. As a result, according to this account, women do not have the necessary time to devote to becoming successful at work. This account predicts that women will leave the professions in greater numbers than men, and that those who remain in the professions will achieve less than men. We find a great deal of evidence to support the first prediction, but not the second.

Before we continue, we note an underlying assumption: achievement is importantly related to hours of work. It is obviously necessary to spend some amount of time working, but we do not know how much time is necessary or what the function is that describes the relation between time and achievement. It is even difficult to decide what counts as work. Does supervising graduate students count? Does reading other people's work count? Does going to a talk on a tangential topic count? Does data analysis count? Does thinking count? Or does only writing count? If they all count as work, is more always better? There is no literature on the relation between time spent working (however defined) and achievement, so the assumption underlying the hypothesis is speculation. We note, however, that creativity benefits from spending some time away from the explicit effort of working on a problem—the "incubation" effect (Sio & Ormerod, 2009).

One kernel of truth to this hypothesis is that women who live with men do more than their share of housework and childcare (Bianchi, Sayer, Milkie, & Robinson, 2012). Among all heterosexual married couples with children in 2009–2010, women averaged 18.3 hours of housework and 13.7 hours of childcare per week. The comparable figures for men were 9.5 and 7.2 (Bianchi et al., 2012). Thus, women were performing almost twice as much housework and childcare as men. Lack of parity holds no matter how much each partner earns. Another kernel of truth is that not enough universities have adequate childcare policies, and those that have them do not necessarily implement them (Ahmad, 2016). Parents are forced to find their own solutions.

The first prediction of this hypothesis is borne out. Women leave the full-time workforce, either to no paid employment or to part-time paid employment, at rates higher than men (Ceci et al., 2014; Goulden, Mason, & Frasch, 2011; for a review, see Ahmad, 2016). Women's exit from the workforce creates losses for them (to the extent that their work ambitions cannot be fulfilled), the institutions where they had worked, the institutions that trained them, and the fields in which they had worked.

The second part of the hypothesis is not borne out. Women who remain full-time in academia work the same number of hours as men, though they do not necessarily divide their time at work in the same way (Ceci et al., 2014). Women appear to spend the same amount of time in research as men around the world (Bentley & Kyvik, 2013). There are few if any productivity differences between women with and without children, though the findings are not completely consistent across studies (Ceci et al., 2014; Fox, 2005; Schroen, Brownstein, & Sheldon, 2004). To the extent that women publish less than men, it does not appear to be due to the presence or absence of children (though men with children may publish more than men without children; Ceci et al., 2014). Women without children, according to this account, should advance as quickly as men, but that is also not the case (Kelly & Grant, 2012, though see Kahn & Ginther, 2017, who outline data suggesting that never-married women without children earn more than never-married men without children, once a suite of controls is introduced; for married men and women with children, controls reduce but do not eliminate a wage gap in the other direction).

Heterosexual women's ability to continue publishing their work despite their greater responsibilities at home may be due to their being a highly selected group. Almost by definition, people who survive in an environment that seems stressful are different from people who do not.

A different kind of responsibility is engagement with one's community. This is work that White women and men and women of color take on more than do White men (see O'Meara, Sandmann, Saltmarsh, & Giles, 2011, for review and discussion). Engagement with one's community can also be reflected in one's work, by, for example, codesigning studies with community members or enlisting community members as participants. Whether community work hinders faculty's research and teaching careers in some ways is not known, but institutions should value efforts by faculty to benefit their communities.

If institutions improved both the availability and accessibility of parental leave and childcare policies (and ensured that parents who took leave cared for their children), there would be less loss of talent and parents would benefit. For the women who do remain in academia, the data do not suggest that having children affects productivity, though having children may affect how women are evaluated and thus how much they are paid.

3. Ability

An account that attributes different professional outcomes to different abilities is periodically popular. In the area of gender, mean differences between males and females on most cognitive tasks are small or nonexistent. Attention has thus shifted from average differences to the ratio of males to females among those most talented at math. The argument here is that men are disproportionately found at the upper tail of scores on standardized math tests and are therefore more likely to excel in fields that require math.

Young males *are* disproportionately represented at the high end of standardized tests of math compared with young females, but the ratio of males to females in the top tenth of a percent of the math SAT shrank from 13.5 in a cohort tested in 1981–1985 to 2.53 in a cohort tested in 2011–2015 (Makel, Wai, Peairs, & Putallaz, 2016).[29] Thus, there is nothing immutable about the distribution of males and females with respect to math skills. Among adults, men are much more highly represented than women in math departments and among winners of math prizes. Some data suggest that girls' math ability is not cultivated to the same extent as boys' (Ellison & Swanson, 2010).

Partially supporting the hypothesis that early evidence of strong math skills is related to later achievement are data showing that people at the uppermost tail of the math SAT distribution as 13-year-olds—the top 1%—have by ages 48–53 amassed a striking number of accomplishments in science and other fields, dramatically more than base rates would predict (Lubinski, Benbow, & Kell, 2014).

One cannot, however, infer from high accomplishments that being in the top 1% of a standardized math test at an early age is necessary, sufficient, or jointly necessary and sufficient for high achievement in the sciences. The lack of sufficiency is apparent from the fact that women superscorers were much more likely to be full-time homemakers than were men, women superscorers made less money than men, women superscorers had fewer achievements than men, and women superscorers were less likely to have careers in the natural sciences than men (Lubinski et al., 2014). It is not enough to be a high scorer.

It is also doubtful that super high math scores on the SAT are necessary for success in math and science fields. The average quantitative GRE score for PhD students in math-intensive fields is around the 75th percentile, suggesting that the much greater percentage of men than women in those fields cannot be attributed solely to differences in math facility (Ceci et al., 2014). (Whether exceptionally high achievement is linked to exceptionally high scores on such standardized tests is not known.) Further, personality variables (such as conscientiousness) predict students' grade point averages above and beyond their test scores (Noftle & Robins, 2007).

Finally, the appeal to differences in math ability as an explanation of the slower advancement of women in math and science fields cannot, presumably, be used to explain the slower advancement of women in the humanities, where women also do not fare as well as men (Ginther & Kahn, 2006).

At present, there are no race or ethnicity studies for academia parallel to these gender studies. As we noted earlier, African Americans are less successful than Whites in obtaining grant funding even after controlling for a variety of characteristics. Thus, while there may be average differences in cognitive test scores,[30] African Americans whose characteristics are equivalent to Whites' do not reap the same benefits.

We have two general criticisms of accounts based on ability differences. The first is that they oversimplify what is necessary for success. No single characteristic, whether it be mathematical or verbal skill,[31] creativity, persistence, hard work, or a conscientious personality, is necessary or sufficient for success in any field. Success is due to a wide range of qualities, including luck, and in any given case it is hard to know how to apportion credit. The second criticism is that ability accounts fail to consider the differential treatment that individuals from different demographic groups receive and the mutability of high scores. If we want people to succeed, we have to have high expectations for them and supply constructive criticism.

4. Productivity

Decisions about hiring, tenure, and promotion are nominally made on the basis of "quality," and quality is generally measured by two values, both of which are imperfectly connected to quality: quantity and citations. We discuss the extent of sex differences in both measures and the extent to which those sex differences in both measures are related to job success.

The most common measure of productivity is number of publications, in part because it is easy to tabulate. The measure has known limitations. For example, researchers can inflate the number of articles they publish by writing very short articles. Several short articles may not be as substantive as one longer article that ties together several approaches, but on a quantity metric they will count more. Work that is new or goes against current thinking may be difficult to publish and require more evidence to publish, especially if one works at an institution that is not among the most prestigious.

Another common measure of productivity is number of citations. This is a measure of the impact—for good or for ill—that one's work has had.[32] The impact a publication has is determined in part by the perceived quality of the work, the prestige of the journal or academic press where the publication appears, the prestige of the person's institution, the number of people in a field, and current fashion.

Someone who writes a manual that changes how medical examinations are performed has clearly produced something of value. That manual may have required a great deal of time, effort, and analysis. However, it may not count as a publication since it may neither be in a journal nor exist as a book. The established metrics miss that. As another example, someone might write a single article on Shakespeare that sparks interest on the part of directors, who now produce plays differently than they would have before the article was published. It is just a single article, and there may be few citations because the impact that the work has is on the performance of Shakespeare's plays rather than on Shakespearean scholarship. Again, the established metrics will fail to capture the value of the work.

Gender Differences in Productivity If we stick with the established metrics, despite their limitations, we can compare men and women on number of publications. There is enormous variability and inconsistency. In some fields, in some countries, at some ranks, at some time periods, women have produced fewer publications than men. In others, there have either been no gender differences or women have published more. One international study of millions of papers reports that women publish less than men and are cited less than men (Larivière, Ni, Gingras, Cronin, & Sugimoto, 2013).[33] What is almost always found is that a higher percentage of men than women are extra prolific.

The finding that women publish somewhat less than men often occurs in studies where type of institution is not controlled in the analysis. Women are disproportionately found in institutions with heavy teaching responsibilities, while men are disproportionately found in research-intensive institutions. After controlling for such factors, Xie and Shauman (2003) conclude that the gender disparity in productivity in science is an artifact of the gender differences in institutional home.

Other factors that have been found to play a role—albeit inconsistently—in gender disparities in number of publications include time spent in research versus teaching, subfield (Ceci et al., 2014), degree of specialization (Leahey, 2006), and the extent to which a field is resource intensive (Duch, Zeng, Sales-Pardo, Radicchi, Otis, Woodruff, & Amaral, 2012). The inconsistencies are more striking than the consistencies. Sometimes, for example, there are no differences in publication rates between male and female psychologists (Joy, 2006), and sometimes there are (Ceci et al., 2014).

Citations are, overall, less likely than publication counts to show gender disparities, though, again, there is inconsistency across studies, often because of inconsistency in what controls are used. Men tend to cite themselves more than women do, but even that finding is not universal across fields. One innovative suggestion for calculating impact via citations is to subtract years when scholars had no publications and to exclude self-citations; once that is accomplished, there are no gender differences in citations in ecology (Cameron, White, & Gray, 2016). Women are more likely than men to experience years with no publications (as are people who are working on a long-term project); women, as mentioned above, are in general less likely to cite themselves than are men.

Importance of Gender Differences in Productivity to Job Success The main question, however, is whether gender differences in productivity determine promotion and salary. This is an even harder question to answer than the question about sex disparities. Independent of gender, the data suggest that productivity is a factor, but only one among many others (Byrnes, 2007; Ceci et al., 2014). An analysis of assistant professors in psychology departments at highly ranked universities found that 25% of those tenured had published less than one paper per year (Byrnes, 2007). One Dutch study found that gender predicted rank above and beyond productivity (van den Besselaar & Sandström, 2016). Departments have many reasons for retaining and promoting faculty. Productivity is one, but not the only one. We do not know of studies comparing Whites and underrepresented minorities.

Our discussion of productivity thus far has concentrated on research productivity, although institutions of higher learning have a mission to educate students. Even in teaching-intensive schools, research productivity is increasingly the principal criterion for hiring, promotion, and tenure. Junior faculty are often informally told that being a bad teacher will hurt their chances for promotion or tenure, but being an outstanding teacher will not suffice to gain promotion or tenure. Research productivity is the primary measure. Since there is evidence that students rate women worse than they rate men as instructors, even after controlling for various factors that could be relevant (Boring, 2017, using data from France; Boring, Ottoboni, & Stark, 2016, examining data from France and the United States; MacNell, Driscoll, & Hunt, 2015, with U.S. data subsequently used by Boring et al.; Wagner, Rieger, & Voorvelt, 2016, with data from the Netherlands), women are at a disadvantage in teaching when schools take students' evaluations into account.

Other forms of productivity can be measured. In acute care hospitals, for example, one can measure the extent to which physicians follow best practices and protocols to reduce errors as well as patient mortality and readmission rates (Tsugawa, Jena, Figueroa, Orav, Blumenthal, & Jha, 2017). Although the differences in performance are small, they significantly favor women. Women follow best practices more than men, and fewer of their patients die or are readmitted with complications. Women are nonetheless paid less and take longer to achieve full professor status (for a summary, see Parks & Redberg, 2017).

5. Interest

As appeal to intellectual disparities has waned, appeal to interest disparities has waxed. According to the different-interests hypothesis, White women, and men and women of color, are less interested in success, traditionally defined, than White men are (e.g., Ceci & Williams, 2010; Lubinski et al., 2014). For that reason they do not pursue challenging and demanding occupations to the same degree, or, even if they are in such occupations, they do not pursue success. Differential interests have also been recruited to explain why women are underrepresented in math, computer science, chemistry, physics, and engineering (Kahn & Ginther, 2017).

We reject an explanation that relies on differential interests if those interests are portrayed as inherent and immutable. First, people's interests and choices can and do change. Second, and more importantly, interests, choices, and goals are affected by the expectations we have of others, the opportunities we give them to succeed and belong, and the information we provide about what different fields have to offer, as research we considered in chapter 3 suggests. Everyone's potential interests are malleable, and most fields are compatible with a range of interests.

Women are often characterized as interested in people while men are characterized as interested in things. This picture is wrong for several reasons: it is too limiting for both groups; it incorrectly places people and things as opposed, instead of complementary; and it oversimplifies the data giving rise to the characterization (Valian, 2014).

Women *are* more interested in helping people than are men, and women have more progressive political stances. Women see their goals, which include helping others, as incompatible with the goals of science (Diekman, Brown, Johnston, & Clark, 2010). Students perceive most natural sciences, math, and engineering as less compatible with goals involving intimacy and altruism than with goals involving power and achievement.

If students have goals that are communal, they are likely to see science as a bad fit. And women are more likely to have such goals than are men. Changing how work in the sciences is portrayed, to make its social benefits clear, is one way to ensure that people with a range of goals will enter it. Similarly, high achievement in any field might look more attractive if it clearly included ways of using the position to make changes one deems beneficial.

We note that congressmen (Iacus, King, & Porro, 2011, confirming Washington, 2008) and male judges (Glynn & Sen, 2015) are more progressive on women's issues if they have daughters than if they have sons. For judges, the effect is particularly strong for judges who have only one child, a daughter. It should not come as news that people change their interests, and that individuals' interests are affected by the people around them. But the idea that free choice (constrained by childbearing and child-rearing) determines people's professional lives has become popular (e.g., Schmidt, 2011; Williams & Ceci, 2015).

Interest in fields like computer science is affected by the environment (Cheryan, Plaut, Davies, & Steele, 2009); women's interest in the sciences is affected by whether they think they belong and can be a valued member of a field (e.g., Cheryan, Ziegler, & Jiang, 2017; Cheryan, Master, & Melt-zoff, 2015; Cheryan & Plaut, 2010; Dasgupta & Stout, 2014; Smith, Lewis, Hawthorne, & Hodges, 2013); both men and women sabotage peers who excel in areas that are not typical for their sex (Rudman & Fairchild, 2004). All fields that show a sex disparity, including childcare, have this problem: people who identify with the sex that is less well represented feel they do not have as much right to be active in that area. It is hard for fathers to play a time-intensive, nurturing role with their children when so few fathers do.

Marie Wilson, speaking of women in politics, said, "You can't be what you can't see." Something like that happens in every field, for both men and women. Seeing people like oneself in a position opens up that position as a possibility. For people of color the situation is more complex. Even if they were to be represented among leaders at rates matching their representation in the population as a whole, no single underrepresented minority would be very numerous. It is difficult for people from small demographic groups to see themselves in many positions. However, it may not be necessary to see people exactly like oneself. A diverse mix of people in a position may be enough of a signal that the position is achievable. You can be what you can't see if you see enough diversity to think there is room for you, too.

One example of the impact of even minor discouragement was reported by the *The Boston Globe* (Bombardieri, 2005). A male economist told a group of students that professors needed to be aware of the great influence that positive or negative signals can have on their students. He said that as a student he had had a genuine interest in economics, but he also went into economics because he had been dissuaded from some other fields "by experiences where I lagged slightly and where I was made to feel inadequate." He described an occasion when he gave the wrong answer to a physics question and "the person who saw my answer looked on with a certain stunned

belief that I could be so stupid." This is a fairly mild example of discouragement, in which there is no explicit negative content, yet it was sufficient
to deter Lawrence Summers (a former president of Harvard University who
speculated about reasons for women's lower representation in the sciences)
from pursuing physics.

Maybe Lawrence Summers would have been a mediocre physicist. Or
maybe he would have been a good one. We will never know. We will similarly never know how many women and underrepresented minorities will
show interest in the natural sciences and math unless we provide them with
the right "opportunity structures" and the perception that they belong. As
one study concludes,

Women's interests are fundamentally shaped by the culture of [STEM] fields. Just
because women are excited to go into other fields does not mean that they would
not have been equally excited to go into computer science, engineering, and physics
if the cultures signaled to them that they belong there. (Cheryan et al., 2017, p. 22)

Similarly, interests are shaped by challenges. Men and women receive
different responses at work (King, Botsford, Hebl, Kazama, Dawson, &
Perkins, 2012). Male and female managers in the energy and health care
industries, for example, reported equal numbers of opportunities to expand
their capabilities, but men received *challenging* opportunities at higher rates
than women did. Experimental work suggested that men and women articulated equal interest in challenging opportunities but that male managers
acted to protect women from possible failure, thus denying them the challenges that might make them more competitive for higher level jobs.

In short, interests change and choices change. By changing people's
environments, we can provide them with more opportunities.

6. Negotiation and Competition

We begin this section with two stories. The first story comes from Karen, in
box 4.1. Karen had tried to negotiate but failed.

The second story comes from Matthew, an African American faculty
member at a public research university, who was offered a distinguished
chair at a well-known historically Black college. While the change would
bring some losses (in the status of the institution employing him and in
having fewer graduate students), it offered some important gratifications,
in particular the chance to teach many gifted African American students.
He talked with his chair about the offer and the possibility of a competing

offer from his current institution. His chair said, "We only make counter-offers when people have offers from peer institutions. We don't think you'll accept this offer." Matthew accepted the other offer. He too had tried to negotiate but failed.

The hypothesis about negotiation is that White women lose out because they do not negotiate well and avoid competition. This hypothesis has only been proffered for gender disparities, not for race and ethnicity dispari-ties. There is a basis for the hypothesis, in that women negotiate less than men (e.g., Babcock & Laschever, 2009) and engage in competition less in some but not all settings (Andersen, Ertac, Gneezy, List, & Maximiano, 2013; Croson & Gneezy, 2009; Mitchell & Hesli, 2013). Two questions to ask are why that is so and whether that accounts for women's slow advancement relative to men's. We suggest that women and men receive different responses to their attempts to negotiate and compete, and that those different responses affect their behavior. In discussing schemas, we reviewed experiments that show that women who are assertive pay a pen-alty in being disliked, and that liking is related to benefits (Heilman, 2012; Heilman & Okimoto, 2007; Ridgeway, 2011; Rudman & Phelan, 2008).

What holds for assertiveness also holds for negotiation: people do not respond as favorably to women as to men when they negotiate for them-selves (Amanatullah & Tinsley, 2013; Bowles, Babcock, & Lai, 2007; Kulik & Olekalns, 2012). Thus, women don't negotiate in part because, when they try to, they are seen as self-aggrandizing or unlikable (Kray & Thompson, 2004; Ridgeway, 1982), and do not get what they want unless they have already achieved high status (Amanatullah & Tinsley, 2013). Women are more likely to negotiate for higher salary if the job description suggests that negotiation is possible, whereas men negotiate regardless of whether the job description suggests that negotiation is possible or not (Leibbrandt & List, 2014).

Women who negotiate on someone else's behalf are generally more suc-cessful than women who negotiate for themselves because in that case they are not promoting themselves; experience with negotiation helps, as does knowing ahead of time what the relevant range of possibilities is (Mazei, Hüffmeier, Freund, Stuhlmacher, Bilke, & Hertel, 2015). Since women in academia can only negotiate for their own salaries, are sometimes doing so at the beginning of their careers when they have had less experience, and generally have only a vague idea of what the relevant salary range is, they will be at a disadvantage compared to men.

There is almost no research on African Americans' or other minority groups' attempts to negotiate or success at negotiation. Audit studies suggest that African Americans are less successful in negotiating with car dealers (Ayres & Siegelman, 1995). Whites bid less online for baseball cards when the hand holding the card is black rather than white (Ayres, Banaji, & Jolls, 2015), and bid less often and with lower amounts for a portable playing device if the hand holding the device is black rather than white (Doleac & Stein, 2013).

Status affects negotiation. If someone has low status because of his or her gender, race, ethnicity, or rank, he or she cannot negotiate successfully in the same way that someone who has high status negotiates. High status legitimizes negotiation. Women are asked more often than men to occupy service roles (O'Meara, Kuvaeva, Nyunt, Waugaman, & Jackson, in press) and accept (O'Meara, Kuvaeva, & Nyunt, 2017), perhaps in part because they suspect they lack the status to refuse. A similar phenomenon holds for competition, as demonstrated by gender differences in competition in matrilineal versus patrilineal societies (Gneezy, Leonard, & List, 2009). In matrilineal societies women are considerably more competitive than they are in patrilineal societies. Further, in both kinds of societies, girls and boys are equally competitive until around age 13, at which point girls in patrilineal societies (but not in matrilineal societies) stop being as competitive as boys. As is the case with interests, negotiation and competition are influenced by the surrounding context.

Willingness to engage in negotiation and competition can be determined by many considerations, including expectations of winning and the perceived (and possibly actual) social acceptability of competing. Women's math performance suffers when they actively compete against men (Niederle & Vesterlund, 2010; for review of gender effects from an economics perspective, see Niederle, 2016), possibly due to stereotype threat (Ben-Zeev, Fein, & Inzlicht, 2005). In line with that suggestion, women are more likely to compete in an experimental setting if the task is a verbal task—where stereotype threat is absent—than if it is a math task; they also produce work with fewer errors than men if there is no time pressure (Shurchkov, 2012). The ratio of male to female job applicants varies significantly depending on fairly subtle differences in the ways jobs are framed and on differences among applicants that are not related to gender. For example, women are more likely to apply for a job in which their pay would be determined by their performance relative to others if they were to work as part of a team. Gender differences are more extreme among younger applicants than older applicants; among older applicants, men and women equally prefer a fixed wage. Women are also less likely than men to apply for jobs that seem "masculine" (Flory, Leibbrandt, & List, 2015).

In sum, men's and women's willingness to negotiate or compete is not all-or-nothing. If the environment sends signals that they can benefit from negotiation or competition, and that there will not be any negative social consequences, the sexes are very similar.

Is competition good? To the extent that competition can help people do their best work, it is beneficial. Recall that our earlier review in chapter 2 of teams, where we considered the benefits of diversity, shows that cooperation is also good. Cooperation helps bring out everyone's talents. Institutions need to strike the right balance in order to maximize applications from a diverse pool of job candidates and to ensure that they bring out the best in all of their employees.

7.   Overt Bias

Overt bias exists in academia, as the all too numerous documented cases of sexual harassment attest. For one example, women in geophysics, and especially women of color, reported disturbing levels of verbal and physical harassment in a 2015 Internet survey of men and women students, researchers, and faculty (Clancy, Lee, Rodgers, & Richey, 2017). Both men and women reported hearing sexist and racist comments, though women and people of color reported hearing them more than did White men. Students reported more instances than did more senior researchers. Since this is a sample of unknown representativeness, and included many more women than men, the data cannot inform us about how common harassment is, only that it occurs.[34] Even one occurrence is one too many. That harassment has consequences is clear from the larger percentage of women than men reporting feeling unsafe and missing professional events at higher levels because of feeling unsafe. Making matters worse is that academia has failed to prevent harassment or to adequately sanction harassers. Overt bias occurs and is damaging, even if there is now less of it and even if it is now more likely to meet with objections when it occurs. Professional societies and academic institutions have a duty to ensure that professional settings provide an environment where everyone is free from harassment or bullying. Some professional groups have taken steps to fulfill that duty, such as the American Geophysical Union, the American Political Science Association, and the Boston University Conference on Language Development. (See, respectively, https://harassment.agu.org/; http://www.apsanet .org/divresources/policyprocedures/; https://www.bu.edu/bucld/conference -info/conduct/.)

However, we argue that overt bias, which may be an extension of the more subtle examples we have described, is not the major determinant for the widespread pattern of sex, race, and ethnic disparities in achievement that we have documented. Even those women and people of color who never or seldom experience overt bias from peers or supervisors (the majority in the study of geophysicists; Clancy et al., 2017) experience the myriad types of subtle undervaluation that we have documented.

Summary

To summarize, we have reviewed seven alternate accounts of the slower progress and lower salaries of women and people of color (demographic inertia, extra-academic responsibilities, ability, productivity, interest, negotiation and taste for competition, and overt discrimination):

• In the cases of negotiation, competition, and productivity, the facts the explanations are based on may themselves be due to unequal treatment of men and women. For example, men negotiate and compete more than women, but men who negotiate and compete are responded to more positively than women who negotiate and compete. Men are slightly more productive than women, but men and women have different access to resources.

• In the cases of ability and interest, there is insufficient evidence to conclude that men and women, Whites and people of color, differ. Here we conclude that the data to support the claims are not solid. In addition, like negotiation, competition, and productivity, skills, and tastes are affected by treatment.

• In the cases of demographic inertia and extra-academic responsibilities, the facts adduced are correct. Demographic inertia exists. But White men's success is greater than demographic inertia alone would predict. Extra-academic responsibilities differ by gender, and they remove women from the workforce, but they play a small role for those who remain.

• Finally, overt discrimination against White women and men and women of color exists and has negative consequences. It is responsible for some portion of the slower advancement of women and people of color. But even women and people of color who do not experience overt discrimination advance more slowly than their White male peers.

We have repeatedly stated that most academics sincerely espouse egalitarian principles. We have also repeatedly stated that a belief in the merit principle makes it difficult for people to see the small ways in which they violate it. In later chapters, we recommend policies and procedures that will help people operate more consistently with their principles.

Notes

1. We thank Francine Blau (personal communication, January 13, 2017) for bringing both points to our attention.

2. Data are from the National Science Board figure 3–31. Estimated salary differences between women and men with highest degree in S[cience]&E[ngineering] employed full-time, controlling for selected characteristics, by degree level: 2013. For BA/BS individuals, the disparity after all controls were entered was 8.4%; for MA/MS individuals, it was 7.8%. Access to the full report is here: https://nsf.gov/statistics/2016/nsb20161/#/report/

3. Data are from the National Science Board figure 3–32. Estimated salary differences between minorities and Whites and Asians with highest degree in S&E employed full-time, controlling for selected characteristics, by degree level, 2013. For BA/BS individuals, the disparity after all controls were entered was 4.9%; for MA/MS individuals, it was 5.5%. Access to the full report is here: https://nsf.gov/statistics/2016/nsb20161/#/report/

4. One study examining academic salaries by rank and subfield found few significant salary differences between men and women for 2010, though differences generally favored men (Ceci et al., 2014). Across the 24 field/rank combinations, 18 showed a numerical difference in favor of men; among research-intensive institutions, 16 of the 24 fields showed a numerical difference in favor of men. One difficulty with tabulating gender disparities separately by subfield and rank is that the reduction in sample size makes the data less stable; another is that the contribution of factors like ethnicity is unknown. There are also difficulties with having a large sample size, in particular that differences by field will be washed out. Why the NSF data, which controlled for field, show a disparity but the study by subfield does not show significant differences is not clear. Our own findings, reported below, also find differences by field.

5. Data are from table 12. Doctorate recipients, by major field of study: Selected years, 1985–2015. Retrieved online January 27, 2018, from https://www.nsf.gov

/statistics/2017/nsf17306/data/tab12.pdf. These are the most recent data available. If nonresident Asians were included, males would be the majority.

6. Calculations are based on NSF tables 19, 20, 21, and 24. Calculations in table 4.1 include only U.S. citizens and permanent residents. If nonresidents were included, the percentage of African Americans and "all others" would be reduced and the percentage of Asians would be increased; the percentage of women would be reduced. Different NSF tables have different types of missing data, resulting in discrepancies in totals from one table to another; the discrepancies are usually small. We include here the numbers and titles of the tables. Table 19: Doctorate recipients, by ethnicity, race, and citizenship status: 2005–15. Retrieved online January 27, 2018, from https://www.nsf.gov/statistics/2017/nsf17306/data/tab19.pdf. Total N for U.S. citizens and permanent nonresidents is 35,117. Table 20: Male doctorate recipients, by ethnicity, race, and citizenship status: 2005–15. Retrieved online January 27, 2018, from https://www.nsf.gov/statistics/2017/nsf17306/data/tab20.pdf. Total N for males who are U.S. citizens or permanent residents is 17,245. Table 21: Female doctorate recipients, by ethnicity, race, and citizenship status: 2005–15. Retrieved online January 27, 2018, from https://www.nsf.gov/statistics/2017/nsf17306/data/tab21.pdf. Total N for females who are U.S. citizens or permanent residents is 17,872.

7. Population data for 2014 were taken from NSF's table 1–2, Resident population of the United States, by sex, race or ethnicity, and age: 2014, retrieved January 27, 2018, from https://www.nsf.gov/statistics/2017/nsf17310/static/data/tab1-2.pdf. We included individuals between the ages of 25 and 64. "All others" include American Indian or Alaska Native, Native Hawaiian or Other Pacific Islander, two or more races, and other or unknown race and ethnicity (the largest subcategory).

8. We do not report statistical tests because (1) we do not have exact counts for the population and (2) some doctorate recipients are younger than age 25 and older than age 64. But the population numbers are so large that, even with the inexact counts, it is clear that were exact counts available, statistical tests would be significant for the comparisons. We computed some values using the population estimates for adults ages 25–64 with a Fisher exact probability test; even the smallest difference with the smallest overall numbers was significant.

9. The percentage of Asian men would be much higher if temporary visa holders were included.

10. Data are from table 14. Doctorate recipients, by broad field of study and sex: Selected years, 1985–2015. Retrieved January 27, 2018, from https://www.nsf.gov/statistics/2017/nsf17306/data/tab14.pdf. Note that this table includes all women, not simply women who were U.S. citizens or permanent residents.

11. Data are from table 23. U.S. citizen and permanent resident doctorate recipients, by broad field of study, ethnicity, and race: Selected years, 1995–2015. Retrieved January 27, 2018, from https://www.nsf.gov/statistics/2017/nsf17306/data/tab23.pdf.

12. Data are from table 9–21. Science, engineering, and health doctorate holders employed full-time in universities and four-year colleges, by 2005 Carnegie classification of academic institution, sex, race, ethnicity, and disability status: 2013; NSF; January 25, 2017, from http://www.nsf.gov/statistics/2015/nsf15311/tables/pdf/tab9 -21.pdf. This table includes a column for missing data—individuals who did not report type of institution. We have subtracted the missing data from the totals that we use as the denominator. Depending on whether gender, ethnicity, or disability status is being examined, there are differing amounts of missing data.

13. Both gender differences are significant by a test of independent proportions. For very high research activity institutions, Males versus Females, $z = 15.03$, $p < 0.0002$; for high research activity institutions, Males versus Females, $z = 16.27$, $p < 0.0002$.

14. For Ethnicity, Whites are compared to every other group via a test of the significance of the difference between two independent proportions. At very high research activity institutions, Whites versus Asians, $z = -26.565$, $p < 0.0002$ (Asians are better represented than Whites); Whites versus African Americans, $z = 21.17$, $p < 0.0002$; Whites versus Hispanics, $z = 1.936$, $p = 0.053$; Whites versus all others, $z = 8.68$, $p < 0.0002$. At high research activity institutions, Whites versus Asians, $z = -8.151$, $p < 0.0002$ (Asians are better represented than Whites); Whites versus African Americans, $z = 3.016$, $p < 0.03$; Whites versus Hispanics, $z = 4.091$, $p < 0.0002$; Whites versus all others, $z = 7.441$, $p < 0.0002$.

We separately compared African Americans with every other group: they have significantly lower representation than any other group. At very high research activity institutions, African Americans versus Asians, $z = -31.836$, $p < 0.0002$; African Americans versus Hispanics, $z = -15.12$, $p < 0.0002$; African Americans versus all others, $z = -5.777$, $p < 0.0002$. At high research activity institutions, African Americans versus Asians, $z = -6.405$, $p < 0.0002$; African Americans versus Hispanics, $z = .5$, ns; African Americans versus all others, $z = 4.569$, $p < 0.0002$.

15. Disability differences are significant by a test of the significance of the difference between independent proportions. At very high research activity institutions, individuals without disabilities are better represented than those with disabilities, $z = 9.429$, $p < 0.0002$; at high research activity institutions, individuals without disabilities are worse represented than those with disabilities, $z = -6.17$, $p < 0.0002$.

16. Data are from table 18. Employed doctoral scientists and engineers in four-year educational institutions, by broad field of doctorate, sex, faculty rank, and years since doctorate: 2013. Retrieved January 27, 2018, from https://ncsesdata.nsf.gov /doctoratework/2013/html/SDR2013_DST18.html. Note that NSF rounds all data to the nearest hundred, resulting in some small discrepancies. In all cases we accepted the values in individual cells and computed subtotals as required.

17. NSF does not provide similar data by race and ethnicity, nor does it present U.S. citizens separately. Although NSF does present data for subfields within science, we

do not look at subfields because several cells are empty because of the small number of people who reach full professor status within ten years.

18. Tests of independent proportions revealed significantly more men than women for the combined ranks of full and associate professors for *all fields*, $z = 10.00$, $p < 0.0002$ and for *science*, $z = 13.32$, $p < 0.0002$; and more women than men for *health*, $z = -2.69$, $p < 0.01$. A test of independent proportions for the associate professor level for *engineering* showed significantly more men than women, $z = 6.01$, $p < 0.0002$.

19. When all individuals in *all fields* are included (N = 101,500) 16% of men and 13% of women are in the top two ranks, a difference which is significant by a test of independent proportions, $z = 11.88$, $p < 0.0002$. For all individuals in *science* fields (N = 80,600), 15% of men and 11% of women are in the top two ranks, a difference which is significant by a test of independent proportions, $z = 16.12$, $p < 0.0002$. The same holds for tenure proportions, presented later. (It is not clear why the totals for tenured plus tenure track individuals are smaller than the totals for full, associate, plus assistant professors.)

20. We conducted separate tests of independent proportions to determine whether there was a significant difference in the percentage of men and women at the associate professor rank. Men are better represented than women at the associate professor rank in *mathematics and statistics*, $z = 11.62$, $p < 0.0002$; the *physical sciences*, $z = 2.043$, $p < .05$; the *biological and agricultural sciences*, $z = 10.49$, $p < 0.0002$; *social science (excluding psychology)*, $z = 4.82$, $p < 0.0002$.

21. Tests of independent proportions showed no difference between men and women in their proportion of achieving the rank of associate professor within ten years in *computer science*, $z = 1.77$, ns, or *psychology*, where the percentages of men and women achieving associate professor rank are identical.

22. See table 21. Employed doctoral scientists and engineers in four-year educational institutions, by broad field of doctorate, sex, tenure status, and years since doctorate: 2013. Retrieved January 27, 2018, from https://ncsesdata.nsf.gov/doctoratework/2013/html/SDR2013_DST21.html. Some totals here differ from totals in table 18. There are a few small rounding inconsistencies in NSF's table 21. In all cases we accepted the values in individual cells and computed subtotals as required.

23. Tests of independent proportions revealed that, for *all fields*, men are significantly more likely than women to achieve tenure within ten years, $z = 2.90$; $p < 0.004$. The same holds for *science as a whole*, $z = 6.57$; $p < 0.0002$. In *engineering* there is no difference, $z = -0.81$, ns. For *health*, women are more likely than men to achieve tenure within ten years, $z = -5.28$, $p = 0.0002$.

24. We computed individual tests of independent proportions for achievement of tenure within ten years for each field. For *computer/information sciences*, there was no gender difference, $z = 1.77$, ns, mirroring the results for achievement of associate

professor rank in ten years. In contrast, for *mathematics/statistics*, men are more likely to achieve tenure, $z=9.21$, $p<0.0002$. The same is true for *physical sciences*, $z=6.04$, $p<0.0002$, and *biological/agricultural/environmental life sciences*, $z=8.07$, $p<0.0002$. There are no gender differences for *social sciences*, $z=-0.599$, ns. In *psychology*, women are more likely than men to achieve tenure within ten years, $z=-2.86$, $p<0.005$.

25. Ceci et al. (2014) adopt a similar strategy of considering different explanations in their case for the underrepresentation of women in the sciences. Some of the explanations they consider overlap with those we consider here. They sensibly conclude that none of the explanations they consider will, on their own, account for women's lower representation. Blau and Kahn (2017) similarly consider a range of different accounts for gender disparities in the workforce as a whole, concluding that measurable human and social capital factors are not sufficient to explain all of the disparities.

26. The pipeline metaphor may incorrectly make it seem as if there is only one route to science and may be demotivating. For discussion, see Cannady, Greenwald, and Harris (2014); Miller and Wai (2015); and Xie and Shauman (2003).

27. As academic salaries become ever more compressed and rise ever more slowly, men might leave in greater numbers than women for more lucrative fields. If women's salaries are depressed no matter what economic sector they are in, they will have less reason to desert academia.

28. If one assumes, as Shaw and Stanton (2012) do, that movement into a tenured position requires that older individuals leave that position, demographic inertia does account for the transition from untenured to tenured faculty member. But since that simplifying assumption is incorrect, the model using it cannot appropriately test the demographic inertia hypothesis for tenure status.

29. In 1981–1985, seventh graders who took the math SAT as a possible entry point to a program for gifted students showed a gender disparity in favor of boys among the top 1% (1.43 times as many boys as girls), top 0.5% (2.61 times as many boys as girls), and top 0.01% (13.5 times as many boys as girls). For the next five-year period, 1986–1990, those ratios were reduced to 1.31, 2.15, and 7.6. For 1991–1995, they were reduced again to 1.26, 1.95, and 3.87, and for 2006–2010, the data showed lower ratios for the 1% (1.10) and 0.5% (1.54) levels and a similar ratio at the 0.01% level (3.83; Wai et al., 2010). The 2011–2015 cohort showed another reduction in the sex ratio at the uppermost end, to 2.53:1 (Makel et al., 2016). ACT math scores have also shown a decline in the ratio at the 0.01% level, from 3.14 in the 1990–1995 cohort to 2.6 in the 2006–2010 cohort. There may be differences in how the SAT and ACT are constructed, or in the percentages of boys and girls who take the tests, since the male:female ratios among top scorers are different.

Two things are notable. One is the rapid increase in the percentage of girls in the far right tail of the SAT distribution. That increase could be an artifact, in that a different sample of girls may have taken the test in the first decade after the 1981–1985 cohort, or the test could have changed (though Wai et al., 2010, argue that the changes are not meaningful). If it is not an artifact, the difference in the male:female ratio for the SAT shows the lability of math scores, as does the ACT reduction to a lesser extent. Apparently, social context influences children's math performance and can rapidly reduce a 13.5 ratio to a 2.53 ratio, even though the reduction is not linear. The same reduction in the sex ratios was found in India (Makel et al., 2016).

30. There are average differences among different racial and ethnic groups in standardized verbal and math scores. There is evidence both that the tests are less valid predictors of performance for African Americans and Hispanics than they are for Whites (Berry, Clark, & McClure, 2011; Berry, Cullen, & Meyer, 2014), and that cognitive tests slightly overpredict how well African Americans and Hispanics will perform (see Berry & Zhao, 2015; for reviews, see Berry, 2015, and Schmitt, 2014).

31. Math and verbal scores are highly intercorrelated; for the sample of gifted 13-year-olds the correlation is 0.55 (Lubinski, Webb, Morelock, & Benbow, 2001). Girls are more likely than boys to have high verbal scores. That asymmetry—girls can succeed in more fields than boys can—might play a role in field choice.

32. There are a number of different measures of citations, such as total number, average number, *h*, and so on.

33. There are a number of technical issues, such as whether means, medians, or distributions should be used in comparing men and women. Male authors tend to dominate the very highest numbers of publications, and women tend to dominate the lowest numbers, so means may overestimate differences. Researchers and scholars at research-intensive universities publish more than do their peers at four-year colleges, where women are more highly represented. Older studies in general show a greater disparity in favor of men; more recent studies show less disparity.

34. One analysis (Greco, O'Boyle, & Walter, 2015) suggests that studies of counterproductive work behavior have lower response rates than other survey studies and are likely to underreport the existence of troubling rates of inappropriate comments, harassment, and the like.

References

Ahmad, S. (2016). Family or future in the academy? *Review of Educational Research, 87*(1), 204–239. doi:10.3102/0034654316631626

Amanatullah, E. T., & Tinsley, C. H. (2013). Ask and ye shall receive? How gender and status moderate negotiation success. *Negotiation and Conflict Management Research, 6*(4), 253–272.

Andersen, S., Ertac, S., Gneezy, U., List, J. A., & Maximiano, S. (2013). Gender, competitiveness, and socialization at a young age: Evidence from a matrilineal and a patriarchal society. *Review of Economics and Statistics*, *95*(4), 1438–1443.

Anghel, B., de la Rica, S., & Dolado, J. J. (2011). The role of institutions in gender differences in science careers. In Ministerio de Ciencia e Innovación (Ed.), *White paper on the position of women in science in Spain*. Retrieved January 27, 2018, from http://www.idi.mineco.gob.es/stfls/MICINN/Ministerio/FICHEROS/UMYC/White Paper_Interactive.pdf

Ayres, I., Banaji, M., & Jolls, C. (2015). Race effects on eBay. *Rand Journal of Economics*, *46*(4), 891–917.

Ayres, I., & Siegelman, P. (1995). Race and gender discrimination in bargaining for a new car. *American Economic Review*, *85*(3), 304–321.

Babcock, L., & Laschever, S. (2009). *Women don't ask: Negotiation and the gender divide*. Princeton, NJ: Princeton University Press.

Benard, S., & Correll, S. J. (2010). Normative discrimination and the motherhood penalty. *Gender & Society*, *24*(5), 616–646.

Bentley, P. J., & Kyvik, S. (2013). Individual differences in faculty research time allocations across 13 countries. *Research in Higher Education*, *54*(3), 329–348.

Ben-Zeev, T., Fein, S., & Inzlicht, M. (2005). Arousal and stereotype threat. *Journal of Experimental Social Psychology*, *41*(2), 174–181.

Berry, C. M. (2015). Differential validity and differential prediction of cognitive ability tests: Understanding test bias in the employment context. *Annual Review of Organizational Psychology and Organizational Behavior*, *2*(1), 435–463.

Berry, C. M., Clark, M. A., & McClure, T. K. (2011). Racial/ethnic differences in the criterion-related validity of cognitive ability tests: A qualitative and quantitative review. *Journal of Applied Psychology*, *96*, 881–906. doi:10.1037/a0023222

Berry, C. M., Cullen, M. J., & Meyer, J. M. (2014). Racial/ethnic subgroup differences in cognitive ability test range restriction: Implications for differential validity. *Journal of Applied Psychology*, *99*(1), 21–37.

Berry, C. M., & Zhao, P. (2015). Addressing criticisms of existing predictive bias research: Cognitive ability test scores still overpredict African Americans' job performance. *Journal of Applied Psychology*, *100*(1), 162–179.

Bertrand, M., Goldin, C., & Katz, L. F. (2010). Dynamics of the gender gap for young professionals in the financial and corporate sectors. *American Economic Journal. Applied Economics*, *2*(3), 228–255.

Bianchi, S. M., Sayer, L. C., Milkie, M. A., & Robinson, J. P. (2012). Housework: Who did, does, or will do it, and how much does it matter? *Social Forces*, *91*(1), 55–63.

Blau, F. D., & Kahn, L. M. (2017). The gender wage gap: Extent, trends, and explanations. *Journal of Economic Literature, 55*, 789–865.

Bombardieri, M. (April 8, 2005). Summers displays new understanding of women's careers. *The Boston Globe.* http://archive.boston.com/news/education/higher/articles/2005/04/08/summers_displays_new_understanding_of_womens_careers/

Boring, A. (2017). Gender biases in student evaluations of teaching. *Journal of Public Economics, 145*, 27–41.

Boring, A., Ottoboni, K., & Stark, P. (2016). Student evaluations of teaching (mostly) do not measure teaching effectiveness. *ScienceOpen Research*, 1–11. https://www.scienceopen.com/document/read?vid=818d8ec0-5908-47d8-86b4-5dc38f04b23e

Bowles, H. R., Babcock, L., & Lai, L. (2007). Social incentives for gender differences in the propensity to initiate negotiations: Sometimes it does hurt to ask. *Organizational Behavior and Human Decision Processes, 103*(1), 84–103.

Box-Steffensmeier, J. M., Cunha, R. C., Varbanov, R. A., Hoh, Y. S., Knisley, M. L., & Holmes, M. A. (2015). Survival analysis of faculty retention and promotion in the social sciences by gender. *PLoS One, 10*(11), e0143093.

Byrnes, J. P. (2007). Publishing trends of psychology faculty during their pretenure years. *Psychological Science, 18*, 283–286.

Cameron, E. Z., White, A. M., & Gray, M. E. (2016). Solving the productivity and impact puzzle: Do men outperform women, or are metrics biased? *Bioscience, 66*(3), 245–252. doi:10.1093/biosci/biv173

Cannady, M. A., Greenwald, E., & Harris, K. N. (2014). Problematizing the STEM pipeline metaphor: Is the STEM pipeline metaphor serving our students and the STEM workforce? *Science Education, 98*, 443–460. doi:10.1002/sce.21108

Ceci, S. J., Ginther, D. K., Kahn, S., & Williams, W. M. (2014). Women in academic science: A changing landscape. *Psychological Science in the Public Interest, 15*(3), 75–141.

Ceci, S. J., & Williams, W. M. (2010). Sex differences in math-intensive fields. *Current Directions in Psychological Science, 19*(5), 275–279.

Cheryan, S., Master, A., & Meltzoff, A. N. (2015). Cultural stereotypes as gatekeepers: Increasing girls' interest in computer science and engineering by diversifying stereotypes. *Frontiers in Psychology, 6*, article 49. doi:10.3389/fpsyg.2015.00049

Cheryan, S., & Plaut, V. C. (2010). Explaining underrepresentation: A theory of precluded interest. *Sex Roles, 63*(7–8), 475–488.

Cheryan, S., Plaut, V. C., Davies, P. G., & Steele, C. M. (2009). Ambient belonging: How stereotypical cues impact gender participation in computer science. *Journal of Personality and Social Psychology, 97*(6), 1045–1060.

Cheryan, S., Ziegler, S. A., & Jiang, L. (2017). Why are some STEM fields more gender balanced than others? *Psychological Bulletin, 143*, 1–35.

Clancy, K. B. H., Lee, K. M. N., Rodgers, E. M., & Richey, C. (2017). Double jeopardy in astronomy and planetary science: Women of color face greater risks of gendered and racial harassment. *Journal of Geophysical Research. Planets, 122*. doi:10.1002/2017JE005256

Correll, S. J., Benard, S., & Paik, I. (2007). Getting a job: Is there a motherhood penalty? *American Journal of Sociology, 112*(5), 1297–1338.

Croson, R., & Gneezy, U. (2009). Gender differences in preferences. *Journal of Economic Literature, 47*(2), 448–474.

Dasgupta, N., & Stout, J. G. (2014). Girls and women in science, technology, engineering, and mathematics: STEMing the tide and broadening participation in STEM careers. *Policy Insights from the Behavioral and Brain Sciences, 1*(1), 21–29.

Diekman, A. B., Brown, E. R., Johnston, A. M., & Clark, E. K. (2010). Seeking congruity between goals and roles: A new look at why women opt out of science, technology, engineering, and mathematics careers. *Psychological Science, 21*, 1051–1057.

Doleac, J. L., & Stein, L. C. (2013). The visible hand: Race and online market outcomes. *Economic Journal (London), 123*(572), F469–F492.

Duch, J., Zeng, X. H. T., Sales-Pardo, M., Radicchi, F., Otis, S., Woodruff, T. K., & Amaral, L. A. N. (2012). The possible role of resource requirements and academic career-choice risk on gender differences in publication rate and impact. *PLoS One, 7*(12), e51332. doi:10.1371/annotation/7f54a3e6-6dcf-4825-9eb9-201253cf1e25

Ellison, G., & Swanson, A. (2010). The gender gap in secondary school mathematics at high achievement levels: Evidence from the American Mathematics Competitions. *Journal of Economic Perspectives, 24*(2), 109–128.

Flory, J. A., Leibbrandt, A., & List, J. A. (2015). Do competitive workplaces deter female workers? A large-scale natural field experiment on job-entry decisions. *Review of Economic Studies, 82*, 122–155.

Fox, M. F. (2005). Gender, family characteristics, and publication productivity among scientists. *Social Studies of Science, 35*(1), 131–150.

Ginther, D. K., & Kahn, S. (November 2006). Does science promote women? Evidence from academia 1973–2001 (NBER Working Paper 12691). Cambridge, MA: National Bureau of Economic Research. http://www.nber.org/papers/w12691

Ginther, D. K., Kahn, S., & Schaffer, W. T. (2016). Gender, race/ethnicity, and National Institutes of Health R01 research awards: Is there evidence of a double bind for women of color? *Academic Medicine, 91*(8), 1098–1107.

Ginther, D. K., Schaffer, W. T., Schnell, J., Masimore, B., Liu, F., Haak, L. L., & Kington, R. (2011). Race, ethnicity, and NIH research awards. *Science, 333*(6045), 1015–1019.

Glynn, A. N., & Sen, M. (2015). Identifying judicial empathy: Does having daughters cause judges to rule for women's issues? *American Journal of Political Science, 59*(1), 37–54.

Gneezy, U., Leonard, K. L., & List, J. A. (2009). Gender differences in competition: Evidence from a matrilineal and a patriarchal society. *Econometrica, 77*(5), 1637–1664.

Goulden, M., Mason, M. A., & Frasch, K. (2011). Keeping women in the science pipeline. *Annals of the American Academy of Political and Social Science, 638*(1), 141–162.

Greco, L. M., O'Boyle, E. H., & Walter, S. L. (2015). Absence of malice: A meta-analysis of nonresponse bias in counterproductive work behavior research. *Journal of Applied Psychology, 100*(1), 75–97. doi:10.1037/a0037495

Hargens, L. L., & Long, J. S. (2002). Demographic inertia and women's representation among faculty in higher education. *Journal of Higher Education, 73*, 494–517.

Heilman, M. E. (2012). Gender stereotypes and workplace bias. *Research in Organizational Behavior, 32*, 113–135.

Heilman, M. E., & Okimoto, T. G. (2007). Why are women penalized for success at male tasks? The implied communality deficit. *Journal of Applied Psychology, 92*(1), 81–92.

Iacus, S. M., King, G., & Porro, G. (2011). Multivariate matching methods that are monotonic imbalance bounding. *Journal of the American Statistical Association, 106*(493), 345–361.

Jagsi, R., Griffith, M. K. A., Stewart, A., Sambuco, M. D., DeCastro, M. R., & Ubel, P. A. (2013). Gender differences in salary in a recent cohort of early-career physician-researchers. *Academic Medicine, 88*(11), 1689–1699.

Joy, S. (2006). What should I be doing, and where are they doing it? Scholarly productivity of academic psychologists. *Perspectives on Psychological Science, 1*, 346–364.

Kahn, S., & Ginther, D. (2017). Women and STEM (NBER Working Paper 23525). Cambridge, MA: National Bureau of Economic Research.

Kaminski, D., & Geisler, C. (2012). Survival analysis of faculty retention in science and engineering by gender. *Science, 335*(6070), 864–866.

Kelly, K., & Grant, L. (2012). Penalties and premiums: The impact of gender, marriage, and parenthood on faculty salaries in science, engineering and mathematics (SEM) and non-SEM fields. *Social Studies of Science, 42*(6), 869–896.

King, E. G., Botsford, W., Hebl, M. R., Kazama, S., Dawson, J. F., & Perkins, A. (2012). Benevolent sexism at work: Gender differences in the distribution of challenging developmental experiences. *Journal of Management, 38*, 1835–1866.

Kray, L. J., & Thompson, L. (2004). Gender stereotypes and negotiation performance: An examination of theory and research. *Research in Organizational Behavior, 26*, 103–182.

Kulik, C. T., & Olekalns, M. (2012). Negotiating the gender divide lessons from the negotiation and organizational behavior literatures. *Journal of Management, 38*(4), 1387–1415.

Larivière, V., Ni, C., Gingras, Y., Cronin, B., & Sugimoto, C. R. (2013). Global gender disparities in science. *Nature, 504*, 211–213.

Leahey, E. (2006). Gender differences in productivity—Research specialization as a missing link. *Gender & Society, 20*(6), 754–780.

Leibbrandt, A., & List, J. A. (2014). Do women avoid salary negotiations? Evidence from a large-scale natural field experiment. *Management Science, 61*(9), 2016–2024.

Lubinski, D., Benbow, C. P., & Kell, H. J. (2014). Life paths and accomplishments of mathematically precocious males and females four decades later. *Psychological Science, 25*(12), 2217–2232.

Lubinski, D., Webb, R. M., Morelock, M. J., & Benbow, C. P. (2001). Top 1 in 10,000: A 10-year follow-up of the profoundly gifted. *Journal of Applied Psychology, 86*(4), 718–729.

MacNell, L., Driscoll, A., & Hunt, A. N. (2015). What's in a name: Exposing gender bias in student ratings of teaching. *Innovative Higher Education, 40*(4), 291–303.

Makel, M. C., Wai, J., Peairs, K., & Putallaz, M. (2016). Sex differences in the right tail of cognitive abilities: An update and cross cultural extension. *Intelligence, 59*, 8–15.

Manning, A., & Swaffield, J. (2008). The gender gap in early-career wage growth. *Economic Journal (London), 118*(530), 983–1024.

Mason, M. A., & Goulden, M. (2004). Marriage and baby blues: Redefining gender equity in the academy. *Annals of the American Academy of Political and Social Science, 596*(1), 86–103.

Mason, M. A., Wolfinger, N. H., & Goulden, M. (2013). *Do babies matter? Gender and family in the ivory tower.* New Brunswick, NJ: Rutgers University Press.

Mazei, J., Hüffmeier, J., Freund, P. A., Stuhlmacher, A. F., Bilke, L., & Hertel, G. (2015). A meta-analysis on gender differences in negotiation outcomes and their moderators. *Psychological Bulletin, 141*(1), 85–104.

Melguizo, T., & Strober, M. H. (2007). Faculty salaries and the maximization of prestige. *Research in Higher Education*, *48*(6), 633–668.

Miller, D. I., & Wai, J. (2015). The bachelor's to Ph.D. STEM pipeline no longer leaks more women than men: A 30-year analysis. *Frontiers in Psychology*, *6*, article 37. doi:10.3389/fpsyg.2015.00037

Mitchell, S. M., & Hesli, V. L. (2013). Women don't ask? Women don't say no? Bargaining and service in the political science profession. *PS, Political Science & Politics*, *46*(02), 355–369.

National Science Board. (2016). *Science and engineering indicators 2016* (pp. NSB-2016–NSB-1). Arlington, VA: National Science Foundation.

Niederle, M. (2015). Gender. In J. H. Kagel & A. E. Roth (Eds.), *The handbook of experimental economics* (Vol. 2, pp. 481–562). Princeton, NJ: Princeton University Press.

Niederle, M., & Vesterlund, L. (2010). Explaining the gender gap in math test scores: The role of competition. *Journal of Economic Perspectives*, *24*(2), 129–144.

Noftle, E. E., & Robins, R. W. (2007). Personality predictors of academic outcomes: Big five correlates of GPA and SAT scores. *Journal of Personality and Social Psychology*, *93*(1), 116–130.

O'Meara, K., Kuvaeva, A., & Nyunt, G. (2017). Constrained choices: A view of campus service inequality from annual faculty reports. *Journal of Higher Education*, *88*(5), 672–700. doi:10.1080/00221546.2016.1257312

O'Meara, K., Kuvaeva, A., Nyunt, G., Waugaman, C., & Jackson, R. (in press). Asked more often: Gender differences in faculty workload in research universities and the work interactions that shape them. *American Educational Research Journal*.

O'Meara, K., Sandmann, L. R., Saltmarsh, J., & Giles, D. E. (2011). Studying the professional lives and work of faculty involved in community engagement. *Innovative Higher Education*, *36*(2), 83–96.

Parks, A. L., & Redberg, R. F. (2017). Women in medicine and patient outcomes: Equal rights for better work? *JAMA Internal Medicine*, *177*, 161.

Ridgeway, C. L. (1982). Status in groups: The importance of motivation. *American Sociological Review*, *47*, 175–188.

Ridgeway, C. L. (2011). *Framed by gender: How gender inequality persists in the modern world*. Oxford, UK: Oxford University Press.

Rudman, L. A., & Fairchild, K. (2004). Reactions to counterstereotypic behavior: The role of backlash in cultural stereotype maintenance. *Journal of Personality and Social Psychology*, *87*, 157–176.

Rudman, L. A., & Phelan, J. E. (2008). Backlash effects for disconfirming gender stereotypes in organizations. *Research in Organizational Behavior, 28*, 61–79.

Schmidt, F. L. (2011). A theory of sex differences in technical aptitude and some supporting evidence. *Perspectives on Psychological Science, 6*, 560–573.

Schmitt, N. (2014). Personality and cognitive ability as predictors of effective performance at work. *Annual Review of Organizational Psychology and Organizational Behavior, 1*(1), 45–65.

Schroen, A. T., Brownstein, M. R., & Sheldon, G. F. (2004). Women in academic general surgery. *Academic Medicine, 79*(4), 310–318.

Shaw, A. K., & Stanton, D. E. (2012). Leaks in the pipeline: Separating demographic inertia from ongoing gender differences in academia. *Proceedings. Biological Sciences, 279*, 3736–3741.

Shurchkov, O. (2012). Under pressure: Gender differences in output quality and quantity under competition and time constraints. *Journal of the European Economic Association, 10*, 1189–1213.

Sio, U. N., & Ormerod, T. C. (2009). Does incubation enhance problem solving? A meta-analytic review. *Psychological Bulletin, 135*(1), 94–120.

Smith, J. L., Lewis, K. L., Hawthorne, L., & Hodges, S. D. (2013). When trying hard isn't natural: Women's belonging with and motivation for male-dominated STEM fields as a function of effort expenditure concerns. *Personality and Social Psychology Bulletin, 39*(2), 131–143.

Sutanto, W., Bell, R. L., Fei, Q., & Scott, J. (2014). Is there a gender pay gap in business schools? *Business Studies Journal, 6*(2), 39–56.

Thomas, N. R., Poole, D. J., & Herbers, J. M. (2015). Gender in science and engineering faculties: Demographic inertia revisited. *PLoS One, 10*(10), e0139767.

Tsugawa, Y., Jena, A. B., Figueroa, J. F., Orav, E. J., Blumenthal, D. M., & Jha, A. K. (2017). Comparison of hospital mortality and readmission rates for Medicare patients treated by male vs female physicians. *JAMA Internal Medicine, 177*, 206–213.

Valian, V. (2014). Interests, gender, and science. *Perspectives on Psychological Science, 9*(2), 225–230.

van den Besselaar, P., & Sandström, U. (2016). Gender differences in research performance and its impact on careers: A longitudinal case study. *Scientometrics, 106*(1), 143–162.

Wagner, N., Rieger, M., & Voorvelt, K. (2016). Gender, ethnicity and teaching evaluations: Evidence from mixed teaching teams. *Economics of Education Review, 54*, 79–94.

Wai, J., Cacchio, M., Putallaz, M., & Makel, M. C. (2010). Sex differences in the right tail of cognitive abilities: A 30 year examination. *Intelligence, 38*(4), 412–423.

Washington, E. L. (2008). Female socialization: How daughters affect their legislator fathers' voting on woman's issues. *American Economic Review, 98*(1), 311–332.

Weeden, K. A., Thébaud, S., & Gelbgiser, D. (2017). Degrees of difference: Gender segregation of US doctorates by field and program prestige. *Sociological Science, 4,* 123–150.

Williams, W. M., & Ceci, S. J. (2015). National hiring experiments reveal 2:1 faculty preference for women on STEM tenure track. *Proceedings of the National Academy of Sciences of the United States of America, 112*(17), 5360–5365.

Xie, Y., & Shauman, K. A. (2003). *Women in science: Career processes and outcomes.* Cambridge, MA: Harvard University Press.

II How to Achieve an Inclusive Academy

5 Recruiting New Faculty: Developing a Diverse Pool and an Equitable Search Process

In this part of this book we will consider practical solutions that have been developed (or in some cases *could* be developed) to address aspects of faculty life in contemporary academic institutions that are often not inclusive. We begin with issues of recruitment of new faculty, and then follow the working lives of faculty who are in fact hired into our institutions.

Faculty and administrators agree that the future of a college or university lies in the new faculty. One provost we knew often said, "The university with the best faculty wins." Always a small minority of the faculty, given the long careers of most academics after tenure and the increased reliance on contingent faculty, the new tenure-track faculty hired as assistant professors bring in new energy and vision, and keep the university alive to new intellectual developments and research techniques. Because the future of the institution—both short and long-term—rests with the new assistant professors (except in a tiny handful of elite institutions that still do most of their hiring at the senior level), recruiting and hiring is a process many faculty care passionately about and are willing to spend considerable time on.

In this chapter we outline the earliest steps in the search and hiring process—defining the position, recruiting the applicant pool, and setting up the search committee process. When these steps are taken thoughtfully and carefully, search committees that have the capacity to make good decisions will be able to review a diverse pool of candidates. The first steps are critical if the department is going to hire faculty who will add diversity to the institution. In the next chapter we will outline procedures to ensure a fair and equitable decision process at the end of a search.

Pursuing Diversity and Excellence

Hiring new faculty can either help change a department in productive ways or maintain the department's status quo. Faculty commitment to recruitment and hiring can become a resource for institutional change efforts or a resource for resistance. Those faculty who hope to see a more inclusive institution that retains or improves its academic standing are readily persuaded that it is important to invest in hiring practices that are not only thoughtful and effective, but relatively unbiased by the cognitive limitations and shortcuts we have outlined. Equally, faculty in under-resourced institutions may be persuaded that more diverse faculty would meet the demands from students and for service to the institution more adequately.

At the same time, the tradition in some institutions of horse-trading for new hires, of turf battles about the definition of positions, of preoccupation with hiring people who will easily "fit in," and of intense debates over the final candidate, is long and familiar. Some faculty believe that their department's excellence depends on those very traditions, and that change in the service of diversity must inevitably risk the hard-won success and collegiality of the department to date. Not surprisingly, in a study of science and engineering departments that were part of an institutional change effort taking place over more than a decade at one research-intensive university, faculty and department chairs who expressed these kinds of beliefs most often came from departments that in fact did not succeed at the broader effort to achieve greater gender diversity in the faculty (Stewart, Malley, & Herzog, 2016).

It is, then, not just helpful but necessary for institutional leaders to explain how and why diversity and excellence are mutually compatible—perhaps even inextricably linked—goals and outcomes. Since attitudes and beliefs are notoriously difficult to change, whether they are explicit or implicit, we emphasize institutionalized structures that promote processes that mitigate the damaging effects of these kinds of beliefs.

Because of the habitual assumption that either excellence or inclusion must be traded off to achieve the other, any effort to develop, implement, and institutionalize new procedures for the recruitment of faculty must clearly maximize both goals. Recruitment efforts must also build on what is known both about how unconscious cognitive shortcuts like relying on people's fit with our expectations and past experience can lead to poor judgments, and about how those errors and schemas can operate within the recruitment process. As a result of decision-making strategies that rely on representativeness and availability, we are likely to picture successful applicants as sharing personal characteristics with the majority of current job occupants (Kahneman, 2011). However, resistance can be lessened in the face of results showing that new procedures pay off in a more diverse junior faculty that is also at least as outstanding in accomplishments as the less diverse one that preceded it.

In this chapter we will focus on overcoming reliance on the cognitive shortcuts discussed earlier, including reliance on the representativeness, availability, and anchoring decision-making strategies, as well as schemas about gender, race-ethnicity, and other characteristics that are not directly job relevant. We will outline procedures we know about from many institutions, but of course the examples most familiar to us will often come from our own two institutions (the University of Michigan and Hunter College).

Preparing the Description of the Position (or "Writing the Ad")

Why the Position Description Matters: Lack of Diversity in Pools of Applicants

To date most "pools of applicants" (i.e., the total set of people who apply for a position) are not diverse in most fields in terms of race and ethnicity, and in some fields in terms of gender (Smith, Turner, Osei-Kofi, & Richards, 2004). The candidates in these "pools" are expected to have a range of skills and talent, and faculty are quite confident of their ability to assess the skill and talent of potential colleagues. But faculty cannot hire individuals who do not apply: if women and minorities are not in the pool of applicants, they cannot become future colleagues. In short, a diverse pool is a precondition for hiring women and minorities. Having a diverse pool of applicants has other advantages: there is considerable evidence that the diversity of the pool of applicants affects how women and minorities in that pool are evaluated, if they do apply (Sackett, Dubois, & Noe, 1991), and whether they are hired (Bilimoria & Buch, 2010; Smith et al., 2004). This matters because, as we have seen, on average, potential employers, including faculty, are not able to judge skill and talent equally well among women and minorities and among White men.

The Impact of Differential Representation of Groups
in the Pool of Applicants

One factor that makes a difference in the process of evaluation is how well represented people from a particular group are in the pool of people being rated. The availability strategy or heuristic leads us to expect success in candidates like those whose success we have seen before—in the case of most university faculty, people who are male and White. Rosabeth Moss Kanter (1977) proposed that the representation of women in corporations might make a difference in women's treatment; she suggested that conditions were particularly problematic when the representation was skewed (less than 15%), that it improved when it was tilted (between 16% and 35%), and best when it was balanced (between 35% and 65%). Parallel reasoning has been suggested for racial-ethnic minorities, though it is recognized that their base rate in the overall population is not roughly half, as is women's. So the relevant indicators of "skew" and "tilt" are different, but the same general point holds: when minorities are very rare in an organization, their situation will be more difficult.

Three scholars from the University of Minnesota (Sackett, DuBois, & Noe, 1991) designed an unusually rigorous assessment of the impact of group representation by gender and by race on evaluations. Using a large database that had been created by the U.S. Employment Service for other purposes, they examined the ratings of employee performance provided by supervisors of employees in hundreds of different jobs that ranged in the representation of women (in one case) or Blacks (in the other case) from 10% to 90%. This database was particularly useful for studying the impact of the ratio of women and minorities in the job because there were other data available: a composite indicator of cognitive ability (based on several different tests assessing general cognitive ability, verbal ability, and numerical ability), psychomotor ability (a composite of motor coordination, finger dexterity, and manual dexterity), education, and firm experience.

With all of these measures in hand, the researchers first assessed the gender and race differences in performance evaluations across all evaluators. Then they considered whether that difference could be accounted for by differences in cognitive and psychomotor ability, education, and experience; finally, they considered whether—after all of those other factors had been controlled—the difference might be the result of the differential representation of women or minorities in the rating group (the proportion of women or the proportion of Blacks). Overall, women were rated only slightly lower than men across all jobs. However, they were rated much lower than men if there were fewer than 50% women in the jobs, and much higher than men if there were more than 50% women in the jobs. It is worth noting that this pattern contains a very important general lesson: the impression of "no difference" can arise from two different underlying patterns that cancel each other out in data that are summed, or aggregated, across the different patterns. While both ability variables and experience—clearly relevant to assessment of performance—played a role in predicting evaluations, so did the representation of women in the job—clearly an irrelevant variable in assessing any individual's performance.

This pattern did not hold for race. Overall, Blacks in all jobs—regardless of their representation in the job group—were evaluated quite a bit lower than Whites, even after the other factors were controlled. The authors suggested that the pervasiveness of racial schemas (sometimes called stereotypes), and the lack of strong schemas associated with jobs as "raced" as opposed to "gendered"—might account for these results (see also Ilgen & Youtz, 1986).

The perceived "fit" of women (and men) to an occupation (presumably the result of gender, race, and occupational schemas and reliance on the representativeness cognitive strategy) is an important factor in evaluations (see Roberson, Galvin, & Charles, 2007, for a review). Similarly, the proportion of minorities in a setting is an important predictor of evaluations (see Reskin, McBrier, & Kmec, 1999; Roberson et al., 2007, for reviews). For example, Kraiger and Ford (1985) combined data from 74 field and laboratory studies of White raters and 14 studies of Black raters and found that at least in field (or "real world") studies race differences in ratings declined as the proportion of Blacks rated increased. For both gender and race, then, there is reason to believe that the diversity of the people represented in the pool matters for evaluations. This does not surprise us, given what we know about our reliance on both representativeness and availability cognitive strategies.

Data like these—drawn from the real world, and involving large numbers of consequential judgments across many people—are often considered the most convincing. However, three issues might undermine our belief that these data are relevant to the recruitment of faculty in universities today: (1) they are mostly based on the inevitably "uncontrolled" situation of people working in the real world rather than controlled laboratory experiments; (2) some of them are based on data collected in the 1980s, so they may reflect dynamics that were present then but are absent now; and (3) they are based on individuals in a range of positions, but none of them in relatively high status, professional positions like those of university faculty. Fortunately, we have a great deal of additional evidence that supports the likelihood that the findings from Sackett et al.—at least with respect to gender—do apply in experimental settings, in recently collected data, and in settings more similar to academia.

In one early study, Madeline Heilman (1980) showed that MBA students evaluating women applicants for relatively high-status managerial positions were affected in their hiring recommendations by the proportion of women in the applicant pool. She used a sophisticated experimental design that required students to make recommendations for pools of 8 applicants, containing 1, 2, 3, 4, or 8 women. Each judge evaluated 8 sets of application materials with applicants randomly identified as either male or female, enabling the experimenters to rule out the possibility that any differences by gender or gender composition were the result of actual differences in the applications. Raters favored men over women only when women constituted 25% of the pool or less, presumably because that low rate triggered the availability and representativeness cognitive strategies. There is similar, more recent, evidence from studies of women in high-ranking military positions (Pazy & Oron, 2001), of women being hired into managerial positions in savings and loan organizations (Cohen, Broschak, & Haveman, 1998), and of men in nursing and women police officers (Hewstone, Crisp, & Turner, 2011)—that is, from assessments of higher status, more professional-level workers—that proportional representation affects evaluations.

Having a Diverse Pool Matters
In short, in addition to our commonsense motivation to develop a diverse pool—that we cannot hope to hire a more diverse faculty if we do not attract more diverse applicants for our positions—there is also a data-based rationale. That is, our capacity to fairly assess women and minorities (and those from rare groups in general) is lower when we have only a very small number of people from those groups in our applicant pools.

A number of explanations have been proposed and studied to account for why this might be so, beyond the cognitive shortcuts we have already discussed. Some scholars have emphasized the "fit" between the schema for the group individuals belong to and the schema for the job (Heilman, 1983) or the similarity or dissimilarity in group membership between judges and applicants (Tsui & O'Reilly, 1989). Both of these approaches assume that an applicant's group membership—which should not be relevant to assessment of an individual's qualifications or performance—is made salient when their group is statistically rare, lower in general social status, or viewed negatively in terms of competence for the particular job or occupation (Roberson, Galvin, & Charles, 2007). If we have a more diverse pool of applicants, we are less likely to rely on group membership in evaluating applicants, and more likely to actually focus on individual accomplishments. Ensuring a broad and diverse pool of applicants is, then, an important focus for search committees. But how can committees change the features of the pool of applicants, especially in a field in which males and/or Whites are numerically dominant?

Defining the Position to Maximize a Diverse Pool of Applicants

A good place to start is with the definition of the position. If the job is defined in narrow terms (a common strategy in many faculty hires), it will focus on a single research area within a discipline or subfield, will require use of particular methods or approaches, and may also dictate specific courses to be taught.

Here is a typical example of this type of faculty advertisement:

The Department of Psychology at Terrific University is seeking an Assistant Professor with a promising program of research in the area of stigma and stereotyping in social psychology. The successful applicant will not only demonstrate excellence in this research area but will be able to teach courses in Social Psychology, Prejudice and Discrimination, and Attitude Change.

Broad or Narrow Qualifications

Every narrow qualification that is specified will have the effect of leading some potential applicants to select themselves *out* of the pool of possible applicants. Moreover, this process of self-selection is probably biased: individuals with privileged statuses (e.g., Whites, men) are likely to feel more entitled to rewards (e.g., money, positions) than are those with subordinate statuses (e.g., people of color, women; see Bylsma & Major, 1992; Hogue & Yoder, 2003; Hogue, Yoder, & Singleton, 2007; Pelham & Hetts, 2001).

For example, Hogue and Yoder (2003) demonstrated women's "depressed entitlement." Undergraduate students were told "I am investigating the effects of verbal reasoning ability on job performance. You will be completing an exercise that is used to measure verbal reasoning ability for future employees." Students were given an example of the task and then asked to project their competence at it and to indicate how much they should be paid for this task from $1 to $15. As is generally found in studies of this phenomenon, women thought they should be paid significantly less than men (on average $7.48) while men thought they should be paid more (on average $10.27). Importantly, this difference in pay existed despite there being no difference in the judged quality of men's and women's work by external judges or by the students themselves. The analogy to a search process is that detailed specifications of desirable features of an applicant may stimulate a process of self-evaluation of "fit" that will lead to a pool that is less diverse. Thus, if women and underrepresented minority potential job applicants, more often than White men, conclude, "I am not what they are looking for" or "I am not qualified" when reviewing the required qualifications for a position, our applicant pools may be unnecessarily homogeneous.

Cues of Belonging

Cues that women or minorities do not "belong" in a setting have powerful effects in raising doubts that individuals have talent (Walton & Cohen, 2007) or should pursue particular fields (Cheryan, Plaut, Davies, & Steele, 2009). If our goal is to increase the chances that a woman or a person of color will consider applying, it will help if we do not provide cues that lead them to feel they do not belong or would not fit the job definition (see Breaugh, 2013; Cheryan et al., 2009; Gaucher, Friesen, & Kay, 2011; Purdie-Vaughns, Steele, Davies, Ditlmann, & Crosby, 2008; Walker, Feild, Giles, Armenakis, & Bernerth, 2009; Yoder, 2002). If we hope to attract a wide range of applicants, jobs should be described in the broadest terms that are accurate (e.g., by listing several alternative topics or approaches) and offer a range of courses that might be taught rather than a specific and limited set. A more inclusive version of the advertisement above might read:

The Department of Psychology at Terrific University is seeking an Assistant Professor with a promising program of research on the dynamics and consequences of power relations between social groups. The successful applicant will not only demonstrate excellence in this research area but will be able to teach courses appealing to undergraduates both in that area and in broader domains of psychology.

It might be even better if the department were willing and able to advertise for a truly "open position":

The Department of Psychology at Terrific University is seeking an Assistant Professor with a promising program of research in any area. The successful applicant will not only demonstrate excellence in this research area but will be able to teach courses appealing to undergraduates both in that area and in broader domains of psychology.[1]

Box 5.1
Sample "Broad" and "Open" Job Descriptions

The "broad" or "open" descriptions listed here were used for actual faculty searches in the humanities, social sciences, and natural sciences at the University of Michigan. They reflect different degrees of "openness" and different strategies for signaling their openness, but they are all more open than traditional job descriptions in these fields.

English Department

The English Department at the University of XX expects to make an appointment in Composition and Rhetoric in [date]. We are particularly interested in innovative scholars at the entering or advanced Assistant or beginning Associate level, and we are excited to consider a broad range of areas of specialization, including, for example, rhetorical theory and/or history, genre studies, technologies of literacy, discourse studies, and new media writing. The successful candidate will contribute to vibrant and expanding programs at the graduate and undergraduate levels.

Send letter of application, c.v., statement of current and future research plans, statement of teaching philosophy and experience, writing sample, and three letters of reference by October 20th, Attention: [address]. The University of XX is an equal opportunity/affirmative action employer and is supportive of the needs of dual career couples. Women and minority candidates are encouraged to apply. All applications will be acknowledged.

(continued)

Box 5.1 (continued)

Philosophy Department

Rank open (tenured or tenure-track) appointment. Begins [date]. Four courses/ academic year (semester system) at all levels, thesis supervision, usual committee and other nonteaching duties. University-year (nine-month) appointment. A[rea] O[f] S[pecialization]: Open. A[rea] O[f] C[oncentration]: Open. Ph.D. prior to appointment (normally). The Department is open to the possibility of interdisciplinary appointments. Salary highly competitive. All applicants should ensure that their dossiers contain a cover letter and current CV. The cover letter should state whether the applicant is applying for a tenured or untenured position. Applicants for a junior position should also include letters of recommendation, samples of written work, a statement of current and future research plans, evidence of teaching excellence, and a statement of teaching philosophy and experience. Applicants for a tenured position may, if they wish, provide references and written work or other supplementary materials. Women and members of minority groups are especially encouraged to apply. The University supports the needs of dual-career couples. Please send all materials to [address]. Acknowledgment of receipt of your materials will be sent via e-mail. Applications must be received by [date] to be assured of full consideration. The University of XX is an equal opportunity/affirmative action employer.

Anthropology Department

The Department of Anthropology invites applications for one or more full-time faculty positions in **sociocultural anthropology**, rank open, to begin in [date], pending administrative approval. We seek creative scholars who integrate ethnography and theoretical analysis, and who deepen our dialogue with other disciplines and debates. Successful candidates will be able to teach introductory and higher level undergraduate courses in addition to graduate seminars, and their research and teaching interests should complement the strengths of our existing faculty (for more information consult our website at [URL]. The PhD must be completed before the beginning of the appointment. Since we expect to conduct some interviews at the [date] meeting of the American Anthropological Association, applications received before [date] will be at an advantage. Please send hard copies only of: (1) a cover letter; (2) a c.v.; (3) a statement of current and future research plans; (4) a statement of teaching philosophy and experience; (5) a sample of scholarly writing; (6) evidence of teaching excellence; (7) and the names and addresses of three

Box 5.1 (continued)

references to: [address]. The University of XX is an affirmative action, equal opportunity employer, supportive of the needs of dual career couples. Women and minorities are encouraged to apply.

Physics Department

The Physics Department anticipates that a tenure-track faculty position will be available with a [date] starting date. We are considering applications in all areas of physics represented in the department: High Energy Physics, Condensed Matter Physics, Atomic Molecular and Optical Physics (AMO), Astrophysics, Biophysics, and Theoretical Physics. We are particularly interested in applicants working in the areas of Theoretical Astrophysics, Condensed Matter Theory, String Theory, AMO Theory or High Energy Theory. Candidates are required to have a doctoral degree in physics. Women and minorities are encouraged to apply.

The successful candidate is expected to establish an independent research program and to contribute effectively to the Department's undergraduate and graduate teaching programs. Applicants should send a curriculum vitae (CV), a brief statement of present and future research plans, a statement of teaching experience and interests, and the names of at least three persons who can provide letters of recommendation.

For full consideration applications should be received between [dates]. The University of XX is a non-discriminatory/affirmative action employer. The University is responsive to the needs of dual career couples.

Cues of belonging can be conveyed by gendered language in job advertisements, such as the use of *dominant* instead of *excellent*. Male-dominated jobs tend to use more masculine terms than female-dominated jobs do, while feminine words are used equally in both types (Gaucher, Friesen, & Kay, 2011). In a laboratory setting, where the same job can be described in different terms, the use of "masculine" words for an administrative assistant job (*boasts, demanding, strong*) attracted women (the only group tested) less than an advertisement with "feminine" or neutral words (*polite, sensitive, capable*) (Gaucher et al., 2011). The lower attraction was not because women did not think they could handle the job. The language was off-putting.

The mention of diversity values in a job advertisement may affect African Americans and Whites differently. African Americans see mention of a moral obligation as suggesting they might be treated well by the institution, while Whites are more attracted by an explanation for diversity that stresses benefits to the institution (Williamson, Slay, Shapiro, & Shivers-Blackwell, 2008).

The Impact of Broad Searches

The opportunity to search "openly" or broadly can arise both if multiple positions are available at the same time or (when hiring opportunities are rare) if departments are willing to search for "the best available candidate" regardless of the area of specialization. At the University of Michigan broad searches have been the long-standing practice of some departments, not because of an historic commitment to recruiting diverse applicant pools, but because of an historic commitment to excellence. However, Michigan's experience shows that it is not enough to have broad searches. Historically, "open searching" did *not* generally benefit candidates like women and racial-ethnic minorities in these departments. That is because those searches still relied on the strategies or heuristics that we know result in biased judgments. This fact underscores the importance of the underlying desire to increase diversity; without that motivation, no procedural change will result in different outcomes.

In contrast to searches lacking a commitment to diversity, in 2006, the Michigan Chemistry Department decided to experiment with an "open searching" approach, with the explicit hope that it could *simultaneously* better its standing in the field and attract a more diverse applicant pool. Happily, the department maintained data about their applicant pool "before" and "after" the new procedure. Between the academic years 2001 and 2004, the "before" period when the department used conventionally narrow advertisements for positions, women candidates submitted about 15 applications each year. Between 2006 and 2009, the "after" period when they adopted a policy of "open searching," women submitted an average of 34 applications each year—more than doubling their previous yield. The percentage of women in the available pool (PhDs obtained five years ago) did not change over this period: roughly 30% to 35% of chemistry PhDs went to women from 1995 to 2005.[2]

In the "before" period, not quite 30% of the department's actual new hires were women (n = 2) and none were underrepresented minorities; in the "after" period, more than 50% of the new hires were women and three were underrepresented minorities. Not only did open searches increase the total applicant pool (as it would simply by broadening the areas of special-ization), it also attracted a more diverse applicant pool. But why? Why did this department's open searching strategy result in a more diverse pool? We believe one main reason is that they proactively sought out diverse applicants at conferences and through colleagues they knew at institutions that have diverse student bodies or who themselves have track records of men-toring students and postdocs from diverse backgrounds. Perhaps most impor-tantly, they adopted review strategies that maximized their ability to make accurate judgments of talent, regardless of the gender or race/ethnicity of the applicant.

There was another, unanticipated benefit of the new procedure: a much larger proportion of the department participated in the hiring process. Rather than delegating the search to those most directly involved and "expert," many people participated and therefore felt some commitment to the can-didates hired. This benefit—greater faculty involvement and investment in new faculty—is quite separate from the obvious benefit in terms of diversity.

Finally, we note that the department's "objective" excellence increased during this period. For example, in 1999 its "average reputation" rating on *U.S. News and World Report*'s 5-point scale was 3.9, while by 2014 it was 4.2, corresponding to a rise in the ranking from 20th to 15th in a little over a decade.[3] It is impossible to know which of the many variables that changed during this period were responsible for the increase in ranking. The improvement cannot be attributed unequivocally to the hiring of women and faculty of color. However, the data suggest at the very least that diver-sifying the faculty is compatible with increasing its excellence. It is clearly worth departments' trouble to experiment with open searches, tracking their efforts, and tracking the results, with respect to both anticipated and unanticipated costs and benefits.

Difficulties to Overcome in Conducting Broad Searches

We recognize some of the value-based and practical difficulties for many departments of deciding to adopt the practice of using broad job definitions even if they would attract a more diverse pool of applicants. Any change in practices is likely to be experienced by some department members as either a repudiation of the past (in which they are invested) or a risky shift away from practices that have "worked." In fact, one aspect of past practices must be repudiated in order to embrace the goal of increasing the diversity of the faculty. Historically, many academic positions have been defined in terms of the previous occupant or a very specific current teaching need. This practice aims at reproduction of past research or curricular needs. An unintended side effect is to reproduce the homogeneous demographics of the past department faculty (Moody, 2004). Searching for someone in an emergent research area could eliminate the latter problem, but it still will not fill a narrowly defined past research or teaching need. Moreover, if the "emergent area" position is defined narrowly, it also is still likely to result in a narrow pool.[4] For this reason, we believe that departments will only alter their practices if they believe that past practices—even if they produced some good outcomes and certainly were not intentionally exclusionary— will not produce an adequately diverse pool and therefore must change.

For two practical reasons, searching more broadly than a department has done before may generate concerns among faculty accustomed to narrowly targeted searches. The first is that narrowly targeted searches permit assessment of applicants according to narrow criteria; what criteria can apply across a much less homogeneous applicant pool? The second is that narrowly targeted searches yield small, manageable applicant pools; how can we manage a large pool of applications? These two concerns indeed point to two practical problems that should not be ignored.

Different review procedures will be entailed by a larger, more diverse pool (e.g., having applications reviewed by two faculty on the search committee first, and then only going to the rest of the committee if they met a threshold evaluation; only inviting applicants to submit letters and papers after an initial screening of CVs, etc.). Our point here is that these practical problems can be addressed and are a natural outcome of the very result we are aiming for: a large, diverse pool of applicants.

In defining the position, the rank of the faculty member sought is also a factor to consider. Pools are likely to be most diverse at the earliest career stages and least diverse for more senior searches (because older scholars are less diverse than younger scholars). In addition, senior searches are most likely to focus on individuals who are "known" (in person or by reputation) to various faculty in the department. This sense of "knowledge" increases the likelihood that some implicit assumptions (e.g., about who will move, and what the conditions are for their moves) might affect faculty deliberations in ways that might limit the diversity of the candidates still further (Maynard & Brooks, 2008). For example, some faculty assume that women will be less likely to move a whole family than men, that parents will be unlikely to disrupt children's lives (or the lives of children of particular ages), that current marriages or relationships are stable, and that women will not move without a high-status position for their partner, but men will (Stewart, Malley, & Herzog, 2016). These assumptions will tend to disadvantage women, the partnered, and parents, regardless of their capacity to improve the excellence of the department and its diversity.

The Impact of Expressed Institutional Values

Assuming that the rank, research focus, and teaching demands can be defined in terms that favor a broader pool of applicants, are there other issues to consider? Smith et al. (2004) found that special hiring programs (including dual career opportunities), family-friendly policies, and job descriptions that mention institutional values that support diversity are more likely to yield diverse hires. We suspect that these results arise because women and minorities are more likely than majority applicants to expect to be judged according to stereotypes (i.e., to experience stereotype threat), leading them—unless there is contrary evidence—to expect rejection, to assume that they may not fit, or to anticipate discrimination absent an explicit signal that the hiring institution will take their application seriously (Steele, 2011). Therefore, evidence that they are being evaluated not because of their demographic characteristics, but on the basis of their professional expertise, is likely to reduce stereotype threat and increase their confidence in the evaluation process (see also Cohen, Steele, & Ross, 1999; Purdie-Vaughns et al., 2008).

Another reason women and minorities may attend to signals about inclusiveness and attention to families is that some institutions may not be thought of as likely to be "friendly" about family issues; applicants may hold institutional schemas about them that are associated with the opposite (e.g., resource poor, or cold, competitive, and intensely aggressive). In such cases, signaling the availability of these policies may provide counterevidence that leads women and minority applicants to consider such schools more seriously. If we consider all of these factors, it seems best to find ways to signal that the institution is committed to fair and inclusive processes in recruitment and hiring (and subsequent evaluations of faculty; see, e.g., Bilimoria & Buch, 2010), as well as to family-friendly policies for all faculty, while simultaneously avoiding any suggestion that the department's primary concern in evaluating potential candidates has to do with anything other than the excellence of the candidate.

Search Procedures Matter

Once a job description exists, it is important to design search procedures that will facilitate a more diverse pool of serious candidates than the current faculty displays. As sociologists Reskin et al. (1999, p. 350) point out, "Demographic patterns tend to be self-perpetuating." They suggest three reasons this happens: (1) potential employees tend to be assessed in terms of their similarity to current "organizational elites" (due to the representativeness strategy or heuristic and our reliance on prestige as a proxy for quality—discussed at length in the next chapter); (2) hiring is often conducted through existing informal networks of current employees (the operation of homophily matters here); and (3) demographic majorities create environments that may feel inhospitable to demographic minorities. Fortunately, there are remedies for each of these factors.

Identifying New Types of Candidates

First, search committees can adopt an explicit goal of identifying candidates who are *different* from existing faculty, and they can develop strategies for attracting those applicants. In pursuing this goal, it is optimal to treat searching as an activity that is engaged in year-round by all faculty members. When faculty attend talks or are at conferences, they can and should be on the lookout for rising young colleagues in the field, paying particular attention to those from underrepresented groups who are impressive in these settings. Approaching women and minorities who give a stimulating paper in the department or at a conference, and discussing it with them, while at the same time encouraging them to stay in touch, is a great way to develop a much more diverse network not only of potential applicants for positions, but of references to other applicants, such as their students. Accumulating this kind of record in a department can lead to a collectively maintained list of "people to watch out for" that can alert all faculty members about potential future colleagues to look for at other meetings.

It can be difficult for faculty to avoid relying on a narrow network of department members' former mentors and colleagues as sources of applicants and references. Moreover, though faculty may be tempted to rely on the prestige of the institution where an applicant was trained, the highest ranked departments (often the ones where existing faculty were trained, but largely composed of "organizational elites") are not necessarily producing the largest numbers of female graduates and are unlikely to be producing the largest numbers of people of color (as chapter 4 documents). Therefore, relying on colleagues in those departments will not yield the most diverse pool of candidates. (We discuss this issue in detail in the next chapter.) Instead, one strategy is to identify individuals who are mentoring women and minority doctoral students at other institutions and consider those faculty for senior positions at one's institution. If one's own institution graduates significant numbers of well-trained women and minorities in fields where they are underrepresented, those graduates become a good source of suggestions for other women and people of color as they move on to graduate, postdoctoral, and faculty or research careers. It may make sense to recruit those graduates back onto the faculty in the future, in addition to relying on them as trusted references for women and minority applicants for faculty positions.

Search Committee Practices

Search procedures after composition of the job ad vary across disciplines and institutions. Each facet of the search process has implications for how candidates will be recruited and assessed. For example, does the committee request full applications from all candidates or only from a subset? If the latter (and numbers may dictate a limited number of full applications), the committee might underestimate the qualifications of some applicants because they have not had room to provide information about their best assets. In requesting candidates' materials, committees can provide some open-ended opportunity for applicants to "make a case" for their fit and relevance to the position, so the committee can avoid having too little information to perceive an applicant's interesting qualifications (see Roberson et al., 2007, on the value of more information in making better judgments). Increasingly, departments ask applicants to submit a statement about their past contributions to diversity and their anticipated contribution at the institution to which they are applying. The Davis campus of the University of California has developed "guidelines" for applicants in preparing such statements (http://academicaffairs.ucdavis.edu/diversity/equity_inclusion/diversity_statements_writing.html). These statements may help committees identify both some faculty who have little interest or commitment to diversity and some with a past track record of mentoring or contributing to institutional change that might matter to the department.

The Search Committee Composition

It is equally important to be careful about choosing who will serve on the committee that screens full applications and will make recommendations for hiring decisions. If the job has been defined broadly, it will be helpful to have broad expertise represented among the reviewers of applications.

Competence of the Committee   It is best if there are individuals on the review committee who are knowledgeable about the operation of implicit biases. Knowledge does not ensure that the biases will not operate, but it does increase the likelihood of self-conscious efforts to use procedures that will minimize the operation of bias. Including as diverse a group of faculty as is feasible is critical to the fairness of the decision-making process, despite the fact that many members of our culture share the implicit biases about gender, race, parental status, and other variables that may affect judgments.

Why is a diverse committee important? In a revealing study of jurors waiting for assignment to trials, Sommers (2006) assessed the quality of the deliberations of racially diverse (two African American and four White "jurors") versus homogeneous (six White jurors) "juries" constructed to fill the waiting period. These juries were shown videotaped testimony for a trial of an African American defendant. Sommers found that the more diverse jury engaged in a more careful and accurate discussion of the evidence than the homogeneous jury. Moreover, the better discussion was *not* driven by the comments of the Black jurors. The White jurors performed better (made fewer factually incorrect assertions, were more likely to correct errors, and discussed the case longer) in the presence of African American peers. This phenomenon—of White group members performing cognitive tasks more carefully in diverse than in homogeneous groups—has been confirmed in a nonjury setting (Sommers, Warp, & Mahoney, 2008). Using very different, mathematical reasoning, Scott Page (2008) has argued that diverse groups—which bring different tools to solving a problem—are likely to come up with more creative and better solutions to problems. The benefits of diversity that we reviewed in chapter 2 are relevant to the performance of search committees.

Credibility of the Committee   Not only is a diverse committee likely to engage in a better deliberative process, but the diversity contributes to the prima facie credibility of the committee's fairness to applicants and the rest of the community. It is important not to assume that a committee with many women or minority group members will be a committee biased in favor of hiring women or minority group members since evidence shows that women and minorities hold implicit attitudes much like those of majority group members. However, a diverse committee composition is likely to reassure both applicants and people in the institution that a range of people's perspectives have influence in decision-making. That is, committee composition can operate as a cue that diversity is welcome (Purdie-Vaughns et al., 2008). And if jury deliberations are analogous to search committee deliberations, a diverse committee is likely to operate with greater explicitness and care about evaluating individuals according to specific criteria.

Educating the Committee Two further procedures may increase the competence of search committees. The first is providing the committee with training and educational resources that increase members' knowledge of the impact of evaluation biases and ways to overcome them. There is increasing evidence that exposure to well-designed, data-based education alters faculty knowledge (see, e.g., Carnes, Devine, Manwell, Byars-Winston, Fine, Ford, et al., 2015) and affects department-level decision-making (Carnes et al., 2015; Sekaquaptewa, 2015) as well as hiring outcomes (LaVaque-Manty & Stewart, 2008). Workshops of this sort have been offered to search committee members at the University of Michigan, the University of Wisconsin, Florida International University, the University of California, Davis, and Northeastern University, among others.

An alternative approach is to identify "equity advisors" who can serve on search committees in departments other than their own and provide input about appropriate procedures. This strategy has been successful at some institutions (e.g., the University of California, Irvine, and Michigan State University), though at others it has carried an unappealing suggestion of surveillance rather than assistance. If the equity advisors are well-educated, have a high degree of credibility, and are not felt merely to be "policing" the process, this model may work as well.

In order to offer either kind of program, institutions must create a small group of senior faculty to take on the task of studying the literature and presenting it to their colleagues or sitting in on search committees. A course release, freedom from some other service burdens, or direct compensation are essential to signal the value of this labor and make it truly feasible.

In addition to such educational approaches, it may be helpful to consider creating "standing" search committees with a term of a few years, composed of individuals who have been educated and are committed to the twin goals of excellence and diversity (see policy adopted by Michigan's College of Engineering: https://adaa.engin.umich.edu/wp-content/uploads/sites/22/2013/07/RH-Presentations-2015.pdf). In this way, the institution may benefit from a slower, more deliberative hiring process and a cadre of well-educated faculty charged with performing it.

Institutional Self-Representation

As the department, and the search committee, seek to attract diverse faculty (and students), they need to consider how the institution and the department represent themselves on websites and in other descriptions and materials candidates might review. Does the department appear to be diverse in its current composition? Open to a range of perspectives? Eager to increase its breadth and inclusion of a range of interests and types of students and faculty? Possessed of policies that support faculty members' personal lives when there are increases in the complexity of responsibilities for family members requiring care?

The philosophy departments at Columbia University and New York University are two examples of philosophy departments that explicitly address inclusiveness on their websites (http://philosophy.columbia.edu/content/minorities-and-philosophy-initiative, http://as.nyu.edu/philosophy/climate.html, respectively). While the intended audience is students rather than faculty, by their concern and their provision of resources, the departments indicate the value they place on diversity and inclusiveness.

If the department's self-descriptions are not complete in providing good information about those issues, consider sending applicants packets of information that will improve their understanding of the institution's commitments. Some institutions have identified women or underrepresented minority faculty who are willing to meet with job applicants outside the hiring department, so they can provide them with information about the institutional and community climate and culture for their group. (Of course, this imposes a service burden on those faculty that needs to be addressed.) As discussed earlier, women and minorities respond to cues that they might fit in or belong to a given field, department, or situation—or that they might not. It is worth the search committee's time to think through how the department can best represent itself and the institution—accurately—in a welcoming and inclusive manner.

Relying on Data

Finally, at the beginning of the search process, in the course of it, and at the end of it, collecting, maintaining, and reviewing accurate data about the pool of candidates and applicants, about the long, medium, and short lists' characteristics, and about the outcomes (offers made, rejected, and accepted) is critical. Collecting and—especially—reviewing data can itself affect both search processes and their success.

One practice that several schools and colleges at the University of Michigan have adopted is to provide every department with annual data about the rate of PhD attainment by women and minorities in the relevant field five years earlier (as a rough and slightly conservative proxy for the demography of the available market) at PhD-granting institutions, at institutions Michigan faculty consider "peers," and at Michigan itself (see box 5.2). In addition, data are provided about the current population of faculty and doctoral students in that department, and space is provided for (required) reporting about the characteristics of the applicant pool, the interview list, and the final short list.

Routine inspection of the figures provided at the outset of the search allows departments (and deans) to notice when PhD production at the institution in that field is a poor guide to peer or national PhD production. That issue can then be examined and addressed. In addition, mistaken assumptions about the potential availability of applicants can be corrected, and realistic aspirations (including aspirations to attract "ahead" of the pool's rate of women and minorities!) can be developed.

Monitoring the demographic makeup of the applicant pool should be accomplished through a process that keeps gender and race reporting separate from the search committee, so those factors will not be made salient and trigger reliance on schemas, threby biasing evaluation of individual dossiers. In the course of the search, these data can be monitored, and deans or provosts can hold search committees accountable for at least attracting

Box 5.2

Pool Data Summary Form for Search Committees

Table 1.

Percentage of doctoral degrees conferred to women and underrepresented minorities in [department] at the University of Michigan, 14 peer institutions, and all R1 institutions with [department] programs: 2000–2011

	2000	2001	2002	2003	2004	2005	2006	2007	2008	2009	2010	2011	Total
University of Michigan													
Total number of doctoral degrees conferred	52	41	47	40	50	44	44	52	48	56	34	33	541
% doctoral degrees conferred to women	8%	10%	9%	18%	6%	5%	9%	19%	15%	11%	18%	27%	12%
% doctoral degrees conferred to URM[1,2]	8%	7%	0%	0%	0%	0%	13%	0%	0%	5%	9%	10%	4%
14 peer institutions													
Total number of doctoral degrees conferred[3]	511	531	471	494	556	552	584	725	723	680	658	730	7,215
% doctoral degrees conferred to women	11%	13%	12%	11%	11%	14%	11%	12%	18%	17%	19%	13%	14%
% doctoral degrees conferred to URM	6%	8%	9%	2%	10%	4%	5%	11%	7%	8%	11%	7%	7%
R1 institutions													
Total number of doctoral degrees conferred[4]	1,192	1,196	1,059	1,058	1,208	1,269	1,505	1,627	1,595	1,486	1,539	1,679	16,413
% doctoral degrees conferred to women	11%	12%	13%	13%	12%	14%	13%	13%	18%	16%	18%	16%	14%
% doctoral degrees conferred to URM	7%	8%	6%	8%	9%	7%	6%	11%	7%	8%	10%	9%	8%

Source: WebCASPAR/IPEDS Completions Survey.

1. African Americans, Hispanic Americans, and Native Americans (including Alaska Natives).
2. Temporary residents were excluded when calculating percent doctoral degrees conferred to underrepresented minorities, as these individuals were not assigned a race-ethnicity code in the WebCASPAR/IPEDS Completions Survey database.
3. The Office of the Associate Dean for Academic Affairs in the [College] provided a list of peer institutions for each department. The peer institutions for this discipline include: [Institution names]. Data for these comparison institutions were mapped to University of Michigan departments based on Classification of Instructional Programs (CIP) code assignments (2000). Because of differences in organizational structures across institutions and how individual institutions assign CIP codes to their respective departments, the mappings were made in a way to be more inclusive rather than exclusive.
4. Includes R1 institutions that conferred doctoral degrees in [department].

Box 5.2 (continued)

Table 2
Faculty search: Applicant pool and candidate pool—Fall 2013/Winter 2014 recruitment season

	Applicant pool	Intermediate list[7]	Intend to invite
Total	134	134	7
% women[5]	9%	9%	29%
% URM[6]	1%	1%	0%
N, unknown sex	114	114	2
N, Unknown race/ethnicity	82	82	6

Source: Departmental Pool Composition Report.

5. When calculating percent female, individuals without an assigned sex code (male or female) were included in the denominator.
6. When calculating percent underrepresented minority (African Americans, Hispanic Americans, and Native Americans), individuals without an assigned race-ethnicity code were included in the denominator; therefore, the proportion of minorities reported in this table may underestimate the actual proportion of minorities comprising the applicant pool and/or candidate pool.
7. The "Intermediate List" category is for candidates who have merited additional consideration, i.e., candidates for whom reference letters and/or papers were requested by the department. Those invited to campus are usually drawn from the intermediate list.

Table 3
Percentage of women and underrepresented minorities on the tenure track (funded) in [department]

	2001	2013
Total faculty[8]	82	57
% women	7% (n = 6)	11% (n = 6)
% URM	4% (n = 3)	5% (n = 3)

Source: M-Pathways Human Resources Data Warehouse (HR01); effective dates: 03/01/2001 and 09/15/2013.

8. Excludes dry appointments; faculty with appointments in more than one department in the [College] (i.e., greater than 0% time equivalence) were counted in each department.

an applicant pool that reflects the diversity of the doctoral degree pool. When such data were first shared with departments at Michigan, many were surprised that they had graduated fewer women and minority PhDs than they thought, and that the pool of available applicants was larger than they had believed. Over time, they came to expect the annual update of information, and at least some departments use the data to challenge themselves to achieve the outstanding and diverse applicant pool they need if they are to hire the kind of faculty they want.

Concluding Thoughts

The steps in the process of *recruitment of candidates* and *preparing the search committee* outlined here are the crucial first steps in most hiring. However, institutions sometimes engage in hiring processes that do not assume a job opening, an advertisement, and recruitment of many candidates. Instead, this kind of hiring is often "person specific." We will discuss that kind of hiring in the next chapter, where we also discuss the evaluation of candidates in general. For now, we note that in most hiring it is important not only to search broadly but to set up a process for *evaluating candidates* that will be truly fair and equitable if a department is to successfully identify the best candidate for a position. It is to that process that we turn in the next chapter.

Finally, we have developed a list of practical recommendations, based on the principles outlined above. We organize the list by the constituency of faculty—administrative leaders, faculty in departments, and applicants for positions. But—of course—all of the recommendations are meant to operate together to support a common goal: attracting a diverse pool of applicants to our institutions.

Recommendations for Practices that Increase the Diversity of Applicant Pools

Provosts, Deans, and Department Chairs

1. Assert the twin goals of excellence in scholarship, teaching, and service and diversity in faculty hiring. Encourage confidence that these two goals are mutually compatible and indeed mutually reinforcing. Rely on data about the benefits of diversity.

2. Encourage the adoption of "open searches," and remind faculty that they can be used to enhance both the diversity and the excellence of applicant pools and subsequent faculty hires.

3. Publicly praise and consider rewarding departments or other units that succeed in increasing the diversity and excellence in their faculty. Describe the ways they accomplished this achievement to encourage others.

4. Provide new resources for hiring that may be needed to increase diversity (e.g., more funding for travel for applicants or costs of providing educational resources to committees, etc.).

5. Establish procedures that hold search committees and departments accountable for their procedures and their outcomes:

a. Ensure that institutional policies that support faculty in various family situations are clear and accessible in institutional self-descriptions (on paper and on the web). This may include dual career support, childcare support, and policies that support modification of duties or paid leaves under conditions of care for new children and/or sick relatives.

b. Establish search committees that are diverse in terms of demographic characteristics and expertise but homogeneous in commitment to proactive, fair, and equitable processes.

c. Provide search committees and/or equity advisors with appropriate educational or training resources to perform their job competently. Consider appointing search committees over multiple years to maximize the development of expertise at searching.

d. Ask search committees to document the procedures they use to maximize the diversity of the applicant pool, the fairness of their procedures, and their outcomes.

e. Provide institutional data on PhD pools and department-level outcomes that search committees and departments can use.

f. Monitor the short lists and approve searches only when they reflect the pool of applicants (and potential applicants).

g. Avoid undermining the work of search committees by overruling their recommendations if they have performed according to appropriate procedures.

h. Support departments' efforts to improve their climates so they will be more welcoming and inclusive.

Search Committees and Departments

1. Define the position as broadly as possible and write the advertisement in correspondingly broad terms:

a. Include reference in the advertisement to your interest in attracting diverse excellent applicants:

i. Ensure that the committee that evaluates applications reflects the breadth of the advertisement and includes at least some individuals with a particular interest in increasing faculty diversity, as well as individuals with different demographic characteristics (gender, race/ethnicity, etc.).

ii. Signal that the institution is committed to providing support to faculty with all kinds of household situations and family members by publicizing policies that provide those kinds of support.

iii. Request application letters that allow candidates to detail their interest in your position, their qualifications, and their special expertise.

iv. Consider requesting a statement from applicants about their interest in, experience with, and capacity to contribute to institutional diversity efforts.

2. Take full advantage of educational resources and/or equity advisors. Promote equitable search committee practices department-wide so all department members understand their motivation and value.

Applicants for Faculty Positions

Everyone seeking a first faculty appointment is, to some extent, underinformed about what matters most to search committees. However, women and minorities are, on average, less likely to have access to mentors and informal networks that demystify the process. We believe the advice here is valuable to all job seekers but is especially important for those who have not been socialized by a deliberate process of professional preparation, mentoring, and network development.

1. Pay attention to the description of the position, for two reasons:

a. Positions that are defined broadly may reflect departmental commitments to consider a broad range of talented individuals, and they may therefore be of particular interest to women and minorities concerned about their own "fit" with a department and about a department's climate for them.

b. Positions that are defined broadly are likely to attract many applicants (relative to those defined more narrowly). As a result, applicants may have to work particularly hard to differentiate themselves from others.

2. Generally, approach the job application process by providing *each* search committee with an account of your qualifications that differentiates you in terms of the following:

a. Your excellent qualities; be sure to provide clear evidence of your accomplishments in your CV and in your cover letter, and in research and teaching statements:

i. Do not assume your record speaks for itself; emphasize the contributions you think are important.

ii. Explain (on your CV or in your research statement or in your cover statement) which of the projects and publications most directly represent your work (and not your advisor's or collaborators'). You can do this by outlining the role of particular projects in your overall program of research and also by describing the different contributions you and others made to a particular project.

iii. Do not overemphasize a particular aspect of the position you may be most passionate about (e.g., teaching or research), when in fact the search committee is looking for evidence of a balanced commitment to multiple domains.

iv. Present your past accomplishments and immediate future work as coherent and integrated. You don't need to mention everything you've ever done, especially if doing so would create an impression that your efforts are not coordinated or organized by clear goals.

b. Your fit with their needs; outline what you might bring to the position that would add something new to the department, as well as what you might bring that would complement or strengthen existing departmental faculty or other resources. If you can include both kinds of contributions, that's helpful!

c. The specific reasons (in terms of type of institution, department, faculty, students, or curriculum) that you are excited about this particular position. Often search committees are engaged in guessing whether applicants are "serious" or would really come if invited; provide them with explicit evidence that you are serious.

It may sound as if you should avoid generic job application materials, and it may also seem that specific applications are a lot of work. That's right! But if you want a position, and you are in a highly competitive field, it stands to reason that you need to provide differentiating evidence that you are the best candidate for the job. This does not mean bragging; it means providing relevant information that will be helpful to the search committee in seeing you as you really are.

3. Help your recommenders provide good evidence to search committees:

a. Even with the best will in the world, it may not be easy for every one of your letter writers to recall the main things they should emphasize about your accomplishments. In addition to providing them with a sample of your application materials (your CV, cover letter template, research and teaching statements), provide them with a bulleted list of things you think they might want to mention. No one of them will mention them all, but this will help all of them pay attention to the things you care most about.

b. Ask recommenders if there is anyone at the institutions you're most excited about whom they might contact with informal input. This is not something that is always appropriate (they may not know anyone or have the kind of relationship that enables them to feel comfortable approaching someone). So you should leave the decision about whether to do anything up to them, but it doesn't hurt to remind them to think about it by asking the question.

4. Disseminate the information you have about yourself in an accessible form; make it easy for someone who is impressed by a talk you give or a paper you publish to find out more about you. A good way to do this is to create a website that posts the material in an accessible and well-organized fashion. Don't forget to mention the website in your cover letter and on your CV.

Notes

1. See box 5.1 for examples of actual advertisements for positions in humanities, social science, and natural science fields. The examples range in terms of how "open" they are, but all of them are broader and signal openness to applicants with a wider range of histories, interests, and accomplishments than the usual advertisements in those fields.

2. IPEDS Completion Survey (https://webcaspar.nsf.gov/).

3. See http://web.mit.edu/ir/rankings/USNews_Grad_Rankings_1994-2017.pdf (p.20) and http://grad-schools.usnews.rankingsandreviews.com/best-graduate-schools/top-science-schools/chemistry-rankings/.

4. This has been an unintended consequence of some faculty hiring programs that aim to hire "clusters" of faculty in emergent interdisciplinary research areas. When—as happened in a program launched at the University of Michigan in 2007—the positions had to be defined in detail in order to be reviewed for approval to search, the unintended result was narrow pools and hires that were not demographically diverse. This outcome was mitigated when changes were made in the level of detail required in defining positions.

References

Bilimoria, D., & Buch, K. K. (2010). The search is on: Engendering faculty diversity through more effective search and recruitment. *Change: The Magazine of Higher Learning*, *42*(4), 27–32.

Breaugh, J. A. (2013). Employee recruitment. *Annual Review of Psychology*, *64*, 389–416.

Bylsma, W. H., & Major, B. (1992). Two routes to eliminating gender differences in personal entitlement: Social comparisons and performance evaluations. *Psychology of Women Quarterly*, *16*(2), 193–200.

Carnes, M., Devine, P. G., Manwell, L. B., Byars-Winston, A., Fine, E., Ford, C. E., et al. (2015). Effect of an intervention to break the gender bias habit: A cluster randomized, controlled trial. *Academic Medicine*, *90*(2), 221–230.

Cheryan, S., Plaut, V. C., Davies, P. G., & Steele, C. M. (2009). Ambient belonging: How stereotypical cues impact gender participation in computer science. *Journal of Personality and Social Psychology*, *97*(6), 1045–1060.

Cohen, G. L., Steele, C. M., & Ross, L. D. (1999). The mentor's dilemma: Providing critical feedback across the racial divide. *Personality and Social Psychology Bulletin*, *25*, 1302–1318.

Cohen, L. E., Broschak, J. P., & Haveman, H. A. (1998). And then there were more? The effect of organizational sex composition on the hiring and promotion of managers. *American Sociological Review*, *63*(5), 711–727.

Gaucher, D., Friesen, J., & Kay, A. C. (2011). Evidence that gendered wording in job advertisements exists and sustains gender inequality. *Journal of Personality and Social Psychology*, *101*(1), 109–128.

Heilman, M. (1980). The impact of situational factors on personnel decisions concerning women: Varying the sex composition of the applicant pool. *Organizational Behavior and Human Performance, 26*, 386–395.

Heilman, M. (1983). Sex bias in work setting: The lack of fit model. *Research in Organizational Behavior, 5*, 269–298.

Hewstone, M., Crisp, R. J., & Turner, R. N. (2011). Perceptions of gender group variability in majority and minority contexts. *Social Psychology, 42*(2), 135–143.

Hogue, M., & Yoder, J. (2003). The role of status in producing depressed entitlement in women's and men's pay allocations. *Psychology of Women Quarterly, 27*, 330–337.

Hogue, M., Yoder, J., & Singleton, S. B. (2007). The gender wage gap: An explanation of men's elevated wage entitlement. *Sex Roles, 56*, 573–579.

Ilgen, D. R., & Youtz, M. A. (1986). Factors affecting the evaluation and development of minorities in organizations. In K. Rowland & G. Ferris (Eds.), *Research in personnel and human resource management* (pp. 307–337). Greenwich, CT: JAI Press.

Kahneman, D. (2011). *Thinking, fast and slow.* New York, NY: Farrar, Straus and Giroux.

Kanter, R. M. (1977). *Men and women of the corporation.* New York, NY: Basic Books.

Kraiger, K., & Ford, J. K. (1985). A meta-analysis of ratee race effects in performance ratings. *Journal of Applied Psychology, 70*(1), 56–65.

LaVaque-Manty, D., & Stewart, A. J. (2008). "A very scholarly intervention": Recruiting women faculty in science and engineering. In L. Schiebinger (Ed.), *Gendered innovations in science and engineering* (pp. 165–181). Palo Alto, CA: Stanford University Press.

Maynard, D. C., & Brooks, M. E. (2008). The persistence of stereotypes in the context of familiarity. *Industrial and Organizational Psychology: Perspectives on Science and Practice, 1*, 417–419.

Moody, J. (2004). *Faculty diversity: Problems and solutions.* New York, NY: Routledge.

Page, S. (2008). *The difference: How the power of diversity creates better groups, firms, schools, and societies.* Princeton, NJ: Princeton University Press.

Pazy, A., & Oron, I. (2001). Sex proportion and performance evaluation among high-ranking military officers. *Journal of Organizational Behavior, 22*, 689–702.

Pelham, B. W., & Hetts, J. J. (2001). Underworked and overpaid: Elevated entitlement in men's self-pay. *Journal of Experimental Social Psychology, 37*, 93–103.

Purdie-Vaughns, V., Steele, C. M., Davies, P. G., Ditlmann, R., & Crosby, J. R. (2008). Social identity contingencies: How diversity cues signal threat or safety for African

Americans in mainstream institutions. *Journal of Personality and Social Psychology, 94*, 615–630.

Reskin, B. F., McBrier, D. B., & Kmec, J. A. (1999). The determinants and consequences of workplace sex and race composition. *Annual Review of Sociology, 25*, 335–361.

Roberson, L., Galvin, B. M., & Charles, A. C. (2007). When group identities matter: Bias in performance appraisal. *Academy of Management Annals, 1*(1), 617–650.

Sackett, P. R., DuBois, C. L., & Noe, A. W. (1991). Tokenism in performance evaluation: The effects of work group representation on male-female and White-Black differences in performance ratings. *Journal of Applied Psychology, 76*(2), 263–267. doi:10.1037/0021-9010.76.2.263

Sekaquaptewa, D. (2015, June). Hiring for diversity: Evaluation of a faculty recruitment workshop to improve faculty diversity and excellence. Poster presented at the National Science Foundation ADVANCE/GSE Program Workshop, Baltimore, MD.

Smith, D. G., Turner, C. S., Osei-Kofi, N., & Richards, S. (2004). Interrupting the usual: Successful strategies for hiring diverse faculty. *Journal of Higher Education, 75*(2), 133–160.

Sommers, S. (2006). On racial diversity and group decision making: Identifying multiple effects of racial composition on jury deliberations. *Journal of Personality and Social Psychology, 90*(4), 597–612.

Sommers, S. R., Warp, L. S., & Mahoney, C. C. (2008). Cognitive effects of racial diversity: White individuals' information processing in heterogeneous groups. *Journal of Experimental Social Psychology, 44*, 1129–1136.

Steele, C. M. (2011). *Whistling Vivaldi: And other clues to how stereotypes affect us.* New York, NY: Norton.

Stewart, A. J., Malley, J. E., & Herzog, K. A. (2016). Increasing the representation of women faculty in STEM departments: What makes a difference? *Journal of Women and Minorities in Science and Engineering, 22*(1), 23–47.

Tsui, A. S., & O'Reilly, C. (1989). Beyond simple demographic effects: The importance of relational demography in superior-subordinate dyads. *Academy of Management Journal, 32*, 402–423.

Walker, H. J., Feild, H. S., Giles, W. F., Armenakis, A. A., & Bernerth, J. B. (2009). Displaying employees' testimonials on recruitment web sites: Effects of communication media, employee race, and jobseeker race on organizational attraction and information credibility. *Journal of Applied Psychology, 94*(5), 1354–1364.

Walton, G. M., & Cohen, G. L. (2007). A question of belonging: Race, social fit, and achievement. *Journal of Personality and Social Psychology, 92*(1), 82–96.

Williamson, I. O., Slay, H. S., Shapiro, D. L., & Shivers-Blackwell, S. L. (2008). The effect of explanations on prospective applicants' reactions to firm diversity practices. *Human Resource Management, 47*(2), 311–330.

Yoder, J. (2002). Understanding tokenism processes and their impact on women's work. *Psychology of Women Quarterly, 26*, 1–8.

6   Evaluating Job Candidates: Choosing the Short List and Treating Interviewees Equitably

Once the recruitment phase has ended, the evaluation phase begins. In this chapter we focus on the process that occurs after the applications are in—the process of evaluation that eventually leads to a new faculty hire. In this context, everyone wants to hire the "best" candidate. Everyone also wants to evaluate people fairly. Most people pride themselves on being impartial and objective observers of other people's competence, independent of the person's gender or race. As we have argued, however, considerable research suggests that evaluations are subject to error. We have outlined experiments that demonstrate that people—from undergraduates to practicing scientists—are likely to overrate men's competence and underrate women's, unless the woman's performance was extraordinary. People are similarly likely to overrate Whites' competence and underrate that of some racial-ethnic minority groups. *Wanting* to be gender and race neutral does not, by itself, prevent people from making decisions influenced by gender and race schemas. We start with an example of the different attributions people can make for the same behavior, depending on the gender of those being observed:

One man said he had noticed that when he saw a paper with a young male scientist as the first author and the man's male supervisor as the second author, he presumed the young man had contributed the main ideas and had led the research. The young man had earned his place as first author. Otherwise, the supervisor would have put his name first. But when he saw a young female scientist as the first author, he assumed that the male supervisor was doing her a favor. Maybe she had earned the position, but equally likely, her mentor was trying to help her.

We like to think that people's records of accomplishment do not really require interpretation, but in fact we make many interpretations along with our judgments. With someone's CV in hand, we think we can judge his or her merits objectively. But we need to consider how we go about assessing merit.

We will argue here that a confluence of factors—gender and race schemas, age schemas, socioeconomic origin schemas, a bias toward high prestige universities, and a superfluity of candidates—results in fewer women and people of color being considered than would be appropriate. Establishing merit is not straightforward, so we need to adopt practices that will increase the likelihood that our judgments are fair and unbiased.

Fairness in Evaluations

The evaluation process divides into four rough stages: initial screening of candidates, construction of a short list (or medium-short list), selection of interviewees from the short list, and decision-making about candidates after the interviews. Some issues will play a role throughout the process. For example, at the initial screening and at all subsequent points, a preference for individuals with a PhD from a high-prestige institution will result in underrating women (slightly) and people of color (more). Another issue throughout will be the likely slight overrating of White men's credentials compared to those of women and people of color. Some issues, however, only arise later in the process, depending on how the institution conducts its searches.

At the interview stage, faculty beyond the search committee are involved: they go to the candidate's talk and may meet with the candidate. For those faculty, who may not have read any of the candidate's work, their impression is based on a very small sample of behavior, much of which is irrelevant to the work itself, such as the faculty member's physical appearance, manner of presentation, and response to questions. Since faculty tend to have high confidence in their evaluation decision, their reliance on interview performance leads to giving insufficient weight to years of past performance and too much weight to a small slice of behavior.

Although everyone wants to be fair (and usually believes they are fair), several factors make fairness somewhat difficult to attain. We review some of those factors here. The belief that it is possible to make gender- and race-neutral decisions can get people in trouble. Some people take their commitment to merit to mean that, *using the criteria that are currently in place*, everyone should be judged in exactly the same way, regardless of their sex or the color of their skin. We too subscribe to the merit principle, and we too subscribe to the principle of treating people similarly, but we do not endorse the idea that our current criteria are the best ones, nor do we endorse the idea that current notions of similar treatment will maximize everyone's potential or be equally revealing.

We have two goals in this section. One is to spell out the problems with using the criteria that are currently in place. The other is to question whether a commitment to the merit principle ensures following it.

Using the Criteria Currently in Place

For any job, if that job has primarily been held by one type of person, with general approval, observers will tend to see those characteristics as necessary for the job. In fact, one way of trying to determine whether individuals are a good fit for a job is by giving them a test to see if they share the interests and characteristics of people currently in the job (Nye, Su, Rounds, & Drasgow, 2012). The logical problem with this is obvious (Valian, 2014). There might be many satisfactory ways to do a job, only a subset of which are displayed by current jobholders. For example, faculty can be surprised by how well a colleague performs as a chair, noticing that his or her focus and style are very different from a previous admired chair's, but equally, if not more, beneficial to a department. Using criteria derived from one set of successful occupants of a position to evaluate new candidates tilts a faculty against innovation.[1] If a prior occupant who was a woman or a member of a minority group was not successful, illusory correlation can bias observers against others who are demographically similar to the person who failed.

Ratings of job performance depend on the raters' conceptions of what the job requires. Those ratings in turn depend in part on the characteristics of the people in the job. A rater can use standards that are irrelevant but in place because they were at one time typical of most successful jobholders (Valian, 1998, 2014). Some criteria that might look right for the job of university professor—ambition, self-promotion, competitiveness, assertiveness—are characteristics that are double-edged swords for White women and minority women and men. Women who are ambitious, self-promoting, competitive, and assertive are seen negatively by both men and other women, as we have discussed in chapter 3. A further point is that as the potential pool for an occupation slowly becomes less demographically homogeneous, raters run the risk of taking extraneous properties that the original, demographically similar, jobholders shared as relevant to job performance. Having seen only a limited number of ways of solving a problem, raters may see those ways as the sole ways to solve a problem. If, for example, a long line of department chairs had a decisive and assertive style, a candidate who was known for being cooperative and likable might not be seen as sufficiently "tough."

One senior professor told us about trying to interest her colleagues in hiring an extremely talented woman at another university. Her colleagues said the woman was "difficult" and were opposed to pursuing her. Later in the year one of her male colleagues proposed hiring an extremely talented man at another university. Our senior professor said that the man was "difficult." Her male colleagues said, "We can work around that." People notice that difficult men are difficult, but their being difficult is not a deal breaker. For women, being "difficult" is a deal breaker, as shown by work on backlash. And that assumes that the same criteria were used for deciding that these two people were difficult. The result for women is that being a good fit is complicated. Even if a woman meets the informal criteria by which men are judged, she will not be seen as positively as a man is.

Setting the Stage for Shifting Standards

In chapter 3 we reviewed experiments demonstrating that people shift their evaluation standards, depending in part on their prior beliefs about who will do a better job in a particular area. Men look right for the job of construction engineer, with the result that whatever attributes that men might possess to a greater degree than women will give men an advantage. Those attributes will come to look as if they are necessary for the job, whether they are actually relevant or not.

Because there are often competing ideas about what a department needs, the stage is set for shifting standards to play a role. It is in the department's interest to determine impartially who will best satisfy the department's needs and interests, but not everyone has the same ideas about what a department's needs and interests are. Even if there is agreement about the overall needs and interests, people differ in which values they weigh more heavily than others. Some may care only about the likelihood that a faculty member will be a star. Some may see a new area as the wave of the future and others may see it as currently fashionable but unlikely to last. Some might value filling an instructional gap more than strengthening an existing area. Some might prefer a new hire if they are likely to collaborate with that person or if they think the new person is likely to support their views about desirable future directions of the department. To the extent that people are successful in arguing for their candidate, they gain power and advantage in their department—another form of the accumulation of advantage. Having a job description (the creation of which can involve difficult conversations, as we detail in chapter 5) is not the same thing as agreeing on what the department needs or *should* need.

Those different preferences set the stage for people to adopt shifting standards. If likelihood of collaboration is the top priority for one member of a search committee, she may ignore information, such as number of publications, that she might otherwise use to evaluate a group of people all or none of whom she might collaborate with. Thus, even before issues of gender and ethnicity come into play, search committee members are likely to differ in what is important to them in a candidate and to use as a measuring rod whatever qualities the person they want happens to have. Only an agreed-upon set of criteria can provide a buffer to shifting standards.

Gender Issues

The combination of gender schemas and, in some fields, much smaller numbers of women than men applicants, can make it very difficult for women to get to the interview stage. Other factors unique to women, such as motherhood, underline women's identity as women, with the result that mothers are perceived more negatively than childless women and are less likely to be offered as good a job (Correll, Benard, & Paik, 2007; Correll, Kelly, O'Connor, & Williams, 2014; Heilman & Okimoto, 2008). In line with gender schemas, it appears to be difficult for us to imagine that mothers can be committed to their jobs. "Working mothers" have a special title, while "working fathers" do not. And if mothers are seen as exceptionally good professionals, they appear to correspondingly be seen as bad parents (Okimoto & Heilman, 2012) and can be viewed negatively for that reason.

Race–Ethnicity Issues

For underrepresented minorities, the situation is even more extreme. As we mentioned in chapter 3, field studies have found that job applicants with names that sounded African American, such as Lakisha, were less likely to be called for an interview than were applicants with names that sounded

"White," such as Emily (Bertrand & Mullainathan, 2003). There is little reason to think that search committees in academia are less subject to such influences than managers in the general workplace.

Parental and Partner Statuses and Their Role in the Evaluation Process

We indicated in chapter 5 that institutions do well to signal their family-friendly policies to applicants. They should not, however, include consideration of applicants' family situation in the hiring process. As one résumé study demonstrated, parental status plays a different role in the evaluation of men compared to women (Correll et al., 2007). For women it results in perceptions of lesser suitability for compensation, advancement, and leadership; for men it results in perceptions of greater suitability for the same outcomes. In short, there appears to be a "motherhood penalty" and a "fatherhood bonus." For this reason, we recommend that job applicants *not* signal their parenthood status in their applications, and that search committees avoid requesting or permitting discussion of any information they may have about either the parenthood or the partner status of applicants. It is illegal to ask for such information.

Often search committees are tempted to discuss the partner status of their applicants, believing that it is important to take account of it in the process of selecting candidates if they are to be successful. While this thinking is logical from the perspective of the hiring institution, acting on it is likely to trigger both gender and parental schemas that may lead committees to underestimate the qualifications of women and overestimate those of men, as we have just described. For an example, see the kinds of schemas expressed by department members in departments that fail to hire women even in the presence of an institutional commitment to doing so (Stewart, Malley, & Herzog, 2016).

Because of the difficulty of remaining unaffected by personal knowledge about applicants, we recommend that information about candidates' personal lives be neither sought nor considered in the course of the selection process. Whether one penalizes mothers (or mothers-to-be) or benefits fathers or fathers-to-be (because they are seen as more serious and responsible, and as needing to do well at their job to provide for their family), it is hard to undo the effects of irrelevant information. It is like telling a jury to disregard information that is not strictly relevant. A qualitative study of twenty-four search committee deliberations at a research-intensive university found that search committees tended to assume that a woman would not accept a position if she had a partner, but that a man would (Rivera, 2017). Women's relationship status was discussed more often than men's, and committee members believed that it was legal to use such information as long as they had not solicited it from the candidate (which it is not). Personal questions also affect applicants' views of the institution. One study of individuals who withdrew from searches late in the process or turned down offers demonstrated that interpretations of even small comments by faculty members in recruiting departments led to counterproductive interpretations of the underlying biases in the departments by candidates, even if those comments were not the direct cause of candidates' withdrawing (http://advance .umich.edu/resources/STEMTurnDownStudy-2009.pdf).

Commitment in Principle versus Commitment in Practice

Commitment to the merit principle as a principle does not entail abiding by it, as we detailed in chapter 3 when we described how schemas work. Worse, the fact that everyone explicitly subscribes to the principle can impair people's ability to discern the extent to which they do not act in accord with it. The dual experience of holding a principle and of having some data that seem to suggest that one abides by it can close one's eyes to data that suggest this isn't true. Everyone wants to think that they act fairly, leading to their paying more attention to confirming data and less attention to disconfirming data.

We reviewed experimental results on moral licensing in chapter 3. A "license" to act contrary to one's explicit beliefs arises if one has recently performed an action that seems to be in accord with those beliefs. We permit ourselves to lapse into more stereotypic thinking if we have recently performed an action that seems fair and nonstereotyped to us. Similarly, it appears that doing any task that reminds us of what a sterling character we are—such as writing a description of ourselves using morally positive words provided by the experimenter—makes us less generous afterward than does writing a story that reminds us of our negative traits. When we write positively about ourselves, we are less generous in giving money to a worthy cause. When we write negatively about ourselves, we are more generous (Sachdeva, Iliev, & Medin, 2009). The effect is not simply due to writing positively or negatively since it does not occur when people write positively or negatively about someone else, only when they write about themselves.

The effect of moral licensing is not limited to an individual's own behavior. Identifying with a group that one believes is moral can provide license to the individual to behave less morally. Moral licensing can even work vicariously (Kouchaki, 2011). In one of a series of studies with undergraduates, participants in the experimental condition were told that students at their university were more moral than students at other universities (Kouchaki, 2011). In the three control conditions, participants were told that students at their university were not more moral than students at other universities, or that they were more competitive, or that they were more intelligent. All participants then read a scenario in which they were a police chief hiring a new officer in a small town and had to judge whether a White or an African American officer would be better for the job. Those in the more moral and more intelligent groups were more likely to choose the White officer over the African American one than were those who were told that students at their university were more competitive or told they were not more moral (Kouchaki, 2011). Although it appears paradoxical, our reminders to ourselves of our positive ethical qualities make us freer to act selfishly and freer to act in ways that are consistent with group stereotypes.

Strategies to Reduce Schemas' Effects

Two types of strategies can help reduce the effects of schemas (see Monteith, Ashburn-Nardo, Voils, & Czopp, 2002, and Moskowitz & Li, 2011, for reviews and discussion). One strategy acknowledges that schemas are easily activated and concentrates on reducing the biased decisions that one might make on the basis of the schemas (e.g., Devine, Forscher, Austin, & Cox, 2012; Forscher, Mitamura, Dix, Cox, & Devine, 2017; Monteith et al., 2002). In some cases the strategy requires training to develop ways of countering schemas, such as learning to think of a person in terms of his or her individual characteristics rather than in terms of his or her group membership (e.g., Carnes, Devine, Baier Manwell, Byars-Winston, Fine, Ford, et al., 2015; Devine et al., 2012). In other cases the strategy might be to explicitly call one's goals to mind—for example, *I want to be fair*—or reflect on times when one didn't act in accord with one's meritocratic aspirations. Those strategies may help neutralize the consequences of the schema. In these *reactive* strategies (Moskowitz & Li, 2011), acknowledging that one responds on the basis of schemas is a precondition for controlling the behavior that might arise from the almost automatic activation of schemas. The two-part model that is invoked here—acknowledge the presence of schemas, and act on controlling them—requires *not* patting oneself on the back for one's principles but acknowledging that one may not always live up to them.

The second type of strategy suggests that it is possible to prevent activation of a schema to begin with, through being routinely motivated to avoid prejudice (Moskowitz & Li, 2011). Individuals with "chronic" goals of that sort are less likely to respond in terms of schemas when judging individuals. Goals to avoid prejudice can also be developed by encouraging someone to recall a failure in living up to a meritocratic goal. Individuals (primarily White) who were primed to recall such a failure showed a reduced tendency to associate African Americans with negative traits, such as *lazy* (Moskowitz & Li, 2011). A "proactive" strategy of this sort reminds people of an instance when they have acted counter to their principles and thus removes the moral license that thinking well of themselves would otherwise bestow.

Is It Good to Be Race "Blind"?

Whites' commitment to a race-blind strategy can backfire. A White person refusing to use race as a category when it is relevant can affect African Americans negatively, rather than being neutral or positive. In one study, Whites were asked to pick out a target photo from an array of photos of African Americans and Whites. They had a partner who knew who the target was. They were to ask their partner questions that would allow them to find the relevant photo in the shortest amount of time. Even though an African American's ethnicity would help to quickly identify the person, Whites tended not to ask about the race of the target person, especially if their partner was African American. Whites wanted to appear race blind (see review in Apfelbaum, Norton, & Sommers, 2012). However, African Americans saw Whites who avoid mentioning race as more biased than those who did mention it—when the mention was appropriate. Most Whites have probably had the experience of failing to mention someone's racial or ethnic identity from a desire for race not to matter. But if you are a member of an underrepresented group, that refusal to recognize the obvious can simply seem insulting.

A commitment to being race blind might make it difficult for Whites to see discrimination when it exists. A study with children suggests how that might work. Children ages 8 to 11 who were provided with different assumptions in thinking about race differences either perceived or failed to perceive actual discrimination, depending on their assumption. The children heard one of two stories about a teacher who wanted to ensure racial equality in her class by having a class performance, either via a color-blind approach or by means of an approach affirming the value of differences (Apfelbaum, Pauker, Sommers, & Ambady, 2010). Then the children heard different vignettes about forms of exclusion or mistreatment and were asked to evaluate them. In one case, the vignette was ambiguous—a White child didn't invite an African American child to a party. That example is very like what happens to underrepresented minorities and White women in departments—they aren't invited to collaborate, they aren't invited to lunch or coffee, they are at the margins—even though there may be no overt intention to exclude. In another case, the vignette was clear. A White child tripped an African American child in order to take a ball away from him during a game and justified his behavior by saying that the African American child played rough because he was African American.

Children were asked to describe each vignette in their own words and to say whether discrimination had taken place (Apfelbaum et al., 2010). The children who heard the color-blind story were much less likely to detect discrimination, even when there was strong overt evidence of it, than were the children who heard the story emphasizing that different races have value. The study suggests that an assumption that discrimination is unlikely can lead to a failure to see it when it occurs. Thus, we caution search committees to remember that race, ethnicity, and gender can affect our judgments, even if we wish they did not, and to realize that congratulating oneself for being gender and race blind can open the door to making biased judgments. The most helpful attitude is to assume at least skepticism about one's ability to make judgments that are unaffected by someone's race, ethnicity, and gender.

Evaluating Applicants to Create a Short List

The First Pass

The first categorization of candidates' applications is usually made on the basis of (1) information that can be gleaned from a curriculum vitae (CV); (2) information that the evaluator may already have about applicants from meeting them, hearing them present their work, or hearing about them from someone else; and (3) letters of recommendation. (Recommendation letters are not always requested as part of someone's initial application packet. Medical schools, for example, often do not request recommendation letters until after the search committee has created a "long" short list.) CVs include the names of the institutions where the person has received his or her training, and, often, the names of the people the person trained with; a list of publications; a list of conference and other presentations; a list of grants, prizes, and awards; and, often, teaching experience and administrative service. The candidate's cover letter, teaching statement, and research statements, if they exist, may also be consulted, especially the cover letter. Some searches may have 50 candidates; others may have 400. Some search committees may have only three members; others may have six or more. A search committee member who is faced with a multitude of applications will look for ways to extract the maximum amount of information with the minimum amount of effort.

At universities and colleges that put a premium on research, research accomplishment is the single most important criterion. That criterion can be evaluated in terms of a person's publications and in terms of his or her success in obtaining funding for research. In the natural sciences, most publications take the form of articles in journals that only accept papers for publication if they have been successfully reviewed by peers. In the social sciences and the humanities, depending on the field, publications may take the form of journal articles, books, book chapters, or all three. At institutions that put a premium on teaching, research will often still be relevant, but teaching experience and dedication will play an important role as well.

The densest and most substantive information about the quality of someone's research is in the publications themselves. But it is time-consuming to read individuals' work when a search committee is faced with 50 applicants, and even more time-consuming when a committee must review 400 applicants. In addition, many search committees, especially in smaller departments, are composed of members with varying degrees of knowledge in different subfields. Committees will thus be tempted to use at the outset markers like prestige of the person's PhD-granting institution or prestige of the person's primary supervisor as criteria for keeping or eliminating candidates. We take up these issues again in chapter 9, where we consider evaluations of faculty for tenure and promotion.

Relying on Proxies in Assessing Quality

When search committee members base their classifications of applicants on CVs and letters of recommendation instead of reading their work directly, they are using proxy information. The information does not directly provide information about the quality of the person's scholarship—how the candidate presents the background to their research and frames the problem or question; the candidate's methods and materials, the research plan, treatment of the raw material (texts or data), conclusions drawn and inferences made about how the analysis changes one's understanding of the initial problem. Direct information about how the candidate approaches a problem is only available through reading the person's work or, to a lesser extent, through hearing the candidate present the work. Similarly, direct information about the person's teaching is typically acquired through proxy information unless the candidate provides an example of teaching.

Time constraints lead search committee members to begin with proxy information—the CV and the judgments of other people. While the CV is a factual record of a candidate's achievements, achievements are themselves dependent not just on the candidate but on other people. Journal editors decide who the reviewers of a paper will be. The editors' knowledge of the authors, or of the authors' institution, or reputation, may influence their choice of reviewers. Journal reviewers, in their turn, may be influenced not only by the paper itself but also by prestige factors—to the extent that they are known or deducible—such as the prestige of a coauthor or the authors' institution. Some journals practice blind review—where reviewers are not told the identity of the author(s), but identity can often be deduced. Search committee members are sensitive to the prestige of the journals in which the candidate has published and the prestige of the candidate's PhD and postdoctoral supervisors.

Relying on proxy information substitutes a history of other people's views of the candidate for one's own independent evaluation. If one believes that all the preceding processes have been impartial and objective, and if one believes that everyone has had the same opportunity to attend the same stellar schools, one will have no qualms about proxy information. If, however, one believes that factors other than merit can influence where someone applies to graduate school, where someone is accepted to be a student, and with whom one studies once at graduate school, one will be less sanguine about the validity of relying of proxy information. Similarly, if one believes that each achievement is independent of prior achievements, one will assess someone's record differently than if one appreciates the power of the accumulation of advantage.

In general, relying on markers of prestige will advantage men over women, and Whites, Asians, and Hispanics over African Americans, because a lower percentage of women than men, and a lower percentage of African Americans than every other ethnic or racial group, have markers of prestige in their histories. Markers of prestige are more difficult for some groups to acquire, and the lack of those markers then makes further markers harder to acquire. Thus some accumulate advantage, while others accumulate disadvantage.

Search committees have a decision to make at the outset. If they want to maximize inclusiveness, they will have to look beyond proxy information because standard proxies for merit generally favor men over women and favor every other race and ethnic group over African Americans. In some cases the disparities are small, but as Gompers and Wang (2017) point out when discussing the lack of women in venture capital, even a small tendency toward homophily will have an effect on binary outcomes. The same result, we suggest, will hold generally for small disparities.

Prestige of Institution

The prestige of the institution where the candidate received their degree or completed their postdoctoral training or had their first professorial job is objective, in the sense that there is good agreement among academics about which institutions are prestigious; the predictors of prestige are known.[2] But if search committees rely on prestige of degree-granting institution to reduce their applicant pool, they are more likely to eliminate African Americans than Hispanics, Whites, or Asian Americans. In 2015, only 50% of African Americans' PhDs were from universities with very high research activity (as rated by the Carnegie Foundation for the Advancement of Teaching, 2005), compared to 72% of Whites', 73% of Hispanics', and 77% of Asians'. Similarly, committees will be more likely to eliminate women than men: also in 2015, 68% of women and 74% of men received their degrees from the most prestigious institutions. All comparisons, save the difference between Whites and Hispanics, are significant.[3] Putting a premium on prestige of degree-granting institution will result in fewer African Americans and women.

A search committee member attending to prestige might object that prestige of prior institution is diagnostic of future success, as it is and could hardly fail to be, since advantages accumulate, and there are more advantages available at high-prestige institutions. But it is hard to disentangle the effects of individual accomplishment from institutional prestige. As long as highly prestigious institutions preferentially employ people from other highly prestigious institutions, which they do (for political science, see Oprisko, Dobbs, & DiGrazia, 2013; for computer science, business, and history, see Clauset, Arbesman, & Larremore, 2015), it will be impossible to know whether someone with a degree from a less prestigious institution would fare well if given the resources of a prestigious institution.

Another reason that it is difficult to assess the diagnosticity of a prestigious degree is that success is not just an outcome of the tangible resources that institutions supply more or less of, but an outcome of the professional networks that an individual has access to in different types of institutions. Individuals who graduate from nonprestigious institutions not only have fewer tangible resources at their disposal but also have networks that are less densely populated with influential people, compared to individuals whose degrees are from prestigious institutions.

An analysis of job success in sociology makes plain how prestige works in at least one field (Headworth & Freese, 2015). Sociology departments were placed into four prestige tiers, based on survey answers by department chairs and directors of graduate programs. Over the period from 2004–2005 to 2008–2009, 2,644 PhDs were granted. About 60% (1,617) of those graduates came from the two lower prestige tiers and about 40% from the top two tiers. Overall, graduates of the most prestigious schools had more advantages; as students, for example, they published more. Students from the top two tiers were also much better represented as authors in sociology's two flagship journals than were students from the bottom two tiers. Such achievements were presumably facilitated by access to resources and knowledgeable faculty (though access may not have been allocated equally to students from all demographic backgrounds).

Throughout their PhD training, then, more advantage accumulated for students in the top-tier institutions, resulting in a higher likelihood of obtaining a desirable job. Perhaps the saddest finding was that of the 1,617 students from the two lowest tiers, only two were hired by schools in the top tier. None of the 1,133 students from the lowest tier were hired by a school at the top tier, and only three were hired by a school at the second-highest tier. That contrasts with the fate of the 663 individuals who graduated with a degree from the top tier—30 of them took a job at a top-tier institution, and another 69 went to the second tier (Headworth & Freese, 2015). Recall that African Americans, in particular, are more likely to get a PhD from a lower tier institution.

In fields where postdoctoral training is the norm, such as biology, prestige can again play a role. An analysis of biology postdoctoral placements found that high-achieving male faculty had fewer women in their labs than did high-achieving female faculty (of whom there are fewer) or other faculty (Sheltzer & Smith, 2014). To the extent that elite male researchers have laboratories that are male dominated, a hiring preference among search committees for individuals with training from elite investigators will be male dominated. There is no reason to assume explicit gender bias on the part of elite investigators or on the part of search committees, but a shortcut that relies on prestige will result in fewer women being hired for academic positions.

Search committees want to maximize the likelihood that their chosen candidate will be productive and will stay at their institution. It is time-consuming and expensive to hire people. In addition to the time and expense of the search, there is the expense of providing new faculty with start-up costs. If the new faculty member leaves, either because he or she is not productive or because he or she receives a better offer elsewhere, the process starts all over again and the department's investment has gone down the drain. Search committees reasonably want to maximize the likelihood of success of someone they are about to hire. Prestige of PhD-granting institution, prestige of the faculty member(s) the candidate worked with, prestige of the journals the candidate published in, how many publications the candidate has—all those variables are interrelated. But if the committee keeps in mind the values that diversity of all sorts brings to academia, as we discussed in chapter 2, they will need more strategies than an initial reliance on prestige in order to find people who can flourish at their institution, while contributing to its excellence.

Reducing Reliance on Prestige

Three specific practices would reduce the reliance on prestige. The first is to limit to three (or fewer) the number of publications that candidates can submit; that would require candidates to submit the work they think is their most important. If the most important paper is short, so much the better.

The second is to ensure that every candidate who fits the basics of the job description has *at least one* of their papers read by *at least one* search committee member. Readers would be on the lookout for work they found particularly creative or deep or substantial. To that end, the job ad might ask the candidate to specify which one of the three papers they submitted they would most like the committee to read. It may be helpful in mitigating bias to take steps to have that paper read without information about the authors' names or institutional setting. In most fields, it is possible to divide up the search committee's labor in that way. With a large number of applications—say 400—and a search committee of five people, that would mean that after an initial cut (always by at least two of the committee members) of those who do not fit the job description well, each person might read about 50 papers. A search committee member might well find that a daunting prospect! In such a case, the first step might be skimming the abstracts and only reading further if the paper seemed noteworthy in some way. Another solution for very large applicant pools is to divide the reading across the department as a whole.[4] In any case, having a rubric against which the reader evaluates each paper would help standardize assessments both within particular readers and across readers.

The third practice is to look for evidence that candidates from lower prestige institutions could thrive at the searching institution by seeing if they have achieved more than would seem to be the norm for the institution where they received their training or started out. For example, have they applied for external funding? Have they presented at conferences?

For departments that want to increase the diversity of their faculty, the goal is to find women and people of color who could be very successful. Some schools' diversity officers review departments' short lists with an eye to seeing whether any women or people of color might have been overlooked and could be added to the short list. While this procedure is better than nothing, because it ensures some attention to diversity, it is not as good as having the department itself take the responsibility to assess talent in the absence of prestige markers.

Numbers of Publications

Quantity is easy to measure and thus a tempting shortcut for search committees. Journal articles can be evaluated in terms of quantitative measures—the number of publications, the impact factors of the journals that the candidate publishes in, and the number of citations the person's publications have accrued. Books can also be quantitatively evaluated: their number, the prestige of the publisher (usually an academic press), and the number of citations. Each of these markers is itself subject to prestige effects where women and people of color are likely to fare slightly worse than White (and sometimes Asian) men.

Analysis of a nationally representative sample of almost 1,600 individuals in research-intensive institutions shows that researchers increasingly published papers while still in graduate school from 1970 to 2000 (Pinheiro, Melkers, & Youtie, 2014). Before 1980, less than half of graduate students had published a paper pre-PhD. By 2000 and later, a majority of students had published a paper before getting their PhD.

In chemistry, biology, computer science, earth and atmospheric sciences, and electrical engineering, greater productivity as a graduate student is correlated with greater productivity as an assistant and associate professor (Pinheiro et al., 2014). Thus, in those fields, counting a candidate's number of publications as a graduate student is a reasonable way of predicting how productive the individual will be as an assistant and associate professor. Here, too, however, there will be an effect of prestige of institution.

Individuals who publish with their advisor (in fields where that is a practice) publish more papers than do those who publish without their advisor (Pinheiro et al., 2014). To some extent, greater productivity among those who publish with their advisors may be due to selection factors: advisors may choose particularly talented students to publish with. High-publishing advisors may also be more likely to include students as coauthors, especially if they are asked to contribute book chapters. Publishing with an advisor potentially benefits a student in multiple ways: the advisor has skills and knowledge the student can learn from and has a network that can help the student. Those who published at least one paper with their advisor as a graduate student had almost a third more publications per year postdegree than did those who did not publish with their advisor (Pinheiro et al., 2014).

Since the 1970s, men have been more likely than women to publish with their advisors, though the gap is narrowing. Whites have been more likely than Asians and other underrepresented minorities to publish with their advisors, though that gap has narrowed (Pinheiro et al., 2014). It is possible that men and Whites are more talented than women and people of color and are chosen by faculty for that reason. A different possibility is that faculty are more likely to *think* that men and Whites are more talented.

Even when controlling for individual productivity, students who had collaborated with advisors had larger publication records postdegree than did those who had not (Pinheiro et al., 2014). That suggests that collaboration with an advisor has benefits above and beyond those that increase publication rate. Junior collaborators acquire academic capital that serves them well in their subsequent careers. In addition, participation in a research "team" that endures over several or many papers may help an individual look "productive" when it is really the collaboration that is productive. Finally, individuals whose parents were academics also have an advantage.

In sum, academic capital, which includes learned skills in the professional activities required in the academy, plays a role in productivity. Individuals with more experience of academia—whether through parents or through advisors—get a leg up that benefits them for the rest of their career. The small advantage that men and Whites accrue in graduate school ramifies, via the accumulation of advantage, in their productivity after graduate school. Search committees that put a premium on numbers of publications may select individuals who will be productive faculty, but they will miss other individuals who could also be productive. The individuals whom they miss are more likely to be women and people of color. Thus, if a search committee wants to increase the diversity of its interview pool, it will have to take into account the lower opportunity that members of some groups have had to accumulate publications. The committee can also remind itself that it cares more about quality than quantity.

Prestige of Publications

Most academics on search committees know the prestige level of the journals in their field (and some institutions require departments to provide a list of the journals in their field that occupy different tiers). One advantage for graduate students who publish with their advisors is that they can acquire knowledge of the prestige ranking of journals and learn how to determine a good match between their paper and a journal. Journal reputation can be assessed via its impact factor, or the average number of times any given paper in a journal is cited, either over the preceding two years or over the preceding five years. Reliance on impact factors is most common in natural and social science fields, despite serious criticism of the practice (see, e.g., the San Francisco Declaration on Research Assessment: http://www.ascb.org/dora/).

Specialized journals in small fields may have impact factors between 1 and 2, meaning that the average paper in that journal over the preceding two or five years was cited 1–2 times. Impact factors differ from year to year but are fairly stable. A broader journal in the same field might have an impact factor ranging from 3–5, while science-wide journals like *Science* and *Nature* have impact factors of 35 and 38, respectively. For small fields with relatively few researchers, impact factors are low because the number of people who might possibly cite a paper is small. Although impact factor is a rough-and-ready guide, it obscures other relevant differences among journals, such as their theoretical orientation or the size of the field or subfield they reflect.

Deciding where to submit a manuscript is a complicated process: Experienced researchers have a great deal of informally obtained knowledge about journals, from the types of articles a given journal publishes, to the difficulty or length of the review process, to whether they themselves read and cite articles in the journal. All of those factors go into informal judgments of the prestige of someone's publications. When search committee members are looking at CVs outside their immediate area of expertise, they may be unable to judge the importance of a journal by these possibly unshared metrics. They may downgrade or ignore the quality of the publications in specialty journals and resort simply to looking at the number of publications.

Since most researchers tend to have publications in a variety of journals, one strategy a search committee member may use is to scan the list to see whether there are at least a few of the widely recognized "top-tier" journals represented. If there are, the presence of papers in lower tier or unknown journals may be less important. One woman who had served on many search committees and promotion committees thought that men and women made different trade-offs. Men, she thought, published a lot, with a mix of papers in top-tier and lower tier journals. Women, she thought, published less and tended to emphasize publications in top-tier journals. In her view, those different trade-offs benefited men because evaluators look for both quality and quantity. As long as there are some papers to indicate quality, quantity helps. She went on to speculate that when men had a paper rejected from a top-tier journal, they immediately went to a lower tier journal, making only minor changes in the manuscript. But when women had a paper rejected from a top-tier journal, they spent time doing extra experiments to buttress their point and then resubmitted to the same journal. Since that is a more time-consuming procedure, people who adopt it will publish less than people who switch quickly to another journal.

Whether those informal observations are correct is difficult to establish. There have been mixed reports in the literature about sex differences in quantity and quality of publications. Overall, women tend to publish less than men, though the gender disparity is smaller than it was in the past, as we outlined in chapter 4, and is smaller in some fields than others. Many studies reporting gender differences in favor of men do not control for prestige of institution (e.g., in academic medicine; Eloy, Svider, Cherla, Diaz, Kovalerchik, Mauro, et al., 2013; Holliday, Jagsi, Wilson, Choi, Thomas, & Fuller, 2014), even though high prestige is related to productivity and affects reviewer judgments positively when prestige is known. Controlling for prestige and other institutional factors has eliminated gender differences in productivity in some studies (Xie & Shauman, 1998). Other studies, such as a Dutch study that used a pool in the social sciences, have found that gender differences in productivity do not exist among active scientists within three years of their degree, but do exist for active scientists within 15 years of their degree (van Arensbergen, van der Weijden, & Van den Besselaar, 2012).

For graduate students, publication rates are linked to prestige of institution, so the fact that a smaller percentage of women and underrepresented minority men and women are at higher prestige schools, compared to White men and Asians, is likely to result in their having fewer publications.

Whether the quality of women's publications (again, as measured in citations) is greater than men's is much more difficult to determine, and reports vary tremendously. For example, one study examined the records of 85 social and personality psychologists whose degrees were completed in 1996 or 1997, who had full-time faculty positions, and who were members of the Social Psychology Network. They found no sex differences in quantity of publications or quality (as measured by the impact factor of the journals they published in), and no sex differences in the number of times their publications were cited. Although quantity and quality were moderately correlated, the correlation was not linear. Rather, at high levels of quantity or quality, the two were negatively correlated, yielding the implication that publishing very frequently takes a toll on quality, and publishing very high quality work takes a toll on quantity.

A cross-national study of number of papers and number of citations in the sciences found that women were cited less than men, and, in papers published collaboratively, those with a female first or last author were cited less than those with a male first or last author (Sugimoto, Lariviere, Gingras, & Cronin, 2013), though many variables that might be correlated with gender, such as age, were not controlled for. A study of citations in international relations that did control for a large number of variables similarly found that men were cited more than women (Maliniak, Powers, & Walter, 2013), in part because women cite themselves less than men cite themselves and because men (who are still the majority of researchers in this field) cite men more than they cite women. By one estimate, men self-cite 56% more than women do (King, Berstrom, Correll, Jacquet, & West, 2016).

In sum, the CV measures of a candidate's quality will tend to give an edge to White men. The measures are objective, in the sense that they are quantifiable. However, they do not allow the evaluator to independently determine the two most important things—(1) the quality of the person's work and (2) the likelihood that the person can succeed and flourish at the hiring institution. Further, search committee members will find it difficult to mentally adjust for prestige. If two candidates are otherwise similar, the nod is likely to go to the candidate with the more prestigious background.

Letters of Recommendation

Search committee members tend to read letters of recommendation (if they have been submitted) after reading a candidate's CV. Women are at a disadvantage, even when their objective characteristics are the equal of men's (Madera, Hebl, & Martin, 2009; Schmader, Whitehead, & Wysocki, 2007; Trix & Psenka, 2003). Studies have varied in the disciplines they examine—academic medicine (Trix & Psenka, 2003), chemistry (Schmader et al., 2007), and psychology (Madera et al., 2009). They have also varied in whether they examine only individuals who have been hired (Trix & Psenka, 2003) or all candidates (Madera et al., 2009; Schmader et al., 2007). Finally, some studies also assessed candidates' objective attributes via CVs (Madera et al., 2009; Schmader et al., 2007).

In the landmark study that originated this line of research, Trix and Psenka (2003) found that letters for women were shorter than those for men, had fewer "standout" terms (expressions like *brilliant, superb, best, outstanding, unique, exceptional*), and more "grindstone" terms (expressions like *responsible, meticulous*).[5] The combination of fewer standout terms and more grindstone terms can make someone seem not terribly talented but hardworking.

In chemistry, letters for male and female candidates were very similar in length, substance, and use of grindstone expressions. There were, however, significantly more standout terms for men than women, even when their objective characteristics (such as number of publications) were the same. "Star" quality is more likely to be conferred on men than women. In psychology, letters of recommendation for assistant professorship positions in psychology included more terms associated with women—those that emphasize women's nurturance and communal characteristics—in letters for women than in letters for men. The letters were similar in length and general substance. Although communal characteristics might seem a plus for professors, they were rated by potential academic employers as actively detrimental (Madera et al., 2009). Thus, there are differences by field in how recommendations for men and women are written; overall the data suggest that women fare less well than men, though details vary from study to study.

Readers of letters are unlikely to be able to perform the kinds of analyses that experimenters do, looking at hundreds of letters from multiple searches. They are also unlikely to know a priori that they might be influenced by the use of standout terms. Standout terms, in our view, even in an era of inflated, say-nothing-bad styles of letter writing, have not yet lost their currency. To the extent that those terms are ones that readers nonconsciously search for and are affected by, women and (by inference) underrepresented minorities will be at a disadvantage.

We have discussed three ways that women and people of color may be at a disadvantage compared to White men during the initial review process: their PhDs are more likely to come from lower prestige institutions, they are less likely to be well-published and well-cited, and their letters of recommendation are likely to be weaker. Each of the effects is relatively small and by no means uniform: some White women and people of color, for example, have degrees from high-prestige institutions, have a strong publication history (which is correlated with being at a high-prestige institution), and have strong letters of recommendation. Equally, some White men do not have those achievements. On average, however, the proxies that are used to estimate quality favor White men.

Buffering against Bias in Creating a Medium-Short List or Short List

The creation of a medium-short list or final short list of candidates can be affected by all the issues we have raised. What can be done to reduce the effects of less diagnostic information when constructing a medium-short and short list? Deciding on who will screen the applications and how they will do it is crucial (see, e.g., Bauer & Baltes, 2002). In some institutions it appears to make sense to have one individual cut the large applicant pool in half by making a fast pass through the files to exclude those who do not meet eligibility requirements. Without a plan, however, that procedure invites, at a minimum, prestige bias: one individual or a small group may screen out individuals from certain kinds of institutions, or people with advisors they have never heard of, and so on. Since, as we have seen, women and people of color have fewer prestige markers, they have a higher chance of being eliminated at the beginning, before their merits are thoroughly reviewed.

Establish Valid Criteria   To buffer against the biases that informal and implicit criteria might introduce, we recommend establishing and using explicit criteria before review of candidates' materials. The process of adopting a consensual set of criteria to rate candidates provides an opportunity for the search committee or the department to be explicit about the relevant bases for judging applicants and potential applicants. The criteria should be valid and thus should relate to what the department wants in a faculty member. Perhaps published work will be considered more important than grant support; perhaps the reverse will be the case; perhaps both will be weighted equally. Perhaps ability to direct an MA or PhD program will be important. It is, of course, not enough to develop criteria. It is necessary to actually use the criteria and to assess applicants in terms of those agreed-upon criteria rather than in terms of some overall impression. All candidates must be evaluated by the same criteria to the same extent. What applies to recruitment (see chapter 5) also applies to the interview: for the formal part of the interview, all candidates must be asked the same questions, even if that seems slightly awkward.

Ensure Accountability   In general, accountability (e.g., to colleagues) and adequate time for making informed judgments are hallmarks of good decision-making processes (Arthur & Doverspike, 2005; Koch, D'Mello, & Sackett, 2015; Roberson, Galvin, & Charles, 2007). To facilitate evaluators' accountability, we recommend a formal list of the criteria on an "applicant evaluation sheet" (see box 6.1) that every reviewer completes for each applicant. The committee can then consider applicants with high average ratings by reviewers on any, some, or all criteria, as well as those rated high by *any* reviewer. That allows applicants whose strengths may be overlooked or underestimated by some reviewers to nevertheless surface in discussion. The tool can be adapted so that it will be appropriate for different searches and for different search stages. One might have a slightly different set of criteria for the first stage than for later stages.

Many institutions have adopted the practice of "short-list review" (see Bilimoria & Buch, 2010), in which search committees share their intended short list with the dean's office or other administrative office, along with a description of their efforts to generate a pool of diverse qualified applicants and information about the demographic makeup of the applicant pool. If the short list is less diverse than the applicant pool, the dean or the dean's delegate can then discuss the reasons for this departure from expectations, and, if it seems appropriate, stop what would otherwise be the next stage of inviting candidates to visit the campus. This form of accountability motivates search committees to ensure that their process is a good one. Further, one or two such actions on the part of the dean communicates the administration's seriousness of purpose and moves less motivated departments to redouble their efforts to attract diverse applicants.

In one case we know of, a department that had a short list with ten male candidates and no females was stopped from inviting any of them and was encouraged to review their pool and short list again. They came back to the dean with a new list that included several women. In the end, their top candidate—and the person they hired—was one of those women added only after the dean's intervention. Such experiences help persuade departments that they have been overlooking talent that was actually there. Deans and provosts can encourage diversity among interviewees by providing funds to invite more candidates to campus if the pool is a diverse pool.

Box 6.1
Applicant Evaluation Tool

The following offers a method for search committee members to provide evaluations of job applicants. It is meant to be a template that they can modify as necessary for their own uses. The proposed questions are designed for junior faculty candidates; however, alternate language is suggested in parentheses for senior faculty candidates. Committees often need two versions of the form, one for screening (based on less material) and one for reviewing full files for the long short list.

Applicant's name:

Please indicate which of the following are true for you (check all that apply):

☐ Read applicant's CV
☐ Read applicant's statements (re research, teaching, etc.)
☐ Read applicant's letters of recommendation
☐ Read applicant's scholarship (indicate what): _____

Please rate the applicant on each of the following:	excellent	good	neutral	fair	poor	unable to judge
Evidence of scholarly productivity						
Evidence of creativity and innovation in research/scholarship						
Potential for [Record of] scholarly impact/tenurability						
Potential for [Record of] funding (if appropriate to field)						
Evidence of strong background in [relevant fields]						
Contribution to breadth of areas addressed in department research						
Evidence of teaching experience and interest (including grad mentorship)						
Potential [Ability] to teach courses in core curriculum						
Potential [Ability] to teach and advise diverse students						
Potential [Ability] to contribute new course coverage to the curriculum						
Potential [Ability] to contribute positively to the collegial work environment of the department						

Other comments?

For more information or additional copies of this resource, please contact the ADVANCE Program at (734) 647–9359 or advanceprogram@umich.edu, or visit the ADVANCE Program's website at http://advance.umich.edu/stride Resources.php

Attend to Pool Composition   Given the risk of underrating women and people of color, we recommend that search committees attend at the outset to the ratio of male and female, and White and non-White, applicants in the applicant pool. If the ratios do not match the availability pool, the committee can investigate why that is the case and try to bring the applicant pool numbers up at least to the levels of the availability pool. Depending on the field, different ways of estimating the pool will be appropriate, as discussed in chapter 5. In some fields, the PhD rate will be appropriate. In others, the postdoctoral fellowship rate will be more appropriate.

Only by continuing to monitor the composition of successive pools can the committee determine whether it might be using irrelevant criteria to filter candidates (Sagaria, 2002). Useful equity benchmarks include the number and percentage of women and underrepresented minorities in each successive pool after the applicant pool: the preinterview pool, the medium-short list pool, the interview pool, the offer pool, and the candidate acceptance pool. Those benchmarks help the committee see what criteria are being used—or misused. If the ratios of male to female, and White to non-White, increase as the pools narrow, that is a reason to assess the criteria and their application. That will take time, and committees often feel pressed for time. It may nevertheless be necessary to alter the timeline and create procedures that will broaden the pool, even at a late date.

The Interview Stage

As electronic means of interviewing people become more feasible, more search committees interview as many as 10–12 candidates using video-conferencing or teleconferences of approximately one-half hour each, with all committee members present for each interview, and with all questions determined ahead of time by the committee. Some schools stack a large number of 30-minute interviews at annual meetings. An advantage of a preinterview is that search committee members may be more willing to include nontraditional, "riskier" candidates in a large set of interviews than in a small set. A preinterview also provides an opportunity for search committees to see whether their medium-short list adequately represents the pool. Finally, preinterviews, because of their brevity and the need to compare many candidates, lend themselves to a structured interview approach that is much less likely to be adopted in the later interview stage. Structured interviews help eliminate demographic effects (Levashina, Hartwell, Morgeson, & Campion, 2014; McCarthy, Van Iddekinge, & Campion, 2010).

If the interview is structured in order to obtain the most job-relevant information from candidates, that information will serve to individuate one candidate from another. The more individuating information interviewers have about applicants, the less likely they are to rely on demographic information (Kunda & Thagard, 1996), although we have reason to believe that gender can survive individuating information (Chan & Mendelsohn, 2010; Mondschein, Adolph, & Tamis-LeMonda, 2000). As a meta-analysis demonstrated, individuating information did not lessen the extent to which decision makers tended to prefer males for male-dominated positions (Koch et al., 2015).

People are not generally motivated to search for individuating information. Everyone is a cognitive miser, hoping to do the most with the least, to make a judgment quickly and with as little effort as possible. Thus, people need external motivation to overcome their internal cognitive miserliness. The presence of panels that perform the structured interviews helps provide that external motivation because panelists are accountable to each other. The benefit of structured interviews can still be limited, however, if a powerful individual on the panel sets a tone that the less powerful individuals on the panel go along with. The benefit can also be limited if the panels themselves are limited. Two White men might find it difficult to treat each candidate similarly in the less quantifiable aspects of their behavior that can affect candidates' performance. Such aspects as speech errors, interruptions, displays of nonverbal dominance, and failure to look at the candidate while he or she is speaking can impair candidates' performance (e.g., Latu & Mast, 2016).

Structured interviews help ensure that every element of the interview is completed for every applicant, which prevents interviewers from stopping the interview too early. In a less structured context, they may be tempted not to complete the interview, or stop the interview early because they already feel confident that the candidate is a good choice or that the candidate is a bad choice. Structured interviews reduce group differences in ratings (Levashina et al., 2014).

Structured Interviews
Both the preinterview and the interview with the search committee during an on-campus visit can be structured. What counts as a good structured interview? One list contains 15 characteristics (McCarthy et al., 2010). We

summarize them in order to demonstrate how few desiderata most interviews of candidates adhere to. Questions in the interview should be targeted to the characteristics that are optimal for success in the job, so that interviewers' attention will be directed to those characteristics rather than demographic characteristics. The intent can be subverted by developing questions that are not genuinely job-success-related ones, so it's best if the questions are developed by a working group that explicitly pays attention to job-relevant characteristics.

Seven of McCarthy et al.'s (2010) characteristics are as follows:

1. the interviews are based on a comprehensive job analysis

2. within the interviews, the same questions are asked of each candidate, and within the experience-based interview, similar questions are asked of each candidate

3. the use of prompts and follow-up questions is limited

4. different questioning techniques are employed (e.g., ones focused on past experience vs. hypothetical situations)

5. each interview allows sufficient time for interviewers to ask several questions

6. ancillary information is controlled

7. candidates are encouraged to ask questions after the structured phase of the interview process is complete

Human resources departments may conduct such job analyses and develop clear and specific questions, but academics seldom go beyond stating that they want someone who will be a productive, grant-funded researcher with good teaching skills and collegial departmental behavior. Once the candidate is on campus, he or she may have several interviews with individual faculty and lunch or coffee with small groups of faculty, in addition to having a meeting with the entire search committee. How the unofficial interviewers acquire information is typically up to each individual to decide. The assembly of information is fairly flexible.

In terms of requirements 1–7, academic interviews generally do well on having enough time (number 5), but perhaps less so on inviting the candidate to ask questions (7) or on limiting prompts and follow-up questions (3), using multiple questioning techniques (4), or even knowing what such techniques are! Results are usually mixed at best on conducting a comprehensive job analysis, asking the same or similar questions across interviews, and controlling ancillary information (1, 2, and 6). This spotty success suggests that interviewing deserves much more care and attention than it currently receives.

Requirements 8–15 from McCarthy et al. (2010) are as follows:

8. interviewers evaluate each dimension using behaviorally anchored rating scales

9. descriptive scale anchors are derived from…definitions [from] previously developed interviews and responses from previous candidates

10. interviewers are trained on the importance of note taking during the interview process

11. a panel of two interviewers evaluates each candidate

12. the same set of interviewers conducts the interviews for each applicant

13. the interviewers do not discuss candidates between interviews

14. all interviewers are extensively trained to ensure proficiency in conducting and scoring the interview

15. statistical procedures (unit weighting) are used to combine ratings within each interview

Who does all of that? We think it is safe to say: no one. Who would be willing to do it? We think it is also safe to say: in academia, pretty much no one. Although it is encouraging to know that one can eliminate demographic effects with a lot of effort, it is sobering to recognize how likely one is to be affected by gender and race without that effort.

On-Campus Interviews

On-campus visits by the candidate typically last at least one day and often last two days. They include a variety of activities, including, at a minimum, a "job talk" in which the candidate covers his or her work. Often three or four candidates are invited to campus over a period of a few weeks. Many faculty (and students) beyond the initial search committee are likely to participate. At the interview visit, candidates in some science fields may be also asked to give a "chalk talk," in which they present more technical material than would be appropriate for a talk that the entire department will attend; at least one member of the search committee typically attends. At many schools, candidates also give a sample lecture to a class in their topic area, a lecture which is attended by at least one member of the search committee. Candidates generally have a session with the entire search committee and are asked an established set of questions. Candidates meet with other faculty, administrators, and undergraduate and graduate students, and they see the facilities. This broader contact, and weaker structure, allows many things to happen that may be irrelevant to assessing the candidate's "merit."

Some people interview beautifully and some interview badly. It is difficult for search committees to properly weigh interview performance against the years of performance testified to by the person's work. The very thin slice of behavior one gets at an interview can dominate the search committee's impression. One can be much more or much less impressed by a candidate in person than one was by their record. Although we know of no way to compensate for our tendency to pay too much attention to an in-person impression, we caution search committees about this tendency. People are very confident about their ability to detect someone's merit. The unstructured interview lends itself to false confirmation because people primarily seek information that will confirm their views. People tend to do worse at predicting behavior when they rely on unstructured information than when they rely on solid information (Dana, Dawes, & Peterson, 2013; Kausel, Culbertson, & Madrid, 2016).

Candidates who come from less prestigious institutions may have been less well prepped for their visit than those who come from more prestigious institutions. Although most candidates know that it's good to practice their talks multiple times ahead of time and develop answers to the questions they might be asked, many fewer candidates, in our experience, undergo mock interviews at their own campus. Some candidates do not know until a few days before the visit what the interview will be like.

Search committees can help level the playing field by posting on their website what a visit will involve and by giving candidates an idea of what they are looking for at each event. Search committees can also suggest how candidates can prepare for their on-campus visit, and they can bring up topics (like disability or lactation needs) that might be difficult for the candidate to raise. At the same time, we acknowledge the value in seeing how a candidate handles an unexpected question. A good search committee will try to bring out the best in each candidate without producing cookie-cutter interviews. It is a delicate balance. Just as there is an art to interviewing well as an interviewee, there is an art to interviewing well as an interviewer.

Especially in the transition from the preinterview (if there is one) to the interview, and in the transition from the interview to the offer, search committee members who differ demographically from the job candidates may be hard-pressed to maintain subtle behaviors that will bring out the best in a candidate. For example, White male interviewers may be less comfortable in interviewing women and people of color compared to other White men. If so, they will be less likely to bring out the qualities that will show the candidate at his or her best and less successful in interpreting a candidate's interest. The very people who come to the interview at a disadvantage, for the reasons we outlined earlier, can also be at a disadvantage because of deficits in interviewers' abilities.

One early study examined White male students' behavior with other students who were, unknown to the participants, confederates of the experimenter (Word, Zanna, & Cooper, 1974). The confederates were White or African American. The students were White. The students' task was to interview the student they were paired with for a job as a peer counselor. Students who were paired with an African American confederate produced more filled pauses (e.g., *uh*, *er*) and other speech errors, sat farther away, and completed the interview faster than did the students who were paired with a White confederate. Although that study was conducted in 1974, recent research suggests that the same processes were at work in 2016, this time in a study that had one student teach another student (Jacoby-Senghor, Sinclair, & Shelton, 2016).

Research in Switzerland suggests that gender schemas play a role when men interview women in a laboratory setting for a fictitious position as a marketing manager (Latu & Mast, 2016; Latu, Mast, & Stewart, 2015). In one suggestive study, men who adopted a dominant style in interviewing, by looking at the female candidate more while he was talking than when he was listening, and by interrupting her more, had an effect on the women who were being interviewed. (Only women were selected to be interviewed.) Both the women's self-evaluation and the men's evaluation of the women were lower when the men were dominant. When women were the interviewers, their dominance level did not have an effect on candidates, but the number of women interviewers was too small to be definitive.

We conclude that White male interviewers are likely to do a worse job of interviewing women than men, and of interviewing African Americans compared to Whites—at least if people use unstructured interviews. Academic interviews are probably less structured than employment interviews in the business sector, in part because so many different individuals participate in job interviews in academia, most of whom have little or no training in interviewing. In highly structured interviews, as we have mentioned, there are no demographic effects (McCarthy et al., 2010). That is, it does not matter what the sex, race, or ethnicity of the interviewers or interviewees is if the interviewers are adhering to highly structured guidelines. It may also be helpful to ensure that all candidate interviews are conducted with at least two people present, so that problematic questions or assertions from an interviewer can be addressed by the other person present.

How the interviewers represent the school will affect that candidate's interest in coming to it. Interviewers must not ask any illegal questions! Candidates know that questions about age, partners, marriage, and plans for children are illegal. Some interviewers, with the best will in the world, think that casual queries over dinner at the end of an interview day are outside the interview proper and do not count. They do count. The interview starts the moment the candidate is contacted and ends only when someone has been hired. Throughout that period, the candidate is in interview mode. At no point is it permissible to ask about someone's personal life. The interviewer may think that knowledge of the candidate's personal needs will make it easier to let the candidate know what accommodations can be made. Nevertheless, it is illegal.

What interviewers do not anticipate is that some personal questions may be very painful for a candidate. The candidate may have recently ended a relationship, or may have a partner, relative, or friend who is ill or recently died, or may have just learned that they are infertile, or may have experienced any one of a number of other difficult life events. Interviewers are not generally thinking about how a question might be upsetting for a candidate, especially since they see themselves as being friendly and sympathetic. But any personal information that a job candidate does not volunteer should be personal information that the interviewer does not ask the candidate to divulge.

The candidate faced with an illegal question is in a quandary. African Americans, for example, may be asked how they would feel about being in a community that is not racially diverse. Women may be asked whether they are married or are planning on having a child. Candidates do not want to appear churlish, but they also do not want their personal life to be part of the interview. The late Denice Denton said that when she was asked such questions, she answered, "Does that matter?" Not everyone has the confidence, or perhaps seniority and standing, to pull that off. Another possible answer that candidates who are just finishing their degrees or post-docs could provide, is, "Oh, I'm under strict orders from my supervisor (or mentor) not to answer any personal questions," said with a smile. We suggest that candidates practice an answer ahead of time, try it out on various colleagues, tweak it if necessary, and be prepared to use it to answer any question that seems personal. But no matter how tactful or friendly such a response is, it runs the risk of alienating interviewers.

What *can* interviewers do if they are interested in attracting women and people of color as faculty? We recommend that interviewers treat all candidates as similarly as possible and indicate to *every* candidate—no matter their gender, or race, or ethnicity, or sexual orientation, or religion—that the department and institution value diversity (if that is true!). Departments benefit from providing that information to everyone, not only White women and minority women and men; everyone needs to know that they are going to be in a community that values diversity (if, of course, it does). Departments and other offices at the institution can indicate the kinds of supports that it provides. Examples would be support to faculty partners in the hiring process, support in the form of childcare resources and family-friendly policies, and techniques for addressing work-family conflicts, such as stop-the-clock policies. In the ideal case, the department will provide every candidate with full information about all types of faculty support policies and resources. It will also schedule a meeting between the candidate and someone who is not in the department, of whom the candidate can ask questions about what it is like to live there, without concerns that his or her questions will be relayed back to the department. Such community ambassadors should be knowledgeable about matters of concern to diverse groups. Those efforts will help convince otherwise skeptical candidates that the department and school is committed to inclusion and diversity.

One issue an African American may have about small towns, for example, is the availability of services. Single women and men may wonder whether the local social life is couple centered or more diverse. Gay men and women can wonder whether the local community accepts individuals who are out and whether there are centers of community for gay men and lesbians. Muslims may be concerned about whether there is a mosque or a halal butcher in the community, as well as whether there are intense pressures to drink alcohol. Jews may wonder about the presence of stores where they can buy kosher food and how far away a synagogue is. Everyone can wonder about something. A school benefits by knowing what it is like for members of different groups to live in their community. One of us was on a site visit to a research-intensive school in a somewhat rural area and heard women faculty talking about what a terrible place it was to be a straight single woman. The culture was couple centered, and there were virtually no straight single men. Straight single women spent a lot of time trying to figure out how to leave—and did leave.

If schools want to increase the diversity of their faculty, they have to spend some time helping to make the community attractive to their faculty. Every location has advantages and disadvantages. Some disadvantages can be ameliorated. For example, a school can advocate with local retail stores for inclusion of a wider range of products for diverse customers, and it can document for faculty and faculty applicants the nearest synagogues, mosques, and community groups that offer cultural support to particular immigrant groups.

Negotiation of the Offer

The final stage of recruitment is critical. It is often the case that issues that arise in the course of negotiations, if not satisfactorily addressed, affect the transition onto campus and future retention success. A good offer takes into account a candidate's needs and desires, is communicated with enthusiasm, and presents terms that can be negotiated.

Person-Specific Hiring

As noted at the end of chapter 5, some faculty recruitment involves person-specific hiring. In such cases—recruiting partners of candidates identified in regular searches or faculty who would bring special diversity and excellence to the department—the goal is to hire someone who will be valued and successful at the institution. For that reason, it is ideal to use procedures that mirror those involved in regular searches as closely as possible. Thus, it is best to engage a group within the department in the process of assessing the candidate's qualifications, using the same kinds of evidence and the same kinds of evaluation tools that are used in regular searches. Similarly, the visit of the candidate to campus should be conducted in exactly the same way that all candidates' visits are handled, and the postvisit decision should be managed in the same way as well. A detailed account of one institution's procedures aimed for this situation is contained in the University of Michigan's Handbook for Faculty Recruitment and Hiring (advance.umich.edu /resources/handbook.pdf). There are other accounts on other institutions' websites, particularly those that have participated in the NSF ADVANCE program.

Summary

Evaluating job candidates requires skill, and whenever there is a demographic imbalance between the search committee members and the candidates, more skill is required. Everyone is likely to be influenced by prestige, gender, ethnicity, and other schemas when making evaluations. The challenge can be met in part by developing procedures that are designed to protect against unintentional error. No set of procedures will accomplish that perfectly, but the better the procedures, the better the likely outcome.

Recommendations for Practices that Increase the Fairness of the Evaluation Process

Provosts, Deans, and Department Chairs

1. Always express the twin goals of (1) excellence in scholarship, teaching, and service and (2) diversity in faculty hiring. Encourage confidence that the two goals are mutually compatible and indeed mutually reinforcing.

2. Consider the adoption of "short-list review"; if adopted, enforce use of diverse pools.

3. Publicly praise and consider rewarding departments or other units that succeed in increasing the diversity and excellence in their faculty. Describe the ways they accomplished this achievement to encourage others.

4. Provide resources for stages of the process if needed to increase diversity and fairness (e.g., more funding for travel for more candidates, development of materials to reflect the institution's values and commitments in the best light, data about past searches, demographic characteristics of units, etc.).

Search Committee Members

1. Be sure your application packet includes what you want and does not include material you do not want, at each stage. Consider limiting the number of papers or writing samples submitted in order to focus on quality.

2. Consider postponing review of letters of recommendation until later in the process (after initial decisions based on review of the actual work).

3. Set out explicit criteria for evaluating candidates early in the process and continually monitor your own and other committee members' comments for evidence of drift from the criteria or differential application of them to different candidates. Be particularly alert to comments that reflect known gender, race, and family status biases.

4. Avoid relying on proxies for assessing the quality of candidates' work. Read the work, and discuss it with your colleagues.

5. When sharing applicants' work, minimize identifying cues that might lead to reliance on prestige or quantity indicators that are only proxies for quality.

6. Be sure decisions about who will be retained in the pool are made by multiple judges at every stage.

7. During preinterviews (if they occur), use structured interview procedures thoughtfully.

8. During interviews, schedule a structured interview between the candidate and the search committee.

9. Design the candidates' on-campus visits carefully, with attention to issues of differential comfort with different situations. Consider ensuring that interviews always involve more than one person. (People monitor themselves differently if there is an observer.)

10. Monitor the pool at all stages of the process; always be open to extending a stage of the process in the interest of ensuring a broad enough pool of candidates to review.

Department Faculty Members

1. It is optimal if all members of a department understand issues of bias and evaluation. Take steps to educate yourself.

2. Participate in a serious way in the visit process. Review the candidates' dossiers in advance, taking special care to read their work. Attend the talk(s) that you can, and participate in interviewing candidates if you can.

Consider interviewing with another colleague or two who have a different background and approach than yours.

3. Be careful to avoid unintended negative effects of asking personal questions.

Applicants for Faculty Positions

1. White women and underrepresented minority candidates can learn how to address the possible deficiencies in their interviewers' styles.

2. Practice expressing your suitability, and show enthusiasm for the job. It is useful to practice with people who deliberately take a laconic approach, and who deliberately take an aggressive approach, including interrupting.

Notes

1. Ratings of job performance depend on the extent of fit between someone's vocational interest profile and the occupation's profile (Nye et al., 2012). Such congruence indices moderately predict ratings of job performance and employee persistence. To create a congruence index, an individual's three major interest categories and an occupation's three major interest categories are compared. A congruence index measures the extent to which the resulting profiles match. When there is high overlap, ratings of job performance are higher. Thus, interest ratings can be helpful for counseling people about what jobs to pursue. Note, however, that the interest ratings for an occupation are based on attributes of the current practitioners of an occupation.

2. This is on the assumption that *U.S. News and World Report* (USNWR) rankings accurately represent prestige. The size and wealth of a university or college, the salary of the faculty, the student-faculty ratio, and the students' SAT scores together account for almost 90% of the variance in USNWR rankings (Volkwein & Sweitzer, 2006). If one assumes that such indicators appropriately assess prestige, then, indeed, the rankings are valid. Other rankings, such as the Shanghai Jai Tong University *Academic Ranking of World Universities*, are responsive to two main, uncorrelated, factors: the number of world-famous researchers and the overall productivity of researchers (Dehon, McCathie, & Verardi, 2010). Those are factors that search committee members are likely to be responsive to, since fame, by definition, means that someone is well-known, and since the more publications an institution produces, the more likely it is that a random search committee member will have come across one. University ranking is complex. The distribution of universities seems to follow a Zipfian curve, with the top 50 or so universities being discriminable, but the mass of universities varies little one from the other in both number of world-famous figures and productivity (Dehon et al., 2010).

3. We computed these percentages from 2015 NSF data (N=55,006) at https://ncses
.norc.org/NSFTabEngine/#TABULATION. Seventy-seven percent of Asians, 72% of
Whites, 73% of Hispanics, and 50% of African Americans received their degrees from
institutions classified by the Carnegie Commission as having very high research
activity. African Americans comprised only 5% of this in 2015. Fifty percent of the
available pool of African Americans would be lost at the outset if search committees used prestige of institution to create their first list of possible candidates. Tests
of independent proportions showed that Hispanics and Whites did not differ, but
Asians were better represented among schools with very high research activity than
were Whites, $z = 11.958$, $p < .0002$. African Americans were significantly less well represented than any other group, z (comparison with Hispanics) $= -18.475$, $p < .0002$. A
higher proportion of men than women received their degrees from very high research
activity universities, $z = 14.789$, $p < 0.0002$.

4. In mathematics it may not be possible to adopt this strategy. One mathemati-
cian told us that he might have to spend hours on a single paragraph in a paper to
understand it and determine its contribution. For most fields that we are familiar
with, that issue doesn't arise.

5. There were too few letters from women to do an analysis of letter writer by gender.

References

Apfelbaum, E. P., Norton, M. I., & Sommers, S. R. (2012). Racial color blindness:
Emergence, practice, and implications. *Current Directions in Psychological Science*,
21(3), 205–209.

Apfelbaum, E. P., Pauker, K., Sommers, S. R., & Ambady, N. (2010). In blind pursuit
of racial equality? *Psychological Science, 21*, 1587–1592.

Arthur, W., Jr., & Doverspike, D. (2005). Achieving diversity and reducing discrimination in the workplace through human resource management practices: Implications of research and theory for staffing, training, and rewarding performance. In
R. L. Dipboye & A. Colella (Eds.), *Discrimination at work: The psychological and organizational bases* (pp. 325–327). San Francisco, CA: Jossey-Bass.

Bauer, C. C., & Baltes, B. B. (2002). Reducing the effects of gender stereotypes on performance evaluations. *Sex Roles, 47*(9–10), 465–476. doi:10.1023/A:1021652527696

Bertrand, M., & Mullainathan, S. (2003). *Are Emily and Greg more employable than
Lakisha and Jamal? A field experiment on labor market discrimination* (Working Paper
9873). Cambridge, MA: National Bureau of Economic Research.

Bilimoria, D., & Buch, K. K. (2010). The search is on: Engendering faculty diversity through more effective search and recruitment. *Change: The Magazine of Higher
Learning, 42*(4), 27–32.

Carnegie Foundation for the Advancement of Teaching. (2006). *The Carnegie Classification of Institutions of Higher Education* (2005 edition). Menlo Park, CA: Author.

Carnes, M., Devine, P. G., Baier Manwell, L., Byars-Winston, A., Fine, E., Ford, C. E., et al. (2015). The effect of an intervention to break the gender bias habit for faculty at one institution: A cluster randomized, controlled trial. *Academic Medicine, 90,* 221–230.

Chan, W., & Mendelsohn, G. A. (2010). Disentangling stereotype and person effects: Do social stereotypes bias observer judgments of personality? *Journal of Research in Personality, 44*(2), 251–257.

Clauset, A., Arbesman, S., & Larremore, D. B. (2015). Systematic inequality and hierarchy in faculty hiring networks. *Science Advances, 1*(1), e1400005.

Correll, S. J., Benard, S., & Paik, I. (2007). Getting a job: Is there a motherhood penalty? *American Journal of Sociology, 112,* 1297–1338.

Correll, S. J., Kelly, E. L., O'Connor, L. T., & Williams, J. C. (2014). Redesigning, redefining work. *Work and Occupations, 41*(1), 3–17.

Dana, J., Dawes, R., & Peterson, N. (2013). Belief in the unstructured interview: The persistence of an illusion. *Judgment and Decision Making, 8*(5), 512–520.

Dehon, C., McCathie, A., & Verardi, V. (2010). Uncovering excellence in academic rankings: A closer look at the Shanghai ranking. *Scientometrics, 83*(2), 515–524.

Devine, P. G., Forscher, P. S., Austin, A. J., & Cox, W. T. (2012). Long-term reduction in implicit race bias: A prejudice habit-breaking intervention. *Journal of Experimental Social Psychology, 48*(6), 1267–1278.

Eloy, J. A., Svider, P. F., Cherla, D. V., Diaz, L., Kovalerchik, O., Mauro, K. M., et al. (2013). Gender disparities in research productivity among 9952 academic physicians. *Laryngoscope, 123*(8), 1865–1875.

Forscher, P. S., Mitamura, C., Dix, E. L., Cox, W. T., & Devine, P. G. (2017). Breaking the prejudice habit: Mechanisms, timecourse, and longevity. *Journal of Experimental Social Psychology, 72,* 133–146.

Gompers, P. A., & Wang, S. Q. (2017). *Diversity in innovation* (NBER Working Paper No. w23082). Cambridge, MA: National Bureau of Economic Research.

Headworth, S., & Freese, J. (2015). Credential privilege or cumulative advantage? Prestige, productivity, and placement in the academic sociology job market. *Social Forces, 94*(3), 1257–1282.

Heilman, M., & Okimoto, T. G. (2008). Why are women penalized for success at male tasks? The implied communality deficit. *Journal of Applied Psychology, 92*(1), 81–92.

Holliday, E. B., Jagsi, R., Wilson, L. D., Choi, M., Thomas, C. R., Jr., & Fuller, C. D. (2014). Gender differences in publication productivity, academic position, career duration and funding among US academic radiation oncology faculty. *Academic Medicine: Journal of the Association of American Medical Colleges, 89*(5), 767–773.

Jacoby-Senghor, D. S., Sinclair, S., & Shelton, J. N. (2016). A lesson in bias: The relationship between implicit racial bias and performance in pedagogical contexts. *Journal of Experimental Social Psychology, 63*, 50–55.

Kausel, E. E., Culbertson, S. S., & Madrid, H. P. (2016). Overconfidence in personnel selection: When and why unstructured interview information can hurt hiring decisions. *Organizational Behavior and Human Decision Processes, 137*, 27–44.

King, M. M., Bergstrom, C. T., Correll, S. J., Jacquet, J., & West, J. D. (2016). Men set their own cites high: Gender and self-citation across fields and over time. *arXiv preprint* arXiv:1607.00376.

Koch, A. J., D'Mello, S. D., & Sackett, P. R. (2015). A meta-analysis of gender stereotypes and bias in experimental simulations of employment decision making. *Journal of Applied Psychology, 100*(1), 128–161.

Kouchaki, M. (2011). Vicarious moral licensing: The influence of others' past moral actions on moral behavior. *Journal of Personality and Social Psychology, 101*(4), 702–715.

Kunda, Z., & Thagard, P. (1996). Forming impressions from stereotypes, traits, and behaviors: A parallel-constraint-satisfaction theory. *Psychological Review, 103*(2), 284–308.

Latu, I. M., & Mast, M. S. (2016). Male interviewers' nonverbal dominance predicts lower evaluations of female applicants in simulated job interviews. *Journal of Personnel Psychology, 15*, 116–124.

Latu, I. M., Mast, M. S., & Stewart, T. L. (2015). Gender biases in (inter)action: The role of interviewers' and applicants' implicit and explicit stereotypes in predicting women's job interview outcomes. *Psychology of Women Quarterly, 39*, 539–552.

Latu, I. M., & Mast, M. S. (2016). Male interviewers' nonverbal dominance predicts lower evaluations of female applicants in simulated job interviews. *Journal of Personnel Psychology, 15*, 116–124.

Levashina, J., Hartwell, C. J., Morgeson, F. P., & Campion, M. A. (2014). The structured employment interview: Narrative and quantitative review of the research literature. *Personnel Psychology, 67*(1), 241–293.

Madera, J., Hebl, M., & Martin, R. (2009). Gender and letters of recommendation for academia: Agentic and communal differences. *Journal of Applied Psychology, 94*(6), 1591–1599.

Maliniak, D., Powers, R., & Walter, B. F. (2013). The gender citation gap in international relations. *International Organization, 67*(4), 889–922.

McCarthy, J. M., Van Iddekinge, C. H., & Campion, M. A. (2010). Are highly structured job interviews resistant to demographic similarity effects? *Personnel Psychology, 63*(2), 325–359.

Mondschein, E. R., Adolph, K. E., & Tamis-LeMonda, C. S. (2000). Gender bias in mothers' expectations about infant crawling. *Journal of Experimental Child Psychology, 77*(4), 304–316.

Monteith, M. J., Ashburn-Nardo, L., Voils, C. I., & Czopp, A. M. (2002). Putting the brakes on prejudice: On the development and operation of cues for control. *Journal of Personality and Social Psychology, 83*(5), 1029–1050.

Moskowitz, G. B., & Li, P. (2011). Egalitarian goals trigger stereotype inhibition: A proactive form of stereotype control. *Journal of Experimental Social Psychology, 47*(1), 103–116.

Nye, C., Su, R., Rounds, J., & Drasgow, F. (2012). Vocational interests and performance: A quantitative summary of over 60 years of research. *Perspectives on Psychological Science, 7*(4), 384–403.

Okimoto, T. G., & Heilman, M. E. (2012). The "bad parent" assumption: How gender stereotypes affect reactions to working mothers. *Journal of Social Issues, 68*(4), 704–724.

Oprisko, R. L., Dobbs, K. L., & DiGrazia, J. (2013). Pushing up ivies: Institutional prestige and the academic caste system. *Georgetown Public Policy Review*. Retrieved from http://gppreview.com/2013/08/21/pushing-up-ivies-institutional-prestige-and -the-academic-caste-system/

Pinheiro, D., Melkers, J., & Youtie, J. (2014). Learning to play the game: Student publishing as an indicator of future scholarly success. *Technological Forecasting and Social Change, 81*, 56–66.

Roberson, L., Galvin, B. M., & Charles, A. C. (2007). When group identities matter: Bias in performance appraisal. *Academy of Management Annals, 1*(1), 617–650.

Sachdeva, S., Iliev, R., & Medin, D. L. (2009). Sinning saints and saintly sinners: The paradox of moral self-regulation. *Psychological Science, 20*(4), 523–528.

Sagaria, M. A. D. (2002). An exploratory model of filtering in administrative searches: Toward counter-hegemonic discourses. *Journal of Higher Education, 73*(6), 677–710.

Schmader, T., Whitehead, J., & Wysocki, V. H. (2007). A linguistic comparison of letters of recommendation for male and female chemistry and biochemistry job applicants. *Sex Roles, 57*, 509–514.

Sheltzer, J. M., & Smith, J. C. (2014). Elite male faculty in the life sciences employ fewer women. *Proceedings of the National Academy of Sciences of the United States of America, 111*(28), 10107–10112.

Stewart, A. J., Malley, J. E., & Herzog, K. A. (2016). Increasing the representation of women in STEM departments: What makes a difference? *Journal of Women and Minorities in Science and Engineering, 22*(1), 23–47.

Sugimoto, C. R., Lariviere, V., Ni, C., Gingras, Y., & Cronin, B. (2013). Global gender disparities in science. *Nature, 504*(7479), 211–213.

Trix, F., & Psenka, C. (2003). Exploring the color of glass: Letters of recommendation for female and male medical school faculty. *Discourse & Society, 14*(2), 191–220.

University of Michigan ADVANCE Program. (2009, May). *Positive and problematic practices in faculty recruitment.* Unpublished report available online: http://advance.umich.edu/resources/PositiveAndProblematic_RecruitmentPractices.pdf

Valian, V. (1998). *Why so slow? The advancement of women.* Cambridge, MA: MIT Press.

Valian, V. (2014). Interests, gender, and science. *Perspectives on Psychological Science, 9*(2), 225–230.

van Arensbergen, P., van der Weijden, I., & Van den Besselaar, P. (2012). Gender differences in scientific productivity: A persisting phenomenon? *Scientometrics, 93*(3), 857–868.

Volkwein, J. F., & Sweitzer, K. V. (2006). Institutional prestige and reputation among research universities and liberal arts colleges. *Research in Higher Education, 47*(2), 129–148.

Word, C. O., Zanna, M. P., & Cooper, J. (1974). The nonverbal mediation of self-fulfilling prophecies in interracial interaction. *Journal of Experimental Social Psychology, 10*(2), 109–120.

Xie, Y., & Shauman, K. A. (1998). Sex differences in research productivity: New evidence about an old puzzle. *American Sociological Review, 63*(6), 847–870.

7 Retaining Faculty: Building Community in the Academic Workplace

Once new faculty members have been hired, it is, of course, critical to retain them—ideally by offering them a good work environment, one that provides them with adequate resources to do their work and a sense of shared purpose and community. If we are more successful at retaining some groups of faculty than others, then we may undo our efforts at diversifying the faculty by failing to keep the very faculty we worked hard to hire. In this chapter we review the issues that arise in retaining faculty with different backgrounds and needs, in the hope that our academic workplaces can become truly inclusive communities.

Should Institutions Retain Every Faculty Member?

We all talk to faculty who are thinking about leaving their positions at any given college or university, and we hear many different kinds of stories. When a colleague leaves one institution for another because the new position offers some gain in location, resources for the faculty member's research, teaching, or administrative aspirations, or her overall family well-being, colleagues often generally support the plan and view the individual's decision-making as rational.

In this chapter we want to consider such perfectly sensible ideas from the perspective of the institution. In every case, the individuals were recruited and hired as a result of great effort and with hope (on the part of at least some people) that a productive and satisfying connection would develop between the person and the institution. Many people (the hiring committee, faculty in the same or related fields, administrators) worked hard to make a wise choice and to provide the individual with the initial resources to make the relationship work. Nevertheless, at some point a faculty member may decide that there is not enough value in the relationship to retain it. Moreover, a faculty member hired to add diversity to a department may experience that department as an unpleasant work environment. Let's consider some stories we have heard along these lines:

A White woman was hired into a science department right out of her PhD program; she was viewed as a rising star in a difficult field, was offered a substantial start-up, and was told about the department's—and university's—resources for supporting the success of all scientists, including women and minorities. Her first year was very successful in terms of her research, including several publications and the securing of major grant support. However, her teaching did not go well; she had never taught before and sought out help from the department and campus teaching support programs. She felt it could go better the next year. At the end of the year she had received a below-average raise and sought out reasons for this decision. She was very angry to learn that her difficulties with teaching completely outweighed her scholarly progress. Efforts to understand what happened led to conversations with senior colleagues in which she felt patronized and dismissed. She started looking around for other positions and eventually left, despite a matching counteroffer.

A male African American senior faculty member was achieving significant recognition in his field and was increasingly noticed by higher university officials as having a lot to contribute. He often talked with friends about the many occasions on which his colleagues had dismissed or belittled his opinions and values, over many years in the department. He worked hard to improve things for women and minorities in his field. Eventually he was appointed to a major leadership role on campus but found that this changed nothing in his department; he felt his departmental colleagues did not respect him, and he concluded they never would. He responded to an invitation to apply for a major leadership role at another institution, and he left.

A woman was hired by a department that prided itself on its high standards. She had a partner in a related field, and they hired him, too. Over many years she maintained the respect of many of her colleagues in the department, but she carried scars. Though generally quiet and reserved, she once held a large audience on campus spellbound while she recounted the story of the discouraging and offensive treatment she endured as a female junior faculty member from senior men who were ostensibly her "mentors." She rarely brought such stories up; however, when asked, she told of many painful interactions in the department. As she rose to prominence in her field, her partner longed for opportunities that would fit his talents better. When he found them, she left as well.

In all of these cases, work relationships that got off to a good start quickly soured and in all three cases ended badly at the original institution. The first story—of the new assistant professor—ended with the departure of the faculty member who had helped diversity, while contributing to the department's excellence in research. The seeds of discontent were planted early, and as her successes accumulated, she chose to leave behind a department that made her feel unwelcome when she was just getting started. Alternatively, the environment's cool response to her first year could instead have set in motion a cascade of self-doubt, lower productivity, and unhappiness of the sort that leads to a failure to thrive professionally and an unsuccessful tenure case. As we have seen from the other stories, scars acquired early last a long time. Without even considering the costs to the individual, both of these outcomes are costly for institutions.

Happily, these kinds of stories can be avoided. Faculty are a precious resource for universities; universities invest time and money in recruiting them. Their teaching, scholarship, and citizenship over many years shape the nature and reputation of the institution. It stands to reason that institutions seek to protect this investment. This does not mean that every faculty member who is recruited will be happy and successful where they are hired, nor that those who are successful will never be interested in pursuing another position elsewhere. What it does mean, though, is that every newly hired assistant professor should be provided with conditions that offer a realistic chance of promotion and tenure, and that all faculty, whether newly hired or not, at all ranks, should operate within institutional conditions that permit them to be productive and satisfied with their work lives. In the best instances, newly hired faculty will feel that they belong to a larger and supportive community, and that the cultural practices of their department or the larger institution deserve their respect and loyalty. The interactions and relationships that occur in any institution collectively make up its culture, and that culture must support the satisfaction and productivity of all of its members. As we will see, as a department diversifies, it may need to pay particular attention to issues that have not previously come up.

The retention of assistant professors hinges on a combination of wise hiring decisions (already discussed in chapters 5 and 6), a productive probationary period, and a fair and judicious tenure review process (to be discussed in chapter 9). Creating the conditions for all of these is the institution's responsibility, though failures are often attributed to the individual junior faculty member rather than the institution. The retention of tenured faculty hinges on these same factors; if there is significant promotion and tenuring from within, the maintenance of a productive work environment as diverse individuals' needs change over the course of a long career deserves considerable institutional attention.

Most college and university administrators recognize that these truths are self-evident (though occasionally—and counterproductively—their rhetoric may imply that faculty are chronically demanding and dissatisfied whiners, or childish). Despite administrators' understanding that faculty productivity and retention are important to the institution and hinge on job satisfaction, many faculty at many institutions report impressions of the institutional commitment to them that range from intentional abandonment ("sink or swim!") to a felt gap between apparently good intentions and painful or inadequate outcomes. Do some faculty have unrealistic expectations of institutional support? Of course. But it is our impression that most faculty do not. Instead, our observations suggest that institutions often fail to provide adequate conditions for faculty to develop and sustain satisfying and productive careers when in fact they could. Fortunately, we believe that success at this task is within the reach of most administrators—and here department chairs play a critical role (see, e.g., Campbell & O'Meara, 2014), but so do senior faculty generally and administrators higher in the hierarchy—at most institutions.

How Does Faculty Diversity Affect What Faculty Need?

Before we turn to a consideration of what faculty need in order to be retained, it is important to ask whether all faculty need the same things. For example, do faculty who bring diversity to the campus (e.g., women and underrepresented minorities) have "special needs" when it comes to retention? Not exactly. Most faculty need very similar things from an institution in order to thrive. At the same time, some of those things are easier for majority faculty (White men) to find than for those from other groups.

Consider, for example, ensuring a sense of inclusion, full participation, and community respect. That may be much easier for those groups that are numerically and traditionally dominant in university settings (Ackelsberg, Hart, Miller, Queeney, & Van Dyne, 2009; Gutiérrez y Muhs, Niemann, González, & Harris, 2012; Guzman, Trevino, Lubuguin, & Aryan, 2010; Harris, 2007; Thompson, 2008; Tokarczyk, 1993; Urry, 2008). Similarly, some processes—of mentoring, networking, and communication—work more easily and with less explicit or formal attention among community members who can rely on preexisting familiarity, comfort, and equality. For those who feel different, less comfortable, or less privileged, these processes may be obscure and alienating (see box 7.1 for examples). For these reasons

Box 7.1
What Do They Feel When Faculty Feel "Different"?

"…the landscape seems dotted with land mines that might blow up in our faces at any time." (Annas, 1993, p. 171)

"Being inside the institution by virtue of having a role. Being outside the institution by not being invited in or not understanding the rules and norms and how things work." (Hart, Grogan, Litt, & Worthington, 2009, p. 73)

"…the first thing that people who were trying to help me did was to take me to coffee or lunch and to tell me exactly how the department is divided. Some people think of it as a divided department in terms of conservative or forward thinking. The stereotype that was passed on to me was that half the department did not want anyone in my field because it is not a real field and it is identity politics." (Ackelsberg, Hart, Miller, Queeney, & van Dyne, 2009, p. 89)

"The one pervasive metaphor…that comes to me is the metaphor of exile, homelessness. It is the sense of being uprooted, of being wrenched from the world of one's parents and siblings, with only a tenuous possibility of ever putting down new roots." (Tokarczyk, 1993, p. 312)

"I got pushed into doing this diversity group with…students, and it was one of the most painful experiences I've ever had with students. This student challenged me all the way down the line. In one meeting the student got so angry [that] she threw down her knapsack and stomped out of the room and slammed the door…. In fact, this student told me that African Americans didn't know much about their own experience…" (Wilson, 2012, pp. 72–73)

"There was a faculty meeting, and I was making comments, and it would be pretty much ignored. A White male would then make the same comment, and then everybody heard it—oh isn't that brilliant." (Wilson, 2012, p. 74)

"I'm talking about my way of being. I have to adjust my way of being…. we have to adjust our way of being to fit into a structure; they don't. They don't have to adjust their way of being to me…. It's like they don't hear me if I'm the way I am." (Moffitt, Harris, & Forbes Berthoud, 2012, p. 89)

"…you may be the only Native person they've ever met in their entire life, so they're curious about you and what you do and your customs…. I try to be patient and answer them and let them know that we're all different…. It's always, always constantly educating people about what Indians are in this country." (Jacob, 2012, p. 246)

(continued)

Box 7.1 (continued)

"To many of us, success never had anything to do with things like rich, famous, published, or funded. Success means helping our people, connecting to others, being real, and making things better for our families and communities." (Boyd, 2012, p. 281)

"Another issue that I face constantly is having my accomplishments minimized systematically, particularly by my department and the institutional administrators. If I get an award, it is never announced in public; I am never officially congratulated, interviewed for the university newspaper, or invited to lunch by the president or the provost, things that happen when other people...receive similar honors." (de la Riva-Holly, 2012, p. 298)

"...the ghost of class identity can show up in a hallway conference conversation with new colleagues. You mispronounce an ordinary, but little-used word; it's a legacy of your underfunded, public school education. No one says anything, but in a split second, you have identified yourself as a member of the unwashed..." (Anthony, 2012, p. 305)

"I was inordinately visible as a minority female in a predominantly White, male department. I was also visible when it was in the department's best interest to have an ethnic scholar, so my name, teaching, and research were brought up during visits of the national program-accrediting association, international scholars, and elected officials of color.... I felt representative of all ethnic/racial minorities and believed the department cared only about the appearance of diversity without actually valuing it." (Flores Niemann, 2012, p. 342)

"...mainstream academics often label those who challenge the status quo—particularly those situated in oppressed groups—as 'not objective.' They question the validity of our scholarship by pointing out our status in outsider groups as indicators of our 'bias.' Yet the objectivity of men, White people, heterosexuals, and/or academics with middle- and upper-class backgrounds is much less likely to be questioned...." (Stockdill, 2012, p. 162)

"...we hit the glass ceiling already and cannot make changes and break out. Ageism hits just when sexism is coming down." (quoted in Rosser, 2012, p. 104)

"Over time, the accumulation of past inequities becomes a very difficult burden and affects relationships with others and sense of self." (quoted in Rosser, 2012, p. 104)

Box 7.1 (continued)

Ackelsberg, M., Hart, J., Miller, N. J., Queeney, K., & van Dyne, S. (2009). Faculty microclimate change at Smith College. In W. Brown-Glaude (Ed.), *Doing diversity in higher education* (pp. 83–102). New Brunswick, NJ: Rutgers University Press.

Annas, P. (1993). Pass the cake: The politics of gender, class, and text in the academic workplace. In M. M. Tokarczyk & E. A. Fay (Eds.), *Working-class women in the academy* (pp. 165–178). Amherst, MA: University of Massachusetts Press.

Anthony, C. G. (2012). The Port Hueneme of my mind: The geography of working-class consciousness in one academic career. In G. Gutiérrez y Muhs, Y. Flores Niemann, C. G. González, & A. P. Harris (Eds.), *Presumed incompetent: The intersections of race and class for women in academia* (pp. 300–312). Boulder, CO: University Press of Colorado.

Boyd, B. G. (2012). Sharing our gifts. In G. Gutiérrez y Muhs, Y. Flores Niemann, C. G. González, & A. P. Harris (Eds.), *Presumed incompetent: The intersections of race and class for women in academia* (pp. 277–282). Boulder, CO: University Press of Colorado.

de la Riva-Holly, F. (2012). Igualadas. In G. Gutiérrez y Muhs, Y. Flores Niemann, C. G. González, & A. P. Harris (Eds.), *Presumed incompetent: The intersections of race and class for women in academia* (pp. 287–311). Boulder, CO: University Press of Colorado.

Flores Niemann, Y. (2012). The making of a token: A case study of stereotype threat, stigma, racism and tokenism in academe. In G. Gutiérrez y Muhs, Y. Flores Niemann, C. G. González, & A. P. Harris (Eds.), *Presumed incompetent: The intersections of race and class for women in academia* (pp. 336–500). Boulder, CO: University Press of Colorado.

Hart, J., Grogan, M., Litt, J., & Worthington, R. (2009). Institutional diversity work as intellectual work at the University of Missouri–Columbia. In W. Brown-Glaude (Ed.), *Doing diversity in higher education* (pp. 61–80). New Brunswick, NJ: Rutgers University Press.

Jacob, M. M. (2012). Native women maintaining their culture in the White academy. In G. Gutiérrez y Muhs, Y. Flores Niemann, C. G. González, & A. P. Harris (Eds.), *Presumed incompetent: The intersections of race and class for women in academia* (pp. 242–265). Boulder, CO: University Press of Colorado.

Moffitt, K. R., Harris, H. E., & Forbes Berthoud, D. A. (2012). Present and unequal: A third-wave approach to voice parallel experiences in managing oppression and bias in the academy. In G. Gutiérrez y Muhs, Y. Flores Niemann, C.G. González, & A. P. Harris (Eds.), *Presumed incompetent: The intersections of race and class for women in academia* (pp. 78–92). Boulder, CO: University Press of Colorado.

Rosser, S. V. (2012). *Breaking into the lab: Engineering progress for women in science*. New York, NY: NYU Press.

Stockdill, B.C. (2012). Queering the ivory tower: Tales of a troublemaking homosexual. In B.C. Stockdill & M.Y. Danico (Eds.), *Transforming the ivory tower* (pp. 145–182). Honolulu: University of Hawai'i Press.

Tokarczyk, M. M. (1993). By the rivers of Babylon. In M. M. Tokarczyk & E. A. Fay (Eds.), *Working-class women in the academy* (pp. 311–321). Amherst, MA: University of Massachusetts Press.

Wilson, S. (2012). They forgot mammy had a brain. In G. Gutiérrez y Muhs, Y. Flores Niemann, C. G. González, & A. P. Harris (Eds.), *Presumed incompetent: The intersections of race and class for women in academia* (pp. 65–77). Boulder, CO: University Press of Colorado.

institutions aiming at diversity and inclusion often make the tacit explicit (written), and the informal (unwritten) formal (see Matthew, 2016, about the importance of this). They do this despite resistance from those faculty who believe that the system has worked just fine—for those of us already here and successful—without all that effort. The good news is that experience shows that everyone—including the majority—benefits when policies and procedures are formalized and made explicit (COACHE, 2008, 2010; Trower, 2010). The system that appeared to work "fine" can work better— for everyone. Improving conditions for newcomers to academia improves conditions for everyone.

If faculty retention turns on faculty productivity and satisfaction, what are the critical features of a satisfactory working environment for faculty? These can be summarized under three broad rubrics: *resources* that support research, teaching, advancement, and career development; institutional structures that promote *fairness* in treatment; and *transparency* about those structures (Waltman & Hollenshead, 2007). We discuss each of these needs in turn, as well as the more "human" needs employees of all kinds have for *respectful interactions* at work as well as *support for their personal lives*. Our point here is that supplying each of those features is both the right thing to do and the smart thing to do. We will conclude with a discussion of how institutions can maximize a positive work environment for a diverse faculty.

The Role of Resources in Faculty Satisfaction

Resources that support research, teaching, advancement, and career development vary greatly by institutional types. Thus, for example, internal resources for research (including time not committed to classroom teaching or student advising; internal funding; competent support for grant management; available shared equipment and research space) are most substantial at research-intensive institutions and sometimes virtually unavailable at teaching-intensive institutions such as community colleges. In contrast, resources to support student learning may be varied and substantial at community colleges and other teaching-intensive institutions and less present at research-intensive institutions.

Stratification of available resources by institution type is reasonable, to the extent that it is reflected in faculty performance demands. That is, demands for research productivity should not require accomplishments that outrun institutional support for that productivity. Equally, support to individual students can only be provided by faculty teaching small classes, or supported by other resources that enable them to assist individual students. Faculty can be very satisfied with careers in institutional settings with many or few resources for supporting any particular activity (research, teaching, etc.), if the demands on them (and the rewards to them) fit the overall structure of institutional resources. A broad mismatch—for example, between institutional demands to increase grant activity or average publication rate without an increase in institutional support for grant-getting or productivity, or between institutional demands for individualized student attention without appropriate institutional support for advising, learning assistance, or pedagogy—can produce serious morale problems among the faculty. Reasonable calibration of demands to resources is one key element in maintaining faculty satisfaction (see Johns, 2006, on work settings generally, and Hermanowicz, 2012, on academia).

Equitable Access to Resources

What is more often a problem for institutions is ensuring that there is full and equitable access to resources for all faculty. Again, institutional intentions are usually good, and the goal is for all faculty to know about all resources. Nonetheless, the distribution of information is often so uneven that administrators are amazed. For example, even the all-important information about tenure criteria and procedures is far from universally known among junior faculty (COACHE, 2008, 2010; Trower, 2010). In fact, in their face-to-face interviews with pretenure faculty at research-intensive institutions, COACHE researchers reported that every single interviewee mentioned "the need for a clearly-defined, reasonable and equitable path to tenure when asked what would aid in their professional success" (COACHE, 2008, p. 8). Clearly those faculty did not feel that information was readily available or clear. Other information with less dire consequences is probably even less uniformly known.

The implications of lack of information about resources are not neutral. Lack of information often translates both into a sense of being "out of the loop" or of not fully "belonging" in the institution and into unequal access to resources—the latter an inevitable effect of differential awareness of them (Gutiérrez y Muhs et al., 2012; Harris, 2007; Ostrove, Stewart,

& Curtin, 2011; Pololi, 2010; Pololi, Civian, Brennan, Dottolo, & Krupat, 2012; Rosser, 2012; Thompson, 2008; Walton & Cohen, 2007).

Thus, even at an institution with the intention of uniform access and an effort at broad dissemination of information, some faculty may feel that they do not have access to the same resources as do some of their colleagues. And those faculty are likely to be disproportionately from underrepresented groups within their unit (like women in some fields, and racial-ethnic minorities in most). Why is that? Because networks of informal communication work most smoothly among people who are, or are perceived to be, most similar (Kanter, 1977; Rankin, Nielsen, & Stanley, 2007). There is a great deal of informal information flow among people who share characteristics. Information flows less easily and automatically to people who are in some way "different." As we noted in chapter 1, homophily governs social interactions; it also controls the flow of information in social networks (McPherson, Smith-Lovin, & Cook, 2001).

To take one example, some universities have bridge funds to support faculty who have lost their grant funding. One woman told us of discovering that resource only after spending 20 years at her university. The availability was not written down anywhere, and none of her colleagues had told her about it. Only a chance encounter with a colleague alerted her. To avoid outcomes like that, institutions can rely on repeated, formal, and direct communication strategies, rather than one-shot, informal, or indirect communication approaches.

The Critical Role of Repeating Information

Corporate management advisors emphasize the importance of repeated communication (e.g., Collins, 2001)—presumably because they have learned how important it is in ensuring broad awareness. In our experience, academic leaders assume everyone is listening, and worry more about irritating people by repetition, even though as teachers we know the value of providing alternate accounts and examples of the same points. Because any one message may be sent at a time that is inconvenient for a given recipient—who is distracted by the pressure of some other personal or professional matter—it is important that the same message, ideally in different formats and contexts, be sent repeatedly. How often it is sent depends on how important it is to the recipient and the institution, not how irritating it may be to some recipients to hear about it multiple times.

One way institutions signal that an issue is important is by articulating it often.

For the same reason, it is a mistake to rely on intermediaries to be the primary messengers. In many institutions, department chairs (and in smaller school or college units, deans) are presumed to be the optimal communicators of all messages. By definition, they cannot be. Being the intermediary for every message that anyone in the institutional hierarchy may send means these leaders are frequently passing on messages that promote actions or policies that they may not fully understand nor fully agree with. Inevitably, they will be ineffective transmitters of some of those messages. From the view at the top, there is the illusion that the message was "sent," but the reality is that some deans or chairs may not have passed it on at all, others may have passed it on with inaccurate or misleading "information," and yet others may have undermined the message intentionally or unintentionally.

It is no doubt important that deans and department chairs know about all of the institutional resource messages their faculty are receiving (they should never be "out of the loop"), and that they have opportunities to gain needed information about important policies and resources affecting their faculty, but it is equally important that they not be expected to convey every message anyone in the institution needs to send. One alternative is for any given administrator to send a regular (but not too frequent—perhaps monthly) message to all faculty with important information outlined very briefly along with links to more detail.

The same logic applies, even more strongly, to relying on senior faculty "mentors" to pass on knowledge and information to junior faculty. They will inevitably be varied in their skill, motivation, and knowledge as messengers; further, their differences from their mentees, in terms of race-ethnicity, or gender, or country of origin, among many other things, may be a barrier to communication. Here, too, homophily matters. Therefore, important information should be signaled in advance (e.g., providing tenure criteria information at the point of hiring a junior faculty member, at the third year, and in the year before the tenure review is initiated), offered on a "just in time" basis (at the point of initiation of a mandatory tenure review process), and at all times conveyed with a strong emphasis on clear information about timing and deadlines. Ideally, crucial information is also posted on a website, with a straightforward access route and labeling.

Forms of Institutional Assistance to Faculty

The single most uniformly important resource for all faculty is direct assistance from the institution when they need it in order to do their job (Jordan & Bilimoria, 2007). A sense of institutional helpfulness (or its absence) applies to the full range of issues faculty face. Some issues are everyday practical problems: How do I get the projector fixed in my classroom? Where is the office that supports grant applications? Can anyone help me with letters of recommendation? Other issues are complex and deeply personal questions, like those of career development, work-life boundary management, and leadership and advancement. When institutions do well, they offer faculty opportunities to develop skills (e.g., grant-writing, teaching large lecture courses or small seminars, using technology in the classroom) and to enhance their professional connections (networks and collaborations). These opportunities include access to other human beings—leaders, peers, and mentors—who can help with all of these tasks.

At the lowest end of the institutional helpfulness scale, faculty have to solve every practical problem by themselves, investing considerable time and effort chasing down solutions that are not visible or widely available. They are likely to feel that the institution is indifferent to their well-being and that of their students. One of us tried for weeks to get burnt-out overhead fluorescent bulbs in an elevator replaced. It was a small irritation faced multiple times by multiple people every day. The bulbs were finally replaced thanks to a chance meeting with the head of facilities. For the sake of efficiency and freeing faculty to do what only they can do, it is in all institutions' interest to make it as easy as possible for faculty to do the jobs expected of them.

At the highest end of the institutional helpfulness scale, institutions may communicate to their faculty that they are willing to provide assistance to their partners in finding jobs in the area. Institutions that provide support for dual-career hiring benefit from the loyalty that is engendered at the time of an individual's first engagement with the institution. Some institutions offer formal incentives and assistance in hiring onto the faculty (see https://oaa.osu.edu/dual-career-hiring-fund.html for one example); others are able to provide professional dual-career services staff; and some join a Higher Education Recruiting Consortium (HERC) in their region. HERC currently operates in 17 regions and involves over 600 institutions relevant to placement and hiring of faculty and their partners (see http://www.hercjobs.org/ for more information). That, of course, supports retention.

Institutional helpfulness includes the provision of resources of expertise (including mentors and advisors) and structured support to facilitate faculty development at all career stages, as we detail further in chapter 8. When institutions offer programs to faculty about how best to develop their professional skills, we hear over and over that faculty are grateful that the institution "cares" about them enough to make this kind of opportunity available to them; some evidence of faculty appreciation for such opportunities can be seen from evaluations of workshops and from some posted data, such as http://nau.edu/faculty-development/ (visited October 15, 2017).

Institutions are not being purely altruistic by providing faculty with skills development. They not only benefit from the gratitude and appreciation of faculty, but they benefit from higher morale, greater job satisfaction, and higher productivity.

Supporting Diverse Families

Increasingly, it is critical that institutions provide all faculty with support for family-related needs, using a broad definition of "family" that includes households headed by single parents, with and without children; households headed by same-sex partners; and households where faculty may be caring for a family member who is ill. Formally recognizing the diversity of family situations our faculty have—and that they change over time in the course of their careers—is one way an institution can signal its commitment to take the diversity of faculty seriously and support faculty facing many different kinds of challenges. To that end, institutions can develop or revise institutional policies and resources to reflect the diverse personal life needs of their faculty at different stages of their careers, and, equally important, advertise the policies and resources throughout the institution so all faculty have equal access to them and information about them. If individual faculty rely on their department head to know and care about their personal situation, some will be provided with strong support in difficult times and others may receive no support at all. Serious institutional commitment to supporting faculty members' careers is communicated by high visibility of policies that do that and by wide and repeated dissemination of those policies, and monitoring of their use, at all levels of the institution.

A recent initiative led by Dr. Kelly Mack, the Gender Values project, helps institutions assess the adequacy of their family-friendly policies according to general principles as well as in comparison with other institutions. Having developed a rubric for assessing dependent care and family leave policies, the project team has assessed and studied their language and coverage at 51 institutions that have received ADVANCE Institutional Transformation awards. The team assessed the degree to which institutions had policies at all (most did), had institutionalized them in a broadly diffused fashion (many had), and had deliberately targeted nonmajority women (most did not; Mack & Soto, 2016).

We want to emphasize, then, that all institutions—regardless of the level of research, teaching, or faculty development and support resources they are able to offer—can calibrate their demands on faculty to fit those resources. In addition, institutions need to make sure that the resources that do exist are well targeted to their faculty needs, are widely known, and are evenly available to groups of faculty.[1]

The Role of Institutional Fairness in Faculty Satisfaction

It is clear from the discussion of resources that perceptions of the fairness of resource distribution matter to faculty. In this way, faculty are similar to employees in all kinds of organizations. The perception of one's workplace as fair maximizes morale and increases commitment to the organization; conversely, perceiving the workplace as not fair not only lowers morale, but maximizes turnover or attrition and reduces productivity (Carr, Schmidt, Ford, & DeShon, 2003; Hebl, Hebl, George, & Matusik, 2010).

Evaluating Institutional Fairness

Organizational fairness has three elements: the fairness of the *goal* or outcome sought, the fairness of the *procedures* used to accomplish the goal or outcome, and *respectful interactions* in the workplace. These three elements ideally stream together to create a "fair" environment: one that aims at equitable outcomes and has procedures to achieve those goals that enhance equity, as well as civil and respectful interactions on the ground. However, it is possible for an environment to have the goal of fair outcomes, but unfair procedures in trying to realize them.

As one example, consider this: a department decides to provide everyone with the space they need for their research—a fair goal—but allocates space based on people's claims about their needs made in private in whatever approach to calculation they choose. Because it is neither systematic nor transparent, such a procedure is open to unfairness. Or, consider a different scenario in which there are unfair outcomes but a nominally fair procedure: people with certain kinds of research needs get more space than people who need as much space but for different research purposes, via procedures that appear fair to the individuals in the process because the application states clearly that one criterion will be the type of research purpose. Or, consider the worst case—unfair goals and unfair procedures, where space is allocated according to the loudness of faculty demands and via an informal, unstandardized process.

And, of course, any of those scenarios could include individuals who are committed to respectful, collegial interactions—or not. The perception that an organization is fair includes not only the first two elements (fair outcomes and fair procedures), but also the likelihood that different kinds of constituencies have an opportunity to contribute to decision-making about both the outcomes and the procedures (Settles, Cortina, Stewart, & Malley, 2007). This is one feature of collegial interactions that feel fundamentally respectful.

Since space is a resource that is finite and often contested in departments, we will focus on that a little longer. One of us participated in departmental discussions about the allocation of space that apparently began with the assumption that some faculty required no research space (i.e., no space beyond their own offices), so a "fair outcome" could be that some faculty would be allocated no research space. That happened because all of the people planning the allocation of research space had very large space needs. They assumed that some—perhaps many—of their colleagues needed no space at all. Once the larger faculty community was included in the conversation, it became clear that although everyone felt that space should be allocated according to need, those faculty with the lowest level of need did not agree that they needed no research space at all. Some felt they needed access to some common resources (e.g., space for research assistants, or testing individuals, which did not need to be privately held but could be shared), and some felt they needed a modest amount of space for storing and analyzing their own and their students' research materials.

Thus, a "fair outcome" in everyone's eyes could be achieved, but only once all kinds of researchers were part of the conversation.

Including all constituencies in the development of both fair outcomes and fair procedures inevitably takes longer than having a small group of the people with the most intense needs make the decision—but the cost in mistrust and resentment of a fast, exclusive process will in the long run outweigh the "advantage" of an initial saving of time.

The Role of Institutional Transparency in Faculty Satisfaction

One element of both well-distributed knowledge about resources and the perception of organizational fairness that deserves special attention is transparency. Often people interpret the call for transparency as literally applying to every tiny detail about how a decision has been or will be arrived at. By defining transparency in that way, they persuade themselves that it is not practical and therefore not desirable. That caricature of transparency is not what is needed to create a work environment that feels meaningfully respectful and inclusive and therefore maximizes productivity and satisfaction. Generally speaking, the kind of organizational transparency that is important is openness about what decisions are going to be made in the near and far term, the reasons those decisions are on the table at this time, and the process by which the decisions will be made. With respect to the process, that includes who will have input, who will participate in actual decision-making, and what criteria will be used for making the decision.

Another obstacle to transparency is the belief on the part of decision makers that it is actually wise—and will help leaders maintain their power and influence, or lower conflict—to conceal information about how resources are allocated and about the principles that are used to govern that allocation. Again, there is a trade-off between benefits and costs. Dictatorships are beneficial to dictators. The cost is suspicion about institutional decisions, fairness, and principles. Using beneficial features of organizational decision-making helps individuals feel that the organization is operating according to some general principles that are intelligible and even admirable, and, even if the final decision is inconsistent with their own preferences, their preferences were taken into consideration.

Once a decision is made, organization members need to understand what it actually is and what its implications are. That is, they need to understand what outcomes or goals are sought and the procedures by which those outcomes will be pursued. Ideally, the decision will be formalized into a policy that is then accessible to all members of the community. This kind of transparency is essential to a sense of inclusion and participation—and the creation of an academic community.

We hope it is clear at this point that institutional helpfulness, fairness, and transparency are not truly distinct features of work environments. Together they create environments (or the climate of any given environment) that feel helpful, just, and inclusive. Helpful, just, and inclusive environments are the ones in which people generally do their best work, and faculty are no exception. Importantly for the institution, people who are doing their best work rarely want to go somewhere else where they might not be able to keep it up.

The Importance of Respectful Interactions
and the Climate for Difference

The varied institutional features that add up to institutional helpfulness, fairness, and transparency are often summarized in the term "climate." This metaphor is intended to describe the "weather" that defines a person's work environment. Imagine for a moment the way in which climates determine what plants and flowers can grow: most do well under "temperate" or "moderate" conditions in which they experience adequate sunshine, water, and warmth (Settles, Cortina, Malley, & Stewart, 2006). A smaller number thrive well under what are thought of as "harsh" conditions (little sunshine, great cold or heat, and extremely wet or dry conditions). Human beings are similar: most thrive when they are provided with environments that are moderately supportive (sunny and warm); a hardy few can thrive even when conditions are very "chilly" or extremely "hot." Resources, fairness, and transparency are the sunshine, water, and warmth of human work environments.

Differences in Experiences of the Climate
Despite commonalities in what creates a good climate, not everyone in a department experiences the same climate. Often people who are in the numerical majority find it confusing when those who are not in the majority report that they find the climate unpleasant. They may even accuse the

minority of being "wrong" about the environment. Typically, men perceive the climate as more supportive than women do (see, e.g., perceptions of academic conference climate, Biggs, Hawley, & Biernat, 2017), and Whites perceive the climate as more supportive than people of color do (see, e.g., Zambrana, Wingfield, Lapeyrouse, Dávila, Hoagland, & Váldez, 2017).

One way they can both be right is that they are not experiencing the same climate. In some cases, the department supports individuals in some demographic categories more than it supports those in other categories. In other cases, the particular features of support are more congenial to some demographic groups than others. Especially when a department has only a single person of color, or a single woman, that person's perceptions may be dismissed (if they are even known) and may wash out in aggregate measures of the climate. But that person's experience matters, even if it doesn't change the average. In short, how an institution—a department, a school, or a university—handles differences among the faculty is revealed in part by discussions of the "climate."

Institutional Cultures That Are Monolithic Preclude Diversity

One way a bad climate for difference gets created is when people talk about the institutional culture in monolithic terms. When it seems to a community that they must protect a "monoculture"—a culture in which everyone has the same preferences, attitudes, and styles—differences are perceived as threatening and dangerous to community cohesion. In settings like these, someone who is different—female, or from an ethnic minority, or gay or lesbian—may still be okay if the person doesn't draw attention to their differentness, if she, say, acts like "one of the guys" (see Yoshino, 2007, on "covering"). So a monoculture can absorb people who are superficially different in some way as long as they go along with the cultural practices and their presence doesn't change anything (see Bilimoria & Stewart, 2009; Ely & Thomas, 2001). The person is included, but at a cost to herself.

Inclusion as a Token versus as a Full Participant

Another way people who are different may get "included" is as tokens (Hebl et al., 2010; Kanter, 1977; Thompson & Sekaquaptewa, 2002; Yoder, 2002). When this happens individuals who are "different" are routinely "marked" as having a particular characteristic that makes them different that requires attention and comment. Thus, they may be asked for the "woman's point of view" or assumed to care about certain things. For example, racial-ethnic minority group members may be assumed to be the ones who care about "diversity" in the department. Equally, women may be assumed to be the people in charge of educating others about sexual harassment.

In one department discussion of the next recruitment priorities and how best to encourage the hiring of women, Martha—the only woman, a junior faculty member, and a person known to have a partner who lived in another state—was asked by the department chair "to tell us what you think" because of her unique perspective. Martha felt singled out as female and as having a "partner problem" (though, of course, many of the senior men in the department had such "problems," too). She wondered if all her opinions about hiring and the field would be viewed as reflecting those personal qualities. When people are treated as members of a group, rather than as valued individual colleagues, the climate feels "chilly."

In contrast, that same department chair sometimes sought out Martha's opinion by telling her that he valued her good scientific judgment and excellent people skills. When he approached her for input on a problem that way, Martha reacted very differently: she felt like a valued colleague with something to contribute to thinking about a problem—not because she was a woman, but because of her unique individual characteristics, and the needs of the situation.

Fortunately, Martha and her chair were able to discuss the different examples because Martha felt there was a reserve of goodwill and respect on both sides. Equally fortunately, when the department chair heard how Martha felt about the first example, he did not suggest that she was overly sensitive (as women and minorities are often told). Instead, he recognized that it was his responsibility to include Martha in what had been a monoculture without treating her as a token member of a group. He worked hard to figure out how better to frame his questions, and invite input, so that his respect for Martha as a colleague was evident. That included not asking her to speak "as a woman" or putting her on the spot in a public setting about a contentious issue. In this case, the department chair was both the problem and the solution.

But often the individuals who create difficulties for those who are "different" are not in positions of authority, but are colleagues, members of one's community. Robert, the only African American member of his department and a full professor, was sitting in a meeting of his colleagues, discussing which doctoral student applicants would be accepted into the program. Pete—someone who often expressed unpopular, even crude opinions— indicated that he supposed "we are under pressure to admit unqualified students because of affirmative action." Robert waited for one of his knowledgeable colleagues to explain that affirmative action did not require anyone to accept unqualified applicants, but no one said anything. The group simply moved on to other comments.

Worrying later that evening about whether he should have spoken up, Robert also wondered how to understand what had happened: did his colleagues really agree with Pete? Did they think Pete was so obviously off-base they didn't see any reason to answer? Did they think Robert should speak because he was the only individual present who was a member of a minority group? Were they embarrassed that Pete had implied that Robert was unqualified? Being left after meetings with uncertainty about what happened is a common experience for those who do not feel part of the dominant group. This kind of rumination is an indication of how little they fit in or belong. And over time, quite apart from feeling overly visible or invisible, like an outsider or a colluder, the labor it takes to interpret such situations creates a powerful incentive to find a less exhausting niche somewhere else. This is an example of a small disadvantage that being different can impose. We discussed earlier the fact that such small disadvantages are nonetheless destructive. They create problems that occupy a mind that we hope will be free for more satisfying scholarly pursuits.

Meeting the Need for Respectful Interactions
Quite apart from the specific aspects of the environment that spotlight difference, work environments vary in how and how much they tolerate overt or covert expressions of sexual harassment, disrespect, or incivility (Cortina, 2008).

Sexual Harassment   Many colleges and universities, over the past several decades, have adopted policies that aim to discourage sexual harassment. It remains, however, a live issue on college campuses—one that affects the work environment both for younger women as students, postdoctoral researchers, and junior faculty, and for senior faculty who are their confidants and advisors and who themselves may be the targets of sexual harassment. Although it is difficult to document the prevalence of harassment, because it is typically underreported, there are studies describing the type and to some extent the frequency of such events (e.g., Cantalupo & Kidder, 2017; Clancy, Lee, Rodgers, & Richey, 2017; Jagsi, Griffith, Jones, Perumalswami, Ubel, & Stewart, 2016).

Every year we face news of eminent "repeat offenders" who have finally been formally accused and found responsible for their actions. The costs for those who have been harassed are, as we describe, extensive, but there are also costs to the institution and to the academy generally of examples of sexual harassment. Although people of any gender can be the object of sexual harassment, young women are the biggest class. Sexual harassment operates at best to distract from the work that those young women want to do and at worst to destroy their careers, their confidence that they have important and valued work to do, and their trust in the fairness of the academy. The academy has a responsibility to provide everyone with an environment that is free of harassment, no matter how "minor."

Brave women, younger and older, have described the corrosive impact of experiences of being treated by respected, powerful figures in their discipline as sex objects or sex partners, instead of as work colleagues or students (for one example, see http://www.slate.com/articles/health_and_science /science/2016/07/sexual_harassment_has_devastating_consequences_on _victims_ability_to_perform.html). It is worth noting that when individuals do not trust their institutional home to "do the right thing" about sexual or other problems, that in turn corrodes their commitment to work and to that organization (Huerta, Cortina, Pang, Torges, & Magley, 2006; Smith & Freyd, 2014; Willness, Steel, & Lee, 2007).

Faculty and colleagues have increasingly begun to express public support for women who have been harassed. They have circulated letters criticizing bad behaviors that are known to have occurred and have spoken publicly about the need to sanction such bad behaviors. Some professional societies, such as the American Astronomical Society, the American Geophysical Union, and the American Political Science Association, have developed explicit anti-harassment policies in an effort to address the inappropriate behavior of, usually, more senior males toward junior females, at conferences. We hope that the responsibility such professional groups are taking will be replicated broadly in other societies and in colleges and universities.[2]

Sexual harassment can take many forms in the academy. Some are explicitly sexualized, ranging from the legally unacceptable "quid quo pro" exchange of some kind of work benefit for sexual acts to sexualized comments or "dirty" jokes. Others are now known as "gender" harassment—comments on one's appearance, especially in reference to a gender-linked standard (e.g., of masculinity or femininity), derogatory comments about women or men, and sexist jokes or comments (Berdahl, 2007a; Leskinen, Cortina, & Kabat, 2011; Reich & Hershcovis, 2012). These kinds of harassment occur in interactions with students, staff, and faculty. Even if they are not pervasive or encountered on a daily basis, their effects are felt by many women (and by some men, especially indirectly when they observe harassment of women). They are experienced by faculty who are straight and gay. One particularly powerful description of sexual harassment of a gay man is provided by E. Patrick Johnson:

A senior colleague, with a repulsive personality, apparently needs to work out his own sexuality through me, the department's resident Black faggot. He does so by trying to bait me while I'm standing at the copier. He places his latest book in my face (the cover is a picture of Greg Louganis in a Speedo diving into a pool) and chants, "Isn't that hot? Wouldn't you like to taste that?" He further shows his affection by groping me in the department office, feeling he is allowed to do this because the LGBT student group has written "Hug a Queer Today" on the sidewalk. (Johnson, 2009, p. 97)

The effects of sexual harassment experiences include increased work stress, decreased life satisfaction, and harm to physical and emotional health (Berdahl & Moore, 2006; Huerta et al., 2006). Younger women and women of color are particularly vulnerable to the impact of these experiences (Berdahl & Moore, 2006), and women faculty of all ages are likely to be sought out as confidantes by students, staff, and faculty who have been targeted.

Some faculty cannot imagine why mere expressions of sexual interest are so harmful. It is the way these expressions, when unexpected and unwanted, undermine someone's confidence in themselves and their chosen field that is so damaging. One articulate complainant described the impact of her experience to her harasser:

…your confession of your romantic feelings changed everything for me. It took away trust, stability, motivation, ambition and the beauty that I had always seen in this place. Yes, I believe I can say it ruined the experience of being [at this institution] to some extent. I am not judging your feelings…but you should never have told me.

When I think back now, thinking that any nice word, any accidental touch, any hug of yours may have been more than that, it makes me sick to my stomach. Nothing appears to be what it seemed anymore. How can I still trust you?...Everything work-related is related to you and therefore to this incident now. And so I cannot help but feel bad and disturbed, and yes, creeped out whenever I think of our projects. (Quoted in the Sexual Harassment Prevention Program in the College of Literature, Science and the Arts at the University of Michigan, January 22, 2013)

In addition to the costs to the person harassed, other people's experience can weigh heavily both on women faculty and on their enlightened—and troubled—male colleagues (Porath, Macinnis, & Folkes, 2010; Reich & Hershcovis, 2012). Many institutions have enacted policies that discourage these kinds of behavior, but people who have been harassed are often reluctant to report their experiences, given both the frequent power differences between harasser and victim and the close communities of people over long periods of time that are typical of academic settings (Berdahl, 2007a; Rudman, Borgida, & Robertson, 1995). It is therefore critical both to have transparent and effective mechanisms for reporting, evaluating, and addressing sexual harassment complaints and to create a climate in which the egalitarian and civil treatment of all members of the community makes sexual harassment unacceptable and unlikely (see Berdahl, 2007b; Cortina, 2008).

In the face of serious incidents that had occurred on the campus of Yale University, a new and more rigorous policy was adopted and information about it was disseminated on the web (http://provost.yale.edu /uwc-procedures), including information about how individuals could get advice and help in formulating their own preferences about what to do (http://sharecenter.yale.edu/). In addition, the policy adopted includes explicit summarizing and reporting of formal grievances and their disposition (without identifying details) and publication to the community twice each year ("Each January and July, the University Title IX Coordinator will publish a statistical abstract of the handling of sexual misconduct complaints at Yale, including a list of disciplinary actions. These abstracts will include no information that would reveal the identities of the parties.") The aim of these practices was clearly to communicate that the institution will not tolerate sexual harassment, though we note that after these steps were taken the institution was faced with complaints about its long-standing neglect and mishandling of complaints of sexual harassment. Adopting policies is not enough; the practices they are intended to promote must become the culture of the institution. It is tempting to think that creating and adopting the policy will solve the problem, but it is only the first step in solving the problem (Ahmed, 2012).

Incivility   Disrespectful treatment is not confined to harassment. It includes actions that are more covert and not necessarily sexualized or aimed at any particular group—"incivility" (Cortina 2008). Some of the literature that examines these issues labels such actions "microaggressions" (see Sue, 2010a, 2010b; see Lilienfeld, 2017, for methodological concerns about how the term is defined). While incivility focuses on the experience of the recipient of the behavior, we want explicitly to note that many of the actions that come under these rubrics are *not* intentional expressions of disrespect or aggression, or at least are not intentionally aimed at any particular group. In addition, some people are rude to everyone, and at some point almost everyone experiences rudeness. That is part of what makes it easy for bystanders and institutions to ignore incivility: it isn't constant and the targets are widespread. Although everyone experiences rudeness at one time or other, women and people of color experience it more than do White men. And the impact of rudeness on recipients is consequential.

We digress for a moment to affirm that disagreement is fundamental to academic discourse. We do not align with those who would suppress disagreement in the interest of unanimity or conformity (see Nader, 2001, on "coercive harmony"). Disagreement is a defining feature of a community of intellectual inquiry, and a strength of academic research. The academy is expected to provide opportunities for meaningful, serious, and profound disagreement—otherwise, environments become stifling and deadly. At the same time, openness to disagreement is not the same as incivility. Bugeja (2002) distinguishes collegiality, which he favors because it requires inclusive participation of all colleagues, from congeniality, which he argues may suppress dissent. We agree that disagreement can always be expressed—in a collegial manner.

Disagreement is sometimes claimed as one motivation for, and as a justification for, incivility (or lack of collegiality). We think everyone can learn to express disagreements constructively. Disagreement is also sometimes used simply as a cover for people who say, implicitly, "I disagree with you, but I don't want merely to point out problems with your argument or your evidence; I want to interrupt you, cast aspersions on your motivations, your talent, and your sincerity; I want to demonstrate how much smarter than you I am while preventing you from finishing your point!" Departments and institutions that have a reputation for this kind of discourse are—no surprise—often experienced by women and minorities as "hostile" climates (Ackelsberg et al., 2009; Guzman et al., 2010; Jayakumar, Howard, Allen, & Han, 2009). Our view is that climates in which hostility is openly expressed are stifling in their own way, by making it difficult for some members of the academy to express their disagreements.

Researchers have differentiated incivility (which is "low intensity" non-congeniality or rudeness) from bullying (which is higher intensity and usually clearly intentional; Keashly & Jagatic, 2003) and workplace abuse (which is even more intense; Richman, Shinsako, Rospenda, Flaherty, & Freels, 2002). While those types are analytically distinct, the differences among them do not have reliably different implications (Hershcovis, 2011). Constructive dissent requires an atmosphere in which the discussants are aiming at a deeper understanding than would be possible without dissent.

In addition to discussion of this issue in terms of workplace incivility (Cortina, 2008), some research focuses specifically on gender or racial or ethnic harassment (Raver & Nishii, 2010). In these cases, scholars argue that any kind of rude or hostile treatment that is due to one's social identities (race or ethnicity, gender, class, international status, sexual orientation, etc.) creates a work environment that is damaging to morale and productivity, and often to mental and physical health (Jayakumar et al., 2009; Porath, 2017; Raver & Nishii, 2010).

Why do these different hostile features of the workplace climate bother women and minorities more than White men? First, they may not, across the board. There are many White men who do not enjoy this form of intellectual combat but who have learned to live with it and not to resist it (see Keashly, 2012). And there are White women and people of color who do not mind hostile dialogue. However, to the extent that workplace incivility does bother women and minorities more, it is probably because the people most likely to engage in uncivil behavior are those with the greatest confidence and certainty that they are right. Of course, this can include individual female or underrepresented minority faculty members. But most often those with the greatest confidence and sense of entitlement are those with the most status-based privilege: powerful senior faculty with years of experience of being taken seriously, regardless of their behavior. Statistically, those individuals are more likely to be White males. And, statistically, the casualties of this kind of incivility, while including some junior White males (perhaps especially those who feel like outsiders for some reason—different in terms of family status, sexual orientation, intellectual perspective, etc.), are more often White women and racial-ethnic minorities.

Some academics expect people to develop a tough skin, a tolerance for the incivility of a few individuals. They express little or no concern about the impact of occasions of incivility on those who feel least welcome in the environment. (In fact the two senior faculty who left institutions in the opening stories heard just those expectations from their colleagues.) Such a climate—of tolerance for incivility—is related to higher levels of work-related stress, and poorer health and well-being, among all kinds of workers, not just White women and racial-ethnic minority men and women (Cortina, 2008; Lim, Cortina, & Magley, 2008; Miner-Rubino & Cortina, 2004). Incivility is also related to poorer worker morale and job performance (Porath & Erez, 2007; Porath & Pearson, 2010). Finally, environments that tolerate incivility are also more likely to tolerate behavior that is even more pernicious and unacceptable, like sexual harassment (Gutek, 1985; Lim & Cortina, 2005).

There is, then, reason for us all to be more effective at requiring our interactions with one another to meet a minimum standard of respectful civility, even as we express vigorous disagreement. The University of Michigan's Center for Research on Learning and Teaching has guidelines for fostering productive discussions in the classroom, many of which are also appropriate for faculty talking to each other (http://www.crlt.umich.edu/examples -discussion-guidelines/). One department's experience in working to create a better climate, motivated by concerns about graduate students, is presented in box 7.2.

Meeting Faculty Members' Human Needs

The climate of our work environments is created in the course of our interactions with our leaders, our peers, our students, and the staff who support our work lives. It is also defined by the quality of the recognition it affords to the human needs we have that go beyond work but affect and are affected by our work lives. These include features like the nature of the community ties that bind us (see Jordan & Bilimoria, 2007). Some academic

Box 7.2

How One Department Addressed a Climate Issue

The impetus for change in one department was the observation that female graduate students were dropping out of the program at a much higher rate than male students were. Climate seemed to be the major problem. Two faculty went to a workshop on gender and, inspired by what their colleagues at other institutions were doing, formed a committee consisting of faculty and graduate students to discuss climate issues in the department. They created a survey based on existing surveys and on comments from the students. One practical issue that took some time to work through was the university's concern that the survey might disclose problems that they would be legally obligated to address. Although the committee had wanted the survey to be completely anonymous, the university required links that would allow it to identify individuals if someone reported any illegal activity. Respondents were informed that the university might identify them if it thought it had a duty to intervene. Developing the survey and reaching agreement with the university took about a year. Because the committee believed in the importance of assessing and changing the climate, they persevered.

The survey combined multiple-choice and short-answer items. The office of institutional research, not the department, analyzed the results in order to preserve the confidentiality of students' responses and forwarded aggregate data to the committee. The committee summarized the data—basic patterns, numerical results, and some quotations—and discussed the results in three meetings: a faculty-faculty meeting, a student-student meeting, and a meeting with the department as a whole.

To ensure receptivity among the faculty, the committee tied the issues to education. For example, if students were not attending colloquia because of the climate, that interfered with the department's educational mission. One surprise was that all students had complaints about the climate. Another surprise was that women were about twice as dissatisfied as men. Faculty were taken aback and concerned by the extent of the problem.

The department developed several faculty-student subcommittees to make recommendations for change. Each subcommittee met four to five times over a two-month period and presented recommendations to the main climate committee. That group created a combined list of recommendations, which ranged from learning about bystander interventions to creating a more respectful climate. The whole department met again to discuss the recommendations.

While not everyone agreed that the recommended changes should be adopted, there was a consensus to take an experimental attitude. Most of the

(continued)

Box 7.2 (continued)

department recognized that there was a problem, respected the work the committees had performed, and were willing to adopt many of the recommendations, with the understanding that, in two years, the department would reassess the climate with a repeat survey and determine the value of the recommendations. The second survey found dramatic improvement on almost every question. Dissatisfaction had been cut roughly in half and greater attrition by women from the program had stopped. A large majority of students thought that the department now had a respectful climate. As with the first survey, the results were presented at a joint meeting of students and faculty.

The subcommittees continue their work, and there will be another survey in a year. Newer students take the current climate to be the norm. Some older students and faculty are still skeptical, but since the department is manifestly a much more congenial place, they are willing to go along.

What we find exemplary about this department's efforts are (1) their recognition that there was a problem; (2) their efforts to find solutions that went against long-standing norms; (3) their persistence in the face of difficulties, including legal constraints imposed by the institution and reluctance on the part of some faculty; (4) their recognition that climate issues cannot be solved in one fell swoop but require ongoing efforts on a number of fronts by a number of people; (5) their commitment to gathering and analyzing data on a regular basis; and (6) their discovery that their department became a better place for almost everyone.

work settings are associated with elaborate social ties outside of work; others have none. Faculty can be happy and productive in both kinds of settings (though individuals may have different preferences), but no one's work life is made more tolerable and productive when a person feels excluded from the social ties that others have.

Experiencing Exclusion from the Community

Sandra was one of two African American faculty members in her department. After her first year in the department, she began to notice that every Wednesday all the women in the department went to lunch together. Except her. No one had ever told her about these lunches; no one ever invited her to participate. But every week she noticed all the other—White—women went to lunch together, with no male colleagues, and without her. This kind of exclusion strained the collegial ties Sandra felt with those women and made every departmental interaction with them charged in a different way than it would have been if they had included her in the weekly lunches.

People who do belong find it difficult to understand, or even perceive, what it is like not to belong. They fail to recognize the cushion of air on which they float, thanks to their integration in the community, a cushion that makes it possible for them to say what they think to each other without worrying about how it will be received. Someone in that position thinks that free and open dialogue is available to everyone in the community, not realizing that their vantage point is not everyone's vantage point.

Variety in the Demands of Private Life
While the social connections between work and social life are important, we all need to be able to feel free of work demands at some times—free to pursue other interests, to relax, to take care of personal business, to have a private life. Family-friendly resources, policies, and practices have increased with the increased representation of women on the faculty, but we underline the fact that support for faculty members' family responsibilities was present long before women's needs were the focus (Girgus, 2011). The availability of benefits like life and health insurance that covered not only a faculty member but his partner and children was not recognized at the time to derive from men's family roles, but it did. Similarly, the once-common provision of paid college tuition for faculty children was a benefit that assumed a particular family arrangement and a particular set of needs.

Academic households are different now than they were in the past, and they will continue to change. There are more and more households made up of individuals not previously imagined in universities' policies: faculty caring for elders, siblings, or partners; or faculty who are lesbian, gay, bisexual, or transgender. The kinds of supports faculty need at different life stages, and as a result of different life situations, varies. Institutions that create environments that not only recognize and address the range of needs faculty have, but are welcoming and provide warm communities, will succeed in retaining a diverse faculty.

Sometimes particular kinds of faculty members are targeted to meet some work-related demands outside of normal work hours precisely because it is assumed that they have less need of this freedom. For example, Jack—a White man—reported that he was expected to take every guest speaker to dinner because he is single, and his colleagues assumed that he had no need for freedom from work demands in the evening. Equally, Elaine—a White woman—reported that she resented the fact that no one seemed to grasp that as a single person and a homeowner she had to cope with every household emergency on her own, unlike her partnered colleagues, who complained about how little their partners helped. No matter how little their partners may have done, to *her* it appeared that her partnered colleagues could count on two sets of hands around the house and not just one. The point here is that we often make assumptions about how much, or how little, our colleagues need firm, clear boundaries that separate the times when they are expected to respond to work demands from time they can control. Work environments vary in how easy they make it for people to articulate their needs in this domain and to have their preferences stick.

All faculty need assistance in meeting the joint needs of work and a personal life. Those needs change at different points in the life cycle. They may be the result of the presence, absence, or illness of a partner, or a parent, sibling, or child for whom one is responsible; or it may be the result of an illness, accident, or infirmity of one's own.

Dual-Career Services and Childcare Resources
The issue of faculty needs for support for their family lives has been addressed most openly around the needs of parents of young children (Mason & Goulden, 2002a, 2002b, 2004) and the needs of two-career households for dual-career services (Schiebinger, Henderson, & Gilmartin, 2008). Faculty have pressed for on-campus childcare facilities and information about other community resources, as well as family-friendly policies for new parents (including parental leaves). There is increasing evidence that the current generation of graduate students, postdocs, and junior faculty is not as willing to sacrifice family for career as previous generations may have been—and that applies to both women and men (see Ecklund & Lincoln, 2016).

Financial Support at Critical Transition Points
Some universities have special funds aimed at supporting faculty who are at a critical point in their careers and have experienced major life events that make it difficult for them to pursue their work effectively. WISELI, at the University of Wisconsin, for example, has Vilas Life Cycle Professorships. A faculty member applies for support, stating both why his or her current

situation counts as a critical juncture and what major life events make it difficult to move forward. The professorships are intended to respond to the large variety of pressing life events that can happen at just the wrong time in someone's career.

The same logic that applies to bridging grants—keep active faculty active—is the logic that applies to any mechanism for supporting faculty. Some universities have internal grants for new work—seed money to help develop new areas of research.

Stop-the-clock and *modified-duty* policies make the route to tenure more flexible. In both types of policies, certain principles hold. First, the policies are available to as wide a group of people as possible. They do not, for example, assume that only women take care of children. Second, the policies are a genuine time out: people are not required in any way to compensate for time that they spent off the clock or in modified duties. Third, there is no penalty for faculty who avail themselves of the policies for which they are eligible.

Stop-the-Clock Policies   In *stop-the-clock* policies, faculty with new responsibilities for children or other family members (such as an ailing partner or parent) may take—but are not required to take—more than the prescribed number of years (usually between five and seven except in medical schools) before being considered for tenure, without there being any increase in the faculty member's expected productivity. If faculty wish to keep the clock running, they are, of course, free to do so. There are two key aspects to such policies when they are successfully implemented. First, everyone—male or female, of any race-ethnicity—is free to opt in or opt out. "Free" means that if a White man wants to be the primary caretaker of a new child, and can demonstrate that he will in fact be the primary caretaker, he can do so without opprobrium.[3] Second, stopping the clock means that faculty are not considered to have had an "extra" year and thus are not expected to demonstrate the productivity of someone who has had an additional year of full-time effort.

It is very important that institutions' policies be easily accessed and well-documented for their faculty. Many institutions' policies are vaguely worded (or refer the reader to another site with a broken link). As is the case with any policy, too little specificity can leave too much discretion in the hands of an unknowledgeable or unreceptive chair or dean. But too much specificity can create a rigidity that is unresponsive to the variety of difficult life situations that people may face. Some universities' policies differ from school to school, while others have a policy that extends across all schools (generally excluding medical schools, and sometimes business schools).

Modified-Duty Policies In *modified-duties* policies, faculty may be considered for tenure at the canonical time but have reduced teaching responsibilities to balance the heavier responsibilities they have in their personal lives. This too is a change that potentially equally benefits all faculty, regardless of sex or race-ethnicity. There are many variants of such policies. In some cases, modified duties are available only with the addition of a new child to a household. (See, e.g., the policy at Northeastern University.) In other cases, although the addition of a child is the expected reason, others are possible. (See, e.g., the policy at the University of South Carolina.) As with stop-the-clock policies, no "make-up" is expected and no penalties are exacted. In addition, a number of schools have formalized language that is used when seeking outside letters so that external reviewers do not inadvertently penalize candidates who have taken advantage of such policies.

An additional feature of one modified-duties program, at the University of Michigan, is the provision of one semester to all new parents, and a second semester of modified duties for a birth mother whose child is in the home. The grounds for this are that only a birth mother experiences the accompaniments of pregnancy, labor, and breastfeeding.

Lactation Rooms

One change that directly benefits only some women is the provision of lactation rooms across campus so that female faculty can express milk at work in a private setting. Although only the woman benefits directly, there are indirect benefits to the woman's household as a whole: for example, the woman's partner does not need to be ferrying the child to the mother's work to be nursed.

The Importance of Time at Work and Home

Feminist legal scholar Joan Williams (2000) argued in her book *Unbending Gender* that the American "ideal worker" and "ideal mother" are each available for work or mothering at all times. The dramatically increased presence of mothers in the labor force has challenged both of these ideals, but institutions vary widely in how actively they have accommodated this change. To the extent that employers retain a notion of a worker who is available at all times for work, parents of young children (increasingly both men and women) will be dissatisfied.

Moreover, Galinsky and Bond (2009) showed that employees who emphasize their family lives over their work lives or put equal emphasis on each "exhibit significantly better mental health, greater satisfaction with their lives, and higher levels of job satisfaction than employees who are work-centric." They conclude, "Although employers [for us, colleges and universities] may want their employees to be work-centric—focusing on work to the exclusion of the rest of their lives—actually achieving this goal could be a pyrrhic victory, especially in light of escalating work stress and its potential cost in health care" (p. 432). Organizational scholars Lotte Bailyn, Rhona Rapoport, Joyce Fletcher, and Bettye Pruitt (2002) showed that organizations can actually increase productivity while addressing demands for improved "work-life balance" if they recognize that far from limiting work performance, policies and practices that address workers' need to balance work and family roles actually enhance it.

Some faculty have successfully encouraged their departments to limit department meetings and functions to specified working hours, so that parents of young children can meet their responsibilities to them. Indeed, some institutions have adopted work-hour policies, which make this freedom something the institution recognizes and therefore something individuals do not have to wrest from the institution; see, for example, Texas A&M (http://dof.tamu.edu/Faculty-Resources/CURRENT-FACULTY/Faculty-Work -Life/BALANCING-WORK,-PERSONAL-AND-FAMILY-ISSUES, visited July 26, 2016); the Microbiology and Immunology Department at the University of Michigan Medical School (personal communication, Professor Michele Swanson, May 6, 2013); the Sociology Department at the University of Iowa (personal communication, Professor Jennifer Glass, May 7, 2013); Oregon State University's "Toolkit for Academic Administrators" (http://academic affairs.oregonstate.edu/sites/academicaffairs.oregonstate.edu/files/pdf /osu_family-friendly_toolkit_final_2015.pdf; see p. 13; visited January 20, 2018); and the College of New Jersey's policy of a set-aside meetings time on Wednesday afternoons (when no classes are scheduled; see p. 5 of the Governance section of the policy manual: http://policies.tcnj.edu/policies/digest .php?docId=9894; visited January 20, 2018).

Departmental and institutional practices about "extra" work meetings (formal and informal), as well as norms about how much "face time" is expected in the corridors, all define the degree to which institutional demands consume all, some, or none of a faculty member's time outside of the classroom, office hours, and required meetings. These norms about time are often tacit, so individuals can run afoul of them without even knowing it—and, of course, those most likely to run afoul of tacit norms are those most "out of the loop" of informal communication: women and minorities.

Not only can institutions (whether departments, schools and colleges, or universities) help faculty by formulating explicit policies about time that are communicated in a transparent way (e.g., on the school or department website; in the faculty handbook), but they can also offer other kinds of supports that assist faculty in meeting the demands associated with their nonwork lives (see Philipsen, 2008, for detailed recommendations).

The Cost of Inadequate Childcare Resources

Increasingly, institutions provide some kind of support for childcare (whether sponsoring it onsite or subsidizing the cost), for dual-career hiring, and for elder care (Bowman & Feeney, 2011). Some faculty without children find institutional attention to those with them excessive. However, as we noted earlier, we believe that is because they feel overlooked in institutional attention. The remedy is not removal of support for those with children, but inclusion of the different kinds of support needed by those without children.

An institution may falsely think that it has "good resources for working parents" even when those resources no longer meet the needs of newly recruited faculty. Hiring more female and male faculty who have egalitarian relationships with their working partners results in more children who need care. A few examples from faculty at one research-intensive university that prides itself on being family-friendly make this clear. Two examples— about one male and one female new recruit—reflect this generation of young faculty's concern about this issue:

A female candidate for an assistant professor position mentioned that she was about four months pregnant during her second visit. She asked me about daycare options at [this institution] and was disappointed to hear that spots were quite limited such that she would be unlikely to get infant care. She told me that the other university she had an offer from had relatively inexpensive, readily available childcare. She ended up accepting a position at the other university.

A junior male faculty member had offers from other universities.... He said that he decided to come to the [university] because it was family friendly.... He had a child about two years after coming to [the university] and expressed great frustration that daycare spots were unavailable for his infant. He felt like this lack of daycare indicated that [the university] wasn't as family friendly as he had originally been led to believe.

Another example points to the chain of disappointments and the cost to a young mother in the early years of her tenure-track career:

We struggled with infant care for our first child. We got on the wait-list when we were about three months pregnant. We were told we were #404 (I will never forget) and that there was no way we would ever get him in.... We enrolled our son at [a community center] but found the care to be below our standards. We moved him to another [center] and were paired up with a wonderful teacher. We had a good experience until our daughter was born. Her teacher at the same school was not that good. It is incredibly stressful to know that your child is not getting "good" care. We made the tough decision to move the older one, and separate him from the teacher he had since he was six months old so that we could get our younger one into the [university]. We played the game...the same way we were thwarted with our first born. Even after moving him, that just moved us "up" on the waiting list. We were #3 in line now for an infant spot. And we had to wait, and wait, for several months before we were able to get our youngest in. At this point, she was 11 months old and spent 8 months in the care of a substandard teacher. And...as both of us were faculty at [the university]...we spent two hours of each day just commuting between the two centers and doing two drop-offs and pick-ups across town. Now that both are in [the nearby on-campus day-care center], our "commute" is a seven-minute walk. Both of us gained about two hours in our work day. And our children are in an amazing, supportive environment.

Another mother outlined her experience this way:

The process was incredibly stressful and time-consuming (all the interviewing and touring) and confusing. It's hard to explain to someone who hasn't gone through this how all-consuming this is. It's your baby! A whole little human being! You end up spending all this workday time figuring this out, rather than writing papers, working on grants, etc. The daycare folks would not even estimate when a spot would open up and were quite literally unwilling to give us our number despite its existence (I now understand that's because they literally don't open up spots for babies hardly ever). I have heard countless similar experiences of withholding of information like spot number, and inability to find daycare spots for infants. And, of course, the burden of finding these spots seems to lie mostly with women faculty even though it shouldn't. So the lack of daycare for infants is a double burden on women faculty here. There has to be a better way.

Finally, one father expressed his frustration this way:

I would hope that the number of spots or new university sponsored daycare centers could be expanded. With the growing emphasis on diversity in academia, STEM fields, and all other endeavors at [the university], certainly one type of diversity is having children or taking care of dependents. The days of single White men with no dependents leading academic fields or filling faculty rosters is over. If [the university] expects to continue to attract top quality researchers and also fulfill their mission of fostering diversity/inclusion issues, it seems reasonable to increase the family-friendly nature of [the university] by increasing access to daycare centers.

Institutions need policies that enable faculty to manage the periods in their lives when nonwork demands are great, even as they are free to benefit from the increased time commitment of faculty during periods when they are not. Moreover, it is best when these "benefits" are available as entitlements rather than as requests that may or may not be granted (commonly referred to as "opt out" rather than "opt in" policies, emphasizing that the choice not to take them up belongs to the individual faculty member; see, e.g., Rosser, 2012). Operating in an environment where these demands are either taboo (cannot be mentioned) or openly disapproved of inevitably limits faculty members' commitment to the institution. Feeling that an institution has provided crucial freedom, flexibility, or assistance during a particularly difficult time engenders loyalty and appreciation, as well as a faster return to full productivity.

Maximizing Faculty Satisfaction and Retention by Building Community

How can an institution maximize faculty satisfaction and retention? We can summarize our discussion: maximize supportive, helpful resources; be fair; be transparent; enhance the warmth and respectfulness of the faculty community; and meet faculty members' human needs. Maximizing satisfaction and retention requires deep and pervasive institutionalization of these features in policy and practice. They should be explicitly articulated as part of the mission and culture of the institution, embedded in official formal policies, and reflected in the procedures adopted to implement policies.

Ideally, institutional leaders at every level underscore these values as issues are discussed and routine business is conducted, and they themselves reflect a helpful stance and a concern with being fair and transparent. This may sound obvious but we have talked with university leaders who spoke dismissively of these issues as not the business of the academy; faculty who hear or hear about this kind of talk are often shocked and demoralized. In any case, ensuring that the institution is experienced as helpful, fair, and transparent requires recruitment of internal leaders (deans and department chairs) who share these values and are well-educated about the policies and practices that reflect them. These values are supported when faculty are invited to have input into decision-making processes early on and are provided with a clear account of the process of decision-making after the input. It is also supported by regular assessment of the institution's progress (success and failure) toward fully enacting these values. This includes assessing and discussing the climate of work environments for various groups of faculty, as well as assessing more concrete features of the work structure, such as salary, space allocation, time in rank, progress to promotion, uses of internal research funding, use of family-friendly policies, and teaching and service assignments. Finally, maximizing these outcomes requires that the institution prevent the stigmatization of faculty who make use of institutional policies.

Regular collection of data, along with discussion of perceived issues they uncover, provide all faculty and administrators with the information they need about institutional success in providing resources, fairness, and transparency to the faculty. Regular assessment of institutional outcomes also provides opportunities for developing and tweaking policies and practices so they are more widely and uniformly experienced as creating and maintaining the kind of institutional workplace that maximizes faculty satisfaction and commitment.

From frequent and serious institutional conversation, individual faculty will emerge who have the personal interest, skills, and talents to suggest better policies and provide leadership in developing enthusiasm for them. By engaging the faculty in the project of improving the institutional work environment, a new generation of faculty leaders will emerge who can make these issues a priority: they will understand fully that a work environment that maximizes the satisfaction and productivity of all faculty provides the best guarantee of institutional excellence over the long term.

Recommendations for Maximizing Faculty Retention and Building Community

Institutional Policies

Create, publicize, and implement policies that

1. link institutional expectations (e.g., for contract renewal, promotion, and tenure) to institutional resources provided to faculty

2. ensure broad access to resources for all faculty

3. guarantee fair and transparent procedures

4. address human needs of faculty throughout the life cycle (e.g., dual career and child and elder care) as faculty entitlements

5. respect the need for boundaries/limits to demands of work and the workplace

Institutional Programs

Create, publicize, and implement

1. formal programs that support development of faculty professional networks inside and outside the institution

2. networks of faculty with similar life situations (e.g., faculty of color, LGBT faculty, women scientists, single parents, etc.)

3. formal programs that increase the likelihood of a climate of civility, respect, and freedom from harassment

4. data collection and regular reporting on issues of equity (salary, work-load, etc.) and climate, as well as policy use; act on findings proactively

Senior Administrators

1. Ensure that all communication about important issues (e.g., tenure criteria and procedures, grievance procedures) takes place through multiple methods of communication (e-mail, websites, snail mail, discussion in formal meetings).

2. Set an institutional norm of zero tolerance for disrespect, incivility, and harassment.

3. Provide educational opportunities for department chairs and deans to learn about how to create and maintain a positive departmental, school, or college climate.

Department Chairs

1. Proactively ensure that all probationary faculty receive information, advice, and assistance.

2. Develop transparent practices of decision-making and allocation of resources based on principles of equity and fairness.

3. Avoid treating any faculty member as a representative of a group.

4. Be alert to evidence of faculty members' isolation or marginalization and proactively seek ways of engaging those faculty members in key departmental activities of interest to them.

5. Set a departmental norm of zero tolerance for disrespect, incivility, and harassment. Interrupt disrespect and incivility as it occurs; address complaints of harassment rapidly and fairly.

6. Adopt departmental meeting times (including colloquium and other speaker times) that are consistent with humane and family-friendly boundaries on workplace expectations.

All Faculty Members

1. Proactively ensure that all probationary faculty receive information, advice, and assistance.

2. Help explain practices of decision-making and allocation of resources and act to ensure that they are based on principles of equity and fairness.

3. Take seriously the need to assist other, less senior, faculty members in finding resources for their work and in identifying an appropriate professional network.

4. Avoid treating any faculty member as a representative of a group.

5. Respect workplace time boundaries even if you personally feel comfortable with meeting times outside those boundaries.

6. Be alert to evidence of faculty members' isolation or marginalization and proactively seek ways of engaging those faculty members in key departmental activities of interest to them.

7. Do not tolerate disrespect, incivility, or harassment when it occurs; intervene to stop it.

Notes

1. It is difficult adequately to assess the impact of these policies on faculty outcomes such as salary, promotion, and retention. Some studies have focused on the impact of any one of these policies. For example, two have examined "tenure clock stopping" (regardless of the presence of modifications of duties or parental leaves). One of these focuses on a single institution but across disciplines, and results are constrained by low numbers, and a single policy formulation and set of practices (e.g., Manchester, Leslie & Kramer, 2013). Another examines a single discipline but across 50 institutions, but obtains no measures of individual policy use and instead attempts to attribute differential gender rates of outcomes to the presence or absence of a policy institution-wide (e.g., Antecol, Bedard & Stearns, 2016). In the absence of better data about the impact of particular policies on faculty outcomes, we base our recommendations on the signal these policies send to faculty that their particular life situation is one the institution recognizes and seeks to support.

2. For the American Astronomical Society, see https://aas.org/policies/anti-harassment -policy/; for the American Geophysical Union, see https://harassment.agu.org/; for the American Political Science Association, see http://www.apsanet.org/Portals/54/goverance /anti-harrassment.pdf?ver=2017-01-26-141514-047&timestamp=1485458151478; for the Boston University Conference on Language Development code of conduct, see https://www.bu.edu/bucld/conference-info/conduct/.

3. Some institutions apply stop-the-clock or modified duties automatically to new mothers and require that new fathers demonstrate that they will be a (or the) primary caretaker. We prefer a system that does not cement stereotypical gender roles but requires either member of a couple to demonstrate that they will be a caretaker.

References

Ackelsberg, M., Hart, J., Miller, N. J., Queeney, K., & Van Dyne, S. (2009). Faculty microclimate change at Smith College. In W. R. Brown-Glaude (Ed.), *Doing diversity in higher education* (pp. 83–102). New Brunswick, NJ: Rutgers University Press.

Ahmed, S. (2012). *On being included: Racism and diversity in institutional life*. Durham, NC: Duke University Press.

Antecol, H., Bedard, K., & Stearns, J. (2016). Equal but inequitable: Who benefits from gender-neutral tenure clock stopping policies. *IZA Discussion papers, No. 9904*. http://ftp.iza.org/dp9904.pdf

Bailyn, L., Rapoport, R., Fletcher, J. K., & Pruitt, B. H. (2002). *Beyond work-life balance: Advancing gender equity and workplace performance*. San Francisco, CA: Jossey-Bass.

Berdahl, J. L. (2007a). Harassment based on sex: Protecting social status in the context of gender hierarchy. *Academy of Management Review, 32*(2), 641–658.

Berdahl, J. L. (2007b). The sexual harassment of uppity women. *Journal of Applied Psychology, 92*(2), 425–437.

Berdahl, J. L., & Moore, C. (2006). Workplace harassment: Double jeopardy for minority women. *Journal of Applied Psychology, 91*(2), 426–436.

Biggs, J., Hawley, P. H., & Biernat, M. (in press). The academic conference as a chilly climate for women: Effects of gender representation on experiences of sexism, coping responses, and career intentions. *Sex Roles.*

Bilimoria, D., & Stewart, A. J. (2009). "Don't ask, don't tell": The academic climate for lesbian, gay, bisexual and transgender faculty in science and engineering. *National Women's Studies Journal, 21*(2), 85–103.

Bowman, L., & Feeney, M. K. (2011, March 28). Laundry and lab time: Do family-friendly policies affect academic work outcomes? SSRN. doi:10.2139/ssrn.1798142

Bugeja, M. J. (2002). Is congeniality overrated? *Chronicle of Higher Education.* Retrieved from http://chronicle.com/article/Is-Congeniality-Overrated-/46162/

Campbell, C. M., & O'Meara, K. (2014). Faculty agency: Departmental contexts that matter in faculty careers. *Research in Higher Education, 55*(1), 49–74.

Cantalupo, N. C., & Kidder, W. C. (2017). Mapping the Title IX iceberg: Sexual harassment (mostly) in graduate school by college faculty. *Journal of Legal Education, 66*(4), 850–881.

Carr, J. Z., Schmidt, A. M., Ford, D. K., & DeShon, R. P. (2003). Climate perceptions matter: A meta-analytic path analysis relating molar climate, cognitive and affective states, and individual-level work outcomes. *Journal of Applied Psychology, 88,* 605–619.

Clancy, K. B., Lee, K., Rodgers, E. M., & Richey, C. (2017). Double jeopardy in astronomy and planetary science: Women of color face greater risks of gendered and racial harassment. *Journal of Geophysical Research. Planets, 122*(7), 1610–1623.

COACHE. (2008). *Perspectives on what pre-tenure faculty want and what six research universities provide.* Cambridge, MA: Harvard University Collaborative on Academic Careers in Higher Education.

COACHE. (2010). *The experience of tenure-track faculty at research universities: Analysis of COACHE survey results by academic area and gender.* Cambridge, MA: Harvard University Collaborative on Academic Careers in Higher Education.

Collins, J. (2001). *Good to great: Why some companies make the leap … and others don't.* New York, NY: HarperBusiness.

Cortina, L. (2008). Unseen injustice: Incivility as modern discrimination in organizations. *Academy of Management Review, 33*(1), 55–75.

Ecklund, E. H., & Lincoln, A. E. (2016). *Failing families, failing science: Work-family conflict in academic science*. New York, NY: NYU Press.

Ely, R. I., & Thomas, D. A. (2001). Cultural diversity at work: The effect of different diversity perspectives on work group processes and outcomes. *Administrative Science Quarterly, 46*(2), 229–273.

Galinsky, E. M., & Bond, J. T. (2009). Generation and gender in the workplace: A new generation at work. In D. R. Crane & E. J. Hill (Eds.), *Handbook of families and work: Interdisciplinary perspectives* (pp. 425–448). Lanham, MD: University Press of America.

Girgus, J. S. (2011, November). *Rebalancing the work-life norm: Providing family-focused resources*. Keynote address at a conference on Constructing Our Future: Exploring the Values, Strategic Processes and Change Mechanisms of Work-Life Policies, University of Indiana Inter-Campus Coalition for the Advancement of Women, Bloomington, IN.

Gutek, B. (1985). *Sex and the workplace*. San Francisco, CA: Jossey-Bass.

Gutiérrez y Muhs, G., Niemann, Y. F., González, C. G., & Harris, A. P. (Eds.). (2012). *Presumed innocent: The intersections of race and class for women in academia*. Boulder, CO: University of Colorado Press.

Guzman, F., Trevino, J., Lubuguin, F., & Aryan, B. (2010). Microaggressions and the pipeline for scholars of color. In D. W. Sue (Ed.), *Microaggressions and marginality: Manifestations, dynamics and impact* (pp. 145–167). New York, NY: Wiley.

Harris, T. M. (2007). Black feminist thought and cultural contractions: Understanding the intersection and negotiation of racial, gendered and professional identities in the academy. In K. G. Hendrix (Ed.), *Neither White nor male: Female faculty of color* (pp. 55–64). San Francisco, CA: Jossey-Bass.

Hebl, E. B., Hebl, M. P., George, J. M., & Matusik, S. F. (2010). Understanding tokenism: Antecedents and consequences of a psychological climate of gender inequity. *Journal of Management, 36*, 482–510.

Hermanowicz, J. C. (2012). The sociology of academic careers: Problems and prospects. In J. C. Smart & M. B. Paulsen (Eds.), *Higher education: Handbook of theory and research* (Vol. 27, pp. 207–247). New York, NY: Springer. doi:10.1007/978-94-007-2950-6_4

Hershcovis, M. S. (2011). "Incivility, social undermining, bullying…oh my!": A call to reconcile constructs within workplace aggression research. *Journal of Organizational Behavior, 32*, 499–519.

Huerta, M., Cortina, L. M., Pang, J. S., Torges, C. M., & Magley, V. J. (2006). Sex and power in the academy: Sexual harassment in the lives of college women. *Personality and Social Psychology, 32*, 616–628.

Jagsi, R., Griffith, K. A., Jones, R., Perumalswami, C. R., Ubel, P., & Stewart, A. (2016). Sexual harassment and discrimination experiences of academic medical faculty. *Journal of the American Medical Association, 315*(19), 2120–2121.

Jayakumar, U. M., Howard, T. C., Allen, W. R., & Han, J. C. (2009). Racial privilege in the professoriate: An exploration of campus climate, retention and satisfaction. *Journal of Higher Education, 80*(5), 538–563.

Johns, G. (2006). The essential impact of context on organizational behavior. *Academy of Management Review, 31*(2), 386–408.

Johnson, E. P. (2009). In the merry old land of OZ: Rac(e)ing and quee(r)ing the academy. In R. Johnson (Ed.), *The queer community: Continuing the struggle for social justice* (pp. 85–103). San Diego, CA: Birkdale.

Jordan, C. G., & Bilimoria, D. (2007). Creating a productive and inclusive academic work environment. In A. J. Stewart, J. E. Malley, & D. LaVaque-Manty (Eds.), *Transforming science and engineering: Advancing academic women* (pp. 225–242). Ann Arbor, MI: University of Michigan Press.

Kanter, R. M. (1977). *Men and women of the corporation*. New York, NY: Basic Books.

Keashly, L. (2012). Workplace bullying and gender: It's complicated. In S. Fox & T. R. Lituchy (Eds.), *Gender and the dysfunctional workplace* (pp. 78–95). Northampton, MA: Edward Elgar.

Keashly, L., & Jagatic, K. (2003). By any other name: American perspectives on workplace bullying. In S. Einason, H. Hoel, D. Zapf, & C. L. Cooper (Eds.), *Bullying and emotional abuse in the workplace* (pp. 31–60). New York, NY: Taylor & Francis.

Leskinen, E., Cortina, L. M., & Kabat, D. B. (2011). Gender harassment: Broadening our understanding of sex-based harassment at work. *Law and Human Behavior, 35,* 25–39.

Lilienfeld, S. O. (2017). Microaggressions: Strong claims, inadequate evidence. *Perspectives on Psychological Science, 12*(1), 138–169.

Lim, S., & Cortina, L. (2005). Interpersonal mistreatment in the workplace: The interface of general incivility and sexual harassment. *Journal of Applied Psychology, 90*(3), 483–496.

Lim, S., Cortina, L., & Magley, V. (2008). Personal and workgroup incivility: Impact on work and health outcomes. *Journal of Applied Psychology, 93*(1), 95–107.

Mack, K., & Soto, M. (2016, June 15). *Gender values: Meeting the challenges for STEM gender diversity*. Presented at Women in Engineering Proactive Network (WEPAN) Change Leader Forum, Denver, Colorado.

Manchester, C. F., Leslie, L. M., & Kramer, A. (2013). Is the clock still ticking? An evaluation of the consequences of stopping the tenure clock. *Industrial & Labor Relations Review*, *66*(1), 3–31.

Mason, M. A., & Goulden, M. (2002a). Do babies matter? The effects of family formation on the lifelong careers of academic men and women. *Academe*, *88*, 21–27.

Mason, M. A., & Goulden, M. (2002b). Marriage and baby blues: Redefining gender equity in the academy. *Annals of the American Academy of Political and Social Science*, *596*, 86–103.

Mason, M. A., & Goulden, M. (2004). Do babies matter (Part II): Closing the baby gap. *Academe*, *90*, 10–15.

Matthew, P. (Ed.). (2016). *Written/unwritten: Diversity and hidden truths of tenure*. Chapel Hill, NC: University of North Carolina Press.

McPherson, M., Smith-Lovin, L., & Cook, J. M. (2001). Birds of a feather: Homophily in social networks. *Annual Review of Sociology*, *27*, 415–444.

Miner-Rubino, K., & Cortina, L. (2004). Working in a context of hostility toward women: Implication for employees' well-being. *Journal of Occupational Health Psychology*, *9*(2), 107–122.

Nader, L. (2001, July 13). Harmony coerced is freedom denied. *Chronicle of Higher Education*. Retrieved from http://chronicle.com/article/Harmony-Coerced-Is-Freedom /20055/

Ostrove, J. M., Stewart, A. J., & Curtin, N. L. (2011). Social class and belonging: Implications for graduate students' career aspirations. *Journal of Higher Education*, *82*(6), 748–774.

Philipsen, M. I. (2008). *Challenges of the faculty career for women: Success and sacrifice*. San Francisco, CA: Jossey-Bass.

Pololi, L. (2010). *Changing the culture of academic medicine: Perspectives of women faculty*. Hanover, NH: Dartmouth University Press.

Pololi, L. H., Civian, J. T., Brennan, R. T., Dottolo, A. L., & Krupat, E. (2012). Experiencing the culture of academic medicine: Gender matters, a national study. *Journal of General Internal Medicine*. doi:10.1007/s11606-012-2207-1

Porath, C. (2017, September 15). The silent killer of workplace happiness, productivity, and health is a basic lack of civility. https://qz.com/1079344/the-silent-killer-of -workplace-happiness-productivity-and-health-is-a-lack-of-basic-civility/

Porath, C. L., & Erez, A. (2007). Does rudeness really matter? The effects of rudeness on task performance and helpfulness. *Academy of Management Journal*, *50*(5), 1181–1197.

Porath, C. L., Macinnis, D., & Folkes, V. (2010). Witnessing incivility among employees: Effects on consumer anger and negative inferences about companies. *Journal of Consumer Research, 37*, 292–302.

Porath, C. L., & Pearson, C. M. (2010). The cost of bad behavior. *Organizational Dynamics, 39*(1), 64–71.

Rankin, P., Nielsen, J., & Stanley, D. M. (2007). Weak links, hot networks, and tacit knowledge. In A. J. Stewart, J. E. Malley, & D. LaVaque-Manty (Eds.), *Transforming science and engineering: Advancing academic women* (pp. 31–47). Ann Arbor, MI: University of Michigan Press.

Raver, J. L., & Nishii, L. H. (2010). Once, twice or three times as harmful? Ethnic harassment, gender harassment and generalized workplace harassment. *Journal of Applied Psychology, 95*(2), 236–254.

Reich, T. C., & Hershcovis, M. S. (2012). Observing sexual harassment at work: A gendered extension of a gendered construct. In S. Fox & T. R. Lituchy (Eds.), *Gender and the dysfunctional workplace* (pp. 120–134). Northampton, MA: Edward Elgar.

Richman, J. A., Shinsako, S. A., Rospenda, K. M., Flaherty, J. A., & Freels, S. (2002). Workplace harassment/abuse and alcohol-related outcomes: The mediating role of psychological distress. *Journal of Studies on Alcohol, 63*(4), 412–419.

Rosser, S. V. (2012). *Breaking into the lab: Engineering progress for women in science.* New York, NY: NYU Press.

Rudman, L. A., Borgida, E., & Robertson, B. A. (1995). Suffering in silence: Procedural justice versus gender socialization issues in university sexual harassment grievance procedures. *Basic and Applied Psychology, 17*(4), 519–541.

Schiebinger, L., Henderson, A., & Gilmartin, S. K. (2008). *Dual-career couples: What universities need to know.* Stanford, CA: Stanford University, Clayman Institute for Gender Research.

Settles, I. H., Cortina, L. M., Malley, J., & Stewart, A. J. (2006). The climate for women in academic science: The good, the bad, and the changeable. *Psychology of Women Quarterly, 30*, 47–58.

Settles, I., Cortina, L., Stewart, A. J., & Malley, J. E. (2007). Voice matters: Buffering the impact of a negative climate for women in science. *Psychology of Women Quarterly, 31*, 270–281.

Smith, C. P., & Freyd, J. J. (2014). Institutional betrayal. *American Psychologist, 69*(6), 575–587.

Sue, D. W. (2010a). *Microaggressions in everyday life: Race, gender, and sexual orientation.* Hoboken, NJ: Wiley.

Sue, D. W. (Ed.). (2010b). *Microaggressions and marginality: Manifestation, dynamics, and impact.* Hoboken, NJ: Wiley.

Thompson, C. Q. (2008). Recruitment, retention, and mentoring faculty of color: The chronicle continues. In N. V. N. Chism (Ed.), *Faculty at the margins* (pp. 47–54). San Francisco, CA: Jossey-Bass.

Thompson, M., & Sekaquaptewa, D. (2002). When being different is detrimental: Solo status and the performance of women and racial minorities. *Analyses of Social Issues and Public Policy (ASAP),* 2(1), 183–203.

Tokarczyk, M. M. (1993). By the rivers of Babylon. In M. M. Tokarczyk & E. A. Fay (Eds.), *Working-class women in the academy* (pp. 311–321). Amherst, MA: University of Massachusetts Press.

Trower, C. A. (2010). A new generation of faculty: Similar core values in a different world. *AAC&U Peer Review: Emerging Trends and Key Debates in Undergraduate Education,* 12(3).

Urry, C. M. (2008). Are photons gendered? Women in physics and astronomy. In L. Schiebinger (Ed.), *Gendered innovations in science and engineering* (pp. 150–164). Stanford, CA: Stanford University Press.

Waltman, J., & Hollenshead, C. (2007). *Creating a positive departmental climate: Principles for best practices.* Report for ADVANCE by Center for the Education of Women, University of Michigan.

Walton, G., & Cohen, J. (2007). A question of belonging: Race, social fit, and achievement. *Journal of Personality and Social Psychology,* 9(1), 82–96.

Williams, J. (2000). *Unbending gender: Why family and work conflict and what to do about it.* New York, NY: Oxford University Press.

Willness, C. R., Steel, P., & Lee, K. (2007). A meta-analysis of the antecedents and consequences of workplace sexual harassment. *Personnel Psychology,* 60(1), 127–162.

Yoder, J. (2002). Context matters: Understanding tokenism processes and their impact on women's work. *Psychology of Women Quarterly,* 26, 1–8.

Yoshino, K. (2007). *Covering.* New York, NY: Random House.

Zambrana, R. E., Wingfield, A. H., Lapeyrouse, L. M., Dávila, B. A., Hoagland, T. L., & Valdez, R. B. (2017). Blatant, subtle, and insidious: URM faculty perceptions of discriminatory practices in predominantly White institutions. *Sociological Inquiry,* 87(2), 207–232.

8 Facilitating Faculty Success

People are not born knowing how to be successful in their work. They learn how to be successful through access to information and opportunities, and especially challenges and opportunities to learn from low-stakes failures. People also learn through the examples of others whom they would like to emulate and think they could emulate. It is to a department's advantage to provide the conditions in which faculty can do their best work. Although departments hire faculty who have survived an elaborate process of selection in graduate school for their intellectual skills, some areas of professional development may have been relatively neglected or may not have been addressed because they were not appropriate for the individual's position as a graduate student or postdoctoral fellow. Because of those lacunae, most faculty benefit from opportunities to learn a wide range of skills not included in their disciplinary education or apprenticeship. Moreover, retention of all faculty is enhanced when institutions have communicated the value of the faculty and expressed support for them by providing professional development opportunities.

The Job Demands of Being a Faculty Member

Being a high-functioning faculty member is a very complex job. The job includes managing time and responsibilities; deciding where to focus one's energies; making intellectual progress in answering the questions one has posed; applying for funding; teaching effectively and efficiently; gaining value and pleasure from attending conferences; presenting good papers; balancing research, teaching, and service responsibilities; balancing work and a personal life; finding collaborators; operating within a diverse community of faculty and students; working with staff; mentoring graduate students and junior colleagues; choosing meaningful ways to contribute to the institution and discipline; continuing to develop intellectually in a variety of roles; and supporting leaders whose vision one values.

Responsibilities and opportunities change as a professional career progresses. We devote most of this chapter to strategies that apply to junior faculty in particular or apply across the board to all faculty, regardless of rank.

Evaluating One's Progress

One of the main features of academic work that makes it appealing—the independence and autonomy it offers—is also what makes it challenging. The job is challenging for everyone, and part of the challenge is realistically evaluating one's pluses and minuses. White women and underrepresented minorities are less likely than White men to receive opportunities to excel in new research areas and less likely to receive recognition for their research achievements (as we have discussed). The feedback that White women and underrepresented minorities receive, if they take it as reasonably informative about their value, will result in their feeling less entitled than is appropriate. White men, who receive more positive feedback and recognition, will also tend to interpret the feedback they receive as informative and will thus feel more entitled than is appropriate, given their performance (Hogue, Yoder, & Singleton, 2007; Pelham & Hetts, 2001). Women tend to boast less than equivalently accomplished men do (Reuben, Sapienza, & Zingales, 2014). It is difficult for people to appraise their own contributions realistically since part of realism requires taking others' reactions into account, and people's reactions are skewed.

Universal Design

In our view, men and women should be treated similarly, as should Whites and people of color. However, that does not mean treating women like men or treating men like women; similarly, it does not mean treating people of color like Whites nor Whites like people of color. Rather, it means that one finds a way to convey the information that will be the same for everyone *and* will take into account the differences in how people are likely to react. It means applying principles of universal design, as described in the preface: that is, the solution should take into account the range of possible human responses and be tailored to include as many people as possible.

Overview of the Chapter

This chapter reviews what everyone needs to know to be successful and presents examples of programs that help ensure that everyone has access to that information. The chapter describes five kinds of faculty development programs that can be successful: classical one-on-one mentoring, circles of advisors, peer mentoring, workshops, and launch committees for new faculty. It is possible for an institution to offer all or only some of them. These programs should be assessed in terms of their success in reducing race and gender gaps in outcomes, including success in obtaining tenure, retention, time in rank before promotion, access to leadership opportunities in rank-appropriate ways, and representation in leadership positions.

Organized faculty development programs and opportunities make it more likely that all faculty will be successful both inside and outside of the institution. Yet few institutions pay more than lip service to faculty development. For example, some institutions claim to have a mentoring program, and they do, but what they mean by mentoring is that a senior faculty member meets with the junior faculty member once or twice a year. Moreover, we have found—and we have heard this from other colleagues too—that the higher the administrative source on how mentoring works in an institution, the more likely it is portrayed positively and as very successful. To know how mentoring is going, it is crucial to gather information from the presumptive "mentees."

We assume that most people have the twin goals of wanting to be as effective as possible in their work and of wanting to enjoy their work and their life as a whole. There are sometimes limitations on how effective a person can be or how enjoyable their work and life can be, due to external life circumstances. For example, someone may have unusual caretaking responsibilities or may have a chair or head who is a tyrant. Time and chance happen to us all.

Nevertheless, there are skills people can acquire that will allow them to work effectively, efficiently, and enjoyably. Those skills require information and practice. We address here the steps faculty can take to acquire the skills to be a successful and fulfilled academic. In the ideal case, the college or university has tested programs in place that will facilitate faculty development, and a faculty member's chair or dean will ensure that all faculty have the opportunity to participate in those programs. Even if institutional support is lacking, faculty themselves can take the lead in obtaining the information and skills they need.

Faculty Development

The Classical Conception of Mentoring

Perhaps the most widely adopted and popular kind of program to increase the success of individual junior faculty is mentoring.

Defining Mentoring Different people mean different things by mentoring— so different that there is no way of determining, just from the term "mentoring," what such a program might include. Some departments assign every new faculty member a "mentor." What that can mean in practice is that the faculty member meets with the mentor once a semester or year, during which time the mentor asks how things are going and the faculty member says that they are going pretty well. This is like the server who stops by your table in a restaurant and says, "Are you enjoying your meal?" Or it can mean that the mentor meets frequently with the faculty member, gives advice on professional and personal matters, advocates for the faculty member, and serves as a professional model. Or it can mean something in between.

The inadequate end of the distribution of possible ways to mentor is exemplified by a department chair who told us that his department had a mentoring program: "Every year I have an annual evaluation session with junior faculty." That yearly evaluation took about 15 minutes. During the meeting he filled out a form, assigning ratings of "satisfactory," "needs improvement," "unsatisfactory," or "not applicable" in three areas, research, teaching, and service. That seems to nail down a procedure that is not actually mentoring at all.

At the other end of the distribution is the idea of the mentor as sage, advocate, career planner and manager, issuer of challenges to do better, emotional supporter, and tireless giver of advice for all aspects of life until such time as the mentee or protégé no longer needs mentoring. We know of mentors like this, but the number of people who can be or want to be that sort of mentor is tiny. Mentoring that requires that much knowledge, dedication, and time is going to be mentoring for the few by the very few. And mentoring, like any interpersonal relationship, includes negative as well as positive aspects (Eby, Butts, Durley, & Ragins, 2010). Any relationship is more likely to endure when people feel positively valued by the other person. In academia, where critical analysis is part of everyday professional practice, that may be hard to achieve.

Formal Mentoring Programs   Most colleges and universities do not have a consistent mentoring program that operates across all departments, and most do not have any training of people who supervise graduate students or postdoctoral fellows. Even fewer have training programs for senior faculty to mentor junior faculty. Colleges and universities train graduate students and postdocs in how to do research. After that, academics are on their own.

Does Mentoring "Work"?   Despite the large literature on mentoring, it is very difficult to determine whether it "works." Mentoring effects can be measured in terms of objective and subjective benefits and costs to the mentee or protégé(e) (Kram, 1985; Kram & Ragins, 2007; see Allen & Eby, 2011, for a suite of articles). Objective benefits or costs might include various measures of career progress, such as number of publications, number of grants, invitations to speak at scholarly events, progress through the ranks, and so on. Those benefits are occasionally measured, but the length of studies does not always allow extended measurements. Subjective benefits or costs might include various measures of attitudes and motivations, and those subjective benefits or costs might in turn lead to objective benefits or costs.

Some people argue for the value of only creating mentoring relationships between people who are of the same gender and/or race. In our view this is both impossible and unwise. First, wherever there are increasing numbers of a group, the small number of senior people in that group will be overburdened by mentoring. Second, this assumes that sharing group membership is always a basis for a relationship of trust and that not sharing group membership is always a basis for a relationship of mistrust. Neither is true. (For a description of mentoring written by a White mentor and an American Indian mentee, see Fryberg & Gerken, 2012.) That said, it is always helpful for young faculty who belong to an outnumbered group (by race, gender, sexuality, disability, etc.) to have access to senior faculty who are like them, not only as mentors but as role models and sources of community. Those people do not need to be their official mentors. They can be members of a network or a circle of advisors they seek out if they are so inclined, and their mentors and department chair can facilitate their meeting such people.

A major difficulty in establishing the effects of mentoring is that there is seldom an adequate control group (for reviews, see Allen, Eby, Poteet, Lentz, & Lima, 2004; Eby, Allen, Evans, Ng, & DuBois, 2008; Kammeyer-Mueller & Judge, 2008; Underhill, 2006). Informal, or spontaneous, mentoring relationships are common among successful individuals (e.g., Blickle, Witzki, & Schneider, 2009), but in such cases the mentees are self-selected and have selected or been selected by their mentor. Such individuals may simultaneously be engaging in a variety of other behaviors that will help their career. In formal mentoring relationships, where individuals are paired through a formal system of some sort—for example, the departmental chair assigns a mentor to a faculty member—there is again no control group. The documented positive effects are usually modest, and the underlying mechanism for their success remains unclear (Baranik, Roling, & Eby, 2010; Egan & Song, 2008). Mentoring may help mentees in part because the mentor becomes more invested in the mentee's success (Dobbin, Schrage, & Kalev, 2015).

Can Mentoring Harm?   Although negligence on a mentor's part is harmful, the worst way to be a bad mentor is to have a destructive and negative style (Eby et al., 2010; for a qualitative assessment, see, e.g., Straus, Johnson, Marquez, & Feldaman, 2013). From the mentee's perspective, a bad mentor is worse than a mentor who is absent and unresponsive because a bad mentor poisons the mentee's aspirations and goals. Negative terms, even though used less often than positive terms, have a disproportionate effect on the listener, creating a general negativity bias (Ito, Larsen, Smith, & Cacioppo, 1998; Rozin & Royzman, 2001).

One of us heard a male colleague mention an early experience as a faculty member: he had spoken to a senior faculty member about the difficulties of managing his research, applying for funding, being a good teacher, and performing service. The senior person said, in effect, if you can't stand the heat, get out of the kitchen. Thirty years later, this man still remembered that comment and its negative effect on him.

Mentoring and Evaluation   Both senior and junior faculty worry that the same people will play two roles in the lives of junior faculty: mentors or advisors and evaluators at critical career reviews. It is inevitable that some individuals will play both roles, but we believe that senior faculty can learn how to separate them, and junior faculty can be sensible about their own actions.

Senior faculty, when they are providing advice to a younger colleague, need to remember that they are providing *advice*, not instruction. Colleagues must make their own decisions. Whether a junior colleague did or did not follow the senior colleague's advice is not an appropriate issue to bring up when evaluating the junior person's success at career assessments. Similarly, it is inappropriate to bring up information that a junior colleague may have disclosed, such as a teaching problem or a difficulty with a collaborator. The focus of evaluations is the individual's career outcomes, not the particulars of the individual's path.

It is helpful for both mentors and mentees to know from the beginning whether they will be expected to play a major role in evaluation (e.g., because their expertise is pertinent). Mentees must discuss some problems in their work lives with their advisors if they are to get relevant assistance, but they can exercise discretion as to when and with whom to discuss those problems. They may choose to discuss some problems only with those colleagues who will not participate in assessment of their professional competence for institutional reviews.

Passive or Active Mentees?   Even if perfect mentors were plentiful, we see other problems with the classical conception of a mentor. For one thing, it implicitly puts the wrong person in the driver's seat. Each individual should be in charge of his or her own professional life, deciding where he or she wants to go next, figuring out which people to ask for advice, information, advocacy, support, and challenges to excel. A study with undergraduates taught them how to find a range of people, so that they had a "composite mentor." The students became more proactive in their education as a result and changed their pretraining idea of a mentor as a single person to a posttraining idea that many people could be usefully consulted in developing their undergraduate trajectory (Packard, 2003).

Mentoring across Academic Careers The traditional conception suggests that there will come a time when someone no longer needs advice, advocacy, support, challenge, and information. Thus, this conception suggests that it is the weak who need a mentor. One woman we know told her chair that she wanted a mentor, and he said, "Oh, you're too good for that; you don't need a mentor." This illustrates an unfortunate connotation that many people have of "mentor": a mentor is needed by people who don't know what they are doing.

We reject that conception. Everyone can benefit from good advice, support, challenge, and information throughout their professional lives, no matter who they are. Everyone can learn more and develop. We also reject a model that suggests that everyone should have a stable, clear idea about his or her goals because that model forecloses growth. Sometimes goals change. People change their research direction or area. They turn to service to the institution or the profession. Even when goals remain stable—to do one's research, teaching, and service well—one's changing status within the institution and the discipline may add new dimensions to those goals. Associate and full professors may find that junior colleagues now ask them for advice. Most faculty are informal mentors, whether or not they want to be, to students. Senior faculty similarly become informal mentors to junior faculty. Yet there are few formal occasions on which faculty can learn how to excel at giving advice, help, and support (i.e., in a way that will actually benefit the person who has asked for advice, help, or support). Who will mentor the mentors, so that they can mentor well?

A Model Mentor Training Program Medical schools have increasingly risen to the challenge of providing training for mentors of medical students, postdoctoral fellows, and junior faculty. A 26-item Mentoring Competency Assessment (MCA) can be used by would-be or current mentors in medical schools to evaluate their mentoring in six areas: maintaining effective communication, aligning expectations, assessing understanding, addressing diversity, promoting professional development, and fostering independence (Fleming, House, Shewakramani, Yu, Garbutt, McGee, et al., 2013). This assessment tool was developed initially through the Research Mentor Training group (http://www.researchmentortraining.org/index.aspx) and subsequently through the Center for Improvement of Mentored Experiences in Research (CIMER, http://cimerproject.org) within the University of Wisconsin. It can be adapted for broader purposes.

One value of the assessment is to show mentors important areas that they may not be thinking about. The category of aligning expectations, for example, includes "setting clear relationship expectations" and "considering mentor-mentee differences." Many supervisors, in our experience, do not consider the possibility that a student may have different goals than they have. We have provided the full set of 26 MCA items in box 8.1, which is also available at the University of Wisconsin website. Their research suggests that people who are highly motivated to be good mentors can develop their skills through training.[1]

On balance, we think that mentoring can be successful, especially if mentors are highly motivated and receive training or support in how to mentor. Many institutions provide handbooks to faculty that can be used by both mentors and mentees and help them identify their joint goals and how they will work together (for one example, see the resources available under career advising at the University of Michigan's ADVANCE website).

Box 8.1
Mentoring Competency Assessment (MCA)

Please rate how skilled you feel you are in each of the following areas: [Think about your skill generally, with all your mentees. Please only choose "not applicable" (N/A) when a skill cannot be applied to any of your mentees.]

1 = not at all skilled
4 = moderately skilled
7 = extremely skilled
n/a = not applicable

1. Active listening
2. Providing constructive feedback
3. Establishing a relationship based on trust
4. Identifying and accommodating different communication styles
5. Employing strategies to improve communication with mentees
6. Coordinating effectively with your mentees' other mentors

(continued)

Box 8.1 (continued)

7. Working with mentees to set clear expectations of the mentoring relationship

8. Aligning your expectations with your mentees'

9. Considering how personal and professional differences may impact expectations

10. Working with mentees to set research goals

11. Helping mentees develop strategies to meet goals

12. Accurately estimating your mentees' level of scientific knowledge

13. Accurately estimating your mentees' ability to conduct research

14. Employing strategies to enhance your mentees' knowledge and abilities

15. Motivating your mentees

16. Building mentees' confidence

17. Stimulating your mentees' creativity

18. Acknowledging your mentees' professional contributions

19. Negotiating a path to professional independence with your mentees

20. Taking into account the biases and prejudices you bring to the mentor/mentee relationship

21. Working effectively with mentees whose personal background is different from your own (age, race, gender, class, region, culture, religion, family composition etc.)

22. Helping your mentees network effectively

23. Helping your mentees set career goals

24. Helping your mentees balance work with their personal life

25. Understanding your impact as a role mode

26. Helping your mentees acquire resources (e.g., grants, etc.)

https://uwmadison.co1.qualtrics.com/SE/?SID=SV_5jMT4fhemifK01n&Q_JFE=0

But the notion of a single mentor, and the notion that mentees are limited to students, postdocs, and junior faculty, is too limiting. For people whose needs and desires for new skills continue, the time at which they no longer need advice, advocacy, support, challenge, and information is—never. If we try to apply the classical notion of a mentor, midlevel and senior people are usually out of luck. They're supposed to already know what they want to do, or they're supposed to figure it out for themselves, or they're supposed to wait for something to drop into their laps. That is an inefficient way to arrange one's next steps. While it's wonderful to already know what one wants to do next, or to be able to figure it out oneself, or for luck to smile, it seems smarter to increase one's methods for acquiring the skills one needs.

In addition to knowing the topics that one can address if one is providing professional or personal information and advice, one can learn how best to provide that information. In box 8.2 we offer suggestions for how to give constructive advice.

Box 8.2
How to Give Advice and Offer Help

Most of us have seen or heard about extraordinary mentors (e.g., Lee, Dennis, & Campbell, 2007), just as most of us have seen or heard about extraordinary teachers. By definition, "extraordinary" is not the norm. Our goal is to widen the group of people who provide advice, information, advocacy, and other mentoring activities. We do so by suggesting that people concentrate on providing the activities and opportunities where they can be most helpful. We offer here some suggestions about how to give advice and other help, based in part on our own experience and on tips from the Internet (e.g., http://www.wikihow.com/Give-People-Advice/).

Preliminaries

1. Decide what you're good at and concentrate on offering advice or help in those areas. Some people, for example, are very good at writing grants and talking to funding agencies. They can provide excellent help in that arena. Other people might be especially good at talking warmly and helping a student or colleague feel part of things. Let your junior colleagues—all of them, not just the ones you have the most rapport with—know what kind of advice or help you are prepared to offer. Be ready to say that you are not the best person to ask about X, and suggest another person who might be better on that topic.

(continued)

Box 8.2 (continued)

2. There are two broad kinds of help one can offer people: help that is directly related to the progress of their career and help that is psychologically tinged and supportive (Kram, 1985). Think carefully ahead of time about which type of help you are competent and comfortable giving. Again, be ready to say that you are not the best person to ask about X, and suggest another person who might be better on that topic.

3. Decide how much time you're willing to spend. You might not be willing to read someone's entire grant proposal because that would be too time-consuming, but you might be willing to spend 15–30 minutes discussing overall strategy, or you might be willing to read their first few introductory paragraphs. As another example, you might invite junior colleagues to have coffee with you—with no agenda other than getting to know the other person and make them feel welcome.

4. Be prepared to look at things from the point of view of the person you're talking to, even if that is not your point of view or approach. There's no value in telling someone to pull up their socks, or suck it up, or get on with it. They would have done that on their own if they could have. Think about what seems possible for that person, given what they have told you about themselves. Then query them about whether they think it would help to try X.

Giving the Advice or Help

1. Listen carefully and attentively to what people say. Paraphrase what they say to make sure you understand what they are asking for.

2. Concentrate on how you can help people reach their own goals. Their own goals may be different from the goals you would like them to have.

3. Don't promise more than you can deliver. Think about the long-term consequences of your willingness to provide advice or help. You don't want to renege on an implied promise. It's better to offer less and deliver reliably than to offer more and be inconsistent.

4. Be constructive. Don't even think about making negative personal remarks. If you don't think you can be constructive, don't do or say anything. One of us heard someone give a talk in a way that started out unnecessarily badly. We knew just what they should have done. But we had only just met the person and there was no approach that would not have made the person feel like an idiot for starting as they had. Some people make people feel bad. Don't be one of those people.

5. Let people know that there are other people whom they can query and that people can differ in their judgments about what the best course of action in a given case is.

Circle of Advisors

Not everyone is cut out to be a classical mentor, as we have already discussed. Ensuring that mentoring actually works, and that it is considerably more positive than negative, requires a consistent investment of time and resources. A different model is increasingly described in the literature in terms like "composite mentor" (Packard, 2003), "mosaic of advisors" (Rosen, Katz, & Morahan, 2009), "mosaic of mentors" (McCauley & Martineau, 1998), "personal leadership board" (Katz, Rosen, & Morahan, 2009), "developmental network" (Higgins & Kram, 2001), and "mentor network" (de Janasz & Sullivan, 2004; de Janasz, Sullivan, & Whiting, 2003). We use the term "circle of advisors," coined by the Hunter College Gender Equity Project (GEP), in order to eliminate the confusion entailed by the differing connotations that accompany "mentor" in its various guises. The circle is a virtual circle; it is possible that none of the people in the circle know one another.

In our workshops on developing a circle of advisors we discuss the various roles and kinds of help that others can offer. One feature of the workshop is having attendees identify people who could play a given role for them and the ways that they might approach the person to provide the advice, information, or help that is needed. For every role that one wants someone to fill, part of the challenge is to find someone who will be constructive rather than destructive. One of the beauties of the circle-of-advisors model is that a destructive person is easily jettisoned. One simply doesn't ask that person for advice or information again. Since one never took up much of the person's time to begin with, there is no unspoken obligation to keep seeing the person. On the classical mentor model, it is difficult to stop contact with someone who is not helpful.

Pursuing "Advisors"   Do faculty announce to someone, "I want you to be in my circle of advisors?" No. They simply approach the person and ask, for example, "I wonder if you could give me some advice about applying for X. I know that you have been successful at X and I think you would have insights that would help me." Although not everyone will say yes, most people will, because most people enjoy talking about the components of their success.

The people in one's circle of advisors will change as one's needs change. Some may be consulted once a month or more often, and some may be consulted once a year or less often. (See box 8.3 for an example of an advisor who is consulted less often than once a year.)

Box 8.3
An Infrequently Consulted Advisor

A woman tells us, I have a two-hour lunch with Ed about once a year or once every two years. This is purely a one-way relationship, which is one reason I don't talk to him more often. I would feel guilty taking up more of his time. We've known each other, though not well, for 40 years. We started out in the same field. I continued in academia, and he eventually became president of a foundation. He understands how every aspect of academia works. He also has an appreciation for unusual ideas and unconventional ways of doing things. He liked an unconventional article that I wrote a long time ago, so I think of him as someone who will be helpful when I want to do something that doesn't fit an established genre. And that's exactly what he is. I have sometimes had an idea that he's supported and sometimes had an idea that he hasn't supported. In each case, what he does—and I don't know how he does it—is ask questions and listen to what I say until *I* think, okay, I don't really want to do X, or, okay, I really do want to do X. He's not a friend, he's not someone whose professional life is similar to mine, but he's been a wonderful advisor.

Identifying Issues to Discuss   Box 8.4 has a sample list of issues that individuals can ask for help with. We developed this list from published material (McCauley & Martineau, 1998)[2] and from suggestions by workshop participants. Although individuals can do this alone, it is helpful to do it within a group so that people can make a variety of suggestions. It is helpful for people to see that they are not alone, whether it be in navigating how to order chemicals, dealing with finding a book publisher, handling the process of finding experimental participants, dealing with rejection, managing one's time efficiently, or attending conferences. Not everyone will want every kind of information or support. In the act of choosing what to concentrate on, each faculty member defines what needs attention for himself or herself.

The list in box 8.4 is not exhaustive, nor is it a list that everyone might want every item from. A given person can fill more than one role, and some roles might be filled by multiple people; the key idea is that no single person can fill every role (McCauley & Martineau, 1998). It's often a good idea to get more than one take on an issue because different people have different kinds of knowledge. We recall one woman who was told that she should not approach multiple book publishers simultaneously, that

Box 8.4
What Members of a Circle of Advisors Might Provide

General and Not Specific to Any Field; Advisor Need
Not Always Be in One's Field or Profession

1. Challenges to do better
2. Encouragement to succeed
3. Sympathetic critiques of one's self-presentational style
4. Sounding board when new opportunities or dilemmas arise
5. Help with time management and procrastination problems
6. Requirements for accountability (holding one's feet to the fire)
7. Service as devil's advocate

Specific and Work Related

1. Names of other people who might provide useful information or help
2. Advocacy on one's behalf
3. Advice on how to handle conflict within one's group
4. Experience with role-playing negotiation scenarios
5. Suggestions of items to negotiate for
6. Strategies for success, tailored to one's circumstances
7. Constructive criticism of written material
8. Knowledgeable critiques of funding proposals
9. Interpretation of negative reviews; analysis of rejection letters
10. Discussion of how to assign credit when multiple contributors are involved
11. Suggestions for how to handle an underperforming assistant
12. Suggestions of places to apply to for funding
13. Suggestions about writing the diplomatic cover letter when resubmitting a manuscript
14. Information about prizes and awards one might be eligible for
15. Information about how to advance into academic leadership positions
16. Information about book publishers

The listed items are starting points. Not all of them may be relevant to a given person, and someone might want to add others for a large group. No issue is too big or too small. If help with it would allow one to become more effective, it's worth including.

(adapted from McCauley and Martineau, 1998)

publishing a book was like publishing at article in a journal. Had she asked more people about this very important decision, she would have learned that it is permissible to approach more than one publisher (of course, letting them know that one is doing so).

In the GEP's first workshop on the topic of a circle of advisors, we included "someone to hold my feet to the fire" among the roles one might want someone to fill (our thanks to Page Morahan). One of the attendees pounced on it: "That's exactly what I need!" Because it was written down as a possibility, it was validated as a problem that people—not just that woman—might have. Even if people think they should not need such help, acknowledging that they do need it frees them to get the help and solve the problem. That particular woman went on to publish an important book. Another role that faculty might think they should be able to play for themselves is "someone to read my letters of rejection with me." In our view, everyone has areas in which he or she can do better. It shows strength to acknowledge and deal constructively with a weakness. It's more of a weakness to put a rejection letter in a drawer for several months than it is to review it with the right person.

Advisors about Life   For what psychologists call "psychosocial support," another academic is not necessary and may not even be desirable. Managing the demands of a personal and professional life is a process many people can be consulted on, and few are likely to have "the" answer. Assembling different strategies is the task for the person seeking advice. Moreover, not all issues are equally appropriate to discuss with academic advisors. For example, we advise people not to freely disclose their self-doubts to individuals who will be writing letters of recommendation for them or evaluating them for tenure and promotion. One's own doubts tend to engender other people's doubts, especially if one is a member of a group that is underrepresented. Some recipients of such information will be unaffected, but others will be negatively affected. One needs to have a great deal of trust in the person to whom one discloses a weakness or needs to be in such a position of strength that disclosure will only make one seem pleasantly human.

Peer Mentoring

In a recent workshop that one of us led for junior faculty, one person described a problem with a senior person that she didn't know how to solve; she didn't know whom she could approach for advice. Another faculty member in the group had had a similar problem and described how she had solved it. She said she would be happy to discuss it further with the first faculty member. (Although the workshop was open to everyone, it was attended by one man and about 15 women.) That sort of positive communication happens frequently in such workshops and reveals the power of groups with diverse experiences. It also demonstrates to faculty that problems they may have thought were unique to them are not uncommon, and that their peers can be a source of information and support. Examples of peer mentoring range from small informal groups who might meet for years (e.g., Daniell, 2006) to large formal groups convened for a shorter period of time (e.g., Pololi & Evans, 2015).

Increasingly, institutions are providing small incentives (e.g., lunch money, funds to purchase books to read together) for groups of faculty in the same career stage to meet and talk about professional issues together and give each other the benefit of their shared experience. This can be expanded to include activities like invitations to senior faculty leaders in the department and outside, who can be invited to meet with the group of junior faculty and answer their questions about a particular topic relevant to the leader's role. This is an efficient use of senior faculty members' time and also ensures that all of the junior faculty hear the same information and advice.

Workshops

The circle-of-advisors workshop is one of a suite of workshops that the Hunter College GEP developed through support from NSF. Workshops are a natural extension of the circle-of-advisors model. They are a form of collective mentoring. The workshops we describe began at Hunter College and, with further NSF funding, were later extended to all the senior colleges of the City University of New York (CUNY). Some of the workshops are currently offered by the CUNY central administration. By providing such workshops to faculty, administrations demonstrate their commitment to faculty success. Many institutions offer orientation sessions to new faculty, covering the mechanics of arranging life in one's institution, and those are valuable for faculty. However, topics like how to negotiate, how to run a meeting, and so on are seldom covered.

Box 8.5 lists most of the topics that the GEP workshops have addressed. Workshops are typically offered in two or three all-day sessions spread across a semester, generally on a Friday. Notice of the workshops is sent to

Box 8.5

Suite of Workshops, Based on Hunter College Gender Equity Workshops

---

Career Development

1. CVs and cover letters
2. Balancing responsibilities: Research, teaching, and service; learning to say "no"
3. Teaching effectively and efficiently
4. Self-presentation
5. Public speaking and presentations; the first three minutes of a talk
6. Attending conferences
7. Entitlement and negotiation
8. Tenure and promotion
9. Nominating oneself for prizes, awards, and other forms of recognition

Writing and Publishing

1. Time management and procrastination
2. Publishing and handling rejection
3. Maximizing research and writing during the summer
4. Grant writing
5. The ally system
6. Professional influences on productivity

"Mentoring"

1. Building and maintaining a circle of advisors
2. Student and assistant management
3. Giving advice to junior colleagues

Balancing Work and a Personal Life

1. Equality and negotiation in personal relationships
2. Balancing work and a personal life
3. The influence of family on productivity

Leadership

1. Lateral leadership
2. Power and politics within one's department and institution
3. Leadership within one's discipline

departments. The number of participants is capped at 25–30, depending on the room that is available. Participants submit their CVs and make a number of commitments: attend all sessions, complete the (minimal) reading and exercises for each day ahead of time, evaluate each workshop day, and be available for follow-up questions. In some versions, participants are asked to complete logs about their productivity.

Although most workshops were led by Hunter College-internal or CUNY-internal speakers, some were led by external speakers who were judged by the GEP staff to be particularly likely to add a valuable perspective, either because they studied the topic (such as division of responsibilities in the household) or because they had personally had extensive or unusual experience (such as running an extremely large laboratory). One advantage of having internal speakers, other than cost, is that people learn how much valuable information is available within their institution.

A workshop series does entail a cost to the institution. There needs to be a central core of people who set up the workshops, find and distribute the reading material, line up speakers, arrange for food, and so on. Those people's time is compensated, and there is a food budget.

An analysis of the productivity of faculty who had attended the GEP workshops showed that they published more papers and submitted more grant proposals after attending the workshops. This is not a controlled experiment since the faculty who participated were motivated to be successful or they would not have attended three all-day workshops and completed the various activities that were required. One could argue that such individuals might have found other ways to get the information they needed to be more successful. Our response is that even if the attendees were already highly motivated, the workshops did add value, or participants would not have increased their productivity over their baseline rate. A somewhat similar program, restricted to women in economics, where participants were randomly assigned to workshops or to a control group, showed similar improvements in outcomes (Blau, Currie, Croson, & Ginther, 2010). Increasingly, professional associations—perhaps especially those where White men predominate—are offering mentoring workshops before, at, or after annual professional conferences. These provide individuals with both advice and feedback and with a broader network of colleagues nationally at their own and other career stages.

Workshops are an efficient way for individuals to learn about their job. Participants' comments in Hunter College's program evaluations, as well as their high ratings, indicated the value of the workshops. One participant commented,

I really appreciate all your guidance, and I think it was particularly useful for me as an instructor who is at the beginning of the process to get all this necessary information up front and be able to form a long view of my goals and strategies. I would love to participate in future workshops if any are held as a follow-up to this one.

Although individuals can provide such information one-on-one, a workshop is not only efficient but, through the questions from the group, allows for greater clarity on points that might be misunderstood.

Another wrote, "For a junior academic, this workshop is the best thing I could be lucky enough to have encountered." When asked about the structure and format of the seminar, participants expressed satisfaction; one responded, "It was *very very* effective! I wouldn't change the format." Another said, "There was great integration of practice and presentation." In one intermediate report, a participant wrote, "I've been more productive in the last two weeks than I have been in last 6 months. I've reached out to peers for support and advisement and have been able to revise and resubmit one grant application." The value of the workshops for junior faculty—the intended audience—was evident: "These workshops are wonderful. It would be very important for new faculty to take them in the first year to avoid making mistakes and gaining all the information from the very beginning," "The GEP was very effective. I believe that my participation has increased my chances of achieving tenure as a professor."

The Hunter College workshops, which both men and women attended, attempted to integrate information about gender and diversity into each workshop and included male and female presenters from different ethnic groups. The negotiation workshop, for example, presented data on differences in reactions to men and women who negotiate, gave tips on how to negotiate so as to reduce possible negative reactions, and had participants act out negotiation scenarios. At some workshops, a department chair would take the role of a department chair that the faculty member wanted to approach about, say, a course reduction, bridging funds, or an increase in salary. In one workshop, an experienced faculty member coached the person trying to negotiate and the group saw how the chair responded.

At a workshop on attending conferences, the presenter was a woman of color. One of the attendees, also a woman of color but a different ethnicity, asked a question about how she could approach a group of White men at a conference. We doubt whether that woman would have felt as free to ask her question if the presenter had been White. Not every workshop needs to be led by a White woman or a person of color, as long as there is a mix that allows everyone to see that being a "different" gender, color, or ethnicity does not reduce someone's knowledge or authority.

Launch Committees

Another form of collective mentoring is "launch committees." When new faculty are hired, whether they are male or female, they have to figure out how things work at their new institution. We recall one productive scientist's estimation that she would lose one to two years when she moved from her current institution to a new one—and that was for a well-funded senior person! The point of launch committees is to smooth junior faculty members' introduction to their new institution and thus speed up how quickly a new faculty member can become a productive contributor. It is in the institution's best interest to help new faculty hit the ground running. Launch committees are a short-term—typically one-year—form of a circle of advisors with a particular mission.

Case Western Reserve University pioneered a pilot version of the launch committee concept for the school of engineering at Case, funded by a grant from the NSF ADVANCE program. A description of the pilot, written by Erin Lavik, Elmer Lindseth, and G. Q. Zhang, can be found on Case's webpage for the program for Institutions Developing Excellence In Academic Leadership (or IDEAL; http://case.edu/provost/ideal/) in their second-year annual report, p. 65. The University of Michigan has adapted and developed the idea in several schools and colleges for humanists, natural scientists, social scientists, and faculty in music, theater, and dance. What follows is an outline of how a launch committee works (http://advance.umich.edu/launch.php). Other institutions (at the moment Florida International University, Michigan Technological University and The Ohio State University) are experimenting with pilot versions of the launch committee program. We describe the University of Michigan's program, but it can be tailored to particular fields and institutions.

Structure of the Committee A committee is formed that includes the individual's department chair or delegate, a senior colleague in the department with related interests, a senior colleague in a different department with related interests, and a specially trained "convener," who is a senior faculty member from outside the department who does not necessarily share any interests or expertise with the launchee. The convener's role is to ensure that key issues are addressed at each meeting even if the launchee or other participants do not raise them. In addition, the convener can press for clarification of departmental and school practices that are unclear or ambiguous (e.g., how to get a graduate student) or how to address or resolve a problem. Because the conveners have specific preparation and follow-up responsibilities that no other committee member has, they are offered an honorarium of $1,000 at the University of Michigan. All other committee participation is voluntary. There is, in addition, some labor required to orient conveners to their role and to track the committees. This labor can be shared with smaller schools and colleges in large universities, but it is helpful to have a centralized office (in Michigan's case, ADVANCE) that monitors the committees and is prepared to orient conveners and troubleshoot difficulties that may arise.

Committee Process The committee works to identify, with all new faculty members, what space and assistance they will need, what funding and collaboration opportunities are available both inside and outside the institution, and who the most important people are for the new faculty member to meet, focusing on teaching, research, community participation, and service. The tension and balance of personal and professional life is always addressed. The committee and the candidate meet formally either in person or electronically on a monthly basis for the first year, sometimes beginning in the summer before the launchee arrives on campus; committee members are available for informal meetings as well. At each meeting the committee follows up on issues raised at previous meetings and tries to address lingering issues. The committee convener provides brief accounts of the discussion of key topics and sends the reports to the committee members and to whoever is overseeing the launch program.

Evidence of Launch Committees' Value In its initial pilot year at the University of Michigan (2011–2012), there were launches in four science departments. A survey for that year collected data from the eight launchees from those four departments and from four comparable departments that did not have launch committees. Launchees overall were more likely than new faculty in comparable departments to have their research space fully functional and were more satisfied with their research equipment than those in comparable departments. Launchees were also more likely to report knowing senior faculty outside their department and expressed greater ease in identifying a senior colleague to help answer a question. In addition, women launchees (but not men) reported significantly higher satisfaction with service and were more likely to agree that their colleagues created a respectful work environment compared to women in comparable departments who were not part of launch programs.

In subsequent years, the launch committee experience has been assessed for all of the committee members, including the launchee and the department chair(s). The 2015 report (covering 2012–2013 through 2014–2015) from the University of Michigan (available at http://advance.umich.edu /resources/LaunchreportFinal.pdf) summarizes evaluations of 79 committees, involving 267 faculty in nine schools and colleges. That report contains evaluation data without comparisons since all new faculty in science and engineering fields received launch committees.

Launchees report very positive experiences in being welcomed, having a good orientation to the campus, and being integrated into their department (all means above 3.4 on a 4-point scale). Launchees were enthusiastic in their satisfaction with their teaching load, the courses they were asked to teach, the mentoring they received, and the department as a place to work: on a 5-point rating scale, the mean was 5.0. On open-ended questions about the best things they experienced, seven mentioned that the networking opportunities were amazing, and seven mentioned their access to chairs. Six expressed appreciation for the time to ask questions, discuss issues of concern, and gain viewpoints from different faculty members, while five mentioned the advocacy, support, and advice they received.

All of the committee members were similarly positive, citing the value to the launchee, the relative ease of the "work" of launching a talented young colleague, and the pleasure of contributing to the next generation. One committee convener noted, "It's very systematic advising, not catch-as-catch-can advising like we so often have here." Another noted that the launch committee "integrates the new faculty member into the University. They meet people, they make friends, they learn about administrative hurdles. They also learn about many opportunities available, but not necessarily easily apparent." Committee members liked the opportunity for a time-limited relationship that could be continued if it was of interest to the two people but which was not mandated beyond the first year.

Department chairs commented that they intended to be available to new faculty, but this program ensured that those intentions were expressed in actual time spent with them. One said, "Even with the best intentioned chair, there can be things that fall through the cracks, and the junior faculty don't always know that they can be asking for help about certain things." Another commented that it enabled "finding out about problems quickly and fixing those problems with minimal delay." One noted that "I think what I like about them is that the committees come up with some ideas that are not necessarily the way that I would do them, but they're good suggestions."

The multiplication of ideas about how to do things both is liberating to the junior faculty members and underscores the fact that, although they need advice and information, they are in charge of making the decisions about their own career. It also demonstrates to senior faculty that there are multiple strategies for solving problems.

New faculty members' careers start well or badly, depending on how quickly they can adjust to a new institution, create a functional laboratory or develop a group of colleagues to talk to, and learn what facilities are available to ease their transition both professionally and personally. It is hard, without a good introduction, to make up for lost time, hard to overcome needless frustrations, and hard to recover from unwitting mistakes. Some people are lucky. But the institution's job is to reduce the importance of luck. Moreover, receiving assistance and attention in this early stage creates a sense that the institution values the new faculty member—an impression that is likely to have long-term consequences for the faculty member's success, retention, and morale. Finally, serving on launch committees has the unintended bene-fit of offering senior faculty a concrete model of what mentoring involves—a model that can change the way they mentor all of their younger colleagues.

Institutional Support for Launch Committees   Widespread adoption of a launch committee requires institutional support. We note the irony that although faculty at Case Western Reserve University originated this excel-lent idea, the experiment ended in 2012 with the end of the grant that funded the original experiment (personal communication, Diana Bilimo-ria, January 7, 2016). Had the University of Michigan not learned of it, the idea might have died. Instead, launch committees have flourished at Michigan and are being tried now in all liberal arts fields as well as some of the professional schools within the university.

This is one example of many we have seen where new programs are developed but are not maintained over time. Sometimes the lack of support is due to a change of leadership; sometimes it is due to the difficulty of convincing ongoing administrative leadership that the program should be continued. We believe that institutions are well-served by maintaining proven programs, rather than continually developing new ones.

Developing a Mentoring Program

Many schools, especially those that have been funded by the National Science Foundation's ADVANCE program to improve the advancement of women in the sciences, have developed different types of mentoring programs for faculty (see, e.g., Bilimoria & Liang, 2012; Stewart, Malley, & LaVaque-Manty, 2007). There are too many to list. We advise searching the web with terms like "faculty development," "career advising," and "faculty mentoring."

Schools can and should take a more active role in faculty development, including via formal mentoring programs like the two models outlined here. What we suggest is that schools start small, with a committee that examines different models and considers what will work well in their context. Of course, committee members should be compensated for their time, either by release time, the provision of a research assistant, or some other means. Since mentoring—or its equivalent—is an important faculty benefit, it makes sense to do it right. A committee of faculty members from a range of departments will be able to evaluate workable models. Independent evidence suggests that committees consisting of faculty, who take on responsibilities additional to their direct faculty roles, help propagate values throughout a community (e.g., Dobbin & Kalev, 2007). Faculty are accepted as credible when staff members are not, faculty have a sense of their colleagues (though it may not always be correct), and faculty can monitor the success of programs.

Midcareer and Senior Faculty

The strategies for faculty development that we have discussed thus far are applicable to faculty at any level, though many of them have been developed most intensively for new faculty. Faculty at different ranks share many of the same concerns but also have their own particular concerns.

Associate professors with tenure (about 34% of full-time faculty at research-intensive schools), especially those who have been at that rank for more than six years, are less satisfied with their position than are assistant or full professors (Mathews, 2014). Such long-term associate professors report being undermentored, underappreciated, and underrecognized at higher rates than any other group (Mathews, 2014). At research-intensive institutions, the normative career pattern is to move from associate professor to full professor status in seven or fewer years, but at some institutions, associate professor status can be an end point. Women and faculty in the humanities are likely to spend more time at associate professor rank than men do (see chapter 4 and, for a range of models, Committee on Gender Differences in Careers of Science, Engineering, and Mathematics Faculty, 2010). Workshops aimed at helping faculty move from associate professor to full professor are offered by the CUNY central office.

Once faculty have achieved tenure, faculty may ask themselves questions about their goals, both at work and in their personal lives, and reassess their aspirations (Bickel, 2016; Neumann, 2009). In some cases it is difficult for faculty to abandon a line of research that they are no longer interested in and that has provided mixed results at best; they feel a commitment to finish what they started. Having a sympathetic senior person point out that it could be better to start something new that one is excited about, rather than continue not making progress in an area that has lost its appeal, might be all someone needs to begin a fresh direction. The opposite pressure is also problematic: sometimes institutions insist on evidence that an individual has developed a wholly new line of work since the last review, when the individual is deeply interested in pursuing the original program of work and pushing it further. In our view institutions would benefit by being less focused on directing faculty scholarly energy in either direction and more focused on supporting faculty members' best ideas about how to deploy their own energy.

Sometimes midcareer faculty want to play more of a role in the institution but are unsure of how to go about it. They may also find themselves the recipient of multiple requests to serve on committees. Now that they are members of the permanent faculty, other faculty and administrators feel free to ask them for more service. Negotiating those requests is tricky.

A survey of 39 institutions found that very few specified support that was directly aimed at midcareer faculty (Canale, Herdklotz, & Wild, 2013), even though such faculty are numerous, and even though it is costly to their institutions if those faculty are not productive. Examples of support are pamphlets detailing requirements for promotion to full professor, coaching sessions to help faculty advance to full professor, internal grants or fellowships for advancing a faculty member's research program, and academic leadership programs designed to help faculty change roles. Except for the last, most programs are intended to help faculty move to the next step—promotion to full professor.

Faculty who have adopted a circle-of-advisors model are in a better position to consider their next steps than faculty who have progressed under a classical mentor model. Those who have adopted the circle-of-advisors model are accustomed to finding people who can provide information, advice, and encouragement about thinking through the opportunities their change in status offers. Institutions can be helpful here in creating a network of individuals that faculty can call on to discuss their next steps. Schools can also undertake a series of workshops along the lines of those for junior faculty but adapted to the needs of midcareer faculty.

Another model is an internal "sabbatical," where a faculty member might choose to develop a new line of research. A scientist, for example, might work in a colleague's laboratory. An historian interested in political science might sit in on advanced courses, have structured discussions with a senior faculty member, and be provided an office in the political science department for a specified period, enabling them to participate in the department community.

Administrative Leadership Programs

Chairs, deans, and provosts are committed to permanent employment of faculty with tenure. It is in the institution's interest to provide faculty with opportunities for leadership, via programs that we list below as well as through internal programs, such as workshops by faculty who have taken on positions of academic leadership or who have participated in leadership programs. Knowledgeable faculty can provide information about whether a program requires that faculty members be nominated by their institutions and about whether a program provides funding.

We have provided a partial list of some programs in appendix 8.1. Administrators or faculty can search the web with terms like "academic leadership training," "academic leadership professional development," and department chair training." As one example, women in academic medicine, if supported by the dean of their medical school, can apply for the year-long program Executive Leadership in Academic Medicine (ELAM), at Drexel

Medical College (McDade, Richman, Jackson, & Morahan, 2004). The Association of American Medical Colleges (AAMC) has several programs that are designed to help medical schools improve faculty effectiveness. Similarly, the American Council on Education (ACE) sponsors a variety of programs for individuals interested in, or already finding themselves in, academic administration. For example, it sponsors two-day workshops for chairs, supplemented by five webinars throughout the year.

Retiring and Retired Faculty

In 1994, mandatory retirement for faculty ended. This boon for those faculty who saw age 70 as an arbitrary stopping point was a problem for universities, concerned as they were that there would not be room for younger faculty if older faculty continued to work into their seventies. That remains a concern for colleges and universities, and there is evidence, based on data from over 1,000 faculty at a large private university in the metropolitan northeast, that faculty indeed have retired later since mandatory retirement ended: 25% continued past age 78 and 15% were estimated not to be retired until age 80 or older, but there was substantial variation from school to school within the university (Weinberg & Scott, 2013). Faculty in professional schools retired at similar ages to those who had been faculty during the mandatory retirement period, possibly because they could earn significant amounts of money outside the university. It was faculty in the humanities, sciences, arts, and education who stayed on, perhaps partly for financial reasons but perhaps also because of the freedom they had in arranging their teaching responsibilities and their research in satisfactory ways (June, 2012; Weinberg & Scott, 2013).

The main effort universities and colleges have made in considering the needs of retiring and retired faculty is to offer faculty financial incentives for retiring. Some also offer financial planning and continued medical benefits. Very few have considered how to make it possible for faculty to continue to contribute to their field or the institution, should they want to, in retirement. (And some schools make it difficult for faculty, by not allowing them to sponsor students in research.) The result is that there are fewer resources for retiring and retired faculty than there are for those at any other point in their careers.

Several institutions have, however, developed programs that are responsive to some faculty needs, many funded by the Mellon Foundation or the

Sloan Foundation (McLaughlin, Duranleau, & Van Ummersen, 2014; Van Ummersen, Duranleau, & McLaughlin, 2013). One category of needs is projects that faculty want to finish but require institutional resources in order to complete. Another category is access to workshops or counselors that explore options for a productive and satisfying retirement. A third category is maintaining a satisfying relationship with the institution. As with institutional benefits for giving faculty what they need at earlier stages in their careers, here, too, institutions will benefit by doing more than providing monetary incentives and benefits, important though those are.

Retired faculty are a potential and greatly underused asset for the college or university. Retiring and retired faculty have a great deal of knowledge about how their institution works and how their field works. Such faculty can be a resource for leading workshops and organizing mentoring programs. With minimal funding, interested retiring faculty could contribute to the professional development of their junior colleagues.

Measuring Progress or Lack Thereof

How can a school or department determine whether its faculty development programs are successful? In the ideal case, a given program will have both an experimental group that receives the benefits of the program and a control group of individuals who were interested in the program but were not enrolled to it. Measures such as faculty productivity and satisfaction will then determine whether to continue the program. Once the program is open to everyone, the quasi-experimental comparison is no longer feasible, but ongoing benchmark data—of two main types—will be informative. The first type is the data that institutions collect on faculty: retention; success at tenure; time in rank before promotion from associate to full professor; salary; grant funding; and climate survey information. The second type is a faculty member's CV, which includes number of publications and awards. Keeping track of and interpreting such data requires institutional resources.

Institutional Benefits of Faculty Development

We have outlined a variety of ways that institutions can promote faculty productivity and well-being. All the methods require an outlay of resources, but we believe that the increases in outside funding and the renown that faculty bring to the institution make the investment worthwhile. We also note that faculty who are actively and happily involved in research are likely to incorporate students into their research projects, thus also providing benefits to undergraduates, who now have the opportunity to get hands-on experience with research.

Summary

In this chapter we have provided an overview of five kinds of programs that can help faculty succeed. In our view, all of them provide some value. It is not necessary for an institution to offer all of them, but it is important that the institution provide access to some of them. Moreover, it is crucial for the institution to provide avenues for experienced faculty to develop skill at providing constructive and appropriate advice in their areas of expertise (via workshops or participation in launch committees where they may learn about their role), and for faculty who are new to a role to develop their ability to seek advice proactively. We encourage institutions to recognize the importance of establishing a culture in which faculty at all career stages recognize the need for career advice and have ways to obtain it. Finally, we note that programs to help faculty succeed, valuable though they are, cannot substitute for the institutional changes we recommend in the other chapters of this book.

Recommendations for Helping Faculty Succeed

Institutional Policies

1. Routinize provision of information to faculty about key milestones in faculty progress (e.g., third-year review, tenure and promotion to full professor). Make the criteria associated with these milestones transparent.

2. Where possible, provide faculty with support to attend national leadership development programs.

Senior Administrators

1. Explicitly articulate the value of faculty development, and contributions to faculty development, to the institution.

2. If no faculty development programs currently exist, set up a faculty committee to evaluate alternatives and create a pilot program in a few departments.

3. Provide financial and time resources to faculty to develop and implement formal programs:

• or new assistant professors (launch committees)

• for all junior faculty (classical mentoring or circles or advisors or peer advising networks)

• for other faculty at key transitions in their careers

• via workshops on faculty professional development and skill-building that are open to all faculty

4. Ensure that there is an oversight process for programs and that data are collected to assess their value.

5. Consider setting up mentoring relationships or encouraging circles of advisors among faculty seeking and holding administrative positions.

Department Chairs

1. Explicitly articulate the value of faculty mentoring and faculty development to the department.

2. Proactively ensure that all untenured faculty receive information, advice, and assistance via classical mentoring, launch committees, a circle of advisors, or peer mentoring.

All Faculty Members

1. Take full advantage of institutional resources supporting faculty development—whether as a provider or beneficiary. Improve your skills in both roles.

2. Take seriously the value of supporting the faculty development of your colleagues. Provide colleagues with information and constructive advice.

Notes

1. The MCA was tested in 16 medical schools, where 283 mentors rated themselves on the 26 items on a 1–7 scale (Fleming et al., 2013). Their scores on individual items ranged from an average low of 4.41 ("Helping your mentee balance work with their personal life") to a high of 6.05 ("Acknowledging your mentee's professional contributions"). The mentees of those mentors were even more positive about their mentors than the mentors were about themselves. Some caution should be used in considering these results, all of which show performance above the midpoint. The people who took the assessment were probably already interested in trying to be a good mentor. They were a convenience sample of about 22% of those initially

contacted. They had apparently been willing not just to be assessed, but to participate in an eight-hour training program to improve their mentoring skills. All of that said, it's clear that those who participated left feeling armed with useful knowledge.

This training program trained facilitators at the 16 sites where they had tested mentoring competency (Pfund, House, Asquith, Fleming, Buhr, Burnham, et al., 2014). The same 283 participants previously tested were divided into an intervention and control group. The control group received no training and no interaction with trainers. In posttests three months after training, the two groups again rated themselves in the six areas. The intervention group showed a greater positive change overall compared to the control group, driven by a greater positive change in three of the six areas, showing at a minimum that individuals who are motivated to change, and who enroll in an intervention designed to improve changes in six specific areas, are likely to perceive themselves as having changed positively. The data from the mentees was equivocal.

2. Our thanks to Page Morahan for initially introducing us to this material.

Appendix 8.1

Partial List of Faculty Development Programs

Workshop Series for Faculty—Gender Equity Project, Hunter College
http://www.hunter.cuny.edu/genderequity/resources/workshopmaterials

Faculty Career Advising Resources—University of Michigan ADVANCE
http://advance.umich.edu/careeradvising.php

Launch Committees—University of Michigan ADVANCE
http://advance.umich.edu/launch.php

ADVANCE Faculty Development Office—Mentoring for New and Pre-Tenure Faculty, Northeastern University
http://www.northeastern.edu/advance/new-pre-tenure-faculty/faculty-mentoring/

ADVANCE Faculty Professional Development—Center for Institutional Change, University of Washington
https://advance.washington.edu/additionalresources/facdevelopment.html

Faculty Professional Development—Northern Arizona University
https://nau.edu/faculty-development/welcome/

Institutional Faculty Development Plan—University of Wisconsin–Madison
https://www.ohr.wisc.edu/grants/InstitutionalFacultyDevelopmentPlan.html

Leadership workshops (all levels, including presidents)—American Council on Education
http://www.acenet.edu/leadership/Pages/default.aspx

Executive Leadership in Academic Medicine—Drexel
   http://drexel.edu/medicine/academics/womens-health-and-leadership/ELAM/

Faculty Forward—Association of American Medical Colleges
   https://www.staging.aamc.org/services/facultyforward/survey/

Group on Women in Medicine and Science—Association of American Medical
Colleges
   https://www.aamc.org/members/gwims/

Northwestern University Clinical and Translational Sciences Institute Education
and Career Development
   https://nucats.northwestern.edu/education-career-development/early-career
   -faculty-development-programs/navigating-translational-research-enterprise
   /schedule-materials

References

Allen, T. D., & Eby, L. T. (Eds.). (2011). *The Blackwell handbook of mentoring: A multiple perspectives approach*. Malden, MA: Blackwell.

Allen, T. D., Eby, L. T., Poteet, M. L., Lentz, E., & Lima, L. (2004). Career benefits associated with mentoring for proteges: A meta-analysis. *Journal of Applied Psychology, 89*(1), 127–136.

Baranik, L. E., Roling, E. A., & Eby, L. T. (2010). Why does mentoring work? The role of perceived organizational support. *Journal of Vocational Behavior, 76*(3), 366–373.

Bickel, J. (2016). Not too late to reinvigorate: How midcareer faculty can continue growing. *Academic Medicine, 91*(12), 1601–1605.

Bilimoria, D., & Liang, X. (2012). *Gender equity in science and engineering: Advancing change in higher education*. New York, NY: Routledge.

Blau, F. D., Currie, J. M., Croson, R. T. A., & Ginther, D. K. (2010). *Can mentoring help female assistant professors? Interim results from a randomized trial* (NBER Working Paper 15707). Cambridge, MA: National Bureau of Economic Research.

Blickle, G., Witzki, A., & Schneider, P. B. (2009). Self-initiated mentoring and career success: A predictive field study. *Journal of Vocational Behavior, 74*(1), 94–101.

Canale, A. M., Herdklotz, C., & Wild, L. (2013). *Mid-career faculty support: The middle years of the academic profession*. Rochester, NY: Faculty Career Development Services, the Wallace Center, Rochester Institute of Technology.

Committee on Gender Differences in Careers of Science, Engineering, and Mathematics Faculty; Committee on Women in Science, Engineering, and Medicine; Policy and Global Affairs; Committee on National Statistics, Division of Behavioral and Social Sciences and Education, the National Research Council of the National Academies.

(2010). *Gender differences at critical transitions in the careers of science, engineering, and mathematics faculty*. Washington, DC: National Academies Press.

Daniell, E. (2006). *Every other Thursday: Stories and strategies from successful women scientists*. New Haven, CT: Yale University Press.

de Janasz, S. C., & Sullivan, S. E. (2004). Multiple mentoring in academe: Developing the professorial network. *Journal of Vocational Behavior, 64*(2), 263–283.

de Janasz, S. C., Sullivan, S. E., & Whiting, V. (2003). Mentor networks and career success: Lessons for turbulent times. *Academy of Management Executive, 17*(4), 78–91.

Dobbin, F., & Kalev, A. (2007). The architecture of inclusion: Evidence from corporate diversity programs. *Harvard Journal of Law & Gender, 30*(2), 279–301.

Dobbin, F., Schrage, D., & Kalev, A. (2015). Rage against the iron cage: The varied effects of bureaucratic personnel reforms on diversity. *American Sociological Review, 80*, 1014–1044.

Eby, L. T., Allen, T. D., Evans, S. C., Ng, T., & DuBois, D. L. (2008). Does mentoring matter? A multidisciplinary meta-analysis comparing mentored and non-mentored individuals. *Journal of Vocational Behavior, 72*(2), 254–267.

Eby, L. T., Butts, M. M., Durley, J., & Ragins, B. R. (2010). Are bad experiences stronger than good ones in mentoring relationships? Evidence from the protégé and mentor perspective. *Journal of Vocational Behavior, 77*(1), 81–92.

Egan, T. M., & Song, Z. (2008). Are facilitated mentoring programs beneficial? A randomized experimental field study. *Journal of Vocational Behavior, 72*(3), 351–362.

Fleming, M., House, M. S., Shewakramani, M. V., Yu, L., Garbutt, J., McGee, R., et al. (2013). The Mentoring Competency Assessment: Validation of a new instrument to evaluate skills of research mentors. *Academic Medicine: Journal of the Association of American Medical Colleges, 88*(7), 1002–1008.

Fryberg, S. A., & Gerken, L. A. (2012). Twins separated at birth? Critical moments in cross-race mentoring relationships. In K. L. Dace (Ed.), *Unlikely allies in the academy: Women of color and white women in conversation* (pp. 149–159). New York, NY: Routledge.

Higgins, M. C., & Kram, K. E. (2001). Reconceptualizing mentoring at work: A developmental network perspective. *Academy of Management Review, 26*(2), 264–288.

Hogue, M., Yoder, J. D., & Singleton, S. G. (2007). The gender wage gap: An explanation of men's elevated wage entitlement. *Sex Roles, 56*, 573–579.

Ito, T. A., Larsen, J. T., Smith, N. K., & Cacioppo, J. T. (1998). Negative information weighs more heavily in the brain: The negativity bias in evaluative categorizations. *Journal of Personality and Social Psychology, 75*, 887–900.

June, A. W. (2012, March 18). Aging professors create a faculty bottleneck. *The Chronicle for Higher Education*. http://www.chronicle.com/article/Professors-Are-Graying -and/131226/

Kammeyer-Mueller, J. D., & Judge, T. A. (2008). A quantitative review of mentoring research: Test of a model. *Journal of Vocational Behavior, 72*(3), 269–283.

Katz, J. K., Rosen, S., & Morahan, P. (2009). What is team coaching, and why use co-coaches? *Academic Physician & Scientist, 5*, 2–6.

Kram, K. E. (1985). *Mentoring at work*. Glenview, IL: Scott, Foresman.

Kram, K. E., & Ragins, B. R. (2007). The landscape of mentoring in the 21st century. In K. E. Kram & B. R. Ragins (Eds.), *Handbook of mentoring at work* (pp. 659–692). Thousand Oaks, CA: Sage.

Lee, A., Dennis, C., & Campbell, P. (2007). Nature's guide for mentors. *Nature, 447*(7146), 791–797.

Mathews, K. R. (2014). *Perspectives on midcareer faculty and advice for supporting them*. Cambridge, MA: The Collaborative on Academic Careers in Higher Education.

McCauley, C. D., & Martineau, J. W. (1998). *Becoming your own best mentor: Selecting a mosaic of mentors. Reaching your developmental goals: Ideas into action guidebooks*. Greensboro, NC: Center for Creative Leadership.

McDade, S. A., Richman, R. C., Jackson, G. B., & Morahan, P. S. (2004). Effects of participation in the Executive Leadership in Academic Medicine (ELAM) program on women faculty's perceived leadership capabilities. *Academic Medicine, 79*(4), 302–309.

McLaughlin, J., Duranleau, L., & Van Ummersen, C. (Eds.). (2014). *Faculty retirement: Best practices for navigating the transition*. Sterling, VA: Stylus.

Neumann, A. (2009). *Professing to learn: Creating tenured lives and careers in the American research university*. Baltimore, MD: Johns Hopkins University Press.

Packard, B. W. L. (2003). Student training promotes mentoring awareness and action. *Career Development Quarterly, 51*(4), 335–345.

Pelham, B. W., & Hetts, J. J. (2001). Underworked and overpaid: Elevated entitlement in men's self-pay. *Journal of Experimental Social Psychology, 37*(2), 93–103.

Pfund, C., House, S. C., Asquith, P., Fleming, M. F., Buhr, K. A., Burnham, E. L., et al. (2014). Training mentors of clinical and translational research scholars: A randomized controlled trial. *Academic Medicine: Journal of the Association of American Medical Colleges, 89*(5), 774–781.

Pololi, L. H., & Evans, A. T. (2015). Group peer mentoring: An answer to the faculty mentoring problem? A successful program at a large academic department of medicine. *Journal of Continuing Education in the Health Professions, 35*(3), 192–200.

Reuben, E., Sapienza, P., & Zingales, L. (2014). How stereotypes impair women's careers in science. *Proceedings of the National Academy of Sciences of the United States of America, 111*(12), 4403–4408.

Rosen, S., Katz, J. K., & Morahan, P. (2009). Making "Personal Leadership Boards" and team- and co-coaching work for you. *Oncology Times, 31*(7), 21–23.

Rozin, P., & Royzman, E. B. (2001). Negativity bias, negativity dominance, and contagion. *Personality and Social Psychology Review, 5*(4), 296–320.

Stewart, A. J., Malley, J. E., & LaVaque-Manty, D. (2007). *Transforming science and engineering: Advancing academic women*. Ann Arbor, MI: University of Michigan Press.

Straus, S. E., Johnson, M. O., Marquez, C., & Feldaman, M. D. (2013). Characteristics of successful and failed mentoring relationships: Qualitative study across two academic health centers. *Academic Medicine: Journal of the Association of American Medical Colleges, 88*(1), 82–89.

Underhill, C. M. (2006). The effectiveness of mentoring programs in corporate settings: A meta-analytical review of the literature. *Journal of Vocational Behavior, 68*(2), 292–307.

Van Ummersen, C., Duranleau, L., & McLaughlin, J. (2013). Faculty retirement transitions revitalized. *Change: The Magazine of Higher Learning, 45*(2), 16–24.

Weinberg, S. L., & Scott, M. A. (2013). The impact of uncapping of mandatory retirement on postsecondary institutions. *Educational Researcher, 42*, 338–348.

9 Evaluating and Promoting Faculty

A group of senior faculty arrived at a two-day workshop aimed at formulating recommendations for institutional policies and practices around "faculty evaluation." One of us was a participant-observer of the process. Although all of the faculty participants were tenured, and most were full professors, they were diverse in terms of their disciplines, their time at the institution, their age, gender, race or ethnicity, and sexual orientation. The workshop began with small groups of the assembled faculty—organized to be diverse in composition—sharing their best and worst experiences of being evaluated or evaluating their colleagues across their careers.

Groups were surprised to discover that most people recounted a "worst" experience, rather than a "best" experience, about an unforgettably painful early career review when they felt invisible, unheard, or unvalued in the context of the review process. Often, these accounts included experiences that seemed like gross inequities or injustices. This was true of both women and men, of White faculty and faculty of color. Although these senior faculty also identified "best" experiences, the positive stories arose mostly from evaluations they had participated in on the *other* side of the fence, as evaluators. In these cases, they had striven to implement practices that improved on the ones employed in their own painful experiences.

Why is it that these successful senior faculty—chosen as opinion leaders on campus—could so readily recall incidents in their careers when efforts to assess their performance felt inadequate, unfair, humiliating, or even degrading? We believe it is because most academic "performance reviews" are conducted by individuals who do not have a clear understanding of the goals of the review process or of how such a process might work to benefit both individual faculty and the institution. These individuals—nearly always faculty members and faculty administrators—are neither stupid nor (usually) aiming to inflict pain (such as humiliation or alienation). However, without a better articulated understanding of the goals of the review process, and an understanding of how best to reach those goals, both faculty reviewers and targets of review may create or participate in reviews that are experienced as either meaningless or harmful. Our aim in this chapter is to offer guidelines for evaluating faculty so that good outcomes and efficiency are maximized, and wasted time and needless pain and alienation are minimized.

Why Do Faculty Get Evaluated?

Quite apart from formal performance reviews, faculty are evaluated frequently in the course of their work lives: their grants and publications are subject to peer review, and their teaching is subject to student and peer evaluations. As a result, many faculty think that they get a lot of feedback—perhaps more than enough!—on the end products of their work but are less likely to think they receive feedback that helps their day-to-day efforts. The labor that is reflected in any given grant proposal or publication, or a given course, takes months or years and usually involves only the indirect or informal feedback that faculty have sought or noticed—for example, by talking ideas or drafts over with colleagues, students, and family.

Institutional evaluation processes—where they exist—occur on a different timetable. They arise not because a project or a course is complete, but because 12 months—or some multiplicative function of 12 months—has occurred since the last evaluation. Moreover, the assessments are not of a single product, but something more, though it is not always clear precisely what. Sometimes they seem like assessments of one's value to the institution, partly because they are tied to salary increases, but also because they are usually presided over—and sometimes conducted by—an institutional official such as a department chair or dean. Alternatively, assessments sometimes seem more like predictions of success at leaping over the next big hurdle, such as looming tenure or promotion reviews. They can also feel, perhaps most often to the least experienced faculty, like measures of one's value as a human being. Some of this ambiguity may be unavoidable, and very personal, but we think it would help for institutions to be as explicit and clear as possible about the *intended* meaning of institutionally mandated evaluations.

Should We Eliminate Faculty Evaluation?

A radical possibility would be to eradicate formal institutional evaluation processes: they take a lot of time, are difficult to do well, and have some counterproductive effects, as the discussion alluded to earlier made clear. While this might seem a tempting solution, it is unlikely to happen. Worker appraisal began to be a regular feature of the U.S. workplace in the 1940s, and faculty evaluation processes followed along. In the 1990s, calls for greater accountability of universities and their faculties were accompanied by more and more intense calls for systematic evaluation of professors (Curry, 2006). Interestingly, though faculty chafe under frequent formal evaluation, they also resent not being evaluated systematically at all. If there is no systematic process of faculty evaluation, it is easy for faculty to feel—and to be—unrecognized for their accomplishments in scholarship, teaching, service, or leadership. In short, to paraphrase Winston Churchill on democracy: while systematic faculty evaluation may be a very bad system, it is better than others that have been tried.

Treating Faculty as Employees

The link between faculty performance reviews and worker evaluation raises another thorny issue: faculty do not generally feel, nor do they want to feel, like employees. We prefer to think of ourselves as "professionals"—more like (self-employed) doctors, lawyers, and entrepreneurs (all of whom are subject to their own evaluative processes, but that's a different issue). Thought about this way, institutional evaluation processes appear to reduce our uniqueness, independence, autonomy, and creativity, both because they treat us as if we are mere workers and not professionals and because they assess everyone with the same metrics on the same timetable. As with the previous issues mentioned, there is some merit to this objection. No faculty member enacts the professor role exactly like any other, and faculty evaluation processes should be sensitive to the differences among us. There are many different ways of doing a good job and of being valuable to the institution.

At the same time, the elements of our work lives do constitute a job, and it should be possible to demonstrate that we are doing that job well—or not. This should be possible for faculty to know for themselves, and it should be possible for the people who evaluate and report on their performance, even if they are temporary leaders among equals, as department chairs and deans. Institutional evaluation processes, done right, could provide crucial feedback both to individual faculty about how they are doing, and to chairs and deans who are responsible for their collective work lives and for maximizing the satisfaction and success of all of their faculty (whether they see it that way or not!).

Evaluation Processes as Feedback Processes

Most senior faculty freely agree that junior or untenured faculty deserve and need feedback about how they are doing (though not all institutions provide systematic evaluations). The stakes are high for untenured faculty (since they may lose their livelihood if they do not secure tenure), and therefore someone should provide them with feedback about how well they are doing at the features of the job that are associated with successful tenure and promotion. This right to feedback and the need for it strikes us—more controversially—as true for all faculty. The stakes in terms of pride in our work, and a sense of being valued and appreciated for our contributions, are high for all faculty, though some may bristle at the idea of the value of feedback from their local colleagues.

Changes across the Faculty Career

Most professors have long careers; their interests, enthusiasms, and accomplishments change over time, as we discussed in chapter 8. There are some persistent beliefs about career paths, including the notion that major breakthroughs, particularly in science fields, occur early in a person's career. Though this idea has been challenged many times, a recent study that considered evidence across disciplines and institutions showed that only one-fifth of faculty—regardless of field—have a productivity pattern consistent with that notion (Way, Morgan, Clauset, & Larremore, 2017). Most faculty do not, and the variability in other patterns is substantial. For that reason, institutions must adopt evaluation procedures that are sensitive to the wide diversity of patterns in productivity among the faculty.

Moreover, changes in knowledge and interests might be fostered and facilitated by an institution that views evaluation as not merely tied to salaries, or as assessments of adequacy, but as a way to think about research support needs and different teaching and service assignments. In short, the process of evaluation is a form of two-way communication between individual faculty and a department, school, or college about an individual's work, communication that can be satisfying and generative, harmful and alienating, or simply absent.

Are Issues of Equity Relevant in Faculty Evaluation Processes?

Evaluation processes involve judgments, and we have seen how subject human judgment is to cognitive biases. It is reasonable to assume, therefore, that faculty evaluations are no less subject to bias than evaluations of job candidates. For that reason, issues of equity are relevant. Thorngate, Dawes, and Foddy (2009) identify three bad cognitive "habits" that could produce inaccurate judgments: relying on memory of past events rather than making a new judgment ("she had a strong tenure case five years ago; she's a star"); making holistic rather than disaggregated or specific judgments ("he's always been terrific"); and being inconsistent in the weighting applied to different criteria (one person assessed as having published enough despite no grant; another as not having a grant despite enough publications). These three habits alone raise questions about how likely it is that faculty evaluations could be accomplished free of error.

The problem of bias, however, is different; it is based on the specific concern that the accomplishments of some groups of people are overestimated and those of others are underestimated. If this is true when faculty are being evaluated, then issues of equity across groups are a concern. We bring in several lines of research suggesting that equity is a concern.

Reviewing Faculty as Individuals or Members of Groups

We have previously discussed individuating information. In principle, the more we know about people, the less likely we should be to judge them as members of their demographic group and the more likely we should be to judge them as individuals (Landy, 2008). Thus, one might argue that evaluations of people we know (our colleagues) are fundamentally different from evaluations of strangers (entry-level job applicants). On that view, we should not be subject to schemas or stereotypes—and therefore equity issues should not arise—when we are assessing someone we know well as an individual since we possess much more information about the individual and that should prevent us from relying on schemas (Landy, 2008).

Biases in Reviewing People We "Know"

There are several reasons to doubt that we can rely on individuation to protect us against judging people on the basis of their gender or other demographic characteristics (Maynard & Brooks, 2008). We have discussed them in detail earlier in the book but provide a brief reminder of them here. First, we do not always know every colleague we evaluate very well. At a minimum, in large departments, or when evaluating faculty in other departments, there is a wide range of familiarity; we may know one individual we review quite well as a mentor or colleague (or think we do), and another person may only be someone we have seen in the halls. Second, and more importantly, if we relied on schemas in our judgments about an individual at the beginning of a relationship (e.g., upon meeting or recruiting the person), as we know is likely, two cognitive processes, anchoring and confirmation bias, will make us unlikely to change our views (Maynard & Brooks, 2008). Anchoring refers to how slowly we alter our initial impressions. Confirmation bias refers to our tendency to notice evidence that confirms our preexisting ideas rather than evidence that does not. While evaluations of colleagues are different in some ways from evaluations of job candidates, schemas can play a major role in both, for somewhat different reasons.

The Problem of Shifting Standards

A different argument has been made by social psychologist Monica Biernat (see Biernat, 2012). In reviewing many years of research on the role of stereotypes in people's judgments, she notes that members of commonly stigmatized groups (women, racial-ethnic and sexual minorities, etc.) are often viewed differently when judged on their performance in stereotype-consistent domains (where they are rated higher) than in stereotype-inconsistent domains (where they are rated lower), given the same performance. Biernat's hypothesis is that members of commonly stigmatized groups are implicitly compared with stereotyped expectations in both cases, resulting in different and inconsistent judgments because of reference to "shifting standards." Thus, women or racial-ethnic minority group members may be judged as competent or talented "for a woman" or a minority, but as incompetent or not that talented when judged in terms of qualifications for tenure.

Attributions of Credit

Finally, research on attributions of credit suggests that both gender and race of the employee affect the judgments of employers. For example, supervisors are less likely to attribute women managers' performance to ability than men's. In addition, they are less likely to attribute African American managers' performance to ability or effort than Whites', and more likely to attribute it to help from others (Greenhaus & Parasuraman, 1993). Women who demonstrate competence and achievement simultaneously suffer by negative judgments, for example, of their likability (Heilman & Okimoto, 2007; Rudman & Glick, 1999). This is sometimes called a "backlash effect" (Phelan, Moss-Racusin, & Rudman, 2008; Phelan & Rudman, 2010).

A particularly relevant study (Heilman & Haynes, 2005) showed that when performance was accomplished through collaboration (as it often is in the academy), the work of a mixed-gender dyad was attributed to the male (with obvious implications for our ability to understand the true contribution of a faculty member). In the study, judges received a packet including a summary of a trained observer's notes describing each of the two workers (one male and one female) and the overall performance on the task. The task chosen was intended to be male sex-typed: each team was to create an investment portfolio that would yield maximum return over 20 years. The two employees were described with characteristics that were equivalent in qualifications (e.g., a degree in accounting-management or accounting-finance).

Judges received ratings of the team's task performance, defined either as "individual assessments" or "group assessments." When the successful performance was the result of joint work (the group assessment), women were rated as less competent, less influential, and as having played less of a leadership role than comparable men. Moreover, because individual performance was also assessed, it was clear that it was the negative impact of collaboration on the women's ratings that drove these results (rather than a positive impact on the men's). In short, there is reason to believe that when it is unclear who did the work (because it was collaborative), men are given the benefit of the doubt and women are not. In a recent field test of the consequences of academic coauthorship among faculty in two fields differing in the ambiguity of contribution, Sarsons (2017) showed that in a field in which coauthorship does not signal degree of contribution (economics), women coauthors fare badly in terms of tenure rates, and in one where it does (sociology), women coauthors do as well as men.

An important study clarifying the limits of "backlash" effects on women showed that they did not apply to African American women, even though they did apply to White women and African American men (Livingston, Rosette, & Washington, 2012). Of course, African American women are subject to other biases (higher levels of invisibility) that do not as often apply to either White women or African American men (see, e.g., Purdie-Vaughns & Eibach, 2008; Sesko & Biernat, 2010).

The Impact of Group Stereotypes

The "stereotype content model" (Fiske, Xu, Cuddy, & Glick, 1999; see also Fiske, 2011) suggests that the trade-off of beliefs about competence and warmth arise not only in gender stereotypes but also in schemas about race-ethnicity, with some groups (e.g., Asian Americans) viewed as competent but not likable, and some as likable but not competent (African Americans and Latinos). Racial and ethnic schemas affect judgments of both people and of occupations—with high-status occupations and leadership roles generally stereotyped as "White." For example, in one study of applicants for high-status jobs, White male judges rated Asian Americans with low-quality credentials as positively as African Americans with high-quality credentials (King, Madera, Hebl, Knight, & Mendoza, 2006).

The existence of so many studies showing that human judgment processes are subject to bad habits that result in error and are saturated with the influence of group-based schemas or stereotypes suggests that we should be attuned to the possibility of inequity in faculty evaluations. There is more direct evidence as well. There is extensive documentation of salary inequity among faculty, in statistical analyses that control for disciplinary, rank, and experience differences (see, e.g., Barbezat, 2002; Jagsi, Griffith, Stewart, Sambuco, DeCastro, & Ubel, 2012; Porter, Toutkoushian, & Moore, 2008; Toutkoushian, Bellas, & Moore, 2007; Toutkoushian & Conley, 2005). If faculty are hired according to the same criteria, then only differential performance should produce salary differences, and there is little evidence for overall performance differences by gender within types of institutions (Xie & Shauman, 2003).

Equally, there is considerable evidence that women spend longer within a particular rank (especially the associate professor rank) than men (Ash, Carr, Goldstein, & Friedman, 2004; Committee on the Status of Women in the Profession, MLA, 2009; Giesler, Kaminski, & Berkley, 2007; Valian, 2000). There is less evidence about the impact of race and ethnicity on salary and on time within rank (but see Barbezat, 2002; Fang, Moy, Colburn, & Hurley, 2000; Hammond et al., 2010; and Castilla, 2008 on race in organizations), but many faculty of color believe that their work is undervalued, including in terms of salary and time to promotion (Stanley, 2006; Stanley, Porter, Simpson, & Ouellett, 2003; Turner, Gonzalez, & Wood, 2008). One woman of color described the experience of Black women this way:

> Most of us feel ourselves obligated to take on certain kinds of tasks. Sometimes you are called upon to be an advisor to a Black student group. You may be asked to serve on a curriculum committee, and you know your presence on the committee will affect the incorporation of certain types of courses into the program, or to be on an admissions committee or review committee where you know that your voice makes a difference. Whether these are undergraduate or graduate students, your voice would make a difference in the discussion. It is very hard to turn some of these things down.... Some of that I don't think you can or should decline. (Harrison, 2016, p. 57)

The experience of faculty evaluation processes is not always the same for faculty of color and White faculty. One scholar describes tenure as a "contact zone" and suggests,

> In this zone, the fate of a professor and the relationships between different ethnic, linguistic, and academic communities with different levels of access to power, knowledge and voice are negotiated through "long-term" and often "intractable" "unequal conflicts," contacts (*encuentros*), and ruptures (*desencuentros*). (Chabram, 2016, p. 95)

It is therefore important that faculty evaluations both *be* fair and *be perceived* to be fair (Curry, 2006).

Principles for Fair Faculty Evaluation Processes

Although there are some specific issues associated with each of the different types of faculty evaluations (annual reviews, third-year or midcareer reviews of assistant professors, tenure and promotion reviews, posttenure reviews), there are common features of faculty evaluation processes that are likely to be fair and to feel fair. Many of these are outlined well by Curry (2006). We will revisit many of these elements as they pertain to particular types of reviews.

First, *the review should be conducted by more than one individual.* Generally, reviews conducted by multiple evaluators are trusted more than those conducted by a single individual: they are subject to consensual validation (Thorngate et al., 2009). The assumption is that the separate formation of impressions by even two evaluators makes it less likely that an individual will form and maintain a biased perspective on the evidence. There is in fact reason to believe that multiple observers may produce more complete and more accurate judgments than a single observer (see, e.g., Vazire & Gosling, 2004, who show that aggregated judgments, based on limited information but multiple observers, are more accurate than those by single observers).

Second, *the review should be based on clearly articulated criteria applied to consistently provided evidence.* Both the faculty member being evaluated and the reviewers should know and understand the criteria that will be used in evaluating the record. This means that the criteria should be explicit and written down so they can be consulted by all parties. Moreover, the criteria should relate directly to larger institutional values and goals (Perna, 2001; Stewart, Dalton, Dino, & Wilkinson, 1996; Tierney & Bensimon, 1996).

Some institutions clearly express expectations in terms, for example, of average student teaching ratings or the number of publications expected before tenure (see, e.g., this table for the University of Michigan Medical School: http://faculty.medicine.umich.edu/appointments-promotions /promotion-process/promotion-benchmarks/, visited October 17, 2017) or the impact factors of the journals that faculty publish in (Ohio State University College of Medicine (https://medicine.osu.edu/faculty/oecrd/Documents/ed _journals20110727.pdf, visited October 17, 2017). Other departments may spell out benchmarks and criteria for achieving positive outcomes (https:// biology.uiowa.edu/sites/biology.uiowa.edu/files/Biology--Faculty%20Promo tion,%20Review%20and%20Assessment%202012.pdf, visited October 17, 2017). Yet other departments claim that precise statements are impossible and that only the broadest possible statement of demands for "quality" or "productivity" can be made. This strikes us as incorrect because it leaves too much of the decision to the discretion of the evaluators and thus risks evaluators' using different standards, depending on whether they are favorably predisposed to the candidate.

Ideally, a department or school strikes a happy medium, being neither vague in a way that encourages evaluation errors nor overspecific by using criteria that may not fit all candidates (e.g., an exact number of publications, particular funding sources, only certain publication outlets). A moderate degree of specificity will make the criteria clear not only to reviewers but to those being reviewed. Sometimes the records of those who were judged favorably in previous years can be provided as information, either in the form of their actual CVs or essays prepared for the review (many of these are password-protected and aimed only at internal faculty) or in terms of averages, modal figures, and the ranges (which often vary widely and therefore are not so helpful) across candidates. In the latter case, information about a range of publications (journal articles, monographs, edited collections) or average teaching ratings can provide guidance about the acceptable ranges that have recently been associated, within a particular institution, with higher raises, reappointment, tenure, or promotion. One medical school posts this sort of information on its website (http://faculty .medicine.umich.edu/appointments-promotions/promotion-process /promotion-benchmarks/, visited January 22, 2018).

The evidence to be reviewed (the candidate's dossier) should include evidence that is pertinent to the evaluation criteria. Guidelines for candidates' preparation of the dossiers should spell out the evidence needed in sufficient detail that all candidates can provide complete information. It is the responsibility of the institution or the evaluators to ensure that the form of the dossier is well-defined for all candidates. It is then the responsibility of the person being evaluated to provide careful, accurate information.

Curry (2006) recommends that evaluations assess performance in the context of an individualized faculty career development plan. Thus, for example, an individual's productivity in a given year might not be in terms of published papers or completed book chapters if that was a year of collecting a large set of data, learning a new technique, or working in an archive on a new project. Instead, progress in those domains (data collection, technical skills, or archival work) might be assessed for that year. A highly individualized review process like this maximizes the likelihood that evaluation criteria are tied to an individual's career stage and personal goals. This may be a particularly appropriate element in reviews that include a serious mentoring element (e.g., the reappointment review or annual reviews). However, it is difficult to imagine that most institutions would be willing to give up reliance on some kind of absolute standard of judgment (not one relative to the individual's goals) for decisions like tenure or promotion.

Third, *the review process should be transparent*. Thus, the reviewers, the procedure, and the steps in the process should all be explicitly defined according to a known timetable that is made clear to both the person being evaluated and the evaluators. Opportunities for input, as well as exclusions of material, should be clearly defined.

Fourth, *service as a faculty reviewer, within the institution and outside, should be understood to be a privilege, and one that requires skill, knowledge, and respect for confidentiality*. All reviewers should be selected or elected based on the judgment that they are capable of fair assessment of the accomplishments of peers. Moreover, they should be willing to be educated—and should in fact *be* educated—about the role of bias in evaluation processes and the steps that must be taken to minimize it. This is obviously the responsibility of the institution with regard to internal reviewers. For outside reviewers, institutions can try to make clear what type of evaluation they want and should pay little or no attention to reviews that have internal evidence of reliance on bias in their review.

Since we have demonstrated that faculty exhibit biases in judgments of each other, it is no surprise that students also express biases in their judgments of faculty (recent studies include Graves, Hoshino-Browne, & Lui, 2017; Storage, Horne, Cimpian, & Leslie, 2016). It is worth noting that in the context of faculty performance reviews, students who provide evaluations of classes are also serving as reviewers of faculty performance, and they are usually uneducated about the ways that group-based biases may enter into their judgments. Some institutions have adopted strategies (e.g., in the directions to students on the actual evaluation forms) that might minimize the intrusion of these biases in the process. In any case, the faculty evaluators should be made aware of the risk of influence of bias in these ratings, particularly for members of some groups.

Fifth, *the review* should not only be conducted according to fair criteria and procedures, but it *should be experienced as fair by the person being reviewed and by those conducting the review*. Reviewers should be held accountable for the quality of their evaluation at the level to which they report (school or college for departments and programs, provost and president for deans).

Sixth, *all faculty who are evaluated should be treated respectfully in the course of the review. This respectful treatment includes thoughtful feedback about their performance, regardless of the decision outcome.* Wherever possible, this feedback should be viewed as providing information that fosters an individual's successful career trajectory (Perna, 2001; Tierney & Bensimon, 1996). Recommendations vary about the value of written or oral feedback from a committee or from an individual, but there is no doubt that explicit, respectful, and detailed feedback increases faculty members' trust and investment in the process.

Finally, *criteria should be periodically reviewed* to determine whether the criteria need to be altered or expanded. In recent years, several institutions have adopted new criteria or expanded their criteria to include elements that had previously been ignored. For example, at Syracuse University, the faculty manual was amended in 2005 to recognize "publicly engaged scholarship" as relevant to tenure reviews along with more traditional approaches:

Syracuse University is committed to longstanding traditions of scholarship as well as evolving perspectives on scholarship. Syracuse University recognizes that the role of academia is not static and that methodologies, topics of interest, and boundaries within and between disciplines change over time. The University will continue to support scholars in all of these traditions, including faculty who choose to participate in publicly engaged scholarship. Publicly engaged scholarship may involve partnerships of University knowledge and resources with those of the public and private sectors to enrich scholarship, research, creative activity, and public knowledge; enhance curriculum, teaching, and learning; prepare educated, engaged citizens; strengthen democratic values and civic responsibility; address and help solve critical social problems; and contribute to the public good. (Syracuse University, 2005, *Faculty Manual*, section 2.34 on Tenure)

The University of California system recommends that criteria must be understood flexibly (see University of California, 2005, Academic Personnel Manual, APM-210, section d):

As the University enters new fields of endeavor and refocuses its ongoing activities, cases will arise in which the proper work of faculty members departs markedly from established academic patterns. In such cases, the review committees must take exceptional care to apply the criteria with sufficient flexibility. However, flexibility does not entail a relaxation of high standards.

The document further specifies that

Teaching, research, professional and public service contributions that promote diversity and equal opportunity are to be encouraged and given recognition in the evaluation of the candidate's qualifications. These contributions to diversity and equal opportunity can take a variety of forms including efforts to advance equitable access to education, public service that addresses the needs of California's diverse population, or research in a scholar's area of expertise that highlights inequalities. (APM-210)

An alternative approach to a similar issue—probably less effective over the long term because not codified in official policy and therefore safely ignored—was taken by the provost at the University of Michigan in 2012 (and restated by later provosts). He sent an e-mail to all faculty pointing out the importance of including attention to "the broad range of entrepreneurial, outreach, and creative activities in which faculty engage" in all faculty review processes. He noted that these included "creating service learning and action-based learning opportunities for students" and "engaging in community-based research," among other examples (Pollack, 2015).

To summarize, fair evaluations require procedures that will buffer evaluators from the errors that evidence suggests can enter the review process. Having multiple reviewers ensures that more features of a candidate will be assessed; having specific criteria guards against emphasizing or deemphasizing criteria depending on who is being evaluated; a fair, transparent, and respectful process gives everyone confidence in the institution; knowledge about the demographically based errors that are inherent in judgments helps evaluators guard against them; periodic review of criteria keeps an institution up-to-date with the range of valuable knowledge that faculty can provide.

Annual Reviews of Faculty

As with all reviews, the purpose of annual reviews should be clear. If, for example, they are to be used as one basis—or the primary one—for allocating merit-based raises, this should be explicit so faculty understand the implications of this evaluation. If the reviews will be used to provide substantive feedback about how well the individual is performing and thus serve as a guideline to the faculty member about whether they are on track for a long-term appointment, then clear criteria must be used to judge performance and detailed feedback must actually be provided. (Many institutions promise feedback but provide such generic feedback that it feels empty and meaningless to the individual.) Finally, if the feedback will be used as a basis for information conveyed to junior or early career faculty about how they are doing, this too should be explicit and should result in direct conversations about how to reach their goals (reappointment or tenure and promotion), as well as the best estimate of whether those goals are attainable.

Who Should Be Reviewed?
Senior faculty may also benefit from periodic reviews if the climate of the department allows for respectful feedback when faculty members are, and perceive themselves to be, at a decision point regarding research, teaching, or service. Such a review cannot be imposed at random or come from

evaluators whom the faculty do not regard true "peers." But for faculty who are facing complex decisions about how to invest their time, an opportunity to share ambivalence and uncertainty and to get feedback from wise colleagues may be valued highly.

Many institutions, but certainly not all, engage in annual reviews of every faculty member. Some require an annual report, described below, from every faculty member, but conduct formal reviews less often and at that time include a review of two or more annual reports. This kind of practice may be warranted when patterns of teaching, scholarship, and service are relatively stable over more than one year, as for more senior faculty. However, it is wise to require faculty to provide reports annually even when they will be reviewed less often so the reports will be less subject to the biases that affect retrospective reports of activities. Annual reports typically include information that may be on a CV (e.g., publications, conference presentations, and service contributions, in a specified time frame) but go well beyond the outcomes covered there, including, for example, research projects under way but not yet yielding conference talks or publications, formal courses taught in that time frame, as well as guest lectures in others' courses, informal teaching through individual tutorials or even small group processes, activities in the community and the discipline, advising of both graduate and undergraduate students, mentoring activities for students and faculty, and contributions to campus and department initiatives that may not be covered by formal committee service.

Annual Activity Reporting

We believe that annual reporting of activities is generally a sensible practice both for individuals and for institutions. It allows individuals to keep track of their activities on a timely basis and it allows institutions to provide formal feedback (in principle via salary adjustments) and informal feedback about how the individual compares with expectations of faculty activity. However, it should not be required of individuals if those reports will not be used by the institution for any purpose that the individual might be expected to value. Thus, if annual reports are never actually read or evaluated, and if feedback is never provided to the individual, requiring the reports is not defensible. In addition, if reports are only used for punitive purposes (e.g., to assign additional teaching to faculty who are not engaged in research activities), there will be little trust or investment in them on the part of the faculty. Institutions must be wise in requiring labor and disclosure from faculty, and that wisdom includes respectful use of the material that is generated by individuals in the form of reports.

The criteria that will be used in annual reviews should be developed in terms of both broad aspects of the larger institutional mission and unit-specific values. A particular department may have a strong mission associated with teaching first- and second-year undergraduates (e.g., composition, required math and science courses, etc.), or as a large major, or a major feeding into a profession. The criteria should reflect such missions. Equally, a department's scholarly mission may be self-understood to involve rapid publication in online journals or, instead, mainly in printed monographs. These disciplinary and departmental differences should be reflected in the articulation of criteria for the review and in the development of a reporting form for faculty to use in describing their annual activities. A clear timetable for reporting, evaluation, and feedback should also be explicitly articulated.

Consistent Format for Reporting
A reasonable balance must be struck between a uniform reporting format that enables consistent application of criteria and the need for individuals to have ways to report unusual or developing activities. It is helpful to be explicit about precisely how information should be reported. For example, should only work actually newly in print during a particular year be reported? Should manuscripts in press or under review be reported but in separate sections? Should projects undertaken but not yet written up be described? If so, where and how? At the same time, in each of the major areas assessed, it may be useful to provide faculty with an opportunity to describe new projects or commitments. However, if a report of new projects is invited, reviewers and the faculty member must have a clear idea of how this information is to be used. The evaluation process must have built in some ways to guard against evaluating different faculty according to different criteria (systematically or idiosyncratically shifting standards).

How Feedback Is Communicated
In the interest of encouraging communication about important issues, it may be helpful to include an opportunity for face-to-face interaction in the process. This interaction might be a one-on-one conversation between a "primary" reviewer and the individual, or it could be a conversation between the committee and the individual. The latter kind of procedure

may, however, disadvantage faculty who feel they lack status or standing in the department. It may also be helpful to ask faculty members to summarize the key points they took away from the review in a postconversation e-mail to ensure that there is agreement on what was said.

If reviews will affect salaries, department chairs must recognize the key role of salary in faculty satisfaction and retention. Judgments and the resulting salaries should reflect the behaviors that a chair hopes to encourage (e.g., good citizenship, selfless contributions to the department, institution, or discipline), and address the trade-off between high-performers-take-all approaches and sharing rewards more broadly across the faculty.

Special Issues in Annual Reviews of Untenured Faculty

Finally, annual review processes for untenured faculty should be accompanied by detailed individual feedback, communicated with the aim of maximizing the individual's chances for reappointment and then promotion and tenure. One vehicle for communicating feedback is a written letter (perhaps drafted by one individual but always shared and revised in a group); another is a face-to-face meeting. Both can be used to good effect. We recommend sending a letter and following up with a meeting in which the inevitable ambiguities of interpretation of feedback can be addressed in person. An example of such a letter and the questions it might elicit from an untenured faculty member is provided in box 9.1. The questions are included to help readers imagine what a junior faculty member may find unclear or confusing even in an explicit letter like this one. Only face-to-face conversation with the chair and perhaps other senior faculty can address the questions that inevitably arise.

Reviews for Reappointment of Junior Faculty

The Goals of Reappointment Reviews

Many institutions have created a review process that assesses junior faculty for reappointment on the tenure track before they are reviewed for tenure and/or promotion. These reviews are often intended to provide both the institution and the individual with information about how the individual is progressing toward tenure and promotion. In some institutions there are two or more two-year reappointment reviews before the tenure review; in others there is one midcareer (third- or fourth-year) review during the "probationary period" as an assistant professor. Reappointment reviews

Box 9.1

Evaluation Letter—Untenured Assistant Professor, Prior to Reappointment

Evaluation Letter	Recipient's Questions
Dear Untenured,	
It is my responsibility to annually evaluate the performance of each faculty member, taking into consideration input from the department advisory committee. The following assessments follow the expectations identified in the letter of offer you received prior to your appointment.	
Teaching: Your primary assignment has been to teach the first year theory sequence and the **two sections of XXX 151**, as well as a graduate seminar. Teaching the theory sequence has been a considerable challenge. We have talked about the student evaluation forms in which your composite overall rating for these courses is 3.5 out of 5.0.	No comments are made anywhere in this report about the two sections of XXX 151; is it going well?
This is below **the department threshold for being considered excellent, which is 4.5**. The examination of your teaching portfolio does indicate that you have put considerable effort into your courses. However, student comments indicate that your lectures seem to lack variety in teaching techniques and could be better organized. The large class setting posed particular difficulties that you continue to work to overcome. Your willingness to consult with others who have experience teaching large required undergraduate courses seems to have been helpful, and I noticed an **improvement in the student evaluation scores in the spring semester**. It was clear from them that you know the material very well and that you are a dedicated teacher. I suggest that you examine closely the comments made by the peer review teaching committee. **Members of the committee would individually welcome a dialogue** with you about these issues. I would also encourage you to continue videotaping class sessions in the coming academic year. With respect to the graduate seminar, all indications from the student evaluation forms suggest that you did an excellent job.	Am I expected to reach that level ("excellent") in all classes? Are the scores obtained this term sufficiently high, if I can maintain them, or are they still too low? Those are all busy people; how can I approach them? Should I?

Box 9.1 (continued)

You should consider whether any of the teaching strategies that work so well in this seminar could be adapted to your other courses, different as they are in level and size. Your teaching performance *has been rated as acceptable*.

How could they possibly work in a large undergraduate class?

That sounds OK; is "acceptable" good enough?

Research: With regard to research, the advisory committee and I agree that you are making good progress. Your article in Journal of MMM and the one accepted in the Journal of RRR are a good start. *These are Tier One journals in our department listing of journals, and you should continue to publish in them.* In looking ahead, however, you need to establish a thematic focus and a research agenda that will be cumulative in building your national reputation. I will ask the mentoring committee to help you in this process. The development of a career plan that includes a *statement about your research direction* would prove helpful here. Your research performance has been rated as excellent.

What department listing? Where is it? Do you mean I have to only publish in these two journals?

Don't these things emerge from my work? I need to just keep publishing and doing projects and the thematic focus will be clear—right?

Service and Outreach: You participate actively in faculty meetings and on the department's admission committee and you were a panel member at this year's major outreach conference. This is a good level of service for a beginning faculty member. Your service performance has been rated as excellent.

Summary and Suggestions, Progress Toward Tenure: Overall you have made a good start. As indicated, you will have to continue to work to improve your teaching in the theory sequence; *good teaching is required for tenure within the department*. Because the tenure decision takes a cumulative look at the total body of your work and its impact on the field, *it is imperative that you articulate your research focus and theme more clearly*. The mentoring committee and I will be glad to help. If this letter does not accurately summarize our discussions, or if you have additional questions or concerns about any of its content, please let me know as soon as possible.

How good? Do I have to be excellent in all kinds of teaching?

I'm not sure how I can articulate a focus when I don't know yet which of my efforts will yield results. Seems to me I should just keep working and the "theme" and "agenda" will emerge as I do. Is that wrong?

Letter reprinted from Curry (2006, p. 11) with permission. Possible questions from junior faculty added.

are generally more extensive and thorough than annual reviews (in part because fewer individuals are reviewed), but there is a great deal of variation in the materials used for these reviews and in the probability of reappointment in different institutions.

The Timing of Reappointment Reviews

The path to a tenure review is only about six or seven years at most institutions that have formal tenure systems (currently about half of higher education institutions; NCES, 2016), and at many schools the tenure decision is a highly consequential "up or out" decision, with no opportunity for rereview (Trower, 2002). We propose that reviews for reappointment are better suited to providing feedback and mentoring to untenured faculty than to making ultimate employment decisions. There may be a small number of faculty whose performance in the early years of a tenure track appointment is so problematic that their department believes they should be terminated before a tenure review. In such cases, it is crucial not only to have a process that allows for a fair and thorough review of the (short) record of accomplishment, but also constructively assesses the prospects for accomplishment in the future. This latter estimate is inevitably based on relatively little data and is therefore subject to significant prediction error: particularly in the early stages of a career, the nature of a faculty member's project and the kind of publication sought may offer little or no reviewable evidence.

Criteria for Reappointment Reviews

Since reappointment reviews are more consequential than annual reviews (if less so than tenure reviews), the criteria for review must be well-defined and clearly communicated to all parties. In addition, as previously noted, candidates need clear guidelines for how to prepare their dossier for review by others. Access to a template or form is often helpful. For example, the University of Vermont offers both general advice about the whole dossier and detailed information about the information that must be provided by the applicant for reappointment (https://www.uvm.edu/~facrsrcs/MASTER _BlueSheetform_Apr2016.docx and https://www.uvm.edu/~facrsrcs/Green BlueSheetInstructions.pdf). Departments, schools, and colleges can often also ask individuals recently successfully reviewed and reappointed to share their dossiers with new applicants so they have a potential model to follow.

The Questionable Role of Outside Letters in Reappointment Reviews

Some institutions include outside letters in interim reviews; many do not. A number of considerations are relevant. One powerful reason not to request external letters is to avoid signaling the trajectory of a highly attractive candidate to individuals at other institutions. The individual at this stage has not yet provided benefits to the institution for the labor and financial investment that has already been made in hiring, recruiting, and support. Another reason is avoidance of adding to the already substantial reviewing burden entailed by tenure and promotion review processes. In addition, external reviews of such an incomplete record of accomplishment may have too much impact on a review process at this stage, when the local institution has much more information than external people have about the junior person's developing career. We will review in the next section how questionable it is to rely on external letters even in the tenure process itself, because of their special vulnerability to biases. For all of these reasons we recommend against reliance on letters at this early stage in a faculty member's career.

The Role of Feedback in Reappointment Reviews

Feedback to the junior faculty member is the single most important element in reappointment reviews (Perna, 2001; Tierney & Bensimon, 1996). We strongly recommend both that feedback be in writing and that it be discussed in a meeting with the candidate. That meeting should include the department chair and at least one senior faculty member other than the chair who knows the faculty member well—ideally someone who has served as an advisor. Early career faculty often have difficulty interpreting feedback, and may both over- and underrespond to what they think they hear. Having seriously engaged senior faculty discuss the feedback with the junior faculty member can help guard against ongoing misinterpretations. Moreover, the senior faculty involved must gauge the relative need of any particular faculty member for both clarity about the seriousness of the criteria for tenure and promotion and their distance from it, and encouragement that the standard can be met. There are large individual and group differences in faculty members' confidence, accuracy of interpretation, and attributions about their own situation (to lack of effort, ability, support, etc.).

Sensitive, attentive senior faculty must take responsibility for trying to convey feedback in a way that fits the receiver and is accurate. Junior faculty have their own responsibilities: to review feedback carefully and to try to calibrate its implications for their efforts. The more constructive the feedback is, in content and style, the more likely it is that the faculty member can interpret it correctly and make use of it. Asking specific questions is the best tactic the faculty member can use to minimize the likelihood of misinterpreting the implications of feedback.

This communication process—like all interpersonal communication—is fraught with complexity. Both senders and receivers are subject to the cognitive biases that we have discussed throughout this volume, but there are some that are particularly likely to be mobilized in this kind of profoundly consequential interaction. Differences in the social groups we all belong to may exaggerate our difficulties: junior faculty are more likely to be women or from another underrepresented minority group (or both) than are senior faculty. Evidence suggests that White women and racial-ethnic minorities are most disposed to trust feedback that conveys that high and transparent standards have been and will be employed, along with confidence that the individual can meet those standards (see Biernat, 2012, for a summary; specific studies include Cohen, Steele, & Ross, 1999; Crocker, Voelkl, Testa, & Major, 1991; Roberts, 1991; Roberts & Nolen-Hoeksema, 1994).

Responsibilities of Evaluators

The senior faculty evaluating the dossier and the individuals conveying the feedback must work to avoid being influenced by group-based schemas in their judgment—either underestimating accomplishments because of reliance on a schema suggesting members of the candidate's group cannot achieve at a high absolute standard or overestimating accomplishments because of reliance on a schema suggesting that the individual is performing better than the group normally would. Low absolute ratings of accomplishment accompanied by high praise from a reviewer should be a red flag that the reviewer is being influenced by using a within-group standard to produce praise and an across-group comparison to provide a low rating. Such a pattern, as mentioned earlier, arises from the influence of group-based stereotypes. Implementation of transparent and consistent standards is the best way to counteract this influence (see Biernat, 2012; Thorngate et al., 2009).

Decisions Not to Reappoint

The painful and infrequent use of reappointment reviews to make a decision not to reappoint must be handled with particular care if confidence in the fairness of the process is to be retained. The fact that this decision must sometimes be made underscores the importance of the composition of the review committee (members must be seen to have the needed expertise and to be fair-minded). In addition, the process must be perceived to have been entirely transparent and based on reasonable criteria if the unsuccessful candidate and the surrounding community of other junior as well as senior faculty are to have confidence in the decision. Finally, humane and considerate treatment of the unsuccessful candidate is crucial, including explicit discussion of the kinds of career advice and mentoring that is still available to them from faculty in the department or school. Decisions not to reappoint inevitably create a rupture between individuals and their colleagues. For that reason, it is crucial to take active steps to ensure that a few individuals are available to provide ongoing support and mentoring as the individual finds an alternate path.

Decisions to Reappoint

Positive decisions to reappoint should also be accompanied by explicit advice about future activities that will maximize the likelihood of tenure and promotion (without suggesting there are any guarantees about future outcomes based on those activities alone). Not only must the feedback about future activities be conveyed carefully and fully, but it is best to outline a plan for the period between the reappointment review and the tenure review. This may be done in consultation with the chair and at least one mentor or by a group of mentors, but it should happen close to the time of the reappointment review and as a result of it.

Tenure and Promotion Reviews

All of the features we have discussed as important in annual and reappointment reviews (e.g., clarity, transparency, fairness of the criteria and the process) apply with special force to tenure and promotion reviews. There is a particular burden on faculty who participate in these high-stakes reviews to be well educated about the potential for biases entering into evaluations of colleagues and for them to be fully capable of committing to conscientious, fair-minded reviews. Thus, both their selection and their "training" or education about bias and fair procedures deserve special attention and care.

Timing of Tenure and Promotion Reviews

We note that it may be valuable to consider whether the tenure and promotion reviews are well-timed at any given institution. Although we assume in our discussion a model that is specifically designed to accommodate the widest possible range of situations, there are alternative unusual models to consider. For example, one model rejects the classic seven-year review cycle. Instead, faculty members have, say, ten years in which to achieve tenure but may put themselves forward at any time. Faculty can submit a maximum of five publications on which they will be evaluated.[1] One faculty member may think she has five noteworthy publications within three years. Another may think he has such a dossier only after ten years. It is the faculty member's choice, in consultation with more senior faculty. On this model, it is not the quantity but the quality of someone's work that is evaluated.

By allowing ten years, the model obviates the need for any policies concerning stopping the clock or modifying duties. Someone can take as much or as little time as they want within their ten-year period. An intellectual benefit is that faculty would be free to consider longer range projects that might take several years to show a result instead of focusing on short-term projects that will maximize quantity. We are not necessarily endorsing this model, but we put it forward as an example of fresh thinking that could stimulate further thinking about the goals of the tenure review and how they should be reflected in the process.

Formation of the Review Committee

Regardless of the timing of the case, it is optimal for members of any tenure review committee to have a discussion of the issue of cognitive biases at the beginning of their deliberations, without reference to any particular case. We recommend that individuals who dismiss the importance of these biases not serve on review committees on the grounds that they are not knowledgeable enough about the cognitive processes underlying evaluations to conduct them fairly and impartially.

Because most faculty assume they are free of bias, it is important that review committee members be educated about specific practices that will minimize the impact of implicit bias. Among other things, this means that all committee members should understand the importance of maintaining consistent standards both across different candidates and in terms of using a set of clear and well-specified (but not overspecified) criteria. It should be viewed as good and appropriate collegial behavior to point out when others are applying different standards to different candidates. The fairness of the review process is the responsibility of every committee member, not just the chair. Some institutions have adopted mandatory (https://aglifesciences.tamu.edu /about/impacts/diversity/) or voluntary (http://fda.fsu.edu/var/ezwebin_site /storage/original/application/c84e2b1b64d1b9269146f092dd21d15f.pdf) educational sessions for tenure review committee members, conducted either online or in person. These seem to be an excellent practice that will likely raise the quality of the tenure review process of any given campus over time, as knowledge and experience implementing improved practices spreads in the community. Some institutions make one committee member responsible for preventing schemas or bias from entering into discussions (http://www.usu.edu/provost/promotion-and-tenure/ombudsperson .cfm). While this may be tempting, we believe it is a mistake to relieve any committee members of the responsibility for a fair review. For that reason, explicit discussion of the issues, recommendation of specific procedures to maximize fairness, and shared responsibility for the review seems a better course.

Specifying Tenure Criteria

Specifying tenure criteria is a complex matter. Many institutions articulate criteria that are too vague ("excellence in scholarship, teaching, and service"), which means they have failed to indicate any standard at all. Some institutions employ overly specific criteria. One overly specific criterion is a particular level of citations. This is not appropriate because citation rate is strongly influenced by time and subfield size, as well as journal impact and other extraneous matters (Hirsch, 2005; Meho & Yang, 2007; Ruscio, Seaman, D'Oriano, Stremlo, & Mahalchik, 2012). Some departments require that candidates include the impact factor of each journal their work appears in. This, too, is inappropriate, as the San Francisco Declaration of

Research Assessment, primarily aimed at evaluation of researchers in the sciences, spells out. (See http://www.ascb.org/dora) This excellent declaration, presented in box 9.2, makes recommendations to funding agencies, institutions, and researchers to limit the use of impact factors. It emphasizes not using proxies, such as journal impact factor, over a paper's quality. Quality, directly assessed, rather than quantity or other metrics, has been stressed by a range of organizations. For example, the Computing Research Association adopted a "best practices" memo in 2015, for evaluating scholarship, and suggested limiting the number of papers considered to one or two for junior scholars being hired and to three to five for consideration for promotion. (See http://cra.org/wp-content/uploads/2016/02/BP_Memo.pdf.)

Another example of overspecificity is requiring particular student teaching evaluation scores. That is not appropriate because those scores are influenced by field, size of class, and complex aspects of discipline, gender, and race composition of the student body, and all interact with the gender and race of the instructor (Bavishi, Madera, & Hebl, 2010), as well as perceived age and "hotness" (Sohr-Preston, Boswell, McCaleb, & Robertson, 2016). In the past studies of student evaluations of teaching have resisted straightforward conclusions because they relied on field data subject to many uncontrolled influences such as self-selection of courses taught by men vs. women. Recently researchers have used inventive techniques to overcome these limitations.

For example, Boring, Ottoboni & Stark (2016) examined one set of data based on evaluations obtained in a 5-year natural experiment in France, in which students were assigned to mandatory first year courses based solely on scheduling considerations, and students were unable to select their instructor; thus instructor gender was "as if" randomly assigned. Data suggested that gender produced significant and large differences in ratings—so large that they could not be used to assess effectiveness. There were, in addition, non-trivial other irrelevant effects (e.g., by discipline), making it impossible to employ a statistical correction. These results were replicated in a US dataset collected under conditions of random assignment in an online course. In another study in which students were randomly assigned to sections taught by men or women, using identical course materials, women were rated significantly lower than men overall; these results were mostly driven by ratings of male students, and were larger for courses

Box 9.2
San Francisco Declaration of Research Assessment

There is a pressing need to improve the ways in which the output of scientific research is evaluated by funding agencies, academic institutions, and other parties.

To address this issue, a group of editors and publishers of scholarly journals met during the Annual Meeting of The American Society for Cell Biology (ASCB) in San Francisco, CA, on December 16, 2012. The group developed a set of recommendations, referred to as the *San Francisco Declaration on Research Assessment*. We invite interested parties across all scientific disciplines to indicate their support by adding their names to this Declaration.

The outputs from scientific research are many and varied, including: research articles reporting new knowledge, data, reagents, and software; intellectual property; and highly trained young scientists. Funding agencies, institutions that employ scientists, and scientists themselves, all have a desire, and need, to assess the quality and impact of scientific outputs. It is thus imperative that scientific output is measured accurately and evaluated wisely.

The Journal Impact Factor is frequently used as the primary parameter with which to compare the scientific output of individuals and institutions. The Journal Impact Factor, as calculated by Thomson Reuters, was originally created as a tool to help librarians identify journals to purchase, not as a measure of the scientific quality of research in an article. With that in mind, it is critical to understand that the Journal Impact Factor has a number of well-documented deficiencies as a tool for research assessment. These limitations include: (A) citation distributions within journals are highly skewed [1–3]; (B) the properties of the Journal Impact Factor are field-specific: it is a composite of multiple, highly diverse article types, including primary research papers and reviews [1, 4]; (C) Journal Impact Factors can be manipulated (or "gamed") by editorial policy [5]; and (D) data used to calculate the Journal Impact Factors are neither transparent nor openly available to the public [4, 6, 7].

Below we make a number of recommendations for improving the way in which the quality of research output is evaluated. Outputs other than research articles will grow in importance in assessing research effectiveness in the future, but the peer-reviewed research paper will remain a central research output that informs research assessment. Our recommendations therefore focus primarily on practices relating to research articles published in peer-reviewed journals but can and should be extended by recognizing additional products, such as datasets, as important research outputs. These recommendations are aimed at funding agencies, academic institutions, journals, organizations that supply metrics, and individual researchers.

(continued)

Box 9.2 (continued)

A number of themes run through these recommendations:

• the need to eliminate the use of journal-based metrics, such as Journal Impact Factors, in funding, appointment, and promotion considerations;

• the need to assess research on its own merits rather than on the basis of the journal in which the research is published; and

• the need to capitalize on the opportunities provided by online publication (such as relaxing unnecessary limits on the number of words, figures, and references in articles, and exploring new indicators of significance and impact).

We recognize that many funding agencies, institutions, publishers, and researchers are already encouraging improved practices in research assessment. Such steps are beginning to increase the momentum toward more sophisticated and meaningful approaches to research evaluation that can now be built upon and adopted by all of the key constituencies involved.

The signatories of the San Francisco Declaration on Research Assessment support the adoption of the following practices in research assessment.

General Recommendation

1. Do not use journal-based metrics, such as Journal Impact Factors, as a surrogate measure of the quality of individual research articles, to assess an individual scientist's contributions, or in hiring, promotion, or funding decisions.

For funding agencies

2. Be explicit about the criteria used in evaluating the scientific productivity of grant applicants and clearly highlight, especially for early-stage investigators, that the scientific content of a paper is much more important than publication metrics or the identity of the journal in which it was published.

3. For the purposes of research assessment, consider the value and impact of all research outputs (including datasets and software) in addition to research publications, and consider a broad range of impact measures including qualitative indicators of research impact, such as influence on policy and practice.

For institutions

4. Be explicit about the criteria used to reach hiring, tenure, and promotion decisions, clearly highlighting, especially for early-stage investigators, that the scientific content of a paper is much more important than publication metrics or the identity of the journal in which it was published.

5. For the purposes of research assessment, consider the value and impact of all research outputs (including datasets and software) in addition to research

Box 9.2 (continued)

publications, and consider a broad range of impact measures including qualitative indicators of research impact, such as influence on policy and practice.

For publishers

6. Greatly reduce emphasis on the journal impact factor as a promotional tool, ideally by ceasing to promote the impact factor or by presenting the metric in the context of a variety of journal-based metrics (e.g., 5-year impact factor, EigenFactor [8], SCImago [9], h-index, editorial and publication times, etc.) that provide a richer view of journal performance.

7. Make available a range of article-level metrics to encourage a shift toward assessment based on the scientific content of an article rather than publication metrics of the journal in which it was published.

8. Encourage responsible authorship practices and the provision of information about the specific contributions of each author.

9. Whether a journal is open-access or subscription-based, remove all reuse limitations on reference lists in research articles and make them available under the Creative Commons Public Domain Dedication [10].

10. Remove or reduce the constraints on the number of references in research articles, and, where appropriate, mandate the citation of primary literature in favor of reviews in order to give credit to the group(s) who first reported a finding.

For organizations that supply metrics

11. Be open and transparent by providing data and methods used to calculate all metrics.

12. Provide the data under a license that allows unrestricted reuse, and provide computational access to data, where possible.

13. Be clear that inappropriate manipulation of metrics will not be tolerated; be explicit about what constitutes inappropriate manipulation and what measures will be taken to combat this.

14. Account for the variation in article types (e.g., reviews versus research articles), and in different subject areas when metrics are used, aggregated, or compared.

For researchers

15. When involved in committees making decisions about funding, hiring, tenure, or promotion, make assessments based on scientific content rather than publication metrics.

16. Wherever appropriate, cite primary literature in which observations are first reported rather than reviews in order to give credit where credit is due.

(continued)

Box 9.2 (continued)

17. Use a range of article metrics and indicators on personal/supporting statements, as evidence of the impact of individual published articles and other research outputs [11].

18. Challenge research assessment practices that rely inappropriately on Journal Impact Factors and promote and teach best practice that focuses on the value and influence of specific research outputs.

References

1. Adler, R., Ewing, J., & Taylor, P. (2008). *Citation statistics*. A report from the International Mathematical Union. Retrieved from http://www.ams.org/notices/200808/tx080800968p.pdf

2. Seglen, P. O. (1997). Why the impact factor of journals should not be used for evaluating research. *BMJ: British Medical Journal, 314*, 498–502.

3. Editorial. (2005). Not so deep impact. *Nature, 435*, 1003–1004.

4. Vanclay, J. K. (2012). Impact factor: Outdated artefact or stepping-stone to journal certification? *Scientometrics, 92*, 211–238.

5. The PLoS Medicine Editors. (2006). The impact factor game. *PLoS Medicine, 3*(6): e291. doi:10.1371/journal.pmed.0030291

6. Rossner, M., Van Epps, H., & Hill, E. (2007). Show me the data. *Journal of Cell Biology, 179*, 1091–1092.

7. Rossner, M., Van Epps, H., & Hill, E. (2008). Irreproducible results: A response to Thomson Scientific. *Journal of Cell Biology, 180*, 254–255.

8. http://www.eigenfactor.org/

9. http://www.scimagojr.com/

10. http://opencitations.wordpress.com/2013/01/03/open-letter-to-publishers

11. http://altmetrics.org/tools/

in mathematics and for more junior female instructors (Mengel, Sauermann, & Zölitz, 2017). These studies suggest that student evaluations of teaching—though often an important part of faculty evaluation--are a very flawed source of evidence.

Reliance on Evidence

It is usually optimal to use multiple forms of evidence for any criterion (thus, not to rely on a single indicator of research or teaching excellence). In the case of teaching, one would consider, for example, the sophistication and creativity of syllabuses and assignments, peer evaluations of teaching as well as student evaluations, the mix of courses offered and evidence of success at different levels (e.g., first- and second-year students vs. upper level students) and in different kinds of courses (e.g., lecture vs. seminar format), attention to individual mentoring of students at various levels, and so on. The particular standard employed should be articulated within fields and units because the nature of the teaching, research, and service demands differs by field. For example, how introductory courses and laboratory or writing-intensive courses are understood and assessed is field specific.

It is worth noting again that evidence of minimal competence tends to be evaluated relatively leniently for "outgroup members" (i.e., White women and racial-ethnic minorities) while evidence of meeting a high standard is likely to need to be higher for those same groups (see Biernat, 2012; Biernat & Kobrynowicz, 1997; Biernat, Ma, & Nario-Redmond, 2008). Moreover, any sign of incompetence or failure on a stereotype-relevant dimension (e.g., female performance in a male-dominated field, minorities' performance in academic settings) is likely to be noticed and weighted heavily (Biernat, Fuegen, & Kobrynowicz, 2010).

Partly because of the subtlety and complexity of these cognitive processes, time pressure militates against fairness. Because the cognitive demands are greater in evaluations of "outgroup" members, time pressure increases reliance on stereotypes or group-based schemas rather than on individual performance (see, e.g., Biernat, Kobrynowicz, & Weber, 2003, in which even judgments of men's and women's heights were influenced by time pressure). Many occasions on which faculty evaluate their junior peers are accompanied by powerful time pressures. Only by minimizing these pressures can one reduce the probability of reliance on group-based stereotypes.

External Letters

Many—perhaps most—institutions rely heavily on external letters from field or subfield experts in the course of tenure and promotion reviews, though they are sought using a variety of procedures (e.g., allowing the candidate to nominate some but not all of the reviewers, ruling out reviewers who are not "arm's length," or alternatively requiring letters from collaborators and/or dissertation and postdoctoral advisors). In addition, some institutions seek a small number of letters, while others seek many (we are aware of a range from at least 3 to 20). Some choices are driven by a desire for objectivity, others by a desire to ensure that the candidate's work is fully understood.

Reliance on external letters from field or disciplinary experts may seem both wise and inevitable—perhaps especially when internal reviewers feel they are not knowledgeable enough about the candidate's area of research to carry out an "expert" assessment. These issues may also feel particularly complicated when individuals work at the intersections of multiple fields or in truly interdisciplinary fields. We agree that there may be special challenges in such cases and reviewers—internal and external—must be selected particularly thoughtfully in those cases.

But we also note that the tenure and promotion decision is always made in part by individuals who are not experts in the field or subfield of the candidate. How do such individuals weigh the accomplishments of an individual in a field they do not know or understand? To some extent they rely on the judgments of those in the unit who are closest in expertise to the candidate (just as they did at the time of hiring), though, of course, the degree of closeness in expertise varies in different cases. However, to a much higher degree at the time of tenure and promotion review, institutions depend on the judgments of individuals outside the institution who are demonstrably (or allegedly!) expert in the same or a related field to assess the scholarly contributions of the candidate.

Despite those good reasons for seeking external opinions, overreliance on letters is an unwise practice. Given the lack of control over the education of external letter writers and their lack of accountability, we are tempted to recommend that departments not request external letters. We understand that it is unlikely that this recommendation will be adopted soon—or perhaps ever. For that reason, we will address in detail the reasons for our skepticism. Our hope is that we will persuade some readers of letters at least to adopt a high degree of skepticism about the weight they should have in the review process. In addition, we strongly recommend adoption of a procedure requiring that at the earliest stages of the review process, individuals within the field at the institution—however incomplete their knowledge of the area of research—should first form their own judgment based on the same material provided to external reviewers, and without any reference to the external reviewers' comments. This procedure will make it more likely that any comments that are inconsistent with the views of the internal reviewers are then subjected to the higher level of scrutiny we believe they merit.

Our reservations about the value of letters in the review process arise first from the fact that these letters are prepared by individuals with unknown education about the cognitive biases outlined in this volume and with unknown capacity for fair-minded assessment. If an institution has—as we hope it has—adopted a set of procedures that makes it likely that *internal* reviewers meet a high standard on these two dimensions, why would it lower the overall quality of the review—to an unknown degree—by adding in material that is generated by individuals who do not meet that standard?

We would not be concerned if there were little or no evidence that external letters are influenced by group-based stereotypes. Unfortunately, the evidence is substantial that they are (Dutt, Pfaff, Bernstein, Dillard, & Block, 2016; Schmader, Whitehead, & Wysocki, 2007; Trix & Psenka, 2003). We reviewed much of this evidence in the context of hiring at the entry level in chapter 6 but it is important specifically to consider the implications for individuals with a longer record of accomplishment, such as tenure candidates. In one key study (Steinpreis, Anders, & Ritzke, 1999), the process of review by external letter writers was mimicked. Thus, raters were sent one CV for an applicant for a job or for early tenure (parallel to material sent to external reviewers). Gender was varied and assigned in advance (by providing a name to the applicant) to records that were otherwise identical. This experiment was conducted with two sets of records, one for a dossier at the entry level and one for a dossier at the point of review for "early tenure."

In the first case, as we might expect, the man's accomplishments—though identical to the woman's—were more highly rated, presumably because of the kinds of schema-related language differences in the letters spelled out in chapter 6. In the second case, of an unusually strong record compatible with review for early tenure, the judges' recommendation for tenure was the same for the man and the woman. However, these recommendations were accompanied by expressions of reservations by raters *four times more often* in the case of the dossier with a female name—perhaps because of the schemas of the judges.

Even when coming to a favorable decision about the female tenure candidate, external reviewers who reviewed her record were especially likely to refer in their comments not to her accomplishments, but to concerns about their source. This finding is consistent with other evidence that, even when associated with positive overall ratings, judgments of women and minorities are influenced by negative stereotype-consistent attributions and memory distortions (see Lord & Taylor, 2009). The reservations expressed by the external reviewers (if summarized in a report) might influence other levels of review, despite the presence of their positive overall judgment. In addition, the expressed reservations may influence internal committee members' own interactions with their colleague, creating a work environment in which in which she must "prove herself" more than her comparably accomplished male counterpart.

In addition to evidence that stereotypes are expressed in external letters, there are other reasons to believe that the letters add little of value to tenure and promotion reviews. External letters are often favorable and therefore provide little differentiation among candidates (Chance, 2012; see also Schneider, 2000). Chance points out that he "will spend much time trying to read what is said and digging deeply for what is not said" (p.3); he recommends that others also do so. We believe that this process of intensive inference about small cues in external letters is another source of unknown error and bias in the review process. Suggestions from review committee members about negative characterizations that may be hinted at or implied by silences in external letters are threats to the fairness of the review process.

The restricted range of opinion expressed in external letters may also limit their value (Thorngate et al., 2009): "With no variability, there can be no predictive validity" (p. 82). Peer reviewers of grant proposals offer views that are only moderately correlated, and disagreement between reviewers is significantly associated with lower judgments of merit regardless of the content of the arguments (Thorngate et al., 2009). Negative inputs are weighted more heavily than positive ones, even though everything we know about cognitive biases suggests that strong inferences from weak cues are not likely to be accurate (Lord & Taylor, 2009).

The Role of Committee Discussion

Group discussions do not automatically ensure fairness in judgment processes even if including more judges is valuable. Discussions in committees making decisions about recommendations to fund or not fund grant proposals (which are, of course, not tenure reviews, but provide an imperfect analogy) do not move members toward greater consensus; the correlation between the average rating given by pairs of primary assessors in advance of discussion and the average rating following discussion was extremely high in the two instances studied: 0.82 and 0.92. Thus, the discussion moved judgments very little. Relying on averaged initial ratings without committee deliberation would have been equally fair and saved a lot of time (Thorngate et al., 2009; see also Pier, Raclaw, Nathan, Kaatz, Carnes, & Ford, 2015, re findings about inconsistency in study section review ratings).

We do not believe that faculty confidence—rightly or wrongly—would be high in a review involving no discussion and collective deliberation, but the results of Thorngate et al.'s research do point to the importance of procedural care in the deliberative process. They recommend, as we have, that planning and preparation establish "clear and concise eligibility rules, merit criteria and [in the case of grant applications] budgeting regulations before an adjudication" (p. 85). They note that committees will generate procedural rules and merit criteria "on the fly" in the absence of prior discussion. Thus, they advocate, as we do, "clearly stated rules" and "clear examples" (p.85), with ongoing feedback from both applicants and evaluators used to improve the clarity of both the stated rules and the examples.

Articulating Best Practices in Letter-Writing Requests

If committees *are* going to request outside letters, we recommend a request along the lines of the template in box 9.3. We note several features about what is and is not being requested in this template. The template acknowledges that people can adopt different approaches to a subject and requests that writers evaluate the candidate independently of whether they agree with the candidate's approach. Although we are somewhat skeptical about reviewers' ability to fully accomplish this, the letter encourages them to try. The letter also specifically asks the reviewers to assess the quality of the person's work and to do so independently of time since degree.

The letter tells reviewers the institution is not asking for a recommendation about tenure or promotion. That is the job of the review committee, based on a full consideration of all of the candidate's qualifications, one of which will be estimates of the quality of the candidate's work. The letter also does not ask reviewers to compare their candidate with any specific people. (Some schools do this: they provide a list of prominent people and ask the reviewer to compare the candidate to those people at comparable stages in their careers, or they ask the reviewer to compare the candidate with their own chosen set of people. This is an invitation to reviewers to let their subjective preferences run wild, with little or no accountability.)

Box 9.3

Template of Request for Outside Letters

Dear Prof. X:

Our department has been reviewing the work of [Dr. ABC]. We make a recommendation to [a divisional meeting] in [month & year] regarding [his or her] [tenure] [promotion to associate professor] [promotion to full professor] [some combination of the above].

I am writing to ask if you would be willing to assist us by providing an evaluation of [Dr. ABC's] scholarly work. We seek impartial evaluations from people such as you, who can comment with knowledge and authority on the scholarly competence and significance of [his or her] research, and who can place [his or her] work in the context of [his or her] particular field.

We are not asking you whether we should or should not recommend [Dr. ABC] for [tenure] [promotion]. Rather, we want you to assess [Dr. ABC's] scholarly achievements and potential and tell us what you see as [his or her] contribution to the field. We are particularly interested in your comments on the quality, rather than the quantity, of [Dr. ABC's] written work and presentations. Assessment of particular articles or chapters in [Dr. ABC's] book, evidence that Dr. ABC brings to bear [if appropriate], and theoretical arguments will be particularly valuable to us.

Finally, please note that at our institution we assess people's suitability for [tenure or promotion] without regard to time in rank or time since degree; please assume that the individual is coming up for review for tenure and promotion at the right time for our institution and refrain from any comment about time.

We recognize that within a field there may be different approaches and controversies; as far as possible, we would like you to address [Dr. ABC's] contributions independent of your own agreement or disagreement with [his or her] approach. We would welcome your comments on all of [Dr. ABC's] work, but you may focus on particular aspects of it.

Our general criteria for evaluating faculty members include their current research and potential for future research, their teaching, and their service to their department and the college. With respect to research, we take into account the fact that [X University is a very high research activity university] [or X College is a liberal arts college where faculty teach as many as three courses a semester at the undergraduate and graduate level, as well as fulfill committee responsibilities] [or some variant]. We do not expect an evaluation of [Dr. ABC's] teaching from you, though [his or her] effectiveness in giving presentations may be something you are familiar with and may wish to comment on.

[Insert here a discussion of the confidentiality and legal status of letters of this kind at your institution and in your state. It is important to provide clear information about who within the institution will have access to the letter, how it will figure in deliberations, and whether the content of the letter and/or its author's identity will or may be divulged to the candidate, and under what circumstances.]

I have enclosed a copy of [Dr. ABC's] curriculum vitae. I do hope you will be able to help us with this important decision. If so, I will send you a more complete dossier, including copies of relevant publications, in electronic or paper format or both, as well as statements by the candidate. Since the Department must review the comments of outside reviewers and submit its recommendation by [date], it would be most helpful if we could receive your signed letter and a copy of your CV in either electronic or paper form by [date].

Promotion to Full Professor

Most institutions separate the award of tenure from promotion to full professor (the final rank of tenure-track faculty). In recent years evidence has
accumulated that promotion to full professor is no more insulated from
equity concerns than any other process. Both analyses within fields and
within institutions across fields indicate a high level of variability in the
timing of promotion to full professor (including that it never happens)
between women and men, and by discipline.

Natural scientists spend the shortest time in the associate professor rank,
social scientists are next, and those in the humanities spend the longest
time in the rank. As we have seen in chapter 4, salary differentials by field
follow the same pattern. This is unsurprising if promotion is accompanied
(as it often is) by a larger raise in salary compared with the size of annual
raises. Given the logic of the accumulation of advantage over time (compound interest), the earlier a raise occurs in a career, the bigger the impact
it will have on the final salary an individual is paid. Considering the gender
distribution across disciplines (more women in the humanities and fewer
in natural science), it is unsurprising that time to promotion is related to
gender (Anderson et al., 2009) and may also be related to race and ethnicity
(Fang et al., 2000). Additional factors beyond distribution by field probably
account for the gender differences since there is also clear evidence of differences in time to promotion within a given discipline, both across and
within institutions (Committee on the Status of Women in the Professions,
MLA, 2009; Giesler et al., 2007).

Specification of Criteria for Promotion
One factor identified by several analyses as a potential explanation for the
disciplinary differences (independent of gender or race and ethnicity) is the
lack of specification of criteria for this promotion beyond those for tenure
and (ordinarily) promotion to associate professor (see Anderson et al., 2009;
Perna, 2001; Tierney & Bensimon, 1996). In the absence of new criteria,
many faculty, trying to assess their own promotability, and many of the
senior faculty they consult, assume that the amount and kind of productivity is roughly identical—there should just be more of both. This assumption may be reasonable in fields in which article publication is the primary
evidence, but in fields that depend on book publication, it is likely to add

time to the period before promotion. The "first book" is normally based not only on scholarship generated during a faculty member's period as an assistant professor, but on the work the faculty member completed for his or her dissertation. The "second book" is unlikely to require less research or integration and must be produced in the context of a full-time job with other responsibilities. Therefore, it is unsurprising that individuals in book fields (the humanities and interpretive social sciences) take longer to accumulate a record for promotion to full professor.

Is it, then, simply inevitable that there must be disciplinary differences in time to promotion? No! Some institutions have adopted a time-based promotion procedure; once faculty members have been in rank some number of years (normally 5–7), their continued scholarly activity and their teaching and service contributions are assessed. If they meet a standard of continued productivity at the level required for adequate performance of a faculty member, they are promoted (see Anderson et al., 2009, pp. 14–15). This approach to the review process requires that "scholarly activity" be measured in terms that may differ from those used at the tenure review. For example, it may be demonstrated in terms of articles that will eventually form part of a monograph, in grant applications, in presentations at national and international meetings, and in partially completed manuscripts.

Recognizing Institutional Demands for Service

Many institutions rely differently on associate professors than on assistant professors for conducting the ongoing work of the institution: taking part in faculty reviews of less experienced faculty, leading committee labor associated with recruitment of faculty and students, curriculum revision, mentoring junior faculty, and so forth. If the job is different, then the weighting of the criteria may need to be adjusted, too, with somewhat greater weight applied to teaching, service, and leadership than at the tenure review (when scholarly accomplishment and promise tend to lead the other criteria and service and leadership are not weighted heavily). As there is considerable evidence that women and minorities carry a disproportionate responsibility for service and leadership, and carry it earlier in their careers (Guarino & Borden, 2017; Misra, Lundquist, Holmes, & Agromavritis, 2011; Turner et al., 2008), a shift to taking all domains into consideration might help eradicate the gender and race and ethnicity differences in time to promotion.

Disproportionate Impact of Ambiguity

Finally, the ambiguity in timing of promotion to full professor is likely to disadvantage those groups that feel the least comfort and acceptance—belonging—within the institution. Feeling like "an outsider within," as women and minority tenured faculty often do, is likely to lead an individual to have less information and less confidence in moving forward with a promotion in the absence of clear guidelines about timing. In some institutions faculty members are not reviewed for promotion to full professor on a timetable; instead, they must "apply" for promotion. Given what we know about the biases in self-evaluation that affect judgments of individuals' own performance, this process is likely to lead to inequities. One way to combat this bias is to create a routinized procedure requiring all individuals at a normative time after tenure (e.g., 3 or 4 years) to be evaluated by their department in terms of the areas that require additional performance in order for promotion to be considered. Individuals can then be encouraged to develop plans for meeting those criteria on a timeline and can review their projects with a mentor or the department chair on an annual basis. In contrast, when individuals seek advice about whether they are "ready" for promotion, that advice is subject to advisors' unexamined schemas and may lead to unnecessary and counterproductive delays. Adoption of this kind of routinized review process would reduce both disciplinary and demographic differences in time to promotion—and therefore in salary.

Similarly, differences would be reduced or eliminated if more institutions accepted more flexible evidence of continued scholarly activity and impact, engaged in more equal weighting of all elements of a tenured faculty member's job, and provided clear and explicit procedures and timing for the promotion review. Some institutions view promotion to full professor as a rare privilege, to be accorded only to the "special few"; they have to live with the resulting demoralization of those faculty not promoted. Moreover, those faculty can become poor role models for junior faculty in their fields, as they withdraw from meaningful participation in the community and may decrease their productivity. Our perspective is that the institution benefits when the individual benefits—and that entails a system in which the assumption is that all faculty can be promoted to full professor, and support is provided to all tenured faculty, enabling that achievement.

Posttenure Reviews

Because many faculty remain full professors for a long period—often more than half of an academic career—some institutions believe that a substantial posttenure review process is helpful in maintaining faculty engagement and accountability. This seems potentially true, particularly in the absence of an effective and trusted annual review process. However, it is often viewed by faculty as imposing an unproductive burden of labor for little benefit. We know of no research demonstrating the value of posttenure reviews in maintaining faculty productivity, though some have argued that the University of California "step system" (which imposes such reviews throughout the academic career) has done just that and also minimizes salary inequities. (Because of the powerful impact of the "counteroffer" culture in academia, with large raises only tied to external offers, we are dubious about the latter claim.)

In any case, we suspect that an effective annual review system that relaxed the timing of the formal reviews of full professors (so that reporting occurred annually but formal reviews less often) might accomplish the goals of a formal posttenure review. In addition, it seems to us most important that faculty throughout their careers have the opportunity to learn which of their efforts are most highly valued by their near colleagues and to benefit from advice at choice points in their careers. Thus, it is the communicative function of reviews that is most likely to be valuable to faculty members, which requires that great care be taken in both the design and the implementation of procedures for these and all other reviews.

Summary

Faculty review and promotion processes are subject to some of the same sorts of evaluation biases as is faculty hiring—and there are some additional pitfalls. Further, the problem of actually lowering faculty productivity by lowering morale is a risk that must be faced. Many of the risks of unfair review are heightened in the instance of review of faculty who bring diversity to departments and institutions. Both individual faculty and institutions are served best by review processes that mitigate the risks of bias, are transparent, and are conducted according to explicit criteria and on a normative but flexible timetable.

Recommendations for Enhancing the Fairness of Evaluation and Promotion Procedures

Senior Administrative Leaders

1. Ensure that there is institution-wide effort to articulate review criteria clearly for every form of faculty review.

2. Establish the norm that review of one's colleagues is a privilege requiring evidence of conscientiousness and fairness, as well as openness to education about how bias influences such reviews and can be mitigated.

3. Develop an educational program for faculty participating in reviews that allows them to reflect on unintended bias as well as on procedures for mitigating it.

4. Monitor review processes for evidence of inequity by discipline and demographic group. Hold units accountable for fair outcomes.

Department Chairs and Deans of Small Schools

1. A precondition for perceived fairness is that criteria and procedures are spelled out adequately and fairly. Make transparency a priority, and post information about both criteria and procedures prominently.

2. The choice of fair and unbiased reviewers—internally and externally—is a critical factor in the perception that a process has been fair to the candidate and the institution. Make these selections carefully.

3. The burden of clear, productive, and respectful communication is substantial. Develop a process for conducting reviews internally that maximizes your success at this part of the job. This may involve sharing it with a senior faculty member appointed to oversee these reviews or including senior faculty mentors in feedback processes. It should also involve seeking and responding to feedback about how well administrators are doing this aspect of the job.

Faculty Evaluators

1. Become familiar with the literature on how cognitive biases influence judgments of others. Ensure that colleague-reviewers do so as well.

2. Take responsibility for fair deliberation within the review process. If some people are adopting or using arbitrary or different standards, or if they are referring to stereotypes rather than evidence, colleagues should hold those reviewers accountable to a higher standard.

3. Try to avoid making decisions in haste. Allocate the time needed to arrive at a fair opinion. Encourage the committee to do the same in its group process.

Faculty Being Reviewed

1. Keep good records of all work-related activity in a format that is compatible with the format(s) required by the review processes in the institution. Good record keeping will reduce the burden of labor when documents are prepared for the review and will minimize the likelihood of forgotten names (of committees, students, etc.) or lack of mention of crucial, time-consuming activities. Consult with senior and just-promoted colleagues about what records are important to keep.

2. Take responsibility for reviewing timetables, guidelines, and review criteria carefully and well in advance. Ask questions about things that are unclear, and encourage revision of materials for future reviews if things were unclear in this one.

3. Make use of any relevant material that illustrates the desiderata of materials submitted for review. This may include examples of previously submitted material shared widely or requests to individual colleagues.

4. Prepare materials carefully and well in advance. Ask trusted, more senior colleagues for feedback on critical elements that may not be familiar forms of writing to some committee members (e.g., statements of research activity, teaching goals, etc.). Build sufficient time into the timeline to use that feedback to revise the final submission.

5. Always bear in mind that key faculty and administrators who review these documents will not be in the field or subfield and will need clear exposition rather than reliance on disciplinary understanding of specialized language. Ask someone outside the subfield, or even the field, to flag instances of reliance on disciplinary codes in the documents.

Note

1. Nothing prevents a reviewer from visiting a faculty member's website to see what other papers are listed and to read as many as he or she might like. But we imagine most reviewers would be delighted to have only a faculty member's top five publications to read.

References

Anderson, E., Collins, C., Fierke, C., Juster, S., Kimeldorf, H., Penner-Hahn, J., et al. (2009, June 15). *Report of the Associate Professor Rank Committee.* Ann Arbor, MI: College of Literature, Sciences and the Arts, University of Michigan. Unpublished report.

Ash, A. S., Carr, P. L., Goldstein, R., & Friedman, R. H. (2004). Compensation and advancement of women in academic medicine: Is there equity? *Annals of Internal Medicine, 141,* 205–212.

Barbezat, D. (2002). History of pay equity studies. In R. Toutkoushian (Ed.), *Conducting salary-equity studies: Alternative approaches to research* (pp. 9–40). *New Directions for Institutional Research, 115.* San Francisco, CA: Jossey-Bass.

Bavishi, A., Madera, J. M., & Hebl, M. R. (2010). The effect of professor ethnicity and gender on student evaluations: Judged before met. *Journal of Diversity in Higher Education, 3*(4), 245–256.

Biernat, M. M. (2012). Stereotypes and shifting standards: Forming, communicating and translating person impressions. *Advances in Experimental Social Psychology, 45.* doi:10.1016/B978-0-12-394286-9.00001-9

Biernat, M., Fuegen, K., & Kobrynowicz, D. (2010). Shifting standards and the inference of incompetence: Effects of formal and informal evaluation tools. *Personality and Social Psychology Bulletin, 36,* 855–868.

Biernat, M., & Kobrynowicz, D. (1997). Gender- and race-based standards of competence: Lower minimum standards but higher ability standards for devalued groups. *Journal of Personality and Social Psychology, 72,* 544–557.

Biernat, M., Kobrynowicz, D., & Weber, D. (2003). Stereotyping and shifting standards: Some paradoxical effects of cognitive load. *Journal of Applied Social Psychology, 33,* 2060–2079.

Biernat, M., Ma, J. E., & Nario-Redmond, M. R. (2008). Standards to suspect and diagnose stereotypical traits. *Social Cognition, 26,* 288–313.

Boring, A., Ottoboni, K., & Stark, P. B. (2016). *Student evaluations of teaching (mostly) do not measure teaching effectiveness.* ScienceOpen Research; 10.14293/S2199-1006.1. SOR-EDU.AETBZC.v1.

Castilla, E. J. (2008). Gender, race, and meritocracy in organizational careers. *American Journal of Sociology, 113*(6), 1479–1526.

Chabram, A. (2016). Tenure in the contact zone: Spanish is our language, too. In P. Matthew (Ed.), *Written/unwritten: Diversity and hidden truths of tenure* (pp. 95–108). Chapel Hill, NC: University of North Carolina Press.

Chance, D. M. (2012, November 14). The idiocy of promotion-and-tenure letters. *Chronicle of Higher Education* http://www.chronicle.com/article/The-Idiocy-of/135740/

Cohen, G. L., Steele, C. M., & Ross, L. D. (1999). The mentor's dilemma: Providing critical feedback across the racial divide. *Personality and Social Psychology Bulletin, 25,* 1302–1318.

Committee on the Status of Women in the Profession, MLA. (2009, April 27). *Standing still: The associate professor survey.* Modern Language Association of America. Retrieved from https://www.mla.org/About-Us/Governance/Committees/Committee -Listings/Professional-Issues/Committee-on-the-Status-of-Women-in-the-Profes sion/Standing-Still-The-Associate-Professor-Survey/

Crocker, J., Voelkl, K., Testa, M., & Major, B. (1991). Social stigma: The affective consequences of attributional ambiguity. *Journal of Personality and Social Psychology, 60,* 218–228.

Curry, T. H. (2006, February). Faculty performance reviews. *Effective Practices for Academic Leaders, 1*(2). Sterling, VA: Stylus.

Dutt, K., Pfaff, D. L., Bernstein, A. F., Dillard, J. S., & Block, C. J. (2016). Gender differences in recommendation letters for postdoctoral fellowships in geoscience. *Nature Geoscience, 9,* 805–809.

Fang, D., Moy, E., Colburn, L., & Hurley, J. (2000). Racial and ethnic disparities in faculty promotion in academic medicine. *Journal of the American Medical Association, 284*(9), 1085–1092.

Fiske, S. T. (2011). *Envy up, scorn down: How status divides us.* New York, NY: Russell Sage.

Fiske, S. T., Xu, J., Cuddy, A. C., & Glick, P. (1999). (Dis) respecting and (dis)liking: Status and interdependence predict ambivalent stereotypes of competence and warmth. *Journal of Social Issues, 55*(3), 473–489.

Giesler, C., Kaminski, D., & Berkley, R. (2007). The 13+ club: An index of non-promotion of full professors. *NWSA Journal, 19*(3), 145–162.

Graves, A., Hoshino-Browne, E., & Lui, K. P. H. (2017). Swimming against the tide: Gender bias in the physics classroom. *Journal of Women and Minorities in Science and Engineering, 23*(1), 15–36.

Greenhaus, J. H., & Parasuraman, S. (1993). Job performance attributions and career advancement prospects: An examination of gender and race effects. *Organizational Behavior and Human Decision Processes, 55,* 273–297.

Guarino, C. M., & Borden, V. M. H. (2017). Faculty service loads and gender: Are women taking care of the academic family? *Research in Higher Education.* doi:10.1007/s11162-017-9454-2.

Hammond, P. T., Bailyn, L., Brown, E., Harris, L., Norford, L., Ortiz, C., et al. (2010). *Report on the initiative for faculty race and diversity*. MIT. Retrieved from http://orgchart .mit.edu/sites/default/files/reports/20100114_Provost_InitFacultyRaceDiversity Report.pdf

Harrison, R. L. (2016). Building a canon, creating dialogue: An interview with Cheryl A. Wall. In P. Matthew (Ed.), *Written/unwritten: Diversity and hidden truths of tenure* (pp. 46–63). Chapel Hill, NC: University of North Carolina Press.

Heilman, M. E., & Haynes, M. C. (2005). No credit where credit is due: Attributional rationalization of women's success in male-female teams. *Journal of Applied Psychology*, *90*(5), 905–916.

Heilman, M. E., & Okimoto, T. G. (2007). Why are women penalized for success at male tasks? The implied communality deficit. *Journal of Applied Psychology*, *92*(1), 81–92.

Hirsch, J. E. (2005). An index to quantify an individual's scientific research output. *Proceedings of the National Academy of Sciences of the United States of America*, *102*(46), 16569–16572.

Jagsi, R., Griffith, K. A., Stewart, A. J., Sambuco, D., DeCastro, R., & Ubel, P. A. (2012). Gender differences in the salaries of physician researchers. *Journal of the American Medical Association*, *307*(22), 2410–2417.

King, E. B., Madera, J. M., Hebl, M. R., Knight, J. L., & Mendoza, S. A. (2006). What's in a name? A multiracial investigation of the role of occupational stereotypes in selection decisions. *Journal of Applied Social Psychology*, *36*(5), 1145–1159.

Landy, F. J. (2008). Stereotypes, bias, and personnel decisions: Strange and stranger. *Industrial and Organizational Psychology: Perspectives on Science and Practice*, *1*, 379–392.

Livingston, R. W., Rosette, A. S., & Washington, E. F. (2012). Can an agentic Black woman get ahead? The impact of race and interpersonal dominance on perceptions of female leaders. *Psychological Science*, *23*(4), 354–358.

Lord, C. G., & Taylor, C. A. (2009). Biased assimilation: Effects of assumptions and expectations on the interpretation of new evidence. *Social and Personality Psychology Compass*, *3*(5), 827–841.

Maynard, D. C., & Brooks, M. E. (2008). The persistence of stereotypes in the context of familiarity. *Industrial and Organizational Psychology: Perspectives on Science and Practice*, *1*, 417–419.

Meho, L. I., & Yang, K. (2007). Impact of data sources on citation counts and rankings of LIS faculty: Web of Science vs. Scopus and Google Scholar. *Journal of the American Society for Information Science and Technology*, *58*(13), 2105–2125.

Mengel, F., Sauermann, J., & Zölitz, U. (2017). Gender bias in teaching evaluations. IZA Institute of Labor Economics Discussion Paper Series 11000. Available at SSRN: https://papers.ssrn.com/sol3/papers.cfm?abstract_id=3037907/

Misra, J., Lundquist, J. H., Holmes, E., & Agromavritis, S. (2011). The ivory ceiling of service work. *Academe, 97*(1), 22–26.

National Center for Educational Statistics. (2016). Table 316.80. Percentage of degree-granting postsecondary institutions with a tenure system and of full-time faculty with tenure at these institutions, by control and level of institution and selected characteristics of faculty: Selected years, 1993–94 through 2015–16. https://nces.ed.gov/programs/digest/d16/tables/dt16_316.80.asp?current=yes/

Perna, L. W. (2001). Sex and race differences in faculty tenure and promotion. *Research in Higher Education, 66*(5), 541–567.

Phelan, J. E., Moss-Racusin, C. A., & Rudman, L. A. (2008). Competent yet out in the cold: Shifting criteria for hiring reflect backlash toward agentic women. *Psychology of Women Quarterly, 32*, 406–413.

Phelan, J. E., & Rudman, L. A. (2010). Prejudice toward female leaders: Backlash effects and women's impression management dilemma. *Social and Personality Psychology Compass, 4/10*, 807–820.

Pier, E. L., Raclaw, J., Nathan, M. J., Kaatz, A., Carnes, M., & Ford, C. E. (2015). Studying the study section: How group decision making in person and via videoconferencing affects the grant peer review process (WCER Working Paper 2015–6). Retrieved from University of Wisconsin—Madison, Wisconsin Center for Education Research website: http://www.wcer.wisc.edu/publications/workingPapers/papers.php

Pollack, M. (2015, April 2). E-mail re: Faculty evaluation: Recognition of entrepreneurial, creative, and outreach activities. Retrieved from http://advance.umich.edu/resources/FASTERThirdYearTenurePromotionGuidelines.pdf

Porter, S., Toutkoushian, R. K., & Moore, J. (2008). Pay inequities for recently hired faculty, 1988–2004. *Review of Higher Education, 34*, 465–487.

Purdie-Vaughns, V., & Eibach, R. P. (2008). Intersectional invisibility: The distinctive advantages and disadvantages of multiple subordination group identities. *Sex Roles, 59*(5–6), 377–391.

Roberts, T. (1991). Gender and the influence of evaluations and self-assessments in achievement settings. *Psychological Bulletin, 109*, 297–308.

Roberts, T., & Nolen-Hoeksema, S. (1994). Gender comparisons in responsiveness to others' evaluation in achievement settings. *Psychology of Women Quarterly, 18*, 221–240.

Rudman, L. A., & Glick, P. (1999). Feminized management and backlash toward agentic women: The hidden costs to women of a kinder, gentler image of middle-managers. *Journal of Personality and Social Psychology, 77*, 1004–1010.

Ruscio, J., Seaman, F., D'Oriano, C., Stremlo, E., & Mahalchik, K. (2012). Measuring scholarly impact using modern citation-based indices. *Measurement: Interdisciplinary Research and Perspectives, 10*(3), 123–146.

Sarsons, H. (2017). Recognition for group work: Gender differences in academia. *American Economic Review, 107*(5), 141–145.

Schmader, T., Whitehead, J., & Wysocki, V. H. (2007). A linguistic comparison of letters of recommendation for male and female chemistry and biochemistry job applicants. *Sex Roles, 57*, 509–514.

Schneider, A. (2000). Why you can't trust letters of recommendation. *Chronicle of Higher Education, 46*(43), A14–A16.

Sesko, A. K., & Biernat, M. (2010). Prototypes of race and gender: The invisibility of Black women. *Journal of Experimental Social Psychology, 46*(2), 356–360.

Sohr-Preston, S. L., Boswell, S. S., McCaleb, K., & Robertson, D. (2016). Professor gender, age, and "hotness" in influencing college students' generation and interpretation of professor ratings. *Higher Learning Research Communications, 6*(3), 3–25.

Stanley, C. A. (2006). Coloring the academic landscape: Faculty of color breaking the silence in predominantly White colleges and universities. *American Educational Research Journal, 43*(4), 701–736.

Stanley, C. A., Porter, M. E., Simpson, N. J., & Ouellett, M. L. (2003). A case study of the teaching experiences of African American faculty at two predominantly White research universities. *Journal on Excellence in College Teaching, 14*, 151–178.

Steinpreis, R. E., Anders, K. A., & Ritzke, D. (1999). The impact of gender on the review of the curricula vitae of job applicants and tenure candidates: A national empirical study. *Sex Roles, 41*(7/8), 509–528.

Stewart, K. D., Dalton, M. M., Dino, G. A., & Wilkinson, S. P. (1996). The development of salary goal modeling: From regression analyses to a value-based prescriptive approach. *Journal of Higher Education, 67*(5), 555–576.

Storage, D., Horne, Z., Cimpian, A., & Leslie, S.-J. (2016). The frequency of "brilliant" and "genius" in teaching evaluations predicts the representation of women and African Americans across fields. *PLoS One.* doi:10.1371/journal.pone.0150194

Syracuse University. (2005, November 20). *Faculty manual.* Section 2.34 on Tenure. Retrieved from http://www.syr.edu/academics/office_of_academic_admin/faculty/manual/pdf/Section2FM.pdf

Thorngate, W., Dawes, R. M., & Foddy, M. (2009). *Judging merit*. New York, NY: Psychology Press.

Tierney, W. G., & Bensimon, E. M. (1996). *Promotion and tenure: Community and socialization in academe*. Albany, NY: State University of New York Press.

Toutkoushian, R. K., Bellas, M., & Moore, J. (2007). The interaction effects of gender, race, and marital status on faculty salaries. *Journal of Higher Education, 78*, 572–601.

Toutkoushian, R., & Conley, V. (2005). Progress for women in academe, yet inequities persist. Evidence from NSOPF:99. *Research in Higher Education, 46*(1), 1–28.

Trix, F., & Psenka, C. (2003). Exploring the color of glass: Letters of recommendation for male and female medical faculty. *Discourse & Society, 14*(2), 191–220.

Trower, C. A. (2002). What is current policy? In R. P. Chait (Ed.), *The questions of tenure* (pp. 32–68). Cambridge, MA: Harvard University Press.

Turner, C. S. V., Gonzalez, J. C., & Wood, L. (2008). Faculty of color in academe: What 20 years of literature tells us. *Journal of Diversity in Higher Education, 1*(3), 139–168.

University of California. (2005). *Appointment and promotion*. Academic Personnel Manual, ADM-210. Retrieved from http://senate.universityofcalifornia.edu/_files /committees/ucaade/apm245.pdf

Valian, V. (2000). *Why so slow? The advancement of women*. Cambridge, MA: MIT Press.

Vazire, S., & Gosling, S. D. (2004). E-perceptions: Personality impressions based on personal websites. *Journal of Personality and Social Psychology, 87*(1), 123–132.

Way, S. F., Morgan, A. C., Clauset, A., & Larremore, D. B. (2017). The misleading narrative of the canonical faculty productivity trajectory. *Proceedings of the National Academy of Sciences of the United States of America, 114*(44), E9216–E9223. Epub 2017 Oct. doi:10.1073/pnas.1702121114.

Xie, Y., & Shauman, K. (2003). *Women and science: Career processes and outcomes*. Cambridge, MA: MIT Press.

10 Recognizing Faculty Accomplishments

If we take as a given the experimental and observational data that we have presented in earlier chapters, it will not be a surprise to learn that women and people of color are underrepresented in formal and official forms of recognition. The same mechanisms that lead to positions at high-prestige institutions and to higher salaries and faster rates of promotion would be expected to play a role in the recognition of accomplishments. In this chapter we consider whether the specific phenomenon of overlooked excellence in research and scholarship, or "missed merit," is more likely in the careers of women and people of color.

There are many ways to formally recognize faculty accomplishments apart from prestige, salary, and promotion. For example, internal awards within a scholar's department or school may be given for exceptional teaching and mentoring, scholarship, or service. Recipients may be selected by colleagues, students, alumni, or administrators of the institution. Disciplinary associations provide awards in a large number of categories, including teaching, mentorship, and research, and honorary degrees recognize a range of accomplishments. Meta-disciplinary associations like the American Academy of Arts and Sciences, the American Association for the Advancement of Science, and the National Academies primarily recognize research accomplishments. Other forms of recognition include invitations to give conference and colloquium talks. We first consider the value of informal recognition to faculty and the academic communities in which we operate, and then consider the costs and benefits of formal recognition for the institution and the person being recognized.

The Significance and Value of Informal Recognition

Scholars receive meaningful personal recognition from students and colleagues. The student who tells a faculty member "I wasn't sure what I wanted to specialize in, but when you gave the guest lecture in the proseminar I thought, 'that's what I want to work on'" gives deep satisfaction. The people who write a faculty member out of the blue to say how much they appreciated a particular article the faculty member wrote provide unalloyed gratification. The student who credits an instructor with the support and guidance needed to finish a degree supplies a feeling of well-being and achievement. The colleague who tells a chair how well the faculty member handled a difficult faculty meeting engenders pride.

For many faculty, the most meaningful comments are those from students suggesting that a course, a lecture, or a conversation has influenced them. Transmitted in many ways—both at the time and sometimes years later—the sense that one's teaching has been valued and recalled is appreciated by all types of faculty and types of institutions. One of us was stopped on an airplane not long ago and asked if we were Professor So-and-So. When we nodded, the man indicated that he had taken a course from us more than 30 years before, and it had influenced him throughout his life. This was not an instance of a student whom the faculty member knew well, but it was a surprising and delightful reminder of the value of one's work to another person. As the example indicates, the value may take a long time to become clear even to the student and may never be communicated to us. That completely unexpected and unplanned meeting might never have occurred—but it made that semester's work much lighter and more joyful and is remembered when moments of doubt or overload threaten to make teaching feel burdensome.

Such examples are no less important for being smaller and less public than the formal recognition that we concentrate on in this chapter. In the course of an academic life, there is the opportunity for many gestures of informal recognition. Requests for technical and career advice from colleagues, and invitations to serve on consequential committees in the institution and in the disciplinary associations, are other examples—in this case, where one's judgment is valued. Learning that a colleague mentioned finding one's advice valuable or insightful can make one's day. Hearing from a colleague that one's contributions to a committee or departmental or institutional discussion were particularly important to their thinking can make one feel that the extra effort one expended was worth it. Some faculty may experience such expressions of regard as nothing special, but work in "positive psychology" and "appreciative inquiry" supports the observation that appreciation promotes well-being (Cantore & Cooperrider, 2013).

One of us recalls during her first year as a faculty member having a senior colleague leave a note in her mailbox indicating that she had read and admired her newly published article based on her dissertation. That new faculty member walked on air for a long time after that, knowing that her senior colleague had noticed her paper, read it, and claimed to like it!

Sometimes informal recognition comes on the occasion of retirement when students and colleagues convey in notes, letters, and conversations the impact of one's thinking and work and the importance of the example one has set. These expressions are deeply meaningful to most faculty, even if they do come late in the career, but it behooves wise administrators to reflect on how to encourage that kind of feedback to faculty more often and at earlier stages in their career.

When an institutional environment is positive and most faculty feel they are part of a community that values everyone, one's colleagues are more likely to feel inclined to convey their positive regard in informal ways. Similarly, there are many ways to encourage students to communicate their regard to the faculty. One high school has created a graduation ceremony in which all students give brief and informal "talks" (they forego more formal speeches to make time for this) about what high school has meant to them. Inevitably, many students talk about things their teachers have said and done that opened their minds to new perspectives and increased their aspirations and ambitions. The habit of reflection on one's education is one worth inculcating, as is the habit of expressing gratitude to others who facilitate one's growth. The students think about their final talks for much of high school. And the teachers look forward to that ceremony every year as a time when they know they will hear about actions of their colleagues and their own that mattered to the people they have most tried to serve.

Not all faculty receive informal recognition on a regular basis, and not all faculty prize all forms of informal recognition. We suspect, however, that people who do receive informal recognition have happier and more meaningful work lives and are themselves able to appreciate others' work as a result. In institutions or departments with high morale, the group is attuned to the contributions and accomplishments of others, and people feel that it is appropriate to express approval and appreciation of others' contributions and accomplishments. Workplaces in which informal recognition of others' successful efforts flow readily are more pleasant and satisfying workplaces for everyone (see Cantore & Cooperrider, 2013; Cooperrider, 1990). Creating the circumstances for this flow of recognition costs little except in the pleasant labor of imagining ways to foster it (like the cost-free high school ceremony outlined above).

It is also possible, and desirable, to develop more formal but virtually cost-free recognition—in end-of-year ceremonies or in letters of reappointment—at every level of an institution. Developing an institutional culture of acknowledging the value of the work people do to ensure that the place functions well increases the well-being of all concerned—both those who are grateful and those who are appreciated (see, e.g., Algoe, Kurtz, & Hilaire, 2016; Jackowska, Brown, Ronaldson, & Steptoe, 2016).

A final point is that we tend to think of influential scholarship as occurring solely through active engagement in research. But faculty also influence thinking in a field through their teaching by introducing concepts and perspectives to students that change their thinking or by clarifying how to use a particular analytic tool. One of us remembers reading Henry Gleitman's presentation of the statistic d' in the first edition of his textbook in psychology. At last—she understood it. (Alas, recent editions eliminated this section.) She was happy to meet him and be able to tell him how much she appreciated that section and benefited from it. And, still, whenever she uses d', she thinks of Professor Gleitman and mentally thanks him.

Benefits—and Costs—of Formal Recognition

Institutional Benefits of Creating Forms of Formal Recognition
For the institution, external formal recognition of faculty brings prestige. Formal recognition—whether external or internal—can be an occasion of community celebration and personal satisfaction. Departments, programs, and larger institutions can benefit from recognizing faculty service, teaching, and scholarship. Knowing that others have noticed and valued one's work enhances its meaning for most people, even when it comes without a financial award. Formal recognition can fall disproportionately on a few—and often those few are White and male. To avoid that, processes of

recognition need to identify the full range of faculty accomplishments, and many people need to participate in nomination and selection processes. Some institutions lack the resources to create monetary awards, and others may lack the faculty and administrative time to administer awards even if they do not carry financial benefits. Some institutions have the resources but wonder if they are worth the investment when there is so much other work to be done. But since there is relatively little cost to providing many kinds of recognition, and since the benefit to overall morale is great, we recommend it.

Senior faculty can be encouraged to help recognize their junior colleagues' accomplishments—a practice certain to foster those colleagues' sense of belonging and value. Equally, senior faculty suffering from doubts about their scholarly path may be recognized for extraordinary accomplishment in other arenas and find that more confidence and community support encourages them to redouble their scholarly efforts rather than withdrawing from them. Creating a feeling of mutual community through ready forms of formal recognition is possible, but it requires serious attention to the risk of creating a feeling or reality of a "chosen few" or an elite and exclusionary group of "the recognized."

Does Formal Recognition Matter for One's Work?
For the individual, formal recognition can provide some of the same benefits as informal recognition: it represents the respect of one's colleagues in one's institution or in the field as a whole. But an individual may also find that recognition is ignored by the local campus community, or, instead, creates envy and distaste in colleagues. It may also discomfit or embarrass the individual being recognized.

Some colleagues have suggested to us that external markers of professional success have little bearing on people's ability to do important and satisfying work. This is reminiscent of the Guerrilla Girls' poster we described in chapter 2 on the "advantages" of being a woman artist, such as working without the pressure of success and not having to undergo the embarrassment of being called a genius (https://www.guerrillagirls.com). The advantages of recognition, however, include the suggestion that one's work is valuable and worth pursuing. Recognition of new work is particularly valuable since new ideas are often criticized or ignored. With the support of a high-prestige funding agency or recognition from prizes and invited talks, a new idea has a better chance of being taken seriously. Formal recognition provides social capital and legitimacy. Recognition that carries or produces financial support can materially help people do their work, especially in fields that require resources such as equipment or research assistance. Funding agencies are more likely to support work that has previously been recognized.

Finally, formal recognition of one's work within one's community may help one's colleagues actually know what we do. Often we are all working away at service, teaching, and scholarship, unaware of the equally interesting and important work of our colleagues. Learning about it can transform our respect for each other and our sense of shared mission. One of us gave a talk to her institution that carried with it a monetary prize that had been donated. The talk was well-advertised and well-attended. Many colleagues outside her department learned about her work for the first time. Her colleagues within her department, who could have given a one-sentence description of her work, now found that the bigger story was genuinely interesting.

Some people, both with and without formal awards and invitations, think that defining success in terms of recognition is at best unimportant and at worst worshipping a false god. We know of one former department chair who did not want his department to receive two special endowed chairs that the dean was offering because he thought that such chairs created invidious distinctions. We agree that success should not be defined solely by recognition. But formal recognition is one marker—among many—of success, as well as of others' appreciation.

Most individuals in academia are there because, as we discuss in chapter 1, they subscribe to the ideals of the university. Many realize that they could make more money elsewhere (although some academics, through the creation of companies, are also successful in purely monetary terms), but their goals are different. We subscribe to the ideals we laid out in chapter 1. We value the variety, autonomy, and flexibility that academia offers. We value our interactions with students and colleagues. We particularly value our freedom to ask and try to answer a range of questions. We also value a full life that includes, but is not limited to, work.

Formal recognition is not essential for personal satisfaction. Indeed, one could argue, along with the former department chair, that a system of formal recognition distracts faculty from the ideals that are most important to their identity, and that it should be abolished. However, that is not going to happen. Systems of formal recognition exist and will continue to exist. Our goal is fair allocation of rewards. There is reason to suspect that allocation is not impartial, and that individuals in certain demographic groups or with certain characteristics get more than their fair share.

Personal Intellectual Benefits from Formal Recognition

We have commented on the deep meaning faculty attach to the sense that their work matters to their institution, to their colleagues, and to their students. This kind of meaning can also be found from formal recognition within the discipline for teaching and mentoring and service to the field (both in disciplinary associations and at the home institution). Many award committees have only a few candidates to consider because few people nominate their colleagues for awards. Departments and institutions can improve their own standing and their faculty's by nominating them for awards and by providing appropriate documentation to support them. Even being nominated for recognition by one's department or institution can make faculty members aware of their colleagues' respect for their work.

A sense of meaning can be derived from seeing the impact of one's work on the field or discipline beyond the home institution. In order to influence the direction of one's field, to play a role in determining what questions will be seen as central to the field, and to make it more likely that theories one thinks are explanatory will be considered by the field at large, it is helpful to be recognized. Good ideas that no one picks up may be enjoyable and stimulating for an individual researcher to develop and work on, but they do not help shape a field or change the world. When people have ideas that could change the direction of their field, or change how people think about an issue, visibility and formal recognition can be the vehicle. The same holds for the arts. If individuals want their music to be heard, their art to be seen, and their literature to be read, they need recognition.

Costs of Recognition

To the extent that academia is a community of equals, recognition of the few may come with a cost to morale and a sense of community for those who are not recognized. Creating classes of faculty—those who have named chairs and those who do not, those who win prizes and those who do not—may have significant costs in the sense of value and belonging among those who are in the unrecognized classes, as the department chair mentioned above had feared. Anticipation of those costs to others leads some individuals to be concerned about being recognized, even given the benefits.

Recognition may lead to increased influence, privilege, and authority. To the extent that it does, it can also lead to ignoring advice from others (Tost et al., 2012). A series of experiments either primed people to see themselves as powerful, by remembering a time when they had power over other people; primed people to see themselves as not powerful, by remembering a time when other people had power over them; or did not involve priming, simply asking people to remember their most recent visit to a grocery store. Those in the high-power condition were less likely to take into account information that could potentially help them, even when the advice was described as coming from experts. People with formal power roles (presidents, provosts, deans, chairs, group leaders), as well as those who achieve informal power via recognition, all run the risk of failing to listen. Power does not, however, have to lead to closed-mindedness. Those with firm moral standards do not succumb to the insensitivity of power (DeCelles, DeRue, Margolis, & Ceranic, 2012).

Role of Diversity

If White women and women and men of color are the principal individuals who do not receive formal recognition, the most visible models in the field will be White men. We have seen that a diverse group of faculty who are successful matters to students. One way that young women and people of color can determine if there is a place for them is by seeing a mix of people in positions of power and prestige (Correll, 2004; Murphy, Steele, & Gross, 2007). White men know there is room for them because they see so many White men.

As we have argued when discussing the benefits of diversity in chapter 2, demographic homogeneity is also likely to result in less innovation. We want the people who receive formal recognition and help shape the field to include those who offer diversity and enhance the possibility of innovation. Thus, we should invite White women and people of color to speak (Valian, 2013).

In sum, the main reason to be concerned about formal recognition is that people who do receive formal recognition are likely to influence what questions are asked and how those questions are asked. While formal recognition is not necessary for personal happiness or a high-morale community, without formal recognition—for our purposes in this chapter, without invitations to give keynote and plenary talks and without awards for one's performance—an individual's voice may not carry. Because of the importance of formal recognition, we recommend that all institutions make an effort to nominate their faculty for external prizes and awards, and make an effort to invite a diverse group of speakers for colloquia and other academic talks. We also recommend that professional societies include a diverse group of members on their awards committees.

Missed Merit

Are women and people of color really "underrepresented" among those who receive formal awards and recognition? Perhaps instead they are represented less than White men for good reason. If one considers typically used markers of accomplishment, such as the impact factors of the journals that prize-worthy individuals publish in or the prestige of the publishers who publish their books, the support they receive from external funding, the amount they have published, or the number of citations their work receives, perhaps White men simply display more excellence. That could be why they are "overrepresented" at high-prestige institutions and why they receive more recognition.

Belief in a just world (Lerner, 1980) suggests that the deserving are rewarded and the rewarded are deserving. According to this logic, White and Asian men receive the most recognition for scholarly achievement because recognition accrues to those who have the greatest ability and make the most strenuous effort, and those people are predominantly White and Asian men (Summers, 2005). If academia is meritocratic, egalitarian, and just, the best people end up at the best institutions and get the most recognition, and excellent work will be rewarded no matter who does it.

Academics, with their commitment to the *idea* of a meritocracy, are likely to find the just-world hypothesis attractive. For one thing, it means that they can take full credit for their own successes. We are not suggesting that the rewarded are *un*deserving (although they may occasionally be so and more than occasionally may be only partially deserving). Nor do we devalue the journals that prominent people publish articles in or the presses that they publish their books with. Nor do we dispute the idea that being cited often suggests that many people found a scholarly work valuable. Instead, we argue that, for every person who is rewarded, there are others, equally deserving, who are not rewarded. That possibility is a logical extension of the arguments we have made about the effect of schemas on our perceptions of others and our perceptions of ourselves and about the accumulation of advantage (see chapter 4 and Perc, 2014).

If nomination and award committees are more likely to expect success in certain groups, and if small successes indeed accumulate over time, the daily small advantages that White men accrue—however unintentionally— will result in a disproportionate number of them receiving formal acco- lades. An appreciation of how advantage accumulates is reflected in the adage "Awards beget awards" (see, e.g., Smith, 2011). Someone is unlikely to receive a major award without already having accumulated less major awards. That appears to be true for Nobel Prize winners (Chan, Gleeson, & Torgler, 2014).

It is difficult for people who are successful to fully recognize the role of factors other than their own merit (a combination of their talent and effort) in their success, and they therefore often feel they are uniquely meritorious. People are privy to their own insights and good ideas more than anyone else is, and they know how hard they have worked. They lack that firsthand knowledge about others, and they cannot easily gauge the importance of their own institutional affiliation, the people they know, or sheer luck.

A few Nobel Prize winners, however, have been aware of the role of luck and privilege in their lives, and its absence in others'. In 2008, when Mar- tin Chalfie and Roger Tsien won the Nobel Prize in chemistry (along with Osamu Shimomura), they invited Douglas Prasher and his wife to attend the ceremony and paid their way. Chalfie and Tsien's work was heavily based on a gene that Prasher had cloned, but Prasher had left academia, discouraged by his isolation and lack of funding. When he left, he gave samples of his gene to Chalfie and Tsien and referred people who asked for the gene to them. Chalfie included Prasher as a coauthor on an important publication that was possible only because of Prasher's gene. Prasher con- tinued doing scientific work for a time, but he never had another profes- sorial position. He was driving a courtesy shuttle for a car dealership until, two years after Chalfie and Tsien received the Nobel Prize, he obtained a job doing scientific work at a research and development firm. After being laid off from that position, Prasher accepted a long-standing invitation to work as a researcher in Tsien's laboratory. Both Chalfie and Tsien thought that Prasher deserved a Nobel Prize for his work, as detailed in an article titled

"How Bad Luck and Bad Networking Cost Douglas Prasher a Nobel Prize" (http://discovermagazine.com/2011/apr/30-how-bad-luck-networking-cost -prasher-nobel/; see also http://www.the-scientist.com/?articles.view/article No/34536/title/What-Ever-Happened-to-Douglas-Prasher-/).

Prasher's story is unusual on two grounds: the lack of recognition he received despite his talent and his achievement and Chalfie and Tsien's steadfast acknowledgment of Prasher's contribution. Prasher's case differs from the better known example of Rosalind Franklin. Franklin's x-rays were important data for James Watson and Francis Crick's discovery of the heli-cal structure of DNA. But her contributions were not explicitly recognized at the time of Watson and Crick's original paper. In accepting the Nobel Prize in 1962, Watson and Crick made no mention of Franklin. She posthu-mously received greater acknowledgment of her contributions (e.g., Mad-dox, 2002), and Watson acknowledged her work in an added epilogue to his memoir about the discovery of DNA (Watson, 1980).

These examples suggest that if we want to guard against missed merit in distributing formal recognition, and if we want to promote the best and most innovative discoveries and insights and ensure that they appropriately influ-ence the field, we need to change institutions so that they will retain, sup-port, and recognize such individuals. People like Prasher and Franklin had enough ability, passion, and perseverance to make valuable discoveries. It is the field's job to make sure that those discoveries are noticed and honored.

Another honor, considerably more frequent than the Nobel Prize but still rare, is membership in the National Academy of Sciences (NAS). There is enormous variation by university in the number of members, even among universities with similar overall rankings. According to summaries on the NAS website for 2016, among state-funded universities Berkeley had three times as many NAS members as did Cornell, five times as many as Michigan, and ten times as many as Stony Brook. It is possible that those differences reflect "merit," but it is also possible that Berkeley's success in part owes something to sophisticated nomination strategies and well-developed professional net-works. Those strategies can be developed by other institutions as well.

A scientist at a research-intensive university told the following story. He hadn't given a second thought to becoming a member of the NAS—because he presumed he didn't have to think about it. His colleagues would nomi-nate him at a suitable time. Then he noticed that some of his younger colleagues were being nominated. He approached one of the more senior members in his department, telling that person that he had waited his turn and expected to be nominated. He *was* then nominated and was accepted as a member.

In thinking about that story, we notice that the scientist had been confident that he would be successfully nominated. He felt entitled. He also felt he needed to wait his turn. But when he saw that younger colleagues were being nominated, he thought it wasn't fair. He had waited his turn, and the others should wait their turn. He also thought that his senior colleagues weren't doing their job properly. Had he not spoken up, his colleagues might never have nominated him.

We suspect that relatively few people have the same sense of entitlement that this individual had. We know from the findings on gender and entitlement that women are likely to feel underentitled and men are likely to feel overentitled (Pelham & Hetts, 2001). Further, powerful people are more likely to feel entitled and to expect fair treatment (Sawaoka, Hughes, & Ambady, 2015). Power heightens sensitivity to unfairness against the self. Had the same faculty member, doing the same research, been a White woman or a person of color at a lower tier institution, that faculty member may not have felt unfairly treated by not being nominated by colleagues to be a member of the National Academy. Nor would colleagues see the lack of nominations as unfair. If people have been viewed as not fully meritorious early in their career, it will be difficult for people to revise their opinion. Once formed, an opinion is difficult to change, even when people learn that it is incorrect (Reuben, Sapienza, & Zingales, 2014, and see our discussion of anchoring in chapter 9).

The Role of Chance

In the cases of Prasher and Franklin, we use the standard benchmarks for recognizing achievement. Our evidence that those individuals were improperly overlooked comes from evidence of people making similar achievements who were not overlooked. There is, however, an additional consideration, namely, the role of chance. Decisions about what accomplishments are considered prizeworthy are in part due to chance, and the many steps leading up to a prize (publications, citations, funding, and so on) are not equally accessible across different demographic groups.

An MIT student, responding to a guest column in *The Tech* about the role of diversity in admissions and hiring at MIT, expressed well the idea that when rewards are scarce and dimensions of merit are various, many factors will determine outcomes.

...The one thing I remember most on my college tour experiences was at Yale when an admissions representative said that they could reject the first 1200 people and take the next 1200 and NO ONE WOULD KNOW THE DIFFERENCE because there is an overabundance of qualified people applying to these prestigious universities. (February 17, 2012, http://tech.mit.edu/V132/N4/briscoe.html?comments#comments/, comment 35; accessed June 3, 2017)

Deciding what counts as merit is an exercise that is similar to deciding who will get into Yale. There are so many dimensions of merit, and the dimensions can be weighted in so many different ways, that there is no single "best." It is not like determining who can run 400 meters the fastest, where there is a single metric. The people who get Nobel Prizes may well deserve them, but there may be many other equally deserving people who do not get them. Fallible humans are serving as gatekeepers at every stage of someone's career.

In a set of interviews with physicists, one sees with surprise that many of them expected, early in their career, to eventually receive a Nobel Prize, despite the extreme rarity of that event. One Nobel physicist articulated the Nobel Prize version of the Yale phenomenon (Hermanowicz, 2009):

[The reward system in science] attempts to be fair. [But] there are many people who do wonderful things who don't get properly recognized. There's no question about that. I think I was lucky that the work we did was recognized. It could have been otherwise. I mean, after all, we got the Nobel Prize. We did the work probably between '67 and '74. We got the Nobel Prize [many years later]. It took close to twenty years to get that recognition. It could have been that we never would have gotten the recognition. We were very fortunate that it came our way because there is uncertainty in that kind of thing. There are many people who do wonderful things who don't get properly recognized. This last Nobel Prize—the three guys who got it for asymptotic freedom in the strong interactions—it took them thirty years, and there was a chance they wouldn't have gotten it. If it takes thirty years, it means that there was a chance that you won't get it, because something has prevented it [from occurring sooner]. (16L)[1]

This individual realized that merit—doing "wonderful things"—is not the only determinant of receiving a Nobel Prize. Many other factors—factors that we frequently call "luck"—come into play (Frank, 2016). And one can ask, "Who gets to be lucky?" Luck is most likely to smile on those who are already "lucky."

Why Missed Merit Occurs—Gender and Prestige;
the Accumulation of Advantage

We present an interconnected account of missed merit. Highly talented, well-trained, and hardworking scholars and researchers are found at all types of academic institutions. Despite the wide distribution of talent and effort, we claim, the achievements of individuals at teaching-intensive institutions are undervalued—because status influences recognition and awards. Prestige or status effects are especially negative for White women and people of color because they are overrepresented at teaching-intensive institutions, an argument familiar from earlier chapters. Finally, status effects operate at every stage in the process of building a career. Of course, there are additional reasons we may miss merit. For example, if White women and minorities have thinner professional networks, they may know less about award and lecture possibilities and may have fewer mentors or colleagues who are high-status White men who can and will advocate for them in recognition processes.

First, we consider the data that make a prima facie case for the underrepresentation of women in general among awardees and invitees. The absence of racial-ethnic minorities among awardees and invitees is even more striking, if less well-documented to date.

Sex Disparities in Awards

It is relatively easy to assess the distribution of recognition within departments or within an institution because one can compare the number of faculty in a particular demographic at a given rank with the awards those groups accrue. One has some means for computing a baseline (although White women and people of color may not have advanced at an appropriate rate). In contrast, the underrepresentation of White women and underrepresented minorities among award recipients of national and international recognition—prizes, plenary talks, and the like—is much harder to assess. It is hard to know what the relevant pool is. In the case of hiring at the junior level, it is possible at least roughly to gauge the composition of the pool by examining the percentage of different groups among PhD recipients and postdoctoral fellows. If, however, advantage and disadvantage accumulate, as we have demonstrated that they do, the pool of women and underrepresented minorities progressively narrows as careers progress. Thus, when we see an all-male or all-White lineup of invited speakers at conferences, we do not know whether such lineups could have occurred by chance, though efforts to evaluate this possibility suggest that women are in fact less frequently represented than would be expected by chance (G. Martin, 2015).[2]

Personal experience offers examples as well. In the middle of the first decade of the twenty-first century, one of us was invited to give a talk on gender to an annual scientific honors society lecture at one of the CUNY colleges. The program listed all the prior speakers—one per year except for a few years when there was no annual meeting—from the 1960s to the present. Every speaker had been a man, definitely not what one would expect by chance. She had been invited by a female colleague who was president of the society that year. And her colleague asked her to speak about gender, not about her research specialty. Presumably, no one was intending to discriminate, in any of the 30-odd years that invitations had been issued, but it was difficult for organizers to see, without aggregating the data, that they were producing a one-sided set of speakers to students. We would like to think that that first woman gave a great talk, but another nine years went by before another woman was invited to speak.

More recent data suggest that women are underrepresented as colloquium speakers at universities across a range of fields, and that the underrepresentation is most severe at the assistant professor level, a career point where visibility is very helpful (Nittrouer, Hebl, Ashburn-Nardo, Trump-Steele, Lane, & Valian, 2018). The lower representation of women was not due to their refusing invitations more often than men did. An analysis of committee membership showed the importance of gender for a subset of the 50 schools that provided data. Whether colloquium decisions were made by a single person or by a committee, the presence of women was associated with a better mix of male and female speakers (Nittrouer et al., 2018).

This is easy to fix if we assume that there are women and people of color worth hearing from. We can invite them to speak. A colleague related the following story. She had just been invited to be a member of board of an international scientific society and was attending the annual business meeting for the first time. One item of business that had not been on the agenda was to develop a list of people to invite to be board members to replace those whose term had finished. As people made nominations, she noticed that all the nominees were male. She suggested that people take some time to think only of women candidates. Her colleagues, the large majority of whom were male, agreed to do that and quickly came up with the names of women who would be suitable. Women's names were apparently not as cognitively available as men's names, but if the pool was restricted, women's names became available. The colleague also recommended that nominations not be made on the fly, but that people come to the annual meeting with suggestions, and with the understanding that they would aim for a broad representation of scientists.

To reiterate: we do not think that inviters or prize awarders intend to exclude any group. Nor do we think that people should be invited because they are women or people of color. We do think, consistent with the data presented earlier in this book, that White men's names are more cognitively available, and that procedures are necessary to neutralize that tendency.

All groups that invite speakers—from organizers of annual events where only one person speaks, to organizers of departmental colloquia where 4–10 individuals speak—should track whom they invite and who speaks (J. L. Martin, 2014). The Committee on the Status of Women of the American Astronomical Society tracked speakers (though not invitations) for 2013 and posted the results, along with data about the percentage of women members, at https://cswa.aas.org/percent.html. Without data, we have only impressions. Data will allow us to measure variation as a function of field, percentage of women or underrepresented minorities in the field, percentage of women and underrepresented minority organizers, and so on.

All-male and all-White lineups of invited speakers at conferences continue to occur. The 2015 International Congress of Quantum Chemistry conference in Beijing initially listed 24 male invited speakers and no women. Three women in chemistry began an online petition to boycott the conference. The petition received about 1,700 supporters. There was a subsequent apology by the president of the society and the conveners, who said that the list was incomplete and had been prematurely posted. Women were subsequently added to the list. Another international conference in theoretical chemistry that took place in Russia in 2014 had 10 invited speakers, all men; an advisory board of 19 scientists, all men; and an international organizing committee of 10 men.

In a study of six conferences in microbiology in two different subfields, there was a difference in how many women were invited to speak at symposia, depending on whether the members of the two-person inviting committees for each symposium were both male or included at least one woman (Casadevall & Handelsman, 2014). In committees of two men, roughly 25% of symposium speakers were women; in contrast; in committees with one or two women, roughly 38% of symposium speakers were women. Further, there were many more all-male symposia in sessions organized by men than in those organized by committees with one or two women. Roughly a quarter of committee members included themselves as speakers, with no gender difference, so it was not the case that women were inviting themselves to speak more or less often than men were inviting themselves to speak. Similar results were found over a 21-year period in primatology talks at meetings of the American Association of Physical Anthropologists (Isbell, Young, & Harcourt, 2012) and in another study of annual conferences (Sardelis & Drew, 2016).

More research is needed to explore the underlying mechanisms for these outcomes, such as the impact of network composition on invitation offers and acceptances by both men and women. One woman suggested, on the basis of her personal experience, that men and women might offer invitations differently to women. She received an invitation that said, "I really hope you can come because the only other woman that we have is X's partner." They expressed no interest in her work, nor did they identify X's partner by name. We would like to think that woman's experience is anomalous! But women may show more enthusiasm than do men when they are inviting women, leading women invitees to be more interested in accepting. Research increasingly suggests that having women on a committee leads to more—and equivalently qualified—women speakers (Klein et al., 2017).

We recommend that all professional societies track data on nominations and final awards and make those data public, as has been accomplished in one study of awards in physics (Lincoln, Pincus, Koster, & Leboy, 2012).

Assessments of Merit

Both structural and psychological factors conspire to place men and women, Whites and people of color, in positions that differ in how likely they are to lead to large quantities of prize-worthy work or to recognition of the prize-worthy work that they do perform. Recognition is intended to celebrate the "best," but the notion of best—despite its obvious attractions—is not tenable without setting a number of background conditions. Without awareness of those conditions, the notion of the best ignores the many dimensions on which quality can be evaluated and it ignores the role of fashion.

For several reasons, it is difficult to define merit or to separate merit from recognition, and different fields use different metrics. In "book" fields, for example, there is often a rough consensus about which publishers offer the "best" lists in a particular field (usually known only to people in that field!), but in some "article" fields there are quantitative indicators. For example, one study attempted to separate merit from recognition by examining papers that were essentially duplicates of each other published in two different journals (which of course should not happen)—one with a high average rate of citation of its publication (or impact factor) and one with a lower rate of citation of its publications (Larivière & Gingras, 2010). Papers were deemed to be duplicates if they had the same title, the same first author, and the same number of references. For each pair of duplicates, the same paper was cited significantly more often—close to twice as often—if published in a higher impact journal.[3]

Some scholarship may end up in a low-impact journal (or be published by a less prestigious press) for a plethora of reasons that have nothing to do with the quality of the work, some of which were described in chapter 6. People may not be particularly conscious of prestige of the publication outlet as critical to their success and may rely on other factors (people they know publish in a particular journal or press, their advisor or colleague suggests it, etc.), so they may not weight prestige in their submission practices. People at low-prestige institutions may have few immediate colleagues in their specialty to ask for advice. Individuals and members of some groups may underestimate their chances of being published in a prestigious outlet. They may also underestimate the chances of their manuscript's being accepted at journals that do not practice double-blind review (where the author's identity and institution are not disclosed to reviewers and the reviewers' identities are not disclosed to authors). Or people, particularly White women and people of color, may receive well-meaning advice to aim for a "safe" publication outlet.

White women and people of color in fields where humans are the object of study may often study gender and race, topics frequently seen as outside the "mainstream" of the field. For that reason they may submit manuscripts to journals and publishers that are known to be receptive to research on these topics, and that are read by others who share their interests, and are thus appropriate outlets. But such outlets may have lower impact scores and thus fail to contribute to an author's prestige. Finally, those at institutions that provide fewer resources may not be willing or able to take the additional time or have the funds to generate additional material to meet demands of high-prestige publication outlets. When reviewers suggest that an additional experiment be run, for example, they are assuming that the authors have the time and funding to run the experiment.

One of us experienced two different "desk rejections" by editors of a highly-ranked journal for two different papers separated by 25 years; the reason given by two different male editors was that the papers relied on a "specialized sample"—college-educated women. A colleague told us about submitting a paper reporting a study that had only used African American participants to a prestigious social psychology journal. The journal declined to publish it on the grounds that there was no White control group. Both psychologists wondered about the thousands of studies with White or college-educated male participants that have no female or Black control groups but make generalizations about humans as a whole. Both published their studies in "specialty" journals. If highly cited, prestigious journals are unreceptive to new subject matter—or to gender- or race-linked subject matter—researchers have no choice but to publish elsewhere.

Finally, people may not know that it is sometimes possible to successfully challenge an editor's rejection (though of course this does not always work!). In our own networks, considerably more White men than White women or people of color report having done this successfully. Moreover, those few White women and people of color we know who have requested reviews of editors' decisions usually only did so after receiving advice from White men.

Inconsistency in Peer Review

Several studies have demonstrated reviewers' fallibility, and their imperviousness to training, at least over the short run. One study asked reviewers of the *British Journal of Medicine* to successively evaluate three previously published papers on general topics; the investigators put in nine major and five minor errors (with the original authors' permission), retitled the papers, and changed identifying details (Schroter, Black, Evans, Godlee, Osorio, & Smith, 2008). A control group received no training; the two experimental groups either received one day of live training in recognizing errors or a self-administered training package. The first paper was evaluated before any training began; the second, two to three months after training; and the third, six months later. Reviewers detected fewer than 30% of the major errors and fewer than 20% of the minor errors. Training was largely ineffective. Similar findings have been obtained in other fields (Peters & Ceci, 1982).

Articles in science and social science fields that report no differences between groups, or no statistically significant effects, are more likely to have their methodology scrutinized, no doubt in part because there are so many possible reasons for these "null" findings. The result, however, is that reviewers are more lenient with papers reporting positive effects, even when there are errors. One study created papers that were identical except for finding either a positive result or no result. Errors that were deliberately inserted in the paper were more likely to be identified in the paper that reported no effects (Emerson, Warme, Wolf, Heckman, Brand, & Leopold, 2010). The higher bar that is maintained for results that show no difference means that positive effects are overreported (Ioannidis, 2005), leading to a higher likelihood of publishing error-ridden papers (see also Franco, Malhotra, & Simonovits, 2014).

The Role of Prestige
Retractions of papers later found to be fraudulent or simply in error are more likely to occur in high-prestige journals (although retractions are extremely rare, there is a strong correlation between impact factor and retraction rate; Cokol, Iossifov, Rodriguez-Esteban, & Rzhetsky, 2007; Fang & Casadevall, 2011).

Prestige plays a role not only at the level of journals, with higher impact journals overreporting positive results, but also at the level of universities. States with higher prestige universities are most likely to produce papers finding positive results (Fanelli, 2010). Thus, individuals who are at lower prestige institutions, whose faculty produce fewer papers than do those at high-prestige institutions, are at a disadvantage.

Biased Peer Review: Gender and Status

The results thus far concern noise: the peer review system contains a lot of inconsistency. However, there are also possible sources of systematic bias in the review process, such as author gender and race or ethnicity; reviewer gender and race or ethnicity; prestige of authors' institutions; prestige of individual authors, particularly first and last authors; reviewers' publication history; and prestige of reviewers' institutions. We concentrate on author gender and author prestige, where there is ample evidence.

An experimental study asked graduate students in communications to evaluate abstracts that had been accepted for conference presentation (Knobloch-Westerwick, Glynn, & Huge, 2013). The authors varied author gender and the subfield "gender" (some subfields are associated more with men than women). Abstracts designated with male authors were rated as having higher scientific quality than the same abstracts designated with female authors, but only in fields that were seen as male. For neutral and female fields, there was no difference in ratings of male and female authors. In addition, abstracts in male fields were seen as having higher scientific quality than abstracts in female or neutral fields, but only when males were the designated authors. There were no differences between male and female participants. Both thought that the highest quality abstracts were those in male subfields with male authors. Participants with progressive attitudes toward women were less likely to favor male authors.

In this experimental study, the authors were able to create conditions where the impact of gender could be isolated from other potential factors. When examining real-life examples, where there are many variables that are not controlled, there is less evidence of gender effects due to author or reviewer. For example, a study of submissions to *Journal of Neurophysiology* (five-year impact factor of approximately 3.5), which rejects a little more than half of its submissions, detected no gender bias in acceptance rates (Lane & Linden, 2009). What is impossible to determine from this and similar observational studies is the merit of the studies rejected and accepted. When men and women, or prestigious and nonprestigious authors, receive equivalent ratings, can we safely assume that the "true" merit is equal? If fewer women or fewer nonprestigious researchers submit their work to a journal, we face the possibility that women and nonprestigious authors submit only papers that they have reason to believe are at the high end of the distribution, while men and prestigious authors may submit papers that occupy a broader range of the distribution. What makes this possibility more than idle speculation are data demonstrating men's overentitlement and women's underentitlement, and men's overestimation of their likely performance, as we discussed earlier in this chapter.

Other studies have compared acceptance and rejection rates as a function of whether or not the reviewers are blind to author characteristics like race or gender. Here, the evidence is mixed. For example, one study compared two similar journals in behavioral ecology, one of which initiated double-blind review (in which both author's and reviewer's gender were concealed in the process) and the other of which continued with single-blind review (in which only reviewer gender is concealed; Budden, Tregenza, Aarssen, Koricheva, Leimu, & Lortie, 2008). The percentage of papers published by female first authors increased in the journal where double-blind review began, while the percentage stayed the same in the other journal. Such a finding could result either from differences in reviewer evaluations or differences in how often women submitted papers to one or another journal. Other data support the second interpretation more solidly than the first: data from the same field suggest that women are more concerned about likelihood of acceptance than men are (Aarssen, Tregenza, Budden, Lortie, Koricheva, & Leimu, 2008). Analyses of acceptance rates at two similar journals that did not practice double-blind review found no differences as a function of author sex (Primack, Ellwood, Miller-Rushing, Marrs, & Mulligan, 2009; Whittaker, 2008). Further, the rate of increase of female authors in other journals in the field of behavioral ecology seems to have been similar to the rate in the journal that instituted the double-blind review (Webb, O'Hara, & Freckleton, 2008).

To reconcile the findings of strong gender effects in laboratory studies with noneffects in the majority of journal experiences, we can suggest several possibilities. We have already mentioned that women may be more selective than men are about submitting to prestigious journals. Another possibility is that, in many fields, most articles have multiple authors of mixed genders and ethnicities, effectively reducing gender cues. Or the laboratory results could be incorrect. We consider further possibilities after discussing effects due to status.

Status effects develop from someone's structural position—whether authors are at high- or low-prestige institutions—and from the extent of their recognition via prizes, awards, and invitations to be keynote or plenary speakers. Both types of status effects may influence how someone's work is received. Status effects are conceptually separable from the "intrinsic" merit of someone's work, but it is difficult in practice to determine whether we think an intellectual or artistic product is of high quality because of features of the work alone or because of the context in which we encounter it. It is also possible that status accrues to individuals as a result of their intrinsic merit—as the just-world hypothesis would claim. However, if recognition is contingent on status effects instead of or in addition to the objective value of someone's research, disciplines run the risk of missing contributions from individuals at low-status institutions and overvaluing those from high-status institutions. In the same way that men get a small boost in professional life just by being men, from judgments by both women and men, individuals from high-status institutions may get a small boost in professional advancement just by being at a high-status institution.

Having a good idea and publishing that good idea does not guarantee positive reception of that good idea. It is similar, though with higher stakes, to making suggestions at a meeting. A woman's suggestion may be excellent, as indicated by her peers' reception of that suggestion when it comes from a male colleague, but not get its due when it comes from her. Conversely, the suggestion may not be so great and get more than its due when presented by a man.

We have noted that academics, in part because of their commitment to the ideal university, would like to think that the just-world hypothesis holds in academia, even if nowhere else. Similarly, individuals at high-status institutions would like to believe that they are there because of their superior performance. It is thus fitting for them to command more attention than people at lower prestige schools: their ideas and work are not just good, but "better" than many other people's ideas and work; they have been properly rewarded for their efforts. For obvious reasons, it is hard to evaluate how reasonable this is.

An analysis of acceptance rates of abstracts submitted for presentation at meetings of the American Heart Association compared reviews of abstracts from two years in which only single-blind reviewing was used to three subsequent years in which double-blind reviewing was used (Ross et al., 2006). The overall acceptance rate was roughly 28%; 41% of abstracts from the United States were accepted in single-blind review, compared to 33% under double-blind review. There were no effects of author gender in either single- or double-blind reviewing. Results on prestige of institution were confined to schools in the United States; three levels of prestige were coded. Under single-blind review, the acceptance rates for the most prestigious institutions averaged 51%; for medium-prestige schools, 43%; and for low-prestige schools, 33%. Under double-blind review, the comparable figures were 39%, 34%, and 29%. Thus, all U.S. academic institutions dropped in their acceptance rates under double-blind review, but the authors from the most prestigious schools showed the largest decline, and acceptance rates from proposers of institutions of different prestige were bunched more closely together under double-blind review. Abstracts from high-prestige institutions continued to show an advantage, but a much smaller one.

Other evidence of prestige effects comes from a study of how often multiauthored proposals of Internet protocols were accepted by a task force that determined how the Internet should be managed. For several years, when the proposals were posted for review, only the first author's name was cited, with the rest labeled as "et al." The investigators examined the difference in acceptance rate depending on whether high- or low-status individuals' names were omitted (Simcoe & Waguespack, 2011). One set of proposals could be designated as general interest: there were many such proposals, and few were chosen. In that case, failure to include a high-status individual's name in the original posting of the material resulted in lower publication. A different set of proposals was posted to one or another technical group; there, hiding a prestigious author's name had no effect. The conclusion is that when there are too many proposals to evaluate easily, readers make use of prestige to decide what to read or read carefully. Status has a signaling effect.

The discussion of prestige suggests an additional reason for a general absence of gender effects in journal paper reviews and in abstract submissions, namely, that gender is less salient than prestige cues. In the laboratory, experimenters can ensure that only gender distinguishes two conditions. The tight controls that laboratory investigations include make it different from real life, where many cues jostle with gender for influence. Prestige is a powerful cue in some contexts.

One woman, who was born and completed her undergraduate education in Japan, came to the United States for graduate study because her professors in Japan had told her there was no future for a woman in science in Japan. The woman received her PhD in the United States in 1990 and obtained a position at a high-prestige research university in the United States. Fourteen years later she also became head of a research laboratory in Japan. Her explanation for her now being welcomed in Japan was not that Japan had changed, but that her age and experience at the U.S. university overcame the disadvantage of being a woman. The more systematic data we have presented suggest that her experience is not unusual. Real life presents us with many different factors simultaneously.

Thus, prestige may overcome gender effects unless we look only at institutions of comparable prestige. One story we savor was told to us by a woman at a very high-prestige university. She was talking to a man who said that the chair of his department was stepping down and there was no one in the department who could replace him. She said, "What about X?," naming a woman in that department who had had a cabinet position in the U.S. government, with thousands of people under her. "Oh," he said, "there's nothing to that job, you have staff who do everything. This is being chair, this is hard!" At institution A, where everyone had high prestige, additional prestige was discounted and gender came to the fore.

Citations

It is close to axiomatic that papers published in prestigious journals will receive more citations than those published in less prestigious journals, and citations lead to perceptions of achievement. This phenomenon is something of a closed loop. If enough people agree that something counts as an outstanding achievement, then it is one. There is no court of higher opinion until history has its say and the historical record changes. If something should have spurred research but did not, was it still an achievement? If a certain path that many people followed turns out to be a dead end, was the achievement of the person who inspired many people to go down that path a genuine achievement or the unfortunate result of someone's being very convincing?

With those caveats in mind, we consider variables that might affect citation rates. One notable example of how the accumulation of advantage works can be seen in status effects, where the rich get richer. It appears, for example, that Leibniz and Newton independently invented calculus (although each had some information about the other's methods and they had some correspondence). Leibniz, in 1684, published his first paper, laying out differential calculus, while Newton did not publish his variant until 1693. Yet Newton commonly receives the credit for inventing the calculus, perhaps because of the prestige of Great Britain's Royal Society.[4]

If we take the example of Leibniz and Newton at face value, it suggests that above and beyond the "objective" value of one's contributions, recognition in the form of prizes and awards or a position at a high-prestige institution affects how one's projects are received by others. A report of a "natural experiment" examined the citation rate for papers that were published before their authors received a prestigious award, namely, becoming a Howard Hughes Medical Investigator (Azoulay, Stuart, & Wang, 2014). For individuals who already had high status, becoming a Howard Hughes Medical Investigator had little effect. But for individuals with lower status, the award increased citations of previously published papers. Thus, upward changes will be particularly important for those with lower status, including women and people of color.

We referred earlier to the problem of null findings. Compounding that problem is that subsequent researchers, especially in some disciplines, are more likely to pay attention to reports of positive findings than to reports of no effects (Fanelli, 2013). The very fact that prestigious journals have a bias to publish positive findings means that positive findings will be over-cited. Across all fields, positive results are cited about 30% more often than negative results (Fanelli, 2013), with large variability by field.

Journal prestige, recency of references, number of references, and degree of citation of highly cited papers appear to be more important factors than author prestige (as measured by prior citations) or prestige of authors' institutions (see reviews by Didegah & Thelwall, 2013; Onodera & Yoshikane, 2015). The fact that papers with more recent and numerous references tend to be cited more often than those with older and fewer references (Onodera & Yoshikane, 2015) may reflect a rational choice on the part of readers (a preference not to cite a paper that is not au courant).

The weaker findings for prestige of author and institution may be due to several factors. One is that some studies have examined the prestige only of the first author, who is not necessarily the lead author. Another is that prestigious journals' authors are already likely to be at high-prestige institutions. There are so many variables that affect a paper's reception, and those variables interact in so many complex ways, that it is difficult to provide a clear answer to the question of what factors determine how frequently a paper is cited. A machine-learning effort to predict citation rates finds variation across discipline in the importance of different factors. For example, the use of highly cited references is more important in biology than physics, as is authors' prestige and institution prestige (Livne, Adar, Teevan, & Dumais, 2013).

Finally, gender disparities in rate of self-citation affect rates of citation overall (King, Bergstrom, Correll, Jacquet, & West, 2016; West, Jacquet, King, Correll, & Bergstrom, 2013). Between 1991 and 2011, men cited their own work 70% more frequently than women cited theirs.

We note in closing this discussion that fields in which the primary scholarly form is journal publication are studied much more intensively than fields in which the primary scholarly form is books. That said, many of the same factors appear to be relevant (though precisely how relevant is not clear). For example, awards for books are coveted, and books are often awarded more than one prize (perhaps a result of the accumulation of advantage), and individuals from prestigious institutions appear to be the winners of the most prestigious awards (for books and also for fellowships). Gender and race and ethnicity play a role in the distribution of individuals in most of those fields at more and less prestigious institutions, and gender and race and ethnicity schemas apply to judgment processes. For these reasons we suspect that prestige, gender, and race and ethnicity are important factors affecting recognition in book fields, despite the dearth of research examining them.

Working at a High-Prestige Institution

Prestige of institution matters to faculty in all fields on a daily basis in the provision of resources, both material and collegial. Consider a thought experiment in which two individuals, A and B, of equivalent talent (which we stipulate for this example even though we think "talent" is insufficiently multidimensional), effort, and achievement, each have offers from the same two schools—one is a research-intensive school and the other a teaching-intensive school. Person A is single and accepts the offer from the research-intensive school. Person B has a partner, C. C is also a talented academic and has an offer from a third school, a research-intensive institution 3,000 miles away from the research-intensive institution that offered B a position. Neither research-intensive school will offer B's or C's partner a position. But C also has an offer from the same teaching-intensive school that offered B a position. B and C decide that they want to live together, rather than commute 3,000 miles on a semiregular basis. They both accept positions at the teaching-intensive school even though they would both prefer, on purely professional grounds, to be at research-intensive schools.

Whose research career, measured in traditional terms—publication and citation in high-prestige outlets, visibility, influencing graduate students and postdocs—is more likely to flourish? It must be A's since A has access to resources that B and C do not have.

Even in fields where research funding—to buy equipment and to hire assistants or fund students—is less important, prestige of institution affects one's ability to do one's work. Research-intensive institutions are, almost by definition, designed to facilitate faculty research, regardless of field. In research-intensive institutions and in highly ranked liberal arts colleges, faculty will be more experienced at writing proposals for the kinds of fellowships and travel and scholarship grants that enable the research necessary for writing books. In addition, the institutional infrastructure is likely to work better at every level: classrooms, offices, and laboratories are better equipped with technology and furniture; the libraries have extensive holdings; the classrooms, offices, and laboratories, are more likely to be clean, bright, free of vermin, warm in winter and cool in summer, and functional. The duplicating machines mostly work. There is an office that will produce posters. The bathrooms are more often free of graffiti or repainted when graffiti appear, the toilets flush reliably, toilet paper and paper towels are replenished as needed. The elevator is more likely to respond by lighting up when the user presses a button. The grounds are more likely to be well-kept. The staff are more likely to be adequately paid and competent. The teaching assistants are more likely to be capable and well supported. Instructors' teaching responsibilities leave them time to perform research and to accommodate undergraduate students as well as graduate students and postdocs in individual projects. The grants office(s) and institutional review boards are at least relatively well run by helpful individuals who understand federal, state, and local requirements and have experience submitting grants and evaluating research.

In addition to the tangible benefits of being at a research-intensive institution are the intangible benefits of being in the company of people who are recognized leaders in their field, of being part of a network of individuals who know people with whom it might be desirable to collaborate or who know techniques or have information that will help one with one's work, and of having graduate students who are already well trained. All of those features, tangible and intangible, help to produce achievements.

There are also negative aspects to very highly research-intensive environments. The environment in such schools can feel oppressive, confining, isolating, and overly pressured. Faculty who care deeply about teaching may feel that teaching is not appreciated. Those who care about creating an inclusive and welcoming academic community for both faculty and students may feel they are in an unappreciated minority. The emphasis in the sciences on attaining funding and publishing frequently can make it difficult for researchers to think more broadly about their work, to go in new directions, or to incubate an idea. And an emphasis on external funding may lead faculty in the humanities and the humanistic social sciences to feel devalued.

The advantages and disadvantages of working at a research-intensive institution are thus two sides of the same coin. Everything is in place for a faculty member to be productive in certain specific terms, such as scholarly publication (Joy, 2006). Faculty who are not productive in those ways or who have other important goals and values may feel, at a minimum, out of place.

Whether the commitment to publication of scholars at research institutions is higher, whether such scholars profit from the advantages that research institutions offer, or some combination of both, cannot be answered by the data we have reviewed. We suggest that the higher publication productivity of individuals at research-intensive institutions is at least a combination of both and, given the facts we have reviewed, is in many cases due to the advantages of a research institution. Other research has attributed the difference in publication quantity between men and women to structural factors like prestige of institution (e.g., Xie & Shauman, 2003).

One objection to that conclusion might be that even if the prestige of an institution affects publication productivity, high-prestige institutions primarily serve an amplifying function: they support the performance of people who are already performing very highly. The benefits of that support compound over time—advantage accumulates. Yet there is evidence that location affects publication productivity as much as or more than publication productivity affects a researcher's institutional location. One study tracked chemists' publication productivity as a function of the prestige of the institutions they taught at. Moves "up" the prestige ladder led to more publications; moves "down" led to fewer (Allison & Long, 1990). Publication productivity contributed to location, but location had an independent effect. More recent research suggests that more productive researchers are more likely to move up than down, and that mobility up increases productivity even further (Fernández-Zubieta, Geuna, & Lawson, 2015).

A study outside academia looked at the short-term effects of arbitrarily bestowed benefits in four different areas (van de Rijt, Kang, Restivo, & Patil, 2014). At a crowdfunding source the researchers randomly chose 100 start-ups to give money to and another 100 to track as a control group. Neither the control nor the experimental start-ups had received any funding 24 days before the date by which their goal would expire. The initial randomly placed benefit led to significantly more subsequent funding. The advantage of this study is that the start-ups were randomly divided into a control and an experimental group. In real life, selection committees do not choose randomly among their top candidates when hiring and bestowing awards. The disadvantage is that the tracking period was relatively short, so long-term benefits could not be assessed. The simulation is imperfect in another way: research-intensive institutions provide a suite of constantly active benefits to individuals rather than a one-time infusion of cash. Nevertheless, the data are valuable because they show that randomly placed benefits prime the pump for more benefits.

Presence at a research-intensive institution does not, however, guarantee that researchers' work will be creative. There is evidence that the pressure for immediate results works against new ideas in a comparison of individuals with funding from the National Institutes of Health (NIH) and individuals with funding from the Howard Hughes Medical Institute (HHMI). The individuals were matched on a variety of characteristics, including receipt of other prestigious awards. The investigators compared the researchers' productivity, likelihood of producing very highly cited papers, and likelihood of producing papers that were seldom cited (Azoulay, Graff Zivin, & Manso, 2011). HHMI investigator awards are for five years, with the possibility of one renewal; NIH awards range from three to five years. HHMI awards are to the person, rather than a particular project, while NIH awards are for a specific set of proposed studies. Investigators are free to ignore the NIH reviews, but, mindful of the need to have results for the next round of funding, are unlikely to do so. In theory, HHMI, more than NIH, provides individuals with time to explore high-risk ideas.

The HHMI investigators indeed took more risks, as measured by the number of their papers with fewer citations than any they had published before receiving the HHMI award (adjusted for date of publication; Azoulay et al., 2011). They also, however, published papers that were more highly cited than those prior to receiving the HHMI award. An examination of the keywords for the HHMI researchers' papers showed that they explored new directions.

We recognize that individuals at both low- and high-prestige institutions have difficulties. Researchers at low-prestige institutions generally lack many resources to do the work that can be done at high-prestige institutions and have higher teaching responsibilities, but they are also free to explore new ideas. Researchers at high-prestige institutions may have the resources they need and have lower teaching demands, but they are also under pressure to conduct fundable research and publish as much as possible.

Our thought experiment about three equivalently talented candidates who took jobs at research-intensive versus teaching-intensive institutions was intended to show that individuals with equal potential can, for reasons external to talent and effort, take jobs at very different types of institutions. There is increasing recognition that many fields are overproducing PhDs for the available academic positions (Ghaffarzadegan, Hawley, Larson, & Xue, 2015). Every top-rated university grants more PhDs every year than there are academic jobs available for those doctorate holders. Where are those newly minted PhDs going to go? In fields that require postdoctoral positions, there is room for many more postdocs than for assistant professors, but there is a similar, if somewhat smaller, glut of postdocs. There are not enough jobs available for them, either. For a fair number of people, then, chance—or extra-academic factors—determines whether they end up at an elite institution, a less prestigious institution, or outside academia. An individual's commitment and ambition could be one factor, but the sheer paucity of positions is an overwhelming consideration.

The paucity of positions at top-rated schools works against a successful job search for any candidate, but especially for women and people of color. A small amount of advantage for White men can make the difference in the type of institution at which a researcher gets his or her first job.

Although people of every description teach at lower prestige institutions, White men are overrepresented as faculty at high-prestige institutions. The slight advantage for White (and, in science, Asian) males results in fewer women and people of color at top-rated institutions. In particular, top-rated institutions hire a smaller percentage of women than they graduate.

For structural and schema-related reasons, White women and people of color are more likely to obtain positions at schools that do not foster the quantity (and perhaps the quality) of research that is required for visibility. At medium levels of quantity, they are less likely to be recognized by the field as a whole. In addition, they often do not have as part of their immediate professional network people who will nominate them for prizes and write effective letters for them. This pattern can be altered, but only if the top-tier institutions recognize the merit they are currently missing and make a serious effort to alter their distribution of faculty with different backgrounds, and only if professional societies encourage and develop opportunities for nominations of people from diverse institutions.

Summary

Informal recognition is a very important part of faculty life, and a culture that supports it can and should be created and enhanced wherever possible. In addition, departments and institutions may benefit, and create higher faculty morale, if they create low-cost forms of recognition of many kinds of faculty labor: teaching, mentoring, community service, institutional service, and scholarship. It is critical that these forms of recognition be distributed fairly; one way to ensure that this occurs is to engage all faculty in the process of nomination and selection of individuals for awards; another is to create procedures that minimize the likelihood of a small group's receiving most forms of recognition.

Formal recognition at national and international levels is demonstrably vulnerable to some nonrational factors that produce biased outcomes. Neither formal award selection nor peer review of publications and applications for funding is reliable, in the technical sense of high consensus among reviewers, except at the extremes. Gender does not seem to play a consistent role in publication and grant acceptance rates, but it may play a role in paper and grant submission rates since submission rates to high-prestige journals and to granting agencies tend to be lower for women than for men.

Prestige clearly plays a role in all of the outcomes for formal recognition. To the extent that White women and people of color are underrepresented at the most prestigious institutions and overrepresented at less prestigious institutions, their work is more likely to go unrecognized. Both advantage and disadvantage will continue to accumulate in the domain of formal recognition unless major effort is invested in reducing the roles of schemas and prestige in awarding formal recognition. Institutions and professional organizations can improve the procedures by which individuals are recognized.

Recommendations for Practices that Improve Faculty Recognition Processes

Administrative Leaders (Presidents, Provosts, Deans, Department Chairs)

1. Administrative leaders can create a climate of informal recognition of faculty accomplishment, in part by practicing recognition themselves— naming particular contributions, thanking individual faculty in writing or orally for them, and holding other leaders accountable for identifying faculty contributions of many different kinds.

2. Administrative leaders can create formal recognition for many kinds of contributions by faculty and can seek funding to include some kind of financial element. The procedures for nominations should allow many faculty to make nominations (including self-nomination) and should engage many diverse faculty in the selection process.

3. Institutions can make a concentrated effort to nominate their faculty— including White women and underrepresented minorities—for disciplinary and meta-disciplinary awards. The more awards faculty have, the better known their department and institution will be, the more likely it is that faculty will be successful in getting grants, and the more likely it is that their letters of recommendations for students will count.

4. If nominators are not knowledgeable about the potential nominees' work, they can confer with them about the names of external people who could be approached about nominating the person. Consulting the letters of recommendation that were written for people when they were hired or the referee letters that were written when they was promoted could be useful. The people who wrote those letters thought well of the potential awardee and might thus be willing to nominate or conominate them. The

chair of a department, or the dean or provost of a school, can also be a nominator, using as a draft a letter that someone else at the institution may have written. The institution's imprimatur will be helpful.

5. Some departments and some schools have committees that are charged with identifying potential awardees and matching them with potential awards. A committee structure helps solve the problem of lack of knowledge of a person's work, makes it more likely that helpful ideas will emerge, and increases everyone's knowledge about awards.

6. Many people may not know how to write a good letter even if they are knowledgeable about the potential nominee's work. To solve that problem, a nominator can write a letter and ask for constructive critiques from others, both inside and outside the institution. A well-crafted letter carries weight.

7. The nomination letter, updated as appropriate, can be submitted again. Many nominees only win on their third round. That, too, is a fact that is not widely known.

8. As with all institutional metrics, it is important to track the distribution of informal and formal awards as well as nominations by gender, race-ethnicity, and field. Regular review of those data can identify underrecognized individuals and fields and can lead to corrections in the process.

Disciplinary and Metadisciplinary Societies (Like the National Academies)

1. Disciplinary societies should track their own data over time by gender and ethnicity in a way similar to what we recommend for evaluating job candidates. If the data can be published without revealing anyone's identity, they should be published:

• Who is nominated? Is the proportion of women and underrepresented minority nominees what would be expected relative to the membership of the society? If not, the society needs to do more to solicit nominations from underrepresented groups.

• Among those who are in the nomination pool, who receives an award? Is the proportion by demographic group what would be expected given the pool? If not, the society needs to examine its evaluation metrics and procedures.

• Are the awards affected by the number or percentage of women and underrepresented minority members on the awards committee? If so, the society needs to probe for the reasons and appoint committees likely to make fair decisions.

• Are the awards affected by the type of institution where nominees are located? If so, the society needs to rethink the basis for its awards.

Conference Organizers and Colloquium Committee Members

1. At conferences, there are generally several invited speakers, or several symposia with invited participants. At graduation ceremonies and departmental colloquia, there are generally several honorary degree recipients or speakers each year. Include members of underrepresented groups among them.

2. Suggestions for organizers can be found in several places: at the Gendered Conference Campaign (https://feministphilosophers.wordpress.com/gendered-conference-campaign/), at the blogspot For Gender Equity at Conferences (http://forgenderequityatconferences.blogspot.com/), and in a range of articles (Casadevall, 2015; J. L. Martin, 2014; Masur, 2015).

3. Especially if you are inviting people from small or teaching-intensive institutions, provide funding for them. If they decline, find out why and see if you can accommodate their needs. Ask other White women and people of color if the first invitees decline.

4. Express enthusiasm and respect in your invitation.

Conference Hosts and Funders

1. Institutions that host conferences and workshops, and funders that sponsor them, can hold organizers accountable for equitable lineups. That means that to receive hosting or funding, organizers present their best estimates of the composition of the pool from which they can draw speakers and detail their plans for issuing invitations and ensuring appropriate representation.

Individual Faculty

1. Contribute to a culture of informal appreciation:

• Express your appreciation of your colleagues' contributions.

• Pass on to your colleagues the positive things you hear about them from students and others.

2. If you are a White female faculty member, or a faculty member of color, accept invitations to speak!

3. If you are a White woman or member of a racial-ethnic or other underrepresented minority in your field, consider organizing symposia. By

organizing a symposium or workshop, you can introduce a theme you think is important; structure it in a way that you think makes sense; and include yourself, a colleague, and/or a student as a presenter.

4. If you are a White man who is invited to speak at conferences, you can ask the organizer some variation of this: "I think it's important to have a gender balance at conferences. You probably do, too. Could you tell me what you are doing to ensure that?" Then you decide whether you think the organizers' efforts are adequate. If not, decline. You may have to forfeit some invitations in order to live according to this principle.

5. Do not be shy about looking for awards you might be eligible for. You can look at the CVs of past awardees and compare it with yours to see whether you are on track. You can draft a sample nomination letter to give to someone else and ask people for tips on what to emphasize and how to bring out what is most important about your work. Ask the most prestigious people you can to nominate you.

6. If you have been the recipient of awards, use your status to nominate those who you know are deserving but may not otherwise be nominated.

Notes

1. Although that interviewee mentioned a long time lag, the average lag between the publication date of the work that is cited as important and the receipt of the prize is 5 years in physics, 9 in chemistry, and 11 in medicine or physiology (Chan & Torgler, 2013).

2. There have been attempts to estimate the percentage of conference speakers who should be female, based on any distribution of males and females who could be invited. There are different ways of making this estimate, and different conclusions to draw depending on what one calculates. One way uses the Poisson distribution and, via an interactive applet from Aanand Prasad (http://aanandprasad.com/diversity-calculator/?groupName=women&numSpeakers=20&populationPercentage=10/), predicts the likelihood of overrepresentation, exact representation, and zero representation, as a function of how one sets different parameters. For example, if women are 10% of available speakers, and there is a random selection of 20 speakers, women should be *overrepresented* 32% of the time, exactly represented 29% of the time, and not represented at all 12% of the time. But with that applet one cannot calculate, say, the probability of having two or fewer speakers, or two or more speakers. Another applet (vassarstats.net; several clicks are required to get to the applet itself) will do that, using the binomial theorem to estimate the likelihood of a given outcome or that outcome plus more extreme outcomes. The probability of obtaining

one or fewer female speakers is 0.39, rather a large percentage. The probability of obtaining two or fewer is 0.68, and the probability of obtaining two or more is 0.61. What one can conclude is that, by chance, one would expect women to be over-represented considerably more often than is the case, but one would also expect to see women underrepresented often, as is the case. For mathematics, Martin (2015) analyzes two conferences, estimating the pool of female speakers at 25%, and finds that women are underrepresented more often than one would expect by chance. The math for Martin's estimates is given here: http://www.laurenbacon.com/how -likely-is-an-all-male-speakers-list-statistically/

The site https://biaswatchneuro.com/ tracks the percentages of female invited speakers to a variety of conferences in topics related broadly to neuroscience. In a helpful move, the site estimates the base rate of women in the field and provides the basis for the estimation. For example, on December 2, 2016, it summarized the gender breakdown for speakers at a conference held in Germany on episodic memory—one woman and six men—and gave a link to the conference. It estimated the pool as 45% female. It stated how they arrived at their estimate: they searched the "NIH RePORTER with keyword 'episodic memory' and counted the ratio of women among the unique researchers in pages 1, 3, 7, 9 and 10 of 10 results pages." And see Schroeder, Dugdale, Radersma, Hinsch, Buehler, Saul, et al. (2013) for information about evolutionary biology.

3. Impact factors are established yearly for journals in some fields, based on the average number of citations in a given year to articles published in the preceding two years. Within the natural sciences, *Science* and *Nature* have very high impact factors (roughly 35 and 38, respectively), reflecting the breadth and importance of articles that they publish, while highly respected specialty journals, such as the suite of physics journals *Physical Review A-E* range from about 2.5–8. Small fields automatically have journals with small impact factors—there are not enough researchers to write enough articles with enough references to yield a high citation count.

4. The full story is considerably more complicated, but it seems relatively clear that Leibniz's and Newton's methods were different, that integral and differential calculus was due to Leibniz, and that infinitesimal calculus was due to Newton. Arguments raged at the time about whether Leibniz saw Newton's notebooks, but their methods were sufficiently different that seeing Newton's notebooks could have done little more for Leibniz than reassure him that he was on the right track.

References

Aarssen, L. W., Tregenza, T., Budden, A. E., Lortie, C. J., Koricheva, J., & Leimu, R. (2008). Bang for your buck: Rejection rates and impact factors in ecological journals. *Open Ecology Journal*, *1*(1), 14–19.

Algoe, S. B., Kurtz, L. E., & Hilaire, N. M. (2016). Putting the "you" in "thank you": Examining other-praising behavior as the active relational ingredient in expressed gratitude. *Social Psychological & Personality Science, 7*(7), 658–666.

Allison, P. D., & Long, J. S. (1990). Departmental effects on scientific productivity. *American Sociological Review, 55*, 469–478.

Azoulay, P., Graff Zivin, J. S., & Manso, G. (2011). Incentives and creativity: Evidence from the academic life sciences. *Rand Journal of Economics, 42*(3), 527–554.

Azoulay, P., Stuart, T., & Wang, Y. (2014). Matthew: Effect or fable? *Management Science, 60*(1), 92–109.

Budden, A. E., Tregenza, T., Aarssen, L. W., Koricheva, J., Leimu, R., & Lortie, C. J. (2008). Double-blind review favours increased representation of female authors. *Trends in Ecology & Evolution, 23*(1), 4–6.

Cantore, S. P., & Cooperrider, D. (2013). Positive psychology and Appreciative Inquiry: The contribution of the literature to an understanding of the nature and process of change in organizatios. In H. S. Leonard, R. Lewis, A. M. Freedom, & J. Passmore (Eds.), *The Wiley-Blackwell handbook of the psychology of leadership, change, and organizational development* (pp. 267–287). New York, NY: Wiley.

Casadevall, A. (2015). Achieving speaker gender equity at the American Society for Microbiology meeting. *mBio, 6*(4), e01146–15. http://mbio.asm.org/content/6/4.toc

Casadevall, A., & Handelsman, J. (2014). The presence of female conveners correlates with a higher proportion of female speakers at scientific symposia. *mBio, 5*(1), e00846–13.

Chan, H. F., Gleeson, L., & Torgler, B. (2014). Awards before and after the Nobel Prize: A Matthew effect and/or a ticket to one's own funeral? *Research Evaluation, 23*(3), 210–220.

Chan, H. F., & Torgler, B. (2013). Science prizes: Time-lapsed awards for excellence. *Nature, 500*(7460), 29.

Cokol, M., Iossifov, I., Rodriguez-Esteban, R., & Rzhetsky, A. (2007). How many scientific papers should be retracted? *EMBO Reports, 8*(5), 422–423.

Cooperrider, D. L. (1990). Positive image, positive action: The affirmative basis of organizing. In S. Srivastva & D. L. Cooperrider (Eds.), *Executive appreciation and leadership* (pp. 91–125). San Francisco, CA: Jossey-Bass.

Correll, S. J. (2004). Constraints into preferences: Gender, status, and emerging career aspirations. *American Sociological Review, 69*(1), 93–113.

DeCelles, K. A., DeRue, D. S., Margolis, J. D., & Ceranic, T. L. (2012). Does power corrupt or enable? When and why power facilitates self-interested behavior. *Journal of Applied Psychology, 97*(3), 681–689.

Didegah, F., & Thelwall, M. (2013). Determinants of research citation impact in nanoscience and nanotechnology. *Journal of the American Society for Information Science and Technology, 64*(5), 1055–1064.

Emerson, G. B., Warme, W. J., Wolf, F. M., Heckman, J. D., Brand, R. A., & Leopold, S. S. (2010). Testing for the presence of positive-outcome bias in peer review: A randomized controlled trial. *Archives of Internal Medicine, 170*(21), 1934–1939.

Fanelli, D. (2010). Do pressures to publish increase scientists' bias? An empirical support from US States Data. *PLoS One, 5*(4), e10271.

Fanelli, D. (2013). Why growing retractions are (mostly) a good sign. *PLoS Medicine, 10*(12), e1001563. doi:10.1371/journal.pmed.1001563

Fang, F. C., & Casadevall, A. (2011). Retracted science and the retraction index. *Infection and Immunity, 79*(10), 3855–3859.

Fernandez-Zubieta, A., Geuna, A., & Lawson, C. (2015). Mobility and productivity of research scientists. In A. Geuna (Ed.), *Global mobility of research scientists: The economics of who goes where and why* (pp. 105–132). San Diego, CA: Academic Press.

Franco, A., Malhotra, N., & Simonovits, G. (2014). Publication bias in the social sciences: Unlocking the file drawer. *Science, 345*(6203), 1502–1505.

Frank, R. H. (2016). *Success and luck: Good fortune and the myth of meritocracy*. Princeton, NJ: Princeton University Press.

Ghaffarzadegan, N., Hawley, J., Larson, R., & Xue, Y. (2015). A note on PhD population growth in biomedical sciences. *Systems Research and Behavioral Science, 32*(3), 402–405.

Hermanowicz, J. C. (2009). *Lives in science: How institutions affect academic careers.* Chicago, IL: University of Chicago Press.

Ioannidis, J. P. (2005). Why most published research findings are false. *PLoS Medicine, 2*(8), e124.

Isbell, L. A., Young, T. P., & Harcourt, A. H. (2012). Stag parties linger: Continued gender bias in a female-rich scientific discipline. *PLoS One, 7*(11), e49682.

Jackowska, M., Brown, J., Ronaldson, A., & Steptoe, A. (2016). The impact of a brief gratitude intervention on subjective well-being, biology and sleep. *Journal of Health Psychology, 21*(10), 2207–2217.

Joy, S. (2006). What should I be doing, and where are they doing it? Scholarly productivity of academic psychologists. *Perspectives on Psychological Science, 1*, 346–364.

King, M. M., Bergstrom, C. T., Correll, S. J., Jacquet, J. J., & West, J. D. (2016). Men set their own cites high: Gender and self-citation across fields and over time. arXiv:1607.00376 [physics.soc-ph]

Klein, R. S., Voskuhl, R., Segal, B. M., Dittel, B. N., Lane, T. E., Bethea, J. R., et al. (2017). Speaking out about gender imbalance in invited speakers improves diversity. *Nature Immunology, 18*(5), 475–478.

Knobloch-Westerwick, S., Glynn, C. J., & Huge, M. (2013). The Matilda effect in science communication: An experiment on gender bias in publication quality perceptions and collaboration interest. *Science Communication, 35*(5), 603–625.

Lane, J. A., & Linden, D. J. (2009). Is there gender bias in the peer review process at *Journal of Neurophysiology*? *Journal of Neurophysiology, 101*(5), 2195–2196.

Larivière, V., & Gingras, Y. (2010). The impact factor's Matthew effect: A natural experiment in bibliometrics. *Journal of the American Society for Information Science and Technology, 61*(2), 424–427.

Lerner, M. J. (1980). *The belief in a just world: A fundamental delusion.* New York, NY: Plenum Press.

Lincoln, A., Pincus, S., Koster, J., & Leboy, P. (2012). The Matilda effect in science: Awards and prizes in the United States, 1990s and 2000s. *Social Studies of Science, 42*(2), 307–320.

Livne, A., Adar, E., Teevan, J., & Dumais, S. (2013, February). Predicting citation counts using text and graph mining. In *Proceedings of the iConference 2013 Workshop on Computational Scientometrics: Theory and Applications.*

Maddox, B. (2002). *Rosalind Franklin: The dark lady of DNA.* London, UK: HarperCollins.

Martin, G. (2015). Addressing the underrepresentation of women in mathematics conferences. *arXiv* preprint arXiv:1502.06326.

Martin, J. L. (2014). Ten simple rules to achieve conference speaker gender balance. *PLoS Computational Biology, 10*(11), e1003903. doi:10.1371/journal.pcbi.1003903

Masur, S. (2015, December). Great meetings require great speakers: Finding the women speakers you need. *American Society for Cell Biology Newsletter.* Retrieved January 27, 2018, from http://www.ascb.org/newsletter/2015-december-newsletter/great-meetings-require-great-speakers-finding-women-speakers-need/

Murphy, M. C., Steele, C. M., & Gross, J. J. (2007). Signaling threat: How situational cues affect women in math, science, and engineering settings. *Psychological Science, 18*(10), 879–885.

Nittrouer, C. L., Hebl, M. R., Ashburn-Nardo, L., Trump-Steele, R. C. E., Lane, D. M., & Valian, V. (2018). Gender disparities in colloquium speakers at top universities. *Proceedings of the National Academy of Sciences, 115*(1), 104–108.

Onodera, N., & Yoshikane, F. (2015). Factors affecting citation rates of research articles. *Journal of the Association for Information Science and Technology, 66*(4), 739–764.

Pelham, B. W., & Hetts, J. J. (2001). Underworked and overpaid: Elevated entitlement in men's self-pay. *Journal of Experimental Social Psychology, 37*(2), 93–103.

Perc, M. (2014). The Matthew effect in empirical data. *Journal of the Royal Society, Interface, 11*(98), 1–15, 20140378.

Peters, D. P., & Ceci, S. J. (1982). Peer-review practices of psychological journals: The fate of published articles, submitted again. *Behavioral and Brain Sciences, 5*(02), 187–195.

Primack, R. B., Ellwood, E., Miller-Rushing, A. J., Marrs, R., & Mulligan, A. (2009). Do gender, nationality, or academic age affect review decisions? An analysis of submissions to the journal *Biological Conservation. Biological Conservation, 142*(11), 2415–2418.

Reuben, E., Sapienza, P., & Zingales, L. (2014). How stereotypes impair women's careers in science. *Proceedings of the National Academy of Sciences of the United States of America, 111*, 4403–4408.

Ross, J. S., Gross, C. P., Desai, M. M., Hong, Y., Grant, A. O., Daniels, S. R., et al. (2006). Effect of blinded peer review on abstract acceptance. *Journal of the American Medical Association, 295*(14), 1675–1680.

Sardelis, S., & Drew, J. A. (2016). Not "pulling up the ladder": Women who organize conference symposia provide greater opportunities for women to speak at conservation conferences. *PLoS One, 11*(7), e0160015.

Sawaoka, T., Hughes, B. L., & Ambady, N. (2015). Power heightens sensitivity to unfairness against the self. *Personality and Social Psychology Bulletin, 41*(8), 1023–1035.

Schroeder, J., Dugdale, H. L., Radersma, R., Hinsch, M., Buehler, D. M., Saul, J., et al. (2013). Fewer invited talks by women in evolutionary biology symposia. *Journal of Evolutionary Biology, 26*(9), 2063–2069.

Schroter, S., Black, N., Evans, S., Godlee, F., Osorio, L., & Smith, R. (2008). What errors do peer reviewers detect, and does training improve their ability to detect them? *Journal of the Royal Society of Medicine, 101*(10), 507–514.

Simcoe, T. S., & Waguespack, D. M. (2011). Status, quality, and attention: What's in a (missing) name? *Management Science, 57*(2), 274–290.

Smith, D. O. (2011). *Managing the research university*. New York, NY: Oxford University Press.

Summers, L. H. (2005, January 14). Remarks at NBER conference on diversifying the science and engineering workforce. https://www.harvard.edu/president/speeches /summers_2005/nber.php/

Tost, L. P., Gino, F., & Larrick, R. P. (2012). Power, competitiveness, and advice taking: Why the powerful don't listen. *Organizational Behavior and Human Decision Processes, 117*(1), 53–65.

Valian, V. (2013). Invite women to talk. *Nature, 495,* 36.

van de Rijt, A., Kang, S. M., Restivo, M., & Patil, A. (2014). Field experiments of success-breeds-success dynamics. *Proceedings of the National Academy of Sciences of the United States of America, 111*(19), 6934–6939.

Watson, J. D. (1980). *The double helix: A personal account of the discovery of the structure of DNA.* New York, NY: Atheneum.

Webb, T. J., O'Hara, B., & Freckleton, R. P. (2008). Does double-blind review benefit female authors? *Trends in Ecology & Evolution, 23*(7), 351–353.

West, J. D., Jacquet, J., King, M. M., Correll, S. J., & Bergstrom, C. T. (2013). The role of gender in scholarly authorship. *PLoS One, 8*(7), e66212.

Whittaker, D. (2008). Journal review and gender equality: A critical comment on Budden *et al. Journal of Biogeography, 23*(9), 478–479.

Xie, Y., & Shauman, K. A. (2003). *Women in science: Career processes and outcomes.* Cambridge, MA: Harvard University Press.

11 Changing Institutions: The Roles of Formal Leaders, Informal Leaders, and All Faculty

In the first chapter of this book we argued that academic higher education institutions generally do not live up to our ideals of meritocracy and inclusion, and that we fail in part because of our reliance on faulty cognitive processes in making academic judgments about entrance into the academy and promotion within it. We have also argued that if we did live up to those ideals in at least one area and achieved a more diverse faculty, we would realize benefits institutionally and for individuals. If all of that is so, then what does it take for an institution to change, or to become more inclusive and truly meritocratic in its judgments? The simplest answer is the most familiar, and it is also true: it takes leadership. But formal leaders cannot do the job by themselves. Why not?

Decisive Visionary Leadership

Let's imagine a new university president, Jack Peters, who is White and male and seems to fit the part; he "looks presidential." He also has become convinced that institutional change is crucial, and that there must be a more diverse faculty at the university. He is a passionate and persuasive speaker, and during his campus visits he laid out his vision of a fully inclusive institution and named institutional change his top priority. At the end of the usual protracted process, he was selected for the job—surely a mandate to begin enacting his vision.

Since change was his top priority, President Peters accepted the resignation of the sitting provost (routinely submitted at this institution with a new president in office) and appointed an African American man as provost. He invited him to revise both the hiring procedures of the institution and the tenure and promotion processes, with issues of fairness, equity, inclusion, and excellence always uppermost in mind. Within a couple of months these revisions were codified in a document that President Peters presented to the governing board of the institution. They were impressed by his quick and decisive development of new policies that were consistent with what he had told them he aspired to during the search process, and they approved them with a unanimous vote. The president announced the new policies and procedures at a campus-wide event, designed to underscore the importance of these changes and their implementation during the next academic year.

To his astonishment, this speech—articulating the fulfillment of the vision he had enunciated throughout the search process—set off a firestorm of administrative and faculty objection. Deans called the provost, outraged that these misguided new procedures were being adopted without their input; chairs called deans to express their distress about how they could possibly implement the new procedures in the next year; the faculty governing body initiated an investigation into the procedure that led to the adoption of these new policies and contacted AAUP for advice; and individual faculty sent e-mails, made appointments, and talked to each other about the outrageous, top-down, totally out-of-touch administrators in charge of the institution.

What went wrong? You can, no doubt, tick off the mistakes President Peters made, and yet his style of leadership—decisive, assertive, and visionary—is the style most often held up as the model for all leaders. There is a sense in which we all hope for the kind of benevolent dictator that he tried to be. However, Americans and especially university faculty also abhor that kind of leadership; we believe in democratic participation, too. So what does that look like?

Shared Governance and Visionary Decisive Leadership

Let's imagine another new university president, Arthur Maxwell, who is also White and male and also "looks presidential." He is a deep believer in the shared governance model of the university and believes that he must implement change in concert with the faculty governance system. In his first meeting with the faculty senate, President Maxwell invites their input on how to change both hiring and tenure and promotion processes on campus. His speech is a version of his campus visit speech, but because he is now actually discussing making changes in these processes, it is met with stiff questioning and opposition from the senators: Is he aware of the reasons behind the current practices, which have secured the outstanding faculty currently on campus? Does he plan to jeopardize the quality of the institution by imposing new standards and processes? This level of risk to the institution's standing is untenable.

President Maxwell, surprised by the vehemence of the response, agrees that he lacks the kind of deep knowledge of the institution that the sitting faculty have and says that he hopes the faculty will participate in designing the best way forward. He asks for the senate's recommendations about how he should best address the important goals of inclusion and meritocracy while at the same time keeping excellence a top priority. The senators are moved by his recognition of their role and agree to provide him with recommendations.

The senate appoints a task force to study the hiring and tenure and promotion practices of the institution and make recommendations to the president. By the end of the next semester, they send a report to the full senate indicating that there are some minor changes in language that could be adopted to signal that inclusiveness is an important value of the institution along with excellence. The senate accepts their report and sends it to the president. They invite him to respond at their next meeting, which will be at the beginning of the next academic year.

Now a full year into his term, President Maxwell attends the fall senate opening and indicates that he appreciates the report and will ask his administrative staff to work through the implications of adopting the language changes they have recommended. At the same time, he indicates that he believes more comprehensive institutional change will be needed than is envisioned in the report. He has decided, over the summer, to appoint a campus-wide committee to discuss these broader changes. Because hiring and tenure and promotion are each complex, he will ask the committee to divide into subcommittees to look into these different domains. He is also asking faculty who are scholars in organizational studies and in other social science fields to serve as consultants to the committees with respect to research that would provide guidance about the kinds of changes that are needed. He outlines his vision of a year-long process in which the entire university is engaged in a discussion of these issues and systematically considers what changes are needed.

President Maxwell's speech is met with a mixed response. Some of the senators are pleased that he has adopted their recommendations and suspect that a faculty committee process will lead to little further change, so they are satisfied. Some of the senators feel that the president has—very politely—delivered a rebuke to them, and they are offended. Still others feel that the president has a dangerous vision that will risk the university's history and assets. And a few are excited at the prospect of a broad university discussion of these very important issues.

In the next few weeks, the committees are appointed, and some faculty begin to engage in the process outlined by the president. Other faculty express the full range of reactions hinted at in the senators' response in faculty meetings, corridor talk, and discussions with their partners at home. A small group of faculty organizes around one of the faculty senators to go to the board of governors with a concern about the danger to the institution that is posed by the president's approach. The board is very concerned about their concern and asks President Maxwell to respond.

You can imagine a variety of outcomes here: the board could support the president's vision and ignore the small group of opposing faculty; the board could ask the president to respond; the board could be persuaded that they must help the president address the faculty's concerns; there could be an eventual vote of no confidence by the faculty, the senate, or the board. In almost all possible scenarios, the process of considering these changes will be protracted and will now involve an explicit need to defend any change against the charge that it poses a risk to the core mission of the institution.

The point in considering these two scenarios is not the outcome of either, but to note that charismatic leadership and a clear vision and mandate, coupled with participatory processes, does not guarantee successful outcomes any more than the same combination of features and benevolent dictatorship does. These two examples show how male leaders might handle their role. The issues are even more complicated for leaders who are women or racial or ethnic minorities, and we will discuss those complications later.

The important point for now is that institutional change is not easy to make. But it is also not impossible. The people at the top—presidents, provosts, and deans—are critical; they must lead. However, they cannot do it alone.

Leading Change

A great deal of ink has been shed about how to "lead change" in businesses and other organizations, including those engaged in higher education (Bolman & Deal, 2003; Bolman & Gallos, 2011; Collins, 1975; Eckel, Green, Hill, & Mallon, 1999; Kotter, 1996; Rost, 1991). Much of the organizational change literature assumes that change must be "led" and led from the top. In one way that makes perfect sense: by definition, leaders have disproportionate influence in an organization. They are visible to the entire organization and to many outside it, and they are officially responsible for articulating a vision, or goals, for the next stage in the organization's history. It makes sense that those goals might include—or even emphasize—change. In many ways, then, formal leaders of organizations are expected to play a critical role in defining desirable changes, motivating people to make those changes, and setting up a process for implementing them. So why isn't the field of higher education filled with examples of leaders successfully arguing for transformative change?

Believing that You Need to Change

Higher educational institutions, especially in the United States, believe they have a very positive record of accomplishment, particularly when considered in an international or global context (Huffington Post, 2012; National Research Council, 2012). For many years, the U.S. higher education community was proud to be at the top of any competitive ranking, and the rate of entry of students from other countries into U.S. higher education institutions spoke for itself (Andrade, 2006; Institute of International Education, n.d.). In short, there was little competitive pressure internationally.

This pattern has shifted, and U.S. higher education is now under new competitive pressures, leading to increased efforts to deliver educational programs in settings abroad and to persuade those in other countries that the price of a U.S. diploma is not too high (*The Economist*, 2012; Lawrence, 2010; National Research Council, 2012). While there still is little pressure from U.S. students choosing to study in other countries, the world population is increasingly viewing education in the United States as a commodity that can be matched in a variety of ways, including internally. To borrow a truism from psychotherapy, higher educational institutions (like individuals with problems) will only change if they want to—and until recently many U.S. institutions of higher education simply did not want to change. And, of course, some alumni, students, and faculty have a stake in keeping things the way they were or are.

Obstacles to Change: Competing Priorities

Even when many faculty, students, and even alumni think that an institution would be well served by making changes, there are reasons that formal institutional leaders may not articulate a "change" agenda as part of their vision. First, the top leadership is responsible to trustees and state legislatures and other governing bodies for revenue generation and responsible fiscal management (Kezar & Lester, 2011). Change can be costly and can incur unknown, hard-to-estimate costs. Since the top leadership will be held accountable first and foremost for the fiscal health of the organization, change may be lower on the list of priorities than the institution's welfare might require. One dean who did have a strong change agenda commented on why it was so difficult to maintain it:

By my third year as dean, I understood why large public universities seemed so stodgy, so resistant to change. It wasn't ossified bureaucracies, administrative ineptitude, or faculty sloth—as legislators and media so often charged. Rather, it was *the endless preoccupation with one budget crisis after another* that was threatening my own college's ability to direct our attention to the goals we had set for ourselves. (Kolodny, 1998, p. 17; emphasis ours)

The power of urgent budget pressures or crises to preclude attention to needed changes should not be underestimated.

The second highest priority set for top leaders in higher education is increasing the prestige or standing of the institution, whatever its current standing (Kezar & Lester, 2011). Accomplishing improvements in prestige or relative rankings is also costly (in terms of developing equipment resources and new buildings on campus, attracting new and high-profile faculty, or altering the mix of curricula and degrees available to attract students). It certainly can be—often is—the primary "change" agenda that an institutional leader takes on (e.g., pursuing a certain ranking or pursuing inclusion in a more prestigious grouping of institutions).

These two missions—revenue generation and prestige increase—are nearly universal demands on the top leaders in higher education (see study of presidents by *Chronicle of Higher Education*, 2013). Seriously addressing them may well crowd out other kinds of changes—changes to make the environment more "ideal" in terms, for example, of diversity and inclusion, the institutional climate, or policies that support faculty growth and development.

For this reason, leaders eager to initiate major changes on campus are most likely to be successful if they tie any change mission to one of the long-standing "core" missions of the university (including, but not limited to, the two mentioned here; others might be serving the citizens of a particular state or city, maintaining the tradition of excellence, etc.). For example, in the 1980s, James Duderstadt at the University of Michigan outlined both *The Michigan Mandate*, in 1988, and the *Women's Agenda* in 1993), two transformational projects aiming at diversifying the campus, but explicitly tied them to maintaining excellence and Michigan's "competitive edge" (Maher & Tetreault, 2011). Formal leaders who can explain why equity and inclusion are important to the pursuit of the core mission of the institution are more likely to be successful in improving their institutions.

Resistance to Imposed Change

At the same time, as we saw in President Peters, change in academic institutions cannot simply be imposed top-down. Academic culture is characterized by deep faculty skepticism about all administrative programs, including suspicion about their true underlying purposes (Kezar & Lester, 2011, p. 132; Kolodny, 1998, pp. 6–7). Gaining faculty trust and commitment to any given program is a project requiring considerable faculty input at the beginning and a long-term process of listening, adjusting, and continuing pressure to focus on the goal. Administrators at all levels (such as chairs and deans) need not openly resist institutional change efforts but can prevent them by "stalling." Because they are experienced and knowledgeable about how the institution works, they can use delay to outlast the effort (Kezar & Lester, p. 160).

Faculty members can also resist by using tactics of hostility, derogation, and irony that make change efforts appear (usually to their colleagues, but sometimes to other important constituencies like alumni, legislators, and students) ill thought out, risky, and ill-advised (Kezar & Lester, 2011, pp. 162ff). Sociologist Myra Ferree (2005) has labeled these kinds of tactics "soft repression," and she includes the use of ridicule—the kind of verbal weapon faculty are particularly well suited to use—as a primary tool for resisting social change. As Ferree notes, ridicule can be the beginning of a war of attrition in which stigmatization of change agents and, eventually, their silencing are the later stages.

It is important also to note that there is considerable evidence that managers (in universities these are most often deans and department chairs) are most likely to respond positively to change efforts when they are positively engaged in the change through efforts at transparency and accountability, and not through "discretion control" (Dobbin, Schrage, & Kalev, 2015). Managers, like faculty, prefer to operate with some independence in choosing how to implement changes, and resent attempts to control their authority. Like everyone, they are more likely to respond to information (transparency) and reward (promised as a result of monitoring processes and outcomes—or accountability).

This problem can be overstated. It is sometimes argued that nothing that is "mandated" or required can "work" (Dobbin & Kalev, 2017, is sometimes interpreted as suggesting this). We propose instead that mandatory exposure to information and advice about good procedures can serve *transparency* (and therefore be accepted), as long as there is no explicit attempt to limit individuals' right (even obligation) to exercise judgment. It is the impression of "thought control" or (more important) decision control that must be avoided.

For a campus change effort to survive, it needs to prevent or address both administrative stalling and faculty ridicule. Academic institutions are not characterized by a single hierarchy with a "boss" or leader at the top (Clark, 1983; Kezar, Carducci, & Contreras-McGavin, 2006). Although they do have a president or chancellor, virtually all institutions of higher education feature a "shared governance" model in which there is both a management or administrative hierarchy and a parallel and quite distinct faculty governance structure with separate powers (to set the curriculum, approve classes, award degrees, make recommendations about tenure and promotion, etc.). Those special features of higher education institutions offer resources for survival (as well as resistance!). The dual authority structure operates according to two separate bases of authority: position for the administrators and expertise for faculty. Because of the dual structure, with different power bases, efforts to make change, as well as attempts to resist it, can arise in multiple locations and employ different tactics, as we saw in the case of President Maxwell.

Convergent Bottom-Up and Top-Down Change

One analysis of the different roles of the different kinds of actors in institutions found that favorable changes in practices like hiring and retention and promotion procedures are most likely to last if efforts are simultaneously top-down (enacted by formal leaders) and bottom-up (supported by faculty experts; Kezar & Lester, 2011). When formal leaders successfully enlist the support and engagement of faculty efforts in a change process, this tends to have good results (Kezar, 2009; Lester, 2009). In contrast, only about one third of the efforts initiated by grassroots or faculty experts end up converging successfully with those of formal leaders (Kezar & Lester, pp. 228–229). It makes sense that it will be difficult to enlist administrators to join in bottom-up change, but without "buy-in" by formal leaders there is unlikely to be lasting change in institutional structures, practices, and policies.

Some Change Can Be Local

Change efforts do not always take place institution-wide. Faculty are generally most preoccupied with the climate and practices within their home department, school, or college. Sometimes the practices are the result of campus-wide policies, but often they are local practices that are open to alteration. A great deal of local-level change can be successfully launched at the departmental level by faculty in alliance with formal department leadership (the chair or head, along with any other faculty who may occupy formal leadership roles in the department). In a study of "grassroots" efforts by faculty and staff, it is noted that "once grassroots leaders were interested in diffusing their effort across the campus, it became clear that they needed to engage campus leadership and gain buy-in" (Kezar & Lester, p.228). Thus, it is the aspiration to move beyond the local that leads grassroots academic leaders to seek convergence with formal holders of administrative positions. A great deal can be done to improve local conditions before that aspiration is formed.

The Importance of Change to the Faculty

Even though it is difficult to accomplish change, many faculty pay close attention to the winds of change—or their absence—in the institution. Some faculty make judgments about the direction that the institution is going in and its ability to embrace changes that seem critical. Those judgments in turn may either drive them into the job market and to investing in their scholarship and professional societies rather than campus institutions, or keep them focused at the home institution. As we discussed in earlier chapters, all faculty are affected by the culture at the level of the department, by a sense that the environment is supportive and inclusive (or not), and that it is possible to have an effective voice in what happens (Settles, Cortina, Malley, & Stewart, 2006; Settles, Cortina, Stewart, & Malley, 2007). Those perceptions shape how faculty feel about staying or leaving. Of course, faculty will draw conclusions not only about the degree to which changes on campus are accepted and implemented, but also about whether the process of decision-making, and the resulting outcomes, are fair.

The Importance of Data: Documenting Where You Are and What Changes

Finally, change may take place—or fail to take place—without even being noticed if no efforts are made to track and monitor data. For example, we know of one department that regularly admitted women to study in their doctoral program; the faculty and chair therefore believed that it was making great strides in accomplishing diversity among the doctoral students. When data were provided showing the rate of PhD *completion* by gender, the department was shocked to discover that not a single female PhD student had completed the degree in over ten years. While women were being admitted in reasonable numbers, they were leaving in equal numbers. No one noticed the pattern because faculty members only knew about the one or two students they worked with in each cohort. The department did not even know it had a problem until the data were compiled and examined in a way that allowed it to see the problem. As we have stressed throughout, all efforts to make institutional change must be accompanied by a process of gathering and reporting data that enables everyone to see what is—and is not—happening.

The Role of Formal Leaders in Creating the Ideal University

As we noted above, formal leaders have disproportionate influence in organizations. Leaders are highly visible and can explain why certain goals (e.g., equity and inclusion) are important and how those goals are tied to other priorities, including the institution's core mission. Leaders also can generate changes in practices, norms, or structures by creating or formalizing procedures. In some cases leaders control critical institutional processes (e.g., the "standard practice guide" or access to the governing board of regents or trustees or to donors). In other cases, leaders can take a practice that has been voluntary (e.g., participation in a peer education program offered by faculty on how to recruit and hire fairly) and make it a precondition for service on a search committee. If a chair, dean, or provost creates that requirement, the peer education program is legitimated and will reach a wider audience. Finally, and not trivially, formal leaders control the resources that are always needed to implement any institutional change.

Formal leaders can also create incentives and rewards to motivate other actors (other formal leaders or individual faculty members) to participate. For example, leaders can establish awards for individuals' engaging in actions they want to encourage (e.g., for undergraduate teaching or mentoring of junior faculty) or for departments to engage in projects that might serve a larger purpose (e.g., improving the departmental climate for women and underrepresented minorities). Leaders can also provide financial support for the creation of positions, staff, and offices or funding of activities (like internal training of faculty by faculty).

The power that formal leaders have is real, even though they often minimize it, stressing the real and imagined constraints on their authority. If we are to attain ideal universities, formal leaders must be able and willing to use the power they do have toward creating and institutionalizing critical changes. Although we earlier discussed the limits on leaders—top-down fiats are rarely successful, and creating partnerships with faculty requires skill— we emphasize that leadership in academia for any purpose involves the development of such partnerships. In our experience, broad institutional change is virtually unimaginable without at least intermittent attention of the top leadership and their articulation of that change as necessary, desirable, and consistent with core values of the institution.

Types of Leaders

Formal leaders are expected to do a great deal in their roles, and some are more effective than others. One study of women college presidents identified nine "tenets of effective leadership," including passion, reflectiveness, competence, communication ability, understanding of the role of culture, physical and emotional stamina, energy and resilience, focus combined with forward thinking, respect and valuing of individuality and credibility (Wolverton, Bower, & Hyle, 2009, p. 150). An academic leader could reasonably feel that this is a tall order.

Among the many typologies of leadership,[1] we will focus on "transformational leaders" in contrast to transactional and laissez-faire leaders (Bensimon, Neumann, & Birnbaum, 1989; Burns, 1978; Kezar et al., 2006; Kouzes & Posner, 2002). One particularly important and influential account identifies specific characteristics of those three kinds of leaders (Eagly & Carli, 2007).

Transformational leaders have qualities that motivate respect; inspire others to productive action; communicate the values, purposes, and importance of the mission; are optimistic; explain new perspectives clearly; and mentor and develop followers. It is, of course, this last quality—mentoring and developing followers—that President Peters did not have. President Maxwell had many of the same strengths, but he too failed to create a process that would be successful at developing followers. He also had some features of a transactional leader.

Transactional leaders provide rewards for performance, attend to mistakes and failures, and wait to address problems until they are serious. President Maxwell did respond to feedback and tried to address problems proactively, but his combination of transformational and transactional qualities was not enough. Finally, *laissez-faire* leaders are often absent and uninvolved in the organization's day-to-day operation; they are the least effective. The most effective style for academia appears to be a combination of transformational and transactional leadership (Bensimon, 1993; Kezar et al., 2006).

Combining transformational and transactional styles may be effective, but leaders (like President Maxwell) may not be equally good at all aspects of these two approaches. No one is good at everything. Effective leaders know their strengths and weaknesses and can recruit others to help them accomplish those aspects of the job that may be the most difficult for them (Bolman & Gallos, 2011). Sharing responsibility for change is useful in another way: goals will remain in focus even when the formal leadership is distracted by crises or other pressures. Sharing responsibility well requires that leaders learn about faculty expertise, experience, and concerns. Leaders may have relatively good access and knowledge about some areas and virtually none about others. Finding ways to acquire knowledge—formally or informally—is critical to adequate framing of the goal, as well as to devising successful implementation plans. Neither of our fictitious presidents knew enough about the institution, a common occurrence. And neither recruited allies who could collaborate in changing the institution. Involving faculty in any initiative not only brings new information into the process (or can, depending on who is invited), but it can also prevent backlash or resistance that would otherwise arise if the initiatives are, or feel, imposed in a top-down manner.

Not only do formal leaders have individual leadership styles, but there are particular challenges associated with being a leader with a particular social identity. In U.S. culture, and in our examples, the concept of a "leader" is ordinarily imagined in a White male body (Rosette, Leonardelli, & Phillips, 2008). As a result, people who are "other" in some way face particular challenges in enacting the role of leader.

White Women and Underrepresented Minorities as Formal Leaders

There are two reasons that White women and underrepresented minorities face unique challenges as leaders. First, as noted above, we have preexisting ideas about leaders. According to those ideas, leaders are competent, decisive, forceful, and assertive. Second, we have gender and racial and ethnic schemas about the qualities that members of various groups have. Both White women and racial and ethnic minorities are stereotyped as not having one or more of the qualities that we expect in leaders. This lack of fit or schema incongruity between the leader schema and the schema of the group creates a demand on individuals to demonstrate that they "measure up" to the leader schema. White male leaders do not face that demand (Cejka & Eagly, 1999; Eagly & Karau, 2002; Glick, Wilk, & Perreault, 1995; Heilman, 1983, 2001).

In addition, White women and underrepresented minorities who demonstrate qualities that are not thought to characterize their group as a whole often face backlash—or hostile reactions to the violation of a group stereotype (Rudman, Moss-Racusin, Glick, & Phelan, 2012). Because White women and members of particular racial-ethnic minorities face different expectations, we will discuss the issues separately, including the issues facing women who are also racial or ethnic minorities versus men who are racial or ethnic minorities. Identities that involve different intersections of race and gender lead to different pressures and different reactions.

Women Leaders

Our shared cultural ideal of women includes some positive qualities that are valued in leaders, such as caring about others and being skilled at interpersonal relationships. At the same time, women are stereotyped as being relatively passive and not particularly competent—major disadvantages in a leader (see, e.g., Prentice & Carranza, 2002; Rudman et al., 2012). There is, then, pressure on women who seek leadership roles to demonstrate that they are competent and capable of strong, decisive action (often referred to as being "agentic"). However, as discussed in chapter 3, when women do demonstrate a high degree of competence or agency, they are often "punished" by being viewed as not very likable (Heilman, Wallen, Fuchs, & Tamkins, 2004). Rudman and her colleagues have labeled this a "backlash" effect or "Catch 22" and have demonstrated that in hiring situations women are either presumed to be less competent than comparable men (though as likable) or—if viewed as equally agentic—then as less likable (Phelan & Rudman, 2010; Rudman et al., 2012). Both processes lead to the same negative outcome: equivalently qualified women are less often viewed as attractive candidates for hiring than men. Either they are assumed not to be competent and assertive enough, or, if they are demonstrably competent and assertive, they are seen as unlikable—a classic double bind in which women are "damned if they do and damned if they don't."

Many women in leadership roles are quite conscious of these cross-pressures. For example, Mildred Garcia, while president of Berkeley College in New York, pointed out, "It's so much harder for women. We are always under a microscope. If you are strong, you are seen as bitchy. Men, in contrast, are seen as assertive; they know what they're doing" (quoted in Wolverton et al., 2009, p. 48). At the same time, it is clear that agency, or strong, decisive action, is required of leaders. So what happens when women in leadership roles act like leaders?

Women Leaders and Subordinates' Efforts to Undermine Them

Laurie Rudman and her colleagues (Rudman, Moss-Racusin, Phelan, & Nauts, 2012, study 5) designed an experiment that compared participants' views of male and female leaders who were described as scoring high on agentic traits (like "I believe I am a strong, confident leader") or as scoring relatively low on those traits. The men who were described as low in agency were still rated high on competence, but only women high in agency were rated high in competence. At least they were viewed as competent if they explicitly described themselves that way!

In order to assess how subordinates responded to having a competent female leader, the experimenters created an opportunity for participants to undermine the leader's success at a task by providing unhelpful clues rather than helpful ones. As expected, the agentic female leaders were sabotaged— that is, their performance was undermined—more often than agentic male leaders were, and more often than low-agency male or female leaders. This experiment demonstrates the double-bind women leaders face: avoid sabotage by understating your competence and risk having people see you as not qualified to be a leader, or demonstrate your competence and risk provoking negative reactions that may be expressed in sabotage of your success.

Atypical Men

Although men are generally given the benefit of the doubt with respect to their fitness to be leaders, men who are not described in racial or ethnic terms and therefore probably presumed to be White suffer when they are viewed as "atypical men" (Heilman & Wallen, 2010). For example, in one study, modest men were rated as less likable, less agentic, and weaker than comparably modest women (Moss-Racusin, Phelan, & Rudman, 2010). In another study, men who requested a family leave (i.e., men who violated the "ideal worker" stereotype which demands that workers have no interfering commitments outside of work) were viewed as weaker and lower on agency than comparison men; moreover, they were rated as poorer workers and were rated as less deserving of economic rewards (Rudman & Mescher, 2013).

No Room for Mistakes

College president Mildred Garcia noted that there is no room for women to make mistakes in leadership roles. She said,

Your first shot out is what they will remember. It's the only shot you have. One mistake and they'll never ask again. The majority of men can do something terrible at an institution, and a month later or six months later, they'll have another presidency. (quoted in Wolverton et al., 2009, p. 47)

Experimental evidence suggests that *both* men and women in high-status jobs that are gender incongruent are given no room to make mistakes.

Women in high-status roles stereotypically associated with men (police chiefs), and men in high-status roles stereotypically associated with women (president of a women's college), were both viewed as less competent than their gender-congruent counterparts (male police chiefs and female presidents of women's colleges) when they made a mistake (Brescoll, Dawson, & Uhlmann, 2010). As these authors note, violating gender stereotypes in high-status positions creates a situation of high risk or "fragile status" for both men and women.

Underrepresented Minorities in Leadership Roles

There is less research on underrepresented minorities in leadership roles than there is on women, but generally speaking two principles appear to characterize the research to date. First, leaders are stereotypically viewed as White (Rosette et al., 2008). In one study, both African American and Hispanic American managers were viewed as having fewer of the characteristics of a "successful manager" than Caucasian managers (Chung-Herrera & Lankau, 2005). Moreover, underrepresented minorities are—like women—stereotyped generally as less competent than Whites and therefore are seen as less suited for leadership roles (Jost & Banaji, 1994; Jost, Banaji, & Nosek, 2004; Pratto & Pitpitan, 2008).

Second, when underrepresented minorities are presented as highly competent, they elicit negative reactions much like those that White women elicit (Dovidio & Gaertner, 1981; Livingston & Pearce, 2009). In short, underrepresented minorities (and most of the research has focused on African Americans, with a little on Latinos or Native Americans) face the same kind of double bind that has been described for women: they must overcome the presumption that they are not competent, but if they do, they are likely to face backlash unless they have also cultivated "likability."

Asians and Asian Americans in Leadership Roles

Asian and Asian American individuals are often described as subject to positive stereotypes captured by the notion of the "model minority." However, the schema for Asians disadvantages them in the areas of some key leadership traits—agency, assertiveness, and social skills—while advantaging them in the areas of academic achievement and overall competence (Chung-Herrera & Lankau, 2005; Lai & Babcock, 2012). Moreover, there is evidence that Asians and Asian Americans are underrepresented in leadership roles even in fields where they are well represented (Mervis, 2005). To examine why this might be so, one experiment used the standard procedure of manipulating Asian-sounding versus European-sounding names and compared perceptions of individuals with otherwise-identical characteristics (Sy and his colleagues, 2010). Leaders with apparently Asian backgrounds were generally viewed as having less leadership potential than leaders with European backgrounds, though this was less true when they were described as being in occupations stereotyped as congruent for Asians (those requiring technical competence).

The Intersections of Race or Ethnicity and Gender

Most studies have examined race without reference to gender, or gender without reference to race. However, there are some important studies that suggest that the two dimensions combine to create unique stereotypes that affect how male and female ethnic minority leaders may be viewed. For example, as we noted in chapter 3, in one study Black female leaders (like White males) were able to "get away" with being agentic (i.e., their agency did not provoke backlash) in contrast to the treatment of White female and Black male leaders (Livingston, Rosette, & Washington, 2012). These results fit the experience of Sullivan County Community College president Mamie Howard-Golladay, who said, "Stereotypes can, however, work in your favor. Because people sometimes expect Black women to be aggressive, we can get away with being the kind of leaders we need to be" (quoted in Wolverton et al., 2009, p. 75).

Similarly, but demonstrating the intersection of race and gender for men, having a "baby face" has a different impact for White and Black male leaders (Livingston & Pearce, 2009). Although having a baby face was a liability for White men, it was an asset for Black male leaders, presumably because it reduced the schema-based perception of Black men as "threatening" and increased ratings of their "warmth" and "likability."

In sum, race and gender (and no doubt other qualities) combine to create specific schemas and, therefore, specific risks and advantages for individuals in leadership positions. This is important for leaders to know, but it is also important for evaluators of leaders to know. People who are not precisely in official or formal leadership roles but are informal leaders or experts are also subject to stereotypes. Individual leaders face different pressures and constraints as they work to decrease the gap between where our institutions are and where our ideals suggest they should be.

The Role of Informal Leaders in Creating the Ideal University

Faculty leaders who do not hold official administrative positions have been recognized as "organizational catalysts" (Sturm, 2007), "grassroots leaders" (Kezar & Lester, 2011), and "tempered radicals" (Meyerson, 2003; Meyerson & Scully, 1995). In all three cases, the faculty are respected on campus and have a strong—even passionate—commitment to making a positive change. These individuals can play a critical role in initiating change and stimulating others—including formal leaders—to take on the issue they care about and institutionalize it. However, people who become informal leaders are often divided in their commitments. They "identify with and are committed to their organizations, and are also committed to a cause, community, or ideology that is fundamentally different from, or possibly at odds with, the dominant culture of their organization" (Meyerson & Scully, 1995, p. 586). This position, combining loyalty and critique, can be uncomfortable for the individual, but it is also a position from which a change effort can be launched.

What Makes Informal Leaders Effective
Some scholars have identified characteristics of successful informal change agents. One stresses that in order to be successful, and avoid isolation, tempered radicals need allies (Meyerson, 2003). Another argues that informal change agents must be "people with knowledge, influence and credibility" (Sturm, 2007, p. 418). Faculty with those characteristics can mobilize knowledge that promotes change (Sturm, 2006). Thus, individuals who have read and understood the scholarly literature about how to achieve fairness, equity, and inclusion can speak knowledgeably to their peers about how to maximize those goals in the recruitment and evaluation of faculty and students. In turn, because informal leaders are influential and credible, formal administrative leaders may seek their input into systematic ways to mitigate bias in hiring and evaluation processes. This process is a critical step, involving "collaborations in strategic locations" (Sturm, 2006, p. 295).

Individuals can move beyond operating as persuasive experts and can foster institutional change when they are able to collaborate with formal leaders with access to formal institutional processes. Finally, organizational catalysts can pressure leaders who are not particularly interested in collaboration (Sturm, 2006, p. 276ff) by increasing campus awareness of important issues and building grassroots faculty support for making changes.

Successful "Bottom-Up" Change Efforts

One empirical study documents the successes and failures of 165 "grassroots campus leaders" drawn from the faculty and staff on five different types of higher education institutions (a liberal arts college, a community college, a research university, a technical college, and a public regional college; Kezar & Lester, 2011). On all of the campuses, the study identified "individuals who do not have positions of authority, are operating from the bottom up, and are interested in and pursue organizational changes that often challenge the status quo of the institution" (p. 8). One case study is that of Janine, a biology faculty member who is concerned about the fact that many students struggle in her courses because of math deficiencies. She makes informal efforts to address the students' needs but quickly realizes that the demand for math support is greater than she can meet on her own. She organizes a group of faculty who also recognize the issue, and they gather data on the positive impact of math support efforts. Within a few years, the group persuades faculty elected leaders and administrators that they have a solution to a real problem; a math support center is created and becomes a campus resource. The study found as follows:

Many faculty and staff talk about Janine's work with pride—she identified a real need and developed a change that made students more successful. While this problem had existed for years on campus, it had never been addressed and maybe never would have been without Janine's efforts. (p. 3)

There are many other kinds of examples of institutional change efforts that began from the "bottom up" on these five campuses. Some of them attracted significant resistance or opposition, but Kezar and Lester (2011) identified successful tactics for overcoming them: flying under the radar until there was evidence to support the change, creating internal and external networks, developing coalitions, obtaining allies in positions of power, recognizing and naming power dynamics, making modest changes in their proposals, and reframing issues (see p. 165). They point out that formal leaders were almost always critical to the success of the efforts that began with informal leaders:

Almost every successful faculty leader mentioned a supportive department chair or faculty member who had worked with him or her to understand that faculty member's scholarly interests and leadership potential and shaped his or her leadership vision.... Grassroots leaders noted these were more than mentors.... Department chairs and other supporters can use a host of practices to help faculty in playing a leadership role, such as legitimizing activities through public acknowledgment, providing resources (course releases or credit for service), and acting as institutional advocates. (p. 271)

The Value of Convergence

When the somewhat frustrated and alienated faculty members initiate a change, they usually believe that formal leaders will not welcome it, but successful changes are likely to find formal leadership support, especially if the financial cost is balanced by gains. Changes met with institutional support create alliances that tend to strengthen the loyalty and commitment of the informal leaders. Those alliances in turn bring along the legitimating authority and the access to incentives that formal leaders possess. Informal leaders may rightly suspect that formal leaders are unlikely to initiate the kinds of institutional changes that make our institutions more "ideal" (Kezar & Lester, p. 233), but informal faculty leaders can be the catalysts for those changes and bring formal leaders along.

A Word about Institutionalizing Change Efforts

Many administrators respond to pressure from alienated or marginalized faculty by creating a position in the president or provost's office exclusively focused on diversity efforts (sometimes a "diversity provost" or "diversity vice president"). Equally, they may appoint a Diversity Council or committee to take up issues of diversity on campus. While both of these gestures can be well-intentioned and necessary, we recommend that they always be carried out with a vision of "convergence" in mind. We have already noted that it is critical that the president or provost remain attentive to, and vocal about, necessary change and the underlying values it reflects. That expressed commitment cannot stop because someone has been delegated major responsibility for the issue.

For change to continue, diversity and inclusion efforts must always be integrated into the mainstream activities of the institution. Therefore, neither a diversity and inclusion "officer" nor a diversity and inclusion committee should be composed exclusively of "advocates," nor should it be tasked to engage in activities unrelated to mainstream institutional practices. Thus, the individual's portfolio should be broader than diversity and inclusion and should focus on some domain of essential practices of the institution (e.g., admissions, faculty recruitment, etc.).

Similarly, the committee or council should include individuals holding formal power roles, as well as diversity advocates, and the committee's activities should include design of ongoing institutional practices, as well as implementation and accountability. Otherwise the risk is that diversity issues are ghettoized, and those most passionate and most marginalized will remain outside the "system," without the power to make real and lasting institutional changes.

The Role of Faculty Members

Many faculty are neither formal nor informal "leaders" with respect to any given change effort. Yet they play a crucial role in either enhancing or limiting the success of those efforts by others. In short, everyone does play a role whether it is recognized—even by individuals themselves—or not.

Resisting Change Efforts of Others

Complete passivity or indifference to a change effort is a form of resistance; not responding at all to calls to recognize a problem is one way to help ensure that the problem is not addressed. Some faculty are extremely skilled at derogating change efforts, using verbal ridicule to undermine any interest in making a change. Many grassroots activists have described experiences of having their efforts discounted by colleagues. They noted that "the constant barrage of microaggressions…led to them coming in and out of leadership roles, retreating for a year or two to restore their energy" (Kezar & Lester, p. 150). So faculty can create significant "drag" on the change momentum both passively and actively—or they can avoid doing that.

Silent Agreement Can Prevent Change

Explicit agreement that something is an issue supports those who want to work on that issue. If faculty sit in tacit agreement with points made, not wanting to prolong a meeting by explicitly stating their support for a point of view, that can lead to an impression that a viewpoint is much less widely shared than it is. We know of a department that was considering making a significant change in its governance procedures in the interest of greater efficiency. Although many faculty felt there was a need to decrease the time demands of the current governance system, many meetings seemed to result in a lack of consensus about moving forward with a new plan. Finally, the department hired someone from outside to interview all faculty members about their views and to tabulate and report back about them. The astonishing result was that all but one faculty member strongly supported the change. Why was it so difficult for them to know that? First, many people said nothing in meetings, simply listening to what was being said; this made it difficult to gauge how strong the support was on either side. Second, everyone was so concerned to be sure that no "minority view" was ignored that everyone paid strict attention to the objections that were expressed. With the consultant's report in hand, the governance structure was rapidly and permanently changed.

Supporting Change Efforts on the Ground

Faculty who are not interested in committing significant time or energy to change efforts can nevertheless serve as crucial allies in the context of everyday faculty life if their positions are secure enough for them to feel they can speak. (We recognize that those on temporary contracts may feel they cannot speak up in some contexts, and we respect their need to make sensible decisions about what they can and cannot do.) For example, nearly all faculty can talk with their passionately committed colleagues about their ideas and help them think through strategies that may make them more likely to be successful. Some may be able to provide helpful data or examples that support the arguments favoring change, provide objections that need to be countered, or clarify the limits the proposed change may have. Faculty allies can also encourage other faculty, who have reasoned reservations about the change, to articulate their reservations clearly. That will help those messages be heard by those seeking change, who can then actually address them in their proposals for a new approach.

When there are public discussions of an issue that might deserve attention, individual faculty can help create and maintain space for people to fully articulate their points of view. For example, one of us witnessed a colleague simply say, "I'd like to hear what Professor X has to say; please let him finish," when someone was interrupted by a colleague who was ridiculing his perspective. This entirely civil request not only resulted in Professor X's making his point, but led to a lively and constructive conversation. Sometimes it is necessary to directly challenge the assertion of a colleague who seems determined to "shoot down" an idea, or it is helpful to reframe an issue in a way that defuses the hostility of another faculty member. Those actions are important contributions to supporting change efforts being led by others.

In short, all faculty members are either supporting efforts to achieve an "ideal university" or are standing in their way. No one is irrelevant.

Where to Start?

Sometimes institutional change efforts are stalled by uncertainty about the "ideal" starting point for making the change. Should we focus on faculty recruitment? Retention? Climate? The tenure process? Sometimes it is clear that one or another beginning point is unlikely to be helpful. For example, many institutions slowed down or stopped faculty recruitment during the economic recession following 2008. That was not a good time to focus on creating change through recruitment of new faculty.

But the good news is it really doesn't matter! Because academic institutions are large interconnected systems of systems, changing any one (major or significant) process is likely to have implications for others. Thus, for example, in many institutions that focused on creating fairer recruitment processes, faculty quickly figured out that it must also be important to think about evaluations of faculty not just during the hiring process, but also during the promotion or tenure process. Equally, recruitment of faculty from groups that are not well represented on the faculty raises questions about how those new faculty will perceive the climate. So improving the recruitment processes, the review processes, and the climate will all be necessary, but changing any of them can be the first step. We have summarized our advice about these matters both in recommendations for different members of the community at the end of this chapter and in a road map for institutional equity as a whole in box 11.1.

Box 11.1
A Road Map to Equity

The Upper Level Administration—Make Visible Commitments

1. Publicly articulate how university or sector will benefit through increasing equity and diversity.

2. State commitment in person to faculty, staff, and students within one's purview.

3. Publicly and personally commit one's section of the institution to equity and diversity.

4. Publicly announce concrete goals, efforts, and successes.

5. Review tenure and promotion decisions for possible inequities by sex or race.

6. Finance the collection and dissemination of data.

7. Finance efforts to improve equity.

8. Reward people who make clear progress on equity and diversity.

Accountability of Deans to Provost

1. Hire deans who have made previous equity and diversity efforts.

2. Evaluation:

a. deans write annual self- and school appraisal, including efforts toward equity and diversity

b. provost and dean meet to discuss dean's performance

c. provost writes brief evaluation

d. dean's and school's benefits are dependent *in part* on progress toward equity and diversity goals (only possible when central administration controls some resources)

Accountability of Chairs (or Heads) to Deans

1. If head system, appointment includes review of previous equity and diversity efforts.

2. Evaluation:

a. chairs/heads write annual self- and department appraisal, including efforts toward equity and diversity—about 7–8 pages in length

b. dean and chair/head meet to discuss chair's/head's performance

c. dean writes 2–3 page evaluation

d. department's benefits and resources are dependent *in part* on progress toward equity and diversity goals

3. Annual review is performed by dean of faculty salaries by sex and ethnicity.

4. Review is performed by dean of start-up packages by sex and ethnicity.

Box 11.1 (continued)

Benchmarks—Up-to-Date Data Provide a Way to Measure Progress toward Goal of Equitable Hiring, Retention, and Promotion

1. Provide data to each department:

a. percentage of female and minority PhDs over last five years—nationally and within school

b. percentage of female and minority postdocs, if known

c. department's history:

i. number of hires per half-decade, presented separately by sex and ethnicity

ii. attrition by sex and ethnicity

iii. years in rank by sex and ethnicity

iv. service on important committees by sex and ethnicity

v. salary by year of degree and sex and ethnicity

vi. start-up packages by sex and ethnicity

vii. where known, comparisons with peer institutions

2. Publish data on university website for each major school or division.

3. Ask department to provide annual equity survey results; provide resources accordingly:

a. nominations for prizes and awards by sex

b. receipt of prizes and awards by sex

c. seminar and colloquium speakers by sex

d. efforts made to support faculty

Needed Resources for Team Responsible for Improving Equity and Diversity

1. Team of faculty and staff:

a. diverse faculty team to develop programs, encourage development of programs, monitor success in meeting goals

b. diverse faculty advisory board with internal and external members

c. institutional research (IR) person to provide and analyze data by department and school and to collect and provide data on availability pool for each department

d. executive assistant, full-time

e. projects manager, full-time to coordinate events, programs, and workshops

f. person to aid with dual-career hires

(continued)

Box 11.1 (continued)

2. Space:

a. office and meeting room in central location with rooms for central faculty, assistants, and IR person

3. Power:

a. authorization to look at any data at any time

b. support of provost and president

c. meetings with president at least two times per term

d. ability to turn down searches

e. authorization to review tenure and promotion decisions when upper level committees meet

When Will We Get There?

Often institutional leaders and faculty hope that after some relatively short and predictable period, the change will have been made. It will be behind us. This is a natural hope and wish, but it is one to resist. As one historian paraphrased in a meeting, "Eternal vigilance is the price of inclusion."

Research and our experience have shown that changing institutions takes a long time (one estimate is that at least ten years is necessary for a large institution to be able to document impact in some areas, like climate; Stewart, 2015). Moreover, short-term changes can be easily reversed if adequate attention is not given to maintaining the new system along with the rationale for the changed practices. For that reason, one cannot promise or expect rapid change. The current practices were the result of decades of development, and their alteration will require sustained attention and commitment.

Nevertheless, the most important thing for those hoping for change to remember is that there have been many successful change efforts in academic institutions—ranging from modest local changes in departmental procedures (that substantially improved faculty members' daily lives) to massive overall institutional changes. These successful changes have nearly always simultaneously engaged three kinds of actors in the collaborative process of identifying a needed change, developing a plan for new procedures, and implementing the plan: formal leaders, informal leaders, and faculty members.

Changes of a significant kind—in which shared norms and everyday practices change—are really changes in culture, and it is cultural change that we are usually aiming for when we talk about institutional change. In order for it to happen, faculty and leaders must work together; as former institution presidents William Bowen and Michael McPherson (2016, p. 70) argued, "Administrators and faculty need to meet together around a bigger table, in a genuinely collaborative mode" to make true institutional changes real. When this kind of change happens, the payoff is that our ideal vision for our institutions gets realized—that we actually have a more inclusive academy. The evidence is that institutional change that increases the diversity and inclusion of higher education can happen much more broadly than it has; and if it does, it not only improves the institution for those who sought it, but is likely to "stick," surviving into the future.

Recommendations for Institutional Change

Formal Leaders

1. Consider whether there are changes you would like to see in the institution that would make it more "ideal." If you do not identify them and articulate them actively and early, you risk being so caught up in pursuit of the goals prescribed by others that you will be unable to pursue these important ones.

2. If you have institutional change goals, explicitly show how they will facilitate the "core mission" and strategic plan of the institution or unit you are leading.

3. Recognize the power of frequent, consistent communication about any important activity or goal.

4. Recognize and resist the tendency only to respond to crises rather than to set an agenda yourself.

5. Develop a process for gaining faculty and other constituencies' input on any change you contemplate. Allow the process to be iterative, involving changes and adaptations in the change plan before it is implemented. Enlist all levels of leadership and faculty involvement in all stages of change making.

6. Ensure that there are adequate longitudinal data maintained in the institution to assess the impact of any change. Monitor the data and report on it to key constituencies, asking them to review it and address any issues they see reflected in the data.

7. Consider the special challenges and opportunities afforded by your particular gender and racial-ethnic identities.

8. Allocate the necessary resources to create and institutionalize the change you hope to see.

Informal Leaders

1. Recognize that informal leaders are often key initiators of institutional change.

2. Identify allies; create and exploit networks of like-minded faculty.

3. Recognize that informal leadership can be costly in stress and fatigue; rely on allies to support you when you are struggling with your own energy or morale.

4. Assume that there will be resistance to change, and avoid demonizing those who oppose your proposals. Instead, create opportunities for others to comment on your proposals for change. Revise your plans based on what you learn from those who are not initially convinced.

5. Enlist the support of formal leaders. Identify appropriate roles for them in the process (e.g., legitimizing the change goal, providing resources or incentives, advocating for change, providing access to institutional data).

All Faculty

1. Recognize that inaction is action, often delaying attention to an important problem or issue.

2. Recognize the damaging role of name-calling, derogation, or ridicule of efforts at change. Avoid engaging in it, and take action to mitigate or challenge it when you observe it.

3. Ask questions and make suggestions that help proposers of changes clarify and improve their proposals. Bring reasoned objections to their attention.

4. Offer explicit rather than tacit support to those leading change efforts.

5. Contribute to the creation and maintenance of open space for consideration of changes in group settings.

6. Provide information (examples, data) that is relevant to change efforts, in the service of improving those efforts.

Note

1. Some, for example, concentrate on the relative weighting of management versus leadership (Aguirre & Martinez, 2006, pp. 75–79).

References

Aguirre, A., & Martinez, R. O. (2006). Diversity leadership in higher education. *ASHE Higher Education Report*, *32*(3).

Andrade, M. S. (2006). International students in English-speaking countries. *Journal of Research in International Education*, *5*(2), 131–154.

Bensimon, E. (1993). New presidents' initial actions: Transactional and transformational leadership. *Journal for Higher Education Management*, *8*(2), 5–17.

Bensimon, E., Neumann, A., & Birnbaum, R. (1989). *Making sense of administrative leadership: The L word in higher education. ASHE Report Series*. Washington, DC: George Washington University.

Bolman, L. G., & Deal, T. E. (2003). *Reframing organizations*. San Francisco, CA: Jossey-Bass.

Bolman, L. G., & Gallos, J. V. (2011). *Reframing academic leadership*. San Francisco, CA: Jossey-Bass.

Bowen, W. G., & McPherson, M. S. (2016). *Lesson Plan: An agenda for change in American higher education*. Princeton, NJ: Princeton University Press.

Brescoll, V. L., Dawson, E., & Uhlmann, E. L. (2010). Hard won and easily lost: The fragile status of leaders in gender-stereotype-incongruent occupations. *Psychological Science*, *21*(11), 1640–1642.

Burns, J. M. (1978). *Leadership*. New York, NY: Harper & Row.

Cejka, M. A., & Eagly, A. H. (1999). Gender-stereotypic images of occupations correspond to the sex segregation of employment. *Personality and Social Psychology Bulletin*, *25*, 413–423.

Chronicle of Higher Education. (2013). *What presidents think: A 2013 survey of four-year college presidents*. Washington, DC: Chronicle of Higher Education.

Chung-Herrera, B., & Lankau, M. (2005). Are we there yet? An assessment of fit between stereotypes of minority managers and the successful-manager prototype. *Journal of Applied Social Psychology*, *35*, 2029–2056.

Clark, R. (1983). *The higher education system*. Berkeley, CA: The University of California Press.

Collins, J. (1975). *Good to great: Why some companies make the leap … and others don't*. New York, NY: HarperBusiness.

Dobbin, F., Schrage, D., & Kalev, A. (2015). Rage against the iron cage: Varied effects of bureaucratic personnel reforms on diversity. *American Sociological Review, 80*(5), 1014–1044.

Dobbin, F., & Kalev, A. (2017). Are diversity programs merely ceremonial? Evidence-free institutionalization. In R. Greenwood, C. Oliver, T. B. Lawrence, & R. E. Meyer (Eds.), *The Sage handbook of organizational institutionalism* (pp. 808–828). London: Sage.

Dovidio, J. F., & Gaertner, S. L. (1981). The effects of race, status and ability on helping behavior. *Social Psychology Quarterly, 44*, 192–203.

Eagly, A., & Carli, L. L. (2007). *Through the labyrinth: The truth about how women become leaders*. Boston, MA: Harvard Business School Press.

Eagly, A. H., & Karau, S. J. (2002). Role congruity theory of prejudice toward female leaders. *Psychological Review, 109*, 573–598.

Eckel, P., Green, M., Hill, B., & Mallon, W. (1999). *Taking charge of change: A primer for colleges and universities*. Washington, DC: American Council on Education.

The Economist. (2012, December 1). Higher education: Not what it used to be. *The Economist*. https://www.economist.com/news/united-states/21567373-american -universities-represent-declining-value-money-their-students-not-what-it/

Ferree, M. (2005). "Soft" repression: Ridicule, stigma and silencing in gender-based movements. In C. Davenport, H. Johnston, & C. Mueller (Eds.), *Repression and mobilization* (pp. 138–155). Minneapolis, MN: University of Minnesota Press.

Glick, P., Wilk, K., & Perreault, M. (1995). Images of occupations: Components of gender and status in occupational stereotypes. *Sex Roles, 32*, 564–582.

Heilman, M. E. (1983). Sex bias in work settings: The lack of fit model. *Research in Organizational Behavior, 5*, 269–298.

Heilman, M. E. (2001). Description and prescription: How gender stereotypes prevent women's ascent up the organizational ladder. *Journal of Social Issues, 57*, 657–674.

Heilman, M. E., & Wallen, A. S. (2010). Wimpy and undeserving of respect: Penalties for men's gender-inconsistent success. *Journal of Experimental Social Psychology, 46*, 664–667.

Heilman, M. E., Wallen, A. S., Fuchs, D., & Tamkins, M. M. (2004). Penalties for success: Reactions to women who succeed at male tasks. *Journal of Applied Psychology, 89*, 416–427.

Huffington Post. (2012, May 14). United States ranked to have best higher education system in the world. http://www.huffingtonpost.com/2012/05/14/united-states-global-ranking_n_1514261.html

Institute of International Education. (n.d.). *Open Doors 2012 fast facts*. Retrieved January 26, 2018, from https://www.iie.org/Research-and-Insights/Open-Doors/Fact-Sheets-and-Infographics/Fast-Facts

Jost, J. T., & Banaji, M. R. (1994). The role of stereotyping in system-justification and the production of false-consciousness. *British Journal of Social Psychology, 33*, 1–27.

Jost, J. T., Banaji, M. R., & Nosek, B. A. (2004). A decade of system-justification theory: Accumulated evidence of conscious and unconscious bolstering of the status quo. *Political Psychology, 25*, 881–919.

Kezar, A. (Ed.). (2009). *Rethinking leadership in a complex, multicultural and global environment: New concepts and models for higher education*. Sterling, VA: Stylus.

Kezar, A. J., Carducci, R., & Contreras-McGavin, M. (2006). Rethinking the "L" word in higher education. *ASHE Higher Education Report, 31*(6).

Kezar, A. J., & Lester, J. (2011). *Enhancing campus capacity for leadership: An examination of grassroots leaders in higher education*. Stanford, CA: Stanford University Press.

Kolodny, A. (1998). *Failing the future: A dean looks at higher education in the 21st century*. Durham, NC: Duke University Press.

Kotter, J. P. (1996). *Leading change*. Boston, MA: Harvard Business School Press.

Kouzes, J. M., & Posner, B. Z. (2002). *The leadership challenge* (3rd ed.). San Francisco, CA: Jossey-Bass.

Lai, L., & Babcock, L. C. (2012). Asian Americans and workplace discrimination: The interplay between sex of evaluators and the perception of social skills. *Journal of Organizational Behavior*. doi:10.1002/job.1799

Lawrence, L. (2010, June 2). US college degrees: Still the best among world's top universities? *Christian Science Monitor*. https://www.csmonitor.com/USA/Education/2010/0602/US-college-degrees-Still-the-best-among-world-s-top-universities/.

Lester, J. (2009). Leadership programs for a family-friendly campus. In A. Kezar (Ed.), *Rethinking leadership in a complex, multicultural and global environment: New concepts and models for higher education* (pp. 151–167). Sterling, VA: Stylus.

Livingston, R. W., & Pearce, N. A. (2009). The teddy-bear effect: Does having a baby face benefit Black chief executive officers? *Psychological Science, 20*(10), 1229–1236.

Livingston, R. W., Rosette, A. S., & Washington, E. F. (2012). Can an agentic Black woman get ahead? The impact of race and interpersonal dominance on perceptions of female leaders. *Psychological Science, 23*(4), 354–358.

Maher, F., & Tetreault, M. K. (2011). Long-term transformations: Excavating privilege and diversity in the academy. *Gender and Education*, *23*(3), 281–297.

Mervis, J. (2005). A glass ceiling for Asian scientists? *Science*, *310*, 5748.

Meyerson, D. E. (2003). *Tempered radicals: How everyday leaders inspire change at work.* Boston, MA: Harvard Business School Press.

Meyerson, D. E., & Scully, M. (1995). Tempered radicalism and the politics of ambivalence and change. *Organization Science*, *6*(5), 585–600.

Moss-Racusin, C. A., Phelan, J. E., & Rudman, L. A. (2010). When men break the gender rules: Status incongruity and backlash toward modest men. *Psychology of Men & Masculinity*, *11*, 140–151.

National Research Council. (2012). *Research universities and the future of America.* Washington, DC: National Academies Press.

Phelan, J. E., & Rudman, L. A. (2010). Prejudice toward women leaders: Backlash effects and women's impression management dilemma. *Social and Personality Psychology Compass*, *4/10*, 807–820.

Pratto, F., & Pitpitan, E. V. (2008). Ethnocentrism and sexism: How stereotypes legitimize six types of power. *Social and Personality Psychology Compass*, *2*, 2159–2176.

Prentice, D. A., & Carranza, E. (2002). What women and men should be, shouldn't be, are allowed to be, and don't have to be: The contents of prescriptive gender stereotypes. *Psychology of Women Quarterly*, *26*, 269–281.

Rosette, A. S., Leonardelli, G. J., & Phillips, K. W. (2008). The White standard: Racial bias in leader categorization. *Journal of Applied Psychology*, *93*(4), 758–777.

Rost, J. J. (1991). *Leadership for the 21st century.* New York, NY: Praeger.

Rudman, L. A., & Mescher, K. (2013). Penalizing men who request a family leave: Is flexibility stigma a femininity stigma? *Journal of Social Issues*, *69*(2), 322–340.

Rudman, L. A., Moss-Racusin, C. A., Glick, P., & Phelan, J. E. (2012). Reactions to vanguards: Advances in backlash theory. *Advances in Experimental Social Psychology*, *45*, 167–227.

Rudman, L. A., Moss-Racusin, C. A., Phelan, J. E., & Nauts, S. (2012). Status incongruity and backlash effects: Defending the gender hierarchy motivates prejudice toward female leaders. *Journal of Experimental Social Psychology*, *48*, 165–179.

Settles, I. H., Cortina, L. M., Malley, J., & Stewart, A. J. (2006). The climate for women in academic science: The good, the bad, and the changeable. *Psychology of Women Quarterly*, *30*, 47–58.

Settles, I., Cortina, L., Stewart, A. J., & Malley, J. E. (2007). Voice matters: Buffering the impact of a negative climate for women in science. *Psychology of Women Quarterly*, *31*, 270–281.

Stewart, A. J. (2015, October). A Long-term Commitment to Institutional Transformation: A Timeline for Change. Presented at National Science Foundation, Washington, DC.

Sturm, S. (2006). The architecture of inclusion: Advancing workplace equity in higher education. *Harvard Journal of Law and Gender*, *29*, 247–334.

Sturm, S. (2007). Conclusion to responses The architecture of inclusion: Interdisciplinary insights on pursuing institutional citizenship. *Harvard Journal of Law and Gender*, *30*, 409–424.

Sy, T., Shore, L. M., Strauss, J., Shore, T. H., Tram, S., Whitely, P., et al. (2010). Leadership perception as a function of race-occupation fit: The case of Asian Americans. *Journal of Applied Psychology*, *95*(5), 902–919.

Wolverton, M., Bower, B. L., & Hyle, A. E. (2009). *Women at the top: What women and university and college presidents say about effective leadership*. Sterling, VA: Stylus.

Conclusion: Making Institutional Changes That Last

We began this book by laying out some general principles for creating a fair and inclusive educational institution. We end by outlining a few general principles for how to create institutional structures that will solidify and enhance desirable changes and, most of all, will make those changes stick—that is, survive turnover in the leadership and the faculty that first tried to encourage movement toward their ideal institution. We have developed these general principles based on our experience trying to implement changes in our own institutions as well as by observing efforts of others at theirs. The principles guided many of our specific recommendations in each of the chapters of part II, but we articulate them here in a more general form because institutional change efforts will inevitably raise issues not covered in this book at all. We hope these general principles will provide an effective framework for thinking through how to make changes that will last.

Six Principles

1. *Change requires a focus on policies and practices.* It can be tempting to treat the issue of creating a fair, equitable, diverse, and inclusive institution (or any other institutional change) either as simply requiring education (changes in knowledge) or as simply requiring attitude changes (which are notoriously difficult to accomplish in a lasting way; see, e.g., Dasgupta & Greenwald, 2001; Eagly & Chaiken, 1995; McGuire, Lindzey, & Aronson, 1985). Institutional changes often do require educating oneself, one's colleagues, and academic leaders about one's institution and about issues, but once a path toward a change has been identified, it is neither practical nor necessary (and is possibly disrespectful) to try to change people's opinions and attitudes. If you believe, as we have argued throughout this book,

that nonconscious schemas and reasoning are playing a role in recruitment and evaluation processes at your institution, then we recommend that you focus on *mitigating* those biases on the ground—in terms of everyday institutional policies and practices—rather than trying to *change* the biases themselves.

That does not mean that we recommend ignorance! We have described at length the data and theories that we hope will become more widely known and appreciated, so that people can understand how and why inequities can persist despite a genuine commitment to merit and inclusion. Knowledge, however, is not enough. As noted above, it is difficult to change attitudes in general (and perhaps nonconscious associations in particular; Stout, Dasgupta, Hunsinger, & McManus, 2011). Over a lifetime we are exposed to many "inputs" (from family members, school experiences, peers, media, etc.) that have provided the informal basis on which we built our associations between social groups and particular roles and traits (see Valian, 1998, for a discussion about why schemas will persist). A workshop, lecture, or program can make us aware of schemas and overly fast thinking and persuade us that we can be led astray in important decisions and judgments. However, only policies and practices aimed at mitigating and buffering the impact of schemas will actually prevent us from being led astray. That strategy has been the hallmark of the recommendations we made throughout this book and undergirds our focus on the social science research that can help us understand what our decision-making limitations are and therefore how to address them. (See Fenstermaker, 2011, for some excellent examples.)

2. *Ground efforts to produce desired institutional outcomes (e.g., fair decision-making) in social science knowledge.* Diversity is actually minimized when we try to change individuals to fit the dominant or status quo model of how something is done. Moreover, changing individuals' beliefs and attitudes is not only difficult, but smacks of a kind of social engineering that is distasteful to most faculty members. A focus on the outcome we are aiming for (a fair and accurate judgment) will lead us to emphasize processes of judgment and decision-making that enhance our ability to deliberate fairly and to minimize our reliance on flawed automatic cognitive processes.

There is considerable research evidence about what kinds of policy changes and "rollout" practices are most and least effective. For example, transparency about policies and broad diffusion of information are critical to policy implementation, as are engaging the key actors, monitoring impact, and demanding accountability (Dobbin & Kalev, 2015; Dobbin, Schrage, & Kalev, 2016; Mitchneck, Smith, & Latimer, 2016). In contrast, workshops that offer only information and discussion of values—without the other features—have less impact. As you consider implementing a policy or policy change, think through what the process of rolling it out will be—how it can be made a high priority for the community in the immediate term. And just as important, consider how you will keep it "fresh" and meaningful through gathering and disseminating data on impact.

3. *Remember that all policies and practices are local.* It is improbable that a policy or practice can be exported wholesale from one institution to another and have the same impact. Universities and colleges have wildly diverse histories, cultures, governance systems, and procedures for adopting and changing policies. We hope you have read about policies and practices in this book that sounded like a good idea. If you try to introduce them into your department, school, college, or university, you will need to adapt them to your local culture. This may require small "tweaks" in language or major alterations. That's desirable! The process of discussing how to adapt a policy or practice allows crucial academic actors—administrators and faculty in this case—to commit to and take responsibility for the policy or practice. And a broad commitment is critical for ensuring that the policy will be implemented.

We discussed some practices as if they were always done in more or less the same way across the institutions that adopt them. But of course they are not. One example is the "short-list review" described in chapter 6. In some institutions, historical information about recent hiring is required for a review of the short list; in others, the short list is reviewed in terms of whether it is diverse on its own terms; in others, diversity of the short list is compared with national pool availability; in some, the dean conducts the review; in others, the chief diversity officer or the provost does so. Those details may or may not matter to the success of the outcome (we lack good cross-institutional data comparing outcomes for similar institutions whose versions of the policy differ in the details), but they matter to the faculty and administrators' confidence in and understanding of how the process fits into the overall faculty recruitment structure of the institution.

Similarly, family-friendly policies use many different concepts and terms at different institutions (leaves, modified duties, reduced workload, etc.), sometimes describing the same practices in different terms and sometimes describing different practices with the same terms. Legal, historical, and cultural meanings are different in different locations, and those meanings often dictate choices of language and links between policies. The important things are that the policies "fit" the institution, are transparent to those who need to use them, and are equitably administered.

The language with which policies are discussed also matters. Language referring to "trailing spouses" and "lead hires"—which inadvertently diminishes the accomplishments and potential of partners of potential hires—is counterproductive. Neither partner will be attracted if the language used diminishes one of them. Equally, language like "extra time" damages those who have time "off" the tenure clock for personal or professional reasons. That time was granted precisely because the individual did *not* have the necessary and appropriate time for their work. To imply that the policy of stopping the clock gave them "extra time" undoes its intent, implicitly suggesting that the person should be held to a higher standard of accomplishment. An accurate description that does not imply an altered standard is "time provided to compensate for time lost."

Changing the language used to discuss such issues is easier than it may seem! The goal is to avoid language that unintentionally excludes or offends some group. For that reason, it is best to make changes based on a broad process of consultation with a wide range of different faculty members. Once the new language is embedded in policy documents that are transparent and widely available, and once campus leaders consistently use the new language, campuses shift to the new terminology almost without noticing it. This kind of change not only affects how decision makers frame individuals and their accomplishments, but also improves the climate of belonging and inclusion that we are aiming to create.

4. *Review the impact of changes in policies and practices for their effects on different constituencies. Use data to assess the differential impact of changes.* Some institutions take up a particular policy for consideration for a variety of immediate reasons: perhaps there is pressure from some group of faculty for more childcare, perhaps there is widespread distress among students

about the lack of faculty of color on campus, or perhaps a new provost or dean wants to achieve a more family-friendly campus. Alternatively, institutions may take up a systematic review of policies that affect faculty all at one time, prompted by a broad consideration of issues of diversity (as the University of Michigan did in 2004; see three reports archived at http://advance.umich.edu/researchreports.php, visited January 24, 2018).

In either case, a review must consider the impact of the policies and practices for everyone, not just the "average" faculty member (which was once and sometimes still is White, straight, and male), and not just the faculty currently at the institution but the faculty it hopes to attract. There is a lot of diversity to consider—race and ethnicity, gender, sexuality, rank, ability status, age, dependent care demands, partner status, health, and more. Only by considering how policies and practices differentially affect different groups of faculty can those policies be altered to fit the needs of most or all the faculty. By consulting individuals from a range of backgrounds, those conducting the review can ensure a more favorable reaction to the resulting document. Recall our principle of universal design: the goal is to benefit as many faculty as possible.

Specifically thinking about how parental leave policies will apply to those who acquire new stepchildren, adopt children, foster children, or are appointed as guardians for children, for example, will ensure that faculty who become new parents outside the more frequent situation of experiencing their own or their partner's childbirth feel included in the vision of the institution. At least as important, faculty who face intense demands for caregiving to sick or dying family members must be recognized and included in policies that are supposed to feel "family friendly."

Here, too, language matters. If accommodations for birth mothers begin from a "sick" or "disability" leave policy, faculty may feel that a natural reproductive process is being labeled as something it is not. Equally, if policies supporting the adjustment to a new child in the household only apply to women, men and their partners may feel that the importance and value of men's childrearing is diminished in value and in fact.

Language also matters in framing goals for inclusion of different races and ethnicities. Majority and minority individuals may respond differently to the same language. For example, one study showed that racial minorities use cues about diversity approaches (e.g., that are "color-blind" or "assimilationist") to assess their safety in an environment and the degree to which they can trust it (Purdie-Vaughns, Steele, Davies, Ditlmann, & Crosby, 2008).

Considering the often-unintended consequences of policy coverage and language, while also considering changes in the policies themselves, is a critical part of a process that ends with a more inclusive policy covering more diverse faculty and resulting in better outcomes.

Finally, the potentially differential impact of any change in policy or practice can only be assessed with data. We have stressed throughout the book the crucial role of institutional data that are fine-grained and disaggregated enough to detect differential impact for different groups, as well as the importance of holding administrators accountable for gathering and monitoring the data and taking appropriate steps to address inequities that are uncovered. All of this should be built into the change process itself.

5. *When possible, adopt policies and practices widely. Provide necessary educational and informational support so that all crucial actors can adopt the policies.* It is common in large institutions to implement a change (e.g., in policies stopping the tenure clock or in recruitment procedures) and to provide substantial information to the relevant community at the time of the change. Ideally, this information will include a thorough explanation of the goals of the policy, the considerations that went into adopting it, and a description of precisely how it will be administered and monitored.

However, updating will also be required. "The community" is constantly changing, with departures of some key actors and arrival of new faculty, new department chairs, and other institutional leaders. Over time, understanding of the policy's goal, as well as the reasons for how and why it was implemented in a particular way, decay in the community. This could lead to a healthy reexamination of the policy, but only if that is based on a full understanding of the thinking behind it. For that reason two things are crucial: (1) full documentation of the rationale and process of developing the policy and (2) frequent and repeated communication about the policy with all of the crucial actors.

It is hard to maintain changed policies when new upper level administrators and faculty arrive. Newcomers may have assumptions or misapprehensions about what the policies are, based in part on their earlier experiences. At the moment of arrival newcomers are overwhelmed by a volume of information they cannot fully assimilate. What will help in maintaining beneficial policies is identifying a set of crucial policies that maintain institutional fairness, diversity, and inclusion; labeling and describing the policies; and recognizing that they need to be explained in a coherent and transparent way—over and over! In order to transfer knowledge about policy beyond the moment of implementing a change, it is helpful to create meaningful educational opportunities for new department chairs and upper level administrators in which they can learn about the rationales underlying all crucial policies and practices and talk together about how to address some of the knotty difficulties in implementing them. Many campuses have workshops to "train" administrators on procedural issues (legal, budget, and other processes). Fewer provide real opportunities for formal leaders to share their questions with each other and learn about best solutions. Increasing those opportunities can be a step toward a more thoughtful policy change process.

6. *Change what you can where you can.* Almost everyone would like to change more things more quickly than is feasible. Moreover, some institutions are more "ready" for change than others, and some leaders are more interested in supporting or making change than others. Whatever your role in your institution (formal leader, informal leader, or faculty member), you will need to make a judgment about where change is most possible. We emphasize that some change is always possible. Sometimes what you "can" change is a small part of a policy rather than all of it. For example, you may hope to make it possible for faculty not only to receive "modified duties" (freedom from teaching) for many kinds of caregiving responsibilities, but also to have the option of changing their appointment from full- to part-time. At some institutions it may be very difficult to do both. At some it will be easier to adopt modified duties for caregiving, and at others to permit faculty to be part-time. We support the idea that some change is better than none, with the provisos that we have already mentioned (such as consulting a wide range of people). Some change often sets a process in motion that leads to more change in the not-too-distant future.

A different approach is to shift the person who will initiate the change. For example, sometimes the fastest way to get a dysfunctional department to develop fair procedures is not to work on the problem inside the department, but instead to have the dean mandate procedures across departments.

We saw that happen when one dean helped a new chair alter the decision-making structure of a department that had relied on a secret powerful committee of the same older White men for decades. The dean mandated school-wide adoption of openly elected committees and transparent procedures. An open process already characterized most departments, so widespread change was not necessary. The problematic department quickly adopted the new policy and practice because it was required, even though its faculty had been unable to come to consensus about doing so for years before.

On the other hand, sometimes the highest level leaders who are relevant are reluctant to make a change. It may nevertheless be possible for one department chair or dean to make that change and to see that change propagate throughout the institution. If that change is successful, even a reluctant dean or provost may be happy to make it known to other department chairs and deans (and in any case the department chair or dean can do that), and in this way to encourage voluntary "bottom-up" change. In another example we know of, a department chair required (not merely encouraged) all faculty on search committees to attend a workshop on fair and equitable faculty recruitment procedures. When the dean of that school learned about that action, he decided that if that chair had survived mandating the workshops, so could he, and he immediately implemented workshops for search committee members college-wide. The school thus reaped the benefit of rapid diffusion of knowledge about practices that mitigate biases in hiring processes.

We recommend a two-step process: assess who or what level of the institution can and will make a change, and work at that level first; then take advantage of opportunities to work at other levels. In one institution we know of, a dean adopted a more generous family leave policy in their small school than was available campus-wide. When other deans indicated that they too were going to adopt the more generous policy, the provost requested that they hold off until the policy could be adopted university-wide. The provost wanted to ensure that the policy would be fairly and equitably available across the university. In this example, bottom-up change was followed by top-down change very rapidly, and a new and more generous policy for the entire institution was adopted over a single summer.

Change often begets more change. When it becomes clear that the academic sky has not fallen when one part of a broadly based set of family-friendly policies is adopted, it is often more possible to imagine adopting the other parts. That is why we suggest simply starting whenever and wherever change is possible.

Sustaining Change and Change Makers

As we noted at the outset of this book, not only have we worked within our own institutions on changes like those we have outlined here, but over the past 15 years we have visited many institutions that have been working on these issues. We have drawn good ideas and confidence from their efforts and have learned a great deal about the goodwill and hope for change that is present in many places in many institutions.

Everywhere we have met individuals with great ideas and hopes for improving their institutions. Some of them have been at places where they found rapid acceptance and implementation for those ideas at many levels, but most have faced some degree of resistance from either administrative leaders or faculty members. Resistance could be due to worries about the potential unintended impact of well-intentioned changes, a reluctance to give up certain privileges of inequality, an impression that the time was not right for pursuing a particular goal, or an objection to the goal itself. Resistance is discouraging—intentionally so. We have been sustained through periods of slow or stalled change by understanding that institutional change is slow, and by our collaborations with others, sometimes at the same institution and sometimes at different institutions. We also have found that respectful, serious engagement with those who do not support change at the outset nearly always helps sharpen our ideas and allows us to improve them. If we meet resistance with openness, the result may be better changes and new allies.

Like our colleagues at other institutions, we have discovered that hand in hand with unexpected resistance, we have met unexpected allies and collaborators in change making both at lower and higher levels of the institutional leadership. That discovery of collaborative partners can itself make the institution feel more inclusive. Working with colleagues helps us to consider more perspectives and contexts and to propose more well-grounded changes than we could do on our own.

We hope that it is clear that we believe that it is possible and worthwhile to make changes in our institutions to bring them into better alignment with our ideals. That is easiest when most people in the institution agree. However, some changes can be made—and can be made to stick!—in almost every institution, even by single individuals and small groups of like-minded people. Keep our six principles in mind as you plan how to move toward the most ideal version of your institution.

Finally, we note that institutional change, even if slow, is in fact inevitable, or, as twentieth-century U.S. President John F. Kennedy said in a speech in Germany in 1963, "the law of life." The question is whether as individuals we will actively engage in making positive change. In our view, engagement in improving our institutions is the only way they will ever become more inclusive and realize our idealistic vision for them. In a speech in 2008, twenty-first-century U.S. presidential nominee Barack Obama said, "Change will not come if we wait for some other person or some other time. We are the ones we've been waiting for. We are the change that we seek." We agree. Hope for the future—that the diverse generations of future faculty and students will find institutions that embrace, affirm, and support their best efforts to make the changes *they* seek—will give us the confidence and determination to make our own worlds better now.

References

Dasgupta, N., & Greenwald, A. G. (2001). On the malleability of automatic attitudes: Combating automatic prejudice with images of admired and disliked individuals. *Journal of Personality and Social Psychology, 81*(5), 800–814.

Dobbin, F., & Kalev, A. (2016, July–August). Why diversity programs fail. *Harvard Business Review*, 52–60.

Dobbin, F., Schrage, D., & Kalev, A. (2015). Rage against the iron cage: The varied effects of bureaucratic personnel reforms on diversity. *American Sociological Review, 80*(5), 1014–1044.

Eagly, A., & Chaiken, S. (1995). Attitude strength, attitude structure and resistance to change. In R. Petty & J. Krosnik (Eds.), *Attitude strength: Antecedents and consequences* (pp. 413–432). Mahwah, NJ: Erlbaum.

Fenstermaker, S. (2011). Ivory towers, playing fields, and glass ceilings: Beyond metaphor to best practices. *Wagadu, 9*, 8–23.

Kennedy, J. F. (1963, June 23). Transcript of Address in the Assembly Hall at the Paulskirche in Frankfurt. Retrieved from http://www.presidency.ucsb.edu/ws/?pid=9303

McGuire, W., Lindzey, G., & Aronson, E. (1985). Attitudes and attitude change. In G. Lindzey & E. Aronson (Eds.), *Handbook of social psychology: Vol. 2. Special fields and applications* (3rd ed., pp. 233–346). New York, NY: Random House.

Mitchneck, B., Smith, J. L., & Latimer, M. (2016). A recipe for change: Creating a more inclusive academy. *Science, 352*, 148–149.

Obama, B. (2008, February 5). Transcript of speech to supporters in *The New York Times*. Retrieved from http://www.nytimes.com/2008/02/05/us/politics/05text-obama.html

Purdie-Vaughns, V., Steele, C. M., Davies, P. G., Ditlmann, R., & Crosby, J. R. (2008). Social identity contingencies: How diversity cues signal threat or safety for African Americans in mainstream institutions. *Journal of Personality and Social Psychology, 94*(4), 615–630. doi:10.1037/0022-3514.94.4.615.

Stout, J. G., Dasgupta, N., Hunsinger, M., & McManus, M. A. (2011). STEMing the tide: Using ingroup experts to inoculate women's self-concept in science, technology, engineering, and mathematics (STEM). *Journal of Personality and Social Psychology, 100*, 255–270. doi:10.1037/a0021385

Valian, V. (1998). *Why so slow? The advancement of women.* Cambridge, MA: MIT Press.

Author Index

Subject Index